The
Great Theatres
of London

The
Great Theatres
of London

New Edition

RONALD BERGAN

and Jane Burnard
Edited by Robyn Karney

ANDRE
DEUTSCH

First published in 1990 by
Prion, an imprint of Multimedia Books Ltd.

This revised edition published in 2004 by
André Deutsch
an imprint of the
Carlton Publishing Group
20 Mortimer Street
London
W1T 3JW

A catalogue record for this book is available
from the British Library

ISBN 0-233-00066-6

Printed and bound in China

Contents

Foreword

Architecture and drama are brother arts, but like many siblings they don't always get along. The perfect performance, if there is such a thing, is the communion of actors, audience and the building itself. The acoustics, the sightlines, the comfort of the seats, the atmosphere of the auditorium, the service at the bars and the size of the dressing rooms all contribute to the success or failure of a production. Sometimes there is too great a contrast between the glamour and the luxury of the front of house and the cramped squalor of backstage. But, for an actor, there is nothing equal to playing before a laughing, weeping, snoring, coughing, shocked or enraptured audience in a space created for the purpose.

After years in the USA, I returned to find the architectural face of London changing rapidly, in some cases for the better. However, it is pleasing to see that the great London theatres, part of the glory of the city, remain virtually untouched by 'progress'. Fortunately, most of them are protected from the clutches of property developers. One doesn't have to believe in ghosts to feel a frisson when one enters these ornate and showy playhouses of yesteryear, the architectural equivalents of how we imagine the flamboyant actor-managers like Tree and Irving to have been.

I have been lucky enough to have played at the Royal Court, which has a tradition going back to the era of Pinero and Shaw, combined with the reputation for radical contemporary drama; and for some years with Sir Laurence Olivier's National Theatre Company at the Old Vic, a theatre with one

As Lambert Le Roux in *Pravda* (1985)

vi

foreword

With Judi Dench in *Antony and Cleopatra* (1987)

of the richest of histories. And I've played at the National Theatre on the South Bank, the concrete proof that modern theatres can have an ambience, excitement and personality of their own. That wonderful Olivier stage on which one can mount a vast battle or play the most intimate of scenes!

Yet we actors 'are the abstracts and brief chronicles of the time', and although Keen and Garrick and other great names that fill the pages of this book have come to dust, most of the theatres they played in still remain. The history of the theatre is also the history of the theatres, a fact that this beautifully illustrated, entertaining and informative book celebrates.

Introduction

Amodern-day Wordsworth, standing upon Westminster bridge, would still be able to contemplate 'ships, towers, domes, theatres and temples', although there are far more theatres than the poet dreamed of in 1807. In fact, London has more mainstream theatres than any other city in the world, most of them dating from the Victorian era, and clustered mainly in the West End, the area bounded by Oxford Street to the north, the Strand to the south, Regent Street to the west and Kingsway to the east, with Shaftesbury Avenue running like an arrow through this heart of the capital's playground.

Apart from the 40 or so theatres in the West End there are the two great government-subsidised companies – the National on the South Bank and the Royal Shakespeare Company at the Barbican in the City – as well as the two famous opera houses, and important theatres at Blackfriars, Hammersmith, Sloane Square, Victoria, Hampstead and in the East End, plus the many fringe theatres that have mushroomed in and around London since the 1970s.

These many hives of theatrical activity are sustained by a standard of acting that has gained a justifiably high international reputation. In other words, theatre is alive and well and living in London, despite bitter economic realities and competition from cinema, TV and video. Continuing queues at the box-office testify to the fact that there is no substitute for live entertainment.

The first playhouse, erected in London in April 1576, was aptly named The Theatre. When it was pulled down in 1597, its timber was used to build the Globe, Shakespeare's famous wooden O. The company there was led by Richard Burbage who was the first Hamlet, Lear and Othello, and one of the first in a long line of actor-managers who ran, and often owned, the theatres in which they performed. Laurence Olivier, in his tenure at the National Theatre at the Old Vic (which he quit in 1974), was probably the last of a species.

It took over a century for the playhouse to emerge from the unroofed, circular Globe into the familiar horseshoe-shaped auditorium with its tiered boxes. It was only in the 18th century that the theatre took on the trappings of pomp hitherto reserved for palaces and churches. In the 19th century, with the rise of the civic-proud middle classes, theatres were erected with porticos and columns echoing Imperial Rome, and decor of florid baroque motifs, a mode that continued until the end of World War I. There was a reaction in the '20s and '30s, when theatres went in for simpler lines and Art Deco interiors, while others were influenced by cinema architecture. The following generation broke away from the tyranny of the proscenium arch, moving towards the open stage and theatre in the round, as well as the more democratic seating of the raked auditorium. From the Theatre Royal, Drury Lane to the Barbican, London encompasses the visible history of theatre architecture.

In the process of reseaching this book, I would often have to visit theatres in the cold light of morning. Without the lights, the curtains or eager audiences, they resembled glamorous but ageing women caught before they were able to dress and make up. Thus it was possible to view the theatres as buildings of instrinsic interest, detached from their function, as one visits a cathedral when no service is in progress. However, an audience is an essential ingredient in making these architectural glories or extravagant follies come alive 'The play's the thing', of course, but spectators are aware of the spacial relationship between the stage and the auditorium, the shape of the theatre and the decor, and the history, which makes theatregoing far more than what is happening over the footlights at a given moment.

I hope that my text, enriched immeasurably by the splendid photography taken for the book by Kirsty McLaren, will increase your pleasure in visiting the great theatres of London.

Ronald Bergan

The Adelphi

The king of musical comedy, George Edwardes, always maintained there was box-office magic in the word 'girl' and he was right – at least as far as the last 80 or so years of the Adelphi's history is concerned. Edwardes himself produced *The Quaker Girl* (1908), which ran here for 536 performances, followed by *The Girl In The Taxi* (1912) and *The Girl From Utah* (1913). The theatre's longest-running success was *Charlie Girl* starring Anna Neagle, which ran from December 1965 to early 1971, despite a lambasting from the critics. The 'Lambeth Walk Musical', *Me And My Girl* (1985), continued in the happy line of 'girl' hits, and ran for an amazing nine years.

The first theatre on the site in the Strand was built for a girl. John Scott, who made a fortune from the invention of a washing blue, built the Sans Pareil in 1806 for his stage-struck daughter. It opened with *Miss Scott's Entertainments* in which the talented Jane Scott sang songs, recited poems, spoke monologues written by herself, and danced. A series of melodramas followed, with Miss Scott usually in the leading role. In 1819, John Scott sold the theatre to two gentlemen called Jones and Rodwell, who gave it a facelift and renamed it the Adelphi. As the Lord Chamberlain's licence given to the theatre did not cover 'straight dramas', they were obliged to put on what were called burlettas, being plays containing no less than five pieces of vocal music in each act. This meant that even *Othello* had to be interrupted every few minutes by a song. This unhappy situation lasted until the monopoly of the Patent Theatres was broken in 1843. Despite this restriction, the Adelphi was one of the most popular theatres in London in the 1820s. William Moncrieff's *Tom And Jerry; Or, Life In London* (1821) ran a record 100 consecutive performances, but was surpassed a few years later by *The Pilot* (1825), adapted from

'His murder marked the passing of the kind of melodrama so long associated with the theatre where he died.'

— Lynton Hudson on William Terriss, *The English Stage*

James Fenimore Cooper's sea novel under the new management of Frederick Yates and Daniel Terry.

Adaptations from novels seemed to be the thing in the 1830s, with Charles Dickens's serials being the favourites. Moncrieff rapidly dramatised *The Pickwick Papers*, calling it *Sam Weller; Or, The Pickwickians* (1837), *Nicholas Nickleby* (1838) and *Oliver Twist* (1839). Dickens called Moncrieff 'the literary gentleman... who had dramatised 247 novels as fast as they had come out – some of them faster than they had come out'. In 1844, the famous French dancer Madame Céline Céleste and the actor-manager Benjamin Webster took over what a contemporary described as 'by far the most fashionably attended theatre in London', where they staged what came to be known as 'Adelphi Dramas', mostly written by John Buckstone. Shaw wrote that 'a really good Adelphi melodrama is of first-rate literary importance because it only needs elaboration to become a masterpiece'.

After Webster became sole manager, he decided to demolish the theatre which had fallen into 'incurable disrepair' and built a larger one in its place in 1858. The New Adelphi was among the first London theatres to evoke the epithet 'luxurious' from the press. During the building's 42 years of existence it saw the successes of Dion Boucicault's *The Colleen Bawn* (1860) and *The Octoroon* (1861), the latter being the first play to treat the Afro-American seriously. From 1879, the handsome and debonair William Terriss, father of the future actress Ellaline Terriss, appeared in a celebrated series of melodramas. On 16 December 1897, life imitated art when he was stabbed to death by a vengeful actor as he was entering the stage door to appear in *Secret Service*.

the adelphi

In 1901 the theatre was extensively altered and the name changed to the Century, but public pressure caused the old name to be restored. Under Otho Stuart, whose 'management was distinguished for its judgement, enterprise and liberality', the Adelphi became the home of Shakespeare and modern poetic dramas from 1904 to 1908. Then musical comedy established itself here, first under George Edwardes and later Alfred Butt. As described above, 'girl' titles were popular, but *The Boy*, a musical version of Pinero's *The Magistrate* (1917), ran 810 performances. Another 'boy' was Peter Pan in the shape of Gladys Cooper at Christmas 1923. After two hit revues starring the husband-and-wife team Jack Hulbert and Cicely Courtneidge, and the musical *Mr Cinders* (1929), the theatre was once again pulled down.

What arose in 1930 was a plain linear terracotta structure designed by Ernest Schaufelberg, with its handsome lettering across the top. (In 1993, when Andrew Lloyd Webber and James Nederlander became the new owners, the Adelphi was lavishly restored, and many of the Art Deco fittings and features were reinstated.)

The 1930s decor was a perfect setting for its opening productions, many of them modern musical comedies and revues produced by Charles B. Cochran, including *Evergreen* (1930) starring Jessie Matthews; Noël Coward's *Words And Music* (1932) with Ivy St Helier, Doris Hare and the 23-year-old John Mills; *Follow The Sun* (1936) with Claire Luce; and *Home And Beauty* (1937) in which Binnie Hale sang the praises of 'A Nice Cup Of Tea'.

During the 1940s there was not much at the Adelphi worthy of the theatrical history books other than Marie Tempest's London farewell in a revival of Dodie Smith's popular family comedy-drama *Dear Octopus* (1940);

A typical Adelphi extravaganza *circa* 1840

13

Robert Lindsay and Emma Thompson in the smash-hit revival of Noel Gay's musical, *Me And My Girl* (1983)

Ivor Novello's *The Dancing Years* (1942), which ran for most of the war; and Vivian Ellis's *Bless The Bride* (1947). For most of the 1950s producer Jack Hylton presented a series of variety shows featuring popular radio and television personalities such as Jimmy Edwards, Vera Lynn, Tony Hancock, Arthur Askey,

the adelphi

Shirley Bassey, and the Tiller Girls, the English equivalent of the Radio City Rockettes.

Before musicals completely dominated the fare at the Adelphi, Beatrice Lillie in *Auntie Mame* (1958) held the stage here for two years. Van Johnson in *The Music Man* (1961) gave way to three home-grown musicals – *Blitz!* (1962), of which a critic commented that 'one comes out humming the sets by Sean Kenny', and *Maggie May* (1963), both by Lionel Bart, and the aforementioned *Charlie Girl*. Broadway returned with *Show Boat* (1971), *The King And I* (1973) and Stephen Sondheim's *A Little Night Music* (1975) starring Jean Simmons, Hermione Gingold, Maria Aitken and Liz Robertson. After Miss Robertson became Alan Jay Lerner's seventh wife, she played Eliza in her husband's *My Fair Lady* (1979). In 1982, the D'Oyly Carte Company made its valedictory appearances, sadly not yet back at its spiritual home, the Savoy across the road. The following year, Stephanie Lawrence had a personal triumph in the musical *Marilyn*, but the show died prematurely, to be replaced by the long-running *Me And My Girl*. *Sunset Boulevard* followed, another great success with 1,500 performances, and now the Adelphi is entertaining audiences with the Broadway hit *Chicago* – winner of 1998's Olivier Award for Outstanding Musical Production. *Chicago's* glamorous, stylish design fits very well with the Adelphi's Art Deco auditorium, and the theatre looks set for another great run.

the adelphi theatre
strand = wc2e

The Albery

Virtually back to back and boasting similar decorative, late-Victorian facades are the Wyndham's Theatre, facing Charing Cross Road, and the Albery on St Martin's Lane. They have more in common than the same architect, W. G. R. Sprague. On entering the foyer of the Albery, one is faced by a bust of Sir Bronson Albery after whom the theatre was named in 1973. For its previous seventy years of existence, it was known as the New Theatre. The change of name was a fitting tribute to the dedicated theatrical dynasty that has played such a significant role in the history of the West End for more than a century.

The dramatist James Albery married sixteen-year-old Mary Moore in 1878. Seven years later, with three children and a husband whose health and income had been ruined by the demon drink, Mary joined actor-manager Charles Wyndham's company at the Criterion Theatre and soon became his leading lady and business partner. This successful collaboration enabled Wyndham to build the theatre that bears his name in 1899 and, four years later, the New on the vacant lot just behind it. After the deaths of James Albery (from cirrhosis of the liver) and Wyndham's first wife, Charles and Mary married in 1916. When his mother died, Bronson Albery (knighted in 1949) took control of the three theatres. His son Donald (knighted in 1977) followed in his footsteps and then Bronson's grandson Ian became managing director of what is called the Maybox Group, expanded to include the Piccadilly and Whitehall theatres.

Sprague, architect of eight extant London theatres, designed the New with a capacity of 877 seats, far larger than Charles Wyndham's other two theatres. It boasts a spacious entrance and a large and attractive dress-circle bar. Above the proscenium can be seen two golden angels, representing Peace and Music, with Cupids on either side. Much of the Louis XVI flavour of the

'Here was a gathering together of 400 years of tradition, and the New seemed alive with distinguished ghosts.'
— Bryan Forbes on the Old Vic tenancy

white and gold decoration has been maintained, but the building lacks the intimacy, atmosphere and prettiness of its near neighbour. What it certainly does not lack is a rich heritage.

The newly knighted Sir Charles Wyndham appeared opposite Mary Moore in the first production at the New in March 1903, a revival of a play called *Rosemary*. They were followed by such luminaries as Forbes Robertson, Mrs Patrick Campbell and Cyril Maude before Fred Terry (Ellen's younger brother) and his wife Julia Neilson took over for six months annually from 1905 to 1913. Among their successes were *The Scarlet Pimpernel, Dorothy O' The Hall* and *Henry of Navarre*, in the latter of which Fred's daughter, Phyllis Neilson-Terry, made her first appearance. Phyllis, a member of another legendary theatrical dynasty, was cousin to John Gielgud, who was to figure so prominently at the same theatre.

In 1915 Dion Boucicault, son of the playwright of the same name, became manager. His first presentation was a revival of *Peter Pan*, which flew high for a further four Christmas seasons, the Peter of 1917 being Fay Compton. Boucicault, known as 'Dot', also distinguished himself by producing a series of plays by leading playwrights such as Somerset Maugham (*Caroline*, 1916; *The Land Of Promise*, 1917), A. A. Milne (*Belinda*, 1918; *Mr Pim Passes By*, 1920), Sir Arthur Wing Pinero (*The Freaks*, 1918) and J. M. Barrie (*The Old Lady Shows Her Medals*, 1917). The distinguished American actress Katharine Cornell made her only London appearance as Jo in *Little Women* (1919) and, in 1920, 21-year-old Noël Coward had a play of his produced in the West End for the first time. Despite a successful first night and good

The great Sybil (later Dame Sybil) Thorndike gave well over 200 performances of her legendary *St Joan* at this theatre in 1924

notices, *I'll Leave It To You*, with Coward himself in the lead, flickered out after five weeks. The failure was blamed on the economy-conscious Lady Wyndham (Mary Moore) who removed half the stage lighting. But she was also responsible for inviting Sybil Thorndike and her husband Lewis Casson to appear in Shelley's *The Cenci* (1922) and *Cymbeline* (1923) among other plays. Then came Sybil's great triumph – her creation of the title role in Shaw's *St Joan* in March 1924, which ran for 244 performances.

Enter 21-year-old John Gielgud as Lewis Dodd (succeeding Noël Coward in the role) in Margaret Kennedy's *The Constant Nymph* (1925). His association with the theatre was resumed in the famous 'black and white' production of *Twelfth Night* (1932), followed by his first popular success in the title role in *Richard Of*

the great theatres of london

Bordeaux (1933) by Gordon Daviot (a pseudonym of Josephine Tay). The actor with the most mellifluous of voices then established himself as a star in *Hamlet* (1934), one of the longest runs ever of the play at 155 performances. After taking the title role in André Obey's *Noah* (1935), Gielgud invited Laurence Olivier to alternate with him as Romeo and Mercutio to Peggy Ashcroft's Juliet, with Edith Evans as the Nurse, and it was during the run that he found his real-life Juliet in Vivien Leigh.

When the Old Vic Theatre and Sadler's Wells were bombed out in 1941, the two companies sought refuge at the New Theatre, which became the site of many glittering evenings. For nine years, youthful queues gathering in the morning at the side of the theatre were a common sight. They were rewarded with such memorable performances as Ralph Richardson in *Peer Gynt* (1944), Olivier and Richardson in *Uncle Vanya* (1946) and Edith Evans in *The Cherry Orchard* (1948). After the Old Vic returned to its renovated home, the high standard at the New was maintained. Female stars such as Katharine Hepburn in Shaw's

Fagin (Ron Moody) surrounded by his young apprentice pickpockets in *Oliver!* Lionel Bart's musical ran for a record-breaking seven years

the albery

The Millionairess (1952), Dorothy Tutin in *I Am A Camera* (1954) and Leslie Caron in *Gigi* (1956) sparkled brightly, before all gave way to the boy *Oliver!*, Lionel Bart's musical version of *Oliver Twist*, which ran from 1960 to 1967, breaking all records for this theatre.

In 1971, Olivier returned as head of the as yet homeless National Theatre company for a season which included his James Tyrone in Eugene O'Neill's *Long Day's Journey Into Night*. The next year, the RSC's production of Boucicault's *London Assurance*, with Donald Sinden and Judi Dench, transferred from the Aldwych and enjoyed a successful run, as did Somerset Maugham's *The Constant Wife* (1974), starring Ingrid Bergman, and *A Month in the Country* with Helen Mirren and John Hurt. The theatre's change of name to the Albery did not alter its policy of presenting quality productions with top-ranking actors. In the 1980s, for example, were three sensitive American plays on serious issues: *Children Of A Lesser God* (1981); *Torch Song Trilogy* (1985); and *The Normal Heart* (1986).

These days, the Albery is gaining a reputation as a venue that presents West End showcases of work by leading producing theatres – such as the National Theatre's acclaimed production of *Baby Doll*; the Donmar Warehouse's *Company* (1996); the RSC's *The Cherry Orchard* with Judi Dench (1995); *An Ideal Husband* by the Peter Hall Company; an extraordinary season in 1998 by the Almeida Theatre Company – opening with Racine's *Phèdre* and *Britannicus* (with Diana Rigg), followed by Sheila Hancock in *Vassa* and Cate Blanchett in David Hare's *Plenty*.

Home to Noël Coward's very first produced play in 1920, the Albery has now brought him into the twenty-first century with the sell-out, award-winning production of *Private Lives*, starring Lindsay Duncan and Alan Rickman.

the albery theatre
st martin's lane = wc2n

The Aldwych

There are few theatres in London that have had three such distinct and diverse reputations as the Aldwych. For the pre-war generation it was the home of the 'Aldwych Farces'; from 1960 the Aldwych is remembered as having been the London base of the Royal Shakespeare Company for 22 glorious years; and since then it has been the home of quality drama with productions such as *The Cherry Orchard* with Judi Dench, Sam Mendes's production of *The Rise and Fall of Little Voice* and *Who's Afraid of Virginia Woolf?* with Diana Rigg and David Suchet.

The Aldwych is the twin of the Strand Theatre on the opposite corner of the same block, not far from Drury Lane and the Royal Opera House. They were opened within seven months of each other in 1905 and designed by W. G. R. Sprague with identical facades and almost the same seating capacity of over 1000. The interior decoration of the Aldwych is a mixture of Georgian and French baroque, the dominant colour being a greyish blue with gilt ornamentation. A dual stairway ascends past three huge mirrors and meets in the handsome plush Circle Bar under chandeliers from where one can look down into the vestibule from a circular ramp. *The Era* magazine in 1905 wrote that 'one of the innovations that will be greatly appreciated by the male members of the audience is a commodious smokers' gallery above the entrance hall'.

The Aldwych was built for actor-manager-dramatist Seymour Hicks in association with the famed American impresario Charles Frohman. Hicks and his wife, the beautiful Ellaline Terriss (born in the Falkland Islands in 1871), starred in the opening productions, often musical comedies such as *Blue Bell* (1905) and *The Gay Gordons* (1907). In 1909 Chekhov's *The Cherry Orchard* was given its first performance in England. Nigel Playfair, who

'It was the happiest of choices for the RSC. A real theatre, not a culture bunker.'
— Janet Suzman

was in the cast, related how the actors had little understanding of their roles, most of the audience walked out, and the critics complained that the play was gloomy and formless. It was to return to the Aldwych triumphantly in Michel Saint Denis's celebrated production for the RSC in 1961.

During the Great War the theatre put on a few popular revivals but was also used for a time as a club for Australian servicemen. In 1920, Sacha Guitry and Yvonne Printemps, the second of his four wives, came from Paris to appear in several of the Frenchman's pieces, including *Nono* (written when Guitry was 16). However, with the transfer of *Tons Of Money* from the old Shaftesbury Theatre (destroyed by bombs in 1941), the Aldwych began its renowned reign as the home of English farce, a title it held until the Whitehall achieved a similar reputation in the '50s. In the main its shows were written by Ben Travers, and relied on mistaken identities, comical coincidences and ludicrous characters played by accomplished comedians such as Tom Walls, Ralph Lynn, Robertson Hare, Mary Brough and Winifred Shotter. *A Cuckoo In The Nest* (1925), *Rookery Nook* (1926), *Thark* (1927), *Plunder* (1928), *A Cup Of Kindness* (1929) and others made the Aldwych one of the most popular places of entertainment in London until 1933.

There followed a lean period, despite the introduction of the Privilege Ticket – two seats for the price of one – until the wartime successes: Lillian Hellman's effective anti-Nazi play *Watch On The Rhine* (1942) starring Diana Wynyard and Anton Walbrook; and Lynn Fontanne and Alfred Lunt in Robert Sherwood's *There Shall Be No Night* (1943), written in response to the German invasion of Finland. This was followed by two fine actors in Shakespeare: Robert Donat in *Much Ado About Nothing*

Janet Suzman as Helen of Troy in John Barton's epic cycle of Greek dramas

(1946); and Michael Redgrave as Macbeth (1947). America was represented strongly in the next few years. Gian Carlo Menotti introduced his opera double bill, *The Medium* and *The Telephone,* in 1948, and there was the first English production of Tennessee Williams's steamy drama *A Streetcar Named Desire* (1949), in which Vivien Leigh, in one of the few great female roles in English-speaking contemporary theatre, proved her powers as never before. The year 1955 saw another American hit, *The Bad Seed* by Maxwell Anderson, but, in the same year, Christopher Fry's long-awaited *The Dark Is Light Enough*, despite Edith Evans's superb performance, was not a success.

Farce returned to the Aldwych in more ways than one in 1958 when Peter Sellers, appearing in the legitimate theatre (for the first and last time) in *Brouhaha*, stumbled onto the stage one night in a state of inebriation and announced, 'I'm sloshed. Do you want my understudy to go on?' A vociferous 'No!' allowed him to give an outrageously funny performance, sometimes from the stalls.

For some years, the Shakespeare Memorial Theatre Company at Stratford-on-Avon had been looking for a second home in London. In 1960, when Peter Hall became artistic director, they acquired the Aldwych. Before moving in on 15 December, 1960 with Peggy Ashcroft in the title role in *The Duchess Of Malfi*, an apron stage (as at Stratford) was created by bringing the forestage forward to the line of the stage boxes and eliminating the curtain. The interior was re-painted a dark olive, with the gilt left intact.

Roger Rees (foreground right) was Dickens' hero Nicholas Nickleby in the RSC's magnificent dramatisation of the novel

the aldwych

During their long tenancy, the Royal Shakespeare Company (so named in 1961) set new standards for Shakespeare production, and for other classical and modern plays, building up a brilliant ensemble company of actors in the hands of inspired directors. Among the multitude of memorable productions were three directed by Peter Brook – a hippy *Midsummer Night's Dream*, a Samuel Beckett-like *King Lear* with Paul Scofield, and the revolutionary *Marat/Sade* which brought Glenda Jackson to the public attention. There was Pinter's *The Homecoming*, Brecht's *The Caucasian Chalk Circle*, the landmark sequence of eight of Shakespeare's history plays, *The Wars Of The Roses*, and their tenure culminated in their greatest hit, *Nicholas Nickleby* in 1979. The Aldwych also played host to Peter Daubeny's World Theatre season every summer from 1964 to 1973.

Since the departure of the RSC for the Barbican in 1982, the theatre has not disappointed. The early '90s saw the magnificent revival of *The Cherry Orchard* with Judi Dench and *The Rise and Fall of Little Voice* with Jane Horrocks, Pete Postlethwaite and Alison Steadman – both productions directed by a very young Sam Mendes, before his stint at the Donmar Warehouse. In 1996 came the Almeida's production of *Who's Afraid of Virginia Woolf?*, starring Diana Rigg and David Suchet; then the acclaimed *Tom & Clem*, with Michael Gambon and Alec McCowen; Simon Gray's *Life Support*, starring Alan Bates; and the Royal National Theatre's *Amy's View* by David Hare, starring Judi Dench. The Andrew Lloyd Webber/Jim Steinman musical, *Whistle Down the Wind*, ran for two and a half years, followed by Mahler's *Conversion* by Ronald Harwood, starring Antony Sher. Next a revival of Caryl Churchill's '80s masterpiece *Top Girls* and a run of the Royal National Theatre's acclaimed adult comedy, *Mother Clap's Molly House* – in fact, it's been winners all the way.

the aldwych theatre
aldwych = wc2b

The Almeida

Islington, North London, is the home of three great theatres, all of which are exceptional in their own right, despite being twenty minutes from the West End – Sadler's Wells, the Kings Head pub/fringe theatre and the Almeida.

The Almeida's astonishing rise to become what *The Times* describes as 'one of the world's greatest theatres' has taken place in just over ten years. Like the Donmar Warehouse under Sam Mendes, the Almeida's reputation has been built on the energies and talent of two men: Jonathan Kent and Ian McDiarmid. But they needed the right space to realise their visions, and the Almeida is perfect. It is a unique arena for public performance, with its curved back wall, which enfolds performers and audiences in an embrace, resulting in an acting area as large as the auditorium is small. The fact that the Almeida is not a purpose-built theatre but a 'found' space has given a particular quality to performances there; something of the building's various pasts lingers.

The Almeida Theatre is on Almeida Street, just off Islington's Upper Street. It was first built in 1837 as reading rooms and a lecture hall for Islington's newly formed Scientific and Literary Institution. The Institution used the space for 35 years, until the society wound up and the contents were sold. In 1874 the building was bought by the Wellington Club to be used more frivolously as a music hall. In 1904 it fell into more sober hands and was taken over by the Salvation Army, but in 1956 frivolity struck once more and the building became a factory and showroom for Becks Carnival Novelties. By the 1960s it was nearly derelict, and in 1971 the building was put on the market again. Interest was shown by several theatre companies, and in 1972 Pierre Audi and his associates, realising its potential as an extraordinary performance

'My experience at the Almeida, both on stage and off, has to rank as the finest in my memory.'

— Kevin Spacey

venue, bought and renovated the building. It finally opened as the Almeida Theatre, under the directorship of Audi, in 1980, with a Grade II listing. The venue gained a high reputation almost immediately, particularly for Audi's renowned International Festival of Contemporary Music, staged every summer, which won the overall Prudential Award in 1989.

Actors Ian McDiarmid and Jonathan Kent both worked at the Almeida under Pierre Audi. One day, he simply asked them if they'd ever thought of running a theatre. The rest, as they say, is history. In 1990, Audi left the Almeida to head the Netherlands Opera, handing over to McDiarmid and Kent as joint Artistic Directors. Since then, the Almeida has become one of the world's leading independent producing theatres and a world-class institution. To date, the theatre has won 45 theatre awards, including a Laurence Olivier Award and an *Evening Standard* Award, both for Outstanding Achievement, taken 15 productions to the West End and a similar number to New York, and created the internationally acclaimed Almeida Opera. As well as the Almeida at Islington, the theatre has experimented with all kinds of different performance space, to brilliant effect: the Hackney Empire; the Gainsborough Studios in Shoreditch; a converted coach station in King's Cross (home to the theatre in 2002, while the Islington building was being refurbished); a year-long season at the Albery Theatre and a season at the Playhouse, as well as touring nationally and internationally.

Turning what had been a receiving house into a producing house was quite a challenge. McDiarmid and Kent started more or less from scratch, and with very little capital. 'We've run a National Theatre repertoire on a twentieth of their budget,' says Kent of the early days at the Almeida. 'We initially announced a

the almeida

season we didn't have money for. And when we opened with Howard Barker's *Scenes From an Execution*, I could never quite believe that its star, Glenda Jackson, would turn up.'

But turn up she did, and world-class performers have been turning up at the Almeida ever since, despite Equity-minimum pay-rates and working conditions described as 'little better than primitive'. Kevin Spacey, Hollywood star and award-winning as Hickey in Howard Davies's brilliant production of O'Neill's *The Iceman Cometh* (1998), said at the time, 'My experience at the Almeida, both on stage and off, has to rank as the finest in my memory. The world that the Almeida creates is a safe environment where work can be tried and where one feels that the best is being asked for and given.' In fact, the past ten years' history of the Almeida could be told solely in glowing tributes

Kevin Spacey in *The Iceman Cometh*

from actors and reviewers and the long list of prizes and Broadway/West End transfers.

In the same year that McDiarmid and Kent took over the theatre, *The Rehearsal* transferred to the West End. The next year, *All for Love* was the first production to tour internationally, Almeida Opera was launched, Anthony Burgess's new version of Griboyedov's *Chatsky* was the first production to have a UK tour, and Harold Pinter's *Moonlight* had its world premiere. In 1994 Diana Rigg's *Medea* was the theatre's first Broadway transfer, followed the next year by Ralph Fiennes's *Hamlet*. In 1997, in the theatrical equivalent of taking coals to Newcastle, the Almeida took Chekhov's *Ivanov* to Moscow, tailed by a Channel 4 documentary crew. In 1998 Jonathan Kent's production of *Naked* with Juliet Binoche, together with the world premiere of *The Judas Kiss* by David Hare, starring Liam Neeson, transferred to the Playhouse, marking the first time that the Almeida produced its own work in the West End. In the same year, the seminal and multi-award-winning production of *The Iceman Cometh*, with magnificent performances all round, notably from Kevin Spacey and Tim Piggott-Smith, transferred to the Old Vic. *Mr Puntila and His Man Matti* by Brecht, in a new version by Lee Hall, was the first Almeida production to open at the Edinburgh Festival, and *Phèdre* and *Brittanicus*, Jean Racine in new versions by Ted Hughes and Robert David MacDonald respectively, were staged to great acclaim, with Diana Rigg and Toby Stephens leading the casts. Both Racine plays and *The Iceman Cometh* were staged in New York the following year. The year 2000 saw a production, directed by the author, of Harold Pinter's *Celebration* and the world premiere of *The Room*, with Keith Allen and Lindsay Duncan, and the British premiere of Arthur Miller's *Mr Peters' Connections*, directed by Michael Blakemore. In 2002, Jonathan Kent directed Anna Friel in the title role in Nicholas Wright's new adaptation of Wedekind's *Lulu*, and David Hare's new version of Chekhov's *Platanov*. In the same year, Neil LaBute's world premiere of *The Distance From Here* and Jonathan Miller's *Camera Obscura* both toured the UK.

the almeida

It was also the year that McDiarmid and Kent left the Almeida for the Royal National Theatre. They left behind them an incredibly rich, 12-year episode of modern theatrical history. They have been a formidable team, their productions full of adventure, irony and sensitivity. They were able to say, on the announcement of their departure: 'The British theatre's oldest phrase was always, "That's impossible." No one ever dares to say that at the Almeida. People now say, "There must be a way."'

the almeida theatre
almeida street
islington = n1

The Apollo

The smallest of the six theatres that greet one on strolling up Shaftesbury Avenue from Piccadilly Circus is the intimate Apollo with its French Renaissance facade. Four angels perched on two domed towers look down on 'London's Broadway' from the Apollo, which was opened in February 1901, a month after the death of Queen Victoria, thus making it the first playhouse of the new Edwardian age.

Henry Lowenfeld, the owner and manager, originally wished to call it The Mascot because of the badge of a clan of German gypsies – featuring a flying lizard supported by lions on a silver chain and buckle – that was incorporated into the decor to bring good luck. This can still be seen on the right-hand side of the main entrance. The emblem's propitious qualities did not have much effect on the opening offering, *The Belle Of Bohemia*, a musical farce that flopped. Thereafter, the theatre has been lucky enough to have enjoyed a string of successes over the years.

Designed by Lewen Sharp, it is entirely without the pillars of its period that continue to obscure some seats in a number of older West End theatres. Another innovation was the orchestra pit, which Lowenfeld claimed to be 'a free adaptation of Wagner's construction of the orchestra at Bayreuth', to provide a clearer, unmuffled sound from the instruments. It was hoped that, despite its 796-seat capacity which made it more suitable for straight plays, musical comedies would be the theatre's main attraction. George Edwardes, the manager, did more to popularise the genre than anyone else: *Kitty Grey* ran for 220 performances and *The Girl From Kay's* (1902) almost doubled the previous run. Further musical comedies and operettas followed, including André Messager's *Veronique* (1904) and Edward German's *Tom Jones* (1907), a long way from Fielding's novel, in which Cicely Courtneidge made her London debut.

'One night during the run [of Home*] at the Apollo a man in the stalls suffered a heart attack... The dream remained unbroken. They continued with the play.'*

— Garry O'Connor in *Ralph Richardson, An Actor's Life*

From 1908 to 1912, Harry Gabriel Pélissier's *The Follies* was staged here, exceeding 500 performances a season. Pélissier, first husband of Fay Compton, who made her debut in his show, wrote most of the music, lyrics and satirical sketches as well as performing with his company, dressed mainly in Pierrot costumes against black and white curtains. It laid the foundations for intimate revue. After Pélissier died in 1913, aged 39, *The Follies* was disbanded. Mostly straight plays occupied the Apollo during the Great War, the most popular being Harold Brighouse's often-revived and twice-filmed working-class Lancashire comedy, *Hobson's Choice* (1916), with Norman McKinnel as the patriarchal shoe shop owner.

Between the wars many theatrical treasures were dug out of a mixed bag. Ian Hay's thrice-filmed comedy, *Tilly Of Bloomsbury* (1919), continued for 400 performances, Phyllis Neilson-Terry appeared in J. B. Fagan's *The Wheel* in 1922 and in a revival of *Trilby* in the same year, while Frederick Lonsdale's *The Fake* (1924) gave way to two revues in 1925. These were *By The Way*, starring Jack Hulbert and Cicely Courtneidge, and *Tricks* with 21-year-old dancer Marjorie Robertson (later Anna Neagle). The American 'borscht' circuit hit, *Abie's Irish Rose* (1927), Edgar Wallace's thriller *The Squeaker* (1928), Sean O'Casey's stylised World War I play *The Silver Tassie* (1929), Ivor Novello's *A Symphony In Two Flats* (1929) – not a musical – and John Van Druten's *There's Always Juliet* (1930) with Edna Best, Herbert Marshall and Cyril Raymond, provided the varied fare. In 1933, after Diana Wynyard, returning from Broadway, played Charlotte Brontë in Clemence Dane's *Wild Decembers*, Polish-born actress Elisabeth Bergner, forced to flee the Nazis, made her triumphant London debut in Margaret Kennedy's weepie, *Escape Me Never*.

Marion Lorne starred in a number of plays written for her by her husband Walter Hackett between 1934 and 1937, the best of which were *Hyde Park Corner* (1934), *Espionage* (1935) and *London After Dark* (1937). The last laugh at the theatre for some time came with Ian Hay's two-year run of *The Housemaster*. During the Munich crisis, Robert Sherwood's Pulitzer Prize-winner, *Idiot's Delight* (1938), with Raymond Massey, warned audiences of the coming of World War II, before they retreated into Patrick Hamilton's absorbing Victorian thriller *Gaslight* (1939).

The Apollo continued to shine dauntlessly through the dark years with *The Light Of Heart* (1940) by Emlyn Williams, *Old Acquaintance* (1941) by John Van Druten, and 670 performances of Terence Rattigan's *Flare Path* (1942). In 1944 was the first major revival of *Private Lives*, with John Clements and his wife Kay Hammond in the roles Noël Coward had written for himself and Gertrude Lawrence 14 years earlier; that year, too, the profitable theatre was taken over by Prince Littler. For the next 40 years, the theatre gained a reputation for being the home of long-running light comedies, the sort to attract 'the tired businessman'. These included the lovable, eccentric Margaret Rutherford as Miss Whitchurch in John Dighton's school farce, *The Happiest Days Of Your Life* (1948), Marie Löhr, Sybil Thorndike and Lewis Casson in *Treasure Hunt* (1949), and Hugh Hastings's service comedy *Seagulls Over Sorrento* (1950), which ran for over three years. Revue came back smartly with *For Amusement Only* (1956) featuring Ron Moody, and Peter Cook's *Pieces Of Eight* (1959) with Kenneth Williams and *(above)* Two great Grand Old Men of the British theatre – Sir Ralph Richardson (left) and Sir John Geilgud – in David Storey's *Home*

(left) Paul Scofield and Howard Rollins triumphed in *I'm Not Rappaport* (1986)

Fenella Fielding. The sequence of 'for amusement only' shows was broken briefly by Christopher Fry's two adaptations from Jean Giraudoux, *Tiger At The Gates* (1955) with Michael Redgrave as Hector, and Vivien Leigh and Claire Bloom in *Duel Of Angels* (1958). In February 1962, Marc Camoletti's sex comedy *Boeing-Boeing* took the theatre over for a record-breaking 2035 performances before flying off to the Duchess in St Martin's Lane.

The theatre was redecorated in 1965, but its repertoire was little renovated. Apart from two visits by John Gielgud as the prudish headmaster in Alan Bennett's nostalgic satire *Forty Years On* (1968) and in David Storey's Pinteresque *Home* (1969) with his old friend Ralph Richardson, Eileen Heckart repeating her Broadway triumph in *Butterflies Are Free* (1970) and Albert Finney in *Orphans* (1986), the main fare was bedroom farces with titles such as *The Mating Game* (1972) and *Shut Your Eyes And Think Of England* (1977). Since then, however, there have been some fine productions to redress the balance – the return of John Gielgud in Hugh Whitemore's *The Best of Friends*, Wendy Hiller in *Driving Miss Daisy* (1988), the National Theatre's *Mrs Klein* with Francesca Annis and Zoe Wanamaker (1989), Peter O'Toole, James Bolan and Tom Conti (successively) in *Jeffrey Bernard is Unwell* (1990) and Rattigan's *The Deep Blue Sea*, starring Penelope Wilton, from the Almeida. In 1997 came a two-year run for Ben Elton's *Popcorn*, in 2000 the Pulitzer Prize-nominated *Side Man* featuring Jason Priestley, then fine productions of Noël Coward's *Fallen Angels*, *Gondoliers* and *Star Quality* – a term which could well be used to sum up the Apollo's last fifteen years.

the apollo theatre
shaftesbury avenue = wlv

Apollo Victoria

Of all the theatres considered in these pages, the only one built specifically as a 'Picture Palace' is the Apollo Victoria, which opened as the New Victoria Cinema in 1930. By becoming an active theatre in 1981, it reversed a lengthy trend of theatres being transformed into movie houses – the Carlton, Dominion (since reclaimed), Leicester Square, London Pavilion, Prince Charles and Saville all went that way. But the Apollo eschewed its cinematic past with a vengeance when the auditorium was drastically reorganised to fit Andrew Lloyd Webber's hit musical on wheels, *Starlight Express* (1984). The multi-tiered set, ramps extending around the theatre and rock music are a far cry from the golden age of cinema when the Mighty Wurlitzer rose up, its multicoloured lights flashing, before the 'big picture'.

The great decade of British cinema design was the 1930s, that of the USA the 1920s. It was said that the New Victoria was the most architecturally important cinema building to have been erected in Britain. W. Lewis, the architect, provided a modern marble and concrete exterior and an auditorium, with a single long balcony, to seat 2,500 people. In those days full houses at weekends would usually cover costs for the whole week. The carefully wrought Art Deco designs and technically ambitious lighting effects created the impression of a sub-aquatic wonderland. It was decorated with fish, shell and sea flora motifs, and walls of marine colours. The circle, reached by a salmon pink staircase, had the design of an ocean liner with portholes on the doors. Despite some crass redecoration by the Rank Organization in the 1950s, some of the original decor can be seen today. Above the Gents lavatory is a seductively reclining bronze mermaid in a Cleopatra hairdo, and in the foyer a nude female figure is in the process of throwing reels of film about.

'People do not want this sort of thing: they want architecture with marble columns, gilt and mirrors. This won't pay.'
— Sidney Bernstein to the architect

When *Starlight Express* steamed in, special listed building consent was sought to construct the multi-tiered set which largely obscured the original look of the auditorium. The '80s were the heyday of the modern musical, epitomised by Andrew Lloyd Webber's productions, and *Starlight Express* was a shining example of the genre. It was an extravaganza of a musical, using every new theatrical device at its disposal: 1000 seats were lost in order to accommodate the roller-skating ramps that spilled into the auditorium; races took place along these ramps and over a railway bridge while large video screens allowed the audience to watch their progress; and small model trains moved along tracks around the theatre. New lighting was installed and the overhang of the circle painted black. In 1992, a new production of *Starlight Express* was launched, and the foyer and exterior (especially on the Wilton Road frontage) were handsomely improved.

It could be said that *Starlight Express* put the Apollo Victoria 'on the map'. Before that, the super-cinema, built at a cost of a quarter of a million pounds, opposite Victoria Station, had a less than glorious past. As a cinema, after the honeymoon cruise was over, it struggled for many years, interrupted occasionally by the London Festival Ballet, pop concerts and cabarets. Its location and size found it failing to compete with first television, then the smaller cinemas and the video boom. The New Victoria closed down in 1976, emerging five years later under its new name when bought by Apollo Leisure (UK) Ltd.

It opened with a Shirley Bassey recital, followed by the revival of Rodgers and Hammerstein's *The Sound Of Music* (1981) with Petula Clark as the singing novice. Another failed attempt to resurrect a hit musical was *Camelot* (1982) starring Richard

Sholom Aleichem's immortal Jewish milkman, Tevye, was given life by Topol (foreground in red cap) in the 1983 revival of *Fiddler on the Roof*

Harris. Dancer Wayne Sleep showed his range in *Dash*, and the Israeli star Topol returned to play Tevye for the second time in London in a short but successful season of *Fiddler On The Roof* (both 1983), before the Apollo was filled with – in the words of Lloyd Webber and Richard Stilgoe's song – 'A Lotta Locomotion'. *Starlight Express* ran for an amazing 18 years, finally closing in 2002, the same year that *Cats* had its last performance at the New London (after a run of 21 years). The Apollo Victoria followed *Starlight Express* with another big Andrew Lloyd Webber musical, *Bombay Dreams*, for which the theatre was again refurbished, with an enlarged auditorium to seat 2,000 (it had previously seated 1,600). *Bombay Dreams* is a romantic comedy, set in India and based on the wonderful world of Bollywood. Let's hope it follows in the successful tracks of *Starlight Express* ...

the apollo victoria
wilton road = swlv

The Arts

In the 1940s and 1950s, the Arts Theatre was described as 'a pocket National Theatre', with one daring theatrical first after another – the British premiere of Beckett's *Waiting for Godot*, the world premiere of Eugene O'Neill's *The Iceman Cometh* and of Christopher Fry's *The Lady's Not For Burning*, as well as staging Harold Pinter and Joe Orton's first plays. It's had its ups and downs since then, but now, with a bright new frontage and auditorium, this little theatre is going into the twenty-first century with a brave new programme of cutting-edge productions and an enthusiastic new management.

The Arts Theatre, with its simple, unpretentious entrance and small auditorium seating 360, is in the heart of the West End on Great Newport Street, between Leicester Square and St Martin's Lane. It opened on 20 April 1927 as the Arts Theatre Club, to provide 'the amenities of a London Club and a congenial place for those interested in the theatre on both sides of the curtain', with an intimate revue called *Picnic*. The Arts Theatre Club was an 'other' theatre, one of many that opened around this time outside the mainstream West End, to stage unlicensed and experimental plays under club conditions. In this way these brave little theatres eluded the heavy hand of the Lord Chamberlain, who at that time had the power to ban or censor anything he considered inappropriate. Along with other experimental 'try-out' theatres, such as the Gate, the Players', Q Theatre and Embassy at Swiss Cottage, the Arts Theatre Club was able to play host to producing groups like the Stage Society, the new Three Hundred Club and later the London International Theatre, as well as actor-based organisations such as the Repertory Players and the Play Actors, in order to stage theatre that would be impossible on the conventional West End stage, being too risky commercially or in content. These 'other theatres' became very

'It is good to have the Arts Theatre, where Beckett's tramps first waited for Godot, back in business.'

— The *Guardian* on the re-opening of the theatre in 2000

useful as try-out spaces, and as springboards to West End runs. The Arts and the Players' Theatre were particularly important, as their locations in the West End gave them a bit more of a toehold geographically.

The Arts' first important production was staged a year after it opened. *Young Woodley*, by John Van Druten, was a slight but charming study of adolescence, first produced in New York in 1925 but unaccountably banned by the censor in England. Produced privately at the Arts by the Three Hundred Club, the play later had a successful run at the Savoy after the ban was removed. Throughout the '20s and '30s a good deal of new plays shown first at the Arts – including Gordon Daviot's *Richard of Bordeaux* (1932) and Norman Ginsbury's *Viceroy Sarah* (1934) – went on to be West End successes. The Arts also played host to progressive foreign artists and companies – La Compagnie des Quinze appeared in 1931, Yvette Guilbert had a season, and Karsavina danced there.

In 1942 the actor Alec Clunes (father of actor Martin) took over as Artistic Director of the Arts Theatre, and with him came a rich new era in the theatre's history. Beginning with a revival of Odet's *Awake and Sing*, his was a tenure rich in stylish revivals and exciting new writing. Clunes was eager to use the Arts Theatre's 'small' status to stage more from the classical repertoire and give leading performers a far wider range of acting opportunities. In this very creative atmosphere, many new young directors and playwrights premiered significant and groundbreaking productions.

Clunes himself produced and directed numerous plays, many of which he also appeared in – taking the title role in *Macbeth* on its hundredth performance, for instance. Productions included revivals of English classics, such as Farquhar's *The Constant Couple*, and new plays, among them the very first performance of *The Lady's Not For Burning* (1948), the play which first brought author Fry into the limelight, and in which Clunes played the part of Thomas Mendip.

However, of the dozen or so such theatres operating in the late 1940s, by 1955 the only notable survivors of the 'try-out' theatres were the Players' and the Arts, and in the early '50s Alec Clunes left the theatre. In 1954 the new management brought in Peter Hall, then only 25, who quickly established his directorial

Billy McElhaney, Michael Moreland, Michael Nardone and John Stahl from the Traverse Theatre/RNT Production of *Gagarin Way* by Gregory Burke reputation with a mix of European and American imports. In 1955, Hall directed the seminal English premiere of an unknown playwright's first play – *Waiting For Godot*, by Samuel Beckett – to a bemused audience (some of whom walked out). Important European plays followed: Anouilh's *The Waltz of the Toreadors* (1956); the world premiere, in 1957, of Genet's *The Balcony*; and a staging of Harold Pinter's first success, *The Caretaker* (1960). In 1956 Hall left the Arts and was invited to the Shakespeare Memorial Theatre in Stratford (soon to become the RSC). Like his predecessor Clunes, Hall had, in an incredibly short amount of time, made theatrical history at the Arts. This noble tradition continued under the artistic direction of another young man, Peter Wood, who directed an Ionesco double-bill and produced the brilliant premiere of *The Iceman Cometh* (1958) and the premiere of Pinter's second play, *The Birthday Party*, in the same year.

But by 1960 the Arts Theatre was struggling financially and lacked a resident artistic director. The theatre still managed to create waves, however – in 1961, when Miss Jeanne Moody appeared naked in a bedroom scene of *Lady Chatterley's Lover*, questions were asked in the House, and the run of the play was extended by several months as a result.

Peter Hall returned to the theatre in 1962 with the fledgling RSC for a major experimental season, introducing the company to works ranging from Thomas Middleton's *Women Beware Women*, David Rudkin's *Afore Night Came* – which transferred to the Aldwych as the RSC's first truly modern success – and Maxim Gorky's *The Lower Depths*, which was later to become one of four plays by the Russian writer to be directed for the RSC by David Jones. Two years later came another important premiere for the Arts, when Joe Orton's first play, *Entertaining Mr Sloane*, was performed here.

From 1966 Caryl Jenner's Unicorn Theatre for Children took over the building for over 30 years, showing matinees for children. There were still some significant adult plays in this time: in 1975 Robert Patrick's *Kennedy's Children* came to the Arts

Theatre from the King's Head, Islington, making it the first Fringe theatre production originating in a public house to transfer to the West End. The play was subsequently performed on Broadway and then toured the US. There was also a double bill by Tom Stoppard, *Dirty Linen* and *New Found Land* (1976), which ran for four years. John Godber's *Bouncers* (1986) and *Teechers* (1988) and the musical *A Slice of Saturday Night* (1989) all did well too. For the following ten years, no adult drama was produced at the theatre.

Then, in 2000, the Arts Theatre was taken up by a consortium of UK and New York producers, who brushed it down and polished it up with a £250,000 refurbishment (including the installation of a brand-new basement restaurant), and reopened it in the same year with a successful new production of *Another Country* by Julian Mitchell, 20 years after it first opened in the West End. This was followed by *Entertaining Mr Sloane* (with Alison Steadman), which won the *Evening Standard's* award for Best Play of the Year – back at the Arts, 36 years on. The Pet Shop Boys and Jonathan Harvey's musical collaboration, *Closer to Heaven,* was a more risky venture, but received good reviews. Then came Eve Ensler's highly acclaimed *Vagina Monologues* and in 2002 the award-winning *Gagarin Way*, a stunning first play by Gregory Burke, which arrived at the Arts in 2002 after two sell-out seasons at the National.

The future is looking bright again for the little theatre with the very important history.

the arts theatre
great newport street = wc2

The Barbican

After emerging from the Barbican underground station, follow the yellow brick line, alongside towering apartment buildings, and you will suddenly come across an artificial lake, fountains and the wonder of a modern arts complex complete with concert hall, art galleries, libraries, cinemas, restaurants, conference halls and theatres. This is Britain's first – and still this country's only – fully integrated arts centre. Until the new Barbican Centre's automatic doors slid open to the public in March 1982, the City, the commercial heart of London that throbs with capitalist activity by day, was a cultural desert by night. Adolf Hitler was indirectly responsible for the creation of this artistic oasis.

Before World War II, Cripplegate, situated north of St Paul's Cathedral and the Bank of England, was a busy area of small streets and warehouses – the home of the rag trade – in the centre of which stood St Giles's Church. In December 1940, the district was bombed unmercifully by the Luftwaffe in an attack that flattened most of the buildings but spared St Giles, which still stands demurely behind the modern centre. The surroundings lay as a neglected bomb site for 12 years before various proposals were put forward for development. Office blocks seemed the inevitable fate of the once lively area until in 1959 Duncan Sandys, the Minister for Housing and Local Development, suggested that 'a genuine residential neighbourhood, incorporating schools, shops, open spaces and other amenities' should be created 'even if this means forgoing a more remunerative return on the land'.

In April 1959, the Corporation of the City of London approved a scheme proposed by architects Chamberlin, Powell and Bon for apartment blocks and an arts centre, including a concert hall and theatre, as the new premises for the Guildhall

'The absence of aisles in the stalls will obviate the horror of actors fooling about in them – a dated practice…that should be forbidden.'

— Victor Gladstone

School of Music and Drama. Three years later it was decided that the Guildhall School 'be planned as a self-contained entity which would not share the use of the theatre or concert hall, so that these two elements would be available for full-time occupation by professional companies'. In 1964 the Royal Shakespeare Company and the London Symphony Orchestra, then sharing the Royal Festival Hall with other orchestras, became involved in the planning of the theatre and concert hall. It was a rare opportunity for the future occupants actually to play a part in the design of their new homes.

Of the two large subsidised theatres, the National company was installed at the Old Vic while waiting for its new building; the RSC was doing its best to function in its rather cramped London quarters at the Aldwych. Peter Hall, then the artistic director, and the stage designer John Bury worked in close contact with the architects. Out of their discussions came the basic fan-shape or 'modified horseshoe' and, as theatre architect Victor Gladstone wrote, 'most dramatically, the entirely novel scheme of shallow balconies, each thrusting forward one over the other; a concept quite unique, as far as I know'. However, it would take 18 years after its inception before the RSC could move in.

There were many construction difficulties to surmount along the way to completion of the vast and daring concept that eventually became the Barbican Centre. The name derives from its location, in proximity to where Roman walls once existed on which were built barbicans or watch towers. Foundations had to be sunk up to 80 feet below ground level without disturbing the foundations of the nearby buildings. Literally crowning it all is the widest unsupported flat roof in Europe.

the barbican

The auditorium of the main theatre, with a total seating capacity of 1,166, consists of raked stalls, and three narrow circles of only two rows each jutting forward one above the other towards the stage – the most distant seat being a mere 65 feet away. There is no permanent orchestra pit, but the first three rows of the stalls can be removed to provide one, and there is provision for a proscenium arch. The interior finish was arrived at after consultation with Trevor Nunn, who became artistic director of the RSC in 1968. He asked that the house lighting 'glitter not dazzle', and for the walls to be darker than the pale yew originally chosen. They were replaced by a sensuous Peruvian walnut. There are no aisles in the stalls and each row leads to its own individual door, held open before the performance and during the intervals by electromagnets. When the house lights dim, all the doors close in unison, creating a theatrical atmosphere even before the stage is lit. As in most modern theatres there is no curtain, but at intervals a huge black stainless-steel fire curtain rises from the floor to meet another descending from the ceiling.

David Troughton and William Houston as Henry IV and Prince Hal in Michael Attenborough's *Henry IV Part I*

In fact, the whole building is a show in itself. One is constantly surprised when wandering around its spacious and comfortable halls – there are often art exhibitions to be seen or musicians to be heard in odd corners. Also worth a visit is the magnificent wood-panelled 2,026-seat concert hall. On a summer's day, one can sit on the Lakeside Terrace, wander in the beautiful glass conservatory, or enjoy a meal in the Cut Above restaurant with its panoramic views of St Paul's and St Giles's Church. All of which gives the lie to those oft-heard derogatory cries of 'airport architecture', although it does have the feel of an 'Arts Hilton'.

In 2002, after a 20-year tenure at the Barbican, the RSC (under the directorship of Adrian Noble) announced that it would be leaving the centre in order to perform in a range of different venues. This new creative phase began in spring 2002 at the Roundhouse in Camden, with three of Shakespeare's late plays – *The Winter's Tale*, *The Tempest* and *Pericles*. The RSC will continue to use the Barbican theatre occasionally, but only as one amongst others. Shortly after announcing this new programme, as well as other changes to the structure of the RSC which will take the company back to being more 'production-led', Adrian Noble left the company. His last task will be to direct Ralph Fiennes in Ibsen's *Brand* in March 2003. But the play's the thing! The RSC's time at the Barbican was very rich. From the opening productions of both parts of *Henry IV* in 1982 to Edward Hall's *Julius Caesar* with Tim Piggott-Smith in 2002, the dust was never allowed to settle on Shakespeare's works. Other memorable evenings which thrust the Barbican into instant theatrical fame were an Edwardian *All's Well That Ends Well* (1982) with Peggy Ashcroft as the Countess, a circus *Comedy Of Errors* (1984), the extraordinarily dextrous crutch-wielding Antony Sher as *Richard III* (1984–1985), Jeremy Irons's poignant *Richard II* (1987), Adrian Noble's *The Plantaganets* (1988), adapted from *Henry VI* and *Richard III*, Kenneth Branagh's brilliant *Hamlet* (1992), directed by Adrian Noble, and Toby Stephens in the lead role in *Coriolanus* (1995), a fresh, contemporary, young take on the play directed by David Sacker. Apart from Shakespeare, there was Judi Dench triumphant as Brecht's Mother Courage, and Derek Jacobi shining as Cyrano de Bergerac, both marathon performances in 1984, and Ibsen's *The Master Builder* in 1989. There was also Trevor Nunn and John Caird's English version of the French musical *Les Misérables* by Alain Boublil and Claude-Michel Schonberg, which turned out to be one of the company's greatest successes, transferring for a long run at London's Palace Theatre and on Broadway. Another hit that started small and moved to the West End and Broadway was Christopher Hampton's skilful adaptation of Laclos's *Les Liaisons Dangereuses* (1986). The latter was originally given at The Pit, the RSC's intimate (200 seats) and flexible studio theatre situated under the main auditorium.

The RSC will be sorely missed, but the Barbican has already established an exciting theatrical reputation of its own. Since 1998, for six months each year, the theatre is home to the Bite season (Barbican International Theatre Event) – which offers a unique and very important space on the London stage for international performance, dance and drama. Bite has hosted companies such as the world-famous Comédie Française, the Steppenwolf Theater Company from Chicago and the Maly Drama Theatre of St Petersburg, as well as the Barbican's first performance by the Royal Ballet and the Beckett Festival from Dublin's Gate Theatre. Productions from as far away as Japan, South Africa, India and Israel have been staged, and there have been some important premieres – amongst them Peter Hall's *Tantalus*.

the barbican theatre
barbican = ec2

The Cambridge

O n a corner where seven streets meet to form what is known as Seven Dials stands the Cambridge Theatre, which has been at the crossroads many times in its 72-year existence. It was the second of six theatres built in London in 1930, each claiming to be more modern than the last. The others were the Prince Edward, the Phoenix, the Whitehall, the Adelphi and the Leicester Square (now a cinema). The claim to modernity of the Cambridge (designed by the firm of Wimperis, Simpson and Guthrie) was its use of concrete and steel, its clean lines, lively gold and silver decor by Serge Chermayeff (much of which was painted over in red in 1950) and its concealed lighting (replaced by gilt candelabras and chandeliers in 1950). The complete overhaul of the theatre by the Stoll Moss group and designer Carl Toms in 1987 resulted in a larger stage, a reconstitution of much of the earlier ambience and a thorough cleaning, leaving the stone facade and interior gleaming. At the entrance, the 1930 mural of nude chorus girls has been retained.

Anton Dolin and Dora Vadimova were among the clothed dancers in Charlot's *Masquerade*, the opening production, which also featured Beatrice Lillie, Florence Desmond and Henry Kendall. France was well represented in the first years by seasons of Sacha Guitry (1932) and the Comédie Française (1934), but the English contingent failed to make a go of the theatre, and it became a venue for trade film shows in the late 1930s. The war years brought it back into circulation with Edith Evans, Robert Donat and Isabel Jeans in Shaw's *Heartbreak House* (1943) and Johann Strauss's operetta *A Night In Venice* (1944). In 1946, Jan Pomeroy founded the New London Opera Company, which made the Cambridge its home for two years before moving to Sadler's Wells. Opera and ballet seemed particularly suitable for the large house of 1,275 seats. Menotti's opera *The Consul* had its

'The Cambridge Theatre...originally decorated with amusing Jazz Age Motifs by Serge Chermayeff, is now covered in dull ox–blood paint.'
— Simon Tidworth, *Theatres,* 1973

British premiere here with a mainly American cast, and Peter Daubeny presented seasons of foreign dance companies between 1951 and 1952. Previously, there were two popular revues, *Sauce Tartare* (1949) and *Sauce Piquante* (1950), the latter having a 21-year-old unknown named Audrey Hepburn in the chorus.

Straight plays returned to the Cambridge in 1952 with *Affairs Of State,* starring Joyce Redman, Coral Browne, Hugh Williams, Basil Radford and Wilfrid Hyde-White, running for 18 months. An even longer run was clocked up by William Douglas Home's *The Reluctant Debutante* (1955), a typically pre-'kitchen sink' drawing room comedy. In 1960, ripples of the New Wave were felt at the Cambridge with John Mortimer's first full-length play, *The Wrong Side Of The Park*, with Margaret Leighton and Robert Stephens; and in the same year 24-year-old Albert Finney starred in Keith Waterhouse and Willis Hall's *Billy Liar*. Other successes of the period were Margaret Lockwood in *Signpost To Murder* (1962); Tommy Steele as Kipps in the British musical *Half A Sixpence* (1963), which earned considerably more than the title;

Ingrid Bergman and Michael Redgrave in *A Month In The Country* (1965)

and Bruce Forsyth playing seven roles in the American musical *Little Me* (1964).

In September 1965, Ingrid Bergman, Michael Redgrave and Emlyn Williams triumphed in Turgenev's *A Month In The Country*, the Redgrave production that had opened the new

Maggie Smith starred in *Hedda Gabler* (1970) in a revelatory production by Ingmar Bergman

Yvonne Arnaud Theatre in Guildford a few months earlier. But the prestige this generated did not sustain the theatre for too long, and a number of flops forced it to become a cinema for six months from September 1967. Then, in 1968, tenor John Hanson rode to the rescue as the Red Shadow in *The Desert Song*, and as the romantic young royal in *The Student Prince*, old-fashioned productions of old-time Sigmund Romberg operettas, which found an audience.

A very different audience converged on the Cambridge in 1970 for the National Theatre Company season, the highlights of which were Maggie Smith in Ingmar Bergman's production of *Hedda Gabler* and Laurence Olivier's Shylock in Jonathan Miller's nineteenth-century updating of *The Merchant Of Venice*. Quality was maintained in 1971, which saw contrasting Hamlets from Alan Bates and Ian McKellen, the return of Ingrid Bergman in Shaw's *Captain Brassbound's Conversion* and Ralph

Richardson and Jill Bennett in John Osborne's *West Of Suez*. But a number of duds and transfers had the Cambridge floundering again until two archetypal British farces – *Two And Two Make Sex* (1973) and *A Bit Between The Teeth* (1974) – brought business back. The '80s offered a variety of entertainment, from Joan Collins in *The Last of Mrs Cheyney* to a brilliant Peter O'Toole in Shaw's *Man and Superman* (1983). Since reopening after refurbishment in 1987 with Lulu and George Cole in *Peter Pan – The Musical*, the theatre has chosen musical entertainment as its mainstay. In 1988 the New D'Oyly Carte Company was launched at the Cambridge, with glorious productions of *Iolanthe* and *The Yeoman of the Guard*. Then came Bob Carlton's Olivier Award-winning *Return to the Forbidden Planet*, with its three-year run. This was followed by the first stage production of *Fame – The Musical* (1995); *Grease*, for three years; the world premiere of Ben Elton and Lloyd Webber's *The Beautiful Game* (2000); and in 2001 *Fame – The Musical* once again, returning to the West End theatre where it first opened.

**the cambridge theatre
earlham street = wc2h**

The Coliseum

O ne of the most eye-catching landmarks of the West End is the spinning globe of the Coliseum, dominating St Martin's Lane. The colourful sphere tops off an enormous square tower with solid columns, bold carved figures at each end representing Art, Music, Science and Literature, and a pride of sculptured lions. Today the globe, lit from within to give the impression of movement, is the beckoning sign for opera lovers – London's largest theatre (with a current seating capacity of 2,358) has been the home of the prestigious and enterprising English National Opera Company since 1974.

This grandiose Edwardian edifice was the dreamchild of the great theatre manager Oswald Stoll. An Australian of Irish parentage, he found himself, on the death of his stepfather, running the family's music hall in Liverpool at the tender age of 14. Stoll was soon controlling an extensive chain of halls throughout the country. In Victorian times the music hall, whose origin lay in the entertainments at taverns in the eighteenth century, had a bawdy and boisterous reputation. Stoll planned to build a theatre where a man could bring his family without fear of shocking them.

The imposing playhouse with its Italian Renaissance-style facade, designed by the renowned Frank Matcham, leading theatre architect of the day, opened its doors on 24 December, 1904. Crowds flocked out of curiosity to see the palace of pleasures as much as from any desire to attend the four-shows-a-day variety programme. The latter contained such delights as The American Sisters Meredith singing 'Oowana', an Indian love song, Madge Lessing accompanied by a troop of Highland soldiers with pipe band, and a Derby finale in which real horses were ridden on the huge revolving stage, the first such in Great Britain.

'In between the matinee and evening performance, the Coliseum stage appeared vaster and more mysterious, like an empty, echoing cathedral smelling faintly of dust.'
— Noël Coward

In the first week, 67,000 people came to marvel at the mosaic and marble walls and ceilings, elaborate Grand Salon and Grand Staircase, and 'the only theatre in Europe which provides lifts to take the audience to the upper parts of the building. . . primarily for elevation to the handsome Terrace Tea Room', as an early programme sheet proclaimed. (The roof garden was pulled down in 1951.) But the novelty of the structure soon wore off, and the shows were not sufficiently good to continue drawing the crowds. By expunging the more ribald elements and substituting decorous spectacles, Stoll lost the working and lower middle-class

Opera-goers fill the beautiful Matcham-designed auditorium

audiences that were the mainstay of music hall. 'Coarseness and vulgarity are not allowed at the Coliseum,' read an unenticing advertisement.

In an attempt to revitalise the box-office, Stoll presented *The Revue* in 1906, 'invented and produced' by Victor de Cottens of the Folies Bergères in Paris. The commère (female compère) was 20-year-old Billie Burke, who was to marry Florenz Ziegfeld, the master of the American revue, seven years later. Despite its success, the 300-cast show cost Stoll a fortune to mount, and he was forced to close the theatre in June of the same year. It remained dark until December 1907, when the globe lit up the London skyline again. Stoll returned, having formed a new syndicate, cut the four shows a day by half and tempted in the great names of the music hall who had previously been put off by the theatre's earlier slogan of *Pro Bono Publico* (For the Public Good). From 1909 to 1931 the 2,358-seat auditorium was packed to the rafters by crowds enjoying such legendary entertainers as Harry Lauder, Little Tich, Harry Tate, Albert Chevalier, Nellie Wallace and male impersonator Vesta Tilley. These acts were interspersed with performing animals, jugglers, acrobats and curiosities like Fräulein Brunnhilde, 'the tallest pianist in the world' at seven feet eleven. Who would have predicted that Wagner's Brunnhilde would appear on the same stage one day?

When Stoll invited Sergei Diaghilev to bring his Russian Ballet to the Coliseum after their sensational visit to Paris in 1909, the famed impresario said, 'The Russian Ballet sandwiched between performing dogs and a fat lady playing a silver-plated trombone! Never! Never!' However, his troupe did leap the boards of the Coliseum in 1917 after their brilliant pre-war period. In fact, it was not unusual for stars of the 'legitimate' theatre to appear between 'performing dogs and a fat lady'. Ellen Terry played Portia in the trial scene from *The Merchant Of Venice* in 1918, Lillie Langtry paid two glowing visits in 1917 and 1918, and Sarah Bernhardt appeared each year between 1910 and 1913. Her last visit in 1916 was after the amputation of her leg forced her to perform sitting down. Opera was first staged here in 1912 when the Beecham Opera Company presented *Hansel And Gretel*, but was not to return for some years.

Despite a range of dazzling artists, including Jack Buchanan, Gertrude Lawrence, Beatrice Lillie, Jack Hulbert, Cicely Courtneidge and Ronald Colman from England and Marie Dressier, Helen Morgan, W. C. Fields and the Marx Brothers from the USA, by 1931 variety was no longer the spice of live theatre. It was time for the Coliseum to change direction. In April, a new policy was instituted with the opening of *White Horse Inn*. The size of the auditorium, never kind to straight theatre, proved ideal for musical comedy, which held centre stage in the theatre's history for the next three decades. *White Horse Inn*, which ran for 651 performances, was followed by *Casanova* in the same lavish vein. Other large-scale productions included a 'real ice' spectacle called *St Moritz* in 1937.

During World War II the theatre remained open, bringing cheer to besieged Londoners. It was twice hit by incendiary bombs, but only minor damage was done. In January 1942, Sir Oswald Stoll (he had been knighted in 1919) died aged 76. The theatre was bought by Prince Littler who revived *White Horse Inn*, *Me And My Girl*, *Maid Of The Mountains*, *The Belle Of New York* and *The Merry Widow*. But on 7 June, 1947 *Annie Get Your Gun* proved that anything the West End could do in musical comedy, Broadway could do better. The energetic, witty and tuneful Irving Berlin show burst onto the London stage, running for three years, the longest in this theatre's history. *Kiss Me Kate* (1951), *Call Me Madam* (1952), *Guys And Dolls* (1953), *Can Can* (1954), *The Pyjama Game* (1955), *Damn Yankees*, *Bells Are Ringing* (both 1957) and *The Most Happy Fella* (1960) proved that the Broadway musical was here to stay. Sadly, because two of the greatest Broadway musicals, *My Fair Lady* and *West Side Story*, with better casts, were occupying Drury Lane and Her Majesty's respectively, the Coliseum found it increasingly difficult to compete. In 1961, MGM, sniffing around for a large theatre in which to instal Cinerama equipment, took a long lease on the building, turning it into a cinema. As the widest of wide screen processes needed three massive projectors to be placed at the back of the stalls, extensive alterations were made to the auditorium. It remained a none-too-successful enterprise until MGM decided not to renew the lease in 1967.

Meanwhile, Sadler's Wells Opera was beginning to find its theatre in Islington too small and too far from the West End. Stephen Arlen, managing director of the company, entered into negotiations with Prince Littler and took a ten-year lease. A great deal had to be done to repair the damage caused by the Cinerama misadventure in order to achieve the warm, welcoming, comfortable opera house, with superb acoustics, that we know today. In 1992 the building was purchased by the Department of Heritage for the company, renamed the English National Opera in 1974. This vastly successful venture has introduced a whole new generation to opera in less elitist and stuffy confines than the Royal Opera House – and at cheaper prices. In each ten-month season, more than 20 works are given, and often four different operas can be seen in a week. An ambitious and confident programme of restoration is now being undertaken, over a four-year period, to bring the Coliseum back to its former glory in time for its centenary in 2004. The Arts Team at RHWL (architects of the new Sadler's Wells building, 1998) plan to recreate many of the original features, including the splendid facade and the glass roof which covered the Terrace Bar.

ENO's policy has been, from the opening production of *Don Giovanni* on 21 August, 1968, to perform a wide range of operas,

including new works, all in English. Each year, the Company aims to stage a world premiere or a British stage premiere, and it also nurtures young British talent through the Eno Jerwood Young Singers programme. Apart from their achievements in the classics of the operatic repertoire, such as a complete and impressive Ring cycle, they have tackled many less familiar operas of merit. Prokofiev's *The Gambler* and his spectacular *War And Peace*, Tchaikovsky's *Mazeppa*, Martinu's *Julietta*, Wagner's *Rienzi* and Spontini's *La Vestale* are examples of the latter. Proving that opera is a living art form, contemporary works have included Ligeti's *Le Grand Macabre*, Philip Glass's *Akhnaten* and Mark-Anthony Turnage's award-winning *The Tassie*, one of the most successful new operas of recent times, while a new slant is given to more traditional operas as in Jonathan Miller's brilliant New York Mafia *Rigoletto*, his production of *The Mikado* with an English 1920s setting – first performed in 1986 and revived to brilliant effect in 2001 and his award-winning *Carmen* (1996). All performed in the inspirational setting of the Coliseum, of which Lord Harwood, the ENO's first managing director, said '[it] combines the sometimes opposing attributes of style and unpretentiousness, beauty and the sort of familiarity which quickly makes one feel at home.'

the coliseum
st martin's lane = wc2n

(facing page) The famous opera singer Willard White performing at the Coliseum

The Comedy

'**P**anton Street in the Haymarket has for very many years past enjoyed a dubious reputation owing to the numerous "night-houses" once existing in this vicinity. Recent improvements in this and the adjacent thoroughfares have now removed altogether the doubtful resorts of the roisterers of other days, and the demolition of a large pile of buildings on the south side has enabled a spacious theatre to be constructed which seems likely to take a prominent place among the West End establishments devoted to public amusement.' So wrote the *Daily Telegraph* on 14 October, 1881 on the opening of the Comedy Theatre.

Today, there are still plenty of 'roisterers' and 'doubtful resorts' in nearby Soho, but the Comedy is coyly tucked away from the hurly-burly in a quiet side street. On visiting it, one enters the past. The pedimented classical facade, with its Greek 'Lady with the Lamp' sculpture above the entrance, is virtually the same as when it was conceived by Thomas Verity over a century ago, but for the addition of a modern wrought-iron canopy. Built in a record time of six months, the building also has one of the few extant pre-1890 auditoria in London, despite some alterations along the way. This has its disadvantages: pillars hold up the Dress Circle, obscuring the view from certain seats, and the stage is the smallest of any theatre of comparable size in London. The dominant colour of the French Renaissance decor – from the exquisite ceiling to the wallpaper – is gold. Many of its productions, too, have been pure gold, with a fair portion of dross in between.

The Comedy's first manager, Alexander Henderson, intended the venue to be a house of comic opera to rival Gilbert and Sullivan's Savoy Theatre, which had opened only five days earlier. The premiere production was an English version of Edmond

'The architect Sir John Summerson wrote that the Comedy Theatre was the best and most originally preserved of London theatres, and I must say that I agree with him.'
— Sir Ralph Richardson

Audran's French operetta, *The Mascotte*. Similar works followed, some of them featuring Violet Melnotte (born Rosenberg in Birmingham), who took over the Comedy for a while before moving into the Trafalgar Square Theatre (later the Duke Of York's) in 1892. In 1887, Herbert Beerbohm Tree had his first big success as actor-manager with *The Red Lamp*, which he later transferred to the Haymarket when he took over the management there. Another legend of the age, Sarah Bernhardt, appeared in Sardou's *Tosca* and *Fédora*, roles written with her in mind.

In the last decade of the century, managers and plays came and went until Lewis Wailer, one of the outstanding romantic actors of the day, rescued the theatre from the doldrums by presenting Booth Tarkington's *Monsieur Beaucaire* (1902), with himself in the title role, for 430 performances. The equally romantic 23-year-old John Barrymore made his first London appearance in *The Dictator* (1905), while the following year E. W. Hornung's *Raffles*, coincidentally played by Barrymore in a 1917 silent film, started the Edwardian craze for 'crook' plays. The glamorous Gerald du Maurier (father of novelist Daphne) portrayed the dapper gentleman burglar, altering tradition by turning the villain into the hero. Somerset Maugham, the darling of the West End, had three plays performed at the Comedy between 1908 and 1911. They starred Marie Tempest (who made her debut here in *Boccaccio* [1895]) in *Mrs Dot* and *Penelope*, and Marie Löhr in *Smith*.

During World War I, Laurette Taylor recreated her New York triumph here in her husband John Hartley Manners's play *Peg O'*

the comedy

The finely detailed auditorium ceiling

My Heart (1914) for 710 performances. Six revues then occupied
the stage until the end of the war, produced by the kings of revue,
Albert de Courville, Charles B. Cochran and André Charlot. It was
in Charlot's *Tails Up* (1918), starring Jack Buchanan, that Noël
Coward's name first appeared in the West End as a lyric writer.
Revues continued to be a significant part of the Comedy's
programmes for the next few decades. Douglas Byng was in *How
D'You Do?* (1933) and *Hi Diddle-Diddle* (1934), the two
Hermiones (Gingold and Baddeley) in *Rise Above It* (1941) and
Gingold in *Slings And Arrows* (1948); there was the Flanders and
Swann *Fresh Airs* (1956), 23-year-old Maggie Smith's West End

73

debut in *Share My Lettuce* (1957) and *The Premise* (1962), an American revue which relied on improvisation.

The Comedy certainly lived up to its name, and dramas were not the theatre's strong point. Then, in 1956, the theatre played a vital part in helping to undermine the archaic censorship laws of Britain. Until 1968, the unlamented Lord Chamberlain had the right to ban plays if the subject or language was deemed unsuitable. Since it was forbidden to portray homosexuality (or even the suggestion of it), a group of West End managers got together to form the New Watergate Club at the Comedy where they could present banned plays under club conditions. By paying a five-shilling subscription, audiences were able to see three American plays refused a licence: Arthur Miller's *A View From The Bridge* (1956); Robert Anderson's *Tea And Sympathy* (1957); and Tennessee Williams's *Cat On A Hot Tin Roof* (1958). Some time later the Lord Chamberlain's office admitted that homosexuality 'is now so widely debated, written about and talked over that its complete exclusion from the stage can no longer be regarded as justifiable'. The club, therefore, became unnecessary.

The newly gained concession allowed Peter Shaffer's first play, *Five Finger Exercise*, with its subtle homosexual thread, to enjoy a two-year commercial run from 1958. The passing of both time and the Lord Chamberlain brought male and female nudity to the same theatre in the prison drama *Fortune And Men's Eyes* and in Nell Dunn's long-running *Steaming* (1980), set in a women's Turkish bath. Other controversial productions included Peter Nichols's *A Day In The Death Of Joe Egg* (1967) – which enjoyed a hugely successful revival in 2002, with Eddie Izzard and Prunella Scales – Christopher Hampton's *Savages* (1973), starring Paul Scofield, and David Hare's *Knuckle* (1974) with Edward Fox.

The Comedy has been an important venue for Harold Pinter's works – *The Caretaker, No Man's Land, Moonlight, The Hothouse* and *The Homecoming* have all been presented in recent years. In the 1990s Alan Bennett appeared with Patricia Routledge in his

Anthony Andrews and Francesca Annis in Ibsen's *Ghosts* (2001)

Talking Heads, and later so did Maggie Smith. There followed a series of star performances: the Donmar Warehouse's *The Glass Menagerie* with Zoe Wanamaker; Edward Fox and Claire Higgins in *A Letter of Resignation*; Ewan McGregor in *Little Malcolm and His Struggle Against the Eunuchs*; Peter Nichol's *Passion Play*; Simon Callow in *The Mystery of Charles Dickens*; Francesca Annis in Ibsen's *Ghosts*; and the brilliant production of Pinter's *The Caretaker* (2000) directed by Patrick Marber and starring Michael Gambon. The Comedy's brave and continuing tradition of staging daring, quality drama has ensured that this theatre enters its third century in great style.

the comedy theatre
panton street = w1y

The Criterion

Opposite the statue of Eros at Piccadilly Circus stands a Second Empire-style facade, in which a tiny entrance leads into one of London's most entrancing and historically important theatres. Apart from the vestibule (where hangs a full-length portrait of actress-manager Mary Moore), the entire theatre, as conceived by Thomas Verity, is underground. To reach the almost perfectly preserved mid-Victorian auditorium, one descends a flight of stairs between striking tiled walls painted with classical figures, muses and the names of famous composers. The mini-maze of corridors, large mirrors and ceilings adorned with cherubs on clouds gives audiences a feeling of space to counteract any claustrophobia. Indeed, for ten years after the opening in 1874 – until the building was enlarged and properly ventilated – it was necessary to pump air into the theatre to prevent the public from suffocating.

It is easy to imagine, when seated and waiting for the curtain to rise, lovely bejewelled ladies and their Victorian toff escorts surrounded by the pink and aubergine decor of the stalls or leaning forward on the curved-front boxes. In the Royal Box, still used for royalty and VIPs, one might have spotted the Prince of Wales applauding his mistress, Lillie Langtry, appearing opposite Charles Wyndham in *The Fringe Of Society* (1892). If they could be brought back to life, they would still recognise the house, but might be a trifle disturbed by the plays. After all, there were gasps of horror when Kate Rorke, playing a rebellious girl in *Fourteen Days*, lit up a cigarette.

What audiences would have seen and enjoyed in 1877 was a French farce, adapted by James Albery, called *Pink Dominoes*. In the cast was Charles Wyndham, who took over the theatre in 1879 and whose initials are seen in decorative monograms on the walls. Enter Albery's wife, Mary Moore (billed as Miss M.

'The Criterion Theatre, transformed from a stuffy band–box to a convenient, handsome and well–ventilated house...'

- Dramatic Notes, 1884

Mortimer), making her first appearance here in *The Candidate* (1884). A woman of great beauty and intelligence, she soon became Wyndham's leading lady (they married in 1916) with such roles as Lady Amaranthe in John O'Keefe's *Wild Oats* and Ada Ingot in Tom Robertson's *David Garrick* (both 1886). A year later the future King Edward VII invited them to give a command performance of the latter play at Sandringham.

Although the theatre gained a reputation for light comedy, it was Arthur Henry Jones's dramas of social criticism that attracted attention in the last years of the century, notably *The Bauble Shop* (1893), *The Case Of Rebellious Susan* (1894) and *The Liars* (1897). In 1899, Wyndham left to go to the theatre that bears his name. He returned eight years later with a production of Hubert Henry Davies's *The Mollusc*, in which Mary Moore's performance was a tour de force, although she barely stirred from a settee throughout. From 1915 to 1919 ran a farce entitled *A Little Bit Of Fluff*, of which Lynton Hudson in *The English Stage, 1850–1950* commented that although 'its illusory suggestion of naughtiness – and one solitary and by modern standards entirely decorous glimpse of a silk-clad shapely leg – dominated the war-time theatre, it would be unfair to blame the innocents who enjoyed this light-hearted fare for a deterioration in public taste'. It ran for an amazing 1,241 performances – a figure which, though impressive, pales into insignificance when compared to the theatre's six-year run of *Run for Your Wife* (1983–89) and the over 2,500 performances of the Reduced Shakespeare Company's *The Complete Works of Shakespeare (abridged)*.

Cyril Maude in *Lord Richard In The Pantry* (1919), Charles Hawtrey in *Ambrose Applejohn's Adventure* (1921), Sybil

Thorndike in *Advertising April* (1923) and Marie Tempest in five plays between 1926 to 1929 enlivened the rather scanty comedies, and brought in the public. At the death of Mary Moore in 1931, her son Bronson Albery took over the running of the theatre. He presented John Gielgud in *Musical Chairs* (1932), by the young and talented Ronald MacKenzie who was killed in a car crash after the play had been running a year. In 1936, 24-year-old Terence Rattigan's *French Without Tears* started its three-year run, making its author rich and famous. Lesley Storm's comedy *Tony Draws A Horse* was the last pre-war success.

During World War II, the Criterion proved to be a perfect underground shelter for a BBC studio to beam light entertainment to the nation. It was from here that the wartime radio hit *ITMA* (*It's That Man Again*) was broadcast. As soon as peace was declared, the theatre opened its doors for business again with Edith Evans a delightful Mrs Malaprop in *The Rivals* (1945). For the next ten years the Criterion offered a number of profitable comedies including *The Guinea* Pig (1946), in which the expression 'kick up the arse' caused audiences to fall about; Gladys Cooper varying her lines from night to night in Peter Ustinov's *The Indifferent Shepherd* (1948) and Rattigan's *Who Is Sylvia?* (1950). A very different kind of play, Samuel Beckett's modern classic, *Waiting For Godot* (1955), surprised everybody by running a year. At one particular performance, when an old bearded gentleman made his way belatedly to his seat, a cry from the gallery went up that Godot had arrived at last. Jean Anouilh's *The Waltz Of The Toreadors* (1956) followed for a long run. Both these plays were directed by 25-year-old Peter Hall, who had transferred them from the Arts Theatre Club. Other 'avant garde' productions included *Three* (1961), a triple bill of plays by Harold Pinter, John Mortimer and N. F. Simpson, and James Saunders's *Next Time I'll Sing To You* (1962) with an unknown Michael Caine in the cast. More conventional hits were the marital comedies, *The Irregular Verb To Love* (1961) with Joan Greenwood, *A Severed Head* (1963), adapted by J. B. Priestley and Iris Murdoch from the latter's novel, and Alan Ayckbourn's *Absurd Person Singular* (1973). In between, Simon Gray's acerbic *Butley* (1971), starring Alan Bates, kept the theatre full. Among the few flops was a revue called *Hulla Baloo* (1972), set in a 'loo', with contributions from two young men named Andrew Lloyd Webber and Tim Rice – perhaps not something they would now wish to remember!

In the few years before the farce *Run For Your Wife!* began its incredible run, quality productions included Ibsen's *A Doll's House* (1973), with Claire Bloom repeating her Broadway triumph, *Bent* (1978) and Dario Fo's *Can't Pay, Won't Pay* (1981). Through the early 1990s productions ranged from *The Flying Karamazov Brothers* to *Misery*, and since 1996 the wacky and improvisational Reduced Shakespeare Company have made the Criterion their London home, providing delighted audiences with all of Shakespeare's 37 plays in 97 minutes.

the criterion

The Reduced Shakespeare Company's comic abridged version of the complete works of Shakespeare has been nominated for the Laurence Olivier Audience Award for the Most Popular Show

The Criterion has weathered many storms in recent times. Its subterranean location makes it susceptible to damp – £45,000 was spent on improvements in 1972. Then in 1985 the theatre suffered extensive flood damage which ruined some of its unique tiles. In the '70s and early '80s the Criterion was under very real threat of closure when the site on which it stands was proposed for redevelopment. Happily, high-profile demonstrations, with campaigners such as John Gielgud, Edward Woodward and Diana Rigg, assured its future. After three years' careful renovation work, the block that stands today was rebuilt around the theatre, preserving it perfectly. And so the Criterion survives and flourishes, continuing to give pleasure to playgoers.

the criterion theatre
piccadilly circus = wlv

The Dominion

'In the opinion of the Board, the most popular form of entertainment today consists of musical productions, which must be staged on so lavish a scale and be of such magnificence that a theatre with a very large seating capacity is required to render the production commercially successful, and there is undoubtedly a large public demand for big spectacular musical productions at popular prices with high class artistes.' This extract from a report on the building of 'A New Super-Theatre in the Centre of London' was issued in February 1928, just before construction began on the 2,800-seat Dominion Theatre, which stands on the busy intersection of Tottenham Court Road and Oxford Street. Despite alterations to the auditorium, the Dominion is still one of the largest theatres in the West End, with a seating capacity of 2,182.

For many years, the Dominion was used as a cinema, or temporary home for short seasons of opera, dance and rock until it re-entered the mainstream of West End theatres with its production of Dave Clark's space-age musical *Time* (1986). But it opened first as a theatre in October 1929 with an American musical comedy on golf by De Sylva, Brown and Henderson called *Follow Through* (*Follow Thru* on Broadway) starring Elsie Randolph, Ivy Tresmand and Leslie Henson. Neither this, nor a follow-up musical, *Silver Wings*, made much impression. So, in 1930, it provided a venue for Lon Chaney's *The Phantom Of The Opera* with dialogue and some new footage added to the 1925 silent movie. The next year, Charlie Chaplin appeared on stage to make a 'thank you' speech after the first showing of his *City Lights*, in the presence of George V. The screen was folded up in 1932 to allow Richard Tauber to move his ample form, from which emanated his dulcet tenor tones, in a revival of Franz Lehar's *The Land Of Smiles*. A number of film stars, including Maurice

the great theatres of london

*'At first sight the interior of the house gives one the
impression it was really meant for a super cinema.'*
— *The Stage*, 1929

Chevalier, Jeanette MacDonald, Sophie Tucker and Judy Garland,
made appearances in variety seasons.

In 1958, Todd-AO equipment was installed for the showing
of the movie musical *South Pacific* which ran four years, a record
surpassed by *The Sound Of Music*, which resounded through the
Dominion from 1965 to 1973. For over a decade thereafter,
blockbuster films shared the auditorium with the Welsh National
Opera, the Georgian dancers from the USSR, Chinese acrobats
and pop groups. In a way, this was reminiscent of the days when
there was a fun fair and a huge tent, where variety shows were
given, on the empty site on which the Dominion was built. Long
before, as far back as the twelfth century, the St Giles Leper
Hospital had stood on the spot. Some six centuries later, a
brewery was built here containing a 22-foot vat of porter ale. In
October 1814, the vat burst, pouring its contents into the streets
and literally drowning eight people in alcohol.

The site was chosen for the theatre 'owing to its central
position, [and] its proximity to the reconstructed Tube station'.
Designed by W. and T. R. Milburn, its broad Portland stone
facade is now obscured by a giant sign announcing the
entertainment within. The interior with its large mirrored lobby,
twin stairways and wide corridors is very much on the lines of
'the modern picture palaces' built in the 1930s. In order to
accommodate *Time*, one of the most expensive stage musicals of
its day, a few alterations had to be made to the theatre's interior.

Since then, the Dominion has been home to several major
musicals – *Grease* (1993), *Scrooge* (1996), Disney's *Beauty and the
Beast* (1997) and *Notre-Dame de Paris* (2000). The production of
Beauty and the Beast, as well as being a huge hit, was particularly

A scene from the 'space-age' musical, *Time*

notable as it marked Disney's first venture into the West End. And in between these big productions, the Dominion continued its tradition of offering all-round entertainment, with one-off pop shows, operas and other entertainments, ranging from a performance of *Swan Lake* by the celebrated dance company Adventures in Motion Pictures to Michael Ball in concert. And the Dominion still occasionally acts as a cinema – *Return of the Jedi* opened here in 1983, as well as London Film Festival Shows. It's also a regular home to the Royal Variety Performance. And so 1929's 'New Super-Theatre' still entertains and impresses audiences.

the dominion theatre
tottenham court road = wlp

The Donmar
Warehouse

What the *New York Times* has described as 'the current epicenter of theatre glamour in London' is deceptively small and simple. Off a narrow, cobbled street in the middle of London's former fruit and vegetable market, Covent Garden, the Donmar Warehouse comprises a two-level square room with seating around three sides of the acting area for an audience of 250 people. Yet this little theatre is a dazzling hotbed of dynamic creativity, attracting the world's finest theatrical and performing talent. The theatre's reputation has been made in an amazingly short amount of time, and centres on the figure of Artistic Director Sam Mendes.

Back in Victorian times, the building which now houses the Donmar was a vat room and hop warehouse for the local brewery. In the 1920s the space was used as a film studio, then, appropriately for its location, as a banana-ripening warehouse. In 1961, theatre impresario Donald Albery (son of theatre manager Sir Bronson Albery) bought the warehouse and converted it into a private rehearsal studio for the London Festival Ballet, a company he formed with his friend, prima ballerina Margot Fonteyn. The amalgamation of their Christian names, and the previous function of the building, gave the space its current title – the Donmar Warehouse.

From 1977 to 1981, the Royal Shakespeare Company made the Donmar its London home to complement the Stratford venue and to present the company's studio work. Among their noted productions here were the stark Ian McKellen/Judi Dench *Macbeth*, *Piaf* and the first performance of Willy Russell's

*'Powerhouses do not come much smaller, nor much
more powerful, than the Donmar Warehouse.'*
— *Sunday Times*

Educating Rita with Mark Kingston and Julie Walters, which was
followed by a long West End run and a subsequent film
adaptation.

When the RSC left to go to its new home at the Barbican, Ian
Albery (Donald's son) and Nica Burns formed a non-profit
making company called Omega to take the Donmar Warehouse
over. At that point, it was the only theatre of its size which was
able to rely wholly on the box-office for its revenue. It survived
through the brilliant administrative skills of Nica Burns, and
through its fast-growing reputation as a home for Britain's most
innovative touring companies, with residences from Cheek by
Jowl and Hull Truck, amongst others. The Donmar presented a
wide spectrum of entertainment, including *Blues in the Night*,
Fascinating Aida and the Annual Perrier Comedy Awards, further
establishing the theatre as a showcase for cabaret and comedy.

In 1989 the Ambassador Theatre Group acquired the
Donmar, with the intention of redeveloping the theatre, and in
1990, 24-year-old Sam Mendes was invited to take up residency
as Artistic Director, with the challenge of presenting an annual
eight-month season of home-produced work. Like the young
Peter Hall at the Arts Theatre back in the '50s, he rose to the
challenge with incredible confidence and panache. Mendes was
already a well-established West End director, having produced
The Rise and Fall of Little Voice at the Aldwych, and Chekhov's
The Sea and *The Cherry Orchard* with Judi Dench. He asked Caro
Newling – Senior Press Representative at the Royal Shakespeare
Company – to join him as Administrative Director. For the next
two years, and on a shoestring budget, Mendes and Newling
oversaw the redesign of the theatre, retaining the distinctive
characteristics of the former warehouse and the unique thrust

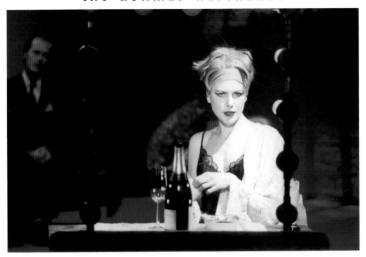

Nicole Kidman in Sam Mendes' production of *The Blue Room* (1998)

stage and adding two bars and significant improvements backstage. In 1992 the theatre reopened as an independent producing house with the triumphant British premiere of Stephen Sondheim's *Assassins*. Its feet have hardly touched the ground since. In 2002 the Donmar celebrated ten years as a producing house under Mendes's artistic direction with, to date, fifteen Laurence Olivier Awards, seven Tony Awards from their Broadway transfers, four *Evening Standard* Awards, six Critics' Circle Awards, and *The Times* Critics' Award for 'epitomising all that is best and boldest about British cultural life'.

The Donmar Warehouse has attracted exceptional directors to its stage. As well as Sam Mendes's own productions (*The Glass Menagerie*, *The Blue Room* and *Cabaret* to name but three), Associate Director Michael Grandage has directed the triple Olivier Award-winning Stephen Sondheim musical *Merrily We Roll Along* (2000), swiftly followed by a brilliant revival of *Passion Play* by Peter Nichols, *Good*, with Charles Dance, and the wartime musical comedy *Privates on Parade* (2002). John Crowley, also an Associate Director, had enormous success with *Juno and the Paycock* (1999) starring Colm Meaney, which transferred to New York, and 2001's *Tales From Hollywood*, a revival of Christopher Hampton's play. In 2001 Nicholas Hytner directed Tennessee Williams's rarely seen *Orpheus Descending*, starring Helen Mirren. Phyllida Lloyd directed *The Threepenny Opera* in 1994, and then the premiere of David Mamet's *Boston Marriage*, starring Zoe Wanamaker (2001), which transferred to the West End. The Donmar has also seen the work of directors such as Robin Lefevre, with *Three Days of Rain* (1999), David Leveaux (*Electra*, 1997), Sean Matthias, Matthew Warchus, Katie Mitchell and James Kerr.

As well as revivals, the Donmar is active in commissioning new work for its intimate auditorium. This has involved collaborations with celebrated playwrights such as David Hare and Frank McGuinness, whose adaptations of *The Blue Room* (1998) and *Electra* respectively became the talk of the town, both during their runs at the Donmar and then again on Broadway. Many of the Donmar's productions have gone on to have West End runs, including Noël Coward's *Design for Living* (1994), *The Glass Menagerie* (1996), *Company* (1996) and *Boston Marriage*; and two have also transferred to Broadway: *The Blue Room* and Tom Stoppard's *The Real Thing* (2000).

With such a range of innovative writing and directing talent, it's not surprising that the Donmar attracts such an amazing number of star performers – Zoe Wanamaker with her exceptional performances in *The Glass Menagerie*, *Boston Marriage* and the title role in *Electra*, Nicole Kidman in *The Blue Room*, Gwyneth Paltrow in *Proof*, Stephen Dillane in *The Real Thing*, Adrian Lester and Sheila Gish in *Company*, Colin Firth in *Three Days of Rain*, William H. Macy in *American Buffalo*, Jim Broadbent, Colin Firth, Brenda Blethyn and Rachel Weisz – to name just a few.

In November 2002, after his magnificent productions of *Uncle Vanya* and *Twelfth Night*, Sam Mendes took his last bow as Artistic Director, leaving to pursue an independent film and theatre career (his film *American Beauty* took five Oscars in 2000, including Best Director), and Michael Grandage became the

Roger Allam in *Privates on Parade*, 2001

Donmar's new Artistic Director. Through his persistence, vision, hard work and creative brilliance, Mendes leaves a space transformed from a fringe venue into what the *Evening Standard* describes as 'a brilliantly innovative, independent producing theatre, exemplifying the very best that London has to offer'. Now the world eagerly awaits the fruits of the Donmar Warehouse's new theatrical era.

the donmar warehouse
earlham street = wc2

The Theatre Royal, Drury Lane

It is ironic that London's oldest, most historically important and most famous theatre does not echo to the sounds of Shakespeare or other great English playwrights, but to the lusty melodies of the Broadway musical. Ever since *Oklahoma!* wowed British audiences in 1947, Drury Lane's large stage and 2,283 seating capacity has housed the best of American musicals including *Carousel* (1950), *South Pacific* (1951) starring Mary Martin (her son Larry 'J. R.' Hagman was in the chorus), *The King And I* (1953), the record-breaking *My Fair Lady* (1958) with Rex Harrison and Julie Andrews – and again in 2001, with Jonathan Pryce and Martine McCutcheon - *Camelot* (1964), Carol Channing in *Hello Dolly!* (1965), *A Chorus Line* (1976), *Sweeney Todd* (1980), *The Best Little Whorehouse in Texas* (1981) and *42nd Street* (1984). In fact, Americans have found it cheaper to see a hit musical here than on Broadway. Indeed, for most of its 324 years of existence (in four different buildings on the same spot), the name of Drury Lane has been synonymous with popular, spectacular shows.

The first playhouse was erected on the site of a riding yard in 1662, two years after the Restoration. The theatre-loving Charles II granted a patent to the company, under Thomas Killigrew, known as The King's Servants. As they were considered part of the Royal Household, the members of the troupe were entitled to wear the scarlet and gold of the royal livery, and this is still worn by the footmen at Drury Lane today. The entire theatre, seating around 700, was about the size of the present stage. Refreshments were supplied by Mrs Mary Meggs, or 'Orange Moll', a widow

'You are come to act in a wilderness of a place.'
— Mrs Siddons to William Dowton in 1796

who had a licence to hawk her fruits to all customers, except those in the upper gallery who might be inclined to throw them at some unfortunate player. One of 'Moll's' girls, Nell Gwynn, made her stage debut at the age of 15 in John Dryden's *The Indian Queen* in 1665. The King, from the Royal Box, fell in love with Nell at first sight, and took her as his mistress. It is likely that the fire that destroyed the building in 1672 was started by an 'orange girl' searching for fruit with a naked flame under the stairs where it was kept.

Sir Christopher Wren designed the second theatre, the foundations of which can still be traced under the present stage. It was more than twice the size of the first, and prospered with the plays of Dryden, William Wycherley, William Congreve and George Farquhar, the cream of Restoration dramatists. After the deaths of Killigrew and King Charles, the Theatre Royal's prestige suffered until the triumvirate of Robert Wilkes, Thomas Doggett and Colley Cibber, all three fine actors, restored its fortunes in 1711. When Charles Fleetwood, a gambler with no money sense, took over, the theatre was led into near bankruptcy, despite an epoch-making *Merchant of Venice* of 1741 in which Charles Macklin raised the role of Shylock from low comedy to a tragic figure. So impressed was George II that he could not get to sleep either during or after the performance. Macklin was a forerunner of a new school of action which David Garrick was to personify.

Garrick, one of the greatest of English actors, became actor-manager in 1747, and spent the next 30 years at Drury Lane. He introduced better lighting and regular rehearsals and removed the public from the boxes at the sides of the stage. Garrick left the theatre in the hands of the celebrated playwright Richard Brinsley Sheridan, whose first important production was his own *The School For Scandal* in 1777. Two years later, Sheridan's *The Critic* exploited the popular taste for spectacle with remarkable scenic effects and lavish costumes. He engaged the superb tragedienne Mrs Sarah Siddons to play Lady Macbeth and her brother John Philip Kemble to make his London debut as Hamlet. However, by 1791, the building had fallen into such a bad state of decay that it was decided to build another in its place. So down went Wren's edifice, and up went one designed by Henry Holland, of which the *Morning Chronicle* of 1794 wrote, 'At length we have an English theatre worthy of our opulence and taste.' On the night of the opening production of *Macbeth*, with Kemble playing opposite his sister, an iron safety curtain was lowered to assure the audience of their protection from fire. Fifteen years later, the theatre burned down. Sheridan sat watching the conflagration with a glass of wine in his hand. When asked how he could do this so calmly, the playwright retorted, 'Can't a man have a drink by his own fireside?'

Drury Lane, more or less as we know it today, was rebuilt with money raised by the brewer Samuel Whitbread. Designed by Benjamin Wyatt on the elegant neo-classical model of the Grand

Theatre of Bordeaux, it opened in 1812 with an address written by Lord Byron. Over the next few decades, several improvements were made. Gas lighting was introduced in 1817, the splendid portico was added in 1820 and the Russell Street colonnade in 1831. Certain things modern audiences take for granted, such as a centre aisle, stuffed and covered seats and a coffee room, were much welcomed. The impressive Rotunda, magnificent

The renowned David Garrick as Tancred (painted by Thomas Worlidge)

Actors gather in the Green Room, *circa* 1820

Grand Salon and the sweeping staircases date from the early nineteenth century. It was on the latter that George III boxed the ears of the reprobate Prince Regent. This resulted in the staircases being called the King's Side and the Prince's Side, names still to be seen on opposite doors.

The new theatre, under the management of Samuel Arnold, introduced the legendary tragedian Edmund Kean to London audiences. He presented his Shylock, was immediately acclaimed a genius, and remained at Drury Lane, playing many of the great Shakespearean roles for five years, his most successful part being Richard III. Of Kean's death scene as Richard, Hazlitt said he 'had a preternatural and terrific grandeur, as if his will could not be disarmed, and the very phantoms of his despair had a withering power'.

After Kean's departure, opera and spectacle were preferred to straight drama under the reign of Alfred Bunn. In 1879, Augustus Harris, a bronze bust of whom sits above a drinking fountain at the north-east corner of the facade, established the theatre's reputation for elaborately staged melodramas and pantomimes. When Harris, known as 'Druriolanus', died in 1896, his right-hand man, Arthur Collins, continued the tradition with even bigger shows. *Ben Hur* (1902) offered a chariot race with real horses, and other productions contained earthquakes, erupting volcanos and shipwrecks. Sensation was piled on sensation, and the public flocked. Drury Lane was also the home for Henry Irving's last season in 1905, Ellen Terry's stage jubilee a year later, in which all the leading theatrical personalities of the day appeared at a mammoth matinee, and Diaghilev's landmark Ballets Russes. Shakespeare's tercentenary in 1916 was celebrated with a production of *Julius Caesar*, after which Frank Benson, who took the title role, was knighted by George V with a property sword in the Royal retiring room.

After 27 years in the job, Collins handed over to Sir Alfred Butt in 1924, who instigated the policy of big musical shows from the USA such as *Rose Marie* (1925), *The Desert Song* (1927), *Show Boat* (1928) and *The New Moon* (1929). Franz Lehar's *The Land Of Smiles* (1931), featuring Austrian-born tenor Richard Tauber, gave way to Noël Coward's patriotic pageant, *Cavalcade*, which ended with the 250-strong company singing the National Anthem and the audience, on its feet, joining in. The multi-talented Ivor Novello dominated Drury Lane in the 1930s as a leading man, composer and writer of *Glamorous Nights*, *Careless Rapture* and *The Dancing Years*, each title aptly describing the sort of entertainment that the Theatre Royal provided and continues to provide. Novello, 'the handsomest man in England', also played the soldier-king in a spectacular revival of *Henry V*.

During World War II 'The Lane' became the headquarters of ENSA, the organisation set up to provide shows for the allied forces at home and abroad. In 1940 considerable damage was done to the upper circles by enemy bombs, an explosion rivalling those the theatre had supplied on stage. Restored to its former glory, it reopened to the public on 19 December, 1946 with Coward's musical *Pacific 1860* starring Mary Martin. It flopped and made way for the arrival of Rodgers and Hammerstein's *Oklahoma!*, which ushered in the golden age of Broadway hit musicals, culminating in 1984's *42nd Street*, with a run of 1,824 performances. The longest run at Drury Lane was an amazing 4,263 performances, and it wasn't a Broadway transfer this time but Cameron Mackintosh's home-grown musical hit *Miss Saigon*, starring Jonathan Pryce (1989).

the theatre royal, drury lane

Audiences that come to Drury Lane find themselves wandering around a veritable theatre museum before entering the auditorium. In the large foyer there is a statue of Shakespeare executed in lead by John Cheere. On the walls behind are a handsome Patent Board with a list of all the holders since 1663 and a mahogany War Memorial with the names in gold of the members of the theatrical profession who fell in the Great War. In the stalls and circle rotunda are statues and busts of Garrick, Kean, Novello, Dan Leno, Forbes-Robertson and the first great black American playwright, Ira Aldridge, as well as a John Northcote painting of Kean as Brutus.

Like a few other old London theatres, Drury Lane has its resident ghosts. One, an eighteenth-century gentleman in a long grey riding cloak, riding boots, sword and three-cornered hat, walks through one wall of the upper circle and disappears on the other side. But he only makes his appearance at matinees and when the house is full. He is thought to have some connection with the skeleton found bricked up in one of the walls with a dagger in his ribs. The other ghost, suspected of being that of the illustrious clown Grimaldi who made his farewell appearance at the theatre in 1828, gives bad actors a kick up the backside from time to time. As the standard of performance at Drury Lane is generally high, this is a rare event.

**the theatre royal, drury lane
catherine street = wc2b**

The Duchess

On the opposite side of Catherine Street from the grandiose Strand and the noble Drury Lane is a small theatre seeking attention with its 'modern Tudor Gothic' facade. Three projecting bays, with a plethora of tiny windows over enamelled panels bearing insignia, give it an elegant air which suits its name – the Duchess. There is not much to catch the eye in the unadorned two-level interior with its hidden lighting effect, enlivened only by two unusual bas-reliefs by the sculptor Maurice Lambert, one each side of the stage. They represent draped figures holding the masks of Comedy and Tragedy above applauding hands. Over the years, hands have applauded plays by J. B. Priestley, Emlyn Williams, Noël Coward and Harold Pinter – and *The Dirtiest Show In Town* and *Oh, Calcutta!*

For most of its existence, the Duchess has been an intimate home for what Priestley called 'the essential Theatre... an institution that cannot safely be despised even by the philosopher'. Priestley, whose *Laburnum Grove* (1933) ran here for 335 performances, managed the theatre from 1934, the year in which two more of his plays were performed. Ralph Richardson, who would be closely associated with the works of Priestley, played an amiable drunkard in *Eden End* and a businessman in *Cornelius*. 'I always see Ralph myself not as a down-to-earth character but as if he is about to float away somewhere,' commented the playwright. Priestley's first play on the concept of time, *Time And The Conways* (1937), ran for over six months; after the war Sybil Thorndike starred in *The Linden Tree* (1947), while *Eden End* was revived in 1948.

Emlyn Williams's links with the Duchess began as an actor in the opening production in November 1929 of a war play called *Tunnel Trench*. He returned as playwright and star in 1935 with *Night Must Fall*, the psychological thriller which contained the

'Ken Tynan had conceived a voyeurs' picnic...called Oh, Calcutta!... Mixing frontery with effrontery it soon found its own public.'
— Raymond Mander and Joe Mitchenson in *Revue*

notorious head in the hatbox. His most popular play, *The Corn Is Green*, ran here from August 1938 until the theatre's closure at the outbreak of war in September 1939. Williams himself played the young Welsh miner who wins a scholarship to Oxford, thanks to his teacher Miss Moffat, a role taken brilliantly by Sybil Thorndike. In 1952, Williams brought his celebrated Dickens recital into the Duchess for a short season.

Although J. B. Priestley and Emlyn Williams were the dominant figures in the theatre's pre-war days, other notable productions were seen here. Nancy Price's People's National Theatre presented Baliol Holloway as Falstaff in *The Merry Wives Of Windsor* and Frank Vosper as Henry VIII in *The Rose Without A Thorn*, both in 1932. In the same year, Jessica Tandy scored a personal success in the all-female play *Children In Uniform*, a translation from the German *Mädchen In Uniform*, set in an oppressive boarding school. It was directed by the Viennese Leontine Sagan, who had filmed it the year before.

During the war years, Noël Coward's 'impossible farce' *Blithe Spirit* (1942) con-

The bronze bas-relief on either side of the proscenium is the only adornment

102

tinued to break records after being transferred here from the Piccadilly and the now defunct St James. In contrast, the shortest run in theatrical history was recorded at the Duchess in 1930 when a revue failed to complete the first night, the audience retreating before the end! Running considerably longer were post-war hits such as Wynyard Browne's *The Holly And The Ivy* (1950) and Terence Rattigan's drama *The Deep Blue Sea* (1952) with Peggy Ashcroft falling for feckless young Kenneth More and attempting suicide. These dramas were examples of the 'well-made play', soon to be discarded by a new school of British writers, of whom Harold Pinter was one of the best. Producer Michael Codron had the courage to bring Pinter's *The Caretaker* into the heart of the West End, and it paid off. This superb comedy of menace with a splendid cast of three – Donald Pleasence, Alan Bates (replaced by Pinter himself) and Peter Woodthorpe – ran for a year. Some years on, Pinter's double bill, *The Basement* and *The Tea Party* (1970) with Pleasence and

Husky-voiced Joan Greenwood and fruity-toned Donald Sinden lent distinction to Terence Rattigan's *In Praise of Love*

Vivien Merchant and Donald Pleasence in Harold Pinter's *Tea Party* (1970), a teasing black comedy

Vivien Merchant (then the author's wife), and his triple bill, *Other Places* (1985), were seen in the vastly changed climate of British theatre.

Raunchy entertainment became the order of the day at the Duchess when it played hostess to *The Dirtiest Show In Town* (1971) for 794 performances, and the revue which merited the above title, *Oh, Calcutta!* (1974), for six years. The legendary *No Sex Please, We're British* transferred here from the Garrick in 1986 after its long run there; *Run For Your Wife* (1990) completed its nine-year West End run at the Duchess; and *Don't Dress For Dinner* transferred from the Apollo and kept audiences happy for a further four and a half years from 1992.

the duchess

Comedies continued into the 1990s with the highly successful *An Evening With Gary Lineker* by Chris England and Arthur Smith (1991) and Maureen Lipman's one-woman show *Live and Kidding*. On a more serious note came the RSC's brilliant production of Peter Whelan's *The Herbal Bed* (1997) and the Royal National Theatre's productions of *Copenhagen* by Michael Frayn (1999) and *Blue/Orange* by Joe Penhall (2001), all showing that the Duchess is a theatre with the capacity to keep on surprising its audiences.

the duchess theatre
catherine street = wc2b

The Duke of York's

This elegant, charming and compact Victorian playhouse was built in 1892, the first of the three theatres in St Martin's Lane – at the time literally a lane, with muddy ditches on either side. The New Theatre (now the Albery) sprang up 11 years later, and the Coliseum soon joined them. With the Garrick backing onto the Duke of York's, and the Wyndham's close behind the Albery, they form a neat cluster of theatres between Shaftesbury Avenue and Drury Lane.

The Duke of York's opened as the Trafalgar Square Theatre, but changed to its present name in 1895 after Henry Dana, the manager, received the following letter from the treasurer of the future King George V.

> I am desired to inform you that HRH the Duke of York has no objection to the Trafalgar Theatre being called The Duke of York's Theatre but to say that this permission gives no authority for the use of the word Royal in connexion with the theatre nor may any reference be made such as 'By permission of HRH the Duke of York.'

Nevertheless, it is a right royal building with a theatrical tradition fit for a king.

It was at the Duke of York's on 27 December, 1904 that Peter Pan flew for the first time on stage. Here, too, a year later, 14-year-old Charlie Chaplin played in *Sherlock Holmes*. On returning in the 1950s with his daughter, Victoria, to see a show, Chaplin was given the Royal Box with its Regency-inspired retiring room designed by Cecil Beaton. The theatre has also been graced over the years by, among others, Marie Tempest, Ellen Terry, Isadora Duncan, Edwige Feuillère, John Gielgud, Glenda Jackson and Al Pacino. Peggy Ashcroft (*Jew Süss*, 1929), John Mills (*London Wall*, 1931) and Joan Plowright (*Moby Dick*, 1955)

'Either he must be the whimsical fairy creature that Nina Boucicault made him, or he must be the lovable tomboy of Pauline Chase. There is no other way.'
— J. M. Barrie on the playing of Peter Pan

all began to make their names here. Plowright played the Cabin Boy to actor-director Orson Welles's Ahab in a production the critic Kenneth Tynan described as 'a sustained assault on the senses, which dwarfs anything London has ever seen since, except perhaps, the Great Fire'. And the theatre has its very own ghost. An iron fire-door which once existed is heard to slam shut every night at ten. Some years ago, an old-fashioned iron key with a tag marked 'Iron Door' dropped at the feet of the manager. A female figure dressed in black has been seen to wander through the circle bar. It is said to be none other than the ghost of Violet Melnotte, the owner, known to everyone as 'Madame'.

The theatre, designed by Walter Emden for 'Madame' and her husband Frank Wyatt, was not a success until she let it on a long lease to the influential American impresario Charles Frohman in 1897. Frohman, 'The Napoleon of the Theatre',

brought fame, prestige and money to the Duke of York's. The first long run under his aegis was Anthony Hope's *The Adventure Of Lady Ursula* (1898), in which Evelyn Millard caused a stir by appearing in male attire. In 1900 she also starred in Jerome K. Jerome's *Miss Hobbs* and in David Belasco's

Pauline Chase as Peter Pan – one of J. M. Barrie's favourites in the role one-act play, *Madame Butterfly*, which accompanied it. Puccini happened to be in the audience one evening, and was inspired to write his opera of the same name four years later. The long and fruitful collaboration between Frohman and James Barrie at the Duke of York's began with *The Admirable Crichton* (1902), a success despite a strike of scene-shifters after the second act on the opening night. Members of the cast, including H. B. Irving (son of Sir Henry), Gerald du Maurier and Irene Vanbrugh, had to move the scenery themselves. *Peter Pan* followed with Nina Boucicault, Hilda Trevelyan and du Maurier as the first ever Peter, Wendy and Hook respectively. Cissie Loftus (1905), Pauline Chase (1906-13) and Madge Titheradge (1914) were the subsequent Peters at this theatre. Hilda Trevelyan continued for some years as Wendy, also proving herself a perfect Barrie heroine in *Alice Sit-By-The-Fire* (1905), alongside Ellen Terry, and as Maggie in *What Every Woman Knows* (1908).

In 1910 Frohman made a brave attempt to mount a repertory season of ten plays, but suffered a heavy financial loss. Among the plays premiered were Galsworthy's *Justice*, Shaw's *Misalliance* and Harley Granville-Barker's *The Madras House*. Five years later, the

Joan Plowright and Orson Welles rehearse for *Moby Dick* in 1955 theatre world on both sides of the Atlantic was stunned by the news that Frohman had drowned on the S.S. *Lusitania*, torpedoed by the Germans. His last words to a survivor were said to have been from *Peter Pan*: 'To die will be an awfully big adventure.'

During the Great War, the theatre's successes were Doris Keane in *Romance* (1915), Renée Kelly in *Daddy Long Legs* (1916) and Mrs Patrick Campbell in *The Thirteenth Chair* (1917). Noël Coward, in his twenties like the century, became the voice of the Bright Young Things. When he was 14, he had appeared as Slightly in the 1913 *Peter Pan*. Now Coward was back with his revue, *London Calling* (1923), in which Gertrude Lawrence sang 'Parisien Pierrot', and two plays, *Easy Virtue* (1926) and *Home Chat* (1927). The latter, despite the casting of two former Peter Pans, Nina Boucicault and Madge Titheradge, was booed on the first night. Coward's connection with the theatre re-emerged years later with *Waiting In The Wings* (1960), featuring a starry geriatric cast, and a 1963 revival of his classic, *Private Lives*.

The 1930s ushered in the Carl Rosa Opera Company, a non-stop season of Grand Guignol (from 2 p.m. to midnight), and the Ballet Rambert and Markova-Dolin dance companies which did so much to popularise ballet in England. The big hit of the 1940s was *Is Your Honeymoon Really Necessary?* (1944), which ran two years. Other long-runners were John Clements and Kay Hammond in *The Happy Marriage* (1952), Flora Robson in *The House By The Lake* (1956), Margaret Lockwood in *And Suddenly It's Spring* (1959), which had its 'first night' for the critics at a matinee, the Kenneth Williams revue, *One Over The Eight* (1961), Donald Pleasence in Jean Anouilh's *Poor Bitos* (1964), *The Killing Of Sister George* (1965), *Relatively Speaking* (1967) – the first of Alan Ayckbourn's multitude of hits – and *The Man Most Likely To...* (1970).

In 1979, Capital Radio bought the building and closed it for refurbishment. It reopened in February 1980 with restored cream and gold decoration, recreating the warm atmosphere of a Victorian theatre while improving the facilities. The quality of

the duke of york's

Glenda Jackson and Brian Cox in Eugene O'Neill's *Strange Interlude*. They had to survive a marathon five hours per performance

productions since then has remained traditionally high, with Glenda Jackson in *Rose* (1980) and *Strange Interlude* (1983), the off-Broadway cast, headed by Al Pacino, in *American Buffalo* (1984), Willy Russell's *Shirley Valentine* (1989), Ariel Dorfman's award-winning *Death And The Maiden* with Juliet Stevenson (1992) and David Mamet's *Oleanna* (1993). In 1996 the Royal Court took up a three-year residence at the Duke of York's. Whilst here they enjoyed a hugely successful two-year run of *The Weir*, which ended its award-winning season in May 2000. *Stones In His Pockets* followed, winning an Olivier Award for Best Comedy, 2001. Violet Melnotte can rest in peace.

the duke of york's theatre
st martin's lane = wc2n

The Fortune

In the shadow of the glorious Drury Lane Theatre, facing its famous colonnade on the stage door side, lies a small theatre that proudly perpetuates the name of a popular Elizabethan playhouse. The architect, Ernest Schaufelberg, based his designs for the exterior on a print of doubtful authenticity of the old Fortune. Like its predecessor as seen in the sketch, it is a square brick building of four storeys, with minimal adornment. The earlier Fortune, situated not far from where the Barbican Centre stands today, had a statue of the Goddess of Fortune over the entrance. This proved rather ineffectual, as the building, the costumes and playbooks went up in flames in 1621. Above the entrance of the present theatre is a nude figure of Terpsichore, the Greek Muse of Dancing. However, the small stage does not lend itself to any but limited displays of the art of dance. What the 440-seat theatre does provide is a cosy intimacy for shows of a diminutive nature. In fact, its biggest successes have been two revues – *At The Drop Of A Hat* (1957) and *Beyond The Fringe* (1961) – with casts of two and four respectively.

The Fortune's principal interest as a building is that it shares its structure with the Scottish National Church. Strangely, it is built over and under the church, whose entrance is cheek by jowl with that of the theatre's. The opening production in November 1924, a play called *Sinners* by Laurence Cowan, the theatre's owner, might have confused churchgoers. There have also been a few plays whose proximity could not have been welcomed by worshippers on the other side of the wall. Nevertheless, it is a rare architectural unity between religion and secularism.

A brass plate in the lobby proclaims, 'There is a tide in the affairs of men, which, taken at the flood, leads on to Fortune.' But it was often 'the slings and arrows of outrageous fortune' that visited this pleasant playhouse in those early days. It was

*'Our theatre was miscalled the Fortune...
After a very short time we slid into the eternal
obscurity of Fatal Fortune.'*

— Dirk Bogarde on the failure of *Power Without Glory*, 1947

two years after its opening before there was anything significant to appeal to lovers of the theatre. The influential producer J. B. Fagan changed that by presenting Sean O'Casey's modern Irish classics *Juno And The Paycock* and *The Plough And The Stars* in 1926. A year later the actor Tom Walls, at the time associated with the Aldwych farces, took over the management of the Fortune. Frederick Lonsdale's *On Approval* (1927), a comedy of manners about a trial marriage, ran for over a year, making it the first and last hit here for some time.

The People's National Theatre, run by Nancy Price, its founder and guiding spirit, found its first London home at the Fortune from 1930 to 1931. Their most noteworthy production was the revival of John Galsworthy's first play, *The Silver Box*. After Nancy Price – and her inseparable pet parrot – left the theatre, Sybil Thorndike paid a brief visit in 1932 with two plays. It was then given over to amateur productions until the war, during which it was used by ENSA, the

A 1920s programme cover depicts the proscenium of the then newly built Fortune organisation formed to provide entertainment for servicemen and women.

After the war, the building returned to the professional fold for a brief period. One of the short-lived productions was *Power Without Glory* (1947), a working-class drama featuring two unknown actors named Kenneth More and Dirk Bogarde. It soon closed 'due to lack of star names on the canopy and the excessive competition from the energetic Americans across the street in *Oklahoma!*', according to Bogarde. It was another ten years before fortune smiled on the little theatre with *At The Drop Of A Hat*. Michael Flanders in a wheelchair and Donald Swann at the piano entertained audiences with comic songs and patter for over two years.

In the autumn of 1961 a revue, written and performed on a bare stage by four young men just down from Oxbridge, took an emergent 'Swinging London' by storm. *Beyond The Fringe* was not only instrumental in starting the 'satire industry', but was the springboard for the exceptional future careers of Jonathan Miller, Peter Cook, Alan Bennett and Dudley Moore. The show ran 1,184 performances before transferring to the Mayfair in 1964. Other shows that ran here include *Mr Cinders*, *Double Double*, *Nunsense* and *Dangerous Obsession*.

But the Fortune is most closely associated with *The Woman in Black*, which has become a West End legend. This enigmatic and brilliant play first took up residence in 1989, and the theatre and show celebrated 5,000 performances in July 2001. In the same year, the theatre became part of the hugely successful Ambassador Theatre Group. Bouncer, the Fortune Theatre's cat, must be delighted!

the fortune theatre
russell street = wc2b

The Garrick

If David Garrick, according to Dr Johnson, had added to 'the gaiety of nations' and 'the public stock of harmless pleasure', then so too has the attractive late Victorian playhouse named after the great eighteenthth-century actor and built exactly 110 years after his death. A copy of the lost Gainsborough portrait of Garrick beside a bust of Shakespeare welcomes one into the theatre at dress-circle level. Cupids holding laurel-decked shields form part of the finely modelled plasterwork on the balcony fronts and from the domed ornamental ceiling held up by caryatids above the boxes hangs a chandelier. The gold leaf of the auditorium was restored in 1986 by the celebrated stage designer Carl Toms. At the same time the distinctive Portland and Bath stone exterior, opposite the statue of Henry Irving, also had a flattering facelift, making the stately colonnade on the first floor come up as good as new.

It was new in 1889 when Walter Emden and C. J. Phipps built it for actor-manager John Hare with the money of W. S. Gilbert, earned from the light operas he wrote with Arthur Sullivan. The construction was delayed when the deep foundations hit an underground river known to the Romans. Today, underground trains run beneath the theatre. A new drama by Pinero entitled *The Profligate,* with Hare, Forbes Robertson, Lewis Wailer and Katie Rorke, inaugurated the building in April 1889. Pinero's connection with the Garrick continued with *Lady Bountiful* (1891) and *The Notorious Mrs Ebbsmith* (1895), the latter living up to its title. During the run of the play, starring Mrs Patrick Campbell and John Hare, a woman named Ebbsmith was found drowned in the Thames, a counterfoil of a ticket for the production in her pocket. Apparently, she had written to a friend that the play had preyed on her mind. In 1896, Hare left the theatre where he had made such a success,

*'The proscenium is created by the pilasters
that frame the stage boxes; this was
a dramatic and simple change.'*
— Victor Glasstone

particularly in the role of Benjamin Goldfinch in Sydney
Grundy's *A Pair Of Spectacles* (1890), an adaptation from a
French farce. In fact, for almost 100 years, until 1987's *When
Did You Last See Your Trousers?* (1987), farce established itself as
the Garrick's dominant mode.

The twentieth century began well for the Garrick when
Arthur Bourchier and his wife Violet Vanbrugh leased it,
beginning a splendid line of productions with J. M. Barrie's *The
Wedding Guest* (1900). There followed Pinero's *Iris* (1901),
Henry Arthur Jones's white-washing *Julia* (1903), Bourchier as
Shylock in *The Merchant Of Venice* (1905), Henri Bernstein's
Samson (1909) and *The Unwritten Law* (1911), a dramatisation
of *Crime And Punishment*. Bourchier had an apartment at the top
of the theatre with a staircase leading directly to the stage. It is
known as the Phantom Staircase because Bourchier's ghost is said

to descend it, sometimes slapping actors on the shoulder in friendly encouragement.

Another husband-and-wife management team, Oscar Asche and Lily Brayton, packed the theatre for the 1911–12 season in which Asche played Falstaff in *The Merry Wives Of Windsor* and Hajj in *Kismet*. Other managements followed in quick succession, and no discernible policy emerged until the 1940s. Between the wars, productions worth mentioning were Austin Page's *By Pigeon Post* (1918), *Cyrano De Bergerac* (1919), Seymour Hicks in *The Man In The Dress Clothes* (1922), Sutton Vane's allegorical drama *Outward Bound* (1923) and Ivor Novello in his own play, *The Rat* (1924). Somerset Maugham preferred to cast Olga Lindo as Sadie Thompson in *Rain* (1925) rather than the more exciting Tallulah Bankhead, who wanted the role. Five years later Tallulah did appear at the Garrick, as another tart with a heart of gold – Marguerite in *The Lady Of The Camellias*.

During a sparse period in the early 1930s, the theatre even resorted to old-time music hall until a play came in which caught the mood of the time, running 391 performances. Walter Greenwood's *Love On The Dole* (1935) dealt with life among unemployed Lancashire cotton workers. It also introduced 23-year-old Wendy Hiller to the London stage, setting her off on a prestigious career. The theatre itself was unemployed from late 1939 until September 1941, when it reopened with a play entitled *Room V* by someone called Peter Wendy. Soon after, some ex-Aldwych farceurs – performers Robertson Hare and Alfred Drayton and writers Vernon Sylvaine and Ben Travers – descended on the Garrick for much of the '40s. In between *Aren't Men Beasts* (1942), *She Follows Me About* (1943) and others, Michael Redgrave was excellent as the timid would-be murderer in *Uncle Harry* (1944), and Beatrice Lillie was hilarious in the revue *Better Late* (1946).

Debonair actor-singer-dancer Jack Buchanan took on the management of the theatre after the war, appearing in Lonsdale's *Canaries Sometimes Sing* (1947) with Coral Browne, and in Vernon Sylvaine's *As Long As They're Happy* (1953). Mainly comedies were presented under Buchanan's distinctive aegis, including Carson Kanin's *Born Yesterday* (1947) with Yolande Donlan, directed by Laurence Olivier; husband and wife Richard Attenborough and Sheila Sim in *To Dorothy A Son* (1951) and Robert Dhéry's French revue, *La Plume De Ma Tante* (1955), which drew mirth-filled audiences for three years. Then came the very English 1958 revue *Living For Pleasure,* starring Dora Bryan, Joan Littlewood's Theatre Workshop production of the Frank Norman/Lionel Bart musical *Fings Ain't Wot They Used To Be* (1960) and the Charles Dyer two-hander *Rattle Of A Simple Man* (1962).

After a closure for redecoration between June 1965 and April 1966, farce re-established itself at the Garrick with the arrival of

Michael Williams and Judi Dench scored another success as Mr and Mrs Pooter in *Mr and Mrs Nobody* (1986), adapted from Grossmith's *Diary of a Nobody*

the garrick

Brian Rix and his team with such plays as *Stand By Your Bedouin*, *Uproar In The House*, *Let Sleeping Wives Lie*, *She's Done It Again* and *Don't Just Lie There, Say Something*. Alan Ayckbourn's *Absent Friends* (1975) and Ira Levin's ingenious thriller *Death Trap* (1978) then took the stage briefly before giving way to *No Sex Please, We're British* in 1982, adding another four years to its 11-year run at the Strand. In 1986 the Garrick had great success with Michael Williams and Judi Dench in *Mr and Mrs Nobody* (adapted from George Weedon Grossmith's *Diary of a Nobody*) and later with two Noël Coward plays: *Easy Virtue* (1988) and *The Vortex* (1989) with Rupert Everett. In 1990 the theatre presented short seasons of *Bent*, with Ian McKellen and Frankie Howerd, and in 1991 Brian Friel's acclaimed *Dancing at Lughnasa* transferred from the Phoenix (after the National) for a two-year run. The year 1995 was the start of another very successful run for the Garrick: the Royal National Theatre's production of *An Inspector Calls*, which ran for five years. A second J. B. Priestley classic, *Dangerous Corner*, followed in 2001. In 2002 the Garrick attracted several young Hollywood actors to its stage with an acclaimed production of *This is Our Youth*, US writer Kenneth Lonergan's first play in which Matt Damon, Casey Affleck (brother of Ben) and Summer Phoenix all starred.

the garrick theatre
charing cross road = wc2h

The Gielgud

The noble domed structure that commands the corner of Rupert Street and Shaftesbury Avenue today has been renamed twice in its illustrious history. The theatre was opened in December 1906 as the Hicks Theatre, after actor-manager Seymour Hicks for whom it was built. Thankfully, the name that suggests a theatre for out-of-towners was changed in 1909 to the Globe Theatre. And so it remained until 1994, when it was renamed the Gielgud Theatre, to honour Sir John Gielgud and to ensure that, with the opening of Sam Wanamaker's reconstruction of Shakespeare's theatre in Southwark, there would only be one Globe Theatre in London.

The architect was the omnipresent W. G. R. Sprague, who conceived it as the first of two similar companion theatres, the other being the Queen's on the Wardour Street corner of the block. The classical four-storey facade is decorated with four giant Ionic columns proclaiming the theatre's importance. The auditorium, too, is in grand, even somewhat pretentious style, with bold Corinthian columns framing the boxes. The Louis XVI ornamentation, and further columns, recur throughout the interior. A circular Regency staircase leads to an attractive oval gallery from which patrons can look down on the spacious foyer. Aside from some inevitable refurbishment and slight structural changes, the Gielgud is an extremely well-preserved Edwardian lady.

Seymour Hicks, who would be knighted in 1935, appeared with his wife Ellaline Terriss in the opening production, *The Beauty Of Bath*. (It was a transfer from the Aldwych, the other theatre owned by Hicks, both in association with American impresario Charles Frohman.) Successful early hits at the Gielgud included *Brewster's Millions* (1907), with Gerald du Maurier superb in the title role of the comedy subsequently filmed six

'If the past theatrical decade had to be represented by a single production, this is the one that many good judges would choose.'

— The Times on The Importance of Being Earnest, 1939

times; George Grossmith and 'Gaiety Girl' Gertie Millar in the Oscar Strauss operetta *A Waltz Dream* (1908); and Henry Ainley and Mrs Patrick Campbell in *His Borrowed Plumes* (1909) by Mrs George Cornwallis-West (the pen name of Lady Randolph Churchill, Winston's American mother). Musical comedies and transfers kept the theatre full until and throughout World War I. In 1917, French music-hall star Gaby Deslys bade farewell to the stage in 'a musical affair' called *Suzette*.

The post-war decade saw the Gielgud under the management of actress Marie Löhr and her producer husband, Anthony Prinsep. Among their achievements were productions of Somerset Maugham's *Love In A Cottage* (1918) and *Our Betters* (1923), A. A. Milne's *The Truth About Blayds* (1921) and *Mr Pim Passes By* (1922), Frederick Lonsdale's *Aren't We All?* (1923) and Noël Coward's *Fallen Angels* (1925), with Tallulah Bankhead and Edna Best as 'those soused sluts' – as one critic called them. On the first night Tallulah, angry with Maugham for not letting her play Sadie Thompson, gazed out of the window and ad-libbed, 'Rain!' It brought the house down. Another funny lady, Jeanne de Casalis, created shock waves by appearing in pyjamas in *Potiphar's Wife* (1927).

Before H. M. Tennant took over the theatre in 1937, the French star Yvonne Arnaud sparkled in J. B. Fagan's *The Improper Duchess* (1931) and in the revival of Fagan's *And So To Bed* (1932). Mlle Arnaud, a favourite with English audiences, had a theatre named after her in Guildford, Surrey in 1965, seven years after her death. In the first year of the Tennant regime, the lovely American actress Ruth Chatterton made her London debut in Maugham's *The Constant Wife*, and Owen Nares and Edith Evans

Gwen ffrancgon-Davies *(left)*, John Gielgud and Edith Evans in the famous 1939 production of *The Importance of Being Earnest*

starred in St John Ervine's *Robert's Wife*. In 1939, John Gielgud directed the classic production of *The Importance Of Being Earnest* with himself as John Worthing, Gwen Ffrangcon-Davies as Gwendolen, Peggy Ashcroft as Cecily and, essaying Lady Bracknell for the first time, Edith Evans in her most popular and famous role. In later years, she began to hate imitations of her celebrated delivery of the line, 'A handbag?' The play was not performed for another ten years. It was a difficult act to follow.

At the beginning of World War II, Evans and Ashcroft, plus Alec Guinness, played in Clemence Dane's *Cousin Muriel* (1940). Plays reflecting the period were Robert Ardrey's anti-isolationist drama *Thunder Rock* (1940) with Michael Redgrave; Robert Sherwood's *The Petrified Forest* (1942), with Owen Nares in his last role before his death aged 55; and J. B. Priestley's *They Came To A City* (1943). But it was a comedy, Terence Rattigan's *While The Sun Shines* (1943), that cheered people up for the remainder of the war.

One of the most prestigious of post-war plays at the Gielgud was Christopher Fry's verse drama *The Lady's Not For Burning* (1949). In the cast were Gielgud (who directed), Pamela Brown, Claire Bloom and a youthful Richard Burton. In the role of the drunken tinker was the great Shavian actor Esme Percy, then in his sixties. One night, during his big scene, his glass eye fell out. When a fellow actor stepped forward to pick it up, Percy said, 'Don't step on it, for God's sake. They're so expensive!' The following year Fry's *Ring Round The Moon*, a translation from Jean Anouilh, starred Paul Scofield in the dual role of hero and villain.

Further memorable but contrasting productions took the Gielgud through the '50s: Alec Guinness in *The Prisoner* (1954) and two Graham Greene plays, *The Potting Shed* (1958), with the indefatigable Gielgud, and *The Complaisant Lover* (1959) with Ralph Richardson, Phyllis Calvert and Paul Scofield. The latter returned a year later in his most celebrated role as Sir Thomas More in Robert Bolt's *A Man For All Seasons*.

Comedies were the staple fare in the '70s and early '80s. These included Maggie Smith and Kenneth Williams in Peter Shaffer's *The Private Ear And The Public Eye* (1962), Donald Sinden in *There's A Girl In My Soup* (1966), Tom Courtenay in Alan Ayckbourn's ingenious trilogy, *The Norman Conquests* (1974), Vanessa Redgrave in Coward's *Design For Living* (1982) and a three-year run of Andrew Lloyd Webber's production of the schoolgirl romp *Daisy Pulls It Off* (1983). In 1987 the Gielgud returned to drama with Glenda Jackson and Joan Plowright leading a cast directed by Spain's Nuria Espert in Lorca's *The House Of Bernarda Alba*.

Since then the Gielgud has presented the premiere performance of Peter Hall's brilliant production of Wilde's *An Ideal Husband* (1992), Ayckbourn's *Communicating Doors* (1995), the con-

The award-winning production of Lorca's *The House of Bernada Alba* boasted magnificent sets and lighting by Ezio Frigerio

troversial *Shopping and F***ing* by Mark Ravenhill (1997), as well as Vanessa and Corin Redgrave in Noël Coward's last play, *Song at Twilight* (1999). The Gielgud entered the new millennium in great form with an enormously successful run of *The Graduate* starring, successively, Kathleen Turner, Jerry Hall, Amanda Donohoe, Anne Archer and Linda Gray, and in 2002 *Humble Boy*, with Felicity Kendal, transferred from the Royal National Theatre. The theatre that bears the name of one of Britain's greatest stage actors has good reason to be proud of itself.

the gielgud theatre
shaftesbury avenue = wlv

The Theatre Royal
Haymarket

There is no theatre that has more epitomised London playgoing for almost three centuries than the stately Haymarket. Only three London theatres are listed Grade 1 under the 1971 Act on the preservation of buildings of great architectural or historic importance, prohibiting rebuilding or demolition: the Haymarket; the Royal Opera House; and Drury Lane. Of these three national monuments, the Haymarket is the only one where 'straight' plays can be seen, the others being given over exclusively to musicals, opera and ballet. Its graceful John Nash portico, its opulent, well-preserved interior, the premieres of plays by Oscar Wilde, seasons given by theatrical knights and a string of glittering all-star productions have made the Haymarket a byword for elegance and sophistication.

However, this most traditional of West End theatres had a rebellious youth. The first playhouse on the site, just adjoining the present structure, was built without licence or patent in 1720 by a carpenter named John Potter, and called the Little Theatre in the Haymarket. Defying the monopoly which forbade the acting of 'legitimate' drama other than at Drury Lane or Covent Garden, Henry Fielding produced his satire on heroic drama, *Tom Thumb The Great*, here in 1730. Further satires by Fielding attacking both political parties and caricaturing the Royal Family, resulted in the passing of the infamous Licensing Act of 1737, which reinforced the monopoly of the patent theatres and led to the official agency under the Lord Chamberlain for the censoring of all plays. This ended Fielding's career as a dramatist and turned him towards writing novels.

*'Mr Oscar Wilde's new play at the Haymarket
is a dangerous subject because he has the
property of making his critics dull.'*
— George Bernard Shaw on *An Ideal Husband*, 1895

When the actor Samuel Foote took over the theatre, he successfully evaded the law by inviting his friends to partake of cups of chocolate with him, and including entertainment in the occasion. In 1766, Foote was thrown during an attempt to ride the Duke of York's unmanageable horse, a result of a practical joke. His leg had to be amputated and the Duke, as compensation, managed to obtain a licence for Foote to perform drama in the summer months when the other two theatres were closed. Thus did London acquire a third Theatre Royal. Foote sold the theatre to George Colman, who carried it into a prosperous period before handing over to his son. Many plays by Colman the Elder and Colman the Younger were performed during their time here, which was marked by two violent incidents. In 1794, at a Royal Command performance, the crowd was so great that 20 people were trampled to death; then, in 1805, hundreds of tailors gathered to protest at a revival of Foote's satire *The Tailors*, which they saw as an offence to their craft. The riot was quelled by troops.

The Little Theatre was closed for a while when Colman the Younger was imprisoned for debt. His brother-in-law David Morris, who took control, left the old building and built the present edifice a little to the south of it. John Nash, one of the principal exponents of nineteenth-century town planning, designed the theatre in 1821 so that its Corinthian portico could be seen from St James Square. The theatre was described by a contemporary as 'in point of architectural beauty the most elegant in London, but for the convenience of seeing and hearing the worst contrived'. This apparently unpleasant auditorium was completely replaced in 1879 when Squire and Mary Bancroft took possession. The changes made were radical. The Bankcrofts created the first picture-frame stage by placing it entirely behind a proscenium arch. This was highlighted by a thick gold painted border. They did away with the pit (the cheap seats near the front) replacing them with the higher-priced orchestra stalls, which caused a riot on the first night. Clearly, audiences were far more vociferous then.

In 1905, the interior was replaced again by that which can still be admired today – a large house of 906 seats in a rich and elaborate Louis XVI style conceived by C. Stanley Peach. Some improvements were made in 1939, including a large and attractive lounge bar which was constructed under the stalls. In 1994 the theatre was completely refurbished inside at a cost of £2.3 million. Joseph Harker's ceiling was restored, the two thousand lead crystals in the central chandelier were cleaned and twenty gilders were employed to work for three months and used over 5,000 books of gold leaf! More recently, and with great difficulty, the theatre has installed an air-conditioning system. Nothing, however, has disturbed its slightly staid, old-world charm.

The great actor-managers of the Haymarket in the nineteenth century were Benjamin Webster (1837–53), J. B. Buckstone (1853–78), whose ghost is said to haunt the theatre, and the Bancrofts (1800–85). Under these three regimes, the Haymarket became the foremost playhouse in London. Famous actors who appeared here were Samuel Phelps in the 1830s as Shylock, Hamlet, Othello and Richard III; William Macready in *Money* (1840); Barry Sullivan as Hamlet (1853); the American Edwin Booth as Shylock (1861), and Edward Sothern repeating his New York triumph as Lord Dundreary in Tom Taylor's *Our American Cousin* (1861). His portrayal of the imbecile lord was so popular that the long side-whiskers he wore became known as 'dundrearies'. Sothern also created the title role in Tom Robertson's *David Garrick* (1864).

In 1887, the theatre passed into the hands of Herbert Beerbohm Tree. His most resounding success was *Trilby* (1895) with himself as Svengali, the profits of which enabled him to build Her Majesty's Theatre just opposite. However, Tree's *Hamlet* of 1892 was a failure, giving rise to Oscar Wilde's comment, 'My dear Herbert, good is not the word.' But when the famous actor-manager produced and played Lord Illingworth in Wilde's *A Woman Of No Importance* (1893), Oscar commented, 'A charming fellow, and so clever: he models himself on me.' On the first night, Wilde arranged the house carefully, placing peeresses next to poets, dowagers beside young men and his wife Constance in a box with Lord Alfred Douglas. There was a slight problem when the Prince of Wales refused to share the Royal Box with his mistress Lillie Langtry. (She had

made her debut at the Haymarket in 1881.) It was on the same night at the Haymarket that a blackmailer caught Wilde at the stage door and offered him, for ten pounds, the original of a love letter the playwright had addressed to him. 'Ten pounds!' cried Oscar. 'You have no appreciation of literature. If you had asked me for fifty pounds, I might have given it to you.' In 1886 another Wilde play, *An Ideal Husband*, had its premiere at the Haymarket. This same play returned to the theatre exactly one hundred years later in a highly acclaimed

Lillie Langtry, mistress to the Prince of Wales, makes her debut at the Haymarket production directed by Peter Hall, with Martin Shaw as Lord Goring.

After Tree planted himself at his new theatre in 1896, Frederick Harrison and Cyril Maude became the managers, sustaining and extending the tradition of fine plays, casts and settings. Maude gave outstanding performances in J. M. Barrie's *The Little Minister* (1897), Sheridan's *The Rivals* and *School For Scandal* (both 1900); and George Colman the Elder's *The Clandestine Marriage* (1903). Other important productions until the death of Harrison in 1926 (Maude had left in 1905) were Maeterlinck's *The Blue Bird* (1910); the first licensed performance of Ibsen's *Ghosts* (1914), which caused a storm of protest; and Barrie's play of the supernatural, *Mary Rose* (1920).

The highlight of the war years was John Gielgud's repertory season of 1944–45. The plays chosen were *Hamlet, A Midsummer Night's Dream*, Congreve's *Love For Love*, Webster's *The Duchess Of Malfi* and Somerset Maugham's *The Circle*. Gielgud featured in all five plays, while Peggy Ashcroft played Ophelia to his Hamlet and Titania to his Oberon. At the war's end, the sequence of civilised entertainments continued unabated, with the American actress Helen Hayes making her London debut as the mother in Tennessee Williams's *The Glass Menagerie* (1948); Ralph Richardson and Peggy Ashcroft in *The Heiress* (1949); Gielgud in N. C. Hunter's *A Day By The Sea* (1953); and Noël Coward and Margaret Leighton in Shaw's *The Apple Cart* (1954), considered by many to be the finest production of the play.

The Haymarket continued to skim the cream of England's acting establishment: Edith Evans and Peggy Ashcroft appeared in Enid Bagnold's *The Chalk Garden* (1956), and Ralph Richardson in *School For Scandal* (1962), *The Rivals* (1966) and *The Merchant Of Venice* (1967); Alec Guinness was T. E. Lawrence in Terence Rattigan's *Ross* (1960), Trevor Howard starred in Anouilh's *The Waltz Of The Toreadors* (1974), and Maggie Smith triumphed in *The Way Of The World* (1984). In the '80s Hollywood came to the Haymarket in the shape of

Rex Harrison and Diana Rigg headed the cast in a glittering production of Shaw's *Heartbreak House* (1983)

Claudette Colbert in *Aren't We All?* and Christopher Reeve in *The Aspern Papers* (both 1984), Lauren Bacall in *Sweet Bird Of Youth*, Liv Ullmann in Harold Pinter's *Old Times* (both 1985), and, most notably, Jack Lemmon – supreme in Jonathan Miller's quick-fire and powerful production of *Long Day's Journey Into Night* (1986). The '90s saw Robert Lindsay as Cyrano de Bergerac, in a performance celebrating the Queen's 40-year reign, in the presence of Her Majesty (1992), the award-winning *Arcadia* by Tom Stoppard (1994) and *A Streetcar Named Desire*, directed by Peter Hall and starring Jessica Lange (1997). The theatre entered the new millennium in fine form with Helen Mirren in Donald Marguiles's *Collected Stories*, and 2002's highly acclaimed production of *The Royal Family*, starring Dame Judi Dench.

In 1998 the theatre set up 'Masterclass', a charitable trust

Vanessa Redgrave and Joely Richardson in Oscar Wilde's *Lady Windermere's Fan*

providing free theatrical classes and workshops for young people. 'Masters' have included Jeremy Irons, Maureen Lipman and Alan Rickman. Other important developments are 2001's initiative, 'Theatre Royal Haymarket Productions', which aims to create more productions for what has been simply a receiving house, and the appointment of Sir Peter Hall as Advisory Director. All in all, the Theatre Royal, Haymarket has a very noble 282-year history.

the theatre royal, haymarket
haymarket = sw17

Her Majesty's Theatre

'**M**y beautiful, beautiful theatre,' is what Herbert Beerbohm Tree always called Her Majesty's... and with some justification! Today, we can still see this grand old playhouse more or less as the great Victorian actor-manager saw it. However, until the early 1960s its proud dome seemed much higher, for now it is dwarfed by the towering New Zealand House where the Carlton Hotel once stood. The theatre and the hotel were conceived by Charles Phipps in 1897 as an integral architectural unit, facing the Theatre Royal, Haymarket across the street. Of Phipps's theatre interior, still virtually intact, George Bernard Shaw wrote, 'He has had the good sense – a very rare quality in England where artistic matters are in question – to see that a theatre which is panelled, and mirrored, and mantelpieced like the first-class saloon of a Peninsula and Oriental liner or a Pullman drawing room car, is no place for *Julius Caesar*; or indeed for anything except tailor-made drama and farcical comedy.' In fact, it is luxurious but restrained, inspired by, but not attempting to equal, the classical forms of Ange-Jacques Gabriel's opera house at Versailles. It has similar triple tiers of boxes, framed by marble Corinthian columns with rich entablatures, a decorated proscenium arch and pretty eighteenth-century style paintings on the ceiling.

From 1992 to 1994 the building was completely refurbished – including the replacement of a roof – without losing one performance of *The Phantom of the Opera*.

This consistently successful and attractive theatre has had three predecessors on the same site and five different names. The

'Tree took unofficial but characteristic action by making Her Majesty's serve some of the functions of a National theatre.'

— George Rowell

first playhouse was built by the celebrated dramatist-architect Sir John Vanbrugh in 1705 and named the Queen's Theatre. It was destroyed by fire in 1789 and rebuilt as the King's Theatre in 1791. It became Her Majesty's in 1837 before being burnt to the ground 30 years later. It re-emerged from the ashes in 1877 as the Italian Opera House, and was demolished in 1891 to give way to the present building. This edifice, in the French Renaissance style with an open loggia, was called His Majesty's from 1902 to the accession of Elizabeth II in 1952. But under whatever name, it has made its mark on theatrical history.

It is highly appropriate that the present-day hit musical, Andrew Lloyd Webber's incredibly successful *The Phantom Of The Opera*, should be housed in a theatre whose origins were mainly as an opera house. On this spot was performed Handel's first opera for England, *Rinaldo* (1711), followed by a number of others by the German master who became an English citizen in 1726. There were also English premieres here of Mozart's *La Clemenza Di Tito* (1806), *Cosi Fan Tutte*, *The Magic Flute* (both 1811), *The Marriage Of Figaro* (1812) and *Don Giovanni* (1817); Beethoven's sole opera, *Fidelio* (1832); Gounod's *Faust* (1863); and Bizet's *Carmen* (1878). 'Swedish Nightingale' Jenny Lind made a sensational London debut in 1847 in *Norma* and other operas, and the first complete performance of Wagner's Ring cycle was given at Her Majesty's in 1882. The venue only became a straight theatre in its fourth incarnation.

Under Beerbohm Tree, Her (His) Majesty's was one of the most distinguished playhouses in Europe. He carried on the Irving tradition of sumptuous, romantic productions of Shakespeare using many visual effects. The playwright Ben Travers described the realism of some of the productions: 'In *A Midsummer Night's Dream* he introduced live rabbits. In *Julius Caesar* the actor who played Caesar was made to wear a bladder of ox blood under his toga so that when he was stabbed he bled profusely.' When Tree produced *Macbeth*, he recruited 50 real guardsmen for the battle scene. They used such force that during a dress rehearsal Tree cried, 'Stop. Never hit a backcloth when it's down.'

Between 1888 and 1914, Sir Herbert Beerbohm Tree (he was knighted in 1909) staged 18 of Shakespeare's plays, as well as melodramatic adaptations of *Oliver Twist* (1905), *David Copperfield* (1914), *Faust* (1908) and the first production of Shaw's *Pygmalion* (1914). The story goes that Tree, as Professor Higgins, kept fluffing his lines on the first night. When Shaw asked him to learn them better, Tree replied, 'But I do know my lines. I do!' – to which the playwright responded, 'Oh, I don't

The renowned Herbert Beerbohm Tree in tragic mode

dispute that for a moment, Sir Herbert. I willingly concede that you do know your lines. But you certainly don't know mine.' Nevertheless, *Pygmalion* was Shaw's greatest commercial success, with Tree and Mrs Patrick Campbell's Eliza winning accolades.

In 1904, Sir Herbert instigated a drama school, which eventually became the Royal Academy of Dramatic Art, in rooms in the dome of the theatre. It was moved a year later to its present home in Gower Street. Sir Herbert's wife, Helen Maud Holt, shared his reign at Her Majesty's, and played in most of the productions. (In 1933, aged 70, Lady Tree returned to this theatre in *The Merry Wives Of Windsor*.) Her husband not only ran the theatre, acted and produced, but found time to have three daughters by his wife and six children by his mistress Beatrice May Pinney-Reed, one of whom was the film director Carol Reed. A busy man indeed! This colourful character died in 1917 aged 64. On the corner of the theatre in Charles II Street, there is a bronze tablet commemorating his contribution to the reputation of Her Majesty's.

The phenomenal success of *The Phantom of the Opera*, which has been running since 1986, was foreshadowed by Oscar Asche and Frederick Norton's 'Musical Tale of the East', *Chu Chin Chow*, which occupied the theatre from 1916 to 1921, the longest known run before *The Mousetrap*. It was, according to theatre writer Lynton Hudson, 'a cunning mixture of music, stage realism, and art pantomime, its constantly refurbished "Folies-Bergerian" mannequin parade in frocks remarkable for their bizarre and gorgeous colour schemes'. It made a deep and lasting impression on the 12-year-old John Gielgud who saw it over ten times. 'I was overwhelmed by the production, which fulfilled my most cherished pictorial enthusiasms,' he wrote. The oriental theme was continued in *Cairo* (1921), Somerset Maugham's *East Of Suez* (1922) and James Elroy Flecker's *Hassan* (1923) with incidental music by Frederic Delius.

C. B. Cochran, who produced Noël Coward's operetta, *Bitter Sweet* (1929), was told, 'It has no comedy, and the hero is killed at the end of the second act.' The fashionable first night audience were, according to Coward, 'as responsive as so many cornflour blancmanges'. There was, however, much cheering at the end,

the great theatres of london

mainly due to Cochran applauding and shouting 'Author!', and Noël in the gods, crying 'Cochran!' The show, containing the ravishing 'I'll See You Again' which was composed in a taxi during a long traffic jam, ran two years.

Further illustrious evenings at Her Majesty's offered J. B. Priestley's *The Good Companions* (1931) with John Gielgud as Inigo Jollifant; the legendary music hall comedian George Robey displaying his versatility as Falstaff in *Henry IV Part 1* (1935); Ivor Novello and Vivien Leigh in Clemence Dane's version of *The Happy Hypocrite* (1936), originally a one-act play by Sir

Andrew Lloyd Webber's musical *Phantom of the Opera* opened in October 1986 and became one of the biggest commercial successes the West End has ever seen

Herbert's half-brother Max Beerbohm; and J. M. Barrie's final play, *The Boy David* (1936), written for and performed by Elisabeth Bergner. The war years saw mainly revivals of popular musical comedies before plays returned in 1947 with Peggy Ashcroft and Robert Morley in the latter's play, *Edward My Son*. Two Broadway hits, *The Tea House Of The August Moon* (1954) and *No Time For Sergeants* (1956), were among the few other plays to interrupt the string of musicals that so often filled the 1,261 seats of the theatre.

Alan Jay Lerner and Frederick Loewe's *Brigadoon* (1949) and *Paint Your Wagon* (1953) preceded Leonard Bernstein's landmark musical *West Side Story* (1958), which ran over two years. Also hailing from Broadway were *Bye Bye Birdie* (1961), *Fiddler On The Roof* (1967), starring Topol as Tevye the milkman and running 2,030 performances, *Company*, *Applause* (both 1972), *Bubbling Brown Sugar* (1980) and the return of *West Side Story* (1984). But now it is the home-grown *Phantom Of The Opera* that continues to attract vast crowds to Her Majesty's. Produced by Cameron Mackintosh, the original cast was led by Michael Crawford and Sarah Brightman. It is the longest-running, most successful production in the theatre's history.

Sir Herbert Beerbohm Tree always disliked long runs, referring to them as 'obstinate successes'. But with *Phantom of the Opera* still playing to capacity audiences, perhaps Her Majesty's present owners, Lord Lloyd Webber's Really Useful Group, might disagree!

her majesty's theatre
haymarket = swly

The Lyceum

On Wellington Street, which runs between Covent Garden and the Strand, stands a magnificent portico. This is the Lyceum – 'The Crown Jewel of the Strand' as it was known in its Victorian heyday. The Lyceum has a truly remarkable history characterised by constant struggle, innovation and transformation. It's amazing that this gutsy theatre has survived into the twenty-first century – so many times has it risen from the ashes (quite literally, on a couple of occasions!).

It all started in July 1771, when the foundation for the very first building was laid in the Strand on part of the gardens of Exeter House. This first theatre was designed by James Payne, and was situated about 100 yards from its present site. It opened in May 1772, and spent its first 30 years as home to an amazing variety of entertainments – as an exhibition hall, for boxing, fencing, concerts, lectures, public debates, travelling curiosities (such as 'Mr Diller and his Philosophical Fireworks'), panorama and phantasmagoria. In 1802, Madame Tussaud held her first waxwork show here.

Then came the first of the fires that was to transform the theatre's history. In 1809 the Theatre Royal, Drury Lane burned down, and the Drury Lane Company arranged to play at the Lyceum until its theatre was rebuilt. This stroke of fate allowed the Lyceum to obtain a proper licence from the Lord Chamberlain for the presentation of plays. When the Drury Lane Company moved back to its new theatre in 1812, the Lyceum held onto this licence for the summer months.

It was decided that this new status required a 'proper' auditorium and in 1815 Samuel Beazley, who was also the architect of the St James Theatre, the colonnade at Drury Lane and London Bridge Station, completely rebuilt the theatre on a scale of great magnificence.

'It became almost a religion to attend the Lyceum, the theatre which had become a temple and a meeting place for the people and the intellectuals alike.'
— J. B. Booth

The history of the Lyceum contains many 'firsts'. It was the first theatre to be lit by gas; the first, in 1817, to experiment at reduced prices with two performances nightly – one at 6.00 p.m., and one at 9.30 p.m; and the first theatre in London to present a one-man show, starring Edmund Kean. However, despite these innovations, the theatre suffered under the licensing laws, which prevented so-called 'minor' theatres from staging drama without a musical interlude. It still managed to play host to Grimaldi, and presented the first performances in England of Weber's *Der Freishutz* in 1824 and Mozart's *Cosi Fan Tutti* in 1828, as well as some Shakespeare.

Fire struck again in 1830, when the theatre, and a large section of Exeter Street, was burnt down. Once again, Samuel Beazley designed a new theatre, which opened its doors on 4 July 1834. It was built slightly to the west of the old building, with the wonderful portico facing the newly created Wellington Street. The new Lyceum was the first theatre in England to incorporate a balcony which projected over the circle and also offered the facility for booking seats in advance. But it wasn't until 1843, when the Licensing Act finally freed all 'minor' theatres from the restrictions which had previously bound them, that the Lyceum was able to get properly into its stride. There were various changes of management for the next 13 years, and the theatre had some successes with burlesques and plays.

In 1856, fire intervened for the third time. Covent Garden went up in flames, and for a while the Lyceum offered the Opera a home, at the time when Adelaide Ristori was enchanting London with his Italian opera.

Innovative director/designer Julie Taymor used masks, puppetry and dramatic designs in her highly original stage version of Disney's *The Lion King*

However, the Lyceum still wasn't having the consistent successes that it needed. And then, in 1871, came the most momentous event in the Lyceum's history. Hezekiah Bateman took over the theatre's management and was persuaded by actor Henry Irving to stage *The Bells*. Irving as Mathias played to overflowing houses for 150 nights (this when 40 to 50 performances was considered a good run). Next year Irving starred in *Charles I*, which ran for 180 nights. By 1878 the actor had taken over the theatre's management. Together with the legendary Ellen Terry, his leading lady, he turned the Lyceum into the most brilliant playhouse in London. Irving's incredible charisma and talent attracted the very best actors, musicians and designers of the time to the Lyceum. All become part of its incredible success. And the public, of every class, came in droves. Irving was knighted in 1895, the first such honour bestowed on an actor.

Sir Henry Irving remained in charge until 1899, presenting one success after another. And then fire intervened again – this time in the theatre's scenery store – destroying almost all of the Lyceum's assets. In the end Irving was forced to sell his control of the theatre to a syndicate. His last appearance at the Lyceum was in 1902, with Ellen Terry at his side, as Shylock in *The Merchant of Venice*. He died shortly after, in 1905.

It was the end of a glorious era, and the Lyceum came very close to being demolished when a new purchaser could not be found. However, it rose again as a music hall, rebuilt by J. Parkinson and designed by Bertie Crewe (Crewe also designed the Phoenix, Piccadilly, Shaftesbury and Saville Theatres). In March 1907 the Lyceum was licensed as a theatre again, and ran successfully for 30 or so years, producing 'popular drama at popular prices' – mostly melodramas and spectacular pantomimes. The annual pantomime became a highly popular star-studded feature, with Ninette de Valois as the *premiere danseuse*. But by 1939 the theatre was struggling again, and was due for demolition to make way for a roundabout. The theatre's final production was *Hamlet*, directed by Ellen Terry's great-nephew, Sir John Gielgud, in June 1939. As the curtain went down, Gielgud proclaimed, 'Long live the Lyceum! Long live Ellen Terry! Long live Henry Irving!'

The intervention of the Second World War saved the Lyceum again – the proposed roundabout was forgotten about. The theatre briefly returned to drama in 1963, with the pantomime *Pinocchio*, but the '60s, '70s and '80s were decades of TV events

the lyceum

and live music – The Who, Bob Marley, The Clash, Iggy Pop and The Kinks all performed here. In 1985 The National Theatre's *The Mysteries* transferred to the Lyceum. At this time, the theatre was described in the *Daily Telegraph* as a 'luscious old playhouse – fluted Tuscan pillars, curved outswelling boxes, plaster figures of maidens and gods, and everywhere balustrades, urns, wrought iron, escutcheons, gilt and Pompeian red – all the long neglect of its Victorian heyday. Everyone asks why can't it all be restored?'

This question remained unanswered until 1994, when the theatre was bought by Apollo Leisure, who restored it to its former opulent glory and introduced state-of-the-art facilities. A triumphant revival of Andrew Lloyd Webber and Tim Rice's *Jesus Christ Superstar* followed, and in 1999 Disney's smash-hit musical *The Lion King*.

The applause that used to greet Sir Henry Irving as he stepped on to the Lyceum's stage was known as the 'Lyceum Roar'. With the successful Lion King in residence, this roar is resounding again. Long live the Lyceum!

the lyceum theatre
wellington street = wc2

The Lyric, Hammersmith

O nce upon a time, an exquisite late Victorian playhouse
was designed by Frank Matcham, the most renowned
and prolific theatre architect of his day, for the London
suburb of Hammersmith. It soon became prosperous and
fashionable, despite its remote location, drawing crowds from the
West End. The Lyric was, according to one expert, 'one of the
best examples of *fin-de-siecle* theatre interiors in greater London
– one designed by a master of the art of theatre building'. In
1972, despite public outrage, the theatre was razed to the ground
to make room for property development. But the story has a
happy ending.

Before the bulldozers could do their destructive work, the
Greater London Council ordered that most of the plasterwork of
the auditorium be preserved and stored. In 1974, the
Hammersmith Council approved plans for a new theatre to be
built as part of a modern development in King Street, not far
from where the original Lyric stood. This was not to be just
another theatre but a complete reconstruction of Matcham's
interior, using some of the original decor. The result is a curious
but rewarding architectural experience.

The commonplace 1979 building which houses the theatre is
located in a mundane suburban shopping centre. At the top of a
stairway, one finds a roomy lounge, bar, self-service restaurant and
large sun-terrace or patio. Airy and relaxed, the venue provides a
pleasant meeting place for people of the area by day and for
playgoers by night. Up another flight of stairs and one enters a time
warp. There it is: the Lyric Opera House of 1895 with only slight

(*above*) Leading London architect Rick Mather's designs for the Lyric's new front door (2003), restoring the theatre's entrance to its rightful place in the heart of Hammersmith

'The Lyric at Hammersmith... was uncomfortable and smelly, the dressing rooms were wretched, but it had a unique atmosphere.'
— Sir John Gielgud

alterations. The obtrusive pillars have been removed from the stalls and the decorated ceiling has been adapted to incorporate contemporary stage lighting and ventilation. The rococo ornamentation on the boxes and two circles has been retained. The traditional masks of Comedy and Tragedy adorn each side of the slightly enlarged proscenium arch.

Comedy and tragedy have played equal roles during the vicissitudes of the theatre's history. The first structure in Bradmore Grove, known as the Lyric Hall, opened in November 1888 with a French marionette show. Two years later, after reconstruction, it became the Lyric Opera House. In 1895,

A sketch of the period shows the original Frank Matcham exterior of what was then called the Lyric Opera House

the lyric, hammersmith

Matcham was commissioned to redesign the building completely. The tireless new manager, John M. East, produced over 400 shows, acted 120 roles, wrote the spectacular annual pantomimes and invited stars like Lillie Langtry and George Arliss to perform here. Alas, when East left in 1904, the theatre's fortunes plummeted, gaining it the sobriquet of the 'Blood and Flea Pit'. This decline was mainly due to a policy of presenting musty melodramas and the rivalry of the new King's Theatre (designed by W. G. R. Sprague and demolished in 1963) nearby.

In 1918, rescued by Nigel Playfair who redecorated it and changed its name to the Lyric Theatre, it became one of London's most popular and exciting playhouses. A poem of the day went:

> No greater name than Nigel Playfair
> Occurs in Thespian lore or myth;
> 'Twas he who first revealed to Mayfair
> The whereabouts of Hammersmith.

Many celebrated productions and performers lit up the Playfair years. His first success was John Drinkwater's chronicle play *Abraham Lincoln* (1919), which ran for a year. Athene Seyler and Herbert Marshall starred in *As You Like It* (1920) before the three and a half years of *The Beggar's Opera* (1921), which Gielgud found 'enchantingly pretty, too pretty perhaps, as the squalid satire of the play was lost... But how wonderfully he did it!' Gielgud himself appeared for Playfair here in *The Cherry Orchard* (1925) and as John Worthing in the 1930 Aubrey Beardsley-inspired black-and-white production of *The Importance Of Being Earnest*, opposite his aunt, Mabel Terry-Lewis, as Lady Bracknell. The later and most famous of all Lady Bracknells, Edith Evans, created a sensation as Millamant in Congreve's *The Way Of The World*. She also appeared in *The Beaux Stratagem* (1927) and *The Old Bachelor* (1931). Sir Nigel (he was knighted in 1928) had a penchant for the eighteenth century and revived Isaac Bickerstaff's comic operas *Lionel And Clarissa* (1925) and *Love In A Village* (1928) as authentically as he could. There is a Sickert portrait of Playfair as an over-age Tony Lumpkin in the present Stalls Foyer.

the great theatres of london

When Nigel Playfair left the Lyric in 1932, brightness left with him. In fact, it was literally dark for most of the period until after the war. Then, once again, playgoers made their way to Hammersmith for exciting productions. Two young actors returned from active service made an impact – Alec Guinness in his own adaptation of *The Brothers Karamazov* (1946) and Richard Burton in Christopher Fry's *The Boy With The Cart* (1950). John Gielgud directed the latter prior to his stunning 1952–53 season of three plays. Gielgud directed Paul Scofield in *Richard II* and *The Way Of The World* with himself as Mirabell, Pamela Brown as Millamant and Margaret Rutherford as Lady Wishfort. The third play was a rare revival of Thomas Otway's Restoration tragedy, *Venice Preserv'd*, directed by a young Peter Brook and starring Scofield and Gielgud.

The Lyric continued to stage diverse and interesting plays for the rest of the decade. Sir Donald Wolfit took on the arduous task of producing and starring in Henri de Montherlant's uncompromising *The Master Of Santiago* and *Malatesta* (both 1957). Challenging, too, were Harold Pinter's first play, *The Birthday Party* (1958), and Ibsen's early work *Brand* (1959). Sandy Wilson's 'high camp' musical, *Valmouth* (1959), was delightfully frivolous and a smash hit.

the lyric, hammersmith

The internationally acclaimed *Shockheaded Peter*

On 18 October, 1979, the Queen officially opened the newly resurrected Lyric. The premiere production, Shaw's *You Never Can Tell*, continued the great tradition of the theatre's previous life. The theatre, which is funded by the Arts Council, has a flexible 110-seat studio underneath the main auditorium and offers lunchtime music, art exhibitions and children's matinees. Among its productions that have transferred to the West End – a sure sign of acclaim – have been Michael Frayn's *Make And Break* and *Noises Off, Charley's Aunt, Miss Julie, Kean* and *The Seagull*. Under the current management, the Lyric has regained its place as a true London original. The boldly programmed repertoire mixes sharp classical revivals with theatrically innovative contemporary work, and attracts a notably young and varied audience. Recent successes have included plays by Marivaux, Kleist and Maugham, the internationally acclaimed *Shockheaded Peter* and a string of strikingly designed Christmas shows, giving a new twist to the theatre's distinguished history.

the lyric, hammersmith
king street = w6

The Lyric, Shaftesbury Avenue

The Lyric, the oldest of the six surviving theatres in Shaftesbury Avenue, blends into a block of buildings in the Renaissance style that stretches from Rupert Street to Great Windmill Street, with only its canopy and sign betraying its function as a theatre. However, the C. J. Phipps interior, redecorated extensively but tastefully in 1932 by Michel Rosenauer, dispenses the charm and atmosphere of a late Victorian playhouse. Giant Corinthian columns frame the boxes, attractive plasterwork decorates the large arch over the proscenium and a handsome pale green and gold circular ceiling encloses the auditorium.

It was built for Henry Leslie, who made a fortune out of the comic opera *Dorothy* by B. C. Stephenson and Alfred Cellier at the Prince of Wales Theatre. Its eight hundred and seventeenth performance opened the Lyric in December 1888. *Doris*, by the same authors, followed in 1889. As befitting the theatre's name, operettas were the principal fare into the 1920s. Many of the early ones featured Marie Tempest, who only forsook singing for straight acting in 1899. W. S. Gilbert, who had quarrelled with Arthur Sullivan, delivered *The Mountebanks* (1892), music by Cellier, and *His Excellency* (1894), music by F. Osmond Carr.

The legitimate drama was strongly represented by the great Italian actress Eleonora Duse, making her debut in England in *La*

> '*It is fortunate that Phipps's interior*
> *(although altered) was not then completely*
> *devastated for the sake of fashion.*'
>
> — John Earl, *Curtains!!!*

Dame Aux Camellias, *Fédora* and *A Doll's House* in 1893. La Duse refused to wear make-up, and was able to blush or pale at will. Three years later, a play with a religious theme brought people to the Lyric who had never before entered a theatre. It was *The Sign Of The Cross* by Wilson Barrett, who himself played the Roman patrician converted to Christianity by his love for a Christian girl. Barrett claimed in private that he was a believer only as far as the box-office was concerned, and continued to present plays of a similar nature, making him the forerunner of Cecil B. De Mille who filmed *The Sign Of The Cross* in 1932.

Not long after Duse appeared here, two of the greatest French actresses arrived in seasons of French plays – Rejane in 1897 and Sarah Bernhardt in 1898. Loïe Fuller danced through nearly 200 performances of *Little Miss Nobody* (1898), and Evie Greene in *Florodoro* (1899) saw the theatre move profitably into the new century. In 1902 Forbes Robertson, considered the greatest Hamlet of his time, repeated the role (he was to play it into his 60s), also taking on Othello and Kipling's *The Light That Failed*. His Desdemona in the former was Gertrude Elliott,

The programme cover for the opening hit, *Dorothy*, in 1888

158

whom he later married despite his affair with Mrs Patrick Campbell. Lewis Waller, known as 'the high priest of dignified tushery' appeared between 1906 and 1910 in *Othello*, *Monsieur Beaucaire*, *Robin Hood*, *Henry V* and *The Rivals*.

Musical entertainments such as Oscar Strauss's *The Chocolate Soldier* (1910), *The Girl In the Taxi* (1912), *Love And Laughter* (1913) and *Mam'selle Tralala* (1914), the latter three with Yvonne Arnaud, led up to the wartime hit *Romance* (1915) starring Doris Keane. In 1919, she went on to play the female lead in *Romeo And Juliet* with the septuagenarian Ellen Terry as the Nurse. John Gielgud, Terry's grand-nephew, recalled, 'She could hardly remember a word, and Basil Sydney and Leon Quartermaine, who were playing Romeo and Mercutio respectively, whispered every line in her ear, and then she said the line herself and it sounded as if she had just thought of it.'

It was back to musical comedy with *Lilac Time* (1922) and *The Street Singer* (1924) before Tallulah Bankhead, the darling of the 'bright young things', drew the crowds in *The Gold Diggers* (1926), *Garden Of Eden* (1927), *Her Cardboard Lover* (1928) and *Let Us Be Gay* (1929). A dazzling sequence of stars and productions epitomising the best in commercial theatre followed: Leslie Howard (just prior to his Hollywood debut) in *Berkeley Square* (1929); J. B. Priestley's ingenious *Dangerous Corner* (1932); Robert Sherwood's high comedy *Reunion In Vienna* with Alfred Lunt and Lynn Fontanne (later replaced by Noël Coward and Yvonne Printemps) in 1934, as well as Edna Ferber and George S. Kaufman's *Theatre Royal* (the English title of *The Royal Family*), which starred Madge Titheradge, Marie Tempest and Laurence Olivier, directed by Coward. Olivier, playing a flamboyant character based on John Barrymore, slipped and fractured two ankle bones while jumping over a banister rail.

Olivier returned with his friend Ralph Richardson in Priestley's 'farcical tragedy', *Bees On The Boatdeck* (1936), which sank after four weeks. Vivien Leigh came to a matinee with Ivor Novello and sat prominently in a box, making Olivier upstage everyone in order to impress the woman he loved. Many years later Leigh herself (now Olivier's wife) held the stage at the Lyric in Coward's *South Sea Bubble* (1956). Critic Harold Hobson wrote, 'Vivien Leigh is the splendour of the production. Her performance shines like the stars, and is as troubling as the inconstant moon.' When she left the cast to have a baby (she subsequently miscarried), the play lost money.

Plays that had good runs without a dependence on big names were Rattigan's *The Winslow Boy* (1946), *The Little Hut* (1950) and the musicals *Grab Me A Gondola* (1956), *Irma La Douce* (1958) and *Robert and Elizabeth* (1964). However, stars such as the Lunts in *Amphitryon 38* – S. N. Behrman's adaptation of Giraudoux (in 1938) – and in Rattigan's *Love In Idleness* (1944); Deborah Kerr in *The Day After The Fair* (1972); Alec Guinness in *Habeas Corpus* (1973); Jessica Tandy and Hume Cronyn in *The Gin Game* (1979), and Glenda Jackson in *Summit Conference* (1982) did no harm to ticket sales. In the latter, a then unknown Gary Oldman had a role. Other future stars were Antony Sher in *John, Paul, George, Ringo... And Bert* (1974), and Bob Hoskins in *Happy End* (1975). In contrast, 90-year-old Ben Travers, master of the Aldwych farce, provided a new hit play called *The Bed Before Yesterday* (1975) in which Joan Plowright (Lady Olivier) and Helen Mirren appeared. Sher returned to the Lyric 23 years later to play Cyrano de Bergerac in the RSC's 1997 production.

John Moffitt, Helen Mirren and Joan Plowright in the hit comedy, *The Bed Before Yesterday* (1975) by Ben Travers

Five Guys Named Moe won the Laurence Olivier Award for Best Entertainment in 1991

Joe Orton's black comedy *Loot* (1984), which features a coffin on stage throughout, was playing to full houses when the lead actor, Leonard Rossiter, tragically died of a heart attack during a performance. The Lyric recovered from the shock and was soon filled with Lerner and Loewe's melodies in *Gigi* (1985) and Clarke Peters's all-singing, all-dancing *Five Guys Named Moe* (which ran for five years from 1990). After a musical revival of *Ain't Misbehavin'*, the Australian dance sensation *Tap Dogs* in 1995 and a transfer of Andrew Lloyd Webber and Alan Ayckbourn's musical *By Jeeves* in 1996, the Lyric returned to drama with a series of leading actresses: Janie Dee in Alan Ayckbourn's *Comic Potential*; Fanny Burney's *A Busy Day* with Stephanie Beacham and Sara Crowe; *Brief Encounter* with Jenny Seagrove; and Eugene O'Neill's masterpiece, *Long Day's Journey Into Night*, starring Jessica Lange. In 2002, after David Warner's return to the stage in *The Feast of Snails*, the Lyric lived up to its name again with a lively revival of the Andrew Lloyd Webber musical, *Daisy Pulls It Off*.

the lyric, shaftesbury avenue
shaftesbury avenue = wlv

The National Theatre

The National Theatre on London's South Bank, overlooking the Thames, opened in 1976. Despite its relatively young status in this location, the theatre has already built up an impressive and vibrant history – a history that actually goes back to the beginning of the last century, when the dream of a state-owned theatre, especially designed for a permanent company, was first discussed. It was a book by critic William Archer and dramatist Harley Granville-Barker, *A National Theatre; Scheme And Estimates*, that sparked off the debate in earnest. In 1913, the first of many proposed sites was acquired in Gower Street for a National Theatre. Another was in South Kensington where George Bernard Shaw 'turned the first sod'. On Friday, 13 June, 1951, Queen Elizabeth (the late Queen Mother) laid the foundation stone of the new building in front of the main entrance to the newly constructed Royal Festival Hall. The site shifted a little further along the South Bank where construction began a mere 18 years later. Meanwhile, the National Theatre Company was set up in 1962 under the directorship of Sir Laurence Olivier, and was housed 'temporarily' at the Old Vic Theatre for almost 13 years.

Finally, the long-awaited building, designed by Sir Denys Lasdun at a cost of £20 million, took its place proudly beside the Royal Festival, Queen Elizabeth and Purcell Concert Halls, the Hayward Gallery and the National Film Theatre as part of an arts centre of international repute, unrivalled in London even by the impressive Barbican Centre inaugurated in 1982. It is certainly situated in one of the most attractive parts of the great capital,

'I think Lasdun's work is triumphant. He has divested concrete of its brutality. It is slender, delicate, and in beautiful geometric patterns. I think the theatre is a masterpiece.'
— Peter Hall

looking out on a splendid reach of the Thames, curving past Somerset House towards St Paul's Cathedral, a scene not all that different from those painted by Turner and Canaletto.

This panoramic view of the noble and busy river can be appreciated from the many jutting terraces, both open and closed, that form an integral part of the bold, unadorned, functional concrete structure. The National Theatre itself is best seen by walking across Waterloo Bridge towards the lights that spell out the day's events, beckoning potential customers over the water. On entering the building, either from the river walk or from the bridge, one is welcomed by the roomy and relaxing foyers, a restaurant, seven bars, five buffets and excellent bookshops. Before each performance, live music is played in the Ground Floor foyer. The building is open all day and members of the public are encouraged to use it as a social centre whether they see a play or not. In 1996, an Arts Council Lottery Fund award allowed the National to develop and expand its foyers, with a new entrance created to include the box-office and bookshop. Although a fairly large building, now housing three theatres, it has an intimacy lacking at the Barbican, London's other large government-subsidised theatre.

Of the four auditoria, the largest and most radical is the Olivier, so called after the company's first artistic director and England's most famous actor. Sadly, Sir Laurence never performed in the theatre that bears his name. Seating 1,160 people, it is fan-shaped with sharply raked seats in the stalls, slightly raised balconies on either side and an upper circle all bearing down on the large apron stage, most suitable for epic theatre of which the opening production in October 1976 was a supreme example. It was a spectacular rendering of Christopher Marlowe's rarely performed masterpiece, *Tamburlaine The Great*, with Albert Finney powerful in the title role.

It was Finney as Hamlet (transferred from the Old Vic) who opened the 890-seat Lyttelton Theatre seven months previously. Named after the National's first chairman Oliver Lyttelton (Lord Chandos), it is of conventional design with an adjustable proscenium stage, part of which can be lowered to form an orchestra pit.

The Cottesloe is a small (approximately 400 seats), simple, flexible, rectangular room with two tiers of galleries on three sides, which can be used for theatre in the round if necessary. This theatre was named after Lord Cottesloe, the chairman of the South Bank Theatre Board. It provides an essential space for experimental or chamber theatre, or as a try-out venue for plays that might transfer to one of the two larger houses. It opened on Saturday 1 March, 1977, the first occasion on which all three main theatres were in use simultaneously.

The fourth theatre, created as part of the National's Transformation season in 2002, is the smallest and most intimate of them all – the Lyttelton Loft, which seats 100 people.

The aims of the National Theatre are to present 'a diversity of repertoire embracing classic, new and neglected plays from the whole of world drama; to present these plays to the very highest standards; to do experimental work, and work for children and young people; to give audiences a choice of at least six different productions at any one time; to take current productions regularly to the regions and abroad; to use fully the unique advantages of the building so that the public is continuously offered, in addition to plays, all kinds of other events.' On the whole, this manifesto has been admirably adhered to. As principal evidence of this, a look at what has been offered over three decades should suffice.

Among the many outstanding productions of classics, both ancient and modern, the National has given us Trevor Nunn's *The*

Broadway came to the South Bank with *Guys and Dolls*. The Salvation Army prayer meeting is here about to begin...

Merchant of Venice (1999); Alan Bennett's *The Wind In The Willows* (1990); Howard Davies's 1988 production of *Cat On A Hot Tin Roof*; Peter Hall's lucid and exciting production of *Coriolanus* (1984), starring Ian McKellen and using members of the audience as extras; and Paul Scofield and Ben Kingsley in *Volpone* (1977). American classics have been represented by Richard Eyre's out-Broadwaying-Broadway production of *Guys And Dolls* (1982), which transferred to the West End for a commercial run, and 2000's superb production of *All My Sons* by Howard Davies, which Arthur Miller acclaimed as the best performance ever of his play. The NT's policy of commissioning established writers to translate and adapt foreign masterpieces has also paid off well. These have included versions of Molière's *Don Juan* (1981) by John Fowles; Chekhov's *Wild Honey* (1984) and Tolstoy's *Fruits Of Enlightenment* (1979) by Michael Frayn; and the vigorously rhythmic and masked Aeschylus trilogy, *The Oresteia* (1981), strikingly adapted by Tony Harrison.

Neglected plays given new life have included 1996's acclaimed version of Ibsen's *John Gabriel Borkman*; Kyd's *The Spanish Tragedy* (1984), the work that most influenced *Hamlet*; Granville-Barker's *The Madras House* (1977); and Maugham's *For Services Rendered* (1979). Some of the new plays presented have been 2002's multi-award-winning *Gagarin Way* by Gregory Burke; *Amy's View*, by David Hare (1997); Tom Stoppard's *Arcadia* (1993); Alan

166

James Hazeldine in Howard Davies's revival of Arthur Miller's modern classic, *All My Sons* (2000)

Bennett's *The Madness of George III* (1991); Howard Brenton and David Hare's brutally funny exposé of Fleet Street, *Pravda* (1985), starring the brilliant Anthony Hopkins; Peter Shaffer's universally acclaimed *Amadeus* (1979), which was first revealed at the Olivier with Paul Scofield as Salieri; Harold Pinter's *Betrayal* (1978); and Alan Ayckbourn's *Bedroom Farce* (1977).

In 1999 Trevor Nunn, the NT's current director, launched a new ensemble of actors with Shakespeare's *Troilus and Cressida*, and two years later the theatre celebrated its twenty-fifth anniversary on the South Bank. In 2002 Transformation – a five month season with reduced ticket prices presenting 13 world premieres - introduced new generations of theatre makers and theatre audiences to one of the best theatres in the world. On 9 March 2002 the National Theatre company staged an astounding and record-breaking 28 performances in 14 different theatres country-wide and in the USA.

And so the noble aims which the National Theatre set for itself over 25 years ago are more than being fulfilled. London's premiere theatre company really has established a triumphant reputation the world over.

the royal national theatre
upper ground, south bank = se1

The New Ambassadors

King: What do you call the play?
Hamlet: *The Mouse-trap.*

Hamlet's sub-title for 'The Murder of Gonzago' lent its name to the Agatha Christie whodunnit which would occupy this dainty and diminutive theatre for over 21 years. From 25 November, 1952 to 25 March, 1974, until it moved a few yards across Tower Court to the St Martin's where it still runs, *The Mousetrap* and the Ambassadors were synonymous. It is a pity, in a way, that many plays and players did not have the opportunity to appear in one of London's most intimate and pretty playhouses during that marathon run.

The Ambassadors and the St Martin's were conceived by their architect, W. G. R. Sprague, as companions born at the same time in 1913, but World War I interrupted the construction of the latter for three years. The Ambassadors is smaller and lower than its neighbour, both conveniently situated opposite the renowned Ivy Restaurant, favourite haunt of the theatrical elite. The theatre has an unfussy classical facade, crowned with a parapet and balustrade decorated with ball-shaped ornaments. Less restrained is the elegant Louis XVI auditorium, the walls of which are festooned with ambassadorial crests. For political reasons these were painted out at the outbreak of war in 1914, and they only reappeared in 1958. A beautiful chandelier shines down from the circular ceiling onto the 453 seats below. The horseshoe-shaped single balcony is reached by a few stairs up from ground level, while the stalls are actually underground.

> 'In a little theatre like the Ambassadors, to have sitting together five or six people who don't laugh or applaud is demoralising.'
> — Charles B. Cochran

Charles B. Cochran recognised that the charming atmosphere and compact size of the Ambassadors would lend itself perfectly to 'intimate' revue when he took a lease on the theatre at the beginning of the war. Here, the great impresario introduced England to what was then a new genre of entertainment from Paris. *Odds And Ends*, starring French actress and singer Alice Delysia, was aimed at more sophisticated audiences than those attending the spectacular revues of the music halls. After 400 performances, it was followed by further Cochran 'miniature revues' called *More (Odds And Ends)* and *Pell Mell*, also with Delysia, between 1915 and 1917. The French connection was continued in 1917 with the presentation of two translated plays, Anatole France's *The Man Who Married A Dumb Wife* and Eugene Brièux's *The Three Daughters Of Monsieur Dupont*.

Many productions of quality were staged during the regime of H. M. Harwood from 1919 to 1932, including his own plays. It was at the Ambassadors that West End audiences first applauded Ivor Novello (in *Deburau*, 1921), 24-year-old Hermione Gingold (in Lord Dunsany's *If*, 1921), Margaret Lockwood in *Family Affairs* (1934) and 22-year-old Vivien Leigh in Ashley Duke's *The Mask Of Virtue* (1935). Miss Leigh created a great impression, as did America's Paul Robeson in Eugene O'Neill's *The Emperor Jones* (1925). When Sydney Carroll took over as manager in 1932, he continued Harwood's good work by presenting revivals of *The Rivals*, *The Country Wife* (1934) and *The Soldier's Fortune* (1935). The last hit before World War II was Margaret Rutherford in *Spring Meeting* (1938).

Hermione Gingold returned to the scene of her adult debut as a fully fledged performer in the vastly successful *The Gate Revue*

(1939), named after the little theatre in Villiers Street, bombed in 1941, from where the show derived. The first revue, which had a young Michael Wilding in the small cast, was followed by *Swinging The Gate* (1940), *Sweet And Low* (1943), *Sweeter And Lower* (1944) and *Sweetest And Lowest* (1946), all with the inimitable Gingold. In 1949, she and Hermione Baddeley used the first major revival of Noël Coward's *Fallen Angels* as a joint showcase for their comic personalities.

A very young Richard Attenborough and his wife, Sheila Sim, as Trotter and Mollie in the original cast of *The Mousetrap* (1952)

the great theatres of london

Nobody ever imagined that a competent little thriller, adapted by Agatha Christie from her own short story *Three Blind Mice*, would enter the record books as the World's Longest Run. The small theatre, the able direction of Peter Cotes, the gripping old-fashioned murder yarn and the snowball effect of a long run helped *The Mousetrap* on its way to becoming a seemingly permanent tourist attraction. Richard Attenborough and his wife Sheila Sim were in the first of generations of casts. When the theatre was finally liberated from *The Mousetrap*, it took some years to catch the habit of success again. This came triumphantly with the transfer of the Royal Shakespeare Company's hit

Lindsay Duncan and Alan Rickman as the sexually decadent and scheming protagonists of *Les Liaisons Dangereuses*, adapted from Laclos's intriguing novel production of Christopher Hampton's *Les Liaisons Dangereuses* (1986) which ran for four years. From 1996 to 1999 the Royal Court leased the theatre for their Royal Court Upstairs, while premises in Sloane Square were renovated. They extended the circle upstairs to create a new theatre, and converted the downstairs into a bar and studio space – and staged landmark productions such as *Shopping and F***ing* by Mark Ravenhill and *East is East* by Ayub Khan-Din. In 1999, when the Royal Court returned to Sloane Square, the theatre was bought by the Ambassadors Theatre Group and renamed the New Ambassadors Theatre. Since then it has continued to present high quality drama with productions like *Krapp's Last Tape*, starring John Hurt, Marie Jones's award-winning *Stones In His Pockets*, Berkoff's *Women, One For the Road,* by and starring Harold Pinter, and David Mamet's acclaimed *Boston Marriage*, from the Almeida.

the new ambassadors theatre
west street = wc2h

The New London

The New London Theatre, built in 1973, lies in the heart of the historic Drury Lane. The very names of the streets surrounding it – Kean, Kemble, Macklin, Betterton, Garrick and Dryden – echo with theatrical history. On the site of the large glass structure, which could pass for a bank or office block, once stood a public house called The Great Mogul, frequented by Nell Gwynn who lived nearby.

In the mid-nineteenth century, the Mogul began to provide entertainment before becoming the renowned Middlesex Music Hall where artistes such as Dan Leno and Marie Lloyd charmed Victorian audiences. Rebuilt by Frank Matcham in 1911, it continued as the New Middlesex Music Hall throughout the Great War, the last of its kind to have a Chairman, the performer who introduced the acts from below the footlights. In 1919, it was taken over by George Grossmith and Edward Laurillard, redecorated and renamed the Winter Garden. Leslie Henson (father of the National's Nicky Henson) returned to the stage from the army to star in the opening production, *Kissing Time*, a musical play by P. G. Wodehouse and Guy Bolton. He continued his association with the theatre in *A Night Out* (1920), an adaptation of Feydeau's farce *L'Hotel Du Libre Echange*, which re-emerged as *Hotel Paradiso* at the Winter Garden in 1956 starring Alec Guinness. Henson also appeared in *Sally* (1921) by Guy Bolton and Jerome Kern, *The Cabaret Girl* (1922) by Bolton, Wodehouse and Kern, and *Primrose* (1925) by Grossmith, Bolton and George Gershwin. Further musical comedies were *Tip Toes* (1926) by Fred Thompson, Bolton and Gershwin, and Sophie Tucker in Vivian Ellis's *Follow A Star* (1930), Rudolf Friml's operetta *The Vagabond King* (1927) and Gracie Fields in the revue *Walk This Way* (1932).

(facing page) Cats – and more cats. It ran and ran...

'The New London is a theatre of the future. It is a theatre that moves; stage, seats, lights – even the walls can be made to change their position.'
— Opening press release, 1973

The lights were out at the Winter Garden for most of the 1930s, coming on again with *Peter Pan* (1942) in which Alastair Sim was Captain Hook for the first time, a role he was to play on and off for 26 years. The theatre was slightly damaged by a bomb shortly after Jack Buchanan and Elsie Randolph appeared in *It's Time To Dance* (1943), but it kept open just the same. Joan Temple's *No Room At The Inn* (1946), which dealt with the wartime evacuation of children, had a surprisingly good run at a theatre noted for much lighter subjects. When *Witness For The Prosecution* (1953) had been running a year, it was one of three Agatha Christie hits in the West End, *The Mousetrap* (at the Ambassadors) and *Spider's Web* (at the Savoy) being the others.

Peter Ustinov *(foreground)* and Brian Bedford in *The Unknown Soldier And His Wife*, which officially opened the theatre in January, 1973

176

the new london

Hollywood star Tyrone Power, who played in the film version of *Witness For The Prosecution*, was dashing as Dick Dudgeon in Shaw's *The Devil's Disciple* (1956). In 1959, the Winter Garden closed its doors forever.

The theatre stood as a hollow shell until 1965, when it was flattened to make room for a complex, incorporating shops, apartments, restaurants... and the New London theatre, designed by Michael Percival. The result is a different environmental experience from the playhouses of yesteryear. Taking on many of the experiments of theatre architecture carried out on the Continent, it gets away from the concept of a fixed space. By having a third of the floor of the auditorium built to revolve, and walls as movable panels, its shape can change from that of an amphitheatre to theatre in the round, from a studio to its utmost capacity of 907 seats, which can be raised or lowered.

The first performance here was a TV recording of Marlene Dietrich's one-woman show in November 1972, two months before the New London opened officially with Peter Ustinov's *The Unknown Soldier And His Wife*, an anti-war play featuring the author and his eldest daughter Tamara Ustinov. Also in 1973, the 25-year-old unknown Richard Gere (prior to his meteoric movie career) played Danny Zuko in the 1950s nostalgia musical *Grease*. Other shows came and went until Andrew Lloyd Webber's music, Trevor Nunn's direction, Gillian Lynne's choreography and T. S. Eliot's minor verse came together to create the legendary *Cats*, which opened in 1981 and has since become the longest-running British musical. But 'even magical things must come to an end' as the slogan went before *Cats*' emotional last performance on 11 May 2002. The question now is, what next for the New London? *Cats* is going to be a hard act to follow...

the new london theatre
drury lane and parker street = wc2

The Old Vic

There is no theatre in London whose history is more imbued with the character of one person than the venerable Old Vic. The spirit of this theatre was embodied by an irritating, God-intoxicated, 'undereducated', unmarried, bespectacled woman who hardly ever saw a play through. Yet Lilian Baylis probably exerted the most profound influence on the performing arts in Britain than anyone else in the twentieth century. And she did it from her tiny office in the theatre she loved and seldom left, away from the mainstream of the West End. It is not too fanciful to argue that without her instinct, indefatigability and religious zeal there would be no National Theatre, Royal Ballet or English National Opera, neither would English acting have acquired the international reputation it enjoys today.

Reputed to have prayed, 'Lord God, please send me a good actor, but send him cheap,' Lilian Baylis was tight-fisted with money but generous with art. She didn't seem to care that patrons would catch their feet in the holes of the carpets as long as there was quality on stage. Such was the prestige and joy of appearing here that the greatest actors would accept miserably low salaries. She treated everyone the same; there were no stars in her heaven. Baylis used to cook bacon and sausages on a gas ring in the wings between, and sometimes during, performances. When Robert Atkins, one of the leading actors and producers in the company, advised her to go out and see what was happening in other theatres, Baylis replied, 'Not keen on plays, dear. Don't know what they're about.'

Tyrone Guthrie, who would become a leading light as producer at the Old Vic, describes a visit he paid to the theatre in 1929 to see Gielgud's Shylock. 'The old house was shabby, even grubby. Rather rude and angry crones shoved a programme into

*'It smells and feels like a theatre, and is
able to transform a collection of human beings
into that curious, vibrant instrument for an
actor – an audience.'*

— Sir John Gielgud

your hands… But the house was packed, and the enthusiasm of
the unspoilt, intelligent audience was infectious…the Old Vic
audience, one felt, was composed of people who you could die to
please, who wanted their horizons enlarged, who would come out
to meet new ideas and new challenges… For the first time in my
life I saw new social possibilities in the theatre.'

How did the Old Vic, as critic Ivor Brown wrote, 'become more
truly Shakespearean in spirit than any regular professional theatre
since the age of the poet himself?' The first hundred years of its
existence gave little indication that it would ever become so. In
1816 it was proposed that a theatre be built in Lambeth on the
South Bank of the Thames. It was to be named the Royal Coburg
in honour of Prince Leopold and Princess Charlotte, who headed
the list of subscribers. The architect was Rudolph Cabanel of
Aachen, and the foundation stone and other materials came from
the recently demolished Savoy Palace at the foot of Waterloo
Bridge, not far from the site. However, building progressed slowly
due to lack of funds until Joseph Glossop, stage-struck son of a
wealthy Soho merchant, put up the money and became manager
when it eventually opened in May 1818.

Owing to the state of the roads and its unfashionable location,
the Royal Coburg soon developed into the home of lurid
melodramas for the local population. According to a
contemporary writer, it was 'the very haunt and refuge of the
melodramatic muse… where murder bares her red arm'.
Nevertheless, none other than Edmund Kean acted here for a
season in 1831, under the management of George Davidge who
insisted that the Monday night working-class audiences were

succeeded in the middle of the week by 'the better classes, the play-going public generally'. In 1833, a redecoration and a change of name – it became officially the Royal Victoria, but known ever since as the Old Vic – did not disguise the fact that it was still a 'Blood Tub', the name given to a theatre staging crude melodramas at very cheap prices. In 1871, it was newly baptised the New Victoria Palace before closing down in 1880. In December of that year, the whole history of the disreputable building was altered.

Emma Cons, a doughty social reformer and the first woman member of the London County Council, bought it and changed the entire interior and the name – to the Royal Victoria Hall and Coffee Tavern. With William Poel as manager, it was used for concerts, operas and scenes from Shakespeare. At the close of the nineteenth century, Miss Cons sent for her 24-year-old niece, then a music teacher in South Africa, to come and assist her. Lilian Baylis, whom Hugh Walpole called a 'first-class Cockney from South Africa', was born in London and went out to the colony with her family in her teens. Although she had had little previous connection with the theatre world, the management passed to her in 1912. Two years later, she began the bold experiment of presenting all of Shakespeare's plays in the First Folio at popular prices. This was achieved with the help of epoch-making producers like Harcourt Williams, Robert Atkins, Ben Greet and Tyrone Guthrie and performers such as Sybil Thorndike, John Gielgud, Laurence Olivier, Ralph Richardson, Peggy Ashcroft, Edith Evans, Charles Laughton, Michael Redgrave, Flora Robson, Alec Guinness and James Mason. In 1923, the production of *Troilus And Cressida* completed the cycle of Shakespeare plays, making the Old Vic the first theatre in the world to achieve this. It must also be noted that opera and ballet performances were being given at the same time until a second house was found at Sadler's Wells in 1931.

Lilian Baylis, 'The Magnificent Tyrant' according to James Agate, died in 1937. After a bomb severely damaged the building in 1941, the theatre was closed for the duration of the war. In

The young Ralph Richardson was a delightful Bottom in *A Midsummer Night's Dream* (1931)

November 1950, the Old Vic Company, after a glittering sojourn at the New Theatre (later renamed the Albery), returned home under the directorship of Michael Benthall. From 1953 to 1958, Benthall followed in Baylis's footsteps by embarking on a 'Five Year Plan' to stage all 36 of Shakespeare's plays in the First Folio once again, beginning with Richard Burton as Hamlet and ending with John Gielgud, Edith Evans and Harry Andrews in *Henry VIII*. Both Burton and the aristocratic-looking John Neville were 'matinee idols' of this period, alternating the parts of Iago and Othello in a 1956 production. Neville broke new ground by playing Hamlet in a white shirt and jeans in 1958.

In 1963, this unofficial national theatre company was disbanded, and the Old Vic became the 'temporary' home (for 13 years) of the newly formed National Theatre under Laurence Olivier, who directed the inaugural production of *Hamlet* starring Peter O'Toole and Michael Redgrave. If, as Voltaire states, 'History is nothing more than a tableau of misfortunes', then the history of the National Theatre at the Old Vic can only be described as a tableau of triumphs. John Dexter and William Gaskill were associate directors and Kenneth Tynan the literary manager, while Olivier's own contribution was tremendous. In addition to his administrative duties, he played 13 roles including Astrov in *Uncle Vanya* (1963), in a cast that boasted Redgrave, Thorndike, Joan Plowright and Fay Compton, as well as Solness in *The Master Builder* and an extraordinarily magnetic pitch-black Othello, both in 1964 and both with Maggie Smith. Among the new plays introduced here were Peter Shaffer's *The Royal Hunt Of The Sun* (1964) and *Equus* (1973), Tom Stoppard's *Rosencrantz And Guildenstern Are Dead* (1966) and *Jumpers* (1974), John Arden's *Armstrong's Last Goodnight* (1964) and Trevor Griffiths' *The Party* (1973).

The first Old Vic production following the departure of the National Theatre in 1976 was *The White Devil* with Glenda Jackson. The following year, the Old Vic became the home of the Prospect Theatre Company directed by Timothy West, with productions including *Hamlet* with Derek Jacobi. The finances of

the theatre were precarious, and in 1982 it was put up for sale. Bought by Canadians Ed and David Mirvish, the Old Vic was restored to its former Victorian splendour. The stone and stucco facade and arched side wall in Waterloo Road were redecorated, and the auditorium with its lyre-shaped balconies was enlarged by 130 to 1078 newly upholstered seats. It was under the Mirvish management that one of the great British

Laurence Olivier (seated) gave one of his many great performances in Strindberg's *The Dance of Death* (1967). Geraldie McEwan was his wife, Robert Lang her brother theatre directors, Jonathan Miller, was made artistic director. Between 1987 and 1990 he directed 17 productions at the Old Vic, collecting five Olivier Awards, including one for *Candide* as Best Musical. At the end of 1997 the Mirvishes announced their decision to sell, and the fate of this historic theatre lay in the balance again. Rumours circulated about plans for a themed pub or - worse – a lap-dancing club. But at the eleventh hour, following pleas from the Government, a non-profit-making trust was formed to buy and save the theatre. The Trust, initially chaired by Alex Bernstein with director Stephen Daldry, actor Kevin Spacey and impresario Sally Greene, undertook to raise the money required and to implement an artistic policy to place the Old Vic once again at the forefront of British Theatre.

Peter O'Toole won great acclaim for his performance in the title role of *Jeffery Bernard Is Unwell*

Since the acquisition of the freehold in 2000, the theatre has been doing just that. The first production under the Trust's ownership was the Almeida's phenomenally successful *The Iceman Cometh*, directed by Howard Davies and starring Kevin Spacey. Subsequent successes have included a new production of *Amadeus* with David Suchet, directed by Sir Peter Hall, a revival of *Jeffrey Bernard is Unwell*, starring Peter O'Toole and directed by Ned Sherrin, Frank McGuinness's new play *Dolly West's Kitchen* and Adventures in Motion Pictures' new production of *The Car Man*, choreographed by Matthew Bourne. In 2002 it was announced that theatre-lover Elton John was to be the new chairman of the Old Vic Theatre Trust – no better figure to help raise funds for renovations and keep the Old Vic in the position it deserves, as one of the greatest theatres in London.

the old vic
the cut, waterloo road = sel

The Palace

'The World's Greatest Artistes Have Passed And Will Pass Through These Doors' is engraved in stone above the stage door of the Palace. The claim is not an idle one, because 'artistes' of the calibre of Sarah Bernhardt, Marie Tempest, Anna Pavlova, Maurice Chevalier, Max Miller, Evelyn Laye, Cicely Courtneidge, Jack Hulbert, Ivor Novello, Jean-Louis Barrault, Laurence Olivier, Judi Dench and Natalia Makarova have played at the Palace, one of London's most glorious monuments to musical theatre.

This High Victorian edifice was built for Richard D'Oyly Carte in 1891 as the Royal English Opera House, to encourage the writing and production of home-grown operas. But to D'Oyly Carte's mortification, only the opening production, *Ivanhoe*, Arthur Sullivan's sole attempt at grand opera, was forthcoming from an English composer. He had to follow it up with André Messager's *The Basoche* from France. After its short run, and a Sarah Bernhardt season during which she played Sardou's Cleopatra, the impresario, who had brought Gilbert and Sullivan together, admitted defeat and sold the building to Augustus Harris in 1892. Harris immediately abandoned any idea of presenting operas here, and renamed the building the Palace Theatre of Varieties.

Although its days as an opera house were short-lived, the theatre retains the air and structure of such a place. In fact, Andrew Lloyd Webber and Tim Rice's rock opera *Jesus Christ Superstar* (1972) and the current musical *Les Misérables*, which began its incredible run in 1985, have been perfectly at home here. Of the latter, Alain Boublil, who wrote the original text, says, 'this book (Victor Hugo's) is already a spoken opera…', and the composer Claude-Michel Schonberg writes, 'after the libretto was written… I decided, when faced with such an epic story, to

> *'The only theatre architecture of the last sixty years in London, or for that matter the provinces, which climbs into the regions of a work of art.'*
> — John Betjeman, 1952

employ a real operatic structure using a mixture of romantic nineteenth-century music with a contemporary mood – I am an opera fan so this exercise was very enjoyable for me.'

The building, occupying a whole block, partly in Shaftesbury Avenue, was designed by C. H. Holloway and decorated by T. E. Colcutt. The striking and unusual Francois I terracotta frontage (restored in 1989) facing Cambridge Circus has three bays filled with dozens of tiny arched windows, and at each corner domed towers rise above the parapet. Inside, a grand marble staircase leads up to the circle bar, also in marble, and down to the extremely attractive Palace Brasserie, looking as it might have done in the last century. The auditorium, seating 1,450, has ornate gold mouldings and mirrors, and the deeply projecting galleries were said to be unparalleled at that time by any theatre in Europe. However, in 1959 John Betjeman wrote, 'Alas, the veined marbles which were so elegant and essential a part of its interior decoration have lately been defaced by a coat of plum-coloured paint.' Fortunately, when Andrew Lloyd Webber's Really Useful Company took over the building in 1982, this paint was scraped off to reveal that the marble and the Mexican onyx panels were undamaged. The Palace is gradually being returned to its former glory in an ongoing project of restoration without affecting performances

Many of the glories of the music hall performed here in variety bills for some years before revues became all the rage. American star Elsie Janis made a hit in *The Passing Show* (1914) in which Clara Beck sang 'I'll Make A Man Of You', one of the most famous recruiting songs of the Great War. In the sequel, *The Passing Show Of 1915*, Basil Hallam introduced the song 'Gilbert The Filbert' before he was killed at the front. Other revues of the period were *Bric-A-Brac* (1915) with Gertie Millar, *Vanity Fair* (1916), *Airs And Graces* (1917) and *Hullo, America!* (1918) in which Elsie Janis partnered Maurice Chevalier. A semi-Pierrot group called *The Co-Optimists*, of whom Stanley Holloway was a founding member, had a good run in 1924.

The tradition of musical comedy at the Palace began in earnest, or rather in frivolity, with Vincent Youmans's *No, No, Nanette* (1925), which ran for 655 performances. Then came *Princess Charming* (1926), *The Girl Friend* (1927), Jerome Kern's *The Cat And The Fiddle* (1932), *The Gay Divorcee* (1933), Cole Porter's *Anything Goes* (1935) and Rodgers and Hart's *On Your Toes* (1937), which returned triumphantly 47 years later. In between these musicals was a Charles B. Cochran revue, *Streamline* (1934), in which Tilly Losch danced exotically, Gilbert and Sullivan were burlesqued, and Florence Desmond played 'The first British mother to fly over the North Pole with her baby'.

From 1938 to 1945 the Palace was almost exclusively occupied by that madcap married couple Cicely Courtneidge and

Jack Hulbert in *Under Your Hat* (1938), *Full Swing* (1942) and *Something In The Air* (1943). They made way for two operettas based on the works of Johann Strauss (*Gay Rosalinda*, 1945) and Edward Grieg (*Song Of Norway*, 1946). During the long run of the latter, the theatre came under the management of Tom Arnold and Emile Littler. Over a year into the run of Ivor Novello's *King's Rhapsody* (1949), its composer-star collapsed and died aged 58.

Coincidentally, the great German playwright Bertolt Brecht, Novello's antithesis, died at the same age in 1956 in East Berlin while his Berliner Ensemble was paying a visit to the Palace on the invitation of impresario Peter Daubeny. Before they left for England, Brecht had told the Ensemble to remember that, as English audiences did not understand German, they were to play it 'quick, light and strong', to dispel any idea the English had that German drama was heavy. Daubeny also brought over other foreign troupes in the 1950s, including the Renaud-Barrault company and Jean Vilar's Theatre Nationale Populaire. The last in a short period of straight plays at the Palace was the transfer from the Royal Court of John Osborne's *The Entertainer* (1957) starring Laurence Olivier with his future wife, Joan Plowright (taking over from Dorothy Tutin), playing his daughter. From then on it was musical entertainment all the way.

Imports from Broadway with British casts were Frank Loesser's *Where's Charley?* (1958) with Norman Wisdom, two Rodgers and Hammerstein hits, *Flower Drum Song* (1960) and *The Sound Of Music* (1961), which ran six sentimental years, and *Cabaret* (1967) with Judi Dench. Among the great big flops were *Two Cities* (1969), a musical derived from the novel *A Tale Of...*, and Betty Grable in *Belle Starr* (1970). Also showing lovely legs was drag artist Danny La Rue, wearing an array of gorgeous gowns for two years in the revue *At The Palace* (1970). Then came *Jesus Christ Superstar* (1972) which, according to Andrew Lloyd Webber, 'kept two then young British lads off the surrounding streets for nine years!' *On Your Toes* (1984) starred Russian ballerina Natalia Makarova, and was directed by 97-year-

Crowd scene in the Cameron Mackintosh production
of *Les Misérables*

old George Abbott, before the Royal Shakespeare Company
brought in *Les Misérables*. Now in its seventeenth year, and
counting, it is the theatre's longest running production.
Nicknamed 'The Glums' by its director Trevor Nunn, *Les
Misérables* has kept the Palace happy for many years.

the palace theatre
shaftesbury avenue = wlv

The Palladium

ife Begins At Oxford Circus And Round About Regent Street, the title of a 1935 Crazy Gang show at the London Palladium, just about summed up what lovers of the music hall felt when approaching this enormous edifice of entertainment. For a variety act to have played the Palladium was equal in theatrical mythology to playing a two-a-day at Broadway's Palace Theatre. A list of all the famous stars who have appeared here would make up a 'Who's Who' of show business.

Until 1865 there stood on the spot a large mansion that belonged to the Dukes of Argyll and Marlborough (hence the names of the two streets that bound the Palladium). After it was demolished a firm of wine merchants built what was known as the Corinthian Bazaar. (The present safety curtain shows what it looked like.) From 1871 to 1887, the building was occupied by Charles Hengler's Circus and then for some years it functioned as a 'Real Ice Skating Rink'. When a syndicate led by the promoter Walter Gibbons (later knighted) acquired the site at a time when business was booming at such places as the Palace, the Hippodrome and the Coliseum, it was decided that a music hall should be built. The architect of the latter two theatres, Frank Matcham, built the Palladium's facade by incorporating parts of the former circus building. With its six giant Corinthian columns on tall pedestals and statues at the centre and either side of the roof it could pass for a neo-Baroque temple, but for the canopy and the neon sign – one of the first to light up a theatre.

The vast, richly adorned and gilded auditorium with its two cantilevered balconies became familiar to millions on TV from the mid-1950s on, with a weekly variety show called *Sunday Night At The London Palladium*. MCs over the years included Tommy Trinder, Norman Vaughan, Bruce Forsyth and Jimmy Tarbuck. The formula was revived for a new generation in 1987

'The Palladium ... attracts a large number of shoppers who patronise the performances before they go home.'
— Ronald Mayes, *The Romance of London Theatres*, 1930

with *Tarbuck's Friends* – who included Howard Keel, Shirley Bassey, Tom Jones and Bruce Forsyth. Bruce himself performed a one-man show at the Palladium for a week in 1991, and on his seventieth birthday in 1998 the theatre staged a special *Sunday Night At The London Palladium* show with Diana Ross.

Those who have had the pleasure of going to this theatre can testify to the surprising intimacy and atmosphere of the place. This People's Palace can claim, with a seating capacity of over 2,300, to be the largest live theatre in London, discounting only the Coliseum – slightly bigger but now an opera house. *The Era* of 1910 noted: 'Perhaps the most unique feature is the box-to-box telephone that has been installed. It will therefore be possible for the occupants of one box, recognising friends in another box, to enter into conversation with them.' Alas, this little convenience no longer exists, and waving and shouting from the paired boxes in arched niches on each level must suffice.

the palladium

The Palladium opened on 26 December 1910 with a variety bill topped by Nellie Wallace, 'The Essence of Eccentricity', Ella Shields and 'Mr Martin Harvey and his full company' in a one-act play called *Conspiracy*. Subsequent programmes mixed farce, ballet, opera, melodrama, song and comedy in two shows each evening and two matinees a week. Variety it was called and variety it was! All the most famous artistes of the music hall appeared here in the first few years: Albert Chevalier entertained with his Cockney coster songs like 'My Old Dutch', and George Robey was elected 'The Prime Minister Of Mirth'. One bill had Thomas Beecham (whose father was an investor in the company running the theatre) conducting operatic excerpts between the comic turns.

In 1912 Charles Gulliver took over the management from Gibbons. Gulliver went in for spectacular revues such as *Whirl Of The Town* (1915), *The Palladium Minstrels* (1921), *Rockets* (1922) and *Whirl Of The World* (1923). The latter starred Nellie Wallace, Tommy Handley – later to come into his own on radio during World War II – and Nervo and Knox, who would return with the Crazy Gang in the 1930s. Revues alternating with the annual pantomime continued until 1928 when George Black reintroduced variety. Black, a theatre manager from the North of England, was the outstanding figure in music hall between the wars.

George Black's opening variety bill featured Gracie Fields, 'The Lancashire Lass making her first Palladium appearance', and Dick Henderson (father of comedian Dickie Henderson), alongside Ivor Novello and Phyllis Monkman in a one-act play entitled *The Gate Crasher*. In 1930, the Royal Variety Show, in aid of the Entertainment Artists' Benevolent Fund, was instigated at the Palladium, the theatre used more often than any other for this annual event. It was also host to the Christmas presentation of J. M. Barrie's *Peter Pan* until 1938. The Peters were Jean Forbes-Hamilton (1930–34 and 1938), Nova Pilbeam (1935), Elsa Lanchester (1936) and Anna Neagle (1937).

The Crazy Gang shows became another Palladium institution from 1932. The three pairs of comedians – Bud Flanagan and Chesney Allen, Charlie Naughton and Jimmy Gold, and Jimmy Nervo and Teddy Knox – brought back the low comedy tradition of 'the halls'. Their outrageous routines kept Londoners laughing in lavish productions, always containing one number with the unprepossessing sextet in drag, until 1938. Some titles were *Okay For Sound* (1936), *London Rhapsody* (1937) and *These Foolish Things* (1938).

The war years were filled with revues: *The Little Dog Laughed* (1940); *Best Bib And Tucker* (1942) starring Tommy Trinder, a favourite Buttons in the pantomime *Cinderella* here for some years; and Irving Berlin's *This Is The Army* (1942) in which the composer himself sang 'Oh, How I Hate To Get Up In The Morning'. On George Black's death in 1946, Val Parnell took over the management and Moss Empires the ownership.

Apart from the Christmas pantos, often running well into the new year, Parnell introduced variety bills topped by big American stars from 1948. Jack Benny, Ethel Merman, Danny Kaye, Bob Hope, Bing Crosby, Fats Waller, Duke Ellington, Frank Sinatra, Tony Martin, Cyd Charisse, Phil Harris, Betty Garrett and Liberace were some of the names to appear on the Palladium's programmes. In 1964, Judy Garland, who had triumphed here in the 1950s, returned with her 18-year-old daughter Liza Minnelli. Judy dominated the show, and Liza's inexperience was cruelly exposed. But in 1973, now a star in her own right, Liza earned a standing ovation from the Palladium audience.

Although the Palladium kept variety alive long after it was said to be dead, there came a time when it had to ring down the curtain on what had been the mainstay of the theatre for most of its history. But *nil desperandum…* musicals were there to save the day. Yul Brynner played his most famous role in *The King And I* (1979), a role replayed by Jason Scott Lee, with Elaine Paige, in 2000. Michael Crawford risked his neck every night for two years in *Barnum* (1981), Tommy Steele attempted to follow Gene Kelly's footwork in *Singin' In The Rain* (1983 and again in 1989); George

the palladium

Yul Brynner played the King of Siam for the umpteenth time in
The King and I (1979). The governess was Virginia McKenna

Hearn and Denis Quilley camped it up in the opulent *La Cage Aux Folles* (1986); Jason Donovan, then Phillip Schofield stopped hearts in a new production of *Joseph and the Amazing Technicolor Dreamcoat* (1991); Sam Mendes directed *Oliver!* with Jonathan Pryce as Fagin in 1994 – the Palladium's longest-running show, with 1,385 performances – and in 2002 Michael Ball took to the air in the Sherman brothers' best-loved musical, *Chitty Chitty Bang Bang*, all in the best Palladium tradition.

the palladium theatre
argylle street = wla

The Phoenix

Champagne corks and flashbulbs popped as London's glitterati poured into the Phoenix Theatre on its opening night, 24 September, 1930. It was not only a special evening because of the launching of Sidney Bernstein's new playhouse, but it was also that most fashionable of premieres – a 'Noël Coward First Night'. *Private Lives*, his brittle and now classic cocktail and dressing-gown comedy, was unveiled, starring the author and Gertrude Lawrence. The pair sparkled as ex-marrieds Elyot and Amanda on honeymoon with their dull spouses, played by the attractive Adrienne Allen and a devastatingly handsome 23-year-old named Laurence Olivier. Few theatres could have had a more glamorous beginning.

Coward wrote *Private Lives* as a vehicle for Lawrence and himself in just four days, while recovering from flu in Shanghai. Of their first love scene on the balcony, Coward's biographer Cole Lesley wrote, 'Gertie and Noël looked so beautiful together, standing in the moonlight, that no one who saw them can ever forget; and they played the scene so magically, lightly, tenderly, that one was for those fleeting moments brought near to tears by the underlying vulnerability, the evanescence, of their love.' The much-revived play got generally good reviews, but Ivor Brown in *Weekend* commented, 'Within a few years, the student of drama will be sitting in complete bewilderment before the text of *Private Lives* wondering what on earth these fellows in 1930 saw in so flimsy a trifle.' Despite full houses, the play closed after three months when it went to Broadway with Jill Esmond, whom Olivier had just married, replacing Adrienne Allen.

In 1936, Noël and Gertie returned to rescue the Phoenix from a bad patch with his programme of nine one-act plays under the title of *Tonight At 8.30*. In one of them, *Hands Across The Sea*, Coward took off Lord and Lady Mountbatten, but sent Lord

'Private Lives *was decked in a glorious sheen of success... and, in addition, was chosen to open the Phoenix Theatre, a smart new ornament to London's theatreland.'*

— Cole Lesley

Louis tickets for the first night. Mountbatten was not amused. 'It was a bare-faced parody of our lives... absolutely outrageous and certainly not worth six free tickets!' (Coward made amends with his 1942 war film, *In Which We Serve*.) On 12 September, 1952, Coward attended *Quadrille*, the Victorian comedy he had written for the Lunts, with gorgeous sets and costumes by Cecil Beaton. It was six days after he had heard that Gertie Lawrence had died of cancer of the liver. He found it difficult to sit through the first night in what he and Gertie used to refer to as 'our theatre'.

Seventeen years later, on 16 December, 1969, the owners of the Phoenix, Gerald and Veronica Flint-Shipman, helped organise a midnight matinee in honour of Coward's seventieth birthday. Coward entered his box on the stroke of midnight, and friends on stage and in the audience, including Princess Margaret, rose to their feet to sing 'Happy Birthday'. A few days before, he had opened the swanky Noël Coward Bar in the foyer, the first thing that greets one on entering this pleasing theatre. A collection of paintings and photos associated with Coward line the walls. He died in 1973, the year that Vanessa Redgrave, Jeremy Brett and John Stride appeared here in a successful revival of *Design For Living*, the play Coward wrote for himself and the Lunts in the 1930s.

The atmosphere of the 1930s still permeates the Phoenix with its Art Deco fittings, mirrored corridors and patterned ceilings conceived by the innovative Russian director and designer Theodore Komisarjevsky (briefly Peggy Ashcroft's second husband). In contrast to the modern, the classical is represented by the painted panels, by Vladimir Polunin, showing reproductions of works by Tintoretto, Titian and Giorgione. The exterior of the Charing Cross Road entrance is also classical in style with its four rather jaundiced columns. This entrance is awkwardly separated from the main entrance in Phoenix Street (next to a newly built cinema) by an unappetising apartment block.

The carefree early days of the theatre receded as the Munich crisis loomed. In 1938, Michel St Denis produced Bulgakov's *The White Guard* and Shakespeare's *Twelfth Night*, both with Michael Redgrave and Peggy Ashcroft, to acclaim. They were followed by a timely revival of Elmer Rice's *Judgement Day* (1939), about the Reichstag trial. The highlight of the war years was John Gielgud's production of *Love For Love* (1943) with himself as Valentine and Yvonne Arnaud as Mrs Frail. The critic W. A. Darlington noted that 'the crowds who flocked to see it

The breakfast table scene from Coward's immortal *Private Lives* (1930) with *(from left to right)* Adrienne Allen, Noël Coward, Gertrude Lawrence and Laurence Olivier were not impelled by a sudden realization of Congreve's excellence as a writer, but by his bawdiness'. It might be remembered that Arnold Bennett called Noël Coward 'the Congreve of our day'. Gielgud returned after the war as Leontes in *The Winter's Tale* (1951) and Benedick in *Much Ado About Nothing* (1952). During the former, Hazel Terry (Fred Terry's granddaughter) accidentally set herself alight and was doused by a fellow actor, the playwright John Whiting. Gielgud remarked before making his entrance, 'I hear cousin Hazel caught fire. The Terrys have always been combustible.'

Failing to catch fire here was Thornton Wilder's 'history of the world', *The Skin Of Our Teeth* (1945), starring Vivien Leigh and presented by her husband Laurence Olivier. This eminent theatrical couple appeared together in Terence Rattigan's Coronation year offering, a Ruritanian tale called *The Sleeping Prince* (1953) – filmed in 1957 as *The Prince And The Showgirl* with Olivier and Marilyn Monroe. Rattigan, on much better form, had been here previously with his double bill of *The Browning Version* and *Harlequinade* with Eric Portman and Mary Ellis in the vastly contrasting pieces. Paul Scofield made a great impact in *Hamlet*, Graham Greene's *The Power And The Glory* and T. S. Eliot's *The Family Reunion* from 1955 to 1956. There was a touch of Hollywood in the 1976 'Phoenix Theatre Season' of four plays – Rock Hudson and Juliet Prowse in *I Do I Do*, Glynis Johns and Louis Jourdan in *13, Rue De Lamour*, Lee Remick in *Bus Stop* and Douglas Fairbanks Jr in *The Pleasure Of His Company*, and in 1992 Dustin Hoffman's memorable Shylock, directed by Sir Peter Hall. This production, and the young Kenneth Branagh's season (1988), with Branagh himself in *As You Like It*, showed that Shakespeare could still be a West End attraction.

The '80s and '90s have seen their share of award-winners - Alan Bleasdale's Elvis musical, *Are You Lonesome Tonight?* (Musical of the Year, 1985) and Brian Friel's *Dancing at Lughnasa* (1991 Olivier Award for Best Play). The Phoenix also continues its tradition for long runs: from *Canterbury Tales* (1968, for five years) to Tom

Stoppard's *Night and Day* (1978 for two years) and the longest run
of all – *Blood Brothers*, the Willy Russell musical, which transferred
from the Albery in late 1991.

the phoenix theatre
charing cross road = wc2h

The Piccadilly

In the souvenir programme that accompanied the opening of the Piccadilly Theatre in April 1928, it was stated that if all the bricks used in its construction were placed end to end in a straight line, they would stretch from London to Paris. This was another way of saying that the theatre was a huge construction, one of the largest built in London in the twentieth century. Designed by Bertie Crewe and Edward A. Stone for the impresario Edward Laurillard, its 1,400-seat auditorium aimed for space and comfort. There were elongated bars on the three levels and beautifully equipped Ladies' Salons with rows of dressing tables and mirrors to assist any necessary facial refurbishment. The fittings and decoration in green and gold were carried out in the modernist Art Deco style by Marc-Henri and Laverdet, as the French designers Marc-Henri Levy and Gaston Laverdet were known. The attractive four-storey Portland stone facade curves gracefully round the corner on which the theatre stands, vaguely influenced by John Nash's classical frontages in Regent Street only a few yards away.

Evelyn Laye, reputedly the most popular musical comedy actress of the time, starred in the first production here, Jerome Kern's *Blue Eyes*, which ran four months before transferring. For the next year, the theatre was used by Warner Brothers for the showing of 'talkies', starting with Al Jolson's second film, *The Singing Fool*. Live theatre returned in November 1929 with a revival of *The Student Prince*. A very mixed batch of productions ensued, failing to give the Piccadilly any distinctive personality or policy.

Up to the outbreak of war, the theatre played host to Cicely Courtneidge in a revue entitled *Folly To Be Wise* (1931), Robert Donat and Ernest Thesiger in James Bridie's *A Sleeping Clergyman* (1933) and Gwen ffrangcon-Davies in *The Barretts Of*

'In May 1973 success arrived at last with Gypsy starring Angela Lansbury.'
— Mander & Mitchenson

Wimpole Street (1935). The character of the Piccadilly was epitomised in a *mélange* called *Choose Your Time*. It consisted of a continuous programme of variety turns, a swing band, newsreels, cartoons and *Talk Of The Devil*, a short play with Yvonne Arnaud and John Mills.

In 1941, Noël Coward's *Blithe Spirit* had its premiere here. The hugely popular 'supernatural' comedy, starring Cecil Parker, Fay Compton, Kay Hammond and Margaret Rutherford as the eccentric clairvoyant Madame Arcati, soon transferred to the St James's (since demolished) and the Duchess to complete an amazing 1997 performances. After touring with *Macbeth* (1942), John Gielgud brought it to the Piccadilly for a few 'exhausting, and not very successful' months. (Incidentally, Ernest Thesiger played the First Witch.) The bad luck said to attend 'the Scottish play' lingered on into 1943, when the theatre was damaged by a flying bomb attack.

In 1945, the year of its reopening, Coward's revue *Sigh No More* was seen. It featured Joyce Grenfell, Cyril Ritchard and Coward's close friend Graham Payn, for whom he wrote the song 'Matelot'. Edith Evans and Godfrey Tearle tackled *Antony And Cleopatra* (1946), and John Van Druten's *The Voice Of The Turtle* (1947) was coldly received. Short runs and transfers occupied the Piccadilly until the interior was completely redecorated in a streamlined, rather anonymous manner in 1955, the red plush seating being reduced to number 1,150.

In the five years leading up to the acquisition of the theatre by Donald Albery (against stiff competition from Bernard Delfont) four comedies stood out: Peter Ustinov in his own *Romanoff And Juliet* (1956); Richard Attenborough, John Clements, Kay Hammond and Constance Cummings in *The Rape Of The Belt*

Paul Thornley and Derek Griffiths in *Noises Off*, the hit comedy by Michael Frayn

(1957) by Cummings's husband Ben W. Levy; *Hook, Line And Sinker* (1958) with Joan Plowright and Robert Morley; and the real-life married couple Clements and Hammond in *The Marriage Go Round* (1959).

It was American drama and musicals that gave the Piccadilly some prestige in the '60s and '70s – Edward Albee's scabrous *Who's Afraid Of Virginia Woolf?* (1964), Claire Bloom in *A Streetcar Named Desire* (1974) and Henry Fonda in his solo performance as Clarence Darrow (1975). The Royal Shakespeare Company brought productions here while waiting for the Barbican to open, including the hit *Educating Rita* (1981) with Julie Walters. The 1990s were a decade of variety, with dance – notably the award-winning *Swan Lake* presented by the contemporary ballet company, Adventures in Motion Pictures; plays – a season directed by Sir Peter Hall; in 1999, a return to the musical – the award-winning *Spend, Spend, Spend* starring Barbara Dickson; and comedy – Michael Frayn's smash-hit comedy *Noises Off*. And the Piccadilly sails on...

the piccadilly theatre
denman street = wlv

The Playhouse

O n the corner of the junction between Northumberland
Avenue and the Embankment, almost tucked beneath
Charing Cross Railway Station, stands a lovely theatre
with a pretty glass canopy. The story goes that the original theatre
was built on this site not because the speculator, Sefton Parry, was
a theatre-lover but because he believed that the South-Eastern
Railway would have to acquire the ground, at a large profit to
Sefton, for an extension scheme to Charing Cross Station.
Thankfully, the hoped-for extension never happened, and the
theatre is now 120 years old, and thriving.

The first building was designed by architects Fowler and Hill
in the French renaissance style, with an elevation of Portland
stone, ornamental carving and statues over the main entrance and
internal decorations of ivory and gold. The auditorium ceiling
featured medallion portraits of famous poets and a handsome
glass chandelier, and the stage had damask draperies and curtains.
To this day, the theatre retains its beautifully painted canvas act
drop (the last in London).

In March 1882, the Avenue Theatre (as it was first known)
opened with a revival of *Madame Favart* by Offenbach. It was the
first of a long series of French comic operas, given under several
managements, which filled the theatre until 1890. Then George
Alexander, before the historic era of his management of the St
James's Theatre, was manager of the Playhouse for a year. His first
production was a great success called *Dr Bill*. In 1894 the theatre
had another big hit, with Shaw's *Arms and the Man*, in a season
given by the actress Florence Farr. Florence was sponsored by
Miss Horniman, a tea heiress, in what is believed to be the first
example of commercial sponsorship in the theatre. The opening
night of Shaw's production – his very first West End play – was a
great success, with Oscar Wilde and W. B. Yates on the guest list.

'The best West End theatre for comedy.'
— Jon Naismith, Producer, BBC Radio 4

Apparently, when Shaw took the stage at the end to take a bow, amongst the cheering came a single 'boo' from the gallery. Shaw responded: 'My dear fellow, I quite agree with you, but what are we two amongst so many?' The Playhouse's auditorium has always been a favourite with actors for its intimacy with the audience.

From 1898 until 1900 the highly popular actor Charles Hawtrey had a run of 544 performances with Ganthony's *A Message From Mars* – quite phenomenal at that time. Other significant productions were Somerset Maugham's early play, *A Man of Honour*, and R. C. Carton's *Mr Hopkinson*, with James Welch. In 1905 Cyril Maude took over the management, leaving the Haymarket where he had been established for some years. He set about reconstructing the theatre. The work was almost completed when on 5 December, 1905 part of Charing Cross Station collapsed onto the theatre. Six people were killed, 26 injured and the theatre badly damaged. After some delay, rebuilding work started. Most of the original exterior was retained, but a completely new interior was constructed, and decorated in rich brown and gold. The new theatre was renamed the Playhouse and it opened on 28 January, 1907. Cyril Maude continued as manager until 1915, presenting a long series of successes. His family's association with the theatre is commemorated today by a stucco cameo of his son John above the foyer bar.

(above) George Bernard Shaw

the playhouse

Frank Curzon then took the theatre, with Gladys Cooper as leading lady. She joined him in management in 1917 and together they were responsible for a series of light, popular shows. In 1927 Gladys became the sole lessee, and there followed a golden period for the Playhouse, with presentations of several plays by Maugham with distinguished casts that included Laurence Olivier, Ivor Novello, Gerald du Maurier, Noël Coward and Raymond Massey.

In the 1930s the Playhouse staged the acclaimed *Libel!* (1934), the professional debut of Alec Guinness, and during 1938 and 1939 the actress and theatre manager Nancy Price ran her People's National Theatre here. On the outbreak of World War II, the theatre closed. It reopened during the war with the Old Vic Company's staging of three productions, including an early play by Peter Ustinov, *Blow Your Own Trumpet*. After the war, the theatre had successes with Bridget Boland's *Cockpit*, *The Perfect Woman* (1948) and Agatha Christie's *Murder at the Vicarage* (1949), with Thora Hird.

A recording of *The Goon Show*

The theatre left the fold in 1951, and was converted to become a BBC radio recording studio. These years were rich with classic comedy – the *Goon Shows* and *Hancock's Half Hour* were presented here, to delighted and packed houses. In 1972 very first episode of *I'm Sorry, I Haven't a Clue* was recorded, and in 2002 the cast and crew were welcomed back to the Playhouse for their historic thirtieth anniversary show.

The BBC left the theatre in 1975, and for the next 25 years the Playhouse changed hands many times. The first new proprietor was Robin Gonshaw, who formed a public company to reopen the Playhouse as a theatre, restoring the auditorium to the original 1907 decor of Maude's era, while refitting the backstage area. The theatre reopened in October 1987 with the musical *Girl Friends*. Shortly afterwards, the politician, novelist and playwright Jeffrey Archer bought a controlling interest in the theatre, and the Playhouse staged various productions featuring Ian McKellen, Donald Sinden, Leo McKern, Jackie Mason and Patricia Routledge. In 1991 the Peter Hall Company made the theatre their new home, with Shakespeare's *Twelfth Night*, Tennesee Williams's *The Rose Tattoo*, starring Julie Walters, and Molière's *Tartuffe* with Felicity Kendal, Paul Eddington and John Sessions. In the same year, an award-winning production of Ibsen's *Hedda Gabler*, directed by Deborah Warner, was presented. In 1992 the legendary Ray Cooney, actor, playwright and producer, bought the Playhouse and presented the highly popular *It Runs in the Family* – a farce written by, directed by and starring Ray Cooney!

Then in 1996 the theatre changed hands again, and had hits with Thelma Holt's *A Doll's House* (subsequent winner of four Tony Awards in New York), *HRH,* starring Amanda Donohoe and Corin Redgrave, and *The Wood Demon* by Chekhov. Two years later, the Almeida Theatre chose the playhouse to produce its own work in the West End for the very first time, with two outstanding plays: *The Judas Kiss* with Liam Neeson, and *Naked* with Juliette Binoche. Since then there have been the critically acclaimed Jackie Mason in his one-man show *Much Ado About*

J. B. Priestley's thriller *An Inspector Calls* has won 19 major theatre awards

Everything, a record-breaking run of *Thunderbirds F.A.B.* and currently the National Theatre's *An Inspector Calls*, which has been running at the Playhouse since September 2001. The success of these last two productions shows that the Playhouse really has established itself again in the West End. In this new, more stable atmosphere, the management have introduced the West End's first theatre crèche, the restaurant has been refurbished, and there are plans for an outdoor café and possibly a theatre bookshop.

The Playhouse has sometimes suffered as a result of being seen as 'out of the way'. So, while we all have good reason to be grateful to the South-Eastern Railway for not building their extension to Charing Cross 120 years ago, we also have good reason to be grateful today to Westminster County Council, whose beautiful new footbridge over the Thames leads pedestrians right up Northumberland Street, straight towards the Playhouse Theatre.

the playhouse theatre
northumberland avenue = wc2

The Prince Edward

For the last 24 years crowds have been making their way past sex shops, pubs and restaurants in the lively, cosmopolitan, rather sleazy area of Soho to a brown-brick building in the shape of an Italian palazzo on the corner of Greek and Old Compton Streets. Behind the sturdy square facade, decorated unostentatiously with four pillars, is the gorgeously plush interior, the result of 1990's daringly impressive refurbishment costing £3.5 million. In fact, the Prince Edward simply reeks of the sleek satisfaction that comes from having had the smash-hit musical *Evita* (1978) here for eight fat years, followed by *Chess* (1986), booking over a year ahead, and 1993's Broadway hit *Crazy For You*, with its three-year run. But this money-making did not come about overnight. Despite the hits of the past 20 or so years, the theatre itself has had an extremely chequered career.

This chameleon of a structure has been variously a theatre, a cabaret-restaurant, a servicemen's club, a trade show cinema and the home of Cinerama. It has staged musicals, revues, variety, pantomimes, floor shows and ballet. It has also had three names. On the spot where it was built in 1930 stood a vast draper's shop known as The Emporium. Although Royalty and other nobs patronised it, it began losing trade in the 1920s and was demolished. The building that arose on the site was the first of four new theatres opened in London in 1930. All of them – the Cambridge, the Phoenix, the Whitehall and the Prince Edward – went for the latest in interior decoration, much of which was what we now call Art Deco. The interior designers, Marc-Henri and Laverdet, went for rectilinear patterns and René

> *'To Evita this evening at the Prince Edward...*
> *It's the cult of kitsch again, inert, calculating,*
> *camp and morally questionable. I felt out*
> *of step with popular taste...'*
> — Sir Peter Hall (Diaries)

Lalique amber glass to frame the proscenium arch. Alas, this has vanished now.

Coincidentally, the theatre that finally came into its own with *Evita* kicked off with another Latin American señorita. The popular Broadway operetta of the 1920s, *Rio Rita*, was chosen as the opening production. Unfortunately, the show that Ziegfeld presented so successfully in the USA failed to take off in the UK. Other short-lived musical comedies followed with only *Nippy* (1930), starring Binnie Hale, managing to get beyond 100 performances. Not even the wonderful black American cabaret artiste Josephine Baker, the toast of Paris, could fill the theatre in 1933. Non-stop revue from 2 p.m. to midnight was tried until the management, admitting defeat, leased the building for the use of trade film shows.

However, thanks to a syndicate which included the theatre's architect, E. A. Stone, it opened in April 1936 as the London Casino, having been converted skilfully, and at a cost of £25,000, into a cabaret-restaurant. A dance floor and stairways from the stalls to the dress circle were constructed. Business boomed as people flocked to dine, dance and watch spectacular stage shows such as *Folies Parisiennes*. But the party was over in 1940, when the London Casino had to close down during wartime and became the Queensbury All-Services Club.

Tom Arnold and Emile Littler changed it back into a theatre, again called the London Casino. *Pick-Up Girl* (1946) retained the air of naughtiness, dispelled by a revival of Ivor Novello's operetta *The Dancing Years* (1947). A mish-mash of variety, ballet, pantomimes and musicals continued for the next few years.

the prince edward

These included the French-style 'Les Girls' show, *Latin Quarter* (1949), Cicely Courtneidge in a revue called *Over The Moon* (1953), and *Wish You Were Here*, a musical set in a holiday camp and the last stage production before the arrival of Cinerama Holiday in 1954. A flashing sign proclaimed the newest big-screen fad, and *How The West Was Won* (1962) as well as *2001: A Space Odyssey* (1968) were shown here.

In 1974, the Delfont Organisation took over the ownership, redecorated the building and used it as a cinema but for the occasional annual pantomime. Reverting to its original name, the Prince Edward opened its doors to *Evita* in 1978, and it was a case of 'Don't cry for me any more'. Andrew Lloyd Webber and Tim Rice's politico-rock musical, with a sensational Elaine Paige, an unknown, in the title role, put British musicals firmly on the map. Eight years later Elaine Paige starred again in *Chess*, and then again, in 1989, in Cole Porter's *Anything Goes*. Tim Rice collaborated with members of the pop group Abba and RSC director Trevor Nunn to create *Chess*. Those same Abba members, Benny Andersson and Bjorn Ulvaeus, have written the Prince Edward's latest show, *Mamma Mia,* a musical based on the songs of this best-loved pop group. Looks like the perfect recipe for another smash hit for the Prince Edward.

the prince edward theatre
old compton street = wlv

The Prince of Wales

If a vote were to be taken on the best location for a theatre in the West End, the key position on the corner of Coventry and Oxendon Streets, where stands the Prince of Wales, would surely win. The crowds of revellers streaming between Piccadilly Circus and Leicester Square cannot fail to see the dominating, once-white artificial-stone building with its huge sign and belfry-like tower. Its favourable position has certainly helped to fill its 1,139 seats since it was built in 1937.

The first theatre on the site, called simply the Prince's, was designed by C. J. Phipps as an exotic affair with a Moorish style foyer and smoking room. It opened in January 1884 with Herbert Beerbohm Tree in W. S. Gilbert's 'Fairy Comedy', *The Palace of Truth*. Tree also appeared in a free adaptation of Ibsen's *A Doll's House* called *Breaking A Butterfly* and in Charles Hawtrey's farce *The Private Secretary*, both in the year of the theatre's inauguration. In 1885, Tree played Joseph Surface to Lillie Langtry's Lady Teazle in *School For Scandal*. 'The Jersey Lily' returned for a season of plays in 1886, the year the Prince's, coincidentally, changed its title to the Prince of Wales, named after the actress's intimate friend. The success of the comic opera *Dorothy* (1887), which ran a year, led the producer, Henry J. Leslie, to build the Lyric, Shaftesbury Avenue from its profits. The appearance of the 'wordless play' *L'Infant Prodigue* from France, with mimes Jane May and Zanfretta, led to the establishment of the first Pierrot troupe in England.

According to the dictionary definition, musical comedy is 'a popular type of light entertainment which derives from a fusion

218

'A curious medley of song, dance and nonsense ...and the very vaguest attempt at satirising the modern masher.'

Sunday Times on In Town, 1892

of burlesque and light opera'. Thus George Edwardes's *In Town* (1892) has the distinction of being considered the first true musical comedy. Another example of the new genre as presented by Edwardes was *The Gaiety Girl* (1893). Apart from musical comedy, Mrs Patrick Campbell and Forbes Robertson performed in Maurice Maeterlinck's symbolist drama *Pelléas et Mélisande* with incidental music by Fauré. Marie Tempest, having deserted Edwardes and musical comedy, played in three adaptations from novels: *English Nell,* from Anthony Hope; *Peg Woffington*, from Charles Read; and *Becky Sharp* from Thackeray's *Vanity Fair*, all between 1900 and 1901. Edwardes's musical comedies returned from 1903 to1910; 'Man-about-town' Charles Hawtrey appeared in comedies from 1912 to 1918, and Beatrice Lillie, Gertrude Lawrence, Jack Buchanan and Jessie Matthews featured in André Chariot revues from 1918 to 1926. Things deteriorated somewhat in the 1930s as the Prince of Wales resorted to 'Non-Stop Revue' which was only halted by the demolition of the theatre in 1937.

The foundation stone of the new house, which opened in October 1937, was laid by Gracie Fields. The architect, Robert Cromie, conceived a large two-tier theatre with the circle front within 21 feet of the orchestra. The auditorium has a slightly cavernous feel, but the enormous stalls bar has room for an impressive archive of playbills of the many shows that have played here. Among them were the successes under the management of George Black in the 1940s. He introduced comedian Sid Field to London audiences in *Strike A New Note* in 1943. Field also shone in *Strike It Again* (1944), *Piccadilly Hayride* (1946) and finally *Harvey* (1949), Mary Chase's Broadway hit about an amiable

Linda Baron was the mature Belle Poitrine in the musical version of Patrick Dennis's *Little Me* (1984)

drunk with an imaginary giant white rabbit as a friend. Sadly, Field died at the age of 46 during its long run. *Harvey* returned to the Prince of Wales in 1975, when Hollywood star James Stewart repeated his New York stage role of Elwood P. Dowd, the drunk, which he had also played on the screen in 1950. Another legendary movie star, Mae West, appeared here briefly in *Diamond Lil* in 1948.

For much of the 1950s the theatre was given over to traditional variety shows, featuring Benny Hill, Frankie Howerd and Norman Wisdom, until *The World Of Suzie Wong* (1959) – called by critic Kenneth Tynan 'The World Of Woozey Song' –

the great theatres of london

arrived for a run of almost three years. American comedies and musicals were to be the principal fare from then on. Neil Simon's first play, *Come Blow Your Horn* (1962), had a good run, but it was Barbra Streisand's dynamic presence in *Funny Girl* (1966) that had the queues collecting in Coventry Street. Streisand was

Cameron Mackintosh's musical adaptation of *The Witches of Eastwick* hit the London stage in 2000

the prince of wales

some months pregnant at the time (by her then husband Elliot Gould), so the show's run was limited. Other imports were the splendid *Sweet Charity* (1967) starring Juliet Prowse, *Promises Promises* (1969), *Same Time Next Year* (1976), *I Love My Wife* (1977) and *Little Me* (1984). Home-grown productions included *The Good Old Bad Old Days* (1972), directed, starring and written (with Leslie Bricusse) by Anthony Newley, *Underneath The Arches* (1982), a tribute to Flanagan and Allen, and *Allo Allo* (1986), a comedy derived from the television series about the French Resistance which vast sections of the population found irresistible. The 1990s was a decade of musical hits, with *Copacabana* (1994), *Smokey Joe's Café* (1996) and *West Side Story* (1999). Now the smash-hit musical *The Full Monty* (2002), based on the highly popular film, is outstripping the West End competition.

the prince of wales theatre
coventry street = wlv

223

The Queen's

In the heart of 'theatreland', on the corner of Shaftesbury Avenue and Wardour Street, stands the modern glass-fronted, red-brick, five-storey building that houses the Queen's Theatre. If one wonders, while contemplating the pleasing but unexceptional 1959 facade, what the 1907 playhouse once looked like, then one has only to walk a few yards to the Gielgud Theatre on the Rupert Street corner of the block. They were designed by W. G. R. Sprague as near-identical twin theatres. Today, they could not be more dissimilar.

Some people may agree with John Earl's views on the Queen's 'outdated, un-theatrelike, and even heartless' exterior, but few can fail to be charmed by the red, white and gold auditorium, with its domed ceiling and Louis XVI-style plaster ornamentation, which creates an elegant Edwardian atmosphere. The reason why the Gielgud's exterior remains little altered from its inception in 1906, while its twin resides in a modern shell, is that a German bomb fell on the unfortunate Queen's in September 1940, destroying much of the facade and the back of the stalls. It is ironic that the first London theatre casualty of the war was a theatre which had had fewer theatrical bombs than most.

However, the Queen's took some years to make its reputation. The opening production, *The Sugar Bowl* (1907), a comedy with Edmund Gwenn, was a flop, allowing Shaw's *The Devil's Disciple* to transfer from the Savoy. H. B. Irving took over the management in 1909, appearing in a number of his famous father Henry's renowned barnstorming parts such as *The Bells*, *Louis XI* and *The Lyons Mail*. But in 1913 blood and thunder gave way to 'Tango Teas' for which the stalls were transformed into a dance floor with tables placed around it so that the patrons could partake of tea and dance the fashionable tango – all for half-a-crown.

*'No doubt in 1957 the restoration of the facade...
was seen as exciting and new. Now it looks outdated,
un–theatrelike, and even heartless.'*
— John Earl in *Curtains!!!*

When the strains of the tango had died away, the sound of applause returned to the building for the American Jewish comedy *Potash And Perlmutter* (1914) and its sequel *Potash And Perlmutter In Society* (1916). In the '20s, the theatre welcomed Alfred Savoir's *Bluebeard's Eighth Wife* (1922), Fred and Adele Astaire in *Stop Flirting* (1923), Owen Nares and Fay Compton in J. M. Barrie's *The Little Minister* (1924) and Edmund Gwenn and Yvonne Arnaud as Mr and Mrs Pepys in *And So To Bed* (1926).

From 1929, the stage of the Queen's held a dazzling array of stars and stars-to-be that elicits the inevitable phrase 'the good old days'. Cedric Hardwicke (knighted in 1934) appeared as Magnus in *The Apple Cart* (1929) and Mr Barrett in *The Barretts Of Wimpole Street* (1930) with Gwen ffrangcon-Davies as Elizabeth; Edith Evans was in *The Apple Cart*, *Heartbreak House*

(1932) and *Once In A Lifetime* (1933); and Marie Tempest, Sybil Thorndike, Margaret Rutherford, Ursula Jeans and Rex Harrison were assembled for Robert Morley's first play, *Short Story* (1935). But it was John Gielgud's presence that dominated the Queen's from 1937 to the outbreak of war.

He made his first appearance in the West End here in his debut performance of *Hamlet*, transferred from the Old Vic in 1930, with Donald Wolfit and Martita Hunt as Claudius and Gertrude. To see a 25-year-old Prince of Denmark was a novelty for audiences used to middle-aged actors tackling the role. It did well even though two other *Hamlet*s were playing in London at the same time. (Henry Ainley at the Haymarket, and Alexander Moissi, in German, at the nearby Gielgud Theatre – then called the Globe.) Gielgud returned in 1937 in a play especially written for him by Emlyn Williams, titled – curiously to our modern ears – *He Was Born Gay*. It ran for 12 nights. Putting that behind him, he brought in a season of four plays for eight months starting in September of the same year. Gielgud not only played Richard II to Michael Redgrave's Bolingbroke, Shylock to Peggy Ashcroft's Portia, Vershinin in *Three Sisters* and Joseph Surface in *School For Scandal*, but also directed the first two.

In addition to the leading actors, Harry Andrews, Dennis Price and Alec Guinness had small parts in all four productions. Redgrave and his wife Rachel Kempson appeared as Charles Surface and Maria in Tyrone Guthrie's *School For Scandal*, little knowing that their one-year-old daughter Vanessa would appear on the same stage with her father in Robert Bolt's *The Tiger And The Horse* (1960), triumph in Ibsen's *The Lady From The Sea* (1961) and as Nina in *The Seagull* (1964), and star with her sisters Lynn and Jemma in the acclaimed *Three Sisters* and *Matador* (1990).

Immediately after this exhausting but rewarding season, Gielgud stepped into modern dress to play opposite Marie Tempest in Dodie Smith's family saga *Dear Octopus* (1938). Dame Marie did not get on with the author, and when Smith took a curtain call on the first night with the company, the actress turned her back on her in full view of the audience. The first night also coincided with Chamberlain's return from Munich. The year's run was broken by the declaration of war, and the Queen's closed down. It reopened in December 1939 with the optimistically titled revue *All Clear* starring Beatrice Lillie, followed by Daphne du Maurier's *Rebecca* with Owen Nares, Celia Johnson and Margaret Rutherford. It was during the successful run of the latter that the bomb fell.

The devastated theatre stood dark and deserted for almost 20 years, a sad reminder of the Blitz, before architects Bryan Westwood and Hugh Casson restored it. It reopened in July 1959, appropriately enough with John Gielgud giving his Shakespeare recital, *The Ages Of Man*. In the same year, the year of his knighthood, Sir Michael Redgrave returned in *The Aspern Papers*, his own adaptation of the Henry James story. Anthony Newley sang 'What Kind Of Fool Am I?' as Littlechap in the allegorical musical *Stop The World I Want To Get Off* (1961) for over a year before moving with it to Broadway.

The big theatrical event of 1966 was the return of Noël Coward to the West End after a 13-year absence. He starred alongside Irene Worth and Lilli Palmer in a trio of new plays which he gave the omnibus title of *Suite In Three Keys*. Although Coward's health was poor and he often 'dried', he felt 'a warmth and a genuine love emanating from the front of the house at every performance'. It was his final stage appearance. 'The Master' died not long after his friend Marlene Dietrich's successful one-woman show at the Queen's and Gielgud's starry production of *Private Lives* with the then married couple, Maggie Smith and Robert Stephens, both in 1972.

The '70s and '80s were successful decades for the Queen's, with Alan Bates in *Otherwise Engaged* (1975), Alec Guinness in *The Old Country* (1978), Tom Courtenay in *The Dresser* (1980), Charlton Heston in *The Caine Mutiny Court Martial* (1985) and Alan Bennett's *Single Spies* (1989). In the same year came a brilliant production of *Shadowlands*, starring Nigel Hawthorne, as C. S. Lewis, and Jane Lapotaire; Hawthorne also directed and starred in

The young Vanessa Redgrave was Nina in Chekhov's *The Seagull* in 1964. Twenty-one years later, she graduated to Arkadina, co-starring with her daughter Natasha Richardson as Nina

The Clandestine Marriage (1994). Acclaimed director Thelma Holt has had two successful Shakespeare productions at the Queen's – *Much Ado About Nothing* with Mark Rylance (1993) and *Macbeth* with Rufus Sewell (1999). In 2000, the Queen's became a Really Useful Theatre when Lord Lloyd Webber and Bridgepoint Capital purchased Stoll Moss Theatres Ltd. Under this new management it opened with a sell-out production of *The Seven Year Itch* starring Daryl Hannah. In 2002 the theatre staged a highly acclaimed South African production of *The Mysteries* – all demonstrating that the Queen's is a venue of continuing quality.

the queen's theatre
shaftesbury avenue = wlv

The Royal
Court

The Establishment-sounding Royal Court Theatre, with its noble brick and stone Italian Renaissance frontage, brazenly stares out on the leafy confines of trendy Sloane Square and the fripperies of the King's Road, Chelsea – a surprising locality in which to find the most radical of all of the great theatres of London, and one that changed the face of British drama in the late 1950s.

In 1956, the year of the Suez Crisis, Britain was forced to re-examine its role on the world stage; youth culture burst onto the scene, and so did the production of *Look Back In Anger* at the Royal Court. 'An angry play by an angry young author... neurotic, exaggerated and more than slightly distasteful,' railed the *Daily Mail*, typical of most of the reviews. One critic's voice came through loud and clear – Kenneth Tynan in the *Observer* wrote, 'I doubt if I could love anyone who did not wish to see *Look Back In Anger*. It is the best young play of its decade.' Whatever one thought of 27-year-old John Osborne's choleric, wittily rhetorical shout against aspects of British society, it advanced the careers of its author, the director Tony Richardson and the actors Kenneth Haigh, Alan Bates and Mary Ure (Osborne's wife-to-be); it gave rise to a movement labelled 'Angry Young Men', and was a landmark in the counterblast against the complacency of the commercial theatre.

The English Stage Company was formed in 1956, with Arts Council subsidy, 'to stage and encourage new writing' under the artistic direction of George Devine (pronounced Deveen). Living up to this pledge, Devine presented a multitude of new works by

'If more plays like tonight's Look Back In Anger are produced, the "Writer's Theatre" at the Royal Court must surely sink.'

— *Birmingham Post*, 1956

British writers in the nine years he was at the Court. His achievement was extraordinary. After his death in 1966, the tradition was admirably continued by his successors, William Gaskill, Stuart Burge and Max Stafford-Clark. Among the many notable productions presented over the years have been Osborne's *Luther* (1961), *Inadmissible Evidence* (1964) and *A Patriot For Me* (1965); Arnold Wesker's *Chicken Soup With Barley* (1958), *Roots* (1959), *I'm Talking About Jerusalem* (1960) and *Chips With Everything* (1962); John Arden's *Serjeant Musgrave's Dance* (1959); Ann Jellicoe's *The Knack* (1962); David Storey's *The Contractor* (1969), *In Celebration* (1969) and *The Changing Room* (1971); Christopher Hampton's *The Philanthropist* (1970) and *(above)* Julie Covington and Tom Wilkinson in *Tom And Viv* (1984), Michael Hastings's searing play about T. S. Eliot's first wife, confined to an asylum

(left) John Osborne's *Look Back In Anger* (1956) changed the face of British theatre forever. Here, Jimmy Porter (Kenneth Haigh, right) vents his spleen on his wife, Alison (Mary Ure), while friends Cliff and Helena (Alan Bates, Helen Hughes) look on.

233

Savages (1973); David Hare's *Teeth 'n' Smiles* (1975); Mary O'Malley's *Once A Catholic* (1977), Nigel Williams's *Class Enemy* (1978), Michael Hastings's *Tom And Viv* (1984); and Caryl Churchill's *Cloud Nine* (1980), *Top Girls* (1982) and *Serious Money* (1987).

Modern foreign greats have not been neglected either, and Brecht, Beckett, Genet, Ionesco and Sartre have been well represented. Even the theatrical knights from the 'other' theatre have not been able to resist the pull of the Royal Court. Sir Alec Guinness played in Ionesco's *Exit The King* (1964) and *Macbeth* (1966); Sir John Gielgud (with Sir Ralph Richardson) in David Storey's *Home* (1970), Charles Wood's *Veterans* (1972) and as Shakespeare in Edward Bond's *Bingo* (1973); and Sir Laurence Olivier in Ionesco's *Rhinoceros* (1960) directed by Orson Welles. After seeing *Look Back In Anger*, Olivier asked Osborne to write a play for him. The result was *The Entertainer* (1957), a triumph in all departments and a turning point in the great actor's career.

Archie Rice, the fifth-rate comedian Olivier played in *The Entertainer*, says, 'Don't clap too hard, lady, it's an old building.' In fact, the present building dates from 1888, although there had been a theatre of the same name on the south side of Sloane Square. After that was demolished in 1887, another, designed by Walter Emden and Bertie Crewe, went up on the east side next to the Metropolitan railway station (now Sloane Square tube). Originally a three-tier theatre with a 642-seat capacity, its interior was reconstructed in 1952, closing off the old gallery and reducing the seating to 401. Further redecorations in 1980 enlarged it somewhat. In 1971, a rehearsal room became the 80-seat experimental Theatre Upstairs. However, by 1994 this historic theatre was threatened with closure as its major structures disintegrated. It closed for redevelopment for four years from 1996, and with great technical difficulty a new theatre emerged from the old, managing to reflect its architectural late-Victorian origins while creating better backstage conditions, updated technical systems, improved audience circulation and a modern front of house. While work was in progress the Theatre Downstairs moved to the Duke of York's, and the Theatre Upstairs relocated to the New Ambassadors. In February 2000, the refurbished theatre at Sloane Square opened again, with both auditoria named after the Jerwood Foundation – the Jerwood Theatre Downstairs and the Jerwood Theatre Upstairs.

Arthur Wing Pinero was the playwright most associated with the Royal Court in its earliest days. His successes here included *The Cabinet Minister* (1890), *The Amazons* (1893) and, particularly, *Trelawny Of The 'Wells'* (1898), which recalled his days as an actor. Also popular was *Under The Clock* (1893), a precursor of intimate revue, in which 22-year-old Seymour Hicks and Charles Brookfield impersonated various theatrical luminaries of the day. But the Court's reputation for advanced drama was established when J. E. Vedrenne and Harley Granville-Barker managed the theatre from 1904 to 1907, presenting a remarkable range of plays, 11 of them by George Bernard Shaw, whose wide renown dates from this memorable season. If the spirit of Shaw haunts any theatre, it would surely be the Royal Court. *You Never Can Tell*, *Man And Superman* and *The Doctor's Dilemma* proved there was a public for intellectual theatre. Not unlike today's Court audience, people came to be stimulated mentally and enjoyed being lectured at. It was Harley Granville-Barker's experience here which led him to espouse the cause of a national theatre.

Shaw returned to the Court, under J. B. Fagan's stewardship, with *Heartbreak House* (1921), his first play since before the war. When Barry Jackson became manager in 1924, he had the courage to present Shaw's mammoth five-part *Back To Methuselah* over four nights. Among Jackson's other achievements were Eden Phillpott's *The Farmer's Wife* (1924), which ran almost three years, and modern dress productions of *Macbeth* and *The Taming Of The Shrew* (both 1927). Twenty-one-year-old Laurence Olivier played small roles in the Shakespeare plays. For most of the latter, he had to sit in a stage box in full view of the audience. According to Olivier, he spent much of the time trying to make Ralph Richardson, who played Tranio, laugh. Every

East is East by Ayub Khan-Kin

night he would pull faces and make gestures to no avail. One night, he did absolutely nothing but stare at Ralph who promptly 'corpsed'. Olivier also appeared in Elmer Rice's expressionist fantasy *The Adding Machine* (1928).

The Royal Court was closed (except for a short period as a cinema) between 1932 and 1952. It then marked time for a few years before the historic arrival of the English Stage Company, which has always invited controversy. There was uproar in some quarters at Edward Bond's *Saved* (1965), which depicted a baby being stoned to death, and the same author's *Early Morning* (1968), which presented Queen Victoria having a lesbian affair with Florence Nightingale. Only on one occasion has the Court been seen to give in to outside pressure. This concerned the last-minute withdrawal of Jim Allen's *Perdition* in 1987, concerning the Holocaust, on the grounds that 'it might offend too many people'.

Under the artistic direction of Stephen Daldry, the theatre flourished throughout the '90s. Key productions were *Oleanna* by David Mamet (1993), *Mojo* by Jez Butterworth, *Blasted* by Royal Court protégé Sarah Kane (1995), *The Beauty Queen of Leenane* by Martin McDonagh (1996) and the notorious *Shopping and F***ing* (1997) by Mark Ravenhill. The same year also saw the stage premiere of *East is East* by Ayub Khan-Din, which became a highly successful film two years later, and *The Weir* by Conor McPherson. In 2000 writer Sarah Kane's *4.48 Psychosis* was performed to great acclaim a year after her death. Under Ian Rickson, the theatre staged *Boy Gets Girl* by Rebecca Gilman (2001) and in 2002 *The Night Heron* by Jez Butterworth. And so the Royal Court Theatre, back home in Sloane Square, continues its grand tradition of daring, enlightened drama by exciting new writers.

the royal court
sloane square = swlw

The Royal
Opera House

Opera houses are generally grandiose, luxurious palaces erected to stage the most expensive theatrical art form ever devised – and the Royal Opera House, Covent Garden can take its place among the world's best. Although less monumental than the Paris Opera or La Scala, its ambience of opulence and enchantment and a sense of occasion are created immediately in the sumptuous lobby. The splendid Grand Staircase on the left rises, between huge allegorical paintings, towards the famous Crush Bar – a great hall with 20-foot-high paintings adorning the walls, beneath a sparkling chandelier. All this even before one enters the majestic auditorium, substantially as it was when new in 1858. From the Orchestra Stalls, Stalls Circle and Grand Tier, the horseshoe-shaped levels move up to the Balcony Stalls and the Valhalla of the Amphitheatre close to the shallow, aquamarine dome. Looking down from this vertiginous height towards the stage, with its famous crimson velvet curtains bearing the Queen's monogram, one notices, above the proscenium, a rustic scene in which Orpheus plays his lyre. Along the gold tier-fronts stand a bevy of bare-breasted maidens behind rows of claret-shaded candelabra. From 1996 to 1999 the Royal Opera House underwent a massive programme of development and refurbishment. The auditorium and original foyers were renovated; the magnificent nineteenth-century glass and iron Floral Hall – the roof of which was destroyed in the 1950s – was restored and incorporated into the main theatre building as the new main audience circulation space, and a new building, which houses additional public areas, new rehearsal studios for the

'A very English place for grand occasions! An odd and endearing mixture of red velvet plush and drawing-room intimacy.'
— Max Loppert

Royal Ballet and Opera and better backstage facilities was constructed.

The first theatre, on the site of what had been a convent garden (hence the name), was built in 1732 for John Rich, who held the patent which permitted only the two Theatre Royals, at Drury Lane and Covent Garden, to perform 'legitimate' theatre legitimately. It was originally, therefore, mainly devoted to drama, though three of Handel's operas, *Alcina* (1735), *Atalanta* (1736) and *Berenice* (1737), had their premieres here. Rich, who was constantly in litigation, and who killed a fellow actor in a fight over a wig, managed the theatre until his death in 1761. John Beard, his son-in-law, took over and presented mainly operas until he was succeeded by Thomas Harris in 1774 when plays became the order of the day. Oliver Goldsmith's *She Stoops To Conquer* (1773) and Sheridan's *The Rivals* (1775) had first performances here. In May 1789 Charles Macklin, playing Shylock in *The Merchant of Venice*, made his last appearance but, being as old as the century, he failed to complete the performance. In contrast, a tragedian aged only 13 made his London debut in 1804. Master Betty, known as the young Roscius, played the great Shakespearean roles and caused a sensation. Parliament even adjourned in order to see his Hamlet. This freakish success ended a year later when his attempt at Richard III was hissed off the stage.

In September, 1808, a fire in which 23 firemen were killed destroyed the building and Handel's organ and scores with it. A mere 12 months later a new theatre, modelled on the Temple of Minerva at the Acropolis, stood in its place. Owing to the cost of rebuilding, seat prices were raised. This action caused riots and disturbances for 61 nights until finally actor-manager John Philip Kemble was forced to lower them again. Kemble's sister, Sarah Siddons, bade farewell to the stage with Lady Macbeth in 1812, and Kemble retired in favour of his younger brother Charles in 1817. Charles Kemble was one of the first actor-managers to bring some historical accuracy to costumes and sets, beginning in 1823 with *King John*, designed by James Robinson Planche. Planche was also the librettist of Weber's *Oberon* (1826), 'the most important English romantic opera'.

In March 1833, Edmund Kean, playing Othello, was taken ill during a scene with Iago, played by his son, Charles. Falling into Charles's arms, Kean cried, 'Oh God! I am dying... speak to them for me.' The greatest actor of the age had made his last exit. One of Kean's rivals was William Charles Macready, who assumed the management of Covent Garden in 1837. He introduced a new calcium light that was to revolutionise stage lighting. 'It was the application of the limelight', wrote Edward Fitzgerald, 'that really threw open the realms of glittering

A contemporary engraving of the tragedienne Rachel at Covent Garden in 1841 fairyland to the scenic artist.' Macready's reign was marked by internal dissension. The remarkable Madame Vestris took over in 1839, and the French actress Rachel made a memorable appearance in *Horace* in 1841. In 1856, fire once again consumed the Theatre Royal.

On 15 May, 1858, the Royal Italian Opera, the building we know today, opened. Sir Edward M. Barry created an imposing structure in the Roman Renaissance style with a raised Corinthian portico. The statues by Rossi on either side of the facade, and the Flaxman bas-reliefs along the front, survive from the 1809 building. Managed by Frederic Gye, the new premises were given over entirely to operas sung in Italian, regardless of their provenance. Opera at that period was more a social than an artistic event and, as before, the lights remained on during performances so that the gentry could see and be seen. Berlioz was once refused entry because his evening coat did not match his trousers.

Things improved when Augustus Harris took over in 1888. As operas were now given in their original language and in English, the 'Italian' was dropped from the name of the house. Harris introduced Edouard and Jean de Reszke and Nellie Melba to London, the latter making her debut in *Lucia di Lammermoor* (1888) and continuing to appear in almost every season here until 1914. Adelina Patti sang 25 consecutive seasons in over 30 roles at around £200 a performance.

In the orchestra pit, Gustav Mahler conducted Wagner's Ring cycle in 1892 and, in 1908, Hans Richter conducted the first Ring in English. Thomas Beecham, backed by his father (Joseph, of pills fame), launched his first season in 1910 with the British premiere of Richard Strauss's *Elektra*. After World War I, during which the opera house was used as a furniture warehouse, Bruno Walter became chief conductor. He concentrated mainly on Wagner, Mozart and Strauss, and his *Der Rosenkavalier* of 1924 (with Lotte Lehmann and Elisabeth Schumann) was a landmark. Beecham returned to take over the baton from 1932 to 1939. Between the wars Italian opera, excepting Puccini's works, was somewhat neglected. For example, not a note of Verdi was heard here for six years.

In 1946 the Covent Garden Opera Company was formed, subsidised by the Arts Council, and would share the house with the Sadler's Wells Ballet Company run by Ninette de Valois. (Both companies became Royal later.) The infant opera company had stormy beginnings, with music director Karl Rankl clashing with the director of productions. The latter was Peter Brook, then only 24 years old, who produced an erotic *Salome*, with sets by Salvador Dali, in 1949. Erich Kleiber contributed greatly to the development of the company between 1950 and 1953. He conducted the first British performance of Alban Berg's *Wozzeck* in 1952. In the same year, Maria Callas made her Covent Garden debut in *Norma*, her grandest tragic role. Highlights of Rafael Kubelik's tenure (1955–58) were Birgit Nilsson's Brunhilde in the Ring (1957), *The Trojans* – given in its entirety for the first time on a single evening, also in 1957 – directed by John Gielgud, and Visconti's production of *Don Carlos* (1958), conducted by Giulini.

English performers, and operas, began to attract attention in the 1950s. There were world premieres of works by native

David Hockney designed *L'Enfant et Les Sortilége*

composers such as Benjamin Britten (*Billy Budd*, 1951; *Gloriana*, 1953), William Walton (*Troilus and Cressida*, 1954) and Michael Tippett (*The Midsummer Marriage*, 1955). The wonderful contralto Kathleen Ferrier gave her last ever performance, while in considerable pain, in Gluck's *Orfeo ed Euridice* in 1953. She did not complete the second performance, and was soon dead. In 1959, Australia's Joan Sutherland became a star overnight in *Lucia di Lammermoor*.

Georg Solti took over in 1961, with such triumphs during his regime as *Fidelio* (1961), conducted by Klemperer; *Tosca* (1964) with Callas and Gobbi in a Zeffirelli production, the second act of which is preserved on film for posterity; *Pelléas et Mélisande* (1969); and *Tristan und Isolde* (1971).

Under Colin Davis (1971–86) there were many great nights at the opera, mention of two or three must suffice – *The Marriage Of Figaro* in 1971, which brought an unknown young Maori

Mikhail Baryshnikov and Antoinette Sibley in MacMillan's *A Month In The Country* (1985)

soprano named Kiri Te Kanawa to fame; *La Fanciulla del West* (1980) with sets by James Bond film designer Ken Adam; and Berg's *Lulu* in 1981. Bernard Haitink became Music Director in 1987. Highlights of his triumphant 15-year tenure included the first performances at Covent Garden of Borodin's *Prince Igor* and Janacek's *Katya Kabanova*, a tour of Japan with an all-Mozart programme, restagings of the Wagner repertory, Luciano Pavarotti singing in a revival of *Tosca* (2001), Placido Domingo in *Die Frau Ohne Schatten* (2001) and Bryn Terfel as Don Giovanni (2002).

Developing parallel to the Royal Opera has been the Royal Ballet, much-travelled and world-renowned. Its reputation took root when the company unveiled the great Margot Fonteyn in *The Sleeping Beauty* to New York audiences in the 1950s. Aside from the traditional classical repertoire – sometimes rechoreographed, as with Rudolph Nureyev's version of *The Nutcracker*, the company's choreographers have enriched the programme with new works too numerous to mention. Examples include John Cranko's *Pineapple Poll*, Frederick Ashton's *Symphonic Variations* and Kenneth MacMillan's *Anastasia*, created for the exciting Canadian-born ballerina, Lynn Seymour. Guest choreographers have included the cream of America – Balanchine, Jerome Robbins, Glen Tetley. All have been served by superlative dancers, among them Fonteyn. Michael Somes, Nadia Nerina, David Blair, Merle Park, Donald Macleary, Antoinette Sibley, Anthony Dowell, Lesley Collier, Wayne Eagling and Stephen Jefferies. Svetlana Beriosova, Nureyev himself and his natural successor Mikhail Baryshnikov have also enhanced this great company.

the royal opera house
floral street = wc2e

Sadler's Wells

The world of tutus and tights, pirouettes and *pas de deux* is conjured up for most people when Sadler's Wells is mentioned, mainly because of the years between 1931 and 1940 that the Vic-Wells (later the Sadler's Wells) Ballet Company spent at the building where the hitherto undreamed-of English Ballet was born. Until then, dancers had to change their names to foreign ones to gain acceptance. It was here, in the north London suburb of Islington, far from the madding West End crowds, that a permanent ballet company was formed. It was created by the formidable Lilian Baylis of the Old Vic, who spent five years raising the money to build the theatre after demolishing the old one, and rapidly went from strength to strength, so that the 'Wells' became known throughout the land. Installed since 1946 at the Royal Opera House, Covent Garden, the company has perpetuated the name in its official title – the Sadler's Wells Royal Ballet.

In 1998, the sixth theatre on the Sadler's Wells site was opened, replacing the functional brick building which had existed since World War II. The new Sadler's Wells Theatre, with its soaring glass facade, is an inspirational modern creation designed by the Arts Team at RHWL, with consultant architects Nicholas Hare Architects. It is as impressive and creative inside as it is outside, with a flexible auditorium adjustable to seat either 1,000 or 1,600 people, a sprung stage, double the previous size, and advanced computer-controlled stage and lighting technology.

The name Sadler's Wells derives from the medicinal spring that was discovered in the grounds of a Mr Thomas Sadler in the year 1683. (The original well can be found under a trap door at the back of the stalls.) The land, then in the open country, became a popular pleasure garden where people could watch various

'A bold, handsome, welcoming theatre – its glass facade invites the passer–by to come in... with spacious public areas and a splendid stage, up to the minute in technology...'
— *Financial Times,* 1998

entertainments and take the waters. A wooden 'Musick House' was erected where concerts and masques could be given. It stood for nearly a century, until a stone theatre was built in its place in 1765 by Thomas Rosoman, who became manager. Tom King, the well-known Drury Lane actor and creator of the role of Sir Peter Teazle, succeeded him in 1772, remaining for ten years until Henry Siddons (the actress Sarah Siddons's husband), in association with dramatist-actor-composer Charles Dibdin and his two sons, took over. In 1801, a small boy called Master Carey performed here; he would become Edmund Kean in adulthood.

'Nautical Drama' drew the crowds to Islington from 1814, when a tank of water, 90 feet long and three feet deep, was placed on the stage in order to simulate naval battles. Swimmers manipulated scale-model ships while cannons fired in plays called *The Siege of Gibraltar* and *Naval Triumph; Or, The Tars Of Old England.* However, with the breaking of the monopoly of the Patent Theatres which prevented legitimate drama being given other than at the Theatres Royal in 1843, a new era dawned at Sadler's Wells. The superb actor-manager Samuel Phelps took a lease on the near-derelict building in 1844 where, in the following 18 years, he produced almost all of Shakespeare's plays, thus making it 'a place for justly representing the works of our great dramatic poet', as Phelps rightly claimed. The location which started as a spa became an oasis of culture.

But 'Oh! What a fall was there!' when Phelps retired in 1862. The theatre was used as a skating rink and a prize-fighting venue before it was closed for repairs in 1878. A year later it was bought by Mrs Bateman, the widow of the owner of the Lyceum. On her death in 1881, it passed into her daughter Isabel's hands. Unfortunately, the theatre developed into the home of crude melodrama where the 'gallery contained the most villainous, desperate, hatchet-faced assembly of ruffians to be found in all London'. No wonder Miss Bateman left the stage to take Holy Orders. The 'Wells' later became a music hall, then an early cinema before closing down in 1906 where it lay, like Aurora in *The Sleeping Beauty*, until Lilian Baylis hacked her way through the tangled financial undergrowth to kiss it into life again.

At first, drama, ballet and opera alternated between the Old Vic and Sadler's Wells. The opening Shakespeare season of 1931–32, in which John Gielgud played Malvolio, Benedick and King Lear, and Ralph Richardson was Sir Toby Belch, Petruchio, Bottom and Henry V, ran two weeks at the 'Vic' and one at the 'Wells'. But this proved too expensive and in 1935 only opera and ballet were given, while drama remained at the Vic. With the help of Nicolas Sergueyev from the Russian Maryinsky, the ballet company, under Ninette de Valois (born Edris Stannus in 1898), was able to build up a classical repertoire that included *Giselle*, *Swan Lake*, *Coppélia* and *The Nutcracker*, and new ballets were commissioned from British choreographers. Frederick Ashton delivered *Facade* (1931), *Apparitions* (1936), *Les Patineurs* (1937) and *Horoscope* (1938), while de Valois choreographed *Job* (1931), *The Rake's Progress* and *Checkmate* (both 1935), most of them still performed. When the leading dancers Alicia Markova (Alice Marks) and Anton Dolin (Patrick Healey-Kay) left to form their own company, Margot Fonteyn (Peggy Hookham) and Robert Helpmann stepped into their ballet shoes. The opera company took a little longer to gain wide recognition, but under the baton of Laurence Collingwood, and with singers such as Joan Cross, Edith Coates, Tudor Davies and Henry Wendon, and a growing repertoire strong on Wagner and Verdi sung in English, it soon blossomed.

In 1938, the year after the parsimonious Baylis died, improvements were carried out by enlarging the stage and building new dressing rooms and a rehearsal room. However, in 1940 the theatre was damaged by a bomb and performances were held at the New Theatre (now the Albery) during the war. Only the opera company returned to its home at Sadler's Wells in 1945 with an historic reopening, the world premiere of Benjamin Britten's *Peter Grimes* with Peter Pears in the title role and Reginald Goodall in the pit. It heralded a new dawn of English opera. Over the years, especially under Norman Tucker from 1948 to 1966, the Sadler's Wells opera grew into a real ensemble, members of which were conductors Alexander Gibson and Colin Davis, producers Denis Arundell, Wendy Toye, Basil Coleman and Glen Byam Shaw, and singers who became internationally famous such as Amy Shuard, David Ward, Peter Glossop, Donald McIntyre, Norman Bailey and Rita Hunter. In 1959, the doubtful acoustics were improved by a canopy suspended over the proscenium.

After the company moved to the Coliseum in 1974 to become the English National Opera, the theatre fell on less exciting times. But under the leadership of Ian Albery, who arrived as Chief Executive and Producer in 1994, Sadler's Wells has really thrived again, with ground-breaking productions like Adventures in Motion Pictures' all-male *Swan Lake* in 1996. Today, in its

A venue for international art, The Wells presented the Japanese Noh Theatre in 1983

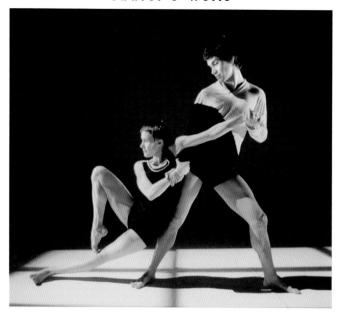

Random Dance's modern masterpiece, *Nemesis*

inspirational new home, it is a dance and lyric theatre of world stature. In the two years since the new Sadler's Wells opened, it has attracted top international choreographers such as Matthew Bourne and Pina Bausch, companies like the Ballett Frankfurt, Mikhail Baryshnikov's White Oak Dance Project, Sankai Juko and Kabuki, as well as the Welsh National Opera, the Royal Ballet and the Royal Opera. In 2001 it was announced that the Random Dance Company (led by the brilliant Wayne McGregor) was to become the Sadler's Wells' Resident Company. Islington's Angel is obviously keeping a good eye on the 'Wells'.

sadler's wells theatre
rosebery avenue = ec1

St Martin's

They make an odd couple, the sober St Martin's and the more frivolous New Ambassadors, a few yards from each other, separated in space by Tower Court and in time by World War I. The pre-war New Ambassadors has a richly adorned interior while the post-war St Martin's avoided fancy plasterwork, opting for the polished wood of the balustraded balcony fronts and Doric columns on pedestals at balcony level, making it seem less intimate than the 550-seat capacity would suggest. Classicism is maintained by the six giant Ionic columns, framing three storeys of large windows, on the stone facade. Links between the two theatres are their common architect, W. G. R. Sprague, the fact that Charles B. Cochran was a lessee of both at their beginnings, and *The Mousetrap*, which ran for 22 years at the Ambassadors, then moved next door to the St Martin's in 1974 for a further interminable run – in 2002 celebrating a record-breaking 50 years!

The theatre that started off on a light note in August 1916 with Gaiety Girl Gertie Millar in Cochran's *Houp La!* soon plunged into the gloom of Eugene Brieux's *Damaged Goods* in the same year. The play, a study of sexually transmitted disease, caused a sensation. After a couple of musical comedies, the theatre returned to 'serious' business with 62-year-old Sir Frank Benson as Hamlet (1920). The director Tyrone Guthrie noted that 'He'd been a very handsome man and proud of his fine physique. It was sad to see this rouged, gaunt ruin of masculine beauty pretending to be Hamlet.'

When the St Martin's was brought under the management of Alec Rea and Basil Dean in 1920, an enterprising series of modern plays was produced. Among the more established writers, John Galsworthy was represented by *The Skin Game*

'Alfred Butt instructed his lieutenants to get the pick of my girls from the St Martin's, even if they cost double the salary of the ordinary chorus girl.'
— Charles B. Cochran, 1925

(1920), *Loyalties* (1922) and *The Forest* (1924); Karel Capek's satire on modern regimentation, *R.U.R.* (1923), made an impact, as did Frederick Lonsdale's *Spring Cleaning* (1925), which had people raising their hands in horror at a 'street walker' being among the dramatis personae. Less controversial was Noël Coward's cardboard Ruritanian drama, *The Queen Was In The Parlour* (1926), with Madge Titheradge, Herbert Marshall and Lady Tree.

Clemence Dane's first play, *A Bill Of Divorcement*, which dealt with the problem of divorce on grounds of insanity, featured a promising young actress called Meggie Albanesi in the role that first brought Katharine Hepburn film fame. Sadly, Miss Albanesi died two years later aged 24, her death being commemorated by a plaque in the foyer of the theatre. Another young actress, 17-year-old Hermione Baddeley, scored a triumph as Florrie Small in Charles McEvoy's study of East End slum life, *The Likes Of Her* (1923). The Great War was the subject of *The White Chateau* (1927) written by Reginald Berkeley while recovering from wounds he received at the front.

The St Martin's continued its policy of dramas on contemporary issues into the 1930s with John Gielgud directing his first modern play, Rodney Ackland's *Strange Orchestra*. Unfortunately, Mrs Patrick Campbell left, after rehearsing for some weeks, because her dog was in quarantine. Of *The Green Bay Tree* (1933) by Mordaunt Shairp, featuring Hugh Williams and Frank Vosper, the critic of the *Star* wrote, 'If the object was to arouse powerful detestation of two abominable people a kind of success may be concluded, but that is all.' The play is possibly the first contemporary drama on the subject of homosexuality, although the word itself is never used.

The first production of J. B. Priestley's oft-revived Yorkshire comedy, *When We Are Married* (1938), was given here, directed by Basil Dean. The author himself took over the role of Henry Ormonroyd, the pickled photographer, when Frank Pettingell was injured in a road accident. He played it for several nights to great applause. Its run was terminated by the outbreak of war. Productions came and went like buses for some years until Edward Percy's murder tale, *The Shop At Sly Corner* (1945), ran 863 performances.

Successes in the '50s and '60s were Joyce Grenfell in the revue *Penny Plain* (1951), American actress Geraldine Page in *The*

The Mousetrap lives on

Keith Baxter (left) and Anthony Quayle in Anthony Shaffer's ingenious *Sleuth* (1970)

Rainmaker (1956), two plays by Hugh and Margaret Williams, *Plaintiff In A Pretty Hat* (1957) and *The Grass Is Greener* (1958), *Guilty Party* (1961), *Where Angels Fear To Tread* (1963), from E. M. Forster's novel, and Eric Portman in *The Creeper* (1965). In preparation for the long years of *The Mousetrap*, Keith Baxter, Anthony Quayle and 'many others' starred in Anthony Shaffer's clever thriller *Sleuth* (1970) for three years. *The Mousetrap* was transferred here on 25 March, 1974, and continues making theatrical history as it enters its 50th year. In 1994 Sir Peter Saunders sold the management of *The Mousetrap* and with it the lease of the St Martin's Theatre to Mousetrap Productions Limited, and the theatre underwent major redecoration to a design by Carl Toms. In 1999, the set of *The Mousetrap* was completely replaced – only the clock on the mantelpiece now remains from the set and props of 1952! Presumably, the news of

st martin's

'whodunnit', despite the play having been seen by over ten million people, has still not reached the eager crowds buying their tickets at the St Martin's.

st martin's theatre
west street = wc2h

The Savoy

The Savoy Theatre, built for impresario Richard D'Oyly Carte from the profits he accrued from Gilbert and Sullivan's light operas, was the very model of a modern major theatre when it opened in October 1881. As *The Times* stated, 'This is the first time that it has been attempted to light any public building entirely by electricity. What is being done is an experiment, and may succeed or fail.' At the opening production, the one hundred and seventieth performance of *Patience*, the electric lights were 'cheered to the very echo'. People have been cheering at the Savoy ever since.

D'Oyly Carte, who had instigated the partnership of W. S. Gilbert and Arthur Sullivan, dreamed of building his own theatre in which to stage their works. A suitable site was found close to the Thames Embankment within the grounds of the old Savoy Palace Hotel, and a theatre, designed by C. J. Phipps, was constructed within a few months. Not only by the 'application of electric light for theatrical purposes' was the Savoy in advance of other theatres of the day. Not for D'Oyly Carte the 'Gingerbread School of Decorative Art' with its elaborate ornamentation and paintings of cherubs and the like. The decoration was composed of cleaner lines and delicate colouring.

The first years were given over almost exclusively to Gilbert and Sullivan's works, which became known as the Savoy operas: *Iolanthe* (1882), *Princess Ida* (1884), *The Mikado* (1885), *Ruddigore* (1887), *The Yeomen Of The Guard* (1888) and *The Gondoliers* (1889) all had first performances here. During the run of the latter, the irascible Gilbert (lyrics) quarrelled with Sullivan (music) and they refused to work with each other again. Sir Arthur, therefore, collaborated with Sydney Grundy on *Haddon Hall* (1892) before the celebrated duo were reconciled. Their thirteenth operetta together, *Utopia Limited* (1893), failed by

'The new Savoy Theatre is the first really outstanding example of modern decoration applied to a public place on a commercial basis.'
— *Country Life*, 1929

trying to hit too many targets in Victorian England at once. Their last work as a team was *The Grand Duke* (1896), also a failure. It marked the end of an era, but not the end of Gilbert and Sullivan at the Savoy. There were seasons of revivals in 1929–30, 1932–33, 1961–62, and two weeks in 1975 celebrating the centenary of their first success, *Trial By Jury*. Full-length portraits of Gilbert and Sullivan stand in the theatre today as a memento of their splendid reign.

In contrast to the melodious music of Sullivan and the witty libretti of Gilbert were Harley Granville-Barker's epoch-making Shakespeare productions between 1912 and 1914. John Gielgud recollected in *A Midsummer Night's Dream*, 'the gold-painted fairies, the swaying green curtains to suggest the wood, the hanging canopy overhead – a kind of chandelier of white and green – and the slim tall figure of Oberon, my cousin Dennis Neilson-Terry. I recall also the slightly bewildered reactions of the audience.' The simple and abstract staging, in contrast to Tree's lavish productions at His Majesty's, received much abuse. Granville-Barker's wife, Lillah McCarthy, played Helena, Viola in *Twelfth Night* and Hermione to Henry Ainley's Leontes in *The Winter's Tale* of whom critic W. A. Darlington commented, 'my first experience of really passionate acting, and it convinced me once and for all that the theatre's first concern was with emotion.'

Between the wars, Gertrude Page's Paddy *The Next Best Thing* (1920) ran for over two years, while Noël Coward's second play, *The Young Idea* (1923), featuring himself, ran only eight weeks causing Coward to remark, 'London is outraged at the play coming off, everyone is talking about it and it's doing me a lot of good.' Playwright John Van Druten first came to prominence with *Young*

Woodley (1928), a study of a schoolboy's infatuation with his teacher's wife, which had unaccountably been banned until then. In 1929 a first play by a then unknown playwright, R. C. Sherriff, a moving and realistic portrayal of men in the trenches called *Journey's End*, was an immediate success. It led to the Hollywood careers of both the director James Whale and the actor Colin Clive. Laurence Olivier, who had created the role of Captain Stanhope in Sunday performances, opted to play in *Beau Geste*, which flopped. After *Journey's End* transferred, the whole of the interior and part of the exterior of the theatre was rebuilt.

The main entrance was shifted from the Embankment side (where the old Phipps facade is still visible) to the courtyard of the new Savoy Hotel. In keeping with the hotel's frontage of stainless steel with its knight in shining armour above the entrance, the theatre decked itself in silver splendour. The interior, designed by Frank A. Tugwell and Basil Ionides, was an Art Deco delight. Many exquisite details on doors, seats and

Paul Eddington, Jan Waters and Patricia Routledge in Michael Frayn's hilarious look at theatre folk, *Noises Off*

walls, a glass screen in the Circle Bar, a group of Egyptian maidens round a large vase and golden Japanese scenes on either side of the stage gave it all an air of chic. Winston Churchill, a constant visitor, would always have a seat in the Royal Box. This was built out for him slightly, thus obscuring a few seats on the side of the circle. When his hearing deteriorated, he would sit in the front row.

The hits of the World War II years were Kaufman and Hart's wicked comedy, *The Man Who Came To Dinner* (1941), in which Robert Morley played Sheridan Whiteside. (The actor's son, critic Sheridan Morley, was named after the character.) Coral Browne also appeared, and would later star in *My Sister Eileen* (1943), *The Last of Mrs Cheyney* (1944) and *Lady Frederick* (1946). Post-war, Margaret Lockwood appeared in Agatha Christie's *The Spider's Web* (1954) for over two years, and in *Subway In The Sky* (1957). Noël Coward renewed his acquaintance with the Savoy with his musical *Sail Away* (1962) in which Elaine Stritch as Mimi Paragon first made herself known to British audiences. *High Spirits* (1964), a musical adaptation of Coward's play *Blithe Spirit* by Hugh Martin and Timothy Gray, limped along for three months, but the Savoy would soon have a string of long runs with plays like *Alibi For A Judge* (1965), two William Douglas Home comedies, *The Secretary Bird* (1968) and *Lloyd George Knew My Father* (1972) with Ralph Richardson and Peggy Ashcroft (afterwards replaced by Celia Johnson) and the controversial *Whose Life Is It Anyway?* with Tom Conti in 1978. Michael Frayn's farce of the theatre, *Noises Off* (1982), ran for over four years.

Then in February 1990, disaster struck – a fire ravaged the auditorium. Three years later, the auditorium and public areas had been faithfully restored to the 1929 vision of Tugwell and Ionides, and the theatre triumphantly reopened with a Royal Gala performed by the English National Ballet, in the presence of HRH The Princess of Wales. Since then, the Savoy has gone from strength to strength with productions such as *The Importance of Being Oscar* with Simon Callow, Edward Fox in *A Letter of*

Gilbert and Sullivan's *Mikado* enjoyed a new audience in 2002 at the Savoy

Resignation and Coward's *Hay Fever* with Geraldine McEwan. The new millennium saw the triumphant return of the D'Oyly Carte season with *The Mikado*, as well as Donald Sutherland's return to the stage in *Enigmatic Variations*. Since then, the D'Oyly Carte Opera Company has returned again to its spiritual home, with acclaimed performances of *The Mikado*, *Iolanthe* and *The Yeomen of the Guard*.

the savoy theatre
savoy court, the strand wc2r

The Shaftesbury

O n 19 July, 1973, just as the Shaftesbury Theatre was about to celebrate the two thousandth performance of the 'flower children' musical *Hair*, part of the ceiling of the auditorium fell in. It seemed as though the theatre's days were numbered as the threat of turning it into an office block loomed over its little roof tower. Would demolition workers really knock down Bertie Crewe's stone frontage that had dominated the corner at the junction of Shaftesbury Avenue and High Holborn since 1911? Would anyone have the heart to wreck the florid interior, with its eight bow-fronted boxes framed by giant Ionic columns? Would a hammer be taken to the life-size statues representing Comedy, Tragedy, Poetry and Music that sit over each upper box? How could the bas-relief of reclining women and Roman soldiers over the proscenium be shattered without compunction? Members of the entertainment industry and Equity, the actors' union, fought a vigorous campaign to keep the theatre open by organising protest marches and getting petitions signed. Happily, in March 1974, the Department of the Environment gave in to the pressure and placed the Shaftesbury on the Statutory List of Buildings of Special Architectural or Historic Interest. Like one of the heroines in the melodramas for which it was built, this pretty Edwardian theatre was saved from a terrible fate in the nick of time.

Under the management of the brothers Walter and Frederick Melville, the New Princes Theatre (as it was originally called until it became the Princes in 1914) housed a series of popular melodramas that have since come to dust. Seymour Hicks's three-year reign began in 1916 with a revival of *Bluebell in Fairyland*. In 1919, Charles B. Cochran took over for a while, the year the great soprano Maggie Teyte appeared in André Messager's light opera *Monsieur Beaucaire*. The Princes also played host to the

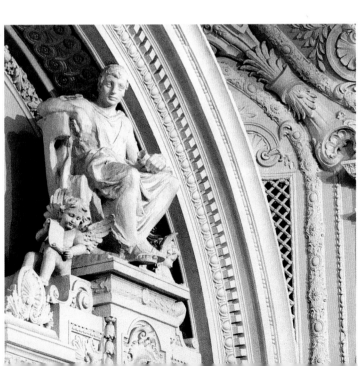

'This particular theatre, because of the ambience of the auditorium... provides an intimate relationship between performer and audience, so necessary for comedy.'
— Ray Cooney

D'Oyly Carte Opera Company when the Savoy was unavailable. Seasons of the works of Gilbert and Sullivan were presented here in the 1920s, '40s and '50s. In fact, the large auditorium of 1,250 (now 1,305) seats has always been suitable for operettas, musicals and ballets. Diaghilev's Russian ballet performed here in 1921 and 1927, and Sadler's Wells Opera and Ballet Company in 1944.

Among the straight plays were *Daniel* (1921), in which Sarah Bernhardt made her final London appearance; *Alf's Button* (1924), a fantasy written by the theatre critic W. A. Darlington; and *Macbeth* (1926), starring Sybil Thorndike and Henry Ainley as the murderous Scottish couple. A gas-pipe explosion in a nearby street interrupted the run of George Gershwin's *Funny Face* (1928), featuring Fred and Adele Astaire and Leslie Henson. Due to 'the impassability of the roadway to vehicular traffic', the theatre was closed for some weeks. In 1929, Firth Shephard blew in as manager, remaining until 1946. The shows under his aegis included Sardou's *Diplomacy* (1933), two adaptations from stories by Edgar Wallace, *The Frog* (1936) and *The Gusher* (1937), and John O'Keeffe's 1791 comedy *Wild Oats* (1938). Although the theatre suffered some bomb blasts in 1940 and 1941, it managed to remain open during the war years.

Ironically, it was in the post-war days that the Princes was dark more often than not. Bright spots were *His Excellency* (1950) with Eric Portman; Michael Redgrave and Peggy Ashcroft in *Antony And Cleopatra* (1953) from Stratford-on-Avon; the American musicals *Pal Joey* (1954) and *Wonderful Town* (1955), and a British one, *Summer Song* (1956), based on the music and life of Dvorak. When the partnership of Charles Clore and EMI bought the theatre in 1962, it was redecorated and renamed the Shaftesbury. Frank Loesser's Broadway hit musical *How To Succeed In Business Without Really Trying* (1963) did for the box-office what the title suggests. In contrast Lionel Bart's Robin Hood musical, *Twangi* (1965), ran for a mere 43 performances. After that, Eric Sykes and Jimmy Edwards in *Big Bad Mouse* (1966) kept the coach parties happy for over a year before the advent of *Hair* in 1968.

Hair was the musical that gave voice to hippiedom, to the anti-Vietnam war and Civil Rights movements, and that opened the day after theatre censorship officially ended, thus allowing audiences the sight of full frontal nudity, both male and female.

After its escape from the bulldozers, the Shaftesbury continued to present musicals, notably Neil Simon and Marvin Hamlisch's *They're Playing Our Song* (1980). The theatre had another facelift in 1986, and again in 1989. It now has a bright and attractive lobby with an array of flowers placed in small alcoves, and the auditorium is a delightful wedding cake of pink and white. It was two years earlier that the Theatre of Comedy company, founded by writer-director Ray Cooney and supported by 30 leading actors, writers and directors, bought the theatre and renamed it, officially, the Shaftesbury Theatre of Comedy.

Among the many highly successful productions presented by the company are founder Ray Cooney's *Run For Your Wife,* Shaw's *Pygmalion* with Peter O'Toole and *See How They Run* (which won founder member Maureen Lipman an Olivier Award). More awards came thick and fast through the '90s: Ray Cooney's *Out of Order* (1990) won the 1991 Olivier Award for Comedy of the Year; the controversial *Kiss of the Spider Woman* won the *Evening Standard* Award for Best Musical 1992, then went on to collect seven Tony awards on Broadway; *Tommy*, by Pete Townsend (1996), won three Olivier Awards, including Outstanding Musical Production; and in 1998 the Shaftesbury was chosen as the London venue for the multi-award-winning musical *Rent*. In 1997 the theatre provided a home for the Royal

The seminal American 'hippy' musical *Hair* made its English home at the Shaftesbury

the shaftesbury

Opera whilst the Royal Opera House Covent Garden underwent major redevelopment. Six operas were performed, including new productions of *Il Barbiere di Siviglia* and the Olivier Award-winning *Paul Bunyan*, directed by Francesca Zambello. Since then, there has been Charles Aznavour's new musical *Lautrec* and the sumptuous *Napoleon*. All in all, a history to be very proud of.

the shaftesbury theatre
shaftesbury avenue = wc2h

Shakespeare's Globe

London's very first playhouse, erected in London in April 1576, was simply called The Theatre. When it was pulled down in 1597, its timber was taken across the River Thames and used to build the Globe – Shakespeare's famous 'wooden O'. The original Globe Theatre was built on the south bank of the Thames in 1599 by an architect named Peter Street, especially for William Shakespeare's company of players. Shakespeare's players (The Chamberlain's Men – later, in 1603, The King's Men) were led by Richard Burbage – the first Hamlet, Lear and Othello, and one of the first in a long line of actor-managers who ran, and often owned, the theatres in which they performed. This noble tradition was echoed in the twentieth century by Sam Wanamaker, actor and director, whose determination and vision created today's modern Globe, and it continues with actor Mark Rylance, the present Artistic Director of the Shakespeare's Globe Theatre.

When the original Globe was built, the South Bank was London's playground – characterised by brothels, bear-baiting and theatre-going. Shakespeare and his contemporaries presented their plays at the Rose, Swan, Hope and Globe theatres – and the Globe was the most popular of them all. But in 1613 a spark from a stage cannon set fire to the thatched roof of the theatre and it was burnt to the ground. A second Globe was built on the same foundations with a tiled roof, and probably a more ornate interior. In 1616 Shakespeare died, and in 1642 the Globe was closed by the Puritans. Two years later, the theatre was destroyed and its foundations buried to make way for tenement buildings.

'...an atmosphere that reflects the ethos of the Globe – informal, infectiously friendly and compellingly inviting.'
— *Time Out* magazine

And there it lay for four hundred years. Then, in 1949, fleeing the artistic oppression of the US's McCarthy era, actor/director Sam Wanamaker came to London and settled there, devoting the rest of his life to realising his vision of bringing Shakespeare's Globe back to life and revitalising world-wide interest in Shakespeare's plays. Central to this vision was the rebuilding of the Globe Theatre as it was in Shakespeare's time, for which Wanamaker tirelessly campaigned to raise money.

In 1970 he established the Globe Playhouse Trust, dedicated to the experience and international understanding of Shakespeare in performance and the celebration of the fact that the greatest dramatic poet in the English language lived in the cradle of English theatre, on Bankside by the River Thames. In the same year, Southwark Council offered the Trust a 1.2-acre site beside the River Thames – a site only 200 yards from the original position of the Globe. This wasn't acquired until 1989, when the foundations of the original building were discovered under a Georgian terrace and Southwark Bridge Road.

shakespeare's globe

Theo Crosby was the architect of Shakespeare's Globe, and he began designs for the site in 1986. Archaeological excavations, panoramas, maps, building contracts, contemporary accounts and remaining buildings each contributed to the body of knowledge that informed the reconstruction. There are no plans or construction drawings that clearly depict the form of the original theatre itself, so its design and construction were quite a challenge. Theo Crosby died in 1994, shortly after the death of Sam Wanamaker. Sadly, neither man had a chance to see their dream fully realised. Since 1994, Crosby's work has been continued by John Greenfield, who first joined the project in 1987, the same year that the site was cleared for ground-breaking and the six-metre-deep foundations were laid.

In 1993 the construction of the theatre itself began on the newly laid Piazza. The next summer, under the supervision of master craftsman Peter McCurdy, the walls were built using traditional methods and traditional components – handmade bricks, lime plaster and 168,000 metres of oak laths. The roof used 6,000 bundles of Norfolk water reed, making the Globe the first thatched building to be built in central London since the Great Fire of 1666.

In 1995, there was a Workshop Season for the new Globe Theatre Company, and in the same year, with funding from the National Lottery, the Globe Theatre was completed, including foyer areas, a restaurant and a café. The theatre is a beautiful, organic building, and its setting is wonderful. Right on the bank of the Thames, it looks towards St Paul's Cathedral across a river spanned by the graceful lines of the Millennium Bridge. To its left is the Tate Modern. The area is full of vibrant landmarks of twenty-first century London, part of a celebration of arts, culture and architecture. On 12 June 1997, in the presence of HM the Queen and HRH Prince Philip, Patron of the Shakespeare Globe Trust, the theatre opened officially with a production of *Henry V*.

The theatre season runs each year from May to September, and audiences at the Globe sit in the gallery or stand informally as 'groundlings' in the yard, just as they would have 400 years

Mark Rylance as Posthumus in *Cymbeline,* 2001

ago. If it rains, the groundlings get wet! But that doesn't seem to put audiences off – each year numbers have been rising, and the theatre's fifth anniversary season was the Company's best attended yet, with nearly a quarter of a million people.

The Globe Theatre Company, under the artistic direction of Mark Rylance, has so far produced 15 of Shakespeare's plays. The three productions of 2001 (*Macbeth, King Lear* and *Cymbeline*) were particularly highly acclaimed. They have also presented the work of Shakespeare's contemporaries: Thomas Middleton, with *A Chaste Maid in Cheapside* (1997) and *A Mad World, My Masters* (1998); Fletcher and Beaumont, with *The Maid's Tragedy* (1997); Richard Brome, with *The Antipodes* (2000); and Thomas Dekker, with *An Honest Whore* (1998). New plays are also commissioned to exploit the theatre's unique audience/actor relationship. Resident playwright Peter Oswald's *Augustine's Oak* (1999) and his version of the epic comedy *The Golden Ass* (2002) were both written especially for the Globe.

The theatre also welcomes international theatre companies. In 1997 it staged *Umabatha*, the Zulu *Macbeth*; in 1998 the Cuban Company Teatro Buendia's version of *The Tempest*; in 1999 the Annette Leday/Keil Company's *Kathakali King Lear*; in 2002 Grupo Galpao's Brazilian *Romeo & Julieta*; and in 2002 the Japanese play *The Kyogen of Errors* (based on *The Comedy of Errors*). The Globe Theatre Company also takes its productions abroad: 2001's *King Lear* ran at the Tokyo Globe for two weeks; *Macbeth* had performances at the Teatro Olimpico, a contemporary of the original Globe Theatre in Vicenza, Italy; and the acclaimed production of *Cymbeline* was performed in New York in 2002. For the past four years the theatre has also been home to the annual WOMAD (World of Music and Dance) festival, and the Comedy Store Players, who play for one riotous night a year.

The Globe isn't just about performances, there's also Globe Education. The theatre devotes six months of each year exclusively to education, running courses on all aspects of Shakespeare and the experience of performing his works as they were originally intended to be performed, for students and teachers throughout the UK and abroad. There is also a permanent and well-attended Exhibition at the Globe – the largest in the world dedicated to Shakespeare and his workplace.

And construction is still going on! An indoor theatre is being built on the site to a design by Inigo Jones (*c*.1616), and a library and education centre are under construction. This unique centre really is a living, working, passionate tribute to the greatest writer in the English language.

shakespeare's globe theatre
new globe walk = se1

The Strand

L ooking at this solid, classical, corner building with its giant columns and pediments, it is difficult to imagine that the Strand was bombed in both World Wars. In each case it continued to function as if nothing had happened. In 1915, during a performance of *The Scarlet Pimpernel*, it suffered a Zeppelin raid. Fred Terry, John Gielgud's great-uncle and an actor-manager in the grand manner, went down among the audience in his Sir Percy Blakeney costume, urging them not to be afraid, before stepping back onto the stage and continuing with the play. During Donald Wolfit's Shakespeare season in October 1940, a German bomb fell on the theatre, damaging the dressing rooms. Having dug out the costumes from the debris, the actors clambered over the ruins to get to the stage. These are two of the most extraordinary examples of the dictum, 'The show must go on.'

Shows have been going on at the Strand non-stop since it opened, in May 1905, with a season of operas alternating with plays given in Italian by the remarkable tragedienne Eleonora Duse and her company. In the same year, a crack in the proscenium arch of his own theatre drove Herbert Beerbohm Tree to bring in *Oliver Twist*, starring himself as Fagin, while it was being repaired. Tree would have found the Waldorf (as the Strand was first called) no less luxurious than His Majesty's. It was built at the same time as and with a facade almost identical to that of the Aldwych Theatre on the opposite corner, separated by the Waldorf Hotel, the architect of both theatres being the renowned W. G. R. Sprague. Although it lacks the delightful oval gallery of its near neighbour, the interior decorations of the Strand are far more impressive.

At the foot of the elegant stairway are twin female figurines holding lamps which throw light upon the highly polished brass

'This mass exhumation of former film stars – British at that – was regarded by the critics as turning the Strand into a disaster area.'
— Michael Denison, 1965

railings and marble walls. In the green and gold 927-seat auditorium are two tiers of boxes, framed in Ionic pilasters and crowned with an ornate sculptural group of cupids. More cupids attend the Sun God in a chariot pulled by four horses, in a vigorous and colourful design above the stage. On the circular ceiling are painted allegorical figures after Le Brun. The Royal Box, used mainly by businessmen wishing to impress their clients or girlfriends, has a large retiring room.

In the years before World War I, apart from Tree and La Duse, many of the great names of the Edwardian theatre appeared at the Strand - H. B. Irving in *Lights Out* (1905), Cyril Maude in *She Stoops to Conquer* (1906) and E. H. Sothem and his wife Julia Marlowe in four Shakespeare plays. Matheson Lang gave the theatre its first long run (403 performances) with *Mr Wu* (1913). So identified did Lang become with the title role that he called his autobiography of 1940 *Mr Wu Looks Back*. During the war, it was the visit of Fred Terry and Julia Neilson in *Henry Of Navarre*, *Sweet Nell Of Old Drury* and *The Scarlet Pimpernel* that held audiences in rapture.

Arthur Bourchier, whose portrait hangs in the foyer, ran the theatre for eight years from 1919. Among his successes were a dramatisation of *Treasure Island*, presented every Christmas from 1922 to 1926; the first British production of Eugene O'Neill's 1903 play *Anna Christie* (1923) with Pauline Lord in the title role; and another American import, *Broadway* (1926) by Philip Dunning and George Abbott. When Bourchier died while touring South Africa in 1927, George Grossmith took over for a couple of years during which he produced Charles Laughton (a year before his film debut) in *Beauty*, and Miriam Hopkins (three years prior to her Hollywood career) in *Bachelor Father* (both 1927).

While farces were still packing them in a few yards away at the Aldwych, comedian Leslie Henson and Firth Shephard produced a rival series of similar entertainments with titles such as *It's A Boy!* (1930), *It's A Girl!* and *Night Of The Garter* (both 1932). After a year's run of *1066 And All That* (1935), 'a comic history with music', farce returned with Aldwych favourites Robertson 'Oh Calamity' Hare and Alfred Drayton in Vernon Sylvaine's *Aren't Men Beasts* (1936) and *A Spot Of Bother* (1937); and Ben Travers's *Banana Ridge* (1938) and *Spotted Dick* (1939).

For most of the war years from 1942, Joseph Kesselring's black comedy *Arsenic And Old Lace*, with Lilian Braithwaite (created a Dame in 1943 during the run), Mary Jerrold, Frank Pettingell and Naunton Wayne, occupied the large Strand. One night, after the performance, Dame Lilian had to take refuge in the ground floor cloakroom during an air raid that lasted many hours. Asked if she was exhausted by the episode, she replied, 'Certainly not! We were fifty pounds up last night.' Braithwaite, the mother of actress Joyce Carey, had been at the Strand 29 years previously in *Mr Wu*.

If the Strand managed to withstand the bombs of two World Wars, then the booming tones of Peggy Mount as Emma Hornett, the battle-axe mother-in-law-to-be in *Sailor Beware* (1955), shook its very foundations for over three years. The 40-

(above) The renowned Italian tragedienne Eleonora Duse graced the Strand with her acclaimed presence

279

Felicity Kendal and Roger Rees starred in *The Real Thing* (1982), Tom Stoppard's highly successful play about contemporary marriage

year-old actress, who had spent years in provincial rep, suddenly found herself a West End star. Aside from a satirical revue, *For Adults Only* (1958), and *The Affair* (1961), an adaptation of C. P. Snow's novel, shows came and went with rapidity for a few years. One, *The Princess* (1960), got such bad notices that the management offered free seats for a week. The experiment failed.

the strand

The opening night of *A Funny Thing Happened On The Way To The Forum* in November 1963 coincided with the news of the assassination of John F. Kennedy. The audience was not much in the mood for laughter, but the musical Roman romp, starring Frankie Howerd, and Robertson Hare as a slave called Erronius, overcame the initial resistance, and the show ran nearly two years.

Alastair Sim and Dora Bryan in Shaw's *Too True To Be Good* and Margaret Lockwood and Richard Todd in *An Ideal Husband* (both 1965) breezed through on their way to other theatres. Peggy Mount returned to the scene of her first triumph in J. B. Priestley's *When We Are Married* (1970), before the incredible run – 11 years – of the farce, *No Sex Please, We're British* (1971), by Anthony Marriott and Alistair Foot, featuring a young Michael Crawford. Like *The Mousetrap*, it became virtually a national institution and ran and ran. When it left for the Garrick and then the Duchess, Tom Stoppard's *The Real Thing* (1984) was able to attract the crowds. *Cabaret* (1986) which followed, with dancer Wayne Sleep as the MC, was ended suddenly a year later by a musicians' strike. The next ten years saw some strong drama and fine actors at the Strand – *Lost in Yonkers* with Maureen Lipman, *The Prime of Miss Jean Brodie*, starring Patricia Hodge, *A View From the Bridge* with Joseph Fiennes, and Imogen Stubbs in *St Joan*. Then, in 1996, came the musical *Buddy*, transferred from the Victoria Palace. It was enormously popular, and finally finished its run in March 2002, making it the most successful rock and roll musical ever with an amazing 5,140 performances, and in the process helping this survivor of a theatre to build a solid foundation for the future.

the strand theatre
aldwych = wc2b

The Vaudeville

This refined, discreet, small theatre in the Strand can lay claim to having launched Henry Irving on his way to becoming the dominant actor-manager during the last 30 years of Queen Victoria's reign. The first theatre on the site was built in 1870 by C. J. Phipps for three of the most popular actors of the day: David James, H. J. Montague and Thomas Thorne, known as the Jew, the Gent and the Gentile. They offered the 32-year-old Irving ten pounds a week to join the company and appear in the opening production, *For Love Or Money*. During the run, he was asked by budding playwright James Albery (the same age as Irving) to read the manuscript of his play *Two Roses*, 'a dainty domestic comedy'. Irving, who had been typecast for years as a villain in trashy plays, was worried that David James (the uncle of David Belasco) might claim the comic role for himself. In the event, Irving played the part of Digby Grant for 15 months before the American impresario, the self-styled Colonel Bateman, installed him at his newly bought Lyceum Theatre round the corner. It was there that Irving made theatrical history.

In 1871, Montague (who was to die two years later aged 34) left the Vaudeville in the hands of his partners. They broke all previous records with H. J. Byron's comedy *Our Boys* (1875), which ran four years. Its popularity was so phenomenal that Strand omnibuses would pull up outside the Vaudeville and the conductors would shout, 'Our Boys!' It was immediately followed by the distaff version called *Our Girls* (1879), which failed. Lightweight entertainments were the main fare, and indeed have been throughout most of the theatre's existence, interrupted by Henry Arthur Jones's 'problem play' *Saints And Sinners* (1884), which shocked some people with its 'religious blasphemies'. The charming Cyril Maude, then in his twenties,

'This little jewel–box of a theatre has, unfortunately, over recent years contained more paste than gems.'
— Clive Hirschhorn, 1986

redressed the balance by appearing in a series of comedies from 1888 until the theatre was reconstructed in 1891.

The compact four-storey Portland stone exterior, with its first-level loggia and French casement windows, could well have passed for the private house of a wealthy Victorian merchant. Today, the facade can be appreciated in its entirety because it only has a small sign over the canopy. Thomas Thorne, the remaining member of the original trio, sold the Vaudeville to the brothers Gatti, whose family continued to own it until 1969. From 1900 to 1906, Agostino and Stephano Gatti shared the management with Charles Frohman, who presented a string of successes starring Seymour Hicks and his wife Ellaline Terriss including *Bluebell In Fairyland* (1901) and J. M. Barrie's *Quality Street* (1902). The couple's last appearance at the Vaudeville was in *The Belle Of Mayfair* (1906) before they moved on to the Aldwych built for them and Frohman. Charles Hawtrey (father of the comedian in the 'Carry On' films) carried on the tradition in several comedies.

For ten years from 1915, the Vaudeville was the home of the Charlot revues. André Charlot had made a name for himself previously as a specialist of the genre at the Alhambra, a famous music hall demolished in 1936. (The Odeon Cinema, Leicester Square, now stands on the site.) Most of the Vaudeville revues had one word titles like *Samples* (1915), *Some* (1916), *Cheep* (1917), *Tabs* (1918), *Snap* (1922), and *Yes* (1923), and were instrumental in helping the careers of Beatrice Lillie, Gertrude Lawrence, Binnie Hale and Stanley Lupino (father of film actress-director Ida Lupino).

In 1926, the theatre was given a completely new interior, keeping the 1892 Phipps frontage intact. The proscenium was

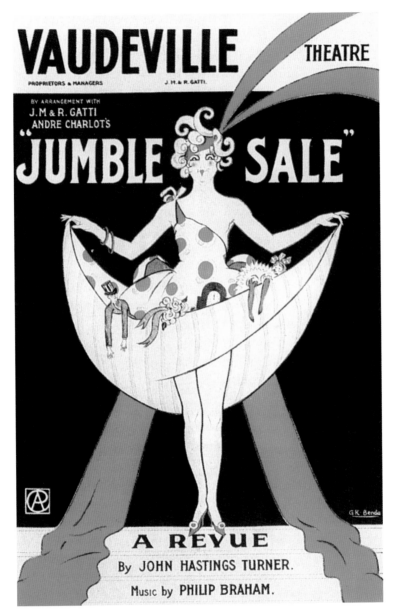

Poster for a Charlot revue, 1920s

the great theatres of london

Left to right: Patricia Hodge, Tim Piggott-Smith, Oliver Cotton and Brenda Blethyn in Michael Frayn's *Benefactors* (1984)

enlarged, new stairways built and the auditorium changed from its horseshoe shape to that of a rectangle with classical ornamentation. It then resumed where it left off – with revues from *Vaudeville Vanities* (1926) to Charlot's *Non-Stop Revue* (1937).

Revue departed, another redecoration ensued, and in came Robert Morley's second play *Goodness, How Sad!* (1938). The wartime successes were three plays by women – *Men In Shadow* (1942) by Mary Hayley Bell, starring her husband John Mills; Enid Bagnold's first play *Lottie Dundass* (1943); and Esther McCracken's *No Medals* (1944), which ran 742 performances.

In 1947, William Douglas Home (brother of future Prime Minister Alec Douglas Home) made a name for himself with the high-life comedy *The Chiltern Hundreds*, which ran for over two years with 78-year-old A. E. Matthews playing a dotty earl. The next long run, in fact the longest in Britain since *Chu Chin Chow*, was a whimsical little English musical by Julian Slade and Dorothy Reynolds called *Salad Days* (1954). Its tinkly but pleasant tunes kept audiences happy for six years. In 1962 the Vaudeville, known mostly for traditional entertainment, had its

286

first whiff of the 'Angry Young Man' school of drama when Arnold Wesker's class-battle air-force play *Chips With Everything* transferred from the Royal Court. But the theatre was soon back to establishment works such as Dorothy Tutin impersonating Victoria in *Portrait Of A Queen* (1965), Sybil Thorndike, Athene Seyler, Richard Briers, Lewis Casson and Julia Lockwood in *Arsenic And Old Lace* (1966) and Leslie Phillips in *The Man Most Likely To...* (1968) which lasted for nearly two years.

In 1969, Peter Saunders bought the theatre from the Gatti family, put in air conditioning and showers in the dressing rooms, and repainted it. The pretty, mirrored entrance with a chandelier leads into the well-preserved auditorium where Moira Lister was seen in boudoir farces *Move Over, Mrs Markham* (1971) and *Key For Two* (1982); Glenda Jackson appeared in tragi-comedies *Stevie* (1977) and *Great And Small* (1983); Michael Frayn's *Benefactors* (1984) was premiered, and the prolific Alan Ayckbourn enjoyed another success with *Woman In Mind* (1986), in which Julia McKenzie won the Society of London Theatres' Best Actress of the Year Award. Other fine performances from women at that time were Pauline Collins in *Shirley Valentine* (1988) and Maureen Lipman in *Re: Joyce* (1989), a tremendous one-woman show based on the life and songs of Joyce Grenfell. The 1990s were a varied decade, with Peter Greenwell's tribute to Noël Coward, *A Talent To Amuse* (1995), the revival of the award-winning David Hare play, *Skylight* (1997), the premiere of the South African musical *Kat And The Kings* (1998) and old favourite *The Chiltern Hundreds* (1999). In 2001 the theatre presented Ray Cooney's sequel to the legendary *Run For Your Wife – Caught in the Net*, starring Eric Sykes and Russ Abbot. And so the Vaudeville continues to supply top-class West End shows in a pleasant setting.

the vaudeville theatre
strand = wc2r

The Victoria Palace

For decades, before air travel became the principal means of transport, most visitors from the Continent would not have had to go far in order to see a supreme example of English theatre architecture. Facing Victoria Station is an imposing and unusual white stone edifice, crowned with giant statues and a Baroque tower and dome. The classical facade, open loggia with Ionic columns high above the entrance and festooned oval windows display the unmistakable touch of master theatre builder Frank Matcham, whose last remaining complete work in London this is.

Two buildings preceded the present Victoria Palace. Moy's Royal Standard Music Hall was demolished in 1886 during the rebuilding of Victoria Station and its environs. A new building on the site continued as a music hall until it, too, was pulled down in 1911. The Victoria Palace, built in the same year for impresario Alfred Butt, must have absorbed the music hall tradition of its antecedents into its very foundation stones for, with large music halls springing up all over the place, this was built to rival them all. The 1,565-seat, richly ornamented auditorium has a domed ceiling (the sliding roof keeps it cool in hot weather) and two tiers of three boxes on either side. Outside, on the pinnacle of the structure, was a gilded metal figure of Pavlova in full flight. It was said that the world's most famous ballerina superstitiously avoided looking at it every time she drove past by drawing the blinds of her car. The statue was taken down to protect it during the Blitz, but its whereabouts today remain a mystery.

'This lovely little theatre is one of the only remaining examples of a great and boisterous era.'
— George Hoare

The Victoria Palace opened in November 1911 with a variety bill and continued in the same fashion, presenting variety and revues until 1934, except for the annual Christmas play *The Windmill Man* from 1920 to 1931. Among the revues were *The Show's The Thing* (1929), starring Gracie Fields, and *The Chelsea Follies* (1930) with Nervo and Knox, prior to them joining the Crazy Gang. In 1934 the notorious patriotic play, *Young England*, turned out to be one of the most curious hits in theatrical history. Walter Reynolds, the play's 83-year-old author, stated, 'I have aimed at providing three hours of clean wholesome entertainment, to put before you a bill of fare made up of the joys, the sorrows, the tears, the laughter, the soft romances and the hard realities of our workaday existence.' But the melodramatic tale of a scoutmaster unjustly accused of theft from the scout funds was greeted with hilarity. Every platitude and sanctimonious situation was jeered, cheered and mocked by the crowds who flocked to see it.

Intentional humour was engendered when Seymour Hicks presented himself in a number of plays, including *The Miracle Man* (1935) in which his wife Ellaline Terriss made her farewell stage appearance at the age of 64. Revue returned in 1936 with *Let's Raise The Curtain,* starring Florence Desmond and the incomparable Elisabeth Welch (still performing, in her eighties, in the 1980s), and *Laughter Over London* with George Robey and Billy Bennett. In December 1937 the musical comedy *Me And My Girl*, with Lupino Lane as Bill Snibson doing the 'Lambeth Walk', started its 1,046 performances, ending when war broke out. Its huge popularity was initially created by a live broadcast of the show made from the theatre. It returned to the Victoria Palace in 1944 for another long run, and proved its appeal at the Adelphi, and on Broadway, over 40 years later.

In 1947 the three comic duos – Flanagan and Allen, Naughton and Gold, and Nervo and Knox – who called themselves the Crazy Gang and had run riot at the Palladium in the 1930s, did the same for 15 years at the Victoria Palace. Joined by 'Monsewer' Eddie Gray, they appeared in *Together Again* (1947), *Knights Of Madness* (1950), *Ring Out The Bells* (1952), *Jokers Wild* (1954), *These Foolish Kings* (1956), *Clown Jewels* (1959) and *Young In Heart* (1960). The much-loved ancient comedians gave their final performance together on 19 May, 1962.

For the next ten years the Victoria Palace was occupied by *The Black And White Minstrel Show*. Variety remained the hallmark through the 1970s with singer-comedian Max Bygraves in two shows (1972 and 1974), and the crude 'Carry On' film team in *Carry On London* (1973) and other revues, until the arrival of the delightful Charles Strouse musical *Annie* (1978), which remained for three and a half years. As at the Palladium, when variety

Brent Bassett and Marin Mazzie in Cole Porter's *Kiss Me Kate*

Stephen Rea and Natasha Richardson in *High Society* (1987), originally a film

faded, musicals tended to fill the bill. The past 20 years have seen many successes: Cyd Charisse flashing her still lovely legs in *Charlie Girl* (1986); Natasha Richardson showing star quality in *High Society* (1987); and Elizabeth Taylor making her London stage debut in Lillian Hellman's drama *The Little Foxes* (1982). In 1989 the hit show *Buddy* began a six-year run that broke the theatre record for the longest-running book musical. Olivier-award-winning musical *Jolson* played for two years from 1995, and was closely followed by *Fame*, a new production of *Annie* and the *New Rocky Horror Show*. A fine revival of Cole Porter's *Kiss Me Kate* opened in 2002, after a production of the successful *Fame*, and so the Victoria Palace is still singing, still dancing into the twenty-first century.

the victoria palace theatre
victoria street = swle

The Whitehall

In the broad avenue of administrative buildings that runs from Trafalgar Square, past the Cenotaph and Downing Street to the Houses of Parliament, stands an incongruous monument to the pursuit of pleasure. The Whitehall Theatre is a white temple-like structure with tombstone-shaped windows, but the straight line of the unadorned facade masks a riotous assembly of Art Deco work within, executed by Marc-Henri and Laverdet. The black walls, an innovation in theatre decoration in England, the silver stripes on black over the proscenium arch and the bold black octagonal shape on the ceiling form an ebony concerto in counterpoint to the sinuous patterns and pastel colours of the murals and motif of musical instruments. Above the stage is a panel in which a nude Aphrodite seems to be trying to extricate herself from the tentacles of a sea-monster. The same tendril theme recurs in the centre of the ceiling and in the lights held in exotic flowers. With the Cubist-influenced murals, the visitor gets a heavy whiff of the fashionable design of 1930, the year the theatre opened.

Fun seems to be the operative word in what the theatre has had to offer in the way of entertainment over the years. The theatre's main claim to fame was as the home for 24 years of what became known as the Whitehall Farces, as distinct from the other Whitehall farces being played in the House of Commons down the road. In April 1961, Brian Rix, who managed the theatre and presented them, broke the Aldwych Theatre's record of staging over 10 years of continuous productions of farce by one management in one theatre.

From its beginnings, comedy has been the main fare of the Whitehall. It was built by Edward A. Stone for the playwright Walter Hackett. He and his wife, Marion Lorne, managed the theatre for the first four years, she acting in the plays he wrote for

*'What it suggests is the atmosphere of combined
comfort and alertness, not without a certain
heartlessness, which becomes the modern comedy.'*
— *The Times,* 1930

her, their relationship illustrated by the title of the opening production – Hackett's *The Way To Treat A Woman* (a transfer from the Duke of York's). Five further successful plays followed, one of them, *Good Losers* (1931), written by Hackett in collaboration with Michael Arlen. From 1934, a string of 'modern comedies' were produced, including St John Ervine's *Anthony And Anna* (1936) and a revival of George Bernard Shaw's *The Doctor's Dilemma* (1939).

During World War II, Alfred Esdaile presented *Whitehall Follies* (1942), a 'Non-Stop Revue' (continuous from 2 p.m. to 9 p.m. daily) featuring Phyllis Dixey, the West End's first stripper. Miss Dixey treated the art of ecdysis with expertise, carrying on a comic dialogue with the audience as she gracefully disrobed down to the last stitch. In fact, total nudity was permitted on stage in those days, provided the artiste did not move her body. Phyllis Dixey would stand frozen (in both senses perhaps) in her naked glory while the audience cheered and applauded.

When Bernard Delfont took over the theatre in 1943, there was a brief return to clothed entertainment, but the public the Whitehall had built up for the revues did not take to Rodney Ackland's *The Dark River* or John Steinbeck's *The Moon Is Down*, the latter about the German occupation of Norway. However, 'England's Queen of Glamour' was soon back in 'Non-Stop Revue Spectacles' like *Good Night Ladies!* So popular were they that Miss Dixey took over the lease of the theatre herself in 1944. Interrupting her revealing shows was R. F. Delderfield's RAF farce *Worm's Eye View* (1945) with Ronald Shiner. After 500 performances it went on tour, returning in 1947 for another 1,745 showings. A new era at the Whitehall had begun.

The farce that followed in 1950 was *Reluctant Heroes* by Colin
Morris, starring Shiner again and Brian Rix, who was to play a
gormless North Country goon forever losing his trousers in many
more hits in the same genre. Far from his stage character, Rix was
astute in the choice of plays he produced, the runs averaging
three years each. They also reached the widest possible public by
being regularly broadcast live on television. In the cast of
Reluctant Heroes was John Chapman who wrote the next two
successes, *Dry Rot* (1954) and *Simple Spyman* (1958). Another
actor in the company, Ray Cooney, provided *One For The Pot*
(1961) – written with Tony Hilton – and *Chase Me Comrade*
(1964). Cooney explained how the latter, originally called *How's*

Your Father, about an escaped convict, came about:

> Brian and I agreed that it was just too old-fashioned – escaped convicts and jewels up the chimney at a time when Harold Pinter was establishing himself! …As I was about to enter the Whitehall Theatre one of the most famous personalities of the day walked by – actually he glided by because it was Nureyev… Suddenly I knew how I could modernise *How's Your Father*. I'd change the whole plot of an escaped convict to a defecting Russian ballet dancer!

The last of the Whitehall Farces was *Uproar In The House* (1967), which ran one and a half years. In 1969 the theatre reverted to the Dixey days, when 'Revue Bar' impresario Paul Raymond took it over to present *Pyjama Tops*, a nudie show prominently featuring Fiona Richmond. After five profitable

Priestley's *When We Are Married* (1986) boasted a superb cast: *(left to right)* Timothy West, James Grout, Brian Murphy, Prunella Scales, Patricia Routledge, Elizabeth Spriggs years, Raymond controversially turned the theatre into a museum of memorabilia of the two World Wars. However, this breached the theatre's licensing conditions, and in 1985 Ian Albery acquired it, refurbished it – retaining the unique art deco features – and began to present live shows again. The tradition of comedy continued with John Wells's *Anyone For Denis?* (1982), in which Margaret Thatcher and her husband were impersonated, a glittering revival of Priestley's *When We Are Married* (1986), *Run For Your Wife* and Alan Ayckbourne's *Absurd Person Singular*. From 1997 to 1999 the theatre was host to radio and television shows and live theatre running concurrently, *The Jack Docherty Show* being just one of these. The hit comedy *Cooking For Elvis* opened in 2000 with rave reviews, followed by (and perhaps continuing the Whitehall's grand 'nude' tradition) *Puppetry of the Penis*, the Edinburgh Festival hit. In spring 2002 this successful theatre staged the two thousand four hundredth performance of *Art*, the multi-award-winning comedy which transferred here from Wyndham's Theatre.

the whitehall theatre
whitehall = swla

Wyndham's Theatre

A s the nineteenth century drew to its close, a delightful new theatre opened its doors to a public who came to gaze on its delicate beauty. Today's audiences can still enjoy this jewel of a Victorian playhouse, named after one of England's finest actor-managers.

Charles Wyndham had long dreamed of building a theatre of his own, despite over 20 successful years of management at the Criterion. The Marquess of Salisbury, then Prime Minister, owned a site between Charing Cross Road and St Martin's Lane which Wyndham thought ideal. However, when he was unable to raise the required amount, Mary Moore, his leading lady (later his wife), asked a number of her friends in high places to stand as guarantors for a bank loan. The Australian-born W. G. R. Sprague was chosen as architect. He also built the New Theatre (now the Albery) for Wyndham on the other half of the same site a few years later and with a similar French classical facade. The French flavour of Wyndham's continues in the splendid Louis XVI decoration of the interior. Boucher was the inspiration for the pretty little ceiling in the foyer depicting angels and cherubs and for the floral design on the circular ceiling above the pale blue and gold auditorium lit by a crystal chandelier. Above the picture-frame proscenium are two male angels holding portraits of Oliver Goldsmith (left) and Richard Brinsley Sheridan (right) in front of a golden-winged bust of what is thought to be Mary Moore. An imposing bust of the theatre's eponymous owner greets one at the entrance, and the monograms C. W. and M. M. adorn each side of the stage.

'Sir Bronson Albery had been old for so long there were rumours... when the pipes in the theatre burst in midsummer... his cold feet were to blame.'
— Peter Ustinov

The theatre opened on 16 November, 1899 in the presence of the Prince of Wales. Charles Wyndham and Mary Moore starred that night in the old Tom Robertson favourite, *David Garrick*. The next productions featured the tall and dashing Wyndham as Rostand's *Cyrano de Bergerac* (1900) and as a lawyer in Henry Arthur Jones's *Mrs Dane's Defence* of the same year.

With Frank Curzon managing on behalf of Wyndham, successes included Mabel Terry-Lewis (Ellen Terry's niece) in *Mrs Gorringe's Necklace*, J. M. Barrie's *Little Mary* (both 1903); *When Knights Were Bold* (1907); and *An Englishman's Home* (1909), written anonymously by 'A Patriot'. In fact, the play, about an invasion of England, was by Gerald du Maurier's soldier brother, Guy, who would be killed in World War I. It caused a flurry of patriotism and increased recruitment into the Territorial Army. When Gerald joined Curzon as manager, he revived his *Raffles* (1914), created the role of the drunken painter in Barrie's *Dear Brutus* (1917), played 'Sapper's' hero *Bulldog Drummond* (1921) with infinite charm and appeared opposite the outrageous American star Tallulah Bankhead, making her London debut, in *The Dancers* (1923).

From 1926, the theatre was given over to the crime dramas of Edgar Wallace until the author's death in Hollywood in 1932. Wallace took an apartment above the theatre, which is now used as an office and still contains the large armchair built to support his portly frame. Audiences chilled to *The Ringer* (1926), *The Calendar* (1929), *On The Spot* (1930), *The Old Man* (1931), *The Case Of The Frightened Lady* (1931) and *The Green Pack* (1932). For *Smoky Cell* (1930), Wallace had the macabre idea of making the public believe they were witnesses to an execution by electric chair in America, even to the issuing of reproduction journalists' cards instead of ordinary theatre tickets.

The Wallace collection gave way to a patchwork of productions under the management of stepbrothers Howard Wyndham and Bronson Albery up to the outbreak of war. In 1934, they presented the imperial drama *Clive Of India*; *The Maitlands*, the second and last play by Ronald MacKenzie, in which John Gielgud played a seedy schoolmaster; and Joyce Carey in her own play *Sweet Aloes*.

The Broadway comedy *Three Men On A Horse* (1936), Gerald Savory's *George And Margaret* (1937) and Esther McCracken's *Quiet Wedding* (1938) blithely followed.

The war years were enlivened by the 1,059 performances of *Quiet Weekend* (1940), the sequel to *Quiet Wedding*, and a 'blitz time afternoon all-star entertainment' called *Diversion* (1939), featuring Edith Evans, Bernard Miles, Dorothy Dickson and two young men who shared a dressing room, Peter Ustinov and Derek Bogerde (Dirk Bogarde). Ustinov's play, *The Banbury Nose* (1944), came in for a few months before *Years Between* (1945) by Daphne du Maurier who, as a child, had watched her father perform from the wings of Wyndham's.

Both Edith Evans (now a Dame) and Peter Ustinov returned to Wyndham's after the war, she in James Bridie's *Daphne Laureola* (1947) and he in *The Love Of Four Colonels* (1951), his first popular success as a playwright. However, for most of the 1950s the theatre was occupied by Sandy Wilson's tuneful '20s musical pastiche called *The Boy Friend* (1954). The show, which

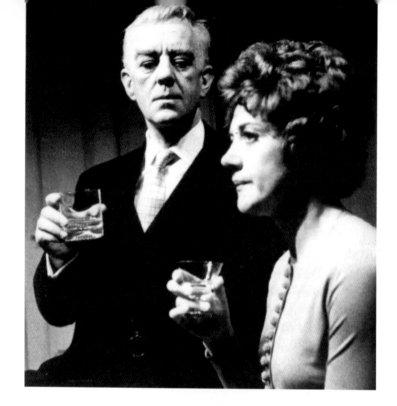

(above) Sir Alec Guinness, here with Eileen Atkins, starred in his own distinguished production of T. S. Eliot's *The Cocktail Party* in 1968

(right) Colin Blakely and Rosemary Harris shone in Arthur Miller's powerful drama, *All My Sons* (1981)

began modestly at the small Players' Theatre, ran a record 2,078 performances and launched Julie Andrews on Broadway. After the flappers left, a flap was caused by Joan Littlewood's controversial Theatre Workshop productions of 20-year-old Shelagh Delaney's *A Taste Of Honey* and Brendan Behan's *The Hostage* (both 1959), bringing Wyndham's sharply back into the contemporary world. The same company would return in 1963 with *Oh What A Lovely War!*, a bitter attack, through song and satire, on the Great War, later filmed by Richard Attenborough.

The Wyndham's stage has been graced over the last three decades by a bevy of fine actresses – Dulcie Gray (*Candida*, 1960); Celia Johnson (*Chin Chin*, 1960; *The Dame Of Sark*, 1974); Vanessa Redgrave (*The Prime Of Miss Jean Brodie*, 1966; *Ghosts*, 1986); Diana Rigg (*Abelard And Heloise*, 1970, and in the hugely successful *Medea*, 1993); Faye Dunaway (*Circe And Bravo*, 1986), and Dame Maggie Smith (*Three Tall Women*, 1996). The religious rock musical *Godspell* (1972) was here for four years, launching stars David Essex, Marti Webb and Jeremy Irons. In 1996 *Art* began its record-breaking run, with Albert Finney, Tom Courtenay and Ken Stott, followed by the enormously successful comedy *The Play What I Wrote*, by Hamish McColl and Sean Foley, directed by Kenneth Branagh, booking a year ahead in 2002. On the door of the star dressing room are scrawled the names of stage luminaries past and present. The history of Wyndham's suggests there will be many more in the future.

wyndham's theatre
charing cross road = wc2h

The Young Vic

The Young Vic Theatre stands on the same road (the Cut, in Waterloo) as the Old Vic, the source from which it sprang in 1970. Young, open, innovative and intimate, the Young Vic was set up to be the natural successor to the Old Vic, following Lilian Bayliss's progressive principles of making good theatre cheaply and freely available to everybody.

The inspiration behind the Young Vic Theatre came from Frank Dunlop, who joined the Royal National Theatre, then based at the Old Vic, as an Associate Director and Administrator in 1967. At this time of great creative innovation and expression from young artists in all fields – music, film, theatre, visual art – Dunlop (who had previously founded the unsubsidised Pop Theatre) proposed to explore a new kind of theatre for the new generation, a theatre that was unconventional, classless, welcoming, circus–like and cheap. Laurence Olivier, the head of the National Theatre at that time, supported his aims, and helped fund Dunlop's programme with the National Theatre's profits. This revenue, plus some assistance from the Arts Council, meant enough money to rent a theatre space for five years. As it was possible to build a custom-made set-up for the same amount of money, it was decided, famously, to build the Young Vic as a temporary structure – designed to last for only five years.

The Young Vic was built on a site just down the road from the Old Vic. On this piece of ground stood an old butcher's shop (the sign outside, the art nouveau tiles and the original hooks are still visible today) which formed the theatre's foyer, with the Main House, built of breezeblock and steel, beside it. A bomb site that had once been a bakery (54 people, sheltering in the cellar, were killed on 17 April 1942, and a plaque listing their names hangs in the theatre's foyer) became the Studio and the café. The auditorium was built to seat 450 in a shallow octagon with a

'We had only sixty thousand pounds to build a temporary structure. We asked for a cross between the Elizabethan Fortune Theatre, Guthrie's Assembly Hall and a circus.'

— Frank Dunlop, founder and first Director of the Young Vic

thrust stage and five simple rows of seats in the stalls and balcony. In 1993 the auditorium was adjusted so that different configurations were possible, such as theatre in the round. At the same time, the Studio, initially a rehearsal room, was converted into a performance space seating 60 to 90 people – also with the possibility of different seating configurations. The audience have a unique relationship with performance at the Young Vic. The current Director, David Lan, calls the auditorium 'a single space in which actors and audience are combined in perfect, relaxed but urgent tension'. The theatre was designed by Bill Howell and built by a church builder from Liverpool called Mercer. It was completed within nine months and opened by an 87-year-old Sybil Thorndike, who lovingly called the Young Vic 'a theatre after my own heart'.

The Young Vic's first production, on 11 September, 1970, was a very free adaptation of Molière's *Les Fourberies de Scapin* called *Scapino*, directed by Frank Dunlop. Dunlop's productions (especially of Shakespeare) were clear, simple and well paced, designed to appeal to a young audience, perhaps unversed in classics or unused to being in a theatre. At that time, the Young Vic had the advantage of sharing National Theatre actors, costumes and other facilities to produce cheaply made, no-frills productions. In addition to plays by Shakespeare, Sophocles, Beckett and Pinter, Dunlop also put on music by Henze, Stomu Yamash'ta and Stravinsky, as well as a free concert by The Who. Outside shows, such as a rock musical from America, *Stomp*, were presented, and radical and experimental theatre companies from elsewhere in the world. The Young Vic was active in commissioning new works for the younger generation too. In its first five years, 11 new plays were produced, many by Denise Coffey, and directed by members of the permanent company, which included Roland Joffe (now known for his film work) and Jeremy James Taylor (founder of the National Youth Music Theatre).

Frank Dunlop's plan worked. The Young Vic was enormously popular, especially with young people, but also (unusually for a modern theatre) with members of the local Southwark community. Tickets were cheaper than the local cinema (the equivalent of today's 20p!), and the hamburgers sold at the café were reputed to be the best in London. Busloads of young people came all the way from Newcastle and Plymouth to see productions.

In 1974 the National Theatre was no longer able unable to support the Young Vic financially. Frank Dunlop remained at the theatre until 1978, when Michael Bogdanov, former director of

the Haymarket and Phoenix Theatres in Leicester, took over. He refurbished the auditorium, bar and backstage area, and produced more extra-vagant productions of classics as well as lunchtime perfor-mances and late-night cabaret shows. But despite some great productions resources soon ran out, and two years later Dunlop returned and imple-

Inika Leigh Wright in
Tripitaka

mented the same policies as before: high-quality, low-budget productions of classics and musicals. By the time he left in 1983, to head the Edinburgh Festival, the theatre was on its feet again.

Dunlop was succeeded by the Director of the Duke's Playhouse in Lancaster, David Thacker. Under him, the Young Vic produced rather less experimental but still challenging, quality theatre, attracting performers such as Vanessa Redgrave, Helen Mirren, Judi Dench, Timothy Dalton and Ian McKellen. Despite the success of the productions, however, by 1990 the Young Vic was financially unstable again, and it took a 'Save the Young Vic' campaign, plus an increased Arts Council grant, to keep the theatre afloat.

In 1992 two young directors, Tim Supple and Julia Bardsley, arrived, with the aim of taking the Young Vic back to being a contentious and alternative production-led theatre. However, the resulting reorganisation was difficult, and after nine months Bardsley resigned and the theatre was again faced with bankruptcy. Then came an upturn in fortunes. Supple's highly

Jude Law attracted much attention for his 2002 appearance in *Dr Faustus*

acclaimed *The Slab Boys*, followed by *Grimm Tales* (1994), proclaimed a new era for the Young Vic. Other successful productions were *The Jungle Book* (1995), *More Grimm Tales* (1997) and RSC productions such as *The Comedy of Errors* (1996) and Ted Hughes's *Tales From Ovid* (1998).

Supple was succeeded by playwright and director David Lan in 2000. Lan had already directed the theatre's *'Tis Pity She's a Whore* (1999) with Jude Law, and adapted Katie Mitchell's production of *Uncle Vanya*. Lan has attracted the best directors to the Young Vic (such as Peter Brook with *Le Costume* and *Hamlet*, starring Adrian Lester, and Richard Jones with Pirandello's *Six Characters Looking For An Author*) and is actively encouraging new young directors with a supportive Young Vic scheme. He has also hosted the Push season (which presented the work of 150 black British artists in theatre, music, film, visual art, comedy and dance), the RSC's Shakespeare's Histories cycle and *Macbeth*, with Antony Sher, and has directed the highly acclaimed *A Raisin in the Sun* (2001) and *Dr Faustus*, with Jude Law (2002).

The Young Vic remains a theatre in which younger artists are supported and younger audiences encouraged with lively and innovative performance. Frank Dunlop's vision is alive and well.

the young vic theatre
the cut = se1

Picture Credits

The publishers would like to thank the following sources and copyright holders for their kind permission to reproduce the pictures in this book:

Alex Von Koettlitz: p21 (bottom), 42, 52 (bottom), 72 (top), 85 (top), 94 (bottom), 98 (bottom), 100, 104, 105, 114, 142, 147

Ambassador's Theatre: p23

Angus McEan (Courtesy of Mander & Mitchenson): p9, 78 (bottom)

BBC Hulton Picture Library: p8, 75, 123, 178

Betram Park: p16

British Travel Association (Britain on View): p19 (top), 43, 98 (top), 117 (top), 130, 141, 157, 161, 167, 183

Catherine Ashmore (Dominic Photography): p40, 44; (Disney): p147

Clive Barda: p144

Clive Totman: p32, 34, 35

Dee Conway: p24 (bottom), 55 (bottom), 72 (bottom), 126, 139 (bottom), 148, 152, 153

Donald Cooper: p13, 17. 20, 28 (top), 36, 48 (bottom), 52 (top), 56, 65 (bottom), 76, 80, 85 (bottom), 90, 101 (bottom), 107, 117 (bottom), 118, 120 (bottom), 122, 129 (bottom), 160 (top), 164, 168 (top), 172, 174 (bottom), 175, 179

Doug McKenzie (Courtesy of Stoll Theatres): p25, 57, 61, 62 (bottom), 121, 138, 147 (top)

Doug McKenzie (Professional Photographic Service): p11, 30 (top), 49, 63, 71, 79, 89, 93, 125 (top), 128, 171, 177 (top)

E.T Archives: p58, 146, 158, 170 (bottom)

Hulton Deutsch: p211

Ivan Kyncl: p31, 167

John Haynes: p6 (bottom)

John Tramper: p274

picture credits

Index

Page numbers in bold indicate an illustration of the subject.

index

index

index

index

index

Frommer's®

Montana & Wyoming

WITHDRAWN

9th Edition

by Eric Peterson

WILEY

John Wiley & Sons, Inc.

Published by:
JOHN WILEY & SONS, INC.
111 River St.
Hoboken, NJ 07030-5774

ISBN 978-1-118-27847-5 (paper); ISBN 978-1-118-33349-5 (ebk); ISBN 978-1-118-33064-7 (ebk); ISBN 978-1-118-33462-1 (ebk)

Editor: Jennifer Polland
Production Editor: Erin Geile
Cartographer: Guy Ruggiero
Photo Editor: Richard Fox
Production by Wiley Indianapolis Composition Services

Front Cover Photo: Overlooking Grinnell Lake beneath Mount Gould and Angel Wing, Many Glacier Region, Glacier National Park, Montana ©James Kay / SCPhotos / Alamy Images
Back Cover Photo: People on horseback riding towards "Hole in the Wall" in Wyoming ©Franco Barbagallo / Hemis / Alamy Images

For information on our other products and services or to obtain technical support, please contact our Customer Care Department within the U.S. at 877/762-2974, outside the U.S. at 317/572-3993 or fax 317/572-4002.

Wiley also publishes its books in a variety of electronic formats. Some content that appears in print may not be available in electronic formats.

Manufactured in the United States of America

5 4 3 2 1

CONTENTS

LIST OF MAPS

HOW TO CONTACT US

In researching this book, we discovered many wonderful places—hotels, restaurants, shops, and more. We're sure you'll find others. Please tell us about them, so we can share the information with your fellow travelers in upcoming editions. If you were disappointed with a recommendation, we'd love to know that, too. Please write to:

Frommer's Montana & Wyoming, 9th Edition
John Wiley & Sons, Inc. • 111 River St. • Hoboken, NJ 07030-5774
frommersfeedback@wiley.com

AN ADDITIONAL NOTE

Please be advised that travel information is subject to change at any time—and this is especially true of prices. We therefore suggest that you write or call ahead for confirmation when making your travel plans. The authors, editors, and publisher cannot be held responsible for the experiences of readers while traveling. Your safety is important to us, however, so we encourage you to stay alert and be aware of your surroundings. Keep a close eye on cameras, purses, and wallets, all favorite targets of thieves and pickpockets.

ABOUT THE AUTHOR

A Denver-based writer, **Eric Peterson** has authored numerous travel guides covering the American West for both Frommer's (including previous editions of *Frommer's Montana & Wyoming* and *Frommer's Colorado*) and Ramble (including *Ramble: A Field Guide to the U.S.A.*), an imprint of Fulcrum Publishing (www.fulcrum-books.com). Peterson has also written for numerous newspapers and magazines, including the *New York Daily News*, *Denver Post*, and *Delta Sky*; he also wrote a winter sports column for Frommers.com. In his free time, he's an avid camper, skier, and hiker; a lifelong Broncos fan; and a part-time rock star (at least in the eyes of his niece Olivia and nephews Mitch and Sam).

FROMMER'S STAR RATINGS, ICONS & ABBREVIATIONS

Every hotel, restaurant, and attraction listing in this guide has been ranked for quality, value, service, amenities, and special features using a **star-rating system.** In country, state, and regional guides, we also rate towns and regions to help you narrow down your choices and budget your time accordingly. Hotels and restaurants are rated on a scale of zero (recommended) to three stars (exceptional). Attractions, shopping, nightlife, towns, and regions are rated according to the following scale: zero stars (recommended), one star (highly recommended), two stars (very highly recommended), and three stars (must-see).

In addition to the star-rating system, we also use **seven feature icons** that point you to the great deals, in-the-know advice, and unique experiences that separate travelers from tourists. Throughout the book, look for:

special finds—those places only insiders know about

fun facts—details that make travelers more informed and their trips more fun

kids—best bets for kids and advice for the whole family

special moments—those experiences that memories are made of

overrated—places or experiences not worth your time or money

insider tips—great ways to save time and money

great values—where to get the best deals

The following abbreviations are used for credit cards:

AE   American Express   DISC   Discover   V   Visa

DC   Diners Club   MC   MasterCard

TRAVEL RESOURCES AT FROMMERS.COM

Frommer's travel resources don't end with this guide. Frommer's website, **www.frommers. com**, has travel information on more than 4,000 destinations. We update features regularly, giving you access to the most current trip-planning information and the best airfare, lodging, and car-rental bargains. You can also listen to podcasts, connect with other Frommers.com members through our active-reader forums, share your travel photos, read blogs from guide-book editors and fellow travelers, and much more.

THE BEST OF MONTANA & WYOMING

A mix of the rugged Wild West, the even more rugged Rocky Mountains, and a few almost-modern cities—or what we might call overgrown cow towns—make the states of Montana and Wyoming delightful vacation spots. This is especially true for people who savor outdoor adventures, but it's also the case for those looking to discover a part of the United States that many of us have seen only in the movies and on television (and that's a rather distorted view). Here you'll find some of the most breathtaking scenery in America; a vast array of wildlife that not only thinks it owns the place, but actually does; and even some first-class Western-style lodges, restaurants, and museums.

Montana

"Big Sky Country" is an apt nickname for **Montana,** with its broad swaths of cloud-dotted blue skies hovering over majestic mountains, forested wilderness, and a seemingly endless sea of plains. Below that picture-perfect sky, there are a lifetime of trails to hike, lakes and rivers to paddle, and wide open spaces to explore. But it is also worth spending some time inside city limits, where several standout restaurants and museums nicely complement the great outdoors. You won't need to pitch a tent here, either: Montana offers first-class Western-style lodges.

Cities **Billings** is the state's largest city, with over 100,000 residents and a bustling industrial center. **Bozeman** and **Missoula** are both college towns, with good bookstores, restaurants, and shops. They are also both tourism centers: Bozeman is a gateway to Yellowstone, and Missoula is a gateway to Glacier National Park. Among the smaller towns in Montana, **Whitefish** is known for superlative outdoor recreation and a fun downtown near Glacier National Park, while **Helena** has a beautiful historic district filled with classic architecture.

Countryside There is nearly endless variety in Montana, from river valleys flanked by the picturesque peaks of the **Rocky Mountains,** to the endless eastern plains, to the geologically gnarled badlands in **Makoshika State Park.** The **Yellowstone, Madison,** and **Missouri rivers** offer incredible boating and fishing opportunities, as does massive **Flathead Lake,** in the state's northwest corner.

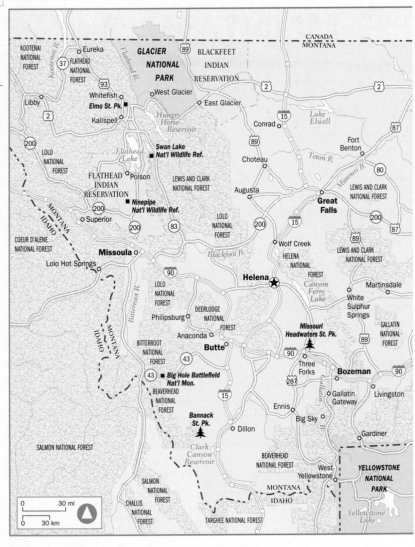

Eating & Drinking   A trip to Montana is a unique opportunity to indulge in the bold, succulent flavors of **big game:** You don't typically find fresh **bison, elk,** and **venison** on a big-city menu. Montana's rivers and streams yield a bounty of **trout, sturgeon, walleye,** and **catfish. Wild huckleberries** are a local delicacy that you'll find in syrup, ice cream, chocolate, and even beer. There are a number of good **microbreweries,** and most bars double as **casinos** with low-stakes gaming.

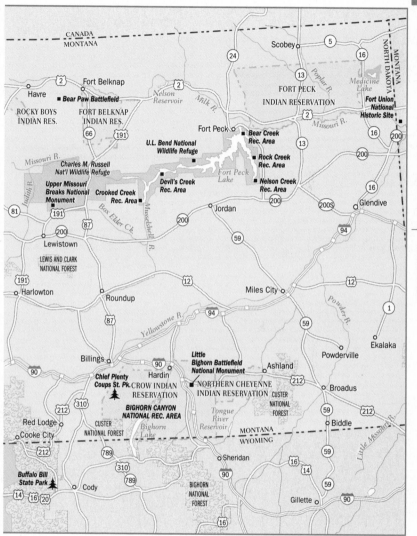

National Parks **Glacier National Park** is one of Montana's can't-miss stops, centered on the awe-inspiring spine of the Rockies. With its soaring peaks, icy lakes and streams, and its multitude of wildlife, it's a paradise for hikers and backpackers. **Yellowstone National Park,** part of which is located in Montana, has forests, lakes, and lots of wildlife, but it is probably best known for its spewing geysers and bubbling, boiling mud. Hike along the **Grand Canyon of the Yellowstone River,** a thousand-foot-deep gorge.

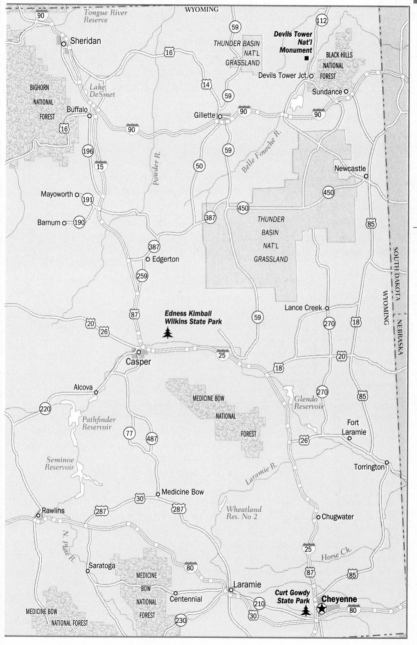

WYOMING

Tongue River
Reserve

90

Sheridan

59

THUNDER BASIN
NAT'L
GRASSLAND

112

**Devils Tower
Nat'l
Monument**

BLACK HILLS
NATIONAL
FOREST

16

14

Devils Tower Jct.

Sundance

Lake
DeSmet

BIGHORN

NATIONAL

FOREST

Buffalo

59

Gillette

90

90

90

16

90

196

59

Newcastle

15

50

Belle Fourche R.

450

Powder R.

Mayoworth

191

387

450

Barnum

190

THUNDER

BASIN

NAT'L

GRASSLAND

85

387

Edgerton

259

Lance Creek

270

18

87

**Edness Kimball
Wilkins State Park**

59

SOUTH DAKOTA

WYOMING

NEBRASKA

20

26

25

18

20

Casper

18

Alcova

MEDICINE BOW

Glendo
Reservoir

270

85

220

NATIONAL

Pathfinder
Reservoir

77

487

FOREST

26

Fort
Laramie

Seminoe
Reservoir

Torrington

Laramie R.

Medicine Bow

30

Wheatland
Res. No 2

Rawlins

287

287

Chugwater

N. Platte R.

25

Horse Ck.

Saratoga

MEDICINE

80

87

85

BOW

NATIONAL

Laramie

628

Centennial

210

**Curt Gowdy
State Park**

Cheyenne

MEDICINE BOW

FOREST

230

30

80

NATIONAL FOREST

Wyoming

The least-populated state in the union, Wyoming is defined by its vast open spaces. Along with ranching, the oil and gas industry is a principal economic driver, as is tourism, largely to Yellowstone and Grand Teton national parks. It's a magnet for outdoor enthusiasts, with great trails to hike in summer and slopes to ski and ride come wintertime.

Cities   With about 55,000 residents apiece, **Cheyenne** and **Casper** vie for the title of most populated city in the least populated state, and serve as worthy stopovers but not vacation destinations. **Laramie** is the home of Wyoming's only four-year university. On the doorstep of Grand Teton National Park, **Jackson** is the hippest, richest, and most active city in the state. **Cody** is also a worthy destination.

Countryside   There are many opportunities for outdoor recreation here, from the **Big Horn Mountains** and the **Wind River Range** to the **North Platte** and **Snake rivers,** not to mention **Yellowstone** and **Grand Teton national parks** and their bounty of active challenges. Mountains mark the state's western and central topography; the eastern side of the state is defined by plains (and coal mines and oil and gas rigs).

Eating & Drinking   Jackson Hole has the best restaurants, but you will find a nice variety of options in the larger cities. The focus is on hearty American fare, but Mexican, Italian, and Asian cuisine is also well represented. Like in Montana, you'll find plenty of game meats on the menus in Wyoming, as well as the occasional basket of Rocky Mountain oysters (deep-fried bull's testicles).

National Parks   If **Yellowstone National Park** is the top attraction in the state, then **Grand Teton National Park** is a close second. Between their collective bounty of peaks, geysers, and wildlife, you have one of the top vacation draws in the Rockies. There is also the first national monument in the United States: the iconic **Devils Tower National Monument,** in the far northeastern corner of the state.

THE best MONTANA & WYOMING EXPERIENCES

- **Hiking the Loop at Glacier National Park** (MT): The best vacation spot in Montana is also the most obvious one. Take the Loop, an 8-mile moderate hiking trail, to see stunning mountain peaks, verdant landscapes, and a surplus of varied plant and animal life; afterward, you can spend the night in the historic Granite Park Chalet. See chapter 5.
- **Seeing Bears and Geysers in Yellowstone National Park** (WY): **Yellowstone** remains the prime attraction in the Rocky Mountains, offering visitors an extraordinary combination of wilderness, wildlife, and geothermal wonders. Take in Old Faithful and the other geysers in the Upper Geyser Basin, and then see if you can spot the less reliable grizzlies and wolves in the Lamar Valley. See chapter 11.
- **Exploring Jenny Lake in Grand Teton National Park** (WY): In this relatively small park, there are magnificent peaks rising from the Snake River plain, alpine lakes, wildflowers, and wildlife. Take the shuttle boat across serene Jenny Lake to hike up Cascade Canyon. After a picnic lunch, descend to the valley floor and hike back around the lake. See chapter 12.

- **Navigating the Missouri River** (MT): Take a multiday paddling adventure down the Missouri River from Fort Benton (p. 176) or a day tour at the Gates of the Mountains near Helena (p. 140). Then stop in at the Lewis & Clark National Historic Trail Interpretive Center in Great Falls (p. 179) to learn how the Corps of Discovery traversed the river in 1805.
- **Trekking the Wind River Range** (WY): Lace up your boots and explore this superlative mountain range that stretches across a vast swath of wilderness in the middle of Wyoming. Use Lander as a base camp, then hike to your content on a trip lasting anywhere from a few hours to a few weeks. See "Wind River Valley" in chapter 13.
- **Yeehawing at the Cody Nite Rodeo** (WY): The Cody Nite Rodeo has the distinction of being the only nightly rodeo in the country in the summertime. Take the time to explore Cody and its strong cowboy culture while in town. See p. 350.

THE best OUTDOOR ADVENTURES

- **Exploring the Bob Marshall Wilderness** (MT): The 1.5-million-acre Bob Marshall Wilderness Complex in northwest Montana is one of America's most spectacular wild places. Lace up your hiking boots, tie on your bandanna, and take to the high country in Montana's northwest corner. See p. 112.
- **Enjoying the Yellowstone Backcountry** (WY): Outfitters from ranches around Yellowstone National Park will take you into the deep wilderness that surrounds the busy attractions at the park's center, and there you'll get a flavor of the wild as rich as the Rockies can offer. If you have experience, you can go on your own—paddling Yellowstone Lake, backpacking along Slough Creek, or Telemark skiing the powder around Shoshone Lake. See chapter 11.
- **Fly-Fishing on the Madison River** (MT): Brown trout aren't native to this area, but no one's asking them to leave; on this popular river running from Yellowstone National Park into Montana, they're the big attraction. The Madison converges with its "holy trinity" counterparts, the Jefferson and Gallatin, near Three Forks, but lots of anglers fish it around Yellowstone. See p. 211 and p. 281.
- **Fishing for Cutthroat Trout on the Snake River** (WY): It seems somehow fitting that the menacing-sounding Snake River is home to a feisty strain of cutthroat trout, making it one of the most satisfying Western rivers to fish. See p. 304.
- **Whitewater Rafting** (MT & WY): The Yellowstone, Snake, Flathead, and Clark's Fork rivers are among the best whitewater-rafting routes in the Rockies.
- **Climbing Devils Tower National Monument** (WY): About 5,000 climbers attempt to summit this 1,267-foot icon every year, but less than 2,000 make it. Hire a guide and see how high you can go. See p. 377.

THE best PLACES TO VIEW WILDLIFE

- **Glacier National Park** (MT): The experience of watching wildlife amid the imposing terrain of Glacier National Park is tough to beat. With a little energy, you can see mountain goats, moose, elk, and other native animals in their natural habitat.

Keep a good distance, and be aware of all bear restrictions and regulations—the grizzly is the park's unofficial mascot. See chapter 5.

o **The Bob Marshall Wilderness Complex** (MT): Just south of Glacier, in the Bob Marshall Wilderness Complex, roam a full complement of Rocky Mountain wildlife—although you have to wander into the backcountry to find it. See p. 112.

o **The Lamar Valley, Yellowstone National Park** (WY): You can see wildlife in many parts of Yellowstone, including the meadows across from the Old Faithful complex. But the richest trove of wildlife is in the park's northeast corner, in the valley nicknamed "The Serengeti of the United States." See chapter 11.

THE best WINTER VACATION EXPERIENCES

o **Skiing at Whitefish Mountain Resort** (MT; www.skiwhitefish.com; © 800/858-3930): With an annual snowfall of 300 inches, a vertical drop of 2,500 feet, a superpipe for the snowboarding crowd, and virtually no lines, Whitefish Mountain is one of the best ski areas in the northwestern United States. See p. 217.

o **Skiing at Big Sky and Moonlight Basin** (MT; Big Sky: www.bigskyresort.com; © 800/548-4486; Moonlight Basin: www.moonlightbasin.com; 877/822-0430): Big Sky and the much newer Moonlight Basin have connected their trail systems, making for a combined 5,300 acres of terrain—the largest ski area in the country, not to mention the one with the most vertical drop. See p. 216 and p. 217.

o **Wintering at Old Faithful** (WY): The chilly season in Yellowstone is increasingly popular, especially since the renovation of the **Old Faithful Snow Lodge** (www.travelyellowstone.com; © 866/439-7375), which is now a handsome, comfortable facility. You can take a snowcoach into the park, or cross-country ski or snowshoe to the Lonestar Geyser and other attractions. See p. 277.

o **Skiing at Jackson Hole Mountain Resort** (WY; www.jacksonhole.com; © 888/333-7766): Jackson Hole offers a vertical drop that will take your breath away. There are a variety of ways to get to the bottom, from double black diamonds to intermediate slopes. Skiers who like a challenge should come here and mix the visit with some ballooning, tours of the elk refuge, and other adventures. See p. 303.

o **Cross-Country Skiing at Lone Mountain Ranch** (MT; www.lonemountainranch.com; © 800/514-4644): One of the top Nordic resorts in the country, Lone Mountain Ranch has about 50 miles of cross-country trails for every skill level. Visit for a day or stay here for a week. See p. 216.

THE best HOTELS & RESORTS

o **Many Glacier Hotel** (Glacier National Park, MT; www.glacierparkinc.com; © 406/892-2525): The best thing about Many Glacier, apart from its elegant mien, friendly service, and cozy rooms, is the setting; it sits along Swiftcurrent Lake and in the shadows of Mount Grinnell and Mount Wilbur. See p. 69.

o **The Pollard** (Red Lodge, MT; www.thepollard.net; © 800/765-5273): You can join Buffalo Bill on the guest register at the Pollard, a historic spot that proves that a hotel doesn't need to sprawl all over the place to set the highest standard of comfort and elegance. See p. 228.

o **Old Faithful Inn** (Yellowstone National Park, WY; www.travelyellowstone.com; © 866/439-7375): If you ever wonder whether there's really art in architecture, look at the way the rustic simplicity and monumental structure of this inn make a perfect fit just across the way from one of nature's most astonishing creations. A lattice of logs climbs to an 85-foot ceiling. You can find peace in the upper balconies or join the convivial crowds around the big stone fireplace below. See p. 294.

- **Four Seasons Resort Jackson Hole** (Jackson, WY; www.fourseasons.com/jacksonhole; ✆ **307/732-5000**): The most deluxe lodging option in Teton Village, the chic Four Seasons has set a new standard for ski-in, ski-out luxury. See p. 312.

- **Jenny Lake Lodge** (Grand Teton National Park, WY; www.gtlc.com; ✆ **800/628-9988**): My favorite property in any national park, this small cabin-resort offers seclusion, top-notch food, and individual attention. The property is a hybrid of mountain-lake resort and dude ranch, with many extras included in its prices. See p. 338.

- **The Chamberlin Inn** (Cody, WY; www.chamberlininn.com; ✆ **888/587-0202**): A block from the center of town, the new and improved Chamberlin Inn is Cody's best lodging option. It features charming historic rooms and apartment units. Consider asking for the Hemingway Suite, where "Papa" stayed in 1932. See p. 351.

- **The Occidental Hotel** (Buffalo, WY; www.occidentalwyoming.com; ✆ **307/684-0451**): Born as a tent in 1878, the Occidental has burned to the ground and been lost in a poker game in its storied history. Today the hotel is a beautifully restored, charming property. See p. 374.

THE best GUEST RANCHES

- **Averill's Flathead Lake Lodge** (Darby, MT; www.flatheadlakelodge.com; ✆ **406/837-4391**): A beautiful log lodge on Flathead Lake surrounded by thousands of acres of forest serves as your home base for all activities, which include horseback riding, boating, and fishing. The Western dude-ranch experience is done right at this place, complete with sing-alongs, campfires, and barn dances. See p. 106.

- **Triple Creek Ranch** (Darby, MT; www.triplecreekranch.com; ✆ **800/654-2943**): This adults-only place is pretty much the perfect guest ranch, where guests are pampered like European royalty, and the prices reflect it. It has all the traditional dude ranch activities, as well as art workshops and wine-tasting weekends. See p. 140.

- **Lone Mountain Ranch** (Big Sky, MT; www.lonemountainranch.com; ✆ **800/514-4644**): Lone Mountain Ranch is a winter and summer resort that has views into the Spanish Peaks Wilderness Area. In winter, there are 45 miles of cross-country trails over terrain that will challenge every level of skier. In summer, you can ride, hike, fish, or simply relax and eat in the popular restaurant. There are bird walks with naturalists and forays into Yellowstone. See p. 219.

- **Lost Creek Ranch & Spa** (Moose, WY; www.lostcreek.com; ✆ **307/733-3435**): Positioned next door to a national park and possessing a beautiful view of the Tetons on one side and the Gros Ventres on the other, Lost Creek layers on the comforts and activities. You can ride, hike, swim, fish, float, play tennis and billiards, shoot skeet, and eat gourmet food. Regulars return every year. There are only 10 cabins, but if you can get a reservation, it's worth it. See p. 315.

- **Eatons' Ranch** (Wolf, WY; www.eatonsranch.com; ✆ **800/210-1049**): The oldest guest ranch in the country, Eatons' is also one of the best. The ranch got its start in North Dakota in 1882 before relocating in 1904 to isolated Wolf Creek Canyon, about 20 miles west of Sheridan. It's a gorgeous location for a dude ranch. See p. 371.

THE best BED & BREAKFASTS

o **The Garden Wall Inn** (Whitefish, MT; www.gardenwallinn.com; ✆ 888/530-1700): This delightful B&B, built in the 1920s, is full of charm—all of the furnishings are period antiques, including claw-foot tubs and Art Deco dressers. Gourmet breakfasts include specialties such as wild huckleberry crepes. See p. 123.

o **The Sanders B&B** (Helena, MT; www.sandersbb.com; ✆ 406/442-3309): Built in 1875, this historically important B&B has been beautifully restored. You'll relax on original furniture under the eyes of portraits hung by the original owner, U.S. Sen. Wilbur Fiske Sanders. See p. 143.

o **Lehrkind Mansion Bed & Breakfast** (Bozeman, MT; www.bozemanbedand breakfast.com; ✆ 800/992-6932): Located in the Historic Bozeman Brewery District, the Lehrkind Mansion looks like something out of a fairy tale. Everything is period, from the rare 1897 Regina music box in the parlor to the many original fixtures in the bathrooms. See p. 207.

o **Wildflower Inn** (Jackson, WY; www.jacksonholewildflower.com; ✆ 307/733-4710): A B&B on 3 acres near Teton Village, the Wildflower Inn features luxurious rooms named after local wildflowers, with private decks, exposed logs, and exceptional privacy. See p. 312.

o **Spahn's Big Horn Mountain Bed and Breakfast** (Big Horn, WY; www.bighorn-wyoming.com; ✆ 307/674-8150): With a 100-mile view from a secluded peak tucked amid the Bighorn Mountains, this rustic hideaway features a massive three-story living area and rooms decorated with country quilts and lodgepole furniture. See p. 371.

o **Nagle Warren Mansion Bed & Breakfast** (Cheyenne, WY; www.naglewarren mansion.com; ✆ 800/811-2610): Originally built in 1888 by famed architect Erasmus Nagle, the mansion was converted into a bed-and-breakfast in 1997. The grand three-story mansion is luxurious and filled with regional antique furniture. It boasts a stately spire that anchors the building's southeast corner. See p. 395.

THE best RESTAURANTS

o **Scotty's Table** (Missoula, MT; www.scottystable.net; ✆ 406/549-2790): The menu is characterized by plenty of excellent local beef, as well as creative spins on French, Italian, and Moroccan standards. Owner-chef Scott Gill moved the eatery to a slick space on the ground level of the historic Wilma Building after a long run south of the river. See p. 92.

o **Cafe Kandahar** (Whitefish, MT; www.cafekandahar.com; ✆ 406/862-6247): The chef here is inspired by French and Creole traditions but also loves to experiment. Local produce and meat dominate the menu; favorite creations include seared elk roulade with forest mushroom, as well as creative seafood and pasta dishes. See p. 127.

o **Second Street Bistro** (Livingston, MT; www.secondstreetbistro.com; ✆ 406/222-9463): In the lobby of the Murray Hotel, this stylish bistro serves a creative,

French-inspired menu. All of the produce in summer comes from the chef's garden, and in winter much comes from a greenhouse. See p. 225.

○ **Snake River Grill** (Jackson, WY; www.snakerivergrill.com; ✆ **307/733-0557**): Locals, including celebs who spend time in the valley, love this place. It's won awards for both its wine list and its menu, which features fresh fish, crispy pork shank, game meat like venison chops, and Idaho trout. See p. 317.

○ **Jenny Lake Lodge Dining Room** (Grand Teton National Park, WY; ✆ **307/733-4647**): The five-course dinners here (from prime rib of buffalo to smoked sturgeon ravioli) are so good you might be distracted from the spectacular scenery just outside the window. You may be roughing it in the park, but you'll need to dress properly at this establishment. See p. 340.

THE best GOLF COURSES

○ **Old Works** (Anaconda, MT): Jack Nicklaus has created a course that is as much fun to play as it is beautiful to look at. The course wonderfully integrates the rocky bluffs, the historic nature of the old copper-processing sites, and prairie grasses and sage. See p. 149.

○ **Teton Pines Resort** (Jackson, WY): You won't find a more beautiful view from any golf course in the country—except maybe the neighboring Jackson Hole Golf & Tennis Club—with the granite Grand Teton looming over every shot. See p. 305.

○ **The Powder Horn** (Sheridan, WY): Under the majestic Bighorn Mountains, this gorgeous 27-hole course mixes Scottish-style golf, wide-open fairways, and some serious target practice. See p. 368.

THE best MUSEUMS

○ **Lewis & Clark National Historic Trail Interpretive Center** (Great Falls, MT; www.fs.fed.us/r1/lewisclark/lcic; ✆ **406/727-8733**): This offers a great perspective on the Corps of Discovery, from its conception back East to its endpoint at the mouth of the Columbia River at the Pacific Ocean. Films, lectures, and demonstrations are among the offerings. See p. 179.

○ **Museum of the Rockies** (Bozeman, MT; ✆ **406/994-2251**): The centerpiece of this first-rate museum is the fabulous dinosaur exhibit. The exhibit, which just had a stellar makeover, has made the place one of the premier paleontological attractions in the world. See p. 205.

○ **Buffalo Bill Historical Center** (Cody, WY; www.bbhc.org; ✆ **307/587-4771**): An art museum, a firearms gallery, the memorabilia of the West's great showman, and exhibits about the Plains Indians comprise the finest museum in the Rocky Mountains. See p. 349.

○ **National Historic Trails Interpretive Center** (Casper, WY; www.blm.gov/wy/st/en/NHTIC.html; ✆ **307/261-7700**): State-of-the-art exhibits give modern travelers an idea of what life on the "road" was like for the emigrants who passed through here in the mid-1800s on the Oregon, Mormon, California, and Pony Express trails. See p. 382.

○ **Old Faithful Visitor Education Center** (Yellowstone National Park, WY; ✆ **307/344-2751**): Stop here to learn about the park's geysers and other thermal features. You'll also find projected geyser-eruption times here, making it a good first stop for those looking to see Old Faithful do its thing. See p. 263.

THE best PERFORMING ARTS & CULTURAL EVENTS

o **International Wildlife Film Festival** (Missoula, MT; www.wildlifefilms.org; © 406/728-9380): This film festival has become a required festival for international filmmakers who specialize in wildlife. It goes for a week, from early to mid-May, and includes panel discussions and workshops, as well as screenings of the world's best wildlife films. See p. 82.

o **Montana Cowboy Poetry Gathering** (Lewistown, MT; © 406/538-4575): Held each year in mid-August, this is a rhyming good time for the bowlegged and horse-drawn set. In addition to a healthy dose of range rhyme, there are booths full of leather and arts-and-crafts shows. See p. 186.

o **Grand Teton Music Festival** (Jackson, WY; © 307/733-3050): Talented musicians from well-known orchestras participate in this summer festival. Tickets can usually be obtained on short notice, especially for the terrific weeknight chamber music performances. See p. 320.

o **Cheyenne Frontier Days** (Cheyenne, WY; © 800/227-6336): The "Daddy of 'em All," Cheyenne Frontier Days is 10 days of parades, rodeo, dances, and concerts. This is the most vivid demonstration of Western hospitality you'll encounter in the modern world. See p. 392.

MONTANA & WYOMING IN DEPTH

S pectacular scenery combines with a genuine frontier history to create what I consider the real American West. The land is mostly uncluttered—even the so-called cities are little more than overgrown cow towns—and the setting is one of rugged beauty, from southeast Yellowstone's Thorofare country (said to be the most remote wilderness in the lower 48 states), to the river valleys where Sacajawea led Lewis and Clark, to the sandstone arroyos of famed outlaw Butch Cassidy's Hole-in-the-Wall country.

There's a little more pavement here than there was in years gone by, but the open horizon and hospitality—along with a pronounced independent spirit among the locals—still exist in Montana and Wyoming. Your first visit will likely be centered on the scenery, the outdoor recreation, and the region's Wild West history, but these two states have even more to offer.

MONTANA & WYOMING TODAY

Since the 1950s, the story of Montana has been an evolving one, with tourism and agriculture playing key economic roles. Primary crops include wheat, cherries, sunflowers, and sugar beets, as well as beef. Growth has emerged as a key, often divisive issue, as areas like Whitefish and Bozeman have attracted wealthy newcomers from out of state and the population has steadily ticked toward 1 million. But large chunks of Montana are far outside the fast track and have remained relatively unchanged for several generations. Likewise, Wyoming depends on agriculture and tourism, but leaned more heavily on oil and gas than its neighbor to the north.

Both states are known for their conservative politics, although Montana has a long and storied history of progressive, labor-oriented politics as well. This makes Montana much more of a swing state when it comes to national elections; many Democrats win elections here.

Unfortunately, mining, logging, and housing developments have impacted the area known as the Greater Yellowstone Ecosystem that surrounds Yellowstone and Grand Teton national parks. The ecosystem is an interdependent system of watersheds, mountain ranges, wildlife habitat, and other components extending beyond the two parks into seven national forests, an Indian reservation, three national wildlife refuges, and nearly a million acres of private land. To put it into perspective, the ecosystem's 18 million acres span an area as big as Connecticut, Rhode Island, and Delaware combined. It is one of the largest intact temperate ecosystems on the planet.

Park officials have the dual—and often contradictory—missions of conserving the natural environment and providing recreational access to three million visitors a year, each with a different definition for the word *wilderness*. The roads and facilities necessary to open the parks to the public are often at odds with the concept of conservation, and the human impact on the environment is no small thing. Recent years have seen record levels of visitors to both parks in spite of difficult economic times, which makes for even more potential conflict between man and wild. In 2011, two visitors to Yellowstone were fatally mauled by grizzly bears—something that had not happened in the park in over 25 years, and a haunting reminder of the inherent dangers that come along balancing conservation and tourism.

Gray wolves, which were eliminated in the 1920s and reintroduced in the 1990s, have been a crucible for conflict. Many ranchers whose lands border the parks have fought the reintroduction tooth and nail, despite the fact that they are compensated when they lose livestock to a wolf. Gray wolves now number about 1,500 in Idaho, Montana, and Wyoming; single animals have turned up in Utah and Colorado, but permanent populations have yet to be established. In 2011, the U.S. Congress passed a spending bill that had a rider attached to it allowing legal wolf hunts to take place in both Montana and Wyoming—despite the endangered status of these wolves. The controversy does not look like it will be going away anytime soon.

Snowmobiles in Yellowstone have also generated their fair share of controversy in the past decade or so. While the machines were to be banned under a plan put in place by the Clinton administration, the Bush administration implemented an alternative compromise of a quota system and best-available technology. The gateway towns of West Yellowstone, Jackson, and Gardiner remain popular jumping-off points for park tours, park officials are still studying the long-term environmental impact of the machines, and snowmobiles still share narrow trails with wildlife during months when the animals' energy levels are at their lowest.

MONTANA DATELINE

11,000 B.C.	Earliest evidence of humans in Montana.
A.D. 1620s	Arrival of the Plains Indians.
1803	The eastern part of Montana becomes a territory through the Louisiana Purchase.
1805–06	Explorers Lewis and Clark journey through the Northern Rockies to and from the Pacific coast.
1864	Montana becomes an official territory. Gold is discovered at Last Chance Gulch in Helena.
1876	Defeat of George A. Custer at the Battle of the Little Bighorn.
1877	Chief Joseph of the Nez Perce tribe surrenders to U.S. soldiers in the Bear Paw Mountains.
1880	The Utah and Northern Railroad enters Montana.
1883	The Northern Pacific Railroad crosses Montana.
1889	Montana, on November 8, becomes the 41st state in the Union.

Though the ranching community has dominated Wyoming politics for most of the past century, the modern economic hammer in the state is undoubtedly the energy industry. The state's fate has been closely tied to oil, gas, and coal, with the economy rising and falling in synch with world prices. But in recent years, the state has tallied billion-dollar surpluses, thanks to the extraction industries. The boom and bust of the energy industry has prompted repeated calls for a more diversified economy, and in recent years, Wyoming's tourism industry has begun to have an impact. This proved critical when drilling slowed when commodity prices plunged in 2008, but the oil and gas industry has bounced back strong as prices have risen in the time since. Nonetheless, Wyoming remains a predominantly rural state—and by far the least populous in the union, with about 570,000 residents as of 2011.

LOOKING BACK: MONTANA & WYOMING HISTORY

Montana

IN THE BEGINNING

The first people believed to have wondered at the land we now call Montana were Folsom Man, who arrived sometime after the end of the last Ice Age about 12,000 years ago and lived here until superseded by the Yuma culture about 6,800 years ago.

Then about 3,000 years ago, a more modern American-Indian culture began to emerge, eventually evolving into the Kootenai, Kalispell, Flathead, Shoshone, Crow, Blackfeet, Chippewa, Cree, Cheyenne, Gros Ventres, and Assiniboine.

EUROPEAN EXPLORERS (18TH C.)

The first European known to enter Montana was Pierre Gaultier de Varennes, sieur de La Vérendrye.

Vérendrye had heard of a river that flowed to the western sea and was looking for the Northwest Passage. He came in 1738 but retreated. Two of his sons, Pierre and François, returned in 1743 and described the "shining mountains," generally believed

1893 The University of Montana in Missoula and Montana State University in Bozeman are founded.	1983 Anaconda Copper Mining Company shuts down.
	1986 Montana spends $56 million on environmental protection programs.
1910 Glacier National Park is established.	
1917–19 Missoula native Jeannette Rankin, a Republican, becomes the first woman elected to U.S. Congress and votes against U.S. participation in World War I.	1995 Wolves are reintroduced into Yellowstone National Park. Daytime speed limits are abolished (but later reestablished).
1940 Fort Peck Dam is completed.	1996 Recluse Theodore Kaczynski, dubbed the Unabomber, is arrested at his cabin near Lincoln and is later sentenced to life in prison for sending a series of mail bombs that killed three people.
1965 Construction of Yellowtail Dam is completed.	
1973 Montana's third state constitution goes into effect.	

continues

to be the Bighorns of southern Montana and northern Wyoming. But threats of a looming Indian war discouraged the brothers, and they returned to Montreal. No other white men are known to have come here for another 60 years.

When they finally did arrive, they were with the expedition of Lewis and Clark. The explorers reached the mouth of the Yellowstone River on April 26, 1805, and pushed upriver to the Shoshone, where they were warmly greeted, the result of having coincidentally brought Shoshone chief Cameahwait's long-lost sister, Sacajawea, with them as one of their guides.

SETTLEMENT (19TH C.)

The first industry in Montana, at least for non-Indians, was trapping. John Jacob Astor, Alexander Ross, and William Ashley brought in their hearty *voyageurs* to clear the country of beaver for the European hat market.

The discovery of gold opened Montana's Wild West era. The lure of easy money, plus the fact that these towns were some 400 miles from official justice, attracted outlaws, con artists, and ladies of the night from all over the West.

In 1864, just as gold was discovered in Last Chance Gulch in present-day Helena, the Montana Territory was formed and Sidney Edgerton became the first territorial governor. The capital was moved to Virginia City, and a constitutional convention was called as the first step toward statehood. A constitution was drafted and sent to St. Louis for printing but was lost somewhere along the way.

In 1884, another constitution was drafted. This one didn't work either, for one reason or another, and in 1889, the now well-practiced delegates came up with a third one. Taking no chances, they prefaced it with the Magna Carta, the Declaration of Independence, the Articles of Confederation, and the U.S. Constitution. Montana finally became a state in November 1889.

TROUBLE BETWEEN THE INDIANS & THE SETTLERS

Montana's Indian tribes were not at first invariably hostile to the whites, and signed a number of treaties signaling their peaceful intentions. But the influx of settlers and the confinement of tribes to reservations resulted in dissatisfaction among the original

1998 The $6-million Lewis & Clark National Historic Trail Interpretive Center opens in Great Falls.

2000–01 A series of forest fires—mostly wildfires, but some caused by careless humans—drive thousands of people from their homes and do millions of dollars in damage.

2003 Wildfires burn 140,000 acres in Glacier National Park.

2005 The grizzly bear is removed from the endangered species list.

2006 A powerful November rainstorm washes out a chunk of Going-to-the-Sun Road in Glacier National Park.

2007–08 Over 1,500 Yellowstone bison are killed as they cross into Montana due to brucellosis fears.

2008 The gray wolf population in the Northern Rockies hits 1,600; the species is no longer listed as endangered.

2009 Montana has its first legal wolf hunting season since reintroduction in 1995.

2010 Separate court rulings return the grizzly bear and gray wolf to the endangered species list.

inhabitants and escalating hostilities against the whites. In 1876, the War Department launched a campaign against the Sioux and Cheyenne. At the end of June that year, this culminated in the **Battle of the Little Bighorn** and the death of all of the command under Gen. George Armstrong Custer.

The Indian victory was only a temporary setback for the whites, however, and by 1880, all the Indians had been forced onto reservations. The last action of the Indian War period occurred in Montana with the heroic flight of Chief Joseph's Nez Perce from their northern Idaho reservation toward Canada in 1877.

INDUSTRIALIZATION (LATE 19TH C.)

When copper was first discovered in the silver mines in Butte, no one could have foretold its effects on Montana's future. When copper wiring became an integral part of several new electrical technologies, Butte copper became an important resource for America. One of the first men to profit was Marcus Daly, an Irish immigrant who arrived in Butte in his mid-30s and purchased his first mine, which yielded incredibly large amounts of the purest copper in the world.

William A. Clark, another copper-mine baron, was a Horatio Alger type. An average youth from Pennsylvania, he rooted around in mines until his efforts took him to Montana. He had a keen business acumen that prompted him to purchase mining operations, electric companies, water companies, and banks. He quickly amassed a great deal of wealth; then his inflated ego drove him to the political arena. His was the major voice in the territorial constitution proceedings in 1884, and when Montana held its last territorial election, Clark was determined to get into public office as Montana's representative.

A war commenced between Daly and Clark, rooted in Clark's determination to hold political office and Daly's unwillingness to see him do it. Montana finally became a state in 1889, after 5 tough years of appeals to the U.S. Congress. The bellicose millionaires were so set on controlling the young state's political interests that they purchased or created newspapers to give themselves a printed voice. They stuffed money into the pockets of voters and agreed on nothing. In Montana's first congressional election, Clark fell three votes shy of his bid, and the legislature adjourned without selecting a second senator, leaving Montana with only half of its due representation in Washington.

The fight for capital status came along in 1894. Helena had been the capital, but the constitution held that the site must be determined by the voters. Daly wanted his newly created Anaconda to be the capital; Clark was happy with the status quo. The fact that Anaconda was ruled by the strong arm of the Anaconda Mining Company caused voters to turn to the diversified ways of Helena. For once in his life, William Clark was not only rich, but also appreciated by the masses. Or so it seemed.

With his thirst for public office revitalized, Clark did his best to buy his way into the U.S. Senate and actually pulled it off. Daly, infuriated by the way his bitter enemy had achieved his seat, demanded an investigation by the Senate. The investigation uncovered a wealth of improprieties on Clark's part, so he resigned. Down but not out, Clark took a deep breath and plunged immediately back into the thick of things. Once when Robert Burns Smith, governor of Montana and hardly an ardent admirer of Clark's, was out of town, Clark arranged for his friend A. E. Spriggs, the lieutenant governor, to appoint Clark to the U.S. Senate. This lunatic act embarrassed the state of Montana, causing Smith to nullify the appointment upon his return. Meanwhile, Daly had sold his Anaconda Copper Company to Standard Oil to form the Amalgamated Copper Company, and Clark was now up against a nameless, faceless opponent.

He chose to link his fate with another, younger copper king, Augustus Heinze, hoping to form an alliance that Amalgamated couldn't match. At this time, Heinze was more influential than the older, less active Clark, and the team of Heinze and Clark soon had complete control of the mining world in Montana. It seemed as if Clark's last wish—to garner the Senate post he had been denied for so long—would be realized with Heinze's help. And so it was—Clark served his state as a senator from 1901 to 1907.

THE 20TH CENTURY

At the beginning of the 20th century, Montana experienced a boom of a different type. The Indian Wars had ended, and white settlers declared the land a safe and fertile haven for farming. The U.S. government helped things along in 1909 when it passed the Enlarged Homestead Act, giving 320 acres to anyone willing to stay on it for at least 5 months out of the year for a minimum of 3 years. Homesteaders arrived from all over the country to stake a piece of land.

Sentiment for the homesteaders was never good, and the generalization that homesteaders were stupid, dirty people became increasingly popular. The truth is that Montana's agricultural backbone was created by these extraordinary people who came west to establish farms. Wheat became—and still is—the major crop in such areas as the Judith Basin, in the center of the state, and Choteau County, north of Great Falls. The mining of copper and other minerals was also strong throughout much of the 1900s, centered on Butte, as was logging in northwestern Montana.

When the Great Depression hit Montana, farming was challenged by severe drought, and jobs were nowhere to be found. Roosevelt's New Deal was a lifesaver. Without the jobs created by the Civilian Conservation Corps and the Works Progress Administration, the state might have never recovered its economic balance. Of particular help was construction of the Fort Peck Dam in the mid-1930s, which employed more than 50,000 workers. The earth-filled dam, the largest of its kind in the world, took almost 5 years to complete.

MODERN MONTANA

After going strong for a century, Montana's copper age came to an end in the early 1980s, when mining ceased at mines in and around Butte. However, the legacy of mineral extraction remains, in the form of environmental degradation and toxic Superfund sites in need of remediation. The Environmental Protection Agency (EPA) has cleaned up (or is cleaning up) many such sites, including ones near Butte and Missoula, but they remain a threat to the groundwater in some areas.

As tourism has grown, largely driven by the national parks, so have the real-estate and service industries. However, the state's ranching legacy or extractive industries certainly have not gone away. In the late 20th and early 21st centuries, logging and mining have remained relatively strong here, but many other industries (including construction, government, and healthcare) employ more people today.

Politically, Montana is known for a progressive history and a libertarian streak, having recently elected Democratic governors and senators and almost going for Barack Obama in 2008. At press time, it was presumed that the state likely would not vote for Obama in the 2012 presidential elections, either, but the race would likely be close.

Wyoming

IN THE BEGINNING

The earliest indications of man in what is now Wyoming date back some 20,000 years. No one knows the identity of these early inhabitants, nor can anyone say with certainty who created the Medicine Wheel in the Bighorn Mountains or the petroglyphs found in various parts of the state. The earliest identified settlers were the Crow, Sioux, Cheyenne, and Arapaho—tribes that came from the east—as well as the Shoshone and Bannock, who came from the Great Basin, more closely related to the peoples of Central America.

The lifestyles of these tribes were greatly changed by the arrival of two European innovations—the horse and the gun. The first white men in Wyoming were fur trappers, and the first of them was John Colter, who left the Lewis and Clark expedition in 1806 to wander south through Yellowstone and possibly Jackson Hole.

SETTLEMENT (19TH C.)

The Oregon Trail and other major pioneer routes west cut right through Wyoming and the territories of the Sioux, Shoshone, Arapaho, and other tribes. Without much regard for the people they were displacing, the non-Indians killed a great deal of the game the Indians depended on; Indian bands, in turn, harassed and sometimes attacked the travelers. Indian tribes were increasingly pushed west into tighter spaces, and there was warfare among tribes.

In a series of treaties, beginning with the Fort Laramie Treaty of 1851, the tribes gave up rights to some of their homelands in return for reservations and other considerations. The discovery of gold in areas like the Black Hills and South Pass, and the routes of settlers, led to numerous treaty violations and continued conflict. Tribes in the east were being evicted and shipped west. Treaties that might have protected Indian rights were modified and broken, and U.S. Army troops were sent in to keep the peace. Some tribal leaders, recognizing the inexorable advance of the whites, decided the only alternative was to fight the invaders.

Local Notables: Famous Folks Who Have Called Montana & Wyoming Home

- Evel Knievel, daredevil, Butte, MT
- Dick Cheney, politician, Casper/Jackson, WY
- William "Buffalo Bill" Cody, scout/showman, Cody, WY
- Gary Cooper, actor, Helena/Bozeman, MT
- Dana Carvey, comedian, Missoula, MT
- David Lynch, filmmaker, Missoula, MT
- Ted Turner, media tycoon, Bozeman, MT
- Chet Huntley, journalist, Cardwell, MT
- Glenn Close, actress, Bozeman, MT
- Peter Fonda, actor, Livingston, MT
- Harrison Ford, actor, Jackson, WY
- Annie Proulx, writer, Saratoga, WY

TROUBLE BETWEEN THE INDIANS & THE SETTLERS

Sitting Bull and Crazy Horse, of the Hunkpapa Sioux, joined forces with members of the Cheyenne and Arapaho tribes along the Little Bighorn River. It was here in June 1876 that a huge gathering of Indians defeated George Custer and his men. Inevitably, this led to a backlash, a series of attacks on Indian communities, culminating in the death of Sitting Bull and the massacre of Spotted Elk and his Sioux followers in 1890 at Wounded Knee, South Dakota. Chief Washakie of the Shoshone was one of the few great Indian leaders still alive, though his star was diminished by his decision to ally his tribe with the whites. That alliance got his people one of the finest reservations in the West, and the only one in Wyoming—Wind River. Then the U.S. Army moved the now-threadbare Arapaho, traditional enemies of the Shoshone, to Wind River "temporarily," and the two tribes began an uncomfortable coexistence that continues to this day.

INDUSTRIALIZATION & THE 20TH CENTURY

Big cattle operators moved into Wyoming in the 19th century, controlling the territory's economy and political scene through such organizations as the Cheyenne Social Club. A couple of severe winters in the 1880s and the influx of new settlers building fences raised tensions. When the cattle barons brought in hired guns to clear out the newcomers, the Johnson County War of 1892 erupted. The wealthy cattlemen claimed the newcomers were rustlers. But that show of muscle was futile in halting the longtime decline of the big livestock owners.

Since 1900, the energy industry has emerged as Wyoming's primary industry. The Teapot Dome Scandal, which involved the bribery of federal officials for drilling rights in Wyoming, was one of the biggest political scandals of its day in the 1920s. The industrialization of public lands in increasingly remote areas of Wyoming in search of fossil fuels followed in subsequent decades, including the eastern side of the state, as well as the Pinedale area in western Wyoming.

The state's remote areas became much easier to visit over the course of the 20th century. Rail and wagon travel dwindled. Airports arrived, along with interstates and

WYOMING DATELINE

18,000 B.C. Earliest evidence of humans in Wyoming.

A.D. 1807 John Colter explores the Yellowstone area, coming as far south as Jackson Hole.

1812 Fur trader Robert Stuart discovers South Pass, the gentlest route across the Northern Rockies.

1843 Pioneers begin traveling west on the Oregon Trail through Wyoming.

1848 The U.S. Army moves into Fort Laramie to protect Oregon Trail travelers from Indians.

1852 The first school in the state is founded at Fort Laramie.

1860 The Pony Express begins its run from Missouri to California, through Wyoming.

1867 The Union Pacific Railroad enters Wyoming.

1868 The Treaty of Fort Bridger creates the Shoshone Reservation in northwest Wyoming. The same year, the Territory of Wyoming is created by Congress.

other highways, making a Yellowstone vacation a more and more popular rite of road-trip passage.

MODERN WYOMING

While agriculture has not faded away entirely in modern Wyoming, it has taken a backseat to the energy economy. Coal, oil, and natural gas are among the state's top exports, as is atmospheric carbon: The state emits more carbon dioxide on a per-capita basis than any of its 49 peers.

In spite of the economic recession (or possibly because of it, in that Wyoming can definitely be visited on a budget), tourism continues to grow, as Yellowstone enjoyed a record-high number of visitors in 2010, followed by another banner year in 2011. This makes for a buoyant economy, but it also fuels more and more demand for sometimes scarce tourism facilities, as well as traffic jams and pollution.

Politically, Wyoming is known as one of the most conservative states, and many vocal locals say they want the federal government involved in their affairs as little as possible. However, with vast tracts of the state's public lands under the purview of federal agencies, this is a sure recipe for controversy and conflict.

MONTANA & WYOMING IN POPULAR CULTURE

Books

In addition to the books discussed below, those planning an extended trip to Yellowstone and/or Grand Teton national parks will find an abundance of information in *Frommer's Yellowstone & Grand Teton National Parks* (John Wiley & Sons, Inc.).

FICTION A. B. Guthrie's *The Big Sky* (Houghton Mifflin, 1947) is now a Montana classic, as is Owen Wister's *The Virginian* (Macmillan, 1929), set in frontier Wyoming. Then move on to contemporary fiction, like the classic fly-fishing novella *A River Runs Through It* (University of Chicago Press, 1976), by Norman Maclean. *Fool's Crow* (Viking Penguin, 1986), by James Welch (a native Montanan), and *Heart*

1869 The Wyoming Territorial Legislature grants women the right to vote and hold elective office.

1870 Esther H. Morris becomes the nation's first female justice of the peace.

1872 Yellowstone National Park is established as the nation's first national park.

1884 The first oil well is drilled in Wyoming.

1886–87 A great blizzard decimates ranches of eastern Wyoming, sending many cattle barons into bankruptcy.

1889 The state constitution is adopted.

1890 Wyoming becomes the nation's 44th state.

1892 The Johnson County War breaks out over a dispute about cattle rustling.

1897 The first Cheyenne Frontier Days rodeo is staged.

1906 Devils Tower is established by President Theodore Roosevelt as the country's first national monument.

continues

Mountain (Viking Penguin, 1989), by Gretel Ehrlich, are fictional stories that revolve around American-Indian and Asian characters. Annie Proulx's *Close Range: Wyoming Stories* (Scribner, 1999) and *Bad Dirt: Wyoming Stories 2* (Scribner, 2004) are recent additions by a fine writer who's spent considerable time around Sheridan. Poet James Glavin's beautifully written *The Meadow* (Henry Holt, 1992) is set in the Tie Siding area of southeast Wyoming.

Montana is fortunate to have the best of its literature compiled in one volume, *The Last Best Place* (University of Montana Press, 1988), the definitive anthology of Montana writings, from American-Indian myths to contemporary short stories.

NONFICTION   Novelist Ivan Doig wrote a beautiful memoir about his youth in Montana, *This House of Sky* (Harcourt Brace Jovanovich, 1978). Gretel Ehrlich's *The Solace of Open Spaces* (Viking Penguin, 1986) is a beautifully written, evocative account of Wyoming ranch life. Paul Schullery's *Searching for Yellowstone* (Mariner Books, 1997) is a great look at the ecology of the world's first national park and mankind's impact on it. Eric Sorg's *Buffalo Bill: Myth and Reality* is an informative read about the man who truly defined the mythos of the West.

If your interests lean more toward geography, check out the *Roadside Geology of Montana* (Mountain Press, 1986), by David Alt and Donald W. Hyndman, and the similar *Roadside Geology of Wyoming* (Mountain Press, 1988), by David R. Largeson and Darwin R. Spearing.

HISTORY   Perhaps the best, and easiest, read about the history and culture of Montana is found between the covers of *Montana, High, Wide and Handsome* (University of Nebraska Press, 1983), written by Joseph Howard and first published in 1944. Another interesting historical tome is Aubrey Haines's two-volume *The Yellowstone Story* (University Press of Colorado, 1977).

Films

Hollywood adapted Norman Maclean's *A River Runs Through It* in 1992 with Brad Pitt; *Rancho Deluxe* (1975) is set in Livingston, Montana, and depicts a rapidly changing place through cattle rustlers played by Jeff Bridges and Sam Waterston; *Little Big Man* (1970) is a revisionist Western that covers Custer's Last Stand and much more.

1910	Buffalo Bill Dam is completed.	1950	National forest and private lands are added to form Grand Teton National Park as it is today.
1925	Nellie Taylor Ross becomes the nation's first female governor.		
1927	A man claiming to be Butch Cassidy visits Wyoming from Washington, suggesting that the outlaw was not killed in Bolivia, as was generally believed.	1965	Minuteman missile sites are completed near Cheyenne.
		1973	The Arab oil embargo sends oil prices skyrocketing, instigating a huge oil-drilling boom in Wyoming.
1929	Grand Teton National Park is established, consisting of only the peaks. That same year, oil thefts are discovered on federal land at Teapot Dome, a scandal that rocks the Harding Administration.	1988	Five fires break out around Yellowstone National Park, blackening approximately one-third of the park.

Wyoming films of note include the made-for-HBO *The Laramie Project* (2001), an adaptation of a stage play about the murder of gay college student Matthew Shepard; *Shane* (1953), the Western classic shot in Jackson Hole; *Heaven's Gate* (1980), the Michael Cimino film about the Johnson County War whose title became synonymous with bloated Hollywood budgets; and *Close Encounters of the Third Kind* (1977), Steven Spielberg's UFO epic that climaxes at Devils Tower National Monument. *Brokeback Mountain* (2005), the acclaimed adaptation of the Annie Proulx short story of the same name, took place in Montana and Wyoming, but most of the movie's Rocky Mountain exteriors were actually shot in Canada.

TV

A number of 1950s and 1960s Western shows were set in Montana and Wyoming, including *Buckskin* (Montana) and *Laramie, The Lawman,* and *The Virginian* (Wyoming). The three national parks in Montana and Wyoming were covered in extensive detail in Ken Burns's 2010 documentary series on national parks, which aired on PBS. However, the states have been ignored by most networks outside of PBS and Animal Planet in recent years.

Music

Country-and-western music is a favorite genre in Montana and Wyoming, but you will also see rock, blues, and jazz bands gracing the stages here. Showcasing primarily the twang of country music, Wyoming has its fair share of legendary music venues, like **Cassie's** (p. 354) in Cody, **Woods Landing** (p. 403) near Laramie, and the **Million Dollar Cowboy Bar** (p. 320) and the **Stagecoach** (p. 320) in Jackson Hole.

Several well-known musicians have called this area home. Late country singer-songwriter Chris LeDoux lived on a ranch in Kaycee, Wyoming. Blackfeet singer-storyteller Jack Gladstone has been called "Montana's troubadour." Grunge-rock pioneers Bruce Fairweather of Mudhoney and Pearl Jam's Jeff Ament both hail from Montana.

1996	The National Park Service institutes a voluntary ban on climbing Devils Tower during June to respect American Indian religious ceremonies.
1998	Gay University of Wyoming student Matthew Shepard is murdered.
2002	The $10-million National Historic Trails Center opens in Casper.
2004	The state enjoys a nearly $1-billion surplus in its annual budget, thanks to increased drilling and mining activity.

2006	The famed tram at Jackson Hole Mountain Resort closes.
2008	A new tram reopens at Jackson Hole Mountain Resort in time for the ski season.
2011	Two visitors are fatally mauled by grizzly bears in Yellowstone, the first such deaths in the park in more than 25 years.

EATING & DRINKING

Montana and Wyoming are probably best known for their beef, but you will also find a lot of local **bison, elk, venison,** and other game meats. (Some say **Rocky Mountain oysters**—deep-fried bull testicles—are a local specialty, but others disagree. They are widely available in both states.) Both states have some great **trout** streams, so be conscious of where yours originated; much of it comes from Idaho.

In Montana, **huckleberries** (purplish wild blueberries that resist commercial production) are a delicacy. Look for them growing wild alongside hiking trails in late summer or in everything from syrup to ice cream at souvenir stands. Northwest Montana also grows some other great crops, including **cherries** and numerous greens, but the biggest crop in the state is wheat, which means that you will find **breads and other baked goods** made from local wheat at the aptly named chain of **Wheat Montana** bakeries statewide.

Missoula and **Bozeman** are both great towns for foodies, as is **Whitefish.** In Wyoming, the best restaurants are undoubtedly in **Jackson Hole,** including the superlative cuisine at **Jenny Lake Lodge** in Grand Teton National Park. Montana's **Flathead Valley** is probably the most fertile spot in either state, with cherry orchards and numerous organic farms.

There are a few wineries in Montana and numerous microbreweries in both states. Top Montana microbreweries include **Bozeman Brewing Company** (p. 210), **Big Sky Brewing Company** and **Kettlehouse Brewing Co.** (Missoula; p. 93), and **Great Northern Brewing Company** (Whitefish; p. 130). Wyoming's standout microbrewery is **Snake River Brewing Co.** in Jackson (p. 319). These breweries produce a wide variety of beers, from Belgian whites to Scotch ales and dark stouts. Note that Montana enforces limited hours and a four-drink maximum at breweries across the state, and keep in mind that most Montana bars double as casinos with live and video poker and other games of chance.

WHEN TO GO

Summer, autumn, and winter are the best times to visit the Northern Rockies. The days are sunny, the nights are clear, and the humidity is low. A popular song once romanticized "Springtime in the Rockies," but that season—or what most people think of as springtime—lasts about 2 days in early June. The rest of the spring season is likely to be chilly with snow or rain; most of the annual moisture in these states falls during March and April.

Eating Native in the Flathead Valley

You will be hard-pressed to find people as fiercely devoted to locally produced food as residents of the Flathead Valley in northwestern Montana. Farms in the valley produce everything from goats to blueberries, and the popular farmers market in Whitefish offers up everything from tomatoes to squash, apples, and grapes. Local restaurants and bed-and-breakfasts such as Cafe Kandahar (p. 127) and the Garden Wall Inn (p. 123) serve local farm-to-table fare. Farm-Hands (www.whoisyourfarmer.org) offers a directory and map of local farms.

Summer is the best season to visit for hiking, fishing, camping, and wildlife-watching. It will be warm during the day and cool at night. In **Montana,** average highs in July run from 79°F (25°C) in **West Yellowstone** to 89°F (32°C) in **Miles City;** lows at night range from 38°F (3°C) to 60°F (16°C). In **Wyoming,** the average high temperatures in July range from 80°F (27°C) to 90°F (32°C)—at high elevations, it almost never gets above 100°F (38°C), and it's dry. The plains tend to get hotter than the mountains.

Fall brings spectacularly clear days; cool, clear nights; and calm winds up until late October, when things get iffy again. Weather is changeable, however, and snow is possible—even likely—in the high country, so don't try an extended backpacking trip unless you are experienced and well prepared. Actually, this is a requirement year-round; you can get caught in mountain snowstorms in July and August.

Winter is a glorious season here, though it can be very cold. Lows in Havre, Butte, West Yellowstone, and Jackson average single digits Fahrenheit (about −15°C) in January. And it can be very windy in some parts of these states, especially on the plains. But the air is crystalline, the snow is powdery, and the skiing is fantastic. If you drive around Montana and Wyoming in the winter, *always* carry sleeping bags, extra food, flashlights, and other safety gear. You need to be prepared to survive if your car breaks down or you get stuck in a blizzard or snow squall. Every resident has a horror story about being caught outside unprepared. Only the north entrance at Yellowstone National Park is open to automobiles in the winter. Lodging is available in the park only at Mammoth and Old Faithful. Ski resort towns, such as Jackson and Kalispell, stay lively all winter, but summer tourist towns, such as Cody, are quiet.

Average Monthly Temperatures in Montana & Wyoming (High/Low)

		JAN	FEB	MAR	APR	MAY	JUNE	JULY	AUG	SEPT	OCT	NOV	DEC
BILLINGS, MT													
	°F	32/14	38/19	45/25	57/34	67/44	77/52	86/58	85/57	72/47	61/37	45/26	36/18
	°C	0/−10	3/−7	7/−3	13/1	19/6	25/11	30/14	29/13	22/8	16/2	7/−3	2/−7
BOZEMAN, MT													
	°F	28/2	34/9	39/15	54/28	65/37	72/44	83/48	82/47	71/39	59/30	43/19	34/10
	°C	−2/−16	1/−12	3/−9	12/−2	18/2	22/5	28/8	27/8	21/3	15/−1	6/−7	1/−12
CODY, WY													
	°F	36/12	40/14	47/21	57/31	66/40	76/47	85/54	83/51	72/42	61/33	46/22	38/15
	°C	2/−11	4/−10	8/−6	13/0	18/4	24/8	29/12	28/10	22/5	16/0	7/−5	3/−9
DEVILS TOWER, WY													
	°F	33/7	40/13	47/19	57/28	68/39	77/48	86/53	86/51	75/41	64/31	45/20	37/12
	°C	0/−14	4/−10	8/−7	13/−2	20/3	25/8	29/11	29/10	23/5	17/0	7/−6	2/−11
HELENA, MT													
	°F	29/9	36/15	44/22	56/31	65/40	74/47	83/52	82/51	70/41	58/31	42/21	32/12
	°C	−1/−12	2/−9	6/−5	13/0	18/4	23/8	28/11	27/10	21/5	14/0	5/−6	0/−11
JACKSON, WY													
	°F	27/5	32/8	41/15	52/24	63/31	72/37	82/40	80/38	71/31	58/23	39/16	28/6
	°C	−2/−15	0/−13	4/−9	11/−4	17/0	22/2	27/4	26/3	21/0	14/−4	4/−9	−2/−14
MISSOULA, MT													
	°F	30/14	37/20	46/25	57/32	66/39	74/46	84/50	83/49	71/40	57/31	40/24	31/17
	°C	−1/−10	2/−6	7/−3	13/0	18/3	23/7	28/10	28/9	21/4	13/0	4/−4	0/−8
YELLOWSTONE, MT & WY													
	°F	22/−2	28/−1	34/3	43/15	52/25	61/32	71/38	71/37	61/29	49/22	34/11	25/3
	°C	−5/−19	−2/−18	1/−16	5/−9	11/−3	16/0	21/3	21/2	16/−1	9/−5	0/−11	−3/−16

Holidays

Banks, government offices, post offices, and many stores, restaurants, and museums are closed on the following legal national holidays: January 1 (New Year's Day), the third Monday in January (Martin Luther King, Jr., Day), the third Monday in February (Presidents' Day), the last Monday in May (Memorial Day), July 4 (Independence Day), the first Monday in September (Labor Day), the second Monday in October (Columbus Day), November 11 (Veterans' Day/Armistice Day), the fourth Thursday in November (Thanksgiving Day), and December 25 (Christmas). The Tuesday after the first Monday in November is Election Day, a federal government holiday in presidential election years (held every 4 years, and next in 2012).

Montana & Wyoming Calendar of Events

For an exhaustive list of events beyond those listed here, check **http://events.frommers. com**, where you'll find a searchable, up-to-the-minute roster of what's happening in cities all over the world.

JANUARY

Montana Pro Rodeo Circuit Finals. Montana's best cowboys compete in the final round of this regional competition in Great Falls. Call ✆ **406222-5473** (www.montana prorodeo.com) for information. Second or third weekend in January.

FEBRUARY

Winter Carnivals. In Whitefish, Montana, there is a parade, a hockey tournament, the "penguin plunge," fireworks, and a dance. Call ✆ **406/862-3548** (www.whitefishwinter carnival.com). First weekend in February. Novelty ski races and other events take center stage during a similar Jackson, Wyoming, event. Call ✆ **307/733-3316.** Mid-February.

Wyoming State Winter Fair. They hold this one indoors in Lander, except for the chariot races. There are booths galore, music, entertainment, a livestock competition, and a big dance. Browse **www.wyomingstatewinter fair.org** for more information. Late February or early March.

MARCH

The Sale to Benefit the C. M. Russell Museum. This is the finest Western art auction in the country, with exhibitors and attendees from around the world. Great Falls, Montana. Call ✆ **406/727-8787** (www. cmrussell.org) for information. Mid-March.

St. Patrick's Day in Butte. This wild and woolly (and often booze-soaked) outdoor party pays homage to Butte, Montana's, Irish heritage. Call ✆ **406/723-3177** for more information. March 17.

APRIL

Montana Storytelling Roundup. Thousands turn out for this annual celebration of storytelling in Cut Bank, Montana. Call ✆ **406/873-0276** (www.montanastorytellers roundup.com) for the schedule. Late April.

MAY

International Wildlife Film Festival. This unique, juried film competition in Missoula, Montana, has more than 100 entries from leading wildlife filmmakers. Call ✆ **406/728-9380** (www.wildlifefilms.org). Early to mid-May.

Miles City Bucking Horse Sale. A "3-day cowboy Mardi Gras," this stock sale in Miles City, Montana, features street dances, parades, barbecues, and, of course, lots of bucking broncos. Call ✆ **406/234-2890** (www.buckinghorsesale.com) for information. Third weekend in May.

Elk Antler Auction. Nearly 10,000 pounds of bull-elk antlers are auctioned off in Jackson's town square. Call ✆ **307/733-3316** (www. jacksonholechamber.com or www.elkfest.org) for information. Third Saturday in May.

JUNE

Plains Indian Museum Powwow. Indian dancers from around the region compete in various dance categories, accompanied by traditional drum groups, on the Robbie Powwow Garden next to the Buffalo Bill Historical Center in Cody, Wyoming. Call © **307/587-4771** (www.bbhc.org) for information. Mid- to late June.

Chugwater Chili Cook-Off. Thousands of hot-food pilgrims come to Chugwater, Wyoming, to taste the spicy contenders in this contest. Call © **307/422-3345** (www.chugwaterchilicookoff.com) for information. Mid- to late June.

Lewis & Clark Festival. Commemoration of Lewis and Clark's journey in and around Great Falls, Montana, with historical reenactments, buffalo roasts, and float trips. Call © **406/452-5661** for information. Late June.

Eastern Shoshone Indian Days Powwow. A celebration of American-Indian tradition and culture that's followed by one of Wyoming's largest powwows and all-Indian rodeos, in Fort Washakie, Wyoming. Call © **307/332-9106** (www.easternshoshone.net) for information. Late June.

JULY

Cody Stampede. There are rodeo nights all summer in Cody, but this long weekend is the big one, and the rodeo ring excitement carries over to street dances, fireworks, and food. Call © **800/207-0744** (www.codystampederodeo.com) for details. July 1 to July 4.

Legend of Rawhide Reenactment. An overeager gold miner comes to an untimely end in this production of the popular Western legend in Lusk, Wyoming. Call © **800/223-5875** (www.legendofrawhide.com) for information. Second weekend in July.

International Climbers Festival. Speakers, music, demonstrations, and climbing at the famed Wild Iris and other rock faces in Fremont County attract rock climbers from around the world to this gathering in Lander, Wyoming. Call © **3443/878-3779** (www.climbersfestival.org). Second weekend in July.

North American Indian Days. The Blackfeet Reservation hosts a weekend of native dancing, singing, and drumming, with crafts booths and games, in Browning, Montana. Call © **406/338-2344** for information. Mid-July.

Grand Teton Music Festival. Fine musicians from around the world join this orchestra every summer. A varied classical repertoire includes numerous chamber concerts and some premieres in Teton Village, Wyoming. Call © **307/733-3050** (www.gtmf.org) for information. Mid-July to the end of August.

Cheyenne Frontier Days. One of the country's most popular rodeos, the "Daddy of 'em All" entertains huge crowds for a full week in Cheyenne, Wyoming. Call © **800/227-6336** (www.cfdrodeo.com) for information. Last week in July.

Evel Knievel Days. Butte, Montana honors its favorite son and one-time problem child, late daredevil Evel Knievel, with parades, stunt shows, and children's events. Call © **406/723-3177** (www.knieveldays.com) for more information. Last week in July.

AUGUST

Sweet Pea Festival. This full-fledged arts festival in Bozeman, Montana, with fine art and musicians, has varied entertainment for all ages. Call © **406/586-4003** (www.sweetpeafestival.org) for information. First full weekend in August.

Grand Targhee Bluegrass Festival. This 3-day celebration of music, arts, food, and entertainment is held at Grand Targhee Resort, near Jackson, Wyoming. Call © **800/827-4433** (www.grandtarghee.com) for information. Mid-August.

Crow Fair. This festival is by far one of the biggest and best American-Indian gatherings in the Northwest, with dancing, food, and crafts in Crow Agency, Montana. Call © **406/638-3700** (http://crowfair.crowtribe.com) for information. Mid-August.

Montana Cowboy Poetry Gathering. This 3-day event features readings and entertainment from the real McCoys in Lewistown,

Montana. Call ☎ **406/538-4575** (www. montanacowboypoetrygathering.com) for information. Mid-August.

SEPTEMBER

Nordicfest. This Scandinavian celebration in Libby, Montana, features a parade, a juried crafts show, headliner entertainment, and an international Fjord horse show. Call ☎ **800/785-6541** (www.libbynordicfest.org) for information. First weekend following Labor Day.

Western Design Conference. Western-style furniture and clothing fashions are displayed on the runway in Cody, Wyoming. Call ☎ **307/690-9719** (www.westerndesign conference.com) for more information. Early or mid-September.

Buffalo Bill Historical Center Art Show and Patrons Ball. With a big art sale to support the museum and a black-tie dinner and ball, this is one of the Rockies' premier (and only) formal social events, in Jackson, Wyoming. For information, call ☎ **307/587-4471** (www.bbhc.org). Late September.

OCTOBER

Hatch. Unspooling over 6 days, this creative arts festival in Bozeman includes film screenings, workshops, filmmaker Q&As, and live music after dark. For information, call ☎ **406/699-7642** (www.hatchexperience. com). Early October.

Glacier Jazz Stampede. This 4-day event brings ragtime, swing, and blues musicians to multiple venues in Kalispell, Montana. Call ☎ **406/755-6088** (www.glacierjazz stampede.com) for more information. Early October.

DECEMBER

Christmas Strolls and Parades. Statewide, Montana and Wyoming. Check with local chambers of commerce for specific dates and locations.

LAY OF THE LAND

In Montana and Wyoming, the earth seems to have turned itself inside out, its hot insides leaking into hot springs and geysers, its bony spine thrust right through the skin of the continent to form the Continental Divide, making it a geologist's dream. And to a biologist, it's heaven, one of the last regions in the United States with enough open space for animals like elk and grizzly bears to roam free.

Plains, basin, and range alternate in this high-altitude environment that is in large part defined by its extremes of weather and climate. These changing landscapes make Montana and Wyoming two of the best vacation spots in the country for travelers who like their scenery dynamic and dramatic.

The western side of both states is mountainous, dragging moisture from the clouds moving west to east and storing it in snowpack and alpine lakes. Because the ridge of the Rockies wrings moisture from the atmosphere, you find deeper, denser forest extending far to the west, while on the east side, the lodgepole pine, spruce, and fir forests give way to the Great Plains, a vast, flat land characterized by sagebrush, native grasses, and cottonwood-lined river bottoms.

But a lot of the landscape dates back more than 100 million years to when the collision of tectonic plates buckled the Earth's crust and thrust these mountains upward. Later, glaciers (of which some vestiges remain) carved the canyons. The tallest peaks in Wyoming are located within the Wind River Range, which rises from the high plains of South Pass and runs northwest to the Yellowstone Plateau. Nine of the peaks in the Winds have elevations over 13,000 feet; **Gannett Peak,** at 13,809 feet, is the highest in the state. Several other mountain ranges are found to the south of Yellowstone—including the Absarokas and the stunning Tetons—and from Yellowstone north into Montana run other dramatic ranges, including the Gallatin,

Yellowstone's Latent Supervolcano

In 2009 and 2010, swarms of earthquakes on the floor of Yellowstone Lake shook the geological community, raising the specter of an eruption on the magnitude of a supervolcano: thousands of times larger than typical eruptions. The Yellowstone caldera has erupted in similarly big ways every 600,000 years for the past 2 million years, and it's about due any century now. However, the hype has a way of overshadowing geological reality: The caldera that sits atop the hotspot responsible for such massive eruptions is not currently anywhere hot enough to produce a cataclysmic blowout like the ones that occurred in eons past. A small eruption could take place at any time, but there will be plenty of warning (in the form of scientific data) before the big one.

Madison, Mission, Bitterroot, Cabinet, and Beartooth, where you'll find Montana's highest point, **Granite Peak,** at 12,807 feet.

The **Continental Divide** enters Montana from Canada and traces a snaking path through the two states. Both Montana and Wyoming have rivers flowing west to the Pacific and east to the Atlantic.

Here you'll also find the headwaters of major river systems—the Flathead and Clark Fork heading west into the Columbia from Montana, along with the Snake from Wyoming; the Yellowstone, North Platte, and Madison joining the Missouri bound east; and the Green from Wyoming emptying into the Colorado heading south. These rivers are the lifeblood of the region, supplying irrigation, fisheries, and power from dams. Montana also boasts the country's largest freshwater body of water west of the Mississippi River: **Flathead Lake. Yellowstone** and **Jackson lakes** are Wyoming's two largest natural bodies of water.

Montana is the greener of these two states, with more abundant alpine wilderness and bigger rivers. Wyoming, however, has been dealt a more interesting hand of natural wonders: waterfalls, geysers, and other geothermal oddities at Yellowstone, as well as the natural landmark of clustered rock columns that rise more than 1,280 feet above the surrounding plains at **Devils Tower National Monument,** near the state's Black Hills region of the northeast. At Wyoming's Red Desert, south of Lander, the Continental Divide splits to form an enclosed basin where no water can escape, and nearby you find **Fossil Butte National Monument,** an archaeological treasure chest of fossilized fish and ancient miniature horses.

The states are characterized by long, cold winters and short summers of hot days and chilly nights. Temperature ranges are dramatic and are largely dependent on elevation. Except along the far western edge of Montana, precipitation here is less than 30 inches a year. It's considerably less as you journey east and south. But the snowpack in the high mountains—more than 300 inches accumulate in some areas—melts through the summer and keeps the rivers running.

RESPONSIBLE TRAVEL

The perpetual debate continues throughout Montana and Wyoming: natural gas drilling and mineral extraction versus recreation and conservation. The Pinedale anticline south of Jackson Hole in Wyoming has been heavily drilled for gas in recent years, sometimes marring the once crystalline Teton views. The Berkeley Pit in Butte,

Montana, is a stark reminder of the price to be paid, a mile-long gash in the earth where a copper-rich mountain once stood.

Numerous lodgings in both states have initiated procedures to be greener, from recycling to water conservation programs. At Teton Village in Wyoming, **Hotel Terra** (www.hotelterrajacksonhole.com; © **800/631-6281**) is the first LEED-certified hotel in the state.

The "localvore" movement is especially strong in Montana in Whitefish, Missoula, and Bozeman.

In Yellowstone and Grand Teton national parks, heavy summer auto traffic and the annual impact of millions of human beings have raised questions about the sustainability of these national parks. But a visit to Yellowstone and Grand Teton national parks can be a relatively green vacation. In Yellowstone, concessionaire **Xanterra Parks & Resorts** (www.yellowstonenationalparklodges.com; © **866/439-7375** or 307/344-7311) has implemented numerous environmental initiatives, including a recycling program, sourcing seafood from sustainable fisheries, and encouraging guests to reuse towels and conserve heat. Campgrounds have recycling bins near the entrance. In Grand Teton, the **Grand Teton Lodge Company** (www.gtlc.com; © **800/628-9988** or 307/543-2811) has also implemented very successful sustainability programs to lessen the human impact on the park. The company purchased wind credits to offset its energy use and diverted 50% of its waste into reusing and recycling everything from aluminum cans, to horse manure, to food waste.

When visiting the national parks of Montana and Wyoming, try to use public or shared transportation whenever possible and minimize the amount of garbage you leave in the park trashcans. Hike as much as possible; you actually get to enjoy the views, and it's one less car on the usually strained roads. One of the best ways to lessen one's impact is to go off the grid on an overnight backpacking trip. **Leave No Trace** (www.lnt.org) is the backpacker's ethic to leave any campsite in the same condition—or better—than when one found it. Backpacking is a refreshing counterpoint to modern life that will give perspective on the issues of sustainability and personal energy dependence.

In addition to the resources for Montana & Wyoming listed above, see frommers.com/planning for more tips on responsible travel.

SUGGESTED MONTANA & WYOMING ITINERARIES

Montana and Wyoming are two of the bigger states in the country, and all of that land and sky makes for something of a blank canvas when it comes to planning a trip to these parts. Most visitors come here to see their natural wonders in general and Yellowstone, Grand Teton, and Glacier national parks in particular, but there is plenty to see beyond their boundaries: top-notch museums; fun college, resort, and authentic Western towns; crystal-clear lakes and rivers for paddling and fishing; and vast tracts of open space.

As far as a time commitment goes, 1 week is a bit short for a trip to Montana and Wyoming, but you can scratch the surface of one region in that time—say, Yellowstone or the Flathead Valley in Montana. Two weeks is much better, giving the opportunity to delve deeper into one region or travel between the Greater Yellowstone Ecosystem and Glacier National Park.

But with all of that real estate, it's important to not stretch yourself too thin: It's better to be out on the trails in the Rockies than behind the wheel of a car. Take time to explore places well off the beaten tourist track and breathe the fresh air, take in the views, and really, truly get away from it all.

THE REGIONS IN BRIEF

Montana

GLACIER COUNTRY & THE NORTHWEST CORNER This includes Glacier National Park, the Flathead Valley and northwest corner of the state, and Missoula, one of Montana's three largest cities. The national park draws millions of visitors annually who come to see its soaring peaks, varied wildlife, and innumerable lakes and streams. The **Going-to-the-Sun Road,** a 50-mile scenic highway that cuts through the heart of the park from southwest to northeast, makes Glacier surprisingly accessible. Elsewhere in the region, the increasingly popular Big Mountain draws downhill skiers, and Flathead Lake is a magnet because of its excellent watersports and quality golf courses. One of the fastest-growing areas in the state, the **Flathead Valley** shelters an interesting mix of residents: Farmers and loggers share ski lifts and trout streams with transplanted urbanites and big-bucks entrepreneurs, all looking for their slice of paradise. On the southern edge of the region is **Missoula,** a vigorous college town with good restaurants, interesting shops, and bits of Montana history.

SOUTHWESTERN MONTANA   This area is extremely diversified. **Helena,** a town centered on arts and politics (though not necessarily in that order), has a beautiful historic district filled with classic architecture and access to tremendous fishing on the Missouri River. **Butte,** on the other hand, is working hard to overcome the decay caused by the exploitation, then abandonment, of its mines. Other areas in this part of the state are full of lore. Vigilantes and corrupt sheriffs dominate the stories of the "ghost towns" of Virginia City and Nevada City, both of which are kept alive today by tourists seeking a realistic glimpse into America's past, and Bannack, an abandoned ghost town that's now a state park.

MISSOURI RIVER COUNTRY   One of the least populated areas in the state, this region stretches from the mountains to the eastern border and is distinguished by prairies that roll along for hundreds of miles. **Great Falls,** the region's largest city, is a mecca for those interested in the story of famed explorers Lewis and Clark. U.S. 2, or the **Hi-Line**—that long stretch of pavement that runs across the northern part of the state—cuts by a series of farms and ranches that perpetuate the homesteader life. New farming equipment and satellite dishes are just modern polish on an old tune.

SOUTH-CENTRAL MONTANA (YELLOWSTONE COUNTRY)   Though this region is almost a twin of the northwest part of the state in many ways—a nearby national park, renowned ski resorts, a university, lots of tourists—it has a unique personality. The city of **Bozeman** is home to Montana State University and a vibrant downtown. Anglers come from all over the world to fish these blue-ribbon trout streams, but the main attraction in this part of the state is **Yellowstone National Park.** Still, even the valleys that lead to it—the Madison, Gallatin, and Paradise—are spectacular destinations themselves.

EASTERN MONTANA   The geography in this part of Montana is similar to its neighboring region to the north, but there are more people and more things to do here. **Billings** is the supply center for eastern Montana and northern Wyoming. It's easily the largest city in Montana and has prospered even without the helpful hand of tourism that the western side of the state has seen. The Bighorn Canyon and the Yellowtail Dam draw their share of visitors, especially hunters and anglers, but this region's main attraction is **Little Bighorn Battlefield,** where Gen. George Armstrong Custer led the 7th Cavalry to defeat at the hands of the Sioux and the Northern Cheyenne.

Wyoming

YELLOWSTONE PLATEAU   Yellowstone sits atop a volcanic caldera that periodically blows its top—once every 600,000 years, give or take—but in the interim provides a largely intact ecosystem in this park of 2.2 million acres. Protected from major development by the National Park Service, Yellowstone provides habitat no longer found elsewhere in the Lower 48 and is home to herds of bison, elk, grizzly bears, trumpeter swans, Yellowstone cutthroat trout, and more subtle beauties such as wildflowers and hummingbirds. The geothermal area is greater than any other in the

The Regions of Montana & Wyoming

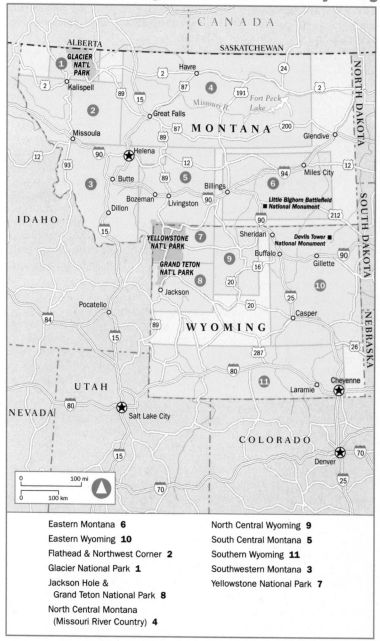

Eastern Montana **6**

Eastern Wyoming **10**

Flathead & Northwest Corner **2**

Glacier National Park **1**

Jackson Hole &
Grand Teton National Park **8**

North Central Montana
(Missouri River Country) **4**

North Central Wyoming **9**

South Central Montana **5**

Southern Wyoming **11**

Southwestern Montana **3**

Yellowstone National Park **7**

world, with mud pots, geysers, and hot springs of all colors, size, and performance, indicative of a complex natural plumbing system that pulls water down into the Earth's crust and regurgitates it at high temperatures. More than three million visitors come here annually, not just to pay homage to Old Faithful, but also to fish, hike, camp, and boat.

THE TETONS & JACKSON HOLE The Tetons are a young range, abrupt and sharp edged as they knife up from the plain below. And while the photogenic peaks get top billing, it's the valley of Jackson Hole that provides the more varied environments and experiences. **Grand Teton National Park** offers some of the most stunning scenery most of us will ever see—shimmering lakes, thickly carpeted forests, and towering peaks that are blanketed with snow throughout most of the year. It's an easy-to-see park—you can catch its breathtaking beauty on a quick drive—but you'll find lakes and waterfalls and even better views and adventures if you leave your car and take to the trails and waterways. The Tetons are especially popular with mountain climbers, who scale its peaks year-round. Elsewhere in the valley, you can float the lively Snake River, visit the National Elk Refuge in the winter, or play cowboy at one of the dude and guest ranches that dot the valley. Skiers and snowboarders have a blast at the resorts here, as well as Grand Targhee on the other side of Teton Pass. And the snug town of **Jackson,** with its antler-arched town square and its busy shops, offers everything from classy art galleries to noisy, two-steppin' cowboy bars.

NORTH-CENTRAL WYOMING This is the sort of basin settlers were looking for when they came this way in the 19th century—mountain ranges on all sides cradling wide, ranchable bottomlands, and some mineral wealth to pay for ranch kids' college educations. More and more, though, the oil and gas development, sheep herding and cattle driving, and beet and wheat growing are giving way to recreation and tourism. The beautiful mountains here—the Wind Rivers, the Owl Creeks, the Absarokas, the east side of the Bighorns—get less attention than the Tetons, but that only makes them more attractive. Historically, the area learned its lessons in tourism from the West's greatest showman, Buffalo Bill Cody, who helped build the fun-loving town that still bears his name. The rodeo and great museum of **Cody** are joined by other attractions, including the **Bighorn Canyon National Recreation Area,** the hot springs of **Thermopolis,** and the **Wind River Indian Reservation,** home to the Shoshone and Arapaho peoples.

EASTERN WYOMING The plains don't begin when you pass east over the Continental Divide; there's another mountain range to cross, and then another—first the Bighorns, then the Black Hills—before you're really out there on the howling flats. The **Bighorns** are a treasure of steep canyons, snow-crowned peaks, good fishing, and good hiking, and at their feet sit two of Wyoming's nicest communities, **Sheridan** and **Buffalo.** Some of the prize ranches in this valley have become some of the best dude ranches in the country. Farther east, across the plains beyond the energy boomtown of Gillette, stands the unmistakable geological landmark that is **Devils Tower,** and along Wyoming's eastern border rise the Black Hills. The region's other claim to fame lies in its history. This is the land of Butch Cassidy and his Hole-in-the-Wall Gang (also known as the Wild Bunch) of cattle rustlers, cowboys, and outlaws.

SOUTHERN WYOMING To the millions of drivers who cross Wyoming on I-80, this is the empty quarter, consisting of mostly barren, wind-swept plains. But it also has its own mountainous corner—the craggy **Medicine Bow**—a lot of history, and mineral wealth of many varieties, from natural gas to trona. More discerning travelers will not see a wasteland: They'll follow the routes of Oregon Trail pioneers (you can still find the wagon-wheel ruts and graves), get off the freeway to visit Fort Laramie, and throw out a fishing line on the North Platte near Saratoga or in Flaming Gorge Reservoir south of Green River. Here you'll find both old and new—from the historic getaway of **Saratoga** to the capital city of **Cheyenne,** where the city throws the biggest rodeo party in the West during July's Cheyenne Frontier Days.

MONTANA & WYOMING IN 1 WEEK

This route brings you to the northwest corner of Wyoming and south-central Montana: the 18-million-acre parcel known as the Greater Yellowstone Ecosystem.

Day 1: Jackson, Wyoming ★★

Start your Rocky Mountain getaway in the world-class resort town of Jackson. Serviced by more airlines than any other town in the state, Jackson is relatively easy to get to and a comfortable launching pad for a Montana/Wyoming vacation. Check out **Town Square,** with its famed antler arches, and the downtown area for window-shopping and lunch, before heading up to the **National Museum of Wildlife Art** (p. 307) for the afternoon. In the evening, drive to **Teton Village** or nearby **Wilson** for dinner, perhaps with a stop to fish on the **Snake River** en route or, if time permits, a ride up the tram at the **Jackson Hole Mountain Resort.** Take your pick of lodgings in and around Jackson. See chapter 12.

Day 2: Grand Teton National Park ★★★

But of course you didn't come to Wyoming for the civilization. Get up early and head immediately for **Grand Teton National Park.** Stop at the visitor center in **Moose** before catching a boat across **Jenny Lake** to the trail leading up **Cascade Canyon;** take it at least to **Hidden Falls** and **Inspiration Point,** but you'll get away from most of the crowds if you continue up the canyon for another mile or two. Either bring lunch with you or come down to one of the numerous eateries in the park. Spend the afternoon ogling the majestic mountains from the numerous overlooks, and take a stroll around **Willow Flats** and look for moose or hike up **Signal Mountain** (you can drive to the summit as well) for a magnificent perspective. For hungry, budget-minded types, I love the nachos at **Deadman's Bar** in Signal Mountain Lodge (p. 341). Spend the night in one of the park's lodgings or campgrounds. See chapter 12.

Day 3: Arrive in Yellowstone National Park ★★★

You got a taste of the in-your-face grandeur of the Tetons; now it's time for the subtler, wilder confines of **Yellowstone National Park** and its amazing amalgam of wildlife, geysers, and hiking trails. You'll drive out of **Grand Teton National Park** through the **John D. Rockefeller, Jr., Memorial Parkway** before entering Yellowstone, and will soon arrive at the trail head to **Lewis River Channel** to Shoshone Lake, the largest backcountry lake in the Lower 48. Pack a lunch or plan for a late lunch at **Old Faithful,** where you'll spend the night after a stop at **West Thumb** en route. In the evening, watch the famed geyser erupt, and then stroll the boardwalks for a glimpse at some of the lesser-known thermal features here: Castle, Grand, and Riverside geysers are all

Montana & Wyoming in 1 & 2 Weeks

Historic
Mining Town

FLATHEAD
VALLEY
9-11 Glacier NP
CANADA
USA

12-13
Flathead
Lake
Big Fork
15

Milk River

Missoula
Great Falls

Missouri River

14
90
Helena
MONTANA

Butte
8

Bozeman
Yellowstone River
94

Nevada
City
7 Livingston
Bannack
6 PARADISE
VALLEY
90

IDAHO
Virginia
City
3-5 Yellowstone
NP

WEEK 1
15
John D. Rockefeller, Jr.
Memorial PKWY
Grand Teton NP

1 Jackson, WY
2
90
25

2 Grand Teton National Park
1
Jackson
WYOMING

3-5 Yellowstone National Park
6 The Paradise Valley
and Bozeman, MT

7 Bozeman, MT
Sweetwater R.
North Platte R.

WEEK 2
80

8 Butte, Helena, and
Great Falls, MT
0   100 mi

9-11 Glacier National Park
0   100 km

12-13 The Flathead Valley
14 Montana's Gold West
Country

awe-inspiring sights to behold. Stay at one of the myriad lodging options at Old
Faithful; eat here as well. See chapter 11.

Days 4 & 5: Yellowstone National Park ★★★

Now that you've whet your Yellowstone appetite, you've got 2 full days to get
your fill of hiking, wildlife-watching, sightseeing, or whatever else might tickle
your fancy. I recommend visitors spend the first half of Day 4 exploring the
Grand Canyon of the Yellowstone area, gawking from the overlooks but also
hiking one of the **rim trails,** visiting **Clear Lake** and **Lily Lake,** or walking
down the metal staircase known as **Uncle Tom's Trail** for an unbeatable perspective of the base of **Lower Falls.** Drive up to Tower-Roosevelt in the afternoon to unwind on the porch at **Roosevelt Lodge** (p. 295), where you'll sleep
in a dinky cabin after enjoying a cookout on the trail. The next day, you're in
prime position for an early start of wildlife-watching in the **Lamar Valley**—"the
Serengeti of North America." Have lunch in Cooke City and perhaps do a little
fishing in Trout Lake or Soda Butte Creek before reversing course for **Mammoth Hot Springs.** After walking the boardwalks here, eat at the **Sawtooth**

Deli or the **Corral Drive-In** (p. 260) in Gardiner, Montana, or have a quick bite at Mammoth before heading to **Boiling River** for a soak before the sun sets. Stay at Mammoth or Gardiner.

Day 6: The Paradise Valley ★★ & Bozeman, Montana ★★

From Mammoth or Gardiner, drive north on U.S. 89 up the idyllic **Paradise Valley** to **Livingston, Montana.** Wander downtown Livingston, visiting one of the town's three museums, check out a gallery or two and have a bite to eat. Next, drive west on I-90 to downtown **Bozeman, Montana,** for the evening. Spend the afternoon strolling **Main Street,** and settle on a restaurant downtown—there are plenty to choose from—and perhaps a watering hole for an after-dinner drink. As for accommodations close to downtown, I can't recommend the **Lehrkind Mansion Bed & Breakfast** enough (p. 207).

Day 7: Bozeman, Montana ★★

After breakfast at the Lehrkind or one of the noshing spots on Main, head south to the **Museum of the Rockies** (p. 205), on the campus of Montana State University. This top-flight museum offers a view into one of the best and brightest paleontology programs in the country and a look at the largest collection of American dinosaurs in the world. Either have lunch at the museum cafe or head back downtown before venturing south into the **Gallatin National Forest** for an afternoon hiking or fishing expedition. For dinner, try **Montana Ale Works** (p. 208) or the **Mint** (p. 208) in nearby Belgrade, a very Montana kind of place.

MONTANA & WYOMING IN 2 WEEKS

Start with the preceding 1-week itinerary. Then from Bozeman, Montana, make your way northwest to Glacier Country, the Flathead Valley, and many more of the natural wonders that give the Treasure State its nickname.

Days 1 to 7: Montana & Wyoming in 1 Week

Follow the itinerary outlined above.

Day 8: Butte, Helena ★ & Great Falls, Montana

This is a big driving day, covering about 80 miles on I-90 W. and another 150 miles on I-15 N. But it also puts you within a relatively short drive of **Glacier National Park** and gives you an opportunity to visit one or both of Great Falls's terrific museums: the **Lewis & Clark National Historic Trail Interpretive Center** (p. 179) and the **C. M. Russell Museum Complex** (p. 178). I'm also a sucker for the **Sip 'n Dip Lounge** (p. 181), the kitschiest watering hole in the West. En route from Bozeman, stop for a peek at the **Berkeley Pit** (p. 150) in Butte and lunch on **Last Chance Gulch** in Helena (p. 139).

Days 9, 10 & 11: Glacier National Park ★★★

Visit another museum in Great Falls or head directly to **Glacier National Park.** Before ascending **Logan Pass** on Going-to-the-Sun Road, stop at Sunrift Gorge for a hike up toward Siyeh Pass, where there's a nice view of a hanging glacier. Camp or stay at one of the many nice hostelries in the park; eat in the park as well. The next day, take your pick of activities: **rafting** out of West Glacier, **hiking** to Avalanche Lake or another trail, or **sightseeing** in Glacier's many nooks and crannies. Stay in the park again on night 10, or take your choice of one of the hostelries in the gateways of East Glacier, West Glacier, St. Mary, Essex, or Polebridge. Explore more of Glacier by car or foot on Day 11 before leaving the park for Whitefish. In Whitefish, stay at the **Garden Wall Inn** (p. 123) and walk downtown for dinner. See chapter 6.

Days 12 & 13: The Flathead Valley ★★

Use Whitefish as a base for exploring the Flathead Valley. After breakfast, take a scenic cruise or fishing charter on **Flathead Lake;** then spend the remainder of the day in **Bigfork,** shopping, strolling, and having dinner at one of the terrific eateries. Perhaps take in a play at the **Bigfork Summer Playhouse** (p. 104). Stay at one of the many lodgings in or around Bigfork for the evening. On the next day, drive south to **Missoula** for a peek at the **Rocky Mountain Elk Foundation Visitor Center** (p. 87) and the University of Montana campus before getting in one last hike in the **Rattlesnake Wilderness Area** just outside of town. In the evening, venture into downtown Missoula for dinner and drinks. See chapter 6.

Day 14: Explore Montana's Gold West Country

You might end your trip in Missoula and spend the final day enjoying a slow start and a good breakfast. But if your schedule allows, take the day for a **scenic drive** through the Bitterroot Valley, south of town via U.S. 93, and over Lost Trail Pass. From there, you'll have an opportunity to visit one of Montana's historic mining towns: **Virginia City, Nevada City,** or **Bannack.** (The latter is a ghost town that's now a state park.) From any of these, you're in a good position to get to Salt Lake City (if you arrived by air) and I-15 (if you're driving home). See chapter 7.

YELLOWSTONE & GRAND TETON NATIONAL PARKS FOR FAMILIES

Yellowstone and Grand Teton national parks can be challenging destinations for families. Many of the recreational activities (particularly hiking) can be taxing for little ones, who might also find too much time in the car a bit of a bore. The following itinerary offers a few tips for everybody to get the most out of a week in the parks.

Day 1: Arrive in Cody, Wyoming ★

Cody is the ideal gateway for a family vacation in Yellowstone: Kids will surely enjoy the shootouts in front of the **Irma Hotel** (p. 352) downtown, and the nightly **Cody Nite Rodeo** (p. 350) has kiddie rides beforehand and a participatory "calf scramble" that allows youngsters to get in on the action and chase a bewildered calf around the arena in between the events. (The kids are trying to grab the coveted ribbon tied to the animal.) Older kids might even like the **Buffalo Bill Historical Center** (p. 349). Try the sushi at **Shiki** (p. 354) or steaks at **Cassie's** (p. 354), and stay at the **Buffalo Bill Village Resort** (p. 351), the **Mayor's Inn** (p. 352), or the **Chamberlin Inn** (p. 351).

Yellowstone & Grand Teton National Parks for Families

Legend:
1. Cody, WY
2. Arrive in Yellowstone National Park
3-4 Explore Yellowstone National Park
5-6 Grand Teton National Park
7. Jackson, WY

Day 2: Arrive in Yellowstone National Park ★★★

Head straight into **Yellowstone** on Day 2, stopping for a picnic along the shore of **Yellowstone Lake** once you've entered. **West Thumb** is an excellent primer for introducing tykes to the park's geothermal underpinnings. Spend the night at **Old Faithful**, where you can see more incredible displays produced by the heat, water, and geology below. See chapter 11.

Days 3 & 4: Explore Yellowstone ★★★

While many hikes in the first itinerary in this chapter may not be suitable for all children, there are two in particular for people of all ages: **Artist Paint Pot Trail,** south of Norris, and the **Forces of the Northern Range Self-Guiding Trail,** near Mammoth (neither trail is detailed in this book, so ask a ranger for more information). Both are short, level, and give a good glimpse at different phenomena that have shaped Yellowstone's ecosystem over the eons. On Day 3, tackle Artist Paint Pot Trail, then wander Norris's boardwalks before making your way to Mammoth for the evening. Get a room, cabin, or campsite here, and hit **Boiling River** (p. 276) for a soak before exploring more thermal features at Mammoth via boardwalk. The next morning, you're in prime position for the Forces of Nature Self-Guiding Trail, which gives a look at the effects of a forest fire, before driving west for an afternoon exploring the Lamar Valley in search of wildlife—the **Yellowstone Association Institute** offers customizable expeditions that will allow Mom and Dad a break from the wheel. Spend the night at **Roosevelt Lodge** (p. 295)—a family favorite—after enjoying a signature chuck-wagon cookout.

Days 5 & 6: Grand Teton National Park ★★★

It's a pretty good drive from Roosevelt to Grand Teton, so plan a stop at the **Grand Canyon of the Yellowstone** and picnic in the southern reaches of the park en route. You'll probably get your first peek at the Tetons in the early afternoon. Pick a base in the park—your choices range from campgrounds to luxury cabins. **Colter Bay Village** (p. 338) is a family-friendly spot and gives you the opportunity to set out to moose-watch in Willow Flats or around Jackson Lake Lodge. The next day, take the boat across **Jenny Lake** and hike as far up Cascade Canyon as you see fit. In the afternoon, take a **scenic cruise** on Jackson Lake. See chapter 12.

Day 7: Jackson, Wyoming ★★

Your last day will be well spent in Jackson. At **Town Square,** there are nightly shootouts and stagecoach rides. You might ride the tram or scale a climbing wall at **Jackson Hole Mountain Resort** (p. 303), or visit the excellent **National Museum of Wildlife Art,** which has kid-oriented interpretation and activities. Grab dinner at **Billy's Giant Hamburgers** at the **Cadillac Grille** (p. 316) and stay at the **Rustic Inn** (p. 310); it has plenty of room to roam on the banks of Flat Creek, but is also within walking distance of Town Square. Jackson has an airport and is an easy drive from I-15 at Idaho Falls. See chapter 12.

EXPLORING THE WILD WEST PAST OF MONTANA & WYOMING

Many visitors come to the region for the sublime views and superb recreation, but many others come in search of the real West that's slowly but surely fading into the history books. There are pockets of fascinating history that shaped the nation's culture and textbooks, vestiges of the Old West amid the developments of the new in Wyoming and Montana.

Day 1: Cheyenne, Wyoming

Begin your day downtown at the beautifully restored Union Pacific Depot and the **Cheyenne Depot Museum** (p. 393) for a look at how the railroad shaped the history of this part of the West. Pick up their brochure *Tracking Trains in Cheyenne,* and dig a little deeper into this fascinating chapter. Another interesting (and intertwined) tale is told at the **Cheyenne Frontier Days Old West Museum** (p. 394). Stay at the historic **Nagle Warren Mansion Bed & Breakfast** (p. 395) downtown after a dinner at **Poor Richard's** (p. 396).

Exploring the Wild West Past of Montana & Wyoming

Historic
Mining Town

Havre
Chinook
CANADA
USA

Bear Paw
Battlefield

Great Falls

Missouri R.

MONTANA

Butte

Yellowstone R.

MONTANA'S GOLD
WEST COUNTRY

IDAHO

Yellowstone NP

Little Bighorn
Battlefield NM

Sheridan **4-5**

7
6 Cody
Buffalo

Snake R.

Hole-in-
the-Wall

WYOMING

Casper
3

Green R.

Sweetwater R.

Laramie
2
Saratoga
Cheyenne
1

0   100 mi
0   100 km

1 Cheyenne, WY
2 Laramie and Saratoga, WY
3 Casper and Buffalo
4-5 Sheridan & vicinity
6 Cody, WY
7 Chief Joseph Scenic Highway

Day 2: Laramie & Saratoga

On your second day, head west into Laramie for a visit to the **Wyoming Territorial Prison State Historic Site** (p. 400), and then continue into the Snowy Range Mountains to visit **Saratoga, Centennial,** and/or **Woods Landing,** and stay for the night. **Brooklyn Lodge** and **Woods Landing** (p. 403) are interesting.

Day 3: Casper & Buffalo ★

Return to Laramie, and drive north through the Shirley Basin on U.S. 287 and Wyo. 487 to Casper and the excellent **National Historic Trails Interpretive Center** (p. 382). Have lunch at the **Wonder Bar** (p. 384) before continuing north to **Hole-in-the-Wall** (p. 374), a hide-out favored by Butch Cassidy and the Sundance Kid. Stay in Buffalo at the **Occidental Hotel** (p. 374). Explore Buffalo's other attractions, Fort Phil Kearny, and the Jim Gatchell Memorial Museum.

Days 4 & 5: Sheridan & Vicinity ★

From Buffalo, continue north on I-25 to Sheridan for a look at its numerous **historic attractions** (p. 369). Use Sheridan as a base for exploring the rest of the area, especially **Little Bighorn Battlefield National Monument** (p. 244), the site of Custer's infamous Last Stand. If you're looking for a knowledgeable guide, Ron Spahn of Spahn's Big Horn Mountain Bed and Breakfast offers daylong **historic and cultural tours** (p. 368) of the area, including spots well off the beaten track.

Day 6: Cody ★

No Old West trip would be complete without a visit to the town founded by and bearing the name of William "Buffalo Bill" Cody. The **Buffalo Bill Historical Center** (p. 349) is a must-visit, with a great look into the life of Cody himself, as well as many other aspects of the area's history. Stay at the **Mayor's Inn** (p. 352) or the **Chamberlin Inn** (p. 351).

Day 7: Chief Joseph Scenic Highway

From Cody, drive north out of town and get on the **Chief Joseph Scenic Highway** (p. 345), which connects to the Beartooth Scenic Byway, an awe-inspiring route into **Yellowstone National Park.** The road follows the route taken by the Nez Perce tribe, which fled the U.S. Army and its attempt to force relocation to Oklahoma. The flight of the Nez Perce in summer 1877 snaked through Yellowstone but ended in Hi-Line country at **Bear Paw Battlefield** (p. 192). From here, you could head in that direction and later hit Butte and Montana's Gold West Country for a look at the region's mining history, or into Yellowstone for an adapted version of the first itinerary in this chapter. The **Yellowstone Association Institute** (p. 268) also offers a number of history-oriented classes and expeditions.

THE ACTIVE VACATION PLANNER

Montana and Wyoming are among the greatest the great outdoors has to offer, in the United States or anywhere in the world. There are literally millions of acres of public spaces where you can cast for native cutthroat trout or herd cattle, go rock climbing or four-wheeling, raft, or ski. These states collectively boast a trio of spectacular national parks, five national monuments, one national recreation area, two national historic sites, five national historic trails, 14 national forests, one national grassland, more than 20 million acres administered by the federal Bureau of Land Management (BLM), and 64 state parks. All things considered, there are many lifetimes of outdoor recreation to be experienced in these parts.

This chapter provides some up-to-date information on visiting Montana and Wyoming's national parks. Following that are descriptions of activities you can pursue, from A to Z. I'll point you to the best places in the state to pursue your interests and give you the information you'll need to get started. You'll find more details in the appropriate regional chapters.

PREPARING FOR YOUR ACTIVE VACATION
What to Pack & What to Rent

Planning for a trip into the great outdoors may conjure images of vacationers loaded down with golf clubs, skis, cameras, tents, canoes, and bikes. If a car or light truck is your mode of transportation, try to keep the heaviest items between the axles and as close to the floor of your vehicle as possible; this helps improve handling. If you have a bike rack on the rear bumper, make sure the bike tires are far from the exhaust pipe; one bike shop owner told me he does a good business replacing exhaust-cooked mountain-bike tires. Those with roof racks will want to measure the total height of their packed vehicles before leaving home. Underground parking garages often have less than 7 feet of clearance.

One alternative to carrying all that stuff is renting it. Many sporting-goods shops in Montana and Wyoming rent camping equipment; virtually all ski areas and popular mountain-bike areas offer rentals; and major boating centers such as Flathead Lake, Jackson Lake, and Lake Flaming Gorge rent boats. You'll find many rental sources listed throughout this book.

In packing for your trip, you'll want to be prepared for all your favorite activities, of course, but you'll also want to be prepared for an unforgiving climate and terrain. Those planning to hike or bike should take more drinking water than they think they'll need—experts recommend at least 1 gallon of water per person, per day on the trail—as well as high-SPF sunscreen, hats and other protective clothing, and sunglasses with ultraviolet protection. Summer visitors should carry rain gear for the typical afternoon thunderstorms, plus jackets or sweaters for cool evenings. Winter visitors will need not only warm parkas and hats, but also lighter clothing—the bright sun at midday, even in the mountains, can make it feel like June.

Staying Safe & Healthy in the Outdoors

The wide-open spaces and rugged landscape that make these states such a beautiful place to explore can also be hazardous to your health, especially if you're not accustomed to the extremes here; see "Health" and "Safety," in the "Fast Facts" section of chapter 16, for details on dealing with wildlife and high altitudes. The isolation of many of the areas that you'll seek out means there may be no one around to help in an emergency, so you must be prepared, like any good scout. See "What to Pack & What to Rent," above, for tips on what to bring. Also be sure to carry a basic first-aid kit. Most important, check with park offices, park rangers, and other local outdoor specialists about current conditions before heading out.

Outdoor Etiquette

Many of the wonderful outdoor areas you'll explore in Montana and Wyoming are quite isolated; although you're probably not the first human being to set foot here, you may feel like you are. Not too long ago, the rule of thumb was to "leave only footprints"; these days, we're trying to not even do that. Being a good outdoor citizen is relatively easy—it's mostly common sense. Pack out all trash, stay on established trails, be careful not to pollute water, and, in general, do your best to have as little impact on the environment as possible. The best among us go even further, packing out trash others have left behind.

TOURS

Academic Trips

In Yellowstone, the **Yellowstone Association Institute ★★★** (www.yellowstone association.org/institute; ✆ **406/848-2400**) offers a slew of guided classes, including daylong hikes to multiday backcountry adventures, often with a historical or scientific bent. Participants can bunk in cabins at the historic buffalo ranch in Lamar Valley or above Gardiner, Montana, in the new Overlook Field Campus, which opened in 2010 and features cabins with shared kitchens and a commanding view.

The **Teton Science Schools ★★**, 700 Coyote Canyon Rd., Jackson, WY 83001 (www.tetonscience.org; ✆ **307/733-1313**), have an excellent curriculum for students of all ages, from integrated science programs for junior-high kids to adult seminars covering everything from botany to astronomy. Classes take place at campuses in Jackson and Kelly, and other locations in Jackson Hole. The school's **Wildlife Expeditions** (✆ **877/404-6626**) offers tours that bring visitors closer to the park's wildlife. These trips range from a half-day to a week, covering everything from big-horn sheep to the wolves of Yellowstone.

Dan Pence of **Great Divide Wildlands Institute** (www.greatdividetours.com; ℂ 406/683-4669) offers a variety of scenic and historical tours, with a special emphasis on the route of Lewis and Clark and the Nez Perce through the Big Hole area. Starting at $250 for two people, the packages include day trips to where Lewis first met the Shoshone and other customized historical and scenic tours in the Big Hole.

Adventure Trips

There are plenty of opportunities for adventure in Montana and Wyoming—and some terrific outfitters to help you plan and execute your trip. You can take part in a cattle drive; thrill to the excitement of white-water rafting on the Snake or Flathead rivers; scale a mountain in Grand Teton National Park; or head out into some of the most spectacular scenery in the country on foot or on bicycle, or in a four-wheel-drive vehicle. The variety of tours available seems almost endless, but the tour operators can help you find the one for you. In many cases, you can work with an operator to plan your own customized trip—all it takes is money.

Below are some of the most respected companies operating in Montana and Wyoming. Most specialize in small groups and have trips geared to various levels of ability and physical condition. They also offer trips in a range of price categories, from basic to luxurious, and of varying length. Numerous local outfitters, guides, and adventure travel companies are discussed throughout this book. For a complete list of outfitters in Montana or Wyoming, as well as a lot of other useful information and Web links, contact **Visit Montana,** P.O. Box 200533, 301 S. Park St., Helena, MT 59620 (www.visitmt.com; ℂ **800/847-4868** or 406/841-2870); or the **Wyoming Business Council Travel & Tourism Division,** 1520 Etchepare Circle, Cheyenne, WY 82007 (www.wyomingtourism.org; ℂ **800/225-5996** or 307/777-7777).

o **AdventureBus,** 375 S. Main St., Ste. 240, Moab, UT 84532 (www.adventurebus.com; ℂ **888/737-5263** or 909/633-7225), offers trips on its customized buses, with an emphasis on outdoor adventures, including multisport and mountain-biking tours in and around the Yellowstone and Grand Teton national parks.

o **Austin-Lehman Adventures,** P.O. Box 81025, Billings, MT 59108 (www.austinlehman.com; ℂ **800/575-1540** or 406/655-4591), offers guided multiday mountain biking, hiking, and combination tours in and around Yellowstone and Grand Teton national parks.

o **Backroads,** 801 Cedar St., Berkeley, CA 94710-1800 (www.backroads.com; ℂ **800/462-2848** or 510/527-1555), offers a variety of guided multiday road biking, mountain biking, and hiking tours in and around Glacier, Yellowstone, and Grand Teton national parks.

o **Escape Adventures,** 8221 W. Charleston Ave., Ste. 101, Las Vegas, NV 89117 (www.escapeadventures.com; ℂ **800/596-2953** or 702/838-6968), offers guided mountain biking and road cycling in Yellowstone National Park and Jackson Hole.

o **Glacier Guides** (www.glacierguides.com; ℂ **800/521-7238** or 406/387-5555) is the exclusive hiking guide service in Glacier National Park. From May through September, it organizes custom trips and offers weekly departures for 3- and 6-day trips. Prices vary, but you can figure on spending $100 to $150 per person, per day. It also rents equipment and can arrange trips on which you stay indoors at night.

- **High Country Adventures** (www.hcamontana.com; ✆ **406/466-5699**) is the oldest backpacking guide company in the country. It's also the Bob Marshall Wilderness Area's only licensed backpacking outfitter, where there are dozens of licensed horse-packing guides. The company organizes three or four trips per summer that cover about 10 miles of trail in an average day, ranging from a week to 12 days.

- **Montana High Country,** 35 miles west of Dillon, at 7501 Pioneer Mountain Scenic By-way, Polaris, MT 59746 (www.mhct.com; ✆ **406/834-3469**), offers year-round guiding services, including fly-fishing, horseback riding, big-game hunting, and snowmobiling. Prices range from $900 for a 3-day, 4-night snowmobiling package to $2,550 for a 6-day, 7-night fishing trip; hunting trips are also available. They also operate a guest lodge.

- **Ski the Rockies,** 4901 Main St., Downers Grove, IL 60515 (www.skitherockies. com; ✆ **800/291-2588** or 630/969-5800), provides customized skiing and snowboarding packages at the major resorts in Montana and Wyoming.

- The **World Outdoors,** 2840 Wilderness Place, Ste. D, Boulder, CO 80301 (www. theworldoutdoors.com; ✆ **800/488-8483** or 303/413-0938), offers a variety of trips, including multisport adventures that include hiking, biking, and rock climbing in Grand Teton and Yellowstone national parks.

Volunteer Trips

For those who want to keep the trails in good shape and get some fresh air and exercise, the **Continental Divide Trail Alliance** (www.cdtrail.org; ✆ **303/278-3177**) organizes numerous volunteer trail crews in both Montana and Wyoming.

Walking Tours

Backroads (www.backroads.com; ✆ **800/462-2848** or 510/527-1555) offers walking/hiking tours of Glacier National Park and Yellowstone and Grand Tetons national parks; tours last about a week, with overnight lodging in various hotels and cabins. **Country Walkers** (www.countrywalkers.com; ✆ **800/464-9255**) has a walking/hiking tour of Yellowstone.

VISITING MONTANA & WYOMING'S NATIONAL PARKS

For many people, including me, the best part of a vacation to Montana and Wyoming is exploring the region's three national parks: **Glacier, Yellowstone,** and **Grand Teton** (www.nps.gov). Unfortunately, these beautiful national treasures have become so popular that they're being overrun by visitors when the federal government is cutting budgets, making it difficult for the parks to cope with their own success.

To get the most out of your national park visit, try to go in the off season. The parks are busiest in summer, when most children are out of school, so try to visit at almost any other time. Fall is usually best. Spring is okay, but it can be windy and there may be snow at higher elevations. Winter can be delightful if you don't mind snow and cold. If you have to travel in summer, be patient. Allow extra time for traffic jams and lines, and try to hike some of the longer and lesser-used trails. Rangers will be able to tell you which trails are best for getting away from the crowds.

PASSES OFFER free admission ON MOST FEDERAL LANDS

Those who enjoy vacationing at national parks, national forests, and other federal lands have opportunities to save quite a bit of money by using the federal government's annual passes. The America the Beautiful—National Parks and Federal Recreational Lands Pass costs $80 for 1 year from the date of purchase for the general public. It provides free admission for the pass holder and those in his or her vehicle to recreation sites that charge vehicle entrance fees on lands administered by the National Park Service, U.S. Forest Service, U.S. Fish and Wildlife Service, Bureau of Land Management, and Bureau of Reclamation. At areas that charge per-person fees, the passes are good for the pass holder plus three additional adults. Children 15 and under are admitted free.

The passes are also available for U.S. citizens and permanent residents 62 and older for a lifetime fee of $10 (Senior Pass), and are free for U.S. residents and permanent residents with disabilities (Access Pass). The Senior and Access passes also provide 50% discounts on some fees, such as camping.

The Senior and Access passes must be obtained in person at national parks, U.S. Forest Service offices, and other federal recreation sites, but the general public version (the $80 one) can be purchased in person, by phone (☎ **888/275-8747,** ext. 1), or online at http://store.usgs.gov/pass, a website that also provides complete information about the passes.

OUTDOOR ACTIVITIES A TO Z

Montana and Wyoming offer a surprisingly wide range of outdoor activities, from desert hiking and rafting to fly-fishing and skiing. Among the many online outdoor recreation information sources are the very informative and user-friendly Public Lands Information Center website, **www.publiclands.org**, and the **GORP** (Great Outdoor Recreation Page) website, at **www.gorp.com**.

Throughout this book, you'll find contact information for national and state parks, national forests, and the like. Here are some key statewide and regional resources. The **U.S. Forest Service** has information about national forests and wilderness areas in Montana, as well as **Bridger-Teton National Forest** in Wyoming, at the Northern Region Office, Federal Building, 200 E. Broadway, Box 7669, Missoula, MT 59807 (www.fs.usda.gov/r1; ☎ **406/329-3511**). The rest of Wyoming's forests, as well as **Thunder Basin National Grassland,** are covered by the Rocky Mountain Region Office, 740 Simms St., Golden, CO 80401 (www.fs.usda.gov/r2; ☎ **303/275-5350**).

The federal **Bureau of Land Management** also manages millions of acres of recreational lands and can be reached at its Wyoming state office, 5353 Yellowstone Rd., Cheyenne, WY 82009 (www.blm.gov/wy; ☎ **307/775-6256**); or its Montana state office, 5001 Southgate Dr., Billings, MT 59101 (www.blm.gov/mt; ☎ **406/896-5000**).

For information on Montana state parks, fishing, and hunting, get in touch with **Montana Fish, Wildlife, and Parks,** 1420 E. 6th Ave., P.O. Box 200701, Helena, MT 59620 (www.fwp.mt.vov; ☎ **406/444-2535**). In Wyoming, contact **Wyoming**

State Parks and Historic Sites, 2301 Central Ave., Cheyenne, WY 82001 (http://wyoparks.state.wy.us; ✆ **307/777-6323**). For hunting and fishing, contact **Wyoming Game and Fish,** 5400 Bishop Blvd., Cheyenne, WY 82003 (http://gf.state.wy.us; ✆ **307/777-4600**).

You'll have no trouble finding detailed topographic maps—essential for wilderness trips—plus whatever equipment and supplies you need. And despite the well-publicized cuts in budgets and workforces in national parks, recreation areas, and forests, every single ranger I encountered was happy to take time to help visitors plan their backcountry trips. In addition, many sporting-goods shops are staffed by area residents who know local activities and areas well, and are happy to help the would-be adventurer. In almost all cases, if you ask, there will be someone willing and able to help you make the most of your trip.

BACKCOUNTRY SKIING There is nothing as thrilling as skiing deep, untracked powder in completely wild terrain. To enjoy this sport, you need a good set of Telemark skis, good information about where to go, and expert knowledge of snow conditions and avalanche risks. One of the best places to pursue this sport is **Togwotee Pass** in Bridger-Teton National Forest in Wyoming (p. 302). Otherwise, check at local ski shops and ask at the headquarters of national forests and state parks. **Jackson Hole Mountain Resort** (p. 303) decided in 1999 to allow skiers to ski beyond the boundaries of areas it grooms and patrols—as long as they sign waivers. Check with other ski resorts about out-of-bounds forest areas that might be accessible for backcountry adventures.

BIKING Mountain biking is a fast-growing sport. Some folks take it easy, pedaling their way to wild country on smooth, easy-grade paths; others are looking for a fast ride down on bumpy, steep trails. Bring your own bike or rent from a local bike shop that will likely assist you in finding the best spots to ride. Bicycling on roads is also popular, but there are limitations: While automobile traffic on many roads is light, there isn't much room because most of the roads have skimpy shoulders—Yellowstone roads are among the worst. Nor are drivers in this region terribly respectful of bicyclists. So be watchful, research your routes so you can keep to the wider roads, and always wear that helmet.

BOATING & SAILING Serious sailors are not likely to live full time at this altitude; even weekend sailors would be wise to look elsewhere for their kind of fun. But if you insist on trying, you'll find a few sails spread on the bigger lakes of these mountains. You can take a pretty big boat on pretty big **Flathead Lake** (p. 99), **Jackson Lake** (p. 327), or even **Yellowstone Lake** (p. 278) if you're careful about the weather. Smaller boats, such as Hobie Cats, in some ways better suit the sudden, swirling winds typical of these mountains.

Powerboating is another matter; if you've got a motor, pack a lunch and head for any of the many lakes that dot Montana and Wyoming's landscape. **Canyon Ferry** (p. 138) is a popular Montana water-skiing spot, and you'll see Wyoming powerboats cruising **Boysen Reservoir** (p. 356) or **Flaming Gorge** (p. 405). Just make sure to check around locally regarding access if you're uncertain about it. All types of boats are available locally for rent.

CAMPING These states are ideal places to camp; in fact, at some destinations, such as Yellowstone National Park, it's practically mandatory. Most communities have at least one commercial campground, and campsites are available at all the national parks and national recreation areas, though these campsites are often crowded in summer. Those who can stand being without hot showers for a day or so can often find free or very reasonable campsites just outside the national parks, in national forests, and on Bureau of Land Management lands. Other good bets are found at state parks.

A growing number of state and federal campgrounds allow visitors to reserve sites, although, more often than not, only in the busy summer months. Throughout Montana and Wyoming, there are more than 100 national forest campgrounds and numerous state parks that will also reserve sites. To check on campground reservation possibilities for many National Park Service, U.S. Forest Service, and other federal properties, contact the new **Recreation.gov** (www.recreation.gov; ℭ **800/444-6777** or 518/885-3639). For information on Montana state parks, get in touch with **Montana Fish, Wildlife, and Parks,** 1420 E. 6th Ave., P.O. Box 200701, Helena, MT 59620 (www.fwp.mt.gov; ℭ **406/444-2535**). In Wyoming, contact **Wyoming State Parks and Historic Sites,** 2301 Central Ave., Cheyenne, WY 82001 (http://wyoparks.state.wy.us; ℭ **307/777-6323**).

CROSS-COUNTRY SKIING If you don't plan to pound down the backcountry powder on Telemark skis, but you want to get out in the snow, cross-country skiing can be practiced on any relatively flat, open meadow or plain where there's snow on the ground, or along old roads in the region's forests. Scores of guest ranches now groom trails for both track and skate skiing, and almost every ski resort in the region has a trail. If you don't want to pay to ski, **Forest Service logging roads** are typically used for cross-country trails. Many golf courses are also regularly groomed for track skiing; some are even lighted for night skiing. The best place to cross-country ski in Montana is **West Yellowstone** (p. 254); in Wyoming, try the **Jackson Hole** area and **Grand Teton National Park** (see chapter 12).

DOWNHILL SKIING There are over 20 downhill ski areas in Montana and Wyoming, scattered amid the towering mountain ranges found, for the most part, in the western parts of both states. Breathtaking summit vistas are standard fare. Usually operating from late November to mid-April, and with comparatively shorter lift lines and less expensive lift tickets than most other ski areas in the country, Montana and Wyoming ski resorts are great values for the ski enthusiast. Don't fret if you're not skiing black-diamond runs; all ski resorts have acres of beginner and intermediate trails, and seasoned instructors provide lessons at extremely affordable prices. More and more often, you'll find Telemark skiers honing their skills on packed resort slopes. The best skiing in Montana can be found at **Big Sky Resort** (p. 216), near Bozeman, which is the biggest ski area in Montana, with runs for all abilities. West of Glacier National Park, **Whitefish Mountain Resort** (p. 121) prides itself on a family atmosphere. In Wyoming, the Jackson Hole area wins hands down, with the **Jackson Hole Mountain Resort, Snow King,** and **Grand Targhee** ski hills just a short drive apart (see chapter 12).

DUDE RANCHES The dude ranch is the fabled Western experience come to life: daily rides by horseback, cowboy coffee beneath an expansive blue sky, campfire sing-alongs, and homemade food served in rustic lodges. Accommodations are usually in a comfortable cabin or lodge. You need not have any riding experience before your visit; ranch hands are trained to assist even the greenest of greenhorns. For additional information on dude ranches in both Montana and Wyoming, as well as other Western states, contact the **Dude Ranchers' Association,** P.O. Box 2307, Cody, WY 82414 (www.duderanch.org; ℭ **866/399-2339**). Some of the best dude ranches can be found in the **Paradise and Gallatin valleys** in southwest Montana, and in the **Sheridan** area and the **Wapiti Valley** west of Cody in Wyoming.

4

THE ACTIVE VACATION PLANNER

Outdoor Activities A to Z

Are You a Dude or a Guest?

A century ago, it was common courtesy in the West for ranches to feed and lodge travelers who stopped by on their treks across the great empty spaces. Gradually, it became acceptable to accept a few dollars from guests, and by the 1920s, a ranch visit was a full-fledged vacation.

When you make your ranch reservations, it's wise to know the difference between a "dude ranch" and a "guest ranch." A dude ranch typically requires a 1-week minimum stay, and they give you the entire package: riding, fishing, trips to the rodeo, and family-style meals. Dude ranchers look down their noses at "guest" ranches, which will take guests staying just 1 night and charge extra for activities such as riding.

FISHING   Montana and Wyoming have long been known for world-class fly-fishing, their streams and creeks teeming with native trout—rainbow, brook, brown, mackinaw, golden, and cutthroat—as well as kokanee salmon, yellow perch, largemouth bass, and northern pike. Warm-water species include sauger, channel catfish, and smallmouth bass. Best places to fish in Montana: the **Madison River** or any one of the world-class, blue-ribbon streams in the southwest part of the state. In Wyoming, head for the waters of the **North Platte River** (p. 402) near Saratoga and the Miracle Mile, the **Snake River** (p. 304), **Flaming Gorge Reservoir** (p. 405), or the high lakes of the **Wind River Indian Reservation** (p. 363).

GOLF   Golfers may be pleasantly surprised at the number of exceptional courses found in both states, particularly in Bigfork and Anaconda, Montana. Summer's long days make this a perfect place to play a round, especially when you take into consideration that average daily temperatures and humidity are much lower here than at destinations in Florida. Reserve tee times well in advance. Best Montana courses: the **Old Works** (p. 149) in Anaconda and **Eagle Bend** (p. 102) in Whitefish. In Wyoming: the **Jackson Hole Golf and Tennis Club** (p. 305) and **Teton Pines** (p. 305) in Jackson, and the **Powder Horn** (p. 368) in Sheridan.

HIKING   Hiking gives you the added bonus of moderate to strenuous cardiovascular exercise while you're seeing the sights. Remember, though, that these are the mountains, and the elevation you gain over the course of the hike is a much better indication of how difficult the hike will be than the actual distance traveled. Be sure to wear comfortable hiking shoes that have been broken in, and if you plan on hiking in prime grizzly country, be sure to carry bear mace and check with rangers for what to do in case you actually see a bear. Best place to take a hike in Montana: **Glacier National Park** (chapter 5). In Wyoming: the **Wind River Mountains** (p. 361) or **Bighorn Mountains** (p. 367).

MOUNTAINEERING: ROCK & ICE CLIMBING   The Northern Rockies provide superb opportunities for climbers to experience the year-round beauty of Montana and Wyoming's mountains, whether you seek a daylong rock climb during the height of summer in Montana's Beartooths or a technical climb up one of the faces of the Tetons. Ice climbing is becoming a hot ticket in the dead of winter, when many of the world's finest climbers congregate in Cody, Wyoming, for unforgettable winter mountaineering. Not for the faint of heart, the sport is highly technical and requires extreme fitness and stamina. Best place to climb in Montana: **Granite Peak,** the state's highest (p. 227). In Wyoming: **Grand Teton National Park** (chapter 12) or **Wild Iris,** south of Lander (p. 362).

SNOWBOARDING   Experienced snowboarders will find Montana and Wyoming ski areas to be snowboard-friendly. If you're really into riding, ask around at local ski shops for winter backcountry options or summer snowboarding—**Glacier Park's Logan Pass** (chapter 5) is a popular destination. Best place in Montana: **Whitefish Mountain Resort** (p. 121).

SNOWMOBILING   With more than 3,000 miles of trails in Montana and 1,300 in Wyoming, snowmobilers have a vast winter playground to explore. Though rental shops are plentiful, machines are in high demand, so you're wise to make a reservation well in advance. Though snowmobiling doesn't require an extreme level of physical fitness, you have to be able to adequately handle the snowmobile and be well versed in safety measures because avalanches are common in the areas some of these trails traverse. Best bets for snowmobiling in Montana: **West Yellowstone** (chapter 11) and the **Seeley Lake Valley** (p. 109). In Wyoming: **Yellowstone National Park** (chapter 11) and the surrounding national forest lands.

WATERSPORTS: CANOEING, KAYAKING & RAFTING   Paddlers have a wealth of choices here. Montana is particularly rich in rivers worth floating: the Flathead, the Blackfoot, the Madison, the Clarks Fork near Missoula, the Dearborn, the Yellowstone, and even the big old Missouri. In Wyoming, there is less variety, but you'll find some fine stretches of river on the Snake, the Platte, the Hoback, and the Clarks Fork through Sunlight Basin. If you choose white-water rafting, leave the driving to someone else (that is, sign up with an outfitter that will provide an experienced person to pilot

fishing LICENSES

Both Montana and Wyoming require fishing licenses, which are available from most sporting goods stores, outfitters, or tackle shops. Yellowstone National Park requires an additional fishing permit (see chapter 11), and American Indian tribes located in the two states have special regulations and may require permits for fishing in their waters.

In Montana, all nonresident anglers 15 and older are required to buy fishing licenses. Those 14 and under do not need a fishing license as long as they are with an adult who has a valid fishing license. A license for the period of March through the following February is $60. A consecutive 2-day license is $15. In addition to fishing licenses, however, nonresident anglers of all ages must also possess conservation licenses, which cost $10 each. For information, contact the **Montana Department of Fish, Wildlife, and Parks,** 1420 E. 6th Ave., Helena, MT 59620 (www.mt.gov; ✆ **406/444-2535**).

You'll also need a Wyoming state fishing license if you plan to fish that state's waters. An adult nonresident license costs $14 per day and $92 for the season. Youth fees (ages 14–18) are $3 per day and $15 for the season. A $13 Conservation Stamp is also required for all licenses except the 1-day variety. No license is required for kids 13 and under, as long as they are accompanied by an adult who has a valid fishing license. You'll also have to check creel limits, which vary from year to year and place to place. Information is available from the **Wyoming Game and Fish Department** (http://gf.state.wy.us; ✆ **307/777-4600**).

your craft), though you may be asked to paddle. The smaller rivers have no dams to regulate flows, which means kayakers seeking fast, scary runs should come during runoff in June, while canoeists wanting to relax and bird-watch can easily handle the upper Snake or Flathead late in the summer. For thrills, try the **Yellowstone River** at Gardiner, Montana (p. 259), and the **Snake River** in Wyoming (p. 306).

THE ACTIVE VACATION PLANNER

GLACIER NATIONAL PARK

Majestic and wild, this vast preserve overwhelms visitors, beckoning with stunning mountain peaks (many covered year-round with glaciers), verdant mountain trails that cry out for hikers, and the sheer diversity of its plant and animal life. The unofficial mascot in these parts is the grizzly, a refugee from the high plains.

Named to describe the slow-moving glaciers that carved awe-inspiring valleys throughout this expanse of over 1 million acres, Glacier National Park exists because of the efforts of George Bird Grinnell, a 19th-century magazine publisher and cofounder of the Audubon Society. Following a pattern established with Yellowstone and Grand Teton, Grinnell lobbied for a national park to be set aside in the St. Mary region of Montana, and in May 1910, his efforts were rewarded. Just over 20 years later, it became, with its northern neighbor Waterton Lakes National Park in Canada, Glacier-Waterton International Peace Park—a gesture of good-will and friendship between the governments of two countries.

Today you'll see nature in a state of constant change: The glaciers are receding, the result of global warming. Storms and avalanches have periodically ravaged Going-to-the-Sun Road, the curving, scenic 50-mile road that bisects the park. And fires in 2003 charred more than 100,000 acres of forest, about 10% of the park's total acreage.

If your time is limited, simply drive along Going-to-the-Sun Road, viewing the dramatic mountain scenery. Visitors with more time will find diversions for both families and hard-core adventurers; while some hiking trails are suitable for tykes, many more will challenge those determined to conquer and scale the park's tallest peaks. Glacier's lakes, streams, ponds, and waterfalls are equally engaging. Travelers board cruise boats to explore the history of the area; recreational types can fish, row, and kayak.

However, to truly experience Glacier requires slightly more effort, interest, and spunk than a drive through. Abandon the pavement for even the shortest and easiest hiking trail, and you'll discover a window into Glacier's soul.

ESSENTIALS
Getting There

The closest cities to the park with airline service are **Kalispell,** 29 miles southwest of the park; **Missoula,** 150 miles south; and **Great Falls,** 150 miles southeast.

Glacier Park International Airport, north of Kalispell at 4170 U.S. 2 (www. glacierairport.com; ℂ 406/257-5994), is serviced by Allegiant, United, Delta, and Alaska Airlines. Great Falls International Airport (www.gtfairport.com; ℂ 406/727-3404) and Missoula International Airport (www.flymissoula.com; ℂ 406/728-4381) are served by these same airlines.

If you're driving, you can reach the park from U.S. highways 2 and 89. Rental cars are available in Kalispell, Great Falls, Missoula, Whitefish, East Glacier, and West Glacier. Avis, Budget, Hertz, and National all have counters at the above airports.

Amtrak's Empire Builder (www.amtrak.com; ℂ 800/872-7245), a Chicago–Seattle round-trip route, stops at West Glacier and Essex year-round and East Glacier from May to October.

Access/Entry Points

There are six paved entrances that provide vehicular access to Glacier National Park, but if you are traveling by car, you will most likely use West Glacier and St. Mary. These entrances are located at either end of Going-to-the-Sun Road, with West Glacier on the southwest side and St. Mary on the east. From the park's western boundary, you can enter at Polebridge to access Bowman and Kintla lakes, or enter at the Camas Creek entrance and take the Camas Road to Going-to-the-Sun. The Many Glacier entrance provides access to the Many Glacier Hotel, Swiftcurrent Lake, and many backcountry trails. The Two Medicine entrance is only about 4 miles north of East Glacier on Mont. 49, with auto access to Lower Two Medicine Lake and Two Medicine Lake, as well as hiking trails to Pumpelly Pillar and over Pitamakan Pass. Four miles south of the Two Medicine entrance, the East Glacier entrance is for hikers only—it is not a paved entry point for cars—for access to trails at the southeastern corner of the park. Essex is strictly a backcountry access point to Scalplock Mountain and backcountry campgrounds along Ole Creek and Park Creek. Cut Bank is a dirt road, closed in winter, with backcountry access only to Triple Divide Pass and the northern route to Pitamakan Pass.

Caution: Entrance to the park is severely restricted during winter months when the alpine section of Going-to-the-Sun Road is closed. See "Driving in the Park," below, for more information.

Visitor Centers

To receive information about the park before your trip, contact the superintendent, Glacier National Park, West Glacier, MT 59936 (www.nps.gov/glac; ℂ 406/888-7800; TDD 406/888-7806). The Glacier Natural History Association offers numerous publications; for a catalog, contact the association at 12544 U.S. 2 E., P.O. Box 310, West Glacier, MT 59936 (www.glacierassociation.org; ℂ 406/888-5756).

For up-to-date information on park activities once you arrive, check in at visitor centers located at Apgar, Logan Pass, and St. Mary. Apgar is open from May through October (and weekends during the winter), Logan Pass from mid-June to late September, and St. Mary from mid-June to mid-October. Park information may also be obtained from the Many Glacier Ranger Station or park headquarters in West Glacier.

Fees & Backcountry Permits

Rangers are on duty at most entry points to collect fees, issue backcountry permits, and answer questions.

Glacier National Park

Apgar Village Lodge **1**	Many Glacier Hotel **7**	Swiftcurrent
Cut Bank Ranger Station **10**	Rising Sun Motor Inn	Motor Inn **10**
Glacier Park Lodge **11**	& Cabins **8**	Village Inn at Agpar **1**
Granite Park Chalet **6**	St. Mary Lodge & Resort **9**	Weeping Wall **5**
Lake McDonald Lodge **2**	St. Mary Visitor Center **9**	
Logan Pass Visitor Center **4**	Sperry Chalet **3**	

FEES Admission to the park for up to 7 days costs $25 per vehicle, $20 per motor-cycle, or $12 per person for those on foot, bicycles, and motorcycles ($10 in winter). An annual park pass costs $35 and allows unlimited entry to Glacier National Park for an entire year. America the Beautiful passes are also honored (see chapter 16). Camping fees are $10 to $23 per night at the park's drive-in campgrounds. A separate entrance fee is charged for visitors to Waterton Lakes National Park (see "A Side Trip to Waterton Lakes National Park," p. 76).

In 2007, the park launched a **free shuttle bus service.** Visitors simply park their car at the Apgar Transit Center on the west side or the St. Mary Visitor Center and take the shuttle to about 20 stops throughout the park, most of them on Going-to-the-Sun Road. The shuttles connecting the two lots run from about 7am to 7pm. For detailed information on the schedule and routes, visit the park's website or check the insert in the free *Glacier Visitor Guide,* available at all entrances and visitor centers. Additionally, Glacier's signature red **"Jammer"** buses are once more in service. For more information, see "Organized Tours & Activities," below.

BACKCOUNTRY PERMITS You must obtain backcountry permits in person from the Apgar Backcountry Office, St. Mary Visitor Center, or the ranger stations at Many Glacier, Polebridge, or Two Medicine. Visitors who enter Glacier's backcountry from the Canadian side (at Goat Haunt or Belly River in Waterton) can get a permit at the Waterton Visitor Reception Centre, but only with a credit card. **During summer months,** permits may be obtained no earlier than 24 hours before your visit. There is a charge of $5 per person, per night for backcountry camping. Permits are good only for the prearranged dates and locations, with no more than 3 nights allowed at a single campground. Campsites are limited. A single site has a maximum occupancy of four persons. Stoves are required in most areas (no open fires), and pets are not permitted on the trails.

To ensure a spot and avoid the hassle, order a backcountry trip planner from **Backcountry Reservations** (✆ **406/888-7800**), GNP, West Glacier, MT 59936; sending them your dates with a check for $30 between June 15 and October 31 will reserve your spot in the wilderness.

Due to lower demand in winter, camping permits are available up to 7 days in advance. A few rules do take effect beginning each November 20, so double-check at visitor centers for details.

Special Regulations & Warnings

Park regulations here are similar to those in other lands administered by the National Park Service and generally prohibit damaging the natural resources. Pets must be leashed and are not allowed on trails. In addition, RVs and other vehicles longer than 21 feet or wider than 8 feet are prohibited on the 24-mile stretch of Going-to-the-Sun Road between Avalanche Campground and Sun Point on St. Mary Lake. Snowmobiling is prohibited in the park.

When to Go

Glacier is magnificent at any time of the year, but it's not always easily accessible. Most visitors come in **summer,** and it seems as if they all drive along Going-to-the-Sun Road. The 52-mile two-lane road is generally open from early June to September or October, depending upon the weather and road-construction projects. During summer months, sunrise is around 5am and sunset at nearly 10pm, so there's plenty of time for exploring. The shoulder seasons of **spring and fall** see budding wildflowers and seasonal colors, but these sights can be viewed only from the park's outer boundaries and on a limited stretch of the scenic highway.

5

Essentials

GLACIER NATIONAL PARK

In **winter,** road access is limited. Going-to-the-Sun Road is plowed to Lake McDonald Lodge on the west side of the park, 12 miles from West Glacier, but the remainder of the road is closed. Snowmobiles are prohibited. All unplowed roads become trails for snowshoers and cross-country skiers, who rave about the vast wonderland. Guided trips are a great way to experience the park in winter, or you can strap on a pair of snowshoes and explore it on your own. A popular skiing expedition is to go as far up Going-to-the-Sun Road as your energy permits. Wintertime temperatures average between 15°F (–9°C) and 30°F (–1°C), but extreme lows can reach 30°F below zero (–34°C). Average winter snowfall is almost 12 feet, and it snows about half of the days from November through February.

Avoiding the Crowds

If you want to avoid the crowds, travel in the off season before mid-June, when the park begins to fill, and after Labor Day, when families traveling with youngsters have returned home (Aug is the busiest month). If that's not possible, consider the following: As most people congregate close to the major hotels, find a trail head that is equidistant from two major points and head for the woods. Also, the entrances not on Going-to-the-Sun Road (such as Polebridge, Camas Creek, and Cut Bank) do not attract nearly as many people.

Going-to-the-Sun Road is nearly always jammed in the summer daylight hours. If you can, make the trip before 8:30am. In July and August, the parking lot at Logan Pass Visitor Center fills to capacity. Try to visit early in the day or late in the afternoon, and make use of the park's free shuttle.

 Especially for Kids

The park has a *Junior Ranger Newspaper* available at the visitor centers that lists seven activities to introduce youngsters between 6 and 12 years of age to the habitats in Glacier. Kids must complete five activities to receive a badge. Children are also welcome on most interpretive activities but should be accompanied by an adult.

Ranger Programs

When you enter the park, you'll be given a copy of the *Glacier Visitor Guide,* which lists the naturalist-led programs offered at Glacier and Waterton. There are a wide variety of hikes, boat trips, campfire programs, family programs, and other activities. Many are accessible for those in wheelchairs. There are also presentations given by members of local tribes. Most programs are free, although those including boat trips may have a small fee associated. For schedules, check the park newspapers or call ✆ **406/888-7800.**

Tips for Travelers with Physical Disabilities

Information on facilities and services for those with disabilities is available at any of the visitor centers in the park, although most of the park's developed areas are fully accessible by wheelchair. The park's "Accessibility in Glacier National Park" publication describes current programs and services for visitors with disabilities.

FOR THE VISUALLY IMPAIRED Audiotapes, park brochure recordings, and tactile nature items are available at the Apgar, Logan Pass, and St. Mary visitor centers. All other park facilities—restrooms, restaurants, campgrounds, gift shops—are accessible with some assistance.

FOR THE MOBILITY IMPAIRED   The Trail of the Cedars, Oberlin Bend Trail, Goat Lick Overlook Trail, and Running Eagle Falls Nature Trail are wheelchair accessible. A bike path at Apgar also provides magnificent views of the park's scenery. Wheelchairs are available for loan at the Apgar, Logan Pass, and St. Mary visitor centers, and almost all of the park's facilities are fully accessible.

FOR THE HEARING IMPAIRED   Interpreters provide written synopses of most slide and campfire programs. If you plan on hiking, note that five of the park's self-guided nature trails have printed brochures available at the trail head. General park information is available by TDD at ✆ **406/888-7806.** An interpreter may be available to sign at ranger programs. Call ✆ **406/888-7930** 2 weeks in advance to make arrangements.

Organized Tours & Activities

Glacier Park Boat Co., P.O. Box 5262, Kalispell, MT 59903 (www.glacierparkboats. com; ✆ **406/257-2426**), offers **narrated boat tours ★★** from Lake McDonald, St. Mary, Two Medicine, and Many Glacier from mid-June to mid-September. These "scenicruises" combine the comfort of an hour-long lake cruise with a short hike or picnic to create an unforgettable experience. Spectacular views of Lake McDonald sunsets, the awe-inspiring Grinnell Glacier, and the panoramic rugged cliffs ringing St. Mary Lake are just a few of the possible photo opportunities you may have while enjoying a cruise. The boats typically depart every hour, usually seven times each day (although schedules are subject to change in late season or if the weather is inclement). Ticket prices top out at $23. Check ahead for a complete listing of prices and departure times. The concessionaire also offers charter service for larger groups and guided hikes in the park.

Unique **"Jammer" coach tours** run along Going-to-the-Sun Road and north to Waterton. Thirty-three classic bright-red coaches from the 1930s, long identified with Glacier, are in service after a restoration project that began in 1999. Drivers provide insightful commentary about the park and its history, and you don't have to worry about how close you may be to the edge of the often-precipitous road! Full-day rates are about $80 for adults and about $40 for children, with tours departing from both sides of the park. Half-day tours (for about half the price) are also available. For schedules, contact **Glacier Park, Inc.** (www.glacierparkinc.com; ✆ **406/892-2525**).

Historical-cultural **25-passenger motorcoach tours** of the Going-to-the-Sun Road conducted by knowledgeable guides from the Blackfeet Nation originate from East Glacier, Browning, and St. Mary. Rates start at $40 for a 4-hour trip. Contact **Suntours** (www.glaciersuntours.com; ✆ **800/786-9220**).

Vehicle Regulations

Park regulations prohibit vehicles more than 21 feet long or 8 feet wide on the 24-mile stretch of Going-to-the-Sun Road between Avalanche Campground and Sun Point on St. Mary Lake. If you are traveling in a vehicle exceeding the 21-foot limit, park it at one of the parking areas located at Avalanche Campground and Sun Point and let someone else do the driving (see "Traveling Through the Park Without a Car," p. 56).

5

Glacier Guides, P.O. Box 330, West Glacier, MT 59936 (www.glacierguides. com; 𝄞 **800/521-7238** or 406/387-5555), organizes backpacking trips into the Glacier National Park backcountry. These include a 3-day "taste" of the park for about $500 per person and 5 days in the wilderness for about $850 per person. The company has been the exclusive backpacking guide service in the park since 1983.

SPECIAL ACTIVITIES

Scenic helicopter tours of Glacier are offered by **Glacier Heli Tours** (www.glacier helitours.com; 𝄞 **800/879-9310**) and **Kruger Helicopters** (www.krugerhelicopters. com; 𝄞 **800/220-6565**). Prices start at about $115 per person for four people for a half-hour trip.

The **Glacier Institute,** 137 Main St. (P.O. Box 1887), Kalispell, MT 59903 (www.glacierinstitute.org; 𝄞 **406/755-1211**), conducts summer field classes that examine the park's cultural and natural resources. These 1- to 4-day courses include instruction, transportation, park fees, and college credit. Highly skilled instructors bring an intimate knowledge of the region and subject matter to each course. The classroom is Glacier National Park and other areas in northwest Montana; courses cover wildflowers, grizzlies, weather systems, and nature photography. Prices range from $65 to $500 per course. (The pricier classes include lodging.) Contact the institute or visit the website for a listing of the current catalog.

DRIVING IN THE PARK

Because of the massive piles of rock that surround a visitor, it is impossible to drive through Glacier without drawing comparisons to Grand Teton. But at Teton, unless you hit the hiking trails, the mountains keep their distance. In Glacier, as you drive, the mountain peaks envelop you.

Going-to-the-Sun Road

If you plan only a day or two in Glacier, the most important thing to do is to drive **Going-to-the-Sun Road,** the 50-mile road that bisects the park between West Glacier and St. Mary. Points of interest are clearly marked along this road and correspond to the park brochure "Points of Interest Along the Going-to-the-Sun Road," which is available at visitor centers.

The road gains more than 3,400 feet in 32 miles and is very narrow in places. Visitors with a fear of heights should take a van tour or shuttle. Because of the road's narrowness, oversize vehicles and trailers must use U.S. 2.

As you begin the drive from the West Glacier entrance, you'll pass the largest of the 653 lakes in Glacier—**Lake McDonald.** Numerous turnouts along the way present opportunities to photograph the panoramic views of the lake with its mountainous backdrop. You can see **Sacred Dancing Cascade** and **Johns Lake** after an easy half-mile hike from the roadside through a hemlock and red cedar forest. The trail head for this hike is 2 miles north of the Lake McDonald Lodge along Going-to-the-Sun Road.

The **Trail of the Cedars** is a short, handicap-accessible boardwalk trail through terrain thickly carpeted in vibrant, verdant hues. This is also the beginning of the Avalanche Lake Trail, a 2.1-mile hike (one-way) to the foot of Avalanche Lake, one of the most popular day hikes in the park. The trail head is about 5½ miles north of Lake McDonald Lodge, just past the Avalanche Creek Campground.

Almost exactly halfway along Going-to-the-Sun is the overlook for Heaven's Peak, the massive snow-covered mountain to the south that you've just driven around. This is also the jumping-off point for the **Loop Trail,** which can take you to the Granite Park Chalet. Just 2 miles farther is the **Bird Woman Falls Overlook.** Bird Woman Falls drops in a wondrous bounty of water from a hanging valley above the road. Next along the road is the oft-photographed **Weeping Wall,** which is a wall of rock with water pouring forth.

At the 32-mile mark from West Glacier is **Logan Pass,** one of the park's busiest areas and the starting point for the hike to **Hidden Lake,** likely the park's most popular trail. There's a visitor center here atop the Continental Divide, with a bookstore and a small display about the wildlife, flora, and geology of the area.

As you continue the drive downhill, you'll reach the turnout for **Jackson Glacier,** the most easily recognizable glacier in the entire park; followed by **Sunrift Gorge** and **Sun Point,** which are accessible via two short trails rife with wildlife.

Note: A 20-year construction plan on Going-to-the-Sun Road will cause delays in the summer and early closures in some years.

WINTER ROAD CONDITIONS   Going-to-the-Sun Road is open seasonally, usually from early June to September or October, depending on weather conditions and road construction projects. Call the park at *©* **406/888-7800** to find out when tentative openings and closings are scheduled. During the winter, you may drive Going-to-the-Sun Road for 10 miles from West Glacier along Lake McDonald to the road closure; this is a popular destination for cross-country skiers.

Other Drives

ALONG THE LOWER EDGE OF THE PARK   Circumnavigating the lower half of the park is easily accomplished in 1 long day. After a leisurely breakfast in West Glacier, you'll be in East Glacier in plenty of time for lunch at the Glacier Park Lodge (see "Where to Stay," in this chapter) and at St. Mary or Many Glacier for dinner.

The road between West Glacier and East Glacier—approximately 57 miles—is a well-paved, two-lane affair that winds circuitously around the western and southern borders of the park and follows the Middle Fork of the Flathead River. As you descend to the valley floor, you'll travel through beautiful, privately owned Montana ranch and farm land. Shortly after entering the valley, look to the north and admire the park's massive peaks. The **Goat Lick** parking lot, on U.S. 2 just east of Essex, gets you off the beaten path and provides a view down into a canyon carved by the Flathead River. If you have time, take the short hike down to the stream.

Beyond East Glacier, as you head east on Mont. 49 and north toward Two Medicine, you'll notice that the earth appears to fall off. The contrast is inescapable—mountains tower in the west, but to the east the Hi-Line begins, sporting a horizon that extends so far and so flat as to seemingly lend credence and legitimacy to the Flat Earth Society. But round a bend on Two Medicine Road, and suddenly you'll find yourself faced with three mountains (Appistocki Peak, Mount Henry, and Bison Mountain) bare of vegetation but as red as their Southwestern counterparts. Ten miles later, continuing the route northward on U.S. 89, you'll come across a wide panorama of mountain peaks, valleys, ridges, and forested mountains that truly characterizes Glacier's personality. Conclude the bottom half of your long loop by wending downward from these high elevations to the village of St. Mary.

TO POLEBRIDGE There are two ways to see the park's western boundary and to access the lesser-visited Polebridge area in the north: One is slow and bumpy, the other slightly faster and more comfortable. The **North Fork Road** from Columbia Falls takes about an hour to negotiate. It's a sometimes-paved, mostly gravel-and-pothole stretch that follows the North Fork of the Flathead River. Not much is there besides water and scenery, but the area around Polebridge is a popular place to take in Montana's natural beauty without modern-day distractions like telephones and TVs.

The **Inside North Fork Road,** just north of Apgar, also runs to Polebridge. However, it's totally unpaved, takes an hour longer, and is much harder on the driver, passenger, and equipment. Take the faster route instead, and spend that extra hour relaxing on a riverbank.

OUTDOOR PURSUITS

BIKING Opportunities for biking in the park are limited, since bikes may be ridden only on established roads, on bike routes, or in parking areas, and are not allowed on trails. Restrictions apply to the most hazardous portions of Going-to-the-Sun Road during peak travel times from around mid-June to Labor Day; call ahead to find out when the road will be closed to bikers. During low-visibility periods caused by fog or darkness, a white front light and a back red reflector are required. A few shared campsites for bicyclists are held until 9pm at Apgar, Sprague Creek, Fish Creek, Many Glacier, Two Medicine, Avalanche, Rising Sun, and St. Mary campgrounds for $5 per person. Before Logan Pass opens and after it closes, Going-to-the-Sun Road is also popular with bikers, provided it is not knee-deep with snow.

From June 15 to Labor Day, bikes are prohibited between Apgar and Sprague Creek campgrounds between 11am and 4pm in both directions, and from Logan Creek to Logan Pass (eastbound) between 11am and 4pm. It takes about 3 hours and 45 minutes to ride from Sprague Creek to Logan Pass.

BOATING You can take advantage of some of those 653 lakes with a boat rental at various spots. Motor size is restricted to 10 horsepower on most lakes, and a detailed list of other regulations is available at park headquarters and staffed ranger stations. Park rangers may inspect or board any boat to determine regulation compliance. At Apgar and Lake McDonald, you will find kayaks, canoes, rowboats, and motorboats. Only human-powered or electric motorboats are available at Two Medicine. At Many Glacier, you can rent kayaks, canoes, and rowboats. For details, call **Glacier Park Boat Co.** at © **406/257-2426,** or browse **www.glacierparkboats.com**.

FISHING Glacier's streams and lakes are habitat for whitefish, kokanee salmon, arctic grayling, and five kinds of trout. Try the North Fork of the Flathead to fish for cutthroat and bull trout, and any of the park's three larger lakes (Bowman, St. Mary, and McDonald) for rainbow, brook trout, and whitefish. State of Montana fishing licenses are generally not required within the park's boundaries, although you will need one on the North Fork and Middle Fork of the Flathead River. Also remember that since the eastern boundary of the park abuts the Blackfeet Indian Reservation, you may find yourself fishing in their territorial waters. To avoid a problem, purchase a $10 use permit from businesses in the gateway towns; the permit covers fishing, hiking, and biking in the reservation. Fishing outside the park in Montana waters requires a state license; check in at a local fishing shop to make certain you're within the law. For equipment or sage advice, or to schedule a guided foray ($325 for two people for a half-day), contact **Glacier Anglers** (www.glacierraftco.com; ✆ **800/235-6781**), at the Glacier Outdoor Center in West Glacier.

HIKING Glacier is a park that is best seen on foot. Its 1,600 square miles have more than 150 trails, totaling more than 750 miles. You can hike more than 100 miles along the Continental Divide alone.

Trail maps are available at outdoor stores in Whitefish and Kalispell, as well as at the major visitor centers and ranger stations in the park. Before striking off into the wilderness, however, check with the nearest ranger station to determine the accessibility of your destination, trail conditions, and recent bear sightings. Also note that the trail maps don't show elevation changes or many terrain features beyond lakes and the tallest peaks. If you plan to do any extensive hiking, it is best to purchase a U.S. Geological Survey (USGS) topographic map, available at outdoor sporting goods stores and the USGS website (www.usgs.gov).

The Park Service asks you to stay on trails to keep from eroding the fragile components of the park. Also, don't traverse snowbanks, especially the steeper ones. You should have proper footwear and rain gear, enough food, and, most important, enough water, before approaching any trail head. A can of pepper spray can also come in handy when you're in grizzly habitat. If you're planning to hike in Canada, be sure the bear spray is USEPA approved.

See "Exploring the Backcountry," below, for information on some of the longer hiking trails and further information on backpacking.

If you plan an extended hike, let someone know your route and your expected time of return. Take a flashlight in case you take longer than you think. Carry a map, rain gear, and extra clothing, and drink lots of water.

Among the park's shorter and easier trails is the **Trail of the Cedars Nature Trail** (.75 miles round-trip; access is across from the Avalanche Campground Ranger Station), an easy, level trail that's wheelchair accessible. It has interpretive signs along the way. The **Hidden Lake Overlook Nature Trail** ★ (3 miles round-trip; accessed from the Logan Pass Visitor Center) is an easy-to-moderate interpretative trail that climbs 460 feet to an overlook of scenic Hidden Lake. It's a popular trail, but by hiking past the overlook to the lake, you'll avoid some of the crowds (and you might even see a mountain goat).

The **Loop** (8 miles round-trip; access is on Going-to-the-Sun Rd., about halfway btw. Avalanche Campground and Logan Pass Visitor Center) offers a moderate hike that climbs to Granite Park Chalet and back. Many people use it as a continuation of the Highline Trail, but this is the section to do if you're not quite so adventurous (the Highline Trail is almost 8 miles long; see "Exploring the Backcountry," below). If you want to spend the night in the chalet, contact **Belton Chalets** for reservations (✆ **888/345-2649**). See the descriptions of the chalets in "Camping," below.

The **Sun Point Nature Trail** (1.4 miles round-trip; access is 9 miles west of St. Mary at the Sun Point parking area) is an easy walk on gentle slopes that presents commanding views of Baring Falls. Among the favorite hikes (because of its beautiful scenery) is the **Iceberg Lake Trail** ★★ (9.6 miles round-trip; access at a trail head in a cabin area east of the Swiftcurrent Coffee Shop and Campstore). This is a moderate hike that traverses flower-filled meadows to a jewel of a high lake backed against a mountain wall. Even in summer, there may be snow on the ground and ice floating in the lake. Look for mountain goats or bighorn sheep on the cliffs above. And as in many of the park's backcountry areas, keep an eye out for the grizzlies.

Swiftcurrent Nature Trail ★ (2.5 miles round-trip; access is at a picnic area half a mile west of the hotel turnoff) is a fun and easy hike along the lake shore, through the woods, and near a marsh, so you may see deer and birds—keep an eye out for blue grouse. If you have time, continue on the trail as it circles Lake Josephine, another easy hike, adding 2.8 miles to the trip. Dramatic Mount Gould towers above the far end of Lake Josephine, and midsummer wildflowers can be spectacular. A longer, 10-mile round-trip trail to Grinnell Glacier, the park's largest, is also accessed from this area.

The very easy **Running Eagle Falls Trail** (.6 mile round-trip; access is 1 mile west of the Two Medicine entrance) winds through a heavily forested area to a large, noisy waterfall. The popular **Twin Falls Trail** (7.6 miles round-trip; accessed from Two Medicine Campground) is an easy hike to scenic Twin Falls. Hikers can walk the entire distance to Twin Falls on a clearly identified trail, or boat across Two Medicine Lake to the foot of the trail head and hike the last mile. The **St. Mary Falls Trail** ★★ (1.6 miles round-trip; accessed from Jackson Glacier Overlook) is a fairly easy walk that takes you to rushing falls of the St. Mary River. The roar of the cascade is prodigious and satisfying.

HORSEBACK RIDING   You can bring your own horses and pack animals into the park, but restrictions apply to private stock. A free brochure detailing regulations regarding horseback riding is available from the National Park Service.

Swan Mountain Outfitters (www.swanmountainoutfitters.com; ℂ **406/888-5121** or 732-4203) provides horseback riding at Lake McDonald, Apgar Village, and Many Glacier. The company offers hour-long ($40) to full-day rides ($160) into the nearby wilderness.

MOUNTAIN CLIMBING   The peaks of Glacier National Park rarely exceed 10,000 feet in elevation, but don't let the surveyors' measurements fool you. Glacier has some incredibly difficult climbs, and you must inquire at the ranger station regarding climbing conditions and closures. In general, the peaks are unsuitable, except for experienced climbers or those traveling with experienced guides; park administration does not recommend climbing because of the unstable nature of the rock.

RAFTING & FLOAT TRIPS   Though the waters in the park don't lend themselves to white-water rafting, the boundary forks of the Flathead River are some of the best in the northwest corner of the state. For just taking it easy and floating along in the summer sun, the North Fork of the Flathead River stretching from Polebridge to Columbia Falls and into Flathead Lake is ideal. The same may be said for the Middle Fork of the Flathead, which forms the southern border of the park.

For white-water voyagers, the North Fork of the Flathead River (classes II and III) and the Middle Fork (class III) are the best bets. Flow rates change dramatically as snow melts or storms move through the area; inquire at any ranger station for details and conditions.

The Middle Fork is a little more severe and isn't the sort of river you enjoy with an umbrella drink in hand. The names of certain stretches of the Middle Fork inspire terror in and of themselves (the Narrows, Jaws, Bonecrusher), and to assuage that terror, several outfitters offer expert, sanctioned guides.

Established in 1975, **Glacier Raft Company,** P.O. Box 210, West Glacier, MT 59936 (www.glacierraftco.com; ℂ **800/235-6781** or 406/888-5454), is Montana's oldest raft company. Offerings include half-day trips ($48 adult, $36 child), full-day excursions ($82 adult, $59 child), 2-day trips ($335 adult, $275 child), and 3-day outings ($455 adult, $370 child). Prices include all necessary equipment and food. The company also offers scenic trips, inflatable-kayak rentals, and other services. Other local raft guides include **Great Northern Whitewater,** 12127 U.S. 2 East (P.O. Box 270), West Glacier, MT 59936 (www.greatnorthernresort.com; ℂ **800/735-7897** or 406/387-5340); **Montana Raft Company,** P.O. Box 330, West Glacier, MT 59936 (www.glacierguides.com; ℂ **800/521-7238** or 406/387-5555); and **Wild River Adventures,** P.O. Box 272, West Glacier, MT 59936 (www.riverwild.com; ℂ **800/700-7056** or 406/387-9453).

SNOWSHOEING & CROSS-COUNTRY SKIING Glacier has numerous cross-country trails, the most popular of which is the **Upper Lake McDonald Trail** to the Avalanche picnic area. This 8-mile trail offers a relatively flat route up Going-to-the-Sun Road, with views of McDonald Creek and the mountains looming above the McDonald Valley. For the advanced skier, the same area presents a more intense 11-mile trip that heads northwest in a roundabout fashion to the Apgar Lookout. The most popular trail on the east side is the **Autumn Creek Trail,** near Marias Pass. However, avalanche paths cross this area, so inquire about current weather conditions. Yet another popular spot is in Essex along the southern boundary of the park at the Izaak Walton Inn (p. 64). In West Glacier, Glacier Outdoor Center (ℂ **800/235-6781**) rents snowshoes and cross-country ski packages for $15 and $18 per day, respectively; guided trips are also available.

Bear Warning!

To remind you yet again: Glacier is grizzly country. Make noise when you hike, don't cook near where you sleep, and don't sleep in the same clothes you cooked in.

EXPLORING THE BACKCOUNTRY

Glacier offers every kind of backcountry experience, from short day hikes to 2-week treks. Consider your fitness level, backcountry experience, and interests, and then get some advice from one of Glacier's rangers. They can provide you with area maps, but a topographical map is highly recommended if you're going for more than a short walk.

Backcountry campgrounds have maps at the entrance to show you the location of each campsite, the pit toilet, food-preparation areas, and, perhaps most important, food-storage areas. If you fish while camping, it's recommended you exercise catch-and-release, so as to avoid attracting wildlife in search of food. If you eat the catch, be certain to puncture the air bladder and throw the entrails into deep water at least 200 feet from the nearest campsite or trail. You will need a permit to camp; see "Backcountry Permits," earlier in this chapter.

GUIDED BACKCOUNTRY TRIPS Glacier Guides (www.glacierguides.com; ℂ **800/521-7238** or 406/387-5555) is the exclusive hiking guide service in the park. From May through September, it organizes custom trips and offers weekly departures for 3- and 6-day trips. Prices vary, but you can figure on spending $150 to $170 per person, per day. It also rents equipment and can arrange trips where you stay indoors at night.

Notable Backcountry Hiking Trails

BOWMAN LAKE TRAIL ★★   This especially scenic trail (14 miles to Brown Pass) is similar to the Kintla Lake hike in difficulty and, like the Kintla Trail, passes a lake on the north. After a hike through the foliage, the trail climbs out of reach of anyone in bad shape, then ascends 2,000 feet in less than 3 miles to join the Kintla Trail at Brown Pass. A left turn takes you to Kintla Lake (23 miles to the Kintla Lake trail head), a right takes you to Goat Haunt at the foot of Waterton Lake (9 miles). To reach the Bowman Lake trail head, go about ¼ mile north of Polebridge, then turn east (right) up the Bowman Creek road. The road ends after 6 miles at the southeast end of Bowman Lake, from which the trails radiate.

DAWSOM-PITAMAKAN LOOP ★   This difficult 19-mile loop traverses Rising Wolf Mountain; at 9,513 feet, it's the area's most prominent feature. There are backcountry campsites at Old Man Lake and at No Name Lake. The trail offers splendid panoramas of the park's interior and of many alpine lakes. You'll encounter lots of steep ups and downs: The elevation change is 2,400 feet. The trail head is at Two Medicine Campground.

THE HIGHLINE TRAIL   This easy-to-moderate 12-mile round-trip hike, which gains only 200 feet in elevation, begins at the Logan Pass Visitor Center and skirts the Garden Wall at elevations of more than 6,000 feet to Granite Park Chalet. Keep an eye on your watch to be certain you'll have enough time for the return hike to Logan Pass. You can continue on from the chalet to "the Loop," the aptly named section of Going-to-the-Sun Road where the trail actually terminates (an additional 3.2 miles), although to make sure you can get back to your car by nightfall, you'll need to plan for a shuttle.

KINTLA LAKE TO UPPER KINTLA LAKE TRAIL   This 24-mile round-trip hike skirts the north shore of Kintla Lake above Polebridge for about 7 miles before climbing a couple of hundred feet. This stretch of the hike is a breeze. However, once you hit Kintla Creek, you may want to reconsider going any farther. With 12 miles under your belt at this point, climbing 3,000 feet may not seem like a great idea. The trail, once it breaks into the clear, offers views of several peaks, including Kinnerly Peak to the south of Upper Kintla Lake. The trail head is located 14 miles north of Polebridge after a drive along a gravel road, at the western tip of Kintla Lake.

PIEGAN PASS TO MANY GLACIER   If you're looking for a longer, tougher hike from Logan Pass, try this one. You pick up the trail at Siyeh Bend, about 3 miles on the east side of Logan Pass Visitor Center. It's a 13-mile walk up over Piegan Pass, past Grinnell Glacier and Grinnell Lake to Josephine and Swiftcurrent lakes before reaching Many Glacier Lodge. There are many long, steep stretches, going both up and down.

QUARTZ LAKE TRAIL   Accessed from the Bowman Creek trail head, the entire loop is 12 miles, running up and over an 1,800-foot ridge and then dropping down to the south end of Lower Quartz Lake. From there, it's a level 3-mile hike to the west end of Quartz Lake, then it's 6 miles back over the ridge farther north (and higher up) before dropping back to Bowman Creek. An interesting aspect of this trail is evidence of the Red Bench Fire of 1988, which took a chunk out of the North Fork area.

CAMPING

Inside the Park

Stop at any ranger station for information on closures and availability, and consult the chart below for information on amenities and fees.

There are a variety of camping opportunities here. Campgrounds accessible by paved roads include **Apgar,** near the West Glacier entrance; **Avalanche Creek,** just up from the head of Lake McDonald; **Fish Creek,** on the west side of Lake McDonald; **Many Glacier,** in the northeast part of the park; **Rising Sun,** on the north side of St. Mary Lake; **St. Mary,** on the east side of the park; and **Two Medicine,** in the southeast part of the park near East Glacier. **Sprague Creek,** near the West Glacier entrance, offers a paved road but does not allow towed vehicles. There are also five campgrounds accessed by narrow dirt roads. Though utility connections are not provided at these sites, fireplaces, picnic tables, washrooms (with sinks and flush toilets), and cold running water are located at each campground. Campsites are available on a first-come, first-served basis, payable by cash or check, except for Fish Creek and St. Mary campgrounds, where sites can be reserved through the **National Park Service Reservation System** (www.recreation.gov; *©* **877/444-6777**).

A few shared sites for bicyclists are held until 9pm at Apgar, Sprague Creek, Avalanche, Fish Creek, Many Glacier, Two Medicine, Rising Sun, and St. Mary campgrounds for $5 per person.

The Campgrounds

Despite its proximity to the center of the hotel and motel activity, the **Many Glacier Campground ★★** is a densely wooded campground with more privacy than you'd expect. The campground has adequate space for small motor homes and pickup truck/camper combinations, but space for vehicles pulling trailers is limited. It is a veritable mecca for tent campers. The **Avalanche Campground** is situated in the bottom of the valley near Lake McDonald in a heavily treed area immediately adjacent to the river. The **Two Medicine Campground ★★** lies in the shadow of the mountains near three lakes and a stream. It is a forested area that has beautiful sites, plenty of shade, and opportunities to wet a fishing line. Two Medicine is a little out of the way of the typical Glacier traveler and may offer a little more solitude. The **Cut Bank Campground** road is not paved, but it's only 5 miles from the pavement to the ranger station and campground. The road and campground are best suited to recreational vehicles 21 feet or shorter.

Chalets

Two of the park's most popular destinations, Granite Park and Sperry Chalets—National Historic Landmarks built by the Great Northern Railway between 1912 and 1914—are subjects of an extensive restoration project. The **Granite Park Chalet** is a hiker's shelter only. Guests must bring their own food, water, cooking and eating utensils, flashlights, and sleeping bags. Rooms and beds are provided, as are a kitchen with a cooking stove and dining room. No public water is available, so bring your own. The chalet has 12 rooms (all single bunk beds) and sleeps two to six per room. Cost is about $148 per night for two people, and the kitchen facilities are shared. To get there, you'll have to walk about 3 miles from the Loop trail head off Going-to-the-Sun Road, or about 6 miles on the trail to Swiftcurrent Pass at the end of Many Glacier Road from the east side.

Amenities for Each Campground in Glacier National Park

Campground	# of Sites	Fee	Max RV Length	Flush Toilets	Disposal Stations	Boat Access
Apgar	192	$10–$20	25 sites; up to 40'	Yes	Yes	Yes
Avalanche	86	$20	50 sites; up to 26'	Yes	Yes	No
Bowman Lake*	48	$10–$15	RVs not recommended	No	No	Yes
Cut Bank*	14	$10	RVs not recommended	No	No	No
Fish Creek	178	$23	3 sites; up to 35'	Yes	Yes	No
Kintla Lake*	14	$10–$15	RVs not recommended	No	No	Yes
Logging Creek*	7	$10	RVs not recommended	No	No	No
Many Glacier	109	$10–$20	13 sites; up to 35'	Yes	Yes	Yes
Quartz Creek*	7	$10	RVs not recommended	No	No	No
Rising Sun	83	$20	3 sites; up to 30'	Yes	Yes	Yes
St. Mary	148	$10–$23	25 sites; up to 35'	Yes	Yes	No
Sprague Creek	25	$20	No towed trailers	Yes	Yes	No
Two Medicine	99	$10–$20	13 sites; up to 32'	Yes	Yes	Yes

Campgrounds are accessible only by narrow dirt roads. RVs are not recommended.

The **Sperry Chalet** is an impressive stone structure in the center of the wilderness. Here you'll get a room (with linens) plus three meals daily, but no bathing facilities except cold water and modern composting toilets located outside. Rates are $305 for two people and include all meals. To get there, walk about 4 miles from the road, up Snyder Creek, then toward Gunsight Mountain. The trail head is opposite the entrance to Lake McDonald Lodge on the lower portion of Going-to-the-Sun Road.

For reservations at either chalet, contact **Belton Chalets** (www.graniteparkchalet.com or www.sperrychalet.com; 📞 888/345-2649).

CAMPGROUNDS IN GATEWAY COMMUNITIES
During the busy season, it's recommended that you reserve a spot at these campsites at least 1 month in advance.

IN EAST GLACIER
Y Lazy R   Situated just off U.S. 2, this campground is conveniently located within walking distance of East Glacier and is the closest to town and its laundry facilities. Plan to arrive early if you want to snag one of the few sites with trees. The Y Lazy R is a great value and an ideal place to plant the RV before heading off to explore the region.

Washington St. and U.S. 2, P.O. Box 13, East Glacier, MT 59434. 📞 **406/226-5505.** 10 tent sites, 20 RV sites. $16 tent; $18 water and electric only; $20 full hookup.

IN ST. MARY
Johnson's of St. Mary   From April through September (depending on the weather), this is where you want to camp if you can get a spot. The campground has showers, an 18-hole miniature golf course, and a laundromat. Campers both inside the park and out come to St. Mary for a good meal at **Johnson's Cafe,** which serves homemade American grub family style (with serving dishes placed on each table) at breakfast, lunch, and dinner daily. Lunches include burgers, sandwiches, and homemade soup (most items $3–$8), and dinners usually include your choice of entrees such as fried chicken, trout, sirloin or T-bone steak, or pork chops, with prices from $10 to $18.

St. Mary, MT 59417. www.johnsonsofstmary.com. 📞 **406/732-4207.** 50 tent sites, 82 RV sites. $25 tent; $36–$39 RV with electricity and water only; $44 full hookup; $29 RV, no hookup. MC, V.

IN WEST GLACIER

Glacier Campground   One mile west of West Glacier on U.S. 2 is the closest campground outside the park. Set in a forested area overgrown with evergreens, it's a quiet, comfortable place to retreat under the shade of the trees, especially on hot days. Most sites have water and electric hookups; the rest are perfect for tent camping. Five rather primitive cabins are also available, with modest furnishings, electricity, beds with mattresses, and use of the campground's bathhouse. Recreational facilities include volleyball, horseshoes, and a basketball court; also on the premises are an excellent cafe, a laundromat, and a small general store.

P.O. Box 477, 12070 U.S. 2, West Glacier, MT 59936. www.glaciercampground.com. © **888/387-5689** or 406/387-5689. 80 tent sites, 80 RV sites, 5 cabins. $19 tent; $22–$29 RV; $35–$55 cabin. AE, DISC, MC, V.

Lake Five Resort   Located 3 miles west of West Glacier and less than a mile from U.S. 2, this cabin and campground arrangement is an alternative to potentially crowded park campgrounds but is still close to the park. The resort is on a 235-acre lake. Seven of the nine cabins are on the lakefront; all are equipped with bathrooms and showers.

540 Belton Stage Rd. (P.O. Box 338), West Glacier, MT 59936. www.lakefiveresort.com. © **406/387-5601.** 9 cabins, 6 tepee lodges; 31 sites with electricity and water, 14 sites with electricity, water, and sewer hookup. $75–$225 cabin; $60 tepee; $40–$45 site. DISC, MC, V.

Backcountry Camping

If it's the backcountry you're bent on seeing, Glacier has more than 65 backcountry campgrounds. Fortunately, many are at lower elevation, so inexperienced backpackers have an opportunity to take advantage of them. For an accurate depiction of your itinerary's difficulty and advice on what may be needed, check with rangers in the area you contemplate visiting. The primary source of danger is bears. Backcountry permits are available at ranger stations, and reservations can be made in person up to 24 hours in advance. There are separate fees for advance reservations ($30) and backcountry camping ($5 per person, per night). See "Backcountry Permits," p. 56.

WHERE TO STAY

Television reception is limited in the Glacier National Park area, so if TV is important to you, check not only that the lodging facility has in-room TVs, but also what channels they get.

Inside the Park

With only one exception, Glacier Park, Inc. (GPI), operates the hostelries in Glacier National Park. Lake McDonald Lodge, Glacier Park Lodge, and Many Glacier Hotel are first-tier properties that have been popular destinations since early in the 20th century. Swiftcurrent Motor Inn is typical of the casual motel-style properties at the other end of the spectrum, providing decent but undistinguished accommodations for less money. Although the lodges have a considerable charm, they don't have spas, air-conditioning, or in-room televisions.

Reserve well in advance. August dates may fill before the spring thaw. For more information on the following properties or to make a reservation, contact **Glacier Park, Inc.,** P.O. Box 2025, Columbia Falls, MT 59912 (www.glacierparkinc.com; © **406/892-2525;** fax 406/892-1375). GPI does not accept pets at any of its facilities.

Apgar Village Lodge The Apgar Village Lodge, on the south end of Lake McDonald, is one of two lodgings in Apgar Village. A less expensive alternative to the park's GPI-managed properties, the log-and-frame cabins have a rustic charm but lack in-room amenities. Many units have multiple bedrooms.

Apgar Village, P.O. Box 410, West Glacier, MT 59936. www.westglacier.com. ℰ **406/888-5484.** 28 cabins, 20 motel rooms. $95–$135 double; $120–$300 cabin. Some units have a 2-night minimum. AE, DISC, MC, V. Closed Oct to mid-May. *In room:* TV, kitchens, no phone.

Glacier Park Lodge ★★ Just outside the southeast entrance at East Glacier, this is the park's flagship inn, an imposing timbered lodge that stands as a stately tribute to the Great Northern Railroad and its early attempts to lure tourists to Glacier. The immaculate lawn and ever-blooming wildflowers frame the grounds in colors that rival the mountain backdrop. The interior features massive Douglas fir pillars, some 40 inches in diameter and 40 feet tall. In fact, stand in the middle of the lobby and look up— beams carved from massive trees are the structural supports for the entire building. Skylights, wrought-iron chandeliers, and a desk hewn from a 36-inch-diameter log add to the Old West flavor. Rooms are nicely furnished, but showers and sinks are very small. There's an immaculately groomed executive-style 9-hole golf course, and some evenings, members of the Blackfeet tribe recount their history and culture around the fireplace.

East Glacier, MT 59434. www.glacierparkinc.com. ℰ **406/892-2525.** Fax 406/892-1375. 154 units. $140–$224 double; $359–$449 suite. AE, DISC, MC, V. Closed Oct to late May. **Amenities:** Restaurant; lounge; 9-hole golf course; outdoor pool.

Lake McDonald Lodge, Cabins & Inn ★★ This place feels like a genuine mountain lodge. Although the two-story building doesn't have the same towering ceilings and open spaces as other park hotels, its wood construction lends it a warm, cozy feel. Lodge rooms, located on the second and third floor (there's no elevator), are pleasantly decorated and have a historic feel. Motel units are simply well-maintained motel rooms. The well-preserved cottages are in multiunit buildings in a wooded area. Situated on the shore of the park's largest lake, the lodge provides a marvelous central base for exploring the western part of the park. The lodge is a center for boating activity; scenic cruises depart daily, and canoe rentals are popular. The lodge houses a dining room, gift shop, and lounge; a coffee shop, post office, and sundries store are also on the grounds. The entire lodge is smoke-free.

Glacier National Park, MT 59936. www.glacierparkinc.com. ℰ **406/892-2525.** Fax 406/892-1375. 62 lodge and motel units, 38 cottage units. $173–$182 lodge room; $134–$141 motel unit; $122–$182 cottage. AE, DISC, MC, V. Closed late Sept to late May. **Amenities:** 2 restaurants; lounge; post office.

Many Glacier Hotel ★★★ Built in 1915 by the Great Northern Railway, this is the largest hotel in the park and our top choice for a place to stay. The alpine-style hotel may be the most-photographed building in the park. When you arrive at Many Glacier after driving along the park's interior road from Babb, it comes slowly into view, as picturesque as a Swiss chalet. In August, after the huckleberries ripen, you can almost count on seeing grizzly bears on the nearby mountains. Rooms, decorated in keeping with the hotel's historic roots, are in the main lodge overlooking the lobby or in the adjoining annex. We like the lakeside rooms, for their views of Swiftcurrent Lake; the smaller units without a view are less expensive. A dining room, coffee shop, gift shop, and lounge are in the hotel. In the evenings (Mon–Sat) starting in midsummer, David Walburn, a Montana singer/songwriter, entertains with his guitar, harmonica, and stories.

If the convenience of staying on Glacier's back porch is important to you, the places listed on the following pages are your best bets. See "Where to Stay" in the Whitefish, Kalispell, and Columbia Falls sections of chapter 6 for listings of places that might be more in line with your needs if the park is merely a 1- or 2-day part of your vacation.

Glacier National Park, MT 59936. www.glacierparkinc.com. © **406/892-2525.** Fax 406/892-1375. 216 units. $152–$236 double. AE, DISC, MC, V. Closed mid-Sept to early June. **Amenities:** Dining room; coffee shop; lounge.

Rising Sun Motor Inn & Cabins   Located 6½ miles from St. Mary, just off Going-to-the-Sun Road, the Rising Sun is a complex made up of a restaurant, a motor inn, cottages, stores, and a service station. The basic rooms are just that—uninspiring motel rooms that are completely adequate for a good night's rest in an excellent location for those who want to explore the eastern side of the park. The cottage rooms (half of a duplex) are more interesting but a bit on the rustic side. All units here are smoke-free.

Glacier National Park, MT 59936. www.glacierparkinc.com. © **406/892-2525.** Fax 406/892-1375. 63 units. $124–$141 double; $128 cottage. AE, DISC, MC, V. Closed mid-Sept to mid-June. **Amenities:** Restaurant.

Swiftcurrent Motor Inn ★ 🦌   The appeal here is for those satisfied with modest prices and decor—primarily active types interested in spending lots of time exploring the backcountry trails. Like Many Glacier, which is just up the street, the inn sits against a mountain backdrop in what is considered a hiker's paradise. Motel rooms have standard decor—functional, but nothing special. Built in 1933, the cabins are a bit more interesting, with one or two bedrooms and perhaps a bathroom (communal facilities are nearby). There's also a coffee shop and restaurant on the premises. All units are smoke-free.

Glacier National Park, MT 59936. www.glacierparkinc.com. © **406/892-2525.** Fax 406/892-1375. 88 units and cabins, some cabins without private bathroom. $124–$141 double in motor inn; $73–$94 double in cabin. AE, DISC, MC, V. Closed mid-Sept to mid-June. **Amenities:** Restaurant. *In room:* No phone.

Village Inn at Apgar   Not to be confused with Apgar Village Lodge (see above), the Village Inn at Apgar is the smallest of the properties GPI operates in Glacier. Located lakeside in Apgar Village, the inn is near the general store, cafes, and boat docks. The Village Inn is comfortably outfitted with modest furnishings, making it a cozy and convenient place. Rooms spread over two floors of the inn; 12 of them have kitchenettes. Second-level rooms have the same lake views as those downstairs, but they have less people traffic. Though there's no in-house dining, the restaurants of Lake McDonald and Apgar are all nearby. Close to the Apgar corral and the docks of Lake McDonald, not to mention a plethora of hiking trails, Apgar Village bustles with activity during the summer. The entire property is smoke-free.

Glacier National Park, MT 59936. www.glacierparkinc.com. © **406/892-2525.** Fax 406/892-1375. 36 units. $136–$236 double. AE, DISC, MC, V. Closed mid-Sept to early June. *In room:* Kitchenette (in some), no phone.

In Gateway Communities

EAST GLACIER

Backpacker's Inn   Low-cost, low-end sleeping accommodations for those willing to share bathroom facilities are what you get at this dorm-style hostel.

29 Dawson Ave. (P.O. Box 94), East Glacier, MT 59434. www.serranosmexican.com. © **406/226-9392.** 8 beds in 1 cabin, 2 private cabins. $12 per person in single-sex dorms; $30 for 1 person, $40 for 2 people in private cabin. AE, DISC, MC, V. Closed mid-Oct to Apr. *In room:* No phone.

Brownies Grocery and AYH Hostel 🛏   Reservations are recommended at this popular grocery store/hostel, which offers comfortable rooms at affordable prices. Dorm and family rooms are on the second floor of a rustic, older log building with several common rooms for guests to share, including a porch, kitchen, bathrooms, and laundry. Family rooms sleep two to six. A bakery and deli (with Internet access) are in the grocery, there's a restaurant next door, and tent sites ($10) are available out back.

1020 Mont. 49 (P.O. Box 229), East Glacier, MT 59434. www.brownieshostel.com. © **406/226-4426.** 10 units, all with shared bathroom, 1 family room, 2 bunk rooms. HI members $16 bunk, $31 double private room, $43 family room; nonmembers $19 bunk, $34 double private room, $46 family room. DISC, MC, V. Closed Oct to mid-May, depending on the weather. *In room:* No phone.

Jacobson's Cottages   In a nicely wooded area, these quaint cottages are small but comfortable. All have cable TV, and one has a kitchen. Entertainment and good food are nearby, and it's a 12-mile drive to the Two Medicine trail.

1204 Mont. 49 (P.O. Box 454), East Glacier, MT 59434. www.jacobsonscottages.com. © **406/226-4422.** Fax 406/226-4425. 12 cottages. $67–$100 double. AE, DISC, MC, V. Closed Oct to mid-May. *In room:* TV, no phone.

ESSEX

Izaak Walton Inn ★★ 🛏   Built in 1939 by the Great Northern Railway, this historic Tudor lodge once served as living quarters for rail crews who serviced the railroad. Located just off U.S. 2 on the southern boundary of Glacier Park, the Izaak Walton is extremely popular with tourists from near and far, many of whom choose to travel by Amtrak train, which stops a mere 100 yards from the front door of the lodge. Both lodge rooms and the converted cabooses offer comfortable and attractive lodging, with wood-paneled walls and various Western touches. And who can pass up the opportunity to sleep in a caboose or the deluxe locomotive? During the winter, this inn is a popular jumping-off spot for cross-country skiers.

290 Izaak Walton Inn Rd., Essex, MT 59916. www.izaakwaltoninn.com. © **406/888-5700.** Fax 406/888-5200. 33 units, 4 caboose cottages, 1 locomotive lodging. $117–$168 double; $235–$255 suite; $230 cabins and caboose cabins; $299 locomotive lodging. 2-night minimum stay in cabins, cabooses, and locomotive. DISC, MC, V. **Amenities:** Restaurant; lounge; sauna; Wi-Fi (free). *In room:* Kitchenette, no phone.

POLEBRIDGE

North Fork Hostel and Square Peg Ranch 🛏   Ideal for the back-to-nature traveler, this lodge sits at the literal end of the road within a stone's throw of the North Fork of the Flathead River, right across the river from the park. Accommodations are ultrarustic, with a mountain-cabin feel—heat is from an old-fashioned woodstove. There are separate facilities for men and women, as well as couples' accommodations, washrooms with hot showers, and clean outhouses. There are also several small cabins suitable for families. Hostel guests should bring linens or sleeping bags (sheets are available for rent) and flashlights. The Ranch offers two rustic log homes, with decor similar to the hostel's, and a few bare-bones, summer-only tepees and campsites for $10 a night. The log homes have solar-heated showers, or guests can use the hostel showers. The hostel and cabins have kitchen facilities, and the former has a relaxing 6-foot-long claw-foot bathtub.

80 Beaver Dr., Polebridge, MT 59928. www.nfhostel.com. © 406/888-5241 or 406/253-4321. 7 bunks, 2 private rooms, 2 cabins, 2 log homes. $20 bunk; $50 cabin; $80 log home. 3-night minimum stay in log home. MC, V. Reservations required in winter. **Amenities:** Bicycle rentals; communal kitchen; Jacuzzi; kayak rentals; Wi-Fi (free). *In room:* No phone.

Polebridge Mercantile and Cabins 🐾 If you can make the trek up the gravelly North Fork Road, then give these bare-bones cabins a try. They don't have running water, let alone bedding—it's BYO sleeping bag at the Merc, which is also home to a fantastic bakery. Each cabin has a propane cooking stove and lights, and the views out over the west side of Glacier National Park make the price a steal, especially if you bring the kids. Polebridge is a happening spot in the summer, when all the river rats and seasonal residents converge for whopping good times and tall tales about running rapids and climbing peaks.

265 Polebridge Loop, Polebridge, MT 59928. www.polebridgemerc.com. © 406/888-5105. 4 cabins. $35–$45 cabin. DISC, MC, V. **Amenities:** Wi-Fi (free). *In room:* Kitchenette, no phone.

ST. MARY

St. Mary Lodge and Resort ★ At the St. Mary end of Going-to-the-Sun Road, this longstanding upscale lodge is newly managed by GPI. The main lodge and rooms are standard Montana fare, with tasteful ironwood furnishings. Lodging is in three different areas near the center of the complex; lodge and motel rooms are nicely done motel-style units that may have two single beds or a queen. The nicest units are the cabins; they boast living areas with dining tables and queen beds in a separate sleeping area, and some have kitchenettes. Most rooms have TVs and air-conditioning. The surrounding complex includes a market, several restaurants, and a lounge.

U.S. 89 and Going-to-the-Sun Rd., St. Mary, MT 59417. www.glacierparkinc.com. © 406/892-2525. Fax 406/892-1375. 115 units. $209–$309 double; $259–$359 cabin. AE, DISC, MC, V. Closed early Oct to late May. **Amenities:** 3 restaurants; 2 lounges; Wi-Fi (free). *In room:* A/C, TV, hair dryer, kitchenette.

WEST GLACIER

Belton Chalets and Lodge ★ A National Historic Landmark, this facility across from the railroad station has been completely restored to the elegance of an early-20th-century hotel. The rooms are small, simple, and old-fashioned. The bathrooms are also small. But the feel of the place is comfortable, and the staff is very friendly. Many of the rooms have private balconies looking out over the rounded timber foothills of Glacier National Park. There is a free shuttle for guests into the park; Wi-Fi is available in the lobby only.

12575 U.S. 2 (P.O. Box 6), West Glacier, MT 59936. www.beltonchalet.com. © 888/235-8665 or 406/888-5000. Fax 406/888-5005. 25 rooms, 2 cottages. Early June to early Sept $155–$325; early Sept to early June $99–$230. DISC, MC, V. **Amenities:** Restaurant (see "Where to Dine," below); lounge; Wi-Fi ($5 per 2 hr.). *In room:* No phone.

Glacier Outdoor Center ★ Built in three stages since 1996, the cabins at the Glacier Raft Company's HQ are delightful, functional, and tasteful, sporting trout, moose, and bears on everything from dishes to lampshades. Backing up to the

Flathead National Forest just west of the park entrance on U.S. 2, the cabins are well off the road, nestled around a grassy glen with a picnic area, volleyball court, and trout pond where casting clinics are held in the summer. Each cabin has a fully equipped kitchen, one to three bedrooms, and a private deck with a barbecue; the two-bedroom units can sleep up to 14 people. There is free Wi-Fi and a full rental/retail/guide operation in the main center, and in the winter, 15km of cross-country ski trails are groomed daily.

12400 U.S. 2, P.O. Box 210, West Glacier, MT 59936. www.glacierraftco.com. ✆ **800/235-6781** or 406/888-5454. 10 cabins. $275–$449 cabin; lower rates in winter. AE, DISC, MC, V. **Amenities:** Wi-Fi (free). *In room:* Kitchen.

Great Northern Chalets ★ This small, rafting-oriented resort near West Glacier offers log chalets that have balconies facing landscaped flower gardens and a pond, with mountain views in the distance. The largest chalet is a beautifully furnished two-story, two-bedroom unit with a full bathroom upstairs and a half-bathroom downstairs. Smaller chalets have one large bedroom upstairs, and a downstairs level with a full-size sleeper sofa and a kitchen with service for six. There's a pond used for fly-fishing instruction.

12127 U.S. 2, West Glacier, MT 59936. www.gnwhitewater.com. ✆ **800/735-7897** or 406/387-5340. Fax 406/387-9007. 5 units. $200–$300 double. DISC, MC, V. Closed late Oct to Mar. **Amenities:** Wi-Fi (free). *In room:* Kitchen.

Vista Motel Perched atop a hill at the west entrance to Glacier National Park, the Vista boasts tremendous views of the mountains. There's a small heated pool, free Wi-Fi in the lobby, and family-size rooms. Accommodations are not luxurious, but the modern motel rooms are clean and comfortable, the customer service is among the best in town, and it's cheaper than the competition.

12340 U.S. 2 E. (P.O. Box 90), West Glacier, MT 59936. www.glaciervistamotel.com. ✆ **877/888-5311** or 406/888-5311. 25 units, including 5 cabins. $95–$155 double. AE, DISC, MC, V. Closed Oct to mid-May. **Amenities:** Seasonal outdoor heated pool. *In room:* No phone.

West Glacier Motel 🗲 Formerly the River Bend Motel, this property has two locations. Half of the units are in West Glacier on Going-to-the-Sun Road, about 1 mile from the park entrance, and a second set of units is a quarter-mile away on forested grounds on a bluff above the river. This 1950s-style motel has small rooms and smaller bathrooms, but the prices are considerably lower than what you'll find in the park. The Western-style cabins are better suited for families; they come with two queen beds and fully equipped kitchens.

200 Going-to-the-Sun Rd., West Glacier, MT 59936. www.westglacier.com. ✆ **406/888-5662.** 32 units. Motel $90–$110 double; cabin $170–$270. AE, DISC, MC, V. Closed late Sept to mid-May. *In room:* Kitchen in cabins, no phone.

WHERE TO EAT

Inside the Park

Food options inside the park are primarily dining rooms operated by GPI. They're convenient, and you're almost always assured of friendly service from a staff of 20-something students from around the country. Breakfasts range from about $5 to $10, lunch entrees are $6 to $15, and most dinner entrees cost $10 to $30.

You'll find above-average food served at above-average prices in the dining rooms at the major properties. Glacier Park Lodge has the **Great Northern Dining Room,** which has Western decor and a menu of beef, barbecued ribs, fish, and chicken, plus a full breakfast buffet; and the **Empire Bar & Grill,** which offers a bar menu of sandwiches and appetizers.

At Lake McDonald Lodge, you'll find **Russell's Fireside Dining Room,** which has a hunting-lodge atmosphere with rough-hewn beams and hunting trophies; it specializes in American standards, including beef tenderloin, roast duckling, seared mountain trout, roast turkey, Alaskan salmon, and steaks. There's also a full breakfast buffet. Also at Lake McDonald Lodge is **Lucke's Lounge,** which serves a bar menu, and the family-oriented **Jammer Joe's Grill & Pizzeria.**

Many Glacier Hotel has the **Swiss Lounge and Interlaken Room,** with a bar menu, and **Heidi's,** a fast-food counter known for its huckleberry frozen yogurt. The dining rooms open with the park and close sometime in September, depending on the facility.

The alternatives include second-tier restaurants in proximity to the hotels, most of which are comparable to chain restaurants in both quality and price. The **Two Dog Flats Grill** at the Rising Sun Motor Inn serves "hearty American fare." The **Swiftcurrent Motor Inn Restaurant** offers lunch and dinner feature combinations of salads, sandwiches, pasta dishes, and create-your-own pizzas. At Apgar, you'll find a deli and a family dining arrangement.

In Gateway Communities

EAST GLACIER & VICINITY

Serrano's MEXICAN   Perhaps the area's best restaurant (although that's not saying too much), Serrano's is just off the highway at the center of town. Serrano's is one of the only eateries in town, so don't be surprised if you encounter masses of people in the dining room and on the outdoor deck at the height of summer. You can expect hearty portions of Mexican food, an ample selection of imported beers and microbrews, and a full bar featuring margaritas.

29 Dawson Ave., East Glacier. www.serranosmexican.com. ⓒ **406/226-9392.** AE, DISC, MC, V. Daily 5–10pm (until 9pm in early May and late Sept). Closed Oct–Apr.

Two Sisters Cafe ★ 📷 AMERICAN   This longstanding favorite serves perhaps the best pie in the area, with a fun atmosphere and a huge license plate collection to boot. Susan and Beth Higgins, the eponymous sisters who run the place, specialize in hearty American fare, with a menu that includes dishes like chili cheeseburgers, hand-battered chicken-fried steak, and big brownie sundaes. As for libations, there are margaritas, microbrews, and a nonalcoholic "lemonade of the day."

4 miles north of St. Mary on U.S. 89, Babb. www.twosistersofmontana.com. ⓒ **406/732-5535.** Most main courses $10–$20. MC, V. Daily June–Sept 11am–10pm. Closed Oct–May.

WEST GLACIER

The Belton Tap Room and Grille ★ AMERICAN   This restaurant, located in restored buildings that were once the Great Northern Railway Chalet, serves respectable food geared toward American tastes—steaks, buffalo, chicken, ribs, trout, and salmon, as well as some vegetarian selections. A large stone fireplace dominates the tap room, which serves several brands of locally brewed beer.

12575 U.S. 2, West Glacier. ⓒ **406/888-5000.** Main courses $13–$34. DISC, MC, V. Daily 5–10pm. Bar open at 3pm, with a limited menu.

Glacier Highland Restaurant AMERICAN   This may be the spot to satisfy your sweet tooth; a baker is on hand, so the pies are worth the stop, and the cinnamon rolls are immense. The Highland Burger is, by any standard, a great hunk of beef, and fresh trout is a dinner specialty.

U.S. 2, West Glacier. ✆ **406/888-5427.** Breakfast items $4–$9; main courses $7–$9 lunch, $8–$20 dinner, $14–$22 pizzas. AE, DISC, MC, V. Daily 7am–10pm, with some seasonal variations. Closed Nov–Apr.

Essential Services

EAST GLACIER   East Glacier has a gas station; a post office; several gift shops; a small market with a limited supply of fresh meats and produce, as well as beer and wine; and a modest supply of fishing and camping accessories.

WEST GLACIER   A gas station, general store, laundromat, photo shop, rafting companies, post office, gift shop, bar, and restaurant are located just outside the West Glacier entrance to the park.

ST. MARY   The **grocery store** (✆ **406/732-4431**) at St. Mary Lodge and Resort will never be confused with a metropolitan-area supermarket, but it's the closest thing you'll find in any of the park's gateway cities except Kalispell, which is 80 miles due west. Fresh produce, canned goods, and beverages, including beer and wine, are found here, but you can expect to pay tourist-town prices. There's also a post office.

A SIDE TRIP TO BROWNING & THE BLACKFEET INDIAN RESERVATION

127 miles NW of Great Falls; 69 miles E of West Glacier; 160 miles W of Havre

According to American Indian legend, the Blackfeet were named by white settlers because their moccasins were blackened with soot from fires or paint. Siksika, the "Blackfooted People," became their tribal name, and they eventually grew into four bands: the Blackfeet in Montana and the Kaina, Pikuni, and Siksika of Alberta, Canada. Today the Blackfeet maintain a humble existence near the beautiful lands that were once their own, with about half of the tribal enrollment of 14,000 living on the reservation near the east side of Glacier National Park. **Browning,** the tribal headquarters, is a gateway town to Glacier, but many visitors pass through quickly in anticipation of the end of the prairies and the beginning of the mountains.

Essentials

GETTING THERE   To reach Browning, follow U.S. 89 south from St. Mary for 32 miles, or take U.S. 2 east from East Glacier for 12 miles. Browning is about 69 miles east of West Glacier on U.S. 2.

SPECIAL EVENTS   Browning holds **North American Indian Days** in mid-July. This 4-day celebration draws visitors from across the region to view American Indian dance competitions, games, and sporting events at the Blackfeet Tribal Campgrounds, which are adjacent to the **Museum of the Plains Indian.**

What to See & Do

The **Museum of the Plains Indian,** U.S. 2 and 89 (© **406/338-2230**), is a fairly modest effort, but it has one of the best collections of Indian garb in the West. It also features some very good art by local Blackfeet artists. The museum is open daily May through September and weekdays year-round. Admission is $3 in summer and free in winter.

A large and eclectic art collection is on display in the **Blackfeet Heritage Center and Art Gallery** (www.blackfeetnationstore.com; © **406/338-5661**), at the intersection of U.S. highways 2 and 89. There are historic artifacts alongside contemporary works, as well as a nicely stocked gift shop. The place is open daily June through October. Admission is free.

A SIDE TRIP TO WATERTON LAKES NATIONAL PARK

190 miles NW of Great Falls; 342 miles S of Edmonton, Alberta, Canada

Waterton Lakes National Park and Glacier are, in many ways, one park separated by an international boundary. The terrain is much the same. But Canada is a foreign country, and you'll be pleasantly reminded of that in a visit to Waterton, where you can still get British high tea and a biscuit, if you're so inclined.

Waterton is where the Canadian mountains meet the vast rolling prairies, so there's an incredible variety of flowers and animals here. As you travel along the high ridge, you'll see meadows and boggy areas that are ideal habitats for moose; later you'll find yourself surrounded by lakes, as the Canadian Rockies fill the horizon. The area is also a haven for elk, mule deer, and bighorn sheep, and both grizzly and black bears are found in the park.

Compared with its counterparts in the Lower 48, Waterton is a tiny park; the total size is only 203 square miles. However, the park has great historical significance: Based on more than 200 identified archaeological sites, historians think that aborigines first populated the area 11,000 years ago.

The parks have been designated the Waterton/Glacier International Peace Park to commemorate the "long history of peace and friendship" between the United States and Canada. Waterton Lakes was made a national park in 1895, with Glacier being designated 15 years later. The joint international designation came in 1932, and in 1995, the peace park became a World Heritage Site.

Essentials

American and Canadian money is freely accepted in both Glacier and Waterton. Stores provide change in the local currency after adjusting for the current exchange-rate differential.

GETTING THERE   From the eastern entrance of Glacier National Park at St. Mary, drive north through Babb until you reach the intersection of Mont. 17—it's very well marked. Head northwest to the Canadian border, where Mont. 17 becomes Alberta 6 (remember that even U.S. citizens need passports to enter Canada). Head down into the valley until you reach the park entrance on your left.

FEES & BACKCOUNTRY PERMITS   Park entrance costs about C$8 per person, with a maximum of about C$20 per vehicle. Day hiking does not require a permit, but backcountry overnight trips do; permits cost about C$10 per person, per day. Permits may be obtained at the visitor center up to 24 hours in advance of your trip, or they may be reserved by calling ☎ **403/859-2224.**

VISITOR INFORMATION The Visitor Reception Centre is just inside the park, on the same road you used coming in (☎ **403/859-5133**). Online, visit www.parks canada.gc.ca/waterton.

Exploring the Park

Unlike most "park villages," Waterton Village actually is a village. As you drive along the perimeter of the lake headed for Waterton Village, you'll pass three large lakes, the habitat of bald eagles that often perch atop the snags of dead trees. The park bears a striking resemblance to Grand Teton National Park in Wyoming, in that its attractions spread across a narrow valley floor. But the valley is narrower and three-fourths of it is surrounded by peaks, so the overall effect is cozier but equally dramatic.

By most standards, it's also windier here—though locals say that they don't acknowledge the wind unless there are whitecaps in the restroom toilets at the Prince of Wales Hotel (see "Where to Stay," below). The Prince of Wales actually does sway noticeably in a high wind, although signs assure you that it is not a concern.

Hiking, biking, and boating on the lake are the most popular pastimes. Most of the 120 miles of trails are easily accessible from town. They range in difficulty from short strolls to steep treks for overnight backcountry enthusiasts.

BIKING All of Waterton's roads are open for bicycling, but because they are shared with automobiles, they are narrow and potentially hazardous. Waterton allows biking on some trails. Check at the visitor center to find out which ones.

HIKING The first thing a lot of people do at Waterton Park is hike the **Bear's Hump Trail ★★**. It is the park's most popular path—but not necessarily the easiest. The trail starts at the visitor center. Only about .75 mile long, it gains 700 feet in elevation from bottom to top. You'll be rewarded with a panoramic view of the park. The hike is called Bear's Hump because of the shape of the mountain, not because you're likely to run into bears—though, of course, you never know.

Right at the edge of Waterton Park, at **Cameron Falls,** Cambrian rocks are exposed from the period 600 million years ago when life exploded on earth. This is the oldest exposed formation in the Rocky Mountains. The falls are spectacular, too.

The 11-mile **Crypt Lake Trail ★★★** has been rated as one of Canada's best hikes—except for those prone to seasickness, since the trail head is reached by taking a 2-mile boat ride across Upper Waterton Lake. Contact **Waterton Shoreline Cruise Company** (www.watertoncruise.com; ☎ **403/859-2362**) for details regarding the boat shuttle. After that, the trail leads past Hellroaring Falls, Twin Falls, and Burnt Rock Falls before reaching Crypt Falls and a passage through a 60-foot rock tunnel. The elevation gain is 2,300 feet, but the hike is doable in 3 hours, one-way.

A second extended tour starts at the marina and heads south across the international boundary to **Goat Haunt,** Montana, an especially popular trip because of the sightings of bald eagles, bears, bighorn sheep, deer, and moose, as well as numerous unusual geologic formations.

The **International Peace Park Hike** is a free guided trip held on Saturdays from the end of June to the end of August. Participants meet at the Bertha trail head at 10am and spend the day on an 8.5-mile trail that follows Upper Waterton Lake. At the end of the trail, hikers return via boat to the main dock.

There is a wonderful nature trail in **Red Rock Canyon,** a short, easy trek through time—.7 mile, 65 million years—to when the shallow sea that once lay here exposed and then oxidized mudstone rock to the color of a merlot. The rocks are banded with white slashes—portions that didn't oxidize because they were not exposed to the air from the receding and returning sea. The Red Rock Canyon Road is also an area of fairly frequent bear sightings.

Where to Stay

Although the Prince of Wales Hotel is clearly the flagship in these woods, a worth-while alternative is the **Waterton Lakes Lodge Resort** (www.watertonlakeslodge. com; ✆ **888/985-6343** or 403/859-2150), with a great location in the heart of Waterton Village. The lodge offers lake and mountain views, and some rooms have fireplaces, whirlpool tubs, and kitchenettes. Other facilities include a health-center spa and indoor pool. Basic lodge doubles start at C$185 in summer.

The Prince of Wales Hotel ★★   The Prince of Wales compares with the finest park hostelries in Montana and Wyoming. Built in 1927 by the Great Northern Rail-way, the hotel boasts soaring roofs, gables, and balconies that convey the appearance of a giant alpine chalet. Rooms, though small, have aged well, with dark-stained, high-paneled wainscoting and heavily upholstered chairs. Bathrooms have European-style tubs with wraparound curtains; one look at the washbasins, and you'd surmise that guests were Lilliputian size when the hotel was first constructed.

The lobby, like those in many of the old railroad hotels, is wood, wood, and more wood—in this case, accented by tufted furniture and carpeting. Two-story-high windows overlook the lake and village, minutes away by footpath. If you don't spend the night at the Prince of Wales, stop in for a traditional **British high tea,** served daily from 2 to 5pm.

Waterton Lakes National Park, AB T0K 2M0. www.glacierparkinc.com. ✆ **403/236-3400** or 406/892-2525 in winter. Fax 403/859-2630. 87 units. C$194–C$299 double; C$599–$799 suite. AE, DISC, MC, V. Closed mid-Sept to early June. **Amenities:** Restaurant; lounge; gift shop.

CAMPING

At the west end of the village is **Townsite Campground ★,** a Parks Canada–oper-ated facility with 235 sites that's an especially popular jumping-off spot for campers headed into the park's backcountry. Prices range from roughly C$16 to C$38; half of the sites have electricity and sewage disposal. Also available on the premises are kitchen shelters, washrooms, and shower facilities. The site perches right on the lake, so views are excellent and trails await evening strollers.

There are also a number of designated **wilderness campgrounds** with dry toilets and surface water, some of which have shelters.

Where to Eat

All of the village's restaurants and retail outlets are within a 4-block area around Waterton Avenue (which the locals call Main St.). So despite the fact that many buildings aren't numbered, you'll have no problem finding places to eat or shop.

The **Royal Stewart Dining Room,** in the lobby of the Prince of Wales Hotel (✆ **403/859-2231**), serves Continental and English fare at breakfast, lunch, and dinner. At Waterton Lakes Lodge Resort, the casual **Vimy's Ridge Lounge and Grill** (✆ **403/859-2150**) serves three meals a day in a room with spectacular views.

MISSOULA, THE FLATHEAD & THE NORTHWEST CORNER

T he northwest corner of Montana is the mythological Montana, the one you probably envisioned when you set out for the Big Sky. This is the country of snowcapped mountains and dense forests and crystal lakes. It's a land of barely explored wilderness and steel-toed lumberjacks, a land peopled with the ghosts of trappers, mountain men, and Blackfeet Indians.

It's also a booming recreational area. The geographic center of the region is Flathead Lake, which boasts the somewhat cumbersome distinction of being the "largest natural freshwater lake west of the Mississippi." The lake was gouged during the last glaciation about 12,000 years ago. It is very deep in places—386 feet out toward the middle—with 128 miles of shoreline, much of it taken up by vacation homes. Anglers will appreciate the fact that trophy trout, salmon, perch, and whitefish populate the lake's depths. And vacationers seeking a quiet getaway will be pleased by the fact that, despite the busy summer season on Flathead Lake, it doesn't feel crowded, and there are plenty of places to get out of earshot of everyone.

Besides the lake, the area from Whitefish to Missoula offers plenty of opportunities for hiking, biking, fishing, boating, golf, parasailing, and nearly every other outdoor activity known to man. In winter, you'll find fine alpine ski areas, excellent cross-country skiing, snowshoeing, snowboarding, and inner-tubing.

Also here is the nation's largest wilderness complex, the **Bob Marshall–Great Bear–Scapegoat Wilderness,** which includes some of the most rugged, beautiful, untrammeled country in the Lower 48 states. The magnificent Chinese Wall, a vast monolith on the spine of the Continental Divide, is a symbol of wilderness in Montana, as is the grizzly bear, the king of the wild even when humans venture in for a visit.

SCENIC DRIVES

Two major cross-country routes intersect in the northwest corner: U.S. 93, which runs north to south, and U.S. 2, which runs east to west. Mont. 200, one of the state's most scenic drives, bisects the lower section of the region.

U.S. 93 heads north from the Bitterroot Valley south of Missoula to the Canadian border. Much of the road slices beneath jagged peaks poking at the skyline. It's especially pretty early in the morning or early evening, when the light softens the rugged landscape. North of Missoula, in the Flathead Valley near St. Ignatius and the spectacular Mission Mountains, the valley opens. At **Polson,** you've reached the southern portion of Flathead Lake, which stretches 28 miles to the north. In some places, it is 8 miles wide. North of the lake are Kalispell, Whitefish, and Columbia Falls, gateway towns to nearby Glacier National Park. The last oasis in Montana is the border village of Eureka, just minutes south of the Canadian border.

MISSOULA ★

200 miles E of Spokane, Washington; 213 miles NE of Lewiston, Idaho; 339 miles W of Billings; 115 miles NW of Helena; 115 miles S of Kalispell

Missoula has been growing by leaps and bounds, and the reason is clear: The city is in a beautiful valley along the Clark Fork River, with a relatively mild climate more influenced by the Pacific Northwest than by the high Rockies. One could say the same about the local culture.

Partly because this is the home of the University of Montana, the crowds in Missoula's vibrant downtown are usually either young and Birkenstocked or grizzled and cowboy-booted. Also in the mix are many prominent Western writers who live in or near the city; the result is an intellectual and cultural outpost.

The great outdoors—be it fly-fishing on Rock Creek, skiing at Snowbowl, hiking in the Selway-Bitterroot or the Rattlesnake Wilderness, or cross-country skiing on Lolo Pass—is probably what most attracts these types to the area. The outdoors figures heavily in area politics as well, with a strong pro-environment sentiment among the populace.

Essentials

GETTING THERE **Alaska/Horizon, Allegiant, Delta,** and **United** all have flights into the **Missoula International Airport** (www.flymissoula.com; © **406/ 728-4381**), northwest of downtown off U.S. 93.

I-90 leads into Missoula from the west (Washington State and Idaho) and the east (Billings and Bozeman). From Salt Lake City, I-15 leads up through Idaho and intersects with I-90 at Butte. For information on **road conditions,** call © **800/226-7623** or **511** for road conditions statewide. Avalanche information can be obtained by calling the **West Central Montana Avalanche Center** (© **800/281-1030** or 406/549-4488).

The **bus terminal,** 1660 W. Broadway (© **406/549-2339**), is served by **Greyhound** (www.greyhound.com; © **800/231-2222**) for national travel, and **Rimrock Stages** (www.rimrocktrailways.com; © **800/255-7655**), which serves intrastate Montana travelers with daily transportation from Missoula to Whitefish.

VISITOR INFORMATION The **Missoula Convention and Visitors Bureau,** 101 E. Main St., Missoula, MT 59802 (www.missoulacvb.org; © **800/526-3465** or

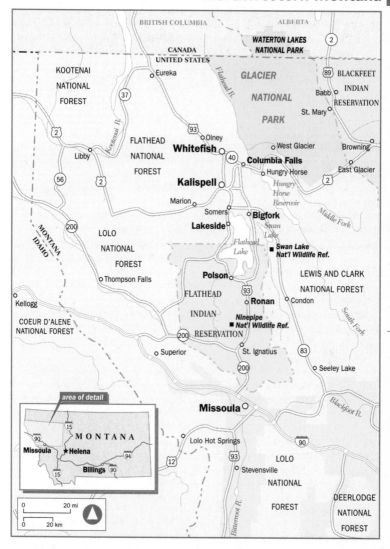

406/532-3250), has brochures, city maps, and area maps for outdoor activities, shopping, dining, and tours for most of northwestern Montana.

GETTING AROUND Alamo (© **800/462-5266** or 406/543-0926), **Avis** (© **800/331-1212** or 406/549-4711), **Budget** (© **800/527-0700** or 406/543-7001), **Enterprise** (© **888/305-8051** or 406/721-2484), **Hertz** (© **800/654-3131** or 406/549-9511), and **National** (© **800/227-7368** or 406/543-3131) maintain counters at the airport; or try **Rent-a-Wreck,** 1905 W. Broadway

(© 800/552-1138 or 406/721-3838). **Airport Shuttler** (© **406/543-9416**) operates a transit service to and from the airport.

Missoula's city bus line is **Mountain Line Transit** (www.mountainline.com; © **406/721-3333**). It doesn't run late at night or on Sunday.

Taxi service is available 24 hours a day through **Yellow Cab** (© **406/543-6644**) and **Green Taxi** (© **406/728-8294**).

ORIENTATION   Missoula's layout is a tad confusing, so make sure you have a good city map. Remember that downtown is bisected by the Clark Fork River, and become acquainted with the locations of the three bridges, which provide access to the university and points south. Trails alongside the river are suitable for strolling, though you'll share them with runners and bikers.

SPECIAL EVENTS   The **International Wildlife Film Festival** ★ (www.wildlife films.org; © **406/728-9380**), founded by internationally known bear biologist Dr. Charles Jonkel in 1977, recognizes scientific accuracy, artistic appeal, and technical excellence through a juried competition. Highlights of the 1-week festival, held annually in early to mid-May, include daily screenings, workshops and panel discussions, a wildlife photo contest, and various wildlife art displays. **Out to Lunch at Caras Park** and **Downtown ToNight** (www.missouladowntown.com; © **406/543-4238**) are popular summer series featuring live entertainment and numerous food vendors from 11am to 2pm every Wednesday and Thursday from 5:30 to 8:30pm June through August. The **Farmers' Market** ★ (www.missoulafarmersmarket.com; © **406/544-1532**) at Market Plaza (located at the north end of Higgins Ave., where it meets with Railroad and Alder sts.) is the place to be during summer for organic vegetables, fresh flowers, and assorted culinary pleasures. It's open Saturday from 8:30am to noon May through late October, as well as Tuesday from 5:30 to 7pm in July and August.

Getting Outside

When you look up in Missoula, it is hard to miss the giant M on Mount Sentinel. The trail to the M is a popular hike, a steep zigzag that rewards the determined hiker with panoramic views of the valley. Mount Sentinel is also a favorite spot for hang gliding. You can obtain information and maps of recreation areas before leaving town at the **Bureau of Land Management,** 3255 Fort Missoula Rd. (© **406/329-3914**).

ORGANIZED ADVENTURES   **Lewis & Clark Trail Adventures,** 912 E. Broadway (P.O. Box 9051), Missoula, MT 59807 (www.trailadventures.com; © **800/366-6246** or 406/728-7609), offers guided hiking and paddling trips in the area.

BIKING

The best place to cycle is at the **Rattlesnake National Recreation Area and Wilderness** (© **406/329-3750**). To get there, drive northeast on Van Buren to Rattlesnake Drive. Be sure to consult one of the free trail maps available at bike shops before setting out. Bikes are prohibited in the wilderness portion of the recreation area. **Montana Snowbowl** ski area also has trails for the serious mountain biker (see "Downhill Skiing," later in this section). To rent bikes, contact **Missoula Bicycle Works,** 708 S. Higgins Ave. (www.missoulabicycleworks.com; © **855/298-2453** or 406/721-6525). Rentals run $18 for a half-day and $25 for a full day.

CROSS-COUNTRY SKIING

There are hundreds of square miles of cross-country ski terrain within 30 miles of Missoula. In nearby Garnet, the absence of gold turned a once-prosperous mining

HOTELS ■
Best Western Grant
  Creek Inn **26**
DoubleTree by Hilton
  Missoula-Edgewater **8**
Goldsmith's Inn **9**
Hilton Garden Inn **25**
Mountain Valley Inn **13**
Ruby's Inn **28**

ATTRACTIONS ●
Aerial Fire Depot and
  Smokejumper Center **24**
Brennan's Wave **4**
Elk Country Visitor
  Center **27**
Historical Museum at
  Fort Missoula **22**
Historic Ninemile Remount
  Depot Visitor Center **29**
Missoula Art Museum **16**
Missoula Carousel **5**

**RESTAURANTS/
NIGHTLIFE** ◆
Bayern Brewing **23**
Bernice's Bakery **3**
Biga Pizza **11**
Catalyst Espresso **10**
Charlie B's **18**
The Depot **19**
Hob Nob **2**
Iron Horse Brew Pub **17**
The Keep **21**

Kettlehouse
  Brewing Co. **1, 20**
The Oxford Cafe **15**
Pearl Café **7**
Red Bird **10**
Scotty's Table **6**
Sean Kelly's **14**
Shack Cafe **12**

Downtown Missoula

town into a ghost town that's now become a magnet for cross-country skiers at the **Garnet Resource Area.** With more than 50 miles of trails and a remote location, this area offers a delightful backcountry experience. And while out there, many like to stay in Garnet's **old-fashioned miner's cabins** (see p. 89). Getting there can be an arduous task in winter. Take I-90 east to Mont. 200, turn east for 5 miles to Garnet Range Road, and then go south along the Forest Service Road.

There are 150 miles of marked cross-country ski trails scattered through the **Lolo National Forest** (© 406/329-3750). Popular areas include **Pattee Canyon, Seeley Lake,** and **Lolo Pass.** The Pattee Canyon Complex, 5½ miles south of town, offers several groomed trails that range in difficulty from a short 1-mile trail to a longer 3.4-mile trail, but the snow level varies from year to year. At Lolo Pass, there's a National Forest information center at the top of the pass with maps and permit sales. To get there, take U.S. 12 west from Lolo for about 30 miles.

Twenty miles from Missoula, the **Lubrecht Experimental Forest** (www.cfc.umt.edu/lubrecht; © 406/244-5524), operated by the University of Montana's forestry department, has six ski trails and numerous logging roads. To reach Lubrecht from Missoula, take I-90 east to exit 109 and follow Mont. 200 northeast to Greenough. Turn right just past the post office, and less than a half-mile down that road is the Lubrecht camp.

DOWNHILL SKIING

Montana Snowbowl   Snowbowl has a vertical drop of 2,600 feet, much of it in the form of steep runs suitable only for experts. There's not a lot of terrain for beginners here, but the hard-core skier will have a ball. Eighty percent of the 1,138 acres are for intermediate, expert, and advanced skiers, with 500 acres of gladed tree skiing. Snowbowl has reasonably priced rooms for rent during the winter, with and without private bathrooms ($42–$126 for two people). Rentals and instruction are also available.

Snowbowl Rd., P.O. Box 8107, Missoula, MT 59807. www.montanasnowbowl.com. © **406/549-9777.** Full-day lift tickets $42 adults, $39 students and seniors, $19 children 6–12, free for children 5 and under; half-day rates available. Late Nov to early Apr 9:30am–4pm (Fri–Sun only in off-peak). Located 12 miles northwest of Missoula. From I-90, exit at Reserve St.; head north on Grant Creek Rd., and turn left on Snowbowl Rd.

FISHING

The **Clark Fork River,** which runs through town, has had its share of environmental problems and concerns over the years. A cleanup effort that began in the 1970s has helped, but it's never going to be an angler's first choice. The **Bitterroot River** and **Rock Creek** are better bets. Though Rock Creek has been known as a blue-ribbon trout stream, the Bitterroot is also a good spot for those who want to pull in a trout or two, and it has multiple public-access areas near the highway. The Missoula office for the **Montana Department of Fish, Wildlife, and Parks** (© 406/542-5500) will direct you to some fine fishing spots, including Siria, a more remote site 30 miles up Rock Creek Road.

Whether guiding you along Missoula's Clark Fork River or helping you pick out the perfect fly, **Grizzly Hackle,** 215 W. Front St. (www.grizzlyhackle.com; © **800/297-8996** or 406/721-8996), can help you with your fly-fishing vacation. Seasoned guides lead you to fishing holes along the Lower Clark Fork, the Bitterroot, the Missouri, and the Blackfoot rivers, as well as Rock Creek, in search of native rainbow, Westslope cutthroat, and brown trout. The company also runs the **Lodge on Butler**

Creek, not far from Missoula, where rooms rent for $165 per night for two, and other overnight accommodations. Grizzly Hackle advocates barbless hooks and catch-and-release fishing, donating heavily to river restoration projects and angling-oriented charities.

GOLF

Farther north, there are a number of great golf courses, but in Missoula, the golf is only average. The 9-hole **Highlands Golf Club,** located at 102 Ben Hogan Dr. (🕿 **406/721-4653**), is a short, hilly public course with wickedly gyrating greens. A round runs $14 to $16. There's also the par-29 executive **Linda Vista,** 4915 Miller Creek Rd. (🕿 **406/251-3655**), with greens fees of $12, and another 9-hole course on the **University of Montana** campus (🕿 **406/728-8629**), with greens fees of $13 to $15. The **Larchmont Golf Course,** 3200 Fort Missoula Rd. (www.larchmont golfcourse.com; 🕿 **406/721-4416**), an 18-hole public course within city limits, is a long, fairly tough track that the big hitters will like. Greens fees are $28 to $30 for 18 holes. A more expensive 18-hole option is the **Ranch Club,** 8501 Ranch Club Rd. (www.ranchclub.com; 🕿 **406/532-1018**), with peak summer greens fees of $95 to walk and $115 to ride. Nonmember access is limited to six rounds a year.

HIKING

Named for a late local newspaper columnist, the **Kim Williams Trail** follows either side of the Clark Fork River for 2.5 miles through downtown. Just north of town is the **Rattlesnake National Recreational Area and Wilderness** (🕿 **406/329-3750**). To get there, drive northeast on Van Buren to Rattlesnake Drive. The Rattlesnake covers 60,000 acres, 33,000 of which are congressionally designated wilderness. Camping is prohibited within 3 miles of the road because of the heavy use the area receives. Drive northeast on Van Buren to Rattlesnake Drive.

There are two state parks in the Missoula area: **Beavertail Hill** (http://fwp. mt.gov/parks; 🕿 **406/542-5500**) is located 26 miles southeast of Missoula on the Clark Fork and is open May through September, with excellent river access and shady cottonwood trees lining the riverbanks. There is a day-use charge of $5 for nonresidents; campers pay $15 per night or $25 for a tipi rental. **Council Grove State Park** (http://fwp.mt.gov/parks; 🕿 **406/542-5500**) is where the Hellgate Treaty establishing the Flathead Indian Reservation was signed. Open for day use only (free), the park has interpretive displays and picnic facilities. Take the Reserve Street exit from I-90 and drive 2 miles south, then 10 miles west on Mullan Road. A third state park at a former Superfund site east of Missoula in Milltown is slated to open in 2013.

Southwest of town, the **Lolo Trail** is an interesting hike. This trail was created by the constant use of the Nez Perce, Salish, and other tribes that lived in the area and moved back and forth across Lolo Pass.

You can explore a half-mile section of the original trail at Howard Creek, 18 miles west of the intersection of U.S. 93 and U.S. 12 in Lolo. Or hike a 5-mile section of the trail from Lee Creek Campground to the Idaho border. The campground is about 26 miles west of the highway intersection in Lolo.

SNOWMOBILING

The areas around Missoula have more than 500 miles of groomed snowmobile trails in a number of popular areas. In Lolo Pass, for instance, there are 150 miles of groomed trails connecting the Lolo and Clearwater national forests. There are four other nearby designated areas—Superior, Skalkaho Pass, Seeley Lake, and Lincoln—each with approximately as many miles of groomed trails. For advice on area snow-mobiling, contact the **Missoula Convention and Visitors Bureau** (✆ **800/ 526-3465**).

WHITE-WATER RAFTING & KAYAKING

Lewis & Clark Trail Adventures, 912 E. Broadway (www.trailadventures.com; ✆ **800/366-6246** or 406/728-7609), offers no-nonsense white-water rafting on the Salmon River during excursions through the heart of the Frank Church No Return Wilderness. The main trip is on a 120-mile stretch of Idaho white water, where you can expect to see mountain goats, bighorn sheep, elk, deer, eagles, and otters. Other excursions take in the Lochsa River, the Alberton Gorge of the Clark Fork River, and the Missouri River (through areas in which Lewis and Clark made their famous trek). Trips run May through September. Hiking, biking, and historical tours on the Lolo Trail are also available. Six-day trips on the Salmon River start at $995 per adult. One-day trips on the Lochsa or through Alberton Gorge range from $75 to $115 per adult. Guided hikes on the Lolo Trail are between $139 (1 day) and $675 (3 days) per adult. Children's rates are about 30% lower.

The Clark Fork, Bitterroot, and Blackfoot rivers are the settings for white-water adventure with **10,000 Waves,** 8080 W. Riverside Dr. (www.10000-waves.com; ✆ **800/537-8315** or 406/549-6670). Half-day and full-day floats feature thrilling white-water rapids along high mountain rivers and through steep, narrow canyons. Half-day trips are $70 per person; full-day floats cost $85 (includes a great lunch), and dinner trips run $115. The company uses self-bailing rafts, which enable the paddler to focus on the sport, not survival. If you want an even bigger thrill, consider a guided kayak trip with instruction. Rates are $160 for a full day or $220 for a 2-day beginner clinic.

Montana River Guides (www.montanariverguides.com; ✆ **800/381-7238** or 406/273-4718) is another good option, offering paddling instruction as well as rafting expeditions. Half-day trips run $55; full-day and dinner trips are $79 and $85, respec-tively. The most gonzo approach is a guided "riverboarding" trip—akin to sledding on the river on a board designed for the purpose—for $85 to $129.

In town, **Brennan's Wave** is a white-water kayaking park on the Clark Fork in the shadows of the Higgins Avenue Bridge. Named for late local kayaking legend Brennan Guth, the world-class park is open to the public and busy with paddlers nearly every day of the year.

Seeing the Sights

You can organize your own tour and check out the architectural highlights of the "Garden City" by contacting the **Missoula Historic Preservation Office** (✆ **406/258-4706**) or downloading a map from www.historicmissoula.org.

Aerial Fire Depot and Smokejumper Center   This is the nation's largest training base for smokejumpers—firefighters who parachute into remote areas of national forests to combat wildfires. This facility offers a fascinating look at the life of a Western firefighter, beginning with the days when pack animals were an impor-tant part of backcountry firefighting, through the 1939 advent of the smokejumper, up to today's heroes. The Aerial Fire Depot Visitor Center features murals, educa-tional videos, a reconstructed lookout tower, and exhibits of firefighters that illustrate

A remarkable community effort, the **Missoula Carousel** (www.carrousel.com; ☎ 406/549-8382) was a project begun with nothing more than unrealistic optimism. During planning, funding, and assembly stages of the project, Missoula relied on the kindness of others to make it happen. The hand-carved and -painted horses are the result of thousands of hours of labor from volunteer workers, most of whom were novices trained in the art of carving and painting. It's a treat for kids, and adults will also marvel at this merry-go-round by the river at downtown's **Caras Park,** which is located at the spot where Higgins Avenue crosses the Clark Fork River. The carousel is open daily year-round from 11am to 5:30pm (until 7pm in summer), with 50¢ rides for children 16 and under and seniors 55 and over, and $1.50 rides for adults. Immediately west of the carousel building is another fun community project: a fantasy-themed playground dubbed **Dragon Hollow.**

the lives and history of these rescue workers. The center also talks about the important role of fire in forest ecology.

5765 W. Broadway, adjacent to Missoula International Airport. ☎ **406/329-4934.** Free admission. Daily 8:30am–5pm. Tours available on the hour beginning at 9am; no tours at noon; last tour begins 4pm. Closed Labor Day to Memorial Day weekend.

Elk Country Visitor Center ★ ☺ Though a relatively young conservation organization, the Rocky Mountain Elk Foundation has made a large contribution to conserving elk and elk habitat. Its visitor center does that contribution proud: Encompassing ecology, biology, game management, and hunting, the center does a nice job telling the story of elk in North America, from their peak population of 10 million to their overhunted low point of just 90,000 (ca. 1900), to their rebound to about a million head today. The exhibits are interactive, covering everything from the unusual elk bugle to conservation legends, and many of them are geared toward children. Many visitors come simply to see the world-record antler racks on display here—one of them measures 448 inches in all. There is a short nature trail on the property. Allow 1 hour.

5705 Grant Creek Rd. (just north of I-90, exit 101). www.rmef.org. ☎ **406/523-4545.** Free admission. May–Dec Mon–Fri 8am–6pm, Sat–Sun 9am–6pm; Jan–Apr Mon–Fri 8am–5pm, Sat 10am–5pm.

Historical Museum at Fort Missoula Fort Missoula, one of Montana's first military posts, was established in 1877, the year Chief Joseph of the Nez Perce led his tribe toward Canada. Now the home of the National Guard and Reserve units, Fort Missoula has as its main attraction this museum, which houses displays that detail the fort's history and rotating exhibits in its indoor galleries. Outside, the campus is also home to several historic buildings moved to the site, including a one-room schoolhouse, a homestead cabin, an 1863 church, and other buildings.

Building 322, Fort Missoula Rd., entrance on South Ave. www.fortmissoulamuseum.org. ☎ **406/ 728-3476.** $3 adults, $2 seniors, $1 students, free for children 5 and under; $10 maximum per family. Memorial Day to Labor Day Mon–Sat 10am–5pm, Sun noon–5pm; rest of year Tues–Sun noon–5pm.

Historic Ninemile Remount Depot Visitor Center This visitor center, along with the Smokejumper Center (above), will educate you in the early methods of rugged firefighting in the northern Rockies. Listed on the National Register of Historic Places, the depot appears today much as it did when the Civilian Conservation Corps constructed it in the 1930s, complete with live pack mules. All tours are self-guided.

20325 Remount Rd., Huson, MT 59846. ℂ **406/626-5201.** Free admission. Daily 9am–5pm. Closed Labor Day to Memorial Day weekend. Drive 22 miles west of Missoula on I-90, then 4 miles north of exit 82.

Missoula Art Museum ★ Located downtown in the historic Carnegie Library (1903) and a new wing (2006), this museum's permanent collection includes about 600 works by about 200 artists, with a special emphasis on contemporary works by Montana and Native-American artists. Changing exhibits feature regional, national, and international art and photography; recent displays showcased works by Ansel Adams and Montana silversmith Haddon Hufford. Associated programs include films, concerts, lectures, tours, and children's events.

335 N. Pattee St. www.missoulaartmuseum.org. ℂ **406/728-0447.** Free admission; donations suggested. Tues–Thurs 10am–5pm; Fri–Sun 10am–3pm.

Shopping

The **Fair Trade Store,** 519 S. Higgins Ave. (www.jrpc.org; ℂ **406/543-3955**), is a project of the Jeannette Rankin Peace Center, selling jewelry, clothing, and musical items from communities around the world. **Butterfly Herbs,** 232 N. Higgins Ave. (www.butterflyherbs.com; ℂ **406/728-8780**), features an eclectic collection of items, including jewelry, coffee mugs, teapots, and handmade paper and candles. If you begin to feel the bohemian spirit and suddenly want your own pair of Birkenstocks, just go next door to **Hide & Sole,** 236 N. Higgins Ave. (ℂ **406/549-0666**), for reshodding. The **Trail Head,** 221 E. Front St. (www.trailheadmontana.net; ℂ **406/543-6966**), is a good outdoors store, with gear for snowshoers, kayakers, and just about everybody in between. There's a second location on the south side of town at Southgate Mall, 2901 Brooks St. (ℂ **406/541-6978**), specializing in gear and clothing for outdoorswomen.

Missoula is home to an impressive literary community, and the city's bookstores are among the state's best, including **Fact and Fiction,** 220 N. Higgins Ave. (www.factandfictionbooks.com; ℂ **406/721-2881**). Vintage, rare, and first-edition books are available from **Bird's Nest Books** (www.birdsnestbooks.com; ℂ **406/721-1125**) at 219 N. Higgins Ave.

Monte Dolack is one of the best-known artists in Montana. His often-humorous posters and prints are available at 139 W. Front St. in the **Monte Dolack Gallery** (www.dolack.com; ℂ **406/549-3248**). The gallery also features works of other prominent Montana artists, including Mary Beth Percival. Other top Missoula galleries include Larry Pirnie's **Pirnie Art Showroom,** 337 E. Broadway (www.pirnieartshowroom.com; ℂ **406/543-2713**), and the **Montana Museum of Art and Culture** in the PAR/TV Building on the campus of the University of Montana (ℂ **406/243-2019**).

Where to Stay

You won't find a whole lot of lodging variety within Missoula's city limits: It's dominated by chains, with a smattering of independents and Victorian-era B&Bs. For a distinctive night's sleep, try roughing it in a historic cabin. Information on rental of **old-fashioned miner's cabins** at the ghost town of Garnet is available by contacting the **Garnet Preservation Association,** 3255 Fort Missoula Rd., Missoula, MT 59804 (www.garnetghosttown.net; ✆ **406/329-3914**). The cabins are available for $30 to $40 a night from December through April, when they are typically accessible only on skis, snowshoes, or snowmobiles. Rustic cabins and lookouts are also available for rent through the **Lolo National Forest** (✆ **406/329-3750**) and the **National Recreation Reservation Service** (www.recreation.gov; ✆ **877/444-6777**).

HOTELS & MOTELS

Best Western Grant Creek Inn ★   Situated close to a freeway off ramp (I-90, exit 101), this Best Western is a solid choice in Missoula. The quality of the rooms and services is what you'd normally associate with a higher-priced chain, with a business center, flatscreen TVs, and near-constant upgrading. There is a good variety of options here. Deluxe suites have a fireplace, a dining area, a desk, a closet, and a nice city view. Conventional rooms are bright and cheery, with two queen-size beds or one king-size bed.

5280 Grant Creek Rd., Missoula, MT 59808. www.bestwestern.com/grantcreekinn. ✆ **888/543-0700** or 406/543-0700. Fax 406/543-0777. 126 units. $115–$159 double; $149–$199 suite. Rates include hot breakfast buffet. AE, DISC, MC, V. **Amenities:** Exercise room; Jacuzzi; indoor pool; sauna. *In room:* A/C, TV, hair dryer, Wi-Fi (free).

DoubleTree by Hilton Missoula-Edgewater ★★   This is the premier hotel facility in Missoula. Located on the north bank of the Clark Fork, the upper-end rooms offer a good deal of space with a beautiful view of the river and the University of Montana. Rooms on the second level have balconies, some overlooking the swimming pool. The property is geared toward business travelers, with meeting rooms and a 24-hour business center. The lobby area is nicely finished, with a gift shop that sells Western souvenirs, clothing, and trinkets. The Finn and Porter restaurant, specializing in steaks, seafood, and chops, is just off the lobby. The wooden deck outside the lounge is a fine spot for a cocktail over the Clark Fork River.

100 Madison St., Missoula, MT 59802. www.missoulaedgewater.doubletree.com. ✆ **800/222-8733** or 406/728-3100. 171 units. $99–$185 double. AE, DISC, MC, V. **Amenities:** Restaurant; lounge; free airport transfers; exercise room; outdoor Jacuzzi; outdoor heated pool. *In room:* A/C, TV, hair dryer, Wi-Fi (free).

Goldsmith's Inn ★   This beautiful 1911 brick building is Missoula's only riverside B&B, right on the Clark Fork River just across from the University of Montana. The home is the relocated former residence of Clyde Duniway, the second president of the University of Montana. Four of the seven rooms are suites with private sitting rooms, and all rooms have private bathrooms and attractive Victorian furnishings. Some also have fireplaces or reading nooks. Request the Clark Fork Suite for your own Japanese soaking bath, complete with a view of the river.

809 E. Front St., Missoula, MT 59802. www.goldsmithsinn.com. ✆ **866/666-9945** or 406/728-1585. 7 units. $124–$159 double; lower winter rates. Rates include full breakfast. DISC, MC, V. *In room:* A/C, TV, hair dryer, Wi-Fi (free).

Hilton Garden Inn ★★   The most comprehensive lodging on Missoula's west side, the six-story Hilton Garden Inn is a convention-oriented facility with terrific rooms. There's more than a hint of "New West" inspiration in the clean and sleek design, and a choice of two queen-size beds or one king. Some feature whirlpool tubs. Facilities include a pair of restaurants (including a good lunch-and-dinner place in the Blue Canyon Kitchen and Tavern), an indoor pool, and easy access to both I-90 and downtown.

3720 N. Reserve St., Missoula, MT 59808. www.hiltongardeninn.com. © **800/222-8733** or 406/532-5300. Fax 406/532-5305. 146 units, including 1 suite. $99–$189 double; $349–$439 suite. AE, DISC, MC, V. **Amenities:** 2 restaurants; lounge; exercise room; indoor Jacuzzi; indoor heated pool. *In room:* A/C, TV, hair dryer, Wi-Fi (free).

The Lodge at Lolo Hot Springs ⛺ This hot-springs resort, 25 miles west of Lolo and only 7 miles from the Montana–Idaho border, is an especially popular winter destination—the cross-country skiing on Lolo Pass is excellent, as is the snowmobiling. There are 18 modern rooms and a large, inviting lobby in the lodge, and 15 in a motel-style unit. The lodge is called the Fort because the design is reminiscent of the fort in the 1948 John Wayne film *Fort Apache.* The motel rooms are large and less expensive than those in the lodge, but they are spare in the decor department. Since the adjacent fabled **Lolo Hot Springs Pool** (www.lolohotsprings.com) is a separate operation, there's a fee to soak in them, but there are two 20-person hot tubs for guest use.

38600 W. U.S. 12, Lolo, MT 59847. www.lololodge.com. © **406/273-2201.** 33 units. $99–$139 double. DISC, MC, V. **Amenities:** Restaurant; lounge; 2 indoor Jacuzzis; Wi-Fi (free). *In room:* A/C, TV/DVD, DVD library, no phone. Located 35 miles southwest of Missoula via U.S. 93 and U.S. 12.

Mountain Valley Inn 🍴 This one-time chain property has evolved into a first-rate independent property, as new ownership has poured money back into the place. Rooms are fresh and clean, with small bathrooms with tub/shower combos; two nicely renovated family suites are available. There's also a small exchange library and guest lounge on the property.

420 W. Broadway, Missoula, MT 59802. www.mountainvalleyinnmissoula.com. © **800/249-9174** or 406/728-4500. 60 units, including 1 suite. $79–$89 double; $119 suite; lower rates fall to spring. Rates include complimentary cookies and full breakfast. AE, DISC, MC, V. **Amenities:** Exercise room. *In room:* A/C, TV, hair dryer, Wi-Fi (free).

Ruby's Inn ★ ☺ Just south of I-90 at the west end of town, Ruby's is hard to miss—just look for the big neon lips. The gaudy sign belies a top-notch independent motel, run by Ruby Erck for more than 25 years, with fresh, clean rooms and a full slate of amenities. Executive rooms are twice as big, and the honeymoon suite has a king-size bed and a two-person hot tub. The best feature might be the "backyard" along Grant Creek with fishing access (and grills to cook your catch) and a creek-side Jacuzzi.

4825 N. Reserve St., Missoula, MT 59808. www.erckhotels.com/rubys. © **800/221-2057** or 406/721-0990. Fax 406/721-0990. 126 units, including 4 suites. $89–$99 double; $119–$129 suite; lower rates fall to spring. Complimentary afternoon refreshments and hot breakfast buffet. AE, DC, DISC, MC, V. Pets accepted ($10 one-time fee). **Amenities:** Free airport transfers; exercise room; outdoor Jacuzzi; seasonal outdoor pool. *In room:* A/C, TV, hair dryer, kitchenette, Wi-Fi (free).

Where to Eat

Missoula is blessed with an excellent variety of restaurants, ranging from organic vegetarian to full-blown carnivorous. In addition to the options discussed below, I suggest the **Hob Nob,** 531 S. Higgins Ave. (© **406/541-4622**), for great breakfasts such as homemade corned beef hash, sourdough flapjacks, and *migas* (an egg and tortilla dish). Also reliable for a scrumptious breakfast and lunch, **Catalyst Espresso,**

111 N. Higgins Ave. (℃ **406/542-1337**), cooks frittatas and scrambles for breakfast and soups, salads, and sourdough for lunch. The historic **Shack Cafe,** 222 W. Main St. (www.theshackcafe.com; ℃ **406/549-9903**), is another local favorite, serving huge omelets known as "buffalo pies" for breakfast and a wide variety of lunch and dinner entrees.

EXPENSIVE

The Depot ★★ STEAKS/SEAFOOD A Missoula institution, the Depot is known for its upscale atmosphere and good food. The decor is along the contemporary cowboy and Western theme, with an inviting brick bar that looks out onto an active rail yard and about 20 colorful paintings by Larry Pirnie. You might try the scallop casserole: scallops and mushrooms in white wine, Swiss cheese, and cream sauce. The beef menu features prime rib, New York strip, and filets; specialties include the garlic-roasted filet and a fresh range veal chop served with fresh mushrooms and heavy cream. There is a huge wine list, including some hard-to-find bordeaux. There's also a more casual pub area called the **Deck,** serving a less expensive array of burgers, sandwiches, and pizzas ($8–$15).

201 W. Railroad Ave. ℃ **406/728-7007.** Reservations recommended. Main courses $17–$37. AE, DISC, MC, V. Sun–Thurs 5:30–9pm, Fri–Sat 5:30–10pm; shorter hours fall to spring. Bar open later.

The Keep ★ STEAKS/SEAFOOD After the landmark Greenough Mansion at the Highlands Golf Club burned to the ground in 1992, this castlelike restaurant, serving some of the area's best food, took its place on the very same foundation. Positioned on the bluffs of southeast Missoula, the Keep has a terrific ambience, heightened by the 30-foot ceiling in the bar and the panoramic views of the city and surrounding mountains. The Keep is known for its rack of lamb and salmon, as well as its rich and decadent desserts. The lounge and terrace offer a more casual setting and a menu of appetizers, salads, and small plates.

102 Ben Hogan Dr. www.thekeeprestaurant.com. ℃ **406/728-5132.** Main courses $27–$40. AE, DISC, MC, V. Daily 5–10pm.

Pearl Café ★★ STEAKS/SEAFOOD/NEW AMERICAN Named for chef/owner Pearl Cash, this swank eatery opened in 2004 and immediately rose into the upper echelon of Missoula's culinary landscape. Cash, who has operated several acclaimed restaurants in the area since the 1970s, delivers a sumptuous menu of creative regional standards, such as grilled filet mignon with a port-roquefort sauce, and duckling with pomegranate-cherry sauce and truffle-shiitake-chèvre flan. Located in the historic former Missoula Mercantile Warehouse, Pearl has three distinct dining areas: a sleek but casual bar area out front, a first-floor dining room with warm peach and brick walls, and an upstairs mezzanine with wrought-iron railings and an air of elegance. The wine list is excellent.

231 E. Front St. www.pearlcafe.us. ℃ **406/541-0231.** Reservations recommended. Main courses $18–$33. AE, MC, V. Mon–Sat 5–9pm.

Red Bird ★★ NEW AMERICAN The small, intimate Red Bird is tucked in the back of the ground floor of the Art Deco Florence Building. Chef Jim Tracey changes the menu monthly, but the entrees are fresh and superbly prepared year-round. One of Tracey's personal favorites is grilled bison tenderloin served with creative presentations that change seasonally. Other dishes include hand-cut beef and lamb plates, as well as killer homemade desserts. A wine bar serves a different menu that includes a gourmet cheeseburger (sharp white cheddar, grilled onions, and shiitake mushrooms) for $13.

111 N. Higgins St., Ste. 100. www.redbirdrestaurant.com. ℂ **406/549-2906.** Reservations recommended. Main courses $26–$36, wine bar menu $12–$22. AE, DISC, MC, V. Tues–Sat 5–9:30pm. Wine bar Mon–Sat 5–10:30pm.

Scotty's Table ★★ NEW AMERICAN/MEDITERRANEAN A chic, upscale bistro just north of the Higgins Avenue Bridge, Scotty's Table uses organic and local ingredients in large part in its menu, which is the perfect balance of Montana and Mediterranean cuisine. The former is characterized by plenty of excellent local beef, served in non-Montanan presentations that respectively include carrot purée and chimichurri sauce; the latter includes creative spins on French, Italian, and Moroccan standards. Owner-chef Scott Gill moved the eatery to a slick space on the ground level of the historic Wilma Building after a long run south of the river.

131 S. Higgins Ave. (lower level). www.scottystable.net. ℂ **406/549-2790.** Reservations recommended. Main courses $10–$12 lunch, $13–$31 dinner. AE, MC, V. Mon–Sat 11am–2:30pm; daily 5–9:30pm. Closed Mon fall to spring.

MODERATE & INEXPENSIVE

Bernice's Bakery ★ BAKERY Bernice's has been one of Missoula's most beloved culinary spots since the late 1970s. This small, out-of-the-way place, known for its delicious baked goods, is a great place for breakfast of the continental variety. In addition to an outstanding soft homemade granola, Bernice's sells buttery croissants filled with flavored cream cheeses, an excellent complement to the freshly brewed organic coffee that's also a staple. Organic juices and teas are available, too. This is also a great dessert spot—the cream puffs are out of this world—and a good choice for lunch as well.

190 S. 3rd St. W. www.bernicesbakerymt.com. ℂ **406/728-1358.** Most items $2–$6. DISC, MC, V. Daily 6am–8pm.

Biga Pizza ☺ PIZZA Biga Pizza cooks up gourmet pies using what's in season locally. The tables are in view of a central open kitchen featuring a colossal brick oven. Among the seasonal options on the menu: in the winter months, the cherry chutney and sausage; and in summer, the Sicilian, with Italian sausage, caramelized onions, and goat cheese.

241 W. Main St. www.bigapizza.com. ℂ **406/728-2579.** Pizzas $12–$19; salads and sandwiches $5–$10. MC, V. Mon–Fri 11am–3pm; Mon–Thurs 5–9:30pm; Fri–Sat 5–10pm.

The Oxford Cafe AMERICAN Even if you don't eat at the Ox, as it's known, you really should go in and look around. Established in 1883, this distinctly Montanan cafe is a Missoula institution, adorned with beer signs, a long bar, a breakfast counter, a bison head, and an endless stream of eccentrics, cowboys, and bikers. Chicken-fried steaks are the specialty of the house; the Ox had sold more than 210,000 all-time at last count. Other restaurants come and go, but the Ox endures, a testament to overflowing breakfast plates, keno, and bottled American beer. As the late proprietor Ralph Baker once put it, "The place hasn't closed in so long, we don't even know where the keys are."

337 N. Higgins Ave. www.the-oxford.com. ℂ **406/549-0117.** Breakfast $4–$13; lunch $3–$8; dinner $6–$13. AE, DISC, MC, V. Daily 24 hr.

Missoula After Dark

WATERING HOLES FOR ANY TASTE

There are plenty of watering holes in Missoula, whether your buzz of choice is alcohol or caffeine induced. **Sean Kelly's,** 130 W. Pine (✆ **406/542-1471**), serves Irish pub–style food—bangers and mash, pot roast, Irish stew—in addition to your alcoholic beverage of choice. The weekend jazz is wonderful, and there are also pool tables in the back. **Iron Horse Brew Pub,** 501 N. Higgins Ave. (✆ **406/728-8866**), has one of the city's best selections of Montana-brewed beer and myriad TVs to watch the game. Bold, bawdy, and bedecked with black-and-white photos of regulars, **Charlie B's,** 428 N. Higgins Ave. (✆ **406/549-3589**), is one of the best dives in the Northwest, serving a cross-section of Missoula: blue-collar types, professionals, and college kids. The exterior doesn't have a sign; just follow the laughter and chatter. The Dinosaur Cafe in the back serves pretty good Cajun plates, including red beans and rice with your choice of sausage. (Live a little—try the alligator.)

There are a number of good breweries in town, with taprooms where they can pour customers a maximum of 48 ounces of beer a day due to Montana state laws. My favorite is the **Kettlehouse Brewing Co. ★★**, 602 Myrtle St. (www.kettlehouse.com; ✆ **406/728-1660**), a neighborhood brewery that supplies excellent craft beer to many local restaurants. Its taproom—open Monday through Saturday from noon to 9pm—is a funky hangout with old couches and a jovial atmosphere. A second location opened in 2009 at 313 N. 1st St. W. with the same phone number and hours. **Big Sky Brewing Company** has a taproom near the airport at 5417 Trumpeter Way (www.bigskybrew.com; ✆ **406/549-2777**), open Monday through Friday from 11am to 6:30pm and Saturday from 11am to 6pm. Touting itself as the only German brewery in the Rockies is **Bayern Brewing,** 1507 Montana St. (www.bayernbrewery.com; ✆ **406/721-1482**), with taproom hours of 10am to 8pm Monday through Friday and noon to 8pm Saturday and Sunday. Wine lovers can also get in on the tasting act in Missoula at **Ten Spoon Winery,** 4175 Rattlesnake Dr. (www.tenspoon.com; ✆ **877/549-8703** or 406/549-8703), typically open Thursday through Saturday nights from 5 to 9pm.

THE PERFORMING ARTS

The **Montana Repertory Theater,** located at the University of Montana campus (www.montanarep.org; ✆ **406/243-6809**), is the state's only Equity company, performing new and classical works. The **Missoula Children's Theater** is the largest touring children's theater in the United States, performing original musical productions and featuring hundreds of talented children from communities across the States, Canada, and the Pacific Rim. The theater season starts early in June and continues through the end of March. The **Missoula Community Theater** provides a year-round calendar of family entertainment. Both the Children's Theater and the Community Theater are located at 200 N. Adams St. (www.mctinc.org; ✆ **406/728-1911** or 728-7529 for the box office).

The **Missoula Symphony Orchestra and Chorale,** 320 E. Main St. (www.missoulasymphony.org; ✆ **406/721-3194**), is composed of university students, Missoula residents, and other regional musicians, who often perform with featured guests in the University Theater on campus. The **String Orchestra of the Rockies,** P.O. Box 8265, Missoula, MT 59807 (www.sormt.org; ✆ **406/493-2990**), a statewide professional string ensemble, is based in Missoula and performs almost exclusively there. At the University of Montana's **Music Recital Hall** (✆ **406/243-6880**), the school's music department often brings in outstanding musicians to perform. Regularly scheduled recitals include solo and ensemble performances by faculty and students.

THE BITTERROOT VALLEY ★

Extends 89 miles S of Missoula to the Idaho border

Although in part a bedroom community for Missoula, the Bitterroot Valley has become a booming second-home and retirement paradise for folks who have fallen in love with the Missoula-area mountains, but not with the Missoula-area traffic. Though not as well known as other areas of the state, the fly-fishing in the Bitterroot River is excellent, making it a preferred destination for anglers in the know.

The Bitterroot has the reputation as Montana's banana belt because the microclimate in the valley offers a long growing season. A lot of Missoula-area golf fanatics head to Hamilton in February because the golf course there greens up for play much earlier than the ones even a few miles farther north.

GETTING AROUND & VISITOR INFORMATION   For maps, brochures, and sage advice about the area and its happenings, consult the **Bitterroot Valley Chamber of Commerce,** 105 E. Main St., Hamilton, MT 59840 (www.bvchamber.com; ☎ **406/363-2400**).

Driving Tours

If you'd like to take a driving tour through the area (see the "Southwestern Montana" map, p. 135), travel south on U.S. 93 to Florence, then cross the Bitterroot River and travel south on Mont. 203/263 through a 32-mile area filled with interesting landmarks, reconnecting with U.S. 93 at Hamilton. On your trip back, take U.S. 93 south through Hamilton, Victor, Darby, and Sula. As an alternative, continue south beyond Sula to Mont. 43, the road that leads to Wisdom. Doing so will take you winding through the valley and canyons of the Bitterroot Mountains, and you'll finally emerge at the Big Hole Battlefield.

If you are feeling very brave, and you don't mind getting your car beaten up on a rough dirt road, take the Skalkaho Pass Road to the east of Hamilton. Pick up Mont. 38 just south of Hamilton—up Skalkaho Creek. The pavement runs out after a few miles, and you'll drive over a rocky, pitted, narrow road up through the Sapphire Mountains. Go slowly—the drop-offs here are as extreme as those along Going-to-the-Sun Road in Glacier National Park, but without the guardrails—but the views of forested hills are unsurpassed. It takes about 2 hours to cover the 54 miles to the **Pintler Scenic Route,** Mont. 1, which you pick up near Georgetown Lake.

Getting Outside

The Bitterroot Valley runs south along the Bitterroot River between the Bitterroot Range to the west and the Sapphire Mountains to the east. The Bitterroot Range is the site of the Selway-Bitterroot Wilderness, which, at 1.3 million acres, is one of the nation's largest wilderness areas. Numerous trail heads are located off major highways between Lolo and Darby. You can get information about hiking in the wilderness from the Bitterroot National Forest's **Darby Ranger District Office,** 712 N. Main St., Darby, MT 59829 (www.fs.fed.us/r1/bitterroot; ☎ **406/821-3913**), open Monday through Friday from 8am to 4:30pm.

The **Lake Como Recreation Area** is a popular day-use and camping area with swimming, hiking, and boating. To get there, go 4 miles north from Darby on U.S. 93. Turn west on Lake Como Road and go about 2½ miles to the area. There are 22 camping units in two different campgrounds for $8 to $16 a night and a "rustic" cabin on the lake for $60 per night. Reservations for the cabin are available through the National Recreation Reservation Service (www.recreation.gov; ✆ **877/444-6777**); the campgrounds are first come, first served.

If it's fly-fishing you're seeking, check out **Chuck Stranahan's Flies and Guides,** 105 State St. (P.O. Box 594), Hamilton, MT 59840 (www.chuck-stranahan. com; ✆ **406/363-4197**), one of the longest-running acts in the Montana guiding business. Owner Chuck Stranahan is a nationally known fly-tier, with a number of his patterns chosen for the Jack Dennis fly-tying book, the bible of the business. He excels in instruction. His company customizes trips for its customers, with an emphasis on the Bitterroot River, though trips also go to other rivers in western Montana. Guided trips cost $400 to $450 per day for one or two people; personal instruction is $165 per person for a full day.

Seeing the Sights

The west side of the valley has fishing access as well as places to shop, eat, and stay. The historic section of the valley is on the east side of the river and is accessible at Florence, Stevensville, Victor, Pinesdale, and Hamilton.

Following are a lot of the attractions you'll come across if you start driving at the north end of Mont. 203/269 and head south.

Eight miles south of Florence on Mont. 203, you'll hit the **Lee Metcalf National Wildlife Refuge** (www.fws.gov/leemetcalf; ✆ **406/777-5552**), which is free and open daily from dawn to dusk. This wetland habitat is the result of dikes and dams that impound the water of several streams. It has helped to improve migratory waterfowl habitats and has created a nesting success, but a number of other species benefit as well, including osprey and deer. A short loop trail, open from mid-July to mid-September, leads around several ponds and blinds in the refuge's southwest corner. The picnic area is open year-round and has 2½ miles of nature trails. Hunting for waterfowl is permitted on designated ponds during the fall duck-hunting season. Bow hunting for deer is also permitted, as is fishing, during their respective seasons. Near the entrance is the well-preserved exterior of the 1885 **Whaley Homestead,** an excellent example of vernacular frontier architecture. You can drive around the refuge on the dirt road and come out in Stevensville, the next stop on the tour.

Stevensville is the oldest town in Montana, the result of the early missionary work of the indefatigable Jesuit Father Pierre DeSmet, who founded **St. Mary's Mission** in 1841. Capped with a bell tower, the mission is a small structure paneled with logs and white boards and an important place in the development of Montana—it was the first permanent structure in the state to be built by European Americans. John Owen bought the mission from the Jesuits in 1850 and established a trading post, Fort Owen. Though the issue of who first found gold in Montana will doubtless never be completely settled, in Owen's diary in 1852, he wrote: "Hunting gold. Found some."

From here, continue south on Mont. 203 to Hamilton and the Marcus Daly Mansion. Montana copper king Marcus Daly never did anything on a small scale, and his house is no exception. The **Marcus Daly Mansion,** 251 Eastside Hwy. (www. dalymansion.org; ✆ **406/363-6004**), is a spectacular Georgian Revival mansion with classical porticoes on a lush 46-acre estate that is now an arboretum and botanic garden. It occupies 24,000 square feet on three floors, with 25 bedrooms, 15 bathrooms, and 7 fireplaces. The mansion was finished in 1910, after Daly's death, and his widow, Margaret, lived there in the summers until her death in 1941. It's typically open 10am to 3pm daily from May through October, as well as on weekends and December. Admission costs $9 for adults, $8 for seniors 50 and over, and $6 for kids 6 to 17 (free for 5 and under).

On the opposite side of the river, the village of Hamilton, several blocks long and 4 blocks wide, is worth a leisurely stroll because most of the businesses here are small, locally owned, and interesting. For outdoor gear, head to **Bob Ward & Sons,** 1120 N. 1st St. (© **406/363-6204**), for a good selection of fishing, skiing, camping, and hunting equipment. Nearby is **Robbins,** 209 W. Main St. (© **406/363-1733**), a nice shop that sells home furnishings, crystal, china, and gourmet kitchen accessories. The **Chapter One** bookstore, 252 W. Main St. (© **406/363-5220**), featuring new and used books and periodicals, adjoins the unusually capitalized **JitterZ,** which sells all manner of espresso drinks. Also worth a look are **Big Sky Candy,** 319 W. Main St. (www.bigskycandy.com; © **406/363-0580**), and **Art City,** 407 W. Main St. (© **406/363-4764**).

Where to Stay

Hamilton Super 8, 1325 N. 1st St., Hamilton, MT 59840 (© **800/800-8000** or 406/363-2940), is a clean, budget-minded motel with a location central to the Bitterroot Valley. Rooms typically run $65 to $85 for two people. The same holds true for the **Best Western Hamilton Inn,** 409 S. 1st St., Hamilton, MT 59840 (© **800/426-4586** or 406/363-2142), though the advantage here is the presentation of an excellent breakfast buffet and the fact that some rooms are equipped with microwaves and refrigerators. Double rooms typically run $85 to $105 per night. Southwest of town, the **Lost Horse Creek Lodge,** 100 Lost Horse Rd., Hamilton, MT 59840 (www.losthorsecreeklodge.com; © **406/363-1460**), abuts national forest land with its 22 cabins and lodge featuring a restaurant and a thoroughly Western 1890s saloon. Double rates in summer are $60 to $120.

Triple Creek Ranch ★★★ This is one of the most elegant, and expensive, guest ranches in the West. The ranch is an adults-only resort that encourages guests to relax and do things according to their own schedules. The luxury cabins have a king-size log-frame bed, complimentary wet bar, wood-burning fireplace, double steam shower, and golf cart for getting around the ranch. Activities include everything from cattle drives to art workshops; tennis rackets, fly-fishing gear, and horses are available to guests. The ranch is the only Montana property to meet the Relais & Châteaux standards. The *Wall Street Journal* called a stay here "roughing it Robin Leach style." The on-site **Triple Creek Dining Room** serves gourmet cuisine for breakfast, lunch, and dinner, featuring a 2,000-bottle wine cellar and dramatic views.

5551 W. Fork Rd., Darby, MT 59829. www.triplecreekranch.com. © **800/654-2943** or 406/821-4600. Fax 406/821-4666. 23 cabins. $750–$2,500 per couple, per night. Rates include meals, drinks, and activities. AE, DISC, MC, V. **Amenities:** Restaurant; bikes; concierge; exercise room; outdoor Jacuzzi; outdoor heated pool; room service; outdoor tennis court. *In room:* A/C, TV, hair dryer, kitchenette, minibar, Wi-Fi (free).

Where to Eat

The **Bitterroot Brew Pub,** 101 Marcus St. (www.bitterrootbrewing.com; © **406/363-7468**), serves pub fare, burgers, tacos, and burritos, as well as its own excellent beers. The **Spice of Life Cafe,** 163 S. 2nd St. in Hamilton (© **406/363-4433**), has creative offerings ranging from a Bitterroot strip steak to Thai curry noodles. A classic diner, the **Kitchen,** 102 S. 2nd St. (© **406/363-0903**), is a local favorite for breakfast and lunch. If all your outdoor activities have you craving a juicy steak, try **Bradley O's Steakhouse,** 1831 U.S. 93 S. (© **406/375-1110**).

A Side Trip: Skiing & Hot Springs at Lost Trail Pass

Lost Trail Pass is a remote and undiscovered corner of Montana about 80 miles south of Missoula on the Idaho border. This area is heavily timbered but not heavily populated. It's also off the beaten path because most travelers use I-15. This corner of the state is very pretty—with pine-covered peaks replacing the forbidding rock crags that dominate the skyline farther north.

With Lost Trail Powder Mountain, Lost Trail Hot Springs, and Camp Creek Inn, this pass area is an unforgettable winter vacation destination for those who loathe big crowds and the attendant ski scene.

Lost Trail Powder Mountain ski area recently expanded into a long, steeper area adjacent to the original hill, with five double lifts serving 1,800 acres in all, as well as three rope tows. Overall, the runs are mostly intermediate, with lots of light powder. If you like to ski the bumps but aren't a fanatic about it, the moguls develop on the intermediate runs in the afternoon, just in time to wear you out completely. The full-day lift ticket prices are an excellent value, at $36 adults, $28 seniors 60 to 69, and $26 children 6 to 12; kids 5 and under ski free, and seniors 70 and over are $13. For more information, contact Lost Trail Powder Mountain, P.O. Box 311, Conner, MT 59827. Ski reports are available during the season at © **406/821-3211** or online at **www.losttrail.com**. The ski area is 90 miles south of Missoula at the Montana–Idaho border, a quarter-mile from U.S. Hwy. 93.

Just down the hill to the north from the ski area is the unpretentious lodge and hot springs, **Lost Trail Hot Springs Resort,** 8221 U.S. 93 S., Sula, MT 59871 (www.losttrailhotsprings.com; © **406/821-3574**). The lodge arranges summer raft trips, horseback riding, and fishing. It isn't fancy by urban standards, but the food in the restaurant, which overlooks the hot-springs pool, is good, especially if you enjoy basic American grub—burgers and pizzas. Nightly rates are $65 to $200 for lodge rooms and $80 to $210 for cabins. If you come just to soak, it's $7.25 for adults, less for seniors and children.

THE FLATHEAD INDIAN RESERVATION & THE MISSION VALLEY

42 miles N of Missoula; 75 miles S of Kalispell

The Confederated Salish & Kootenai tribes make their home on the Flathead Indian Reservation, with tribal headquarters for the 1.3-million-acre reservation in Pablo. The tribes, however, own only slightly more than 50% of the land within reservation boundaries.

The change in culture for the tribes came quickly when fur traders, homesteaders, and the missionaries of the Catholic Church headed west. Founded in the early 1850s by Jesuit priests, the town of **St. Ignatius** (located 32 miles north of Missoula on U.S. 93) is nestled in the heart of the Mission Valley. One of the valley's larger small towns, St. Ignatius has a modest Flathead Indian Museum and trading post on the highway. In Pablo, you'll find another museum and gift shop, the **People's Center,** 53253 U.S. 93 (www.peoplescenter.org; *C* **406/883-5344**), open Monday through Friday (and summer Saturdays) from 9am to 5pm; adult admission is $5.

Wildlife conservation and land management have played big parts in the lives of the tribal members. The **Mission Mountains Tribal Wilderness** was the first wilderness area officially designated as such by a tribe in the United States. Hiking in the wilderness area requires the purchase of a tribal permit from the **Flathead Reservation Confederated Salish & Kootenai Tribes,** 42487 Complex Blvd., Box 278, Pablo, MT 59855 (www.cskt.org; *C* **406/675-2700**). The Mission Mountains Wilderness is located in the Mission Mountain Range, east of U.S. 93. Numerous gravel roads lead up to the trail heads.

The **St. Ignatius Mission,** 300 Beartrack Ave., P.O. Box 667, St. Ignatius, MT 59865 (*C* **406/745-2768**), was established in 1854 as an offshoot of the missionary work of the famous Jesuit Father Pierre DeSmet. A Father Hoecken began the mission in a small log cabin, which is still on the premises and serves as the visitor center. In 1891, the mission added this magnificent brick church in its ministry to the Indians. The ceiling is decorated with 58 murals, depicting scenes from the Old and New Testaments, by Brother Joseph Carignano, an Italian Jesuit without formal art training. The mission is 2 blocks off U.S. 93; visitor hours are 9am to 5pm daily.

The **National Bison Range ★** (www.fws.gov/bisonrange/nbr; *C* **406/644-2211**), just west of St. Ignatius on reservation land, is 7 miles southwest of Charlo on C.R. 212. The 18,500 acres here contain between 350 and 500 bison, the remnants of a national bison herd that once totaled 60 million. The visitor center has a small display about the history and ecology of bison in America. The 19-mile Red Sleep Road goes through four different habitat types—grasslands, riparian, montane forest, and wetlands. In addition to the bison, you'll see deer, bighorn sheep, antelope, and maybe an occasional coyote or black bear. There's a trail here for people with physical disabilities. Gates are open from 7am to dusk daily year-round; the visitor center is open from 8am to 6pm weekdays, 9am to 6pm weekends in summer, and 8am to 4pm weekdays in winter. Cost is $5 per car (free in winter).

If you're more interested in feathers than in fur, check out the **Ninepipe National Wildlife Refuge** (www.fws.gov/bisonrange/ninepipe; *C* **406/644-2211**), which is next to U.S. 93, 5 miles south of Ronan. Established in 1921, the refuge has more than 2,000 acres of water, marsh, and grassland for the double-crested cormorant and the great blue heron, among other migrating birds. The refuge is open daily from dawn to dusk, although portions are closed during the fall and early winter hunting season and the bird-nesting season in spring and early summer. Admission is free. Fishing is permitted in some areas of the adjacent Pablo Reservoir, but a tribal permit is required. For information on tribal fishing regulations, call *C* **406/675-2700.**

The **Ninepipes Museum of Early Montana,** 40962 U.S. 93, Charlo, MT 59824 (www.ninepipesmuseum.org; *C* **406/644-3435**), contains early Western art, American-Indian beadwork, wildlife displays, a life-size diorama of an Indian camp scene, and other displays on the area's history. Admission costs $5 for adults, $4 for students, and $2.50 for children 6 to 12, and is free for children 5 and under. Call for current hours; the museum is closed in winter.

Where to Stay & Eat

Ninepipes Lodge   Located across from the Ninepipe National Wildlife Refuge is this pleasant motel, with 25 standard motel rooms decorated with lodgepole furniture and a wildlife/nature theme. Your choice of king-size, queen-size, double, or twin beds is offered, and all units have TVs and telephones. There is also a restaurant on the premises, offering American selections for all three meals.

41000 U.S. 93, Charlo, MT 59824. www.ninepipeslodge.com. *C* **406/644-2588.** 25 units. $70–$92 double. AE, DISC, MC, V. **Amenities:** Restaurant; bar. *In room:* TV, hair dryer, Wi-Fi (free).

A Side Trip to Hot Springs

Hot Springs is a funky little town of hand-painted signs and potholed streets, tucked into a cul-de-sac of low Montana mountains. Lots of visitors swear by the local waters' therapeutic qualities, especially as a palliative for arthritis. Situated southwest of Polson, just off Mont. 28, the tiny community is about 1½ hours from Flathead Lake.

The 1928 **Symes Hotel ★**, 209 Wall St. (www.symeshotsprings.com; *C* **888/305-3106** or 406/741-2361), is a vaguely pink, Alamo-like structure that aspires to be Art Deco. You can rent rooms or just tubs in stalls that can be filled with the famous waters. Some rooms have their own tubs, and there are two small pools and a large soaking tub outside ($7 adult). Rooms run from about $50 to $140 a night, in a bewildering combination of options (you get claw-foot tubs and the occasional TV, but no phones). There's also a day spa, a yoga studio, and a restaurant on the property. A funky 1935 motel with housekeeping apartments, **Alameda's Hot Springs Retreat,** 308 N. Spring St. (www.alamedashotsprings.com; *C* **406/741-2283**), is a better option. Many of its rooms have soaking tubs; rates range from $50 to $100, including continental breakfast.

Wild Horse Hot Springs (*C* **406/741-3777**), 5 miles northeast of town, offers a rather primitive soak in blue concrete tubs. This place is located several miles down a dirt road. The private rooms are each outfitted with a "plunge" (private pool), toilet, shower, steam room, and furniture that your grandmother would have found old-fashioned. But some people swear by the place and come back every year. There are only two kitchenette rooms to sleep in here, priced at about $80 to $100 a night. A soak costs $6 an hour per person.

For more information, contact the **Hot Springs Chamber of Commerce,** P.O. Box 627, Hot Springs, MT 59845 (www.hotspringsmtchamber.org; *C* **406/741-2662**).

THE FLATHEAD LAKE AREA: SOMERS, POLSON & BIGFORK ★★

Bigfork: 92 miles N of Missoula; 15 miles SE of Kalispell

This is one of the most beautiful areas in Montana. Glacier National Park's towering peaks rise from the valley floor on the east, and the mountains of the Flathead National Forest define the edge of the valley to the west. This is a land of forests, cattle, and alfalfa—with a velvet-green valley floor, green and granite mountains, and, on a sunny day, a dramatic deep-blue ceiling.

This part of Montana seems to offer something for everyone, whether your interests lie indoors or out. There are watersports on the lake and hikes that lead to sparkling mountain streams with views. But if you want to shop or see a play, you can easily spend your day inside the boutiques, galleries, and theater of Bigfork.

With much of this area lying within the tribal lands of the Salish and Kootenai, there is also a long-standing American-Indian heritage.

Essentials

GETTING THERE Bigfork is located near the northeastern shores of Flathead Lake, 15 miles southeast of Kalispell by car, at the intersection of Mont. 35 and Mont. 83. Polson is at the southern tip of the lake, 33 miles southwest of Bigfork via Mont. 35 and 60 miles north of Missoula via U.S. 93. The nearest airports are **Glacier Park International Airport** (www.iflyglacier.com; ☎ **406/257-5994**), north of the lake between Kalispell and Columbia Falls, and the **Missoula International Airport** (www.flymissoula.com; ☎ **406/728-4381**) in Missoula. Bigfork is just a little more than a 30-minute drive from Glacier Park International; Polson is roughly midway between the two airports. For rental cars, **Avis** (☎ **800/230-4898**), **Budget** (☎ **800/527-0700**), **Hertz** (☎ **800/654-3131**), and **National** (☎ **800/227-7368**) maintain counters at each airport.

VISITOR INFORMATION Your best bet for information on the south end of the lake is the **Polson Chamber of Commerce,** 418 Main St., Polson, MT 59860 (www.polsonchamber.com; ☎ **406/883-5969**). For goings-on north, contact the **Bigfork Chamber of Commerce,** P.O. Box 237, Bigfork, MT 59911 (www.bigfork. org; ☎ **406/837-5888**). The **Flathead Convention and Visitor Bureau** (www. fcvb.org; ☎ **800/543-3105** or 406/756-9091), **Travel Montana** (www.travelmt. com; ☎ **800/847-4868**), and **Glacier Country** (www.glaciermt.com; ☎ **800/338-5072**) can supplement this information.

Getting Outside

The Flathead is one of those rare places where you see the serious golfer and the serious backpacker in the same spot, sometimes in the same body. The golfing is excellent on several courses, and the backpacking, hiking, and fishing are even better. Fishing, boating, and yachting are popular sports for those who can afford to practice them. If your plans take you to one of the lakes or trails on the Salish and Kootenai reservation, don't forget to buy a tribal permit.

BIKING

Rentals and guided tours are available from **Mountain Mike's,** 417 Bridge St., Bigfork (☎ **406/837-2453**).

BOATING

With Flathead Lake being the largest natural freshwater lake west of the Mississippi River, you can bet that this is a big boating destination. Boat rentals are available at the **Kwa Taq Nuk Resort** in Polson (☎ **800/882-6363**), and to the north at **Bigfork Marina and Boat Center** (☎ **406/837-5556**), **Bayview Resort and Marina** (☎ **406/837-4843**), and **Marina Cay Resort** (☎ **406/837-5861**).

Fixed-keel sailboats can be launched at the state parks around Flathead Lake. Big Arm, Yellow Bay, and Somers have fishing access. Because winds may blow hard during the afternoon, only ballasted boats are recommended on the main portion of the lake.

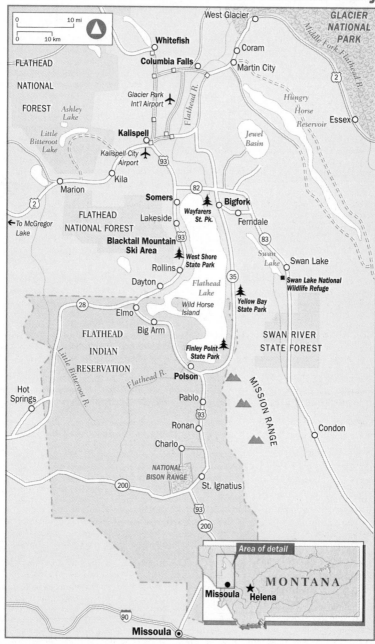

The Montana Department of Fish, Wildlife, and Parks has designated a **Flathead Lake Marine Trail,** showing point-to-point campsites and landing points that a human-powered craft like a canoe or kayak can reach in 1 day. You can obtain a brochure on the trail from the **MFW&P** (www.fwp.mt.gov; *€* **406/752-5501**) or from the **Flathead Convention and Visitor Bureau** in Kalispell (*€* **406/756-9091**).

CRUISES

Excursion cruises are a good way for visitors to check out Flathead Lake. The 65-foot *Far West* (www.flatheadlakeboattour.com; *€* **406/844-2628**) is one of the area's oldest, with daily scenic cruises and occasional Sunday brunch cruises. **Pointer Scenic Cruises** (www.wildhorseislandboattrips.com; *€* **406/837-5617**) offers charter rides on high-speed powerboats that cruise to ancient pictographs viewable only by boat; this company also offers explorations of Wild Horse Island, dinner cruises, and custom tours. The *Shadow* cruise boat (*€* **406/883-3636**) takes a 90-minute tour every day from the Kwa Taq Nuk resort marina in Polson, as well as dinner cruises on Wednesday and Sunday nights A sailboat excursion is available from **Averill's Flathead Lake Lodge** (*€* **406/837-4391**) on two classic racing sloops designed by L. Francis Herreshoff. Fewer than a dozen of these 51-foot "Q-Boats" remain in the world. There are a couple of 2-hour cruises daily from June to mid-September for $39 to $44 adults and $32 for kids 11 and under.

FISHING

Fishing the southern half of Flathead Lake requires a Salish and Kootenai tribal permit, which you can purchase at stores in Polson or at the tribal headquarters in Pablo. The brochure "Fishing the Flathead" is available from the **Flathead Convention and Visitor Bureau** (*€* **406/756-9091**). It provides information on a number of different fishing opportunities, as well as an outline of the licensing and catch-and-release regulations. This brochure includes information on Whitefish, Flathead, and Swan lakes, and several lesser-known lakes where you can catch fish but avoid crowds. To increase your odds of snagging something besides a log, contact **Glacier Fishing Charters** (*€* **406/892-2377**). **A-Able Fishing** (www.aablefishing.com; *€* **406/257-5214**) will also outfit a fishing trip with guides who know the area.

GOLF

There are two golf courses—one terrific, the other just pretty good—overlooking the shores of Flathead Lake. In Polson, the 27-hole **Polson Bay Golf Club** public course is the pretty good one, situated just off the lake on U.S. 93 (www.polsonbaygolf.com; *€* **406/883-8230**). A round of 18 holes is $36 to $47. The course is fairly short—just more than 7,000 yards from the tips and about 6,000 from the white tees—but it's very pretty and beautifully maintained.

The terrific course is **Eagle Bend Golf Club ★★** (www.eaglebendgolfclub.com; *€* **800/255-5641** or 406/837-7310), a challenging Jack Nicklaus–designed track with views of Flathead Lake and the surrounding mountains, located in Bigfork just off the highway on Holt Drive. The 18-hole course is about 6,300 yards from the white tees, but it's extremely challenging. There are 27 excellent holes of golf here. Greens fees range from $38 to $95 for 18 holes, depending on the time of year. *Golf Digest* has called this one of the country's top 50 courses. Be sure to call ahead for a tee time.

There are several other courses in the area. Contact the **Flathead Valley Golf Association** (www.golfmontana.net; *€* **800/392-9795**) for a free visitor's guide and information regarding all of the courses.

HIKING

This is bear country, and hikers should work to avoid confrontations by making noise and being watchful. Don't surprise them, and they won't surprise you.

Besides strolling by the lake at one of the marinas or state parks, the best bet for trekking is in the **Jewel Basin,** a designated hiking area north of Bigfork. More than 30 miles of trails make it a great place for day hiking as well as overnights. Before dropping into the actual basin, you'll get a great look at the Flathead Valley and Flathead Lake. For free maps of some of the more popular trails, inquire locally at one of the **Forest Service** offices in Kalispell (✆ **406/758-5200**) or Bigfork (✆ **406/837-7500**). To reach the head of the hiking area, take Mont. 83 from either Bigfork or Somers, turn north onto Echo Lake Road, and follow the signs.

A short hike, not far from Bigfork and about 45 minutes from the trail head, will take you to **Estes Lake.** Take County Road 209 out of Bigfork. Turn south at the Ferndale fire station. When the road forks, take the right fork, C. R. 498. It's about a 7-mile drive from there to the parking area.

A slightly more ambitious but still short hike goes up to **Cold Lakes** in the **Mission Mountains Tribal Wilderness.** Take Mont. 83 south to C.R. 903. Turn right (west), then follow the road to the trail head. The hike is about an hour each way.

RAFTING

The **Flathead Raft Company** (www.flatheadraftco.com; ✆ **800/654-4359** or 406/883-5838) runs half of its outfit from Polson at Riverside Park on U.S. 93 and half from Bigfork. Tours go down the South Fork of the Flathead River and include a swing through the Buffalo Rapids and Kerr Dam. Half-day white-water trips are $39 to $45, and full-day scenic trips range from $65 to $80. Meals and overnight trips are also available, as are guided kayaking expeditions.

SKIING

The **Blacktail Mountain Ski Area** (www.blacktailmountain.com; ✆ **406/844-0999**) is working hard to make the Flathead Lake region a full-blown year-round resort area. There's an average annual snowfall of 250 inches, which ought to be enough. The area is on more than 1,000 acres of national forest, served by two double chairs, a triple lift, and a handle tow. The hill is excellent for beginner and intermediate skiers, with 1,440 vertical feet of drop. Beginner terrain makes up 15% of the runs, 70% are rated intermediate, and 15% are for experts. There are two restaurants, a lounge, ski rental, a ski school, and a terrain park. Lift tickets for adults cost $36 full day, $30 half-day; children ages 13 to 17 cost $25 full day, $21 half-day; ages 8 to 12 are $16 for full day, $13 half-day; seniors 70 and older are $16 half- or full day; and children 7 and younger are free. Lifts open at 9:30am and close at 4:30pm Wednesday through Sunday and holidays (closed Mon–Tues). The area is located 14 miles west of Lakeside on Blacktail Mountain Road.

Exploring the Area

Bigfork Museum of Art and History This small but nicely staged museum in the village center offers a downstairs gallery with rotating art exhibits and an upstairs primer on the area's history. The art in the gallery is often local and changes on a monthly basis; the historical exhibits include a nice collection of black-and-white photographs and cover the region's cherry farming, the log-rolling laborers that were known as "river pigs," lake ice harvests, and, of course, wild huckleberries.

525 Electric Ave., Bigfork. www.bigforkmuseum.org. ℂ **406/837-6927.** Free admission. Summer Tues–Sat 10am–5pm; winter Tues–Sat 11am–5pm.

Bigfork Summer Playhouse   For over 50 years, Bigfork has earned a fine regional reputation for its summer stock theatrical productions, performed by rising college-age stars. Performances of Broadway shows are scheduled from the end of May until early September. Recent productions include *SHOUT!*, *Guys and Dolls*, and *Happy Days*.

526 Electric Ave., Bigfork. www.bigforksummerplayhouse.com. ℂ **406/837-4886** for showtimes and reservations. Ticket prices vary but are usually around $25.

Miracle of America Museum and Pioneer Village   This eccentric but often interesting museum contains an extensive collection of odds and ends dedicated to explaining the development of America, with specific attention to the Constitution and the Bill of Rights. Like most of these efforts, the place is heavily weighted toward the military side of the story, with plenty of guns, uniforms, and battle memorabilia. But unlike a lot of the roadside museums, there is at least some effort to explain what you're looking at. There's also a collection of antique Harley-Davidsons, dating as far back as 1912, and odds and ends ranging from comic books and Bibles to a two-headed calf trophy and a statue of a winged monkey.

58176 U.S. 93, Polson. www.miracleofamericamuseum.org. ℂ **406/883-6804.** $5 adults, $4.50 seniors, $2 for children 3–12, free for children 2 and under. Summer daily 8am–8pm; rest of year Mon–Sat 8am–5pm, Sun 1:30–5pm.

The Mission Mountain Winery   Montana's only winery is located here on Flathead Lake, producing award-winning merlot along with chardonnay and pale ruby champagne. Tours of the small facility are free and take about 15 minutes. The winery produces 6,500 cases of wine a year. Although most of the wines produced here are white, the winery considers the reds to be the finer vintages. The pinot noir and pinot gris grapes are grown in vineyards around Flathead Lake.

82420 U.S. 93, Dayton. www.missionmountainwinery.com. ℂ **406/849-5524.** May–Oct tastings daily 10am–5pm.

Shopping

Bigfork's main street, Electric Avenue, is littered with a variety of galleries, gift shops, boutiques, and bookstores—and it's only 4 blocks long. **Twin Birch Square,** 459 Electric Ave., is a two-level, pine-log shopping mall where you'll find **Artisans** (www. bigforkart.com; ℂ **406/837-2789**), featuring functional art from all over the country.

The **Eric Thorsen Sculpture Gallery,** 547 Electric Ave. (www.thorsengallery. com; ℂ **406/837-4366**), handles artwork from the well-known sculptor. He is best known for the sculptures he has created for Trout Unlimited, the Wild Turkey Federation, and Ducks Unlimited (at last count, more than 12,000 fundraising pieces in total). His two-level gallery is a display case for bronze and wood creations; on the second level is the artist's studio, where visitors are encouraged to observe the artist at work. Doors away is the gallery of **Ken Bjorge** (www.bjorgesculpturegallery.com; ℂ **877/837-3839**), 603 Electric Ave., who also creates life-size studies of wildlife in bronze. Don't be surprised to find yourself standing next to a 6-foot-tall crane or eagle while he works his craft in your presence.

Two River Gear, 603 Electric Ave. (www.tworivergear.net; ℂ **406/837-3474**), deals in fly-fishing equipment and info, and Patagonia wear. **Artfusion,** 471 Electric

Wild Horse Island, one of the largest islands in the inland United States at 2,000 acres, is run as a wildlife preserve by the Montana Department of Fish, Wildlife, and Parks (http://fwp.mt.gov; ☏ 406/752-5501). It contains one of the last remnants of Montana's endangered Palouse prairie plant and provides a habitat for bighorn sheep, mule deer, coyotes, and a few wild horses. The island was originally created more than 17,000 years ago as a result of heavy glacial activity that formed the entire area. Sensitivity by the human visitors who visit this unusual environmental preserve is essential—please leave no traces of your visit. The park is open for day use only and can be reached only by boat. Several boat tours go to Wild Horse Island as well. You can take one from Bigfork with **Pointer Scenic Cruises** (☏ 406/837-5617). **Note:** There are no visitor services on the island.

Ave. (☏ **406/837-3526**), is an eclectic gallery that represents more than 60 contemporary Montana artists and craftspeople. Around the corner, at **Bay Books & Prints,** 350 Grand Dr. (☏ **406/837-4646**), there are rare books and first editions. The owners carry an extensive collection of books about the explorers Lewis and Clark, some very rare and in good condition.

If you're looking for an authentic yet unusual gift item with a Western theme, visit **Electric Avenue Gifts** (☏ **406/837-4994**), 490 Electric Ave. For delectable jams and syrups, try **Eva Gates Homemade Preserves,** 456 Electric Ave. (www.eva gates.com; ☏ **406/837-4356**), which has been in the business since 1949.

Shopping in **Polson** at the other end of Flathead Lake is less of an upscale experience, but **Three Dog Down,** 48841 U.S. 93 (www.threedogdown.com; ☏ **800/364-3696**) sells comforters, coats, pillows, duvets, and other cold-weather gear. Owner Robert "Bronco Bob" Ricketts is a former opera singer who moved from Cincinnati to Polson to start a low-key dream business. Prices for high-quality down goods are lower here than in more fashionable metropolitan stores.

Where to Stay

There are five campgrounds in **Flathead Lake state parks,** each located at a different point around the lake: Big Arm (☏ **406/849-5255**) and West Shore (☏ **406/844-3044**) on the west side of the lake; and Finley Point (☏ **406/887-2715**), Yellow Bay (☏ **406/982-3034**), and Wayfarers (☏ **406/837-4196**) on the east shore. The phone numbers are operational only in summer. You can also call ☏ **406/752-5501** for information on any of these state park campgrounds, most of which are open May through September, charging $23 ($15 for Montana residents) per night.

Accommodations on and near the lake include guest ranches, water-oriented resorts with the gamut of recreational opportunities, and basic motels that offer clean but modest rooms. Of the last category, a good option is **America's Best Value Port Polson Inn,** 502 U.S. 93 E., Polson, MT 59860 (www.portpolsoninn.com; ☏ **800/654-0682** or 406/883-5385), with an excellent view of the lake. Rates run $129 to $150 double rooms, and $225 to $300 for a family apartment with a kitchenette; rates are lower in winter.

Averill's Flathead Lake Lodge ★★★ ☺   This is the best all-around vacation experience on the lake. A beautiful log lodge surrounded by thousands of acres of forest serves as your home base for all activities, which include horseback riding, boating, and fishing. The Western dude ranch experience is done right at this place, complete with sing-alongs, campfires, and barn dances. The location and the atmosphere of this place (the Averills perfectly combine a ranching lifestyle with the summer vacation experience) make this one of the top picks in the state. Scattered around the property are 20 two- and three-bedroom cabins, featuring simple Western-style furnishings. Inside the lodge are 19 guest rooms, just as woodsy but smaller, which sleep up to four and have queen-size beds and a pair of twin beds in a loft. Meals are served family style in the main lodge—the food is top-notch.

P.O. Box 248, Bigfork, MT 59911. www.flatheadlakelodge.com. 📞 **406/837-4391.** Fax 406/837-6977. 19 lodge rooms, 20 cabins. $3,248 per adult, per week (based on 1-week minimum stay); $1,358–$2,394 children 3–18; $170 children 2 and under. Rates include all meals and ranch activities. AE, MC, V. **Amenities:** Babysitting; children's program; 4 tennis courts; extensive watersports equipment; Wi-Fi (free). *In room:* No phone.

Best Western Plus Kwa Taq Nuk Resort ★   This Best Western affiliate is a top-draw resort managed and owned by the Salish and Kootenai Indian tribes. It's the nicest property on the Polson end of the lake and offers a restaurant, marina, and art gallery. It's also the best decorated, with interesting and artful American-Indian works on the walls. Lakeside rooms have commanding views, enhanced by decks furnished with chairs and cocktail tables. All the rooms are large and amply furnished. The main lobby level is home to both a lounge and a casino, with stunning lakeside views. The lower level has a restaurant as well as a comfortable sitting area and a swimming pool. This is the most expensive property on this end of the lake, but the amenities make it worth the extra money.

303 U.S. 93, Polson, MT 59860. www.kwataqnuk.com. 📞 **800/882-6363** or 406/883-3636. Fax 406/883-5392. 112 units, including 1 suite. $156–$171 double; $215 suite; lower rates fall to spring. AE, DISC, MC, V. **Amenities:** Restaurant (steakhouse); lounge; concierge; Jacuzzi; indoor and outdoor pools; watersports rentals. *In room:* A/C, TV, hair dryer, Wi-Fi (free).

Bridge Street Cottages ★★   Nestled into a nicely wooded area adjacent to the Swan River, these cottages are very clean and comfortable, sporting original art, granite countertops, and terrific attention to detail. The units sleep from two to six guests, ranging from hotel-like "cottage suites" to charming "river cottages," with full kitchens, laundry rooms, and porches fronting the river. All in all, this is a terrific base for couples and families alike, and the nicely landscaped property balances privacy with easy walking access to the village center.

309 Bridge St., Bigfork, MT 59911. www.bridgestreetcottages.com. 📞 **888/264-4974** or 406/837-2785. 12 units. Summer $185–$295 double; rest of year $95–$245 double. AE, DISC, MC, V. *In room:* A/C, TV w/VCR or DVD, kitchen, Wi-Fi (free).

The Candlewycke Inn ★ 👔   Tucked away on 10 acres of pine forest at the foot of the Swan Mountains in dinky Ferndale, this luxurious and large B&B is a modern home that innkeeper Megan Ward converted into a first-rate inn. The parlor, with 30-foot ceilings and an exposed pine staircase, draws you into a comfortable living space bedecked with an attractive selection of folk art. The large rooms have private bathrooms (two have hot tubs) and range from the somewhat frilly Botanical (with a canopied king-size bed, large bathroom, and private entry) to the rugged Wilderness (adorned with animal hides and two queen-size beds). There's a trail system on the property, an immaculate lawn, and all sorts of little touches—such as antlers converted to backscratchers. The breakfasts, anything from orange-cheese blintzes to spinach-artichoke-mushroom Italian eggs, are tailored to the dietary needs of guests.

311 Aero Lane, Bigfork, MT 59911. www.candlewyckeinn.com. © **888/617-8805** or 406/837-6406. 5 units. $135–$185 double; $265 suite. Rates include full breakfast. MC, V. *In room:* A/C, TV, fridge, hair dryer, Wi-Fi (free).

Marina Cay Resort ★   Boasting the most protected harbor on the lake, Marina Cay is a nice resort right on the water on the outskirts of Bigfork. The recently remodeled rooms are very large, and most open to a view on the water. The place attracts a few celebrities, including basketball legend Shaquille O'Neal, whose size 23 shoes are on display in the restaurant. Rooms here are sizable, and there is a wide variety to choose from, but the walls in the older buildings are on the thin side and noise carries from room to room. The restaurant, **Champs,** serves food in the summer, with a sports-bar atmosphere. The summer-only **Tiki Bar** serves drinks by the pool under flaming gas lamps.

180 Vista Lane, Bigfork, MT 59911. www.marinacay.com. © **800/433-6516** or 406/837-5861. Fax 406/837-1118. 115 units. $135–$210 double; $249–$379 condo. Lower rates in off season. AE, DISC, MC, V. **Amenities:** Restaurant (American); lounge; concierge; 2 Jacuzzis; outdoor pool; extensive watersports rentals. *In room:* A/C, TV, hair dryer, kitchenette, Wi-Fi (free).

Mountain Lake Lodge ★★   Unlike many of its peers, Mountain Lake Lodge focuses on accommodations, not recreation, and its single-mindedness shows. The highlights of the hotel, located 5 miles south of Bigfork, are the idyllic courtyard—with a pool, a waterfall, and the best view on the lake—and the rooms, each with a sitting area, fireplace, lake view, and deck or patio. Located in one of five buildings, all have a king-size bed in an imposing log frame and a queen-size sofa sleeper; many have Jacuzzis. The restaurant, **Terra,** serves steak and seafood, or you can grab a wood-fired pizza in the pub. The entire property is nonsmoking.

1950 Sylvan Dr., Bigfork, MT 59911. www.mountainlakelodge.com. © **877/823-4923** or 406/837-3800. Fax 406/837-3861. 30 units, including 15 suites. $239 double; $239–$285 suite. Lower rates in off season. AE, DISC, MC, V. **Amenities:** Restaurant; lounge; exercise room; outdoor Jacuzzi; seasonal outdoor pool. *In room:* A/C, TV, fridge, hair dryer, kitchen, Wi-Fi (free).

Swan River Inn ★   Located in the heart of Bigfork, the Swan River Inn has a decidedly European feel, injected with a fair amount of whimsy to boot. Each of the eight rooms is quite distinctive. The large log-cabin suite is decorated to resemble, well, a log cabin. The Arabian suite is an Aladdin-style fantasy come to life. The Art Deco suite hearkens back to the 1920s. All have beautifully restored bathrooms. Upstairs, the **Swan River Dinner House** serves steak, pork loin, rack of lamb, and a number of chicken and pasta dishes. The second dining room (served from the same kitchen), the **Grotto,** is a lounge transformed into a beautiful French-inspired facility complete with heavy wood furniture, stucco walls, and wrought-iron fixtures. The inn also manages several off-site condos and log homes for $195 to $400 nightly.

360 Grand Ave., Bigfork, MT 59911. www.swanriverinn.com. © **406/837-2220.** Fax 406/837-2327. 8 units. $145–$350 summer; $115–$250 fall to spring. DISC, MC, V. **Amenities:** Restaurant; bar; rooftop garden cafe. *In room:* A/C, TV, no phone, Wi-Fi (free).

Where to Eat

Bigfork has cornered the market on fine dining on the lake. Flathead residents from Whitefish and Kalispell routinely make their way to Bigfork to eat and take in a play

The Flathead Lake Area: Somers, Polson & Bigfork

at the Bigfork Summer Playhouse. Aside from the options below, the restaurant at the **Swan River Inn** (see above) is also recommended.

La Provence ★★ FRENCH/MEDITERRANEAN   Marc Guizol, the affable chef/owner of La Provence, made his way to Bigfork after his culinary career took him to the Ritz-Carlton in Naples and Caesars Palace in Las Vegas. In his own eatery, Guizol's experience shines. The dinner menu is filled with lovingly prepared French standards, from escargot on a puff pastry to roasted duck and grilled filet mignon. He also seasonally mixes in a few game dishes and classic European desserts. The room itself is an airy, pleasant space with a simple country French flair. For lunch, the restaurant's deli serves light fare: quiche, pastries, and sandwiches.

408 Bridge St., Bigfork. www.bigforklaprovence.com. ✆ **406/837-2923**. Reservations recommended. Main courses $8–$10 lunch, $17–$29 dinner. AE, MC, V. No credit cards at lunch. Mon–Sat 11am–2pm; daily 5–9pm. Closed Sun–Mon in winter.

Pocketstone Cafe ★ AMERICAN   A busy, homey, and picture-perfect cafe, the Pocketstone fits the bill for breakfast and lunch. Early risers will love the omelets, egg dishes, grits and oversize cinnamon rolls, while lunch-goers can't miss with the burgers or fry-bread tacos, or big salads. The homemade soups are out of this world (servers are sometimes asked if the cafe specializes in soups); Pa's Montana Chicken Noodle Soup is superlative, but ask about the soup of the day as well.

444 Electric Ave., Bigfork. www.pocketstonecafe.com. ✆ **406/837-7223**. Main courses $5–$10 breakfast, $7–$11 lunch. AE, DISC, MC, V. Daily 6am–3pm.

ShowThyme ★★ NEW AMERICAN   When you ask locals what the best restaurant in town is, they'll more often than not tell you ShowThyme—the restaurant that's located next to the summer playhouse. The atmosphere is a little bit New York, a little bit Montana. With a chef named Blu Funk and a manager named Rose Funk, you know the food has to be colorful. And it is: The Funks serve up everything from rack of lamb to sirloin steaks to *chiles rellenos*, plus nightly specials, all with a touch of creative flair. The king salmon is excellent, as is the filet mignon.

548 Electric Ave., Bigfork. www.showthyme.com. ✆ **406/837-0707**. Reservations recommended. Main courses $15–$29. AE, DISC, MC, V. Tues–Sat 5–9pm. Often closed for several weeks in Jan and/or Feb.

Tiebuckers Pub and Eatery 🍴 AMERICAN   Located in the old railroad depot in the sleepy town of Somers, Tiebuckers is a good restaurant that is prized by the locals. The fresh fish and steamed clams keep the crowds coming, but the menu also offers a good variety of beef and pasta. The chicken in Grandpa's Sauce (a family secret) are also excellent. There's also a selection with sandwiches and other inexpensive dishes.

75 Somers Rd., Somers. ✆ **406/857-3335**. Reservations recommended for parties of 6 or more. Main courses $7–$25. DISC, MC, V. Wed–Sat 5–9pm.

THE SWAN VALLEY

Extends 91 miles S of Bigfork; southern end: 33 miles E of Missoula; 90 miles W of Helena

The 50-mile stretch of Mont. 83 from Columbia Falls to Swan, Condon, and Seeley lakes is isolated from Flathead Lake's tourist attractions. Though less traveled, the road boasts vistas even more lovely than those seen from U.S. 93, its federal cousin to the west. Opportunities for watching wildlife are quite good, and Seeley, Summit, and Alva lakes—all excellent recreational areas—lie close to the highway.

Swan Valley seems more authentically "Montana" than other, busier areas, perhaps because the area isn't developed for tourists. Though some think the timber industry clear-cuts are an eyesore, the remainder of this thinly populated area is crowned with snowcapped mountains and accessible lakes. Swan Valley seems remote compared to the nearby larger towns—an hour from Missoula, 2 hours from Helena—and it looks like it will remain relatively undiscovered for some time. In winter, snowmobiling, cross-country skiing, and even sled-dog mushing are the sports of choice in this out-of-the-way wonderland. Be sure to watch out for deer year-round along Mont. 83, especially at dawn and dusk—and remember, they usually travel in small groups.

Seeley Lake is one of the places where you can see loon. Henry David Thoreau described the bird's call as a "long-drawn, unearthly howl, probably more like that of a wolf than any other bird." The loon is a symbol of north-country wilderness, and an appropriate one for this quiet and beautiful area.

Essentials

GETTING THERE Other than being air-dropped, the only way to get into the Swan Valley is by motor vehicle via Mont. 83. The **Glacier Park International Airport** (© 406/257-5994) and the **Missoula International Airport** (© 406/728-4381) are almost equidistant from the Swan. The town of Seeley Lake is 48 miles from Missoula. Take Mont. 200 east from Missoula 33 miles to Mont. 83 north. It's 42 miles from Kalispell to Swan Lake in the northern portion of the valley. Take U.S. 93 south to Mont. 82 east, then Mont. 83 south. For weather reports, call © 800/226-7623 or 511 (mobile) for road conditions statewide.

VISITOR INFORMATION The Swan Valley isn't exactly a self-promoter. Though several businesses rely on tourists, the valley-wide tendency is to remain small. The **Seeley Lake Chamber of Commerce,** P.O. Box 516, Seeley Lake, MT 59868 (www.seeleylakechamber.com; © 406/677-2880), can send you information on local happenings. For general information about Glacier Country, which includes the Swan Valley, check out www.glaciermt.com or call © 800/338-5072.

Getting Outside

Densely forested and marked by a sparkling chain of lakes, the Seeley–Swan Valley offers a variety of activities for the outdoor enthusiast, with a vast network of Forest Service trails providing year-round recreational opportunities for hiking, mountain biking, fishing, cross-country skiing, and snowmobiling. The **Seeley Lake Ranger District,** 2583 Mont. 83, Seeley Lake (www.fs.usda.gov/lolo; © 406/677-2233), will provide you with a detailed map of these trails upon request. The district office is 3 miles north of Seeley Lake, near mile marker 18 of Mont. 83. One of the most popular summer activities is the **Clearwater River Canoe Trail,** a 3½-mile lei-surely run down the river to the north end of Seeley Lake. The put-in is at the end of Forest Service Road 17597 and ends at the canoe landing at the ranger station.

The Forest Service publishes a brochure that outlines a number of hikes in the national forest and wilderness areas. You can pick up a copy at the Lolo National Forest ranger district office, located at 3583 Mont. 83 just north of the town of Seeley Lake, or request one by phone (© 406/677-2233). For a fairly short and interesting family hike, try the **Morrell Falls Trail,** a 2.5-mile hike from the trail head to a series of cascades, the largest of which drops 90 feet. From Clearwater Junction, travel north on Mont. 83 for 15 miles. Turn east on Cottonwood Lakes Road 477 and go 1¼ miles. Turn north on West Morrell Road 4353, then go 6 miles. Turn east on

Pyramid Pass Road 4364 and go a quarter-mile. Turn north on Morrell Falls Road 4364 and go a mile to the trail head.

OUTFITTERS & GUIDES   Swan Valley is home to several experienced guides who know parts of this vast territory like the toughened backs of their leathery hands. Guided pack trips on horseback usually run from $175 to $250 per person per day, with a normal trip into the Bob Marshall Wilderness usually lasting a week. **Buck Creek Guide Service** (www.buckcreekguideservice.com; (*C*) **406/754-2471**) offers trips that focus on natural history and local culture, as well as big-game-hunting expeditions. **JM Bar Outfitters** (www.jmbaroutfitters.com; (*C*) **406/544-5249**) offers trail rides and fishing trips in the summer and hunting trips in the fall and winter. Call for prices. In Clearwater, **Monture Crick Outfitters** (www.montana outfitter.com; (*C*) **888/420-5768** or 406/244-5763) offers summer backpacking trips, hunting, and fishing in the Bob Marshall Wilderness. Near Ovando, **Lake Upsata Outfitters** (www.upsata.com; (*C*) **406/552-9540** or 406/210-1301) can take you on horseback riding, hiking, fishing, and hunting trips.

Where to Stay

The Lodges on Seeley Lake ★ 🎒   One of only two lodges right on Seeley Lake, this 1920 lodge-and-cabins operation is secluded and offers plenty of space to stretch out. The cabins are spacious and beautifully decorated, complete with upholstered chairs and queen-size beds. All the rooms have televisions, kitchens, fireplaces, and private bathrooms; some have in-room Jacuzzis. Fortunately, the modern conveniences have been added without sacrificing the rustic feeling of the lodge. The best thing here, though, remains the peaceful views of the lake from the beachfront and of the wilderness beyond. The lodges have complimentary boats for guests to take out for fishing or recreation. Four miles east of the lake, **Eagle Port Lodge** is under the same ownership and offers similar amenities and rates, with a tower suite with stunning views.

2156 Boy Scout Rd., P.O. Box 568, Seeley Lake, MT 59868. www.lodgesonseeleylake.com. (*C*) **800/900-9016.** Fax 406/677-3806. 15 units. $159–$298 for up to 8 people. DISC, MC, V. **Amenities:** Watersports equipment. *In room:* TV, kitchen, no phone, Wi-Fi (free).

GUEST RANCHES & RESORTS

Double Arrow Resort ★   Double Arrow is 2 miles south of Seeley Lake off of Mont. 83, near the Bob Marshall Wilderness Area. The resort has just about any activity that a Montana-bound vacationer could want—golf, fishing, horseback riding, hiking, and mountain biking. There are also guided fly-fishing and float trips available on the Blackfoot River. In the winter, there's cross-country skiing, snowmobiling, and sleigh riding. You can get accommodations suited to nearly any taste, from relatively inexpensive rooms in the main lodge, to cabins, to a full-size, four-bedroom lodge all to yourself. The cabins are large and comfortably furnished, with sitting areas featuring upholstered chairs and sofas. Rides to trail heads in the wilderness area offer opportunities for guests to explore Clearwater Valley, Horseshoe Hills, and the Morrell Falls National Recreation Trail. Two all-weather tennis courts and an enclosed pool with a hot tub keep guests busy afterward. There's also an 18-hole golf course.

East of Mont. 83, P.O. Box 747, Seeley Lake, MT 59868. www.doublearrowresort.com. (*C*) **800/468-0777** or 406/677-2777. Fax 406/677-2922. 26 units. $100–$200 double; $200–$800 2- to 4-bedroom lodge. AE, DISC, MC, V. **Amenities:** Restaurant; lounge; golf course; indoor Jacuzzi; indoor pool; tennis courts; watersports equipment. *In room:* Kitchen, no phone, Wi-Fi (in some).

The Resort at Paws Up ★★ Opened in 2005—199 years after Meriwether Lewis climbed Sentinel Rock on the property—this cattle-ranch-turned-ultraposh-resort is situated along 7 miles of the Blackfoot River on 37,000 pristine and rugged acres. Lavish accommodations come in several varieties, ranging from two-bedroom units to the historic 1908 Morris Ranch House next to Elk Creek, which sleeps eight. With 300-thread-count linens, outdoor hot tubs, and DVD libraries among the standard amenities, the common thread is luxury, which even extends into Paws Up's "luxury tents," where roughing it includes feather beds, electricity, and running water. It's certainly not cheap, but the Paws Up's rate includes three meals a day and other perks. For recreation, there's hiking on the resort's 25 miles of trails; horseback riding; sport shooting; ATV rides; boating and watersports; and snowmobiling, cross-country skiing, and sleigh rides in winter. There are special packages for anglers, couples, and equestrians.

40060 Paws Up Rd., Greenough, MT 59823. www.pawsup.com. ℂ **800/473-0601** or 406/244-5200. Fax 406/244-5242. 52 units. $845–$2,735 double. Rates include all meals and activities. AE, DC, DISC, MC, V. About 30 miles east of Missoula via Mont. 200. **Amenities:** 2 restaurants; concierge; exercise room; room service; spa; extensive watersports equipment; Wi-Fi (free). *In room:* A/C, TV/DVD, movie library, hair dryer, kitchenette.

Tamaracks Resort ★ 📷 Tamaracks started out as a homestead in 1916 and became a resort in 1930. It is right on Seeley Lake, with 1,700 feet of lakefront. The resort has a 1940s feel to it, with lots of room between the cabins, screened-in porches, and an attached campground (sites run $35 a night). The cabins are clean and comfortable, and there is also a trio of full-fledged log homes for those needing more space (the largest is 2,500 sq. ft.). Every cabin and home has a full kitchen. The resort offers boat, canoe, and kayak rentals (as well as launch and moorage facilities); a basketball court, horseshoe pits, and volleyball in the summer; and cross-country ski, skate, and snowmobile rentals in winter.

Mont. 83, Mile 17, P.O. Box 812, Seeley Lake, MT 59868. www.tamaracks.com. ℂ **800/477-7216** or 406/677-2433. Fax 406/677-3503. 17 cabins, including 4 log homes. $130–$320 cabin; $295–$450 log home. Lower rates Oct–May. MC, V. **Amenities:** Watersports equipment. *In room:* TV/VCR or DVD, kitchen, no phone, Wi-Fi (some units, free).

Where to Eat

In Seeley Lake, the locals' choice for breakfast or lunch is the **Filling Station Restaurant and Bar,** 3183 Mont. 83 N. (ℂ **406/677-2080**), and the best fried takeout option is undoubtedly the **Chicken Coop,** 645 Pine Dr. (ℂ **406/677-2980**). **Littlebird's Schoolhouse,** 110 Larch Lane (ℂ **406/677-3663**), serves breakfast, lunch, and coffee drinks every day but Sunday and gourmet dinners on Fridays and Saturdays. Both restaurants are in the heart of town. In Swan Lake, try the restaurant at the **Laughing Horse Lodge,** on Mont. 83 (ℂ **406/886-2080**), which serves hearty meals and uses fresh, locally grown ingredients. Open in summer only, the lodge also has double rooms for $85 to $145.

Lindey's Prime Steak House ★ STEAKS A carbon copy of a sister restaurant in Minnesota that has achieved national acclaim, Lindey's makes ordering easy: There are only three dinner choices—chopped sirloin, prime sirloin, and special sirloin—all of which are accompanied by the restaurant's excellent greaseless hash browns plus a tossed green salad. Seating is in a comfortable glass-enclosed space with views overlooking the lake and the seaplane landing area. Bay Burgers is the lunch outlet, serving juicy burgers and little else.

Mont. 83, Seeley Lake. © **406/677-9229.** Main courses lunch $5–$8, dinner $13–$30. DISC, MC, V. May–Sept daily 11am–10pm; Oct to mid-Apr Thurs–Mon 11am–3pm and 5–9pm. Closed mid-Apr to late Apr.

THE BOB MARSHALL WILDERNESS COMPLEX ★★

45 miles S of Big Fork; 78 miles NE of Missoula; 80 miles W of Great Falls

The Bob Marshall Wilderness Complex is the largest wilderness area in the Lower 48 states, covering 1.5 million acres, or about 2,400 square miles. I hate to keep picking on Rhode Island for these comparisons, but the Bob, as it is usually called, is more than twice the size of that state.

The complex includes the Bob Marshall Wilderness proper and the Great Bear and Scapegoat wilderness areas. It abuts Glacier National Park, creating a huge area of relatively untouched country extending nearly half the width of Montana from the Canadian border. Marshall himself was one of the earliest advocates of wilderness for its own sake in the U.S., and the wild lands that bear his name were among the areas designated by the federal Wilderness Act of 1964. The Great Bear and Scapegoat areas were set aside in the 1970s.

Just south of Glacier National Park, the complex occupies nearly the entire territory that lies between the boundaries of U.S. 2 to the north, Mont. 83 to the west, Mont. 200 to the south, and U.S. highways 287 and 89 to the east. Access points along these roads occur infrequently and are poorly marked, so keep your eyes peeled.

The wilderness area has become very popular with hikers and horse-packers over the years, leading to a curious pattern of trail deterioration. Federal budget austerity allows the U.S. Forest Service little funding for trail maintenance, and while heavy traffic on the most popular trails has led to their erosion, many of the secondary trails have virtually disappeared. Quite a few trails that are marked on topographical maps of the area are faint or nonexistent on the ground. You should know fundamental trail-finding and direction skills—how to read a topo map—in case a trail dies out or is covered by snowbanks.

Exploring the Area

For information, maps, and advice about traveling in the Bob Marshall Wilderness Complex, contact one of the ranger stations monitoring the wilderness. In the **Lewis and Clark National Forest:** Rocky Mountain Ranger District, 1102 Main Ave. NW, Box 340, Choteau, MT 59242 (www.fs.usda.gov/lewisclark; © **406/466-5341**). In the **Flathead National Forest:** the Glacier View and Hungry Horse Ranger Districts, 10 Hungry Horse Dr., Hungry Horse, MT 59919 (© **406/387-3800**). In the **Swan Lake Ranger District:** 200 Ranger Station Rd., Bigfork, MT 59911 (www.fs.usda.gov/flathead; © **406/837-7500**). In the **Lolo National Forest:** Seeley Lake Ranger District, HC 31 P.O. Box 3200, Seeley Lake, MT 59868 (www.fs.usda.gov/lolo; © **406/677-2233**). In the **Helena National Forest:** Lincoln Ranger District, 1569 Mont. 200, Lincoln, MT 59639 (www.fs.fed.us/r1/helena; © **406/362-7000**). The **Bob Marshall Wilderness Foundation,** P.O. Box 190688, Hungry Horse, MT 59919 (www.thebmwf.org; © **406/387-3808**), is a good resource as well.

The most popular destination in the Bob is the **Chinese Wall,** a striking rock formation that stands more than 1,000 feet tall and stretches for 22 miles through the wilderness on the western boundary of the **Sun River Game Preserve.** One of the more well-traveled trails and easy accesses to the Chinese Wall is along the South Fork of the Sun River on the Holland Lake–Benchmark Trail (see below). From the east, reach the Chinese Wall by taking Trail 202 at Benchmark for 5 miles to Trail 203, then continue on this trail for roughly 11 miles before taking the Indian Creek Trail, Trail 211, to the south end of the Chinese Wall at White River Pass, elevation 7,590 feet. The Chinese Wall is unmistakable and is one of the most recognizable geologic formations in Montana. The USGS topographical maps for the trip are Slategoat Mountain, Prairie Reef, and Amphitheatre Mountain.

The high meadows at the base of the wall are very fragile, and overnight camping is prohibited along the base between Cliff and Salt mountains, so plan your trip to allow time to reach a camping area away from this section of the wall.

Towering peaks run great lengths through the Bob and stand as some of the tallest, and certainly the most dramatic, sites in the northwest part of the state outside Glacier National Park. **Holland Peak,** just north of Holland Lake on the wilderness area's western boundary, is a spectacular 9,356-foot giant that can be seen from afar but cannot be accessed directly. A short day hike is available from the Holland Lake Lodge (see "Advice for Day-Trippers," below, for directions to the lodge) into the wilderness to **Holland Falls.** The distance from the trail head to the falls is only about 1.5 miles, an easy hike with only 240 feet of elevation gain. This trail is designated for hikers only; bikes, horses, and other pack animals are prohibited.

Once inside the wilderness area, **Big Salmon Lake** is a wonderful destination for photographers, capturing the length and the beauty of Holland Peak's east face. To reach Big Salmon Lake, take Trail 42 from the Holland Lake Lodge on the west side of the Bob to Trail 110. It's a very long day hike and a reasonable 2-day hike through the Swan Range to Big Salmon Lake.

Located one-third of the way in on the **Holland Lake–Benchmark Trail** (a 60-mile trail across the midsection of the Bob that, following a series of shorter trails, takes roughly a week to traverse), Salmon Lake is simple purity without sight or sound of civilization. This trail also runs just south of the Chinese Wall.

North, in the Great Bear, is the impressive **Great Northern Mountain.** This 8,705-foot peak towers over the northeast part of the Great Bear Wilderness and can be viewed from many different points along the roadsides near the wilderness areas.

 Advice for Day-Trippers

Day hiking is best done near **Holland Lake.** Take Mont. 83 south 61 miles from Bigfork or north 20 miles from Seeley Lake to reach the **Holland Lake Lodge** (www.hollandlakelodge.com; ✆ **877/925-6343** or 406/754-2282) and the trails. Trail 42, from the north side of Holland Lake, connects with Trail 110 to reach the Necklace Lakes just inside the Wilderness boundaries. To reach the Holland Lake Falls and Upper Holland Lake before crossing the Wilderness boundary at Gordon Pass, take Trail 415 a short way until it joins Trail 35. This trail, taken to its end, stretches from the western boundary into the center of the park near the South Fork of the Flathead River (not a day hike). Rooms at the lodge run $125 to $145 per person, double occupancy, all meals included.

Ericaceae Vaccinium: The Huckleberry

The key ingredient in everything from vinegar, to fudge, to jelly beans in Montana's northwestern corner, the wild huckleberry grows in similar climates around the world. In Montana, it was a sweet and tart staple for Native Americans and early settlers, and remains a favorite of the grizzly bear to this day. Humans harvest them from the state's public lands—the plants can't be commercially cultivated—and no permit is necessary. Harvest season begins in July at lower elevations (around 3,000 ft.) and continues into September (at elevations around 7,000 ft.). Look for blueberry-like berries on bushes with oval leaves—and try to resist eating them until the picking is done.

You'll need a couple of vehicles if you don't have someone who can pick you up where you exit the Bob at the end of your journey. Park at Holland Lake if you plan on making it your terminus, or at Benchmark, west of Augusta, if you plan on ending there.

If you begin on the east side, the Holland Lake–Benchmark Trail follows the South Fork of the Sun River on trails 202 and 203 before moving west along Indian Creek on Trail 211. This takes you to the south end of the Chinese Wall at White River Pass. From there, you'll take Trail 138 along the South Fork of the White River until you reach the White River and Trail 112. This trail takes you to the South Fork of the Flathead River at White River Park. Across the river, you'll find Murphy Flats and Trail 263 along the river to Trail 110. This long trail takes you along Big Salmon Lake and the Swan Range, and then to Holland Lake outside the Bob's western boundary.

To reach the summit of Great Northern, you'll have to do some off-trail hiking—8 miles, if you make a round-trip. From Martin City, just northeast of Columbia Falls on U.S. 2, take the East Side Reservoir Road (38) for just more than 15 miles to Highline Loop Road (1048). Take this road for just more than a half-mile across the bridge to the trail head. Start along the left side of the creek until the landscape opens up. Trudge up to the ridge, then along it, to Great Northern's summit.

The majestic **Scapegoat Mountain** is the dominating jewel of the Scapegoat Wilderness Area. Surrounded by cliffs, this 9,200-foot summit is easily the most prominent feature in the southern part of the wilderness complex.

Wildlife abounds in the Bob, with grizzly bears being the most feared and the most difficult to spot. Moose and deer are common. Elk gather each fall for mating at the base of the Chinese Wall in the Sun River Game Preserve on the wilderness's east side. There are lots of birds, including the ptarmigan, a brown quail-like bird that changes the color of its plumage each winter to snow white.

HELPFUL TIPS Some things to remember when camping: Before you set out, consult a ranger at one of the district ranger stations mentioned above about distances, the wisdom of your itinerary, and restrictions. You can also pick up a topographical map. Carry plenty of water and water containers. Remember when loading up your pack that this is the weight you'll likely endure for a week or so. Restrictions are few. No vehicles are allowed in the area, including bicycles. To get around in the Bob, you either walk or ride on an animal's back. It might also help to remember, too, that hunting is allowed in many areas, making backpacking in the Bob a little less inviting in the fall. Wear bright colors and make lots of noise.

A RECOMMENDED OUTFITTER   A Montana native, Choteau-based Bill Cunningham has been guiding backpacking expeditions into the Bob Marshall Wilderness since 1973, and that makes his **High Country Adventures** (www.hcamontana. com; © **406/466-5699**) the oldest backpacking guide company in the country. It's also the Bob's only licensed backpacking outfitter, where there are dozens of licensed horse-packing guides. Cunningham goes on every trip, as does his wife, Polly. The company organizes three or four trips per summer that cover about 10 miles of trail in an average day, ranging from a week to 12 days. Breaking up the hiking are good meals, good company, and a layover day for a little fishing or mountain climbing. Trips start at $900 per person, per week. Rates include shuttle from airport, food, and community gear.

KALISPELL ★

115 miles N of Missoula; 249 miles E of Spokane, Washington

Located smack-dab in the center of Montana's primary vacation and tourism region, Kalispell isn't as much a destination for recreational visitors as are Whitefish and Bigfork, but it is a good base for exploring the area and has a number of attractions in its own right. The city, which is also a business and industrial center, is in a beautiful setting and conveniently located for visits to Flathead Lake, skiing in Whitefish, or hiking and touring in Glacier National Park. If you come to Kalispell after visiting Glacier or the Bob Marshall Wilderness, it will seem positively urban. It has all the modern inconveniences, including malls and long waits at traffic lights. But it has managed to preserve a good deal of its historical character and has a colorful arts-and-dining scene.

Essentials

GETTING THERE   **Glacier Park International Airport** (www.iflyglacier.com; © **406/257-5994**) is located north of town at 4170 U.S. 2. **Alaska/Horizon, Allegiant, Delta,** and **United** provide service.

U.S. 2 will get you here from the east or west. From Missoula, U.S. 93 leads north into town on a scenic 120-mile route that takes you past Flathead Lake. The drive usually takes a solid 2½ hours, no matter what the season. RVs amble along the gradually curving road during summer, to the frustration of most other drivers, and icy conditions warrant added caution and reduced speeds during the winter.

Amtrak (www.amtrak.com; © **800/872-7245**) stops at the Whitefish depot, just 15 miles north of Kalispell. The bus terminal is located at 1305 1st Ave. E. (© **406/755-4011**).

VISITOR INFORMATION   The **Flathead Convention and Visitor Bureau** (www.fcvb.org; © **800/543-3105** or 406/756-9091) not only offers practical information concerning Kalispell, but provides information on year-round lodging, activities, and attractions, including Glacier National Park, Whitefish Mountain Resort, and Flathead Lake.

GETTING AROUND   Rental-car companies **Avis** (© **800/831-2847**), **Budget** (© **800/527-0700**), **Hertz** (© **800/654-3131**), and **National/Alamo** (© **800/227-7368**) maintain counters at the airport.

For taxi service, call **Flathead-Glacier Transportation** (© **406/892-3390**).

Getting Outside

Kalispell itself isn't exactly a destination for the person looking for outdoor recreation, but its location between Glacier National Park and Flathead Lake makes it a good home base for those exploring this region during both the summer and ski seasons.

BIKING   Since motor vehicle traffic on U.S. 2 or U.S. 93 makes them less than ideal for bike riding, cyclists usually head to the back roads. **Whitefish Stage Road** runs parallel to U.S. 93 (from U.S. 93, go east on Reserve St. to reach it) and offers some great views of the mountains in a bucolic environment. For area information, as well as all kinds of bicycle accessories, try **Wheaton's**, 214 1st Ave. W. (www.wheatonscycle.com; ✆ 406/257-5808). The **Great Northern Historical Trail** (www.railstotrailsofnwmt.com) features a number of old railroad routes converted to walking/cycling trails in and around Kalispell.

FISHING   There is good fishing on the main Flathead River between Columbia Falls and Kalispell for trout and whitefish. There is good shore access at Pressentine, which is 5 miles north of Kalispell on U.S. 2 (follow the fishing access signs). Or you can float from Pressentine downriver to Old Steel Bridge.

GOLF   **Buffalo Hill** (www.golfbuffalohill.com; ✆ 888/342-6319 or 406/756-4530), just off U.S. 2 north of town at 1176 N. Main St., is an older course that's very hilly, with lots of trees and lots of memorable holes that can have serious golfers brushing up on their cursing. Cost is $49 to $65 for 18 holes, depending on the time of day. Carts are $28 to $34.

HIKING   **Lone Pine State Park** (http://fwp.mt.gov; ✆ 406/755-2706) is an attractive park with a few hiking trails. Go west on U.S. 2. At the intersection with Meridian, you'll see signs for the park sending you left (south). Take this road for about 5 miles (in the curve to your right, the road becomes Foys Lake Rd.) to the park. Once you're there, take in the views of the valley below or hike on the trails. The day-use fee is $5.

Seeing the Sights

Woodland Park, on the east edge of town at Woodland Park Drive, is a little spot that offers visitors a place to sit down in the sun and relax if they want to kill a few hours outside without killing themselves. There's a lagoon with ducks and a swimming pool. Walking tracks skirt the park. Another worthwhile attraction is the **Museum at Central School,** 124 2nd Ave. E. (www.yourmuseum.org; ✆ 406/756-8381), dedicated to preserving Kalispell's history. Admission is $5 adults, $4 seniors, and kids are free.

Conrad Mansion Museum ★   This 26-room Victorian mansion takes up most of a city block. Built in 1895 by Missouri River freighter Charles E. Conrad, the mansion has been beautifully restored and outfitted with the original furnishings. All tours of the mansion are guided and last about an hour; tour guides are dressed in Victorian costume and explain the history of Conrad and his palatial home. Some highlights: an amazing collection of dolls and toys from three generations of the Conrad family, meticulously kept clothing from the 19th century, and the annual Christmas bazaar in late October. The beautiful grounds also make for a peaceful locale for a short walk or a picnic.

330 Woodland Ave. www.conradmansion.com. ✆ **406/755-2166.** Tours $8 adults, $7 seniors, $3 children under 12. Mid-May to mid-Oct daily 10am–5pm; Christmas tours offered in Dec Wed–Sun 1–4pm. Last tour begins an hour before closing. Located 6 blocks east of Main St.

Hockaday Museum of Art ★   The charming Hockaday contains art formerly located in the Carnegie Library. The museum focuses on the works of Montana artists, both contemporary and historic, including Russell Chatham, Ace Powell, and Robert Scriver. There are tours, a gift shop, and an "Arts in the Park" program each July. The Hockaday has a very fine regional reputation for the quality of its programs.

302 2nd Ave. E. www.hockadaymuseum.org. © **406/755-5268.** $5 adults, $4 seniors, $2 students, free for children 11 and under. Tues–Sat 10am–5pm.

Shopping

Although not a major shopping destination, Kalispell has enough to offer if your money is burning a hole in your pocket. The **Kalispell Center Mall,** 20 N. Main St. (www.kalispellcentermall.com; © 406/751-5052), has more than 40 stores and restaurants. Just up the street, downtown Kalispell has a few stores of its own. **Norm's News,** 34 Main St. (© 406/756-5466), has the latest newspapers from around the globe, as well as a comprehensive magazine rack and espresso bar. **Blacktail Books** (© 406/257-5573) is the downtown bookshop on 42 1st Ave. W. Toys and games are available from the **Imagination Station,** 132 Main St. (© 406/755-5668). The **Western Outdoor Store,** 48 Main St. (© 406/756-5818), has a vast collection of Western gear for sale—4,000 pairs of cowboy boots, sterling silver Western belt buckles, and, for the wannabe dude, cowboy hats in all sizes and shapes. There's also an antiques store in the basement. The **Rocky Mountain Outfitter,** 135 Main St. (© 406/752-2446), has all the gear you'll need for hiking nearby trails and scaling the peaks. You can also rent kayaks and canoes if you want to head out on the water on your own. **Mark Ogle Gallery,** 101 E. Center St. (© 406/752-4217), features a selection of wildlife paintings and prints by its same-named owner.

Where to Stay

Beyond the choices listed below, there are a number of reliable chain properties in Kalispell, including **Travelodge,** 350 N. Main St., Kalispell MT 59901 (© 800/578-7878 or 406/755-6123), with summer rates of $99 to $189 double; and **Holiday Inn Express & Suites,** 275 Treeline Rd., Kalispell MT, 59901 (www.kalispellhie.com; © 888/465-4329 or 406/755-7405), with rates of $99 to $209 double.

Hampton Inn ★   A top-flight chain property, Kalispell's Hampton Inn is an attractive three-story brick structure surrounded by lovely landscaping. The fairly large rooms have one king-size or two queen-size beds. The lobby has a comfortable sitting area in front of a large dome fireplace, enhanced by colorful log furniture with leather cushions. A business center provides computers, copy machines, and a printer.

1140 U.S. 2 W., Kalispell, MT 59901. www.hamptoninn.com. © **800/426-7866** or 406/755-7900. Fax 406/755-5056. 120 units. $110–$180 double; $175–$250 suite. Rates include continental breakfast. AE, DISC, MC, V. **Amenities:** Exercise room; indoor Jacuzzi; indoor pool. *In room:* A/C, TV, fridge, hair dryer, Wi-Fi (free).

The Kalispell Grand Hotel ★   The Kalispell Grand is a historic hotel (1912) done in the Old West tradition. Located downtown, the hotel has been beautifully remodeled, right down to the pressed-tin ceiling and elegant oak staircase. By today's standards, the rooms are small, as are the bathrooms, but the historical ambience and fresh feel more than compensate for the lack of space. The lobby is the hotel's centerpiece, with cherrywood walls, a small art gallery, and an air of historic elegance.

100 Main St., Kalispell, MT 59901-4452. www.kalispellgrand.com. ✆ **800/858-7422** or 406/755-8100. Fax 406/752-8012. 40 units. June–Sept $100–$150 double; Oct–May $80–$125 double. Rates include continental breakfast. AE, DC, DISC, MC, V. Pets accepted (free). **Amenities:** Restaurant; lounge. *In room:* A/C, TV, hair dryer, Wi-Fi (free).

Where to Eat

MODERATE

Capers ★★ NEW AMERICAN   Recently renamed after a long run as Cafe Max, Capers brings a dash of big city–style culinary glitz to the Flathead Valley. Owned by Doug and Vonnie Day, the place is small, stylish, and popular. The food is excellent; the chef, Doug, serves a broad menu of elegantly prepared and presented dishes. While the menu changes often, two standbys are the Rocky Mountain rainbow trout and the grilled filet mignon. There are also some salad entrees, as well as brick-oven pizzas, including one with rattlesnake sausage. The restaurant serves beer and wine only, but its eclectic wine list is one of Kalispell's best.

121 Main St. www.capersmontana.com. ✆ **406/755-7687.** Reservations recommended. Main courses $10–$33. AE, MC, V. Mon–Sat 5–9pm. Closed Sun in winter.

North Bay Grille ★ STEAKS/SEAFOOD   A relatively new entry in the Kalispell dining landscape, this restaurant is easily one of the city's best. Thanks to a diverse menu that focuses on steaks and seafood but also includes jambalaya and chicken Marsala, the Grille has quickly become a local favorite. The approach is to bring in fresh seafood and excellent beef, and prepare it with more flair than the Kalispell norm. For lunch, all entrees are $9.95, including fish tacos, Asian chicken salad, and a Texas-style brisket sandwich. The dinner menu focuses on seafood, with Asian, Cajun, and Italian influences, as well as barbecue, steaks, and poultry. There is a full bar and a long and varied martini list.

139 1st Ave. W. www.nbgrille.com. ✆ **406/755-4441.** Reservations recommended. Lunch main dishes $10; dinner main dishes $12–$35. AE, DISC, MC, V. Mon–Thurs 11:30am–9pm; Fri–Sat 11:30am–11pm; Sun 4–9pm. Bar open later.

INEXPENSIVE

Alley Connection CHINESE   The best place in the valley for Chinese cuisine, the Alley Connection took several years to reach its current state of grace. What started out as a small, one-room operation has become two tastefully but simply decorated dining rooms that serve up excellent fare. Meals of chow mein, sweet-and-sour pork, and Szechuan chicken may be ordered separately or in the more popular family style. Lunch is a great deal for less than $6, and service is always quick and dependable.

22 1st St. ✆ **406/752-7077.** Reservations recommended. Lunch $3.75–$6; dinner $8–$13. DISC, MC, V. Mon–Fri 11am–2:30pm; Sat 11:30am–2:30pm; Mon–Thurs 5–9pm; Fri–Sat 5–9:30pm.

Norm's News ☺ BURGERS   Established in 1938, Norm's is a classic old-fashioned soda fountain, with racks of magazines and newspapers and an assortment of 300 kinds of candy, which should perk up the kids after a long day. It's quite a sight, from the Rock-ola jukebox to the ornate back bar carved from Mediterranean cypress. The menu is as basic as it gets: burgers, hot dogs, pork chop sandwiches, and French fries, plus a wide variety of sundaes, shakes, ice-cream sodas, and ice cream.

34 Main St. ✆ **406/756-5466.** Reservations not accepted. Most items $3–$6. DISC, MC, V. Mon–Sat 9am–7pm; Sun 11am–5pm.

Rising Sun Bistro ★ 🍴 FRENCH/AMERICAN   This pleasant, sunny cafe in a converted house just north of downtown Whitefish is decked out with French maps and photos and a nice variety of seating options on the hardwoods. The food, likewise, has its Gallic influences: croissants and parfaits for breakfast; great quiches and crepes (as well as juicy burgers) for lunch; and classic dishes like steak frites and short ribs, as well as nightly vegetarian specials, for dinner. Beer and wine are available.

25 2nd Ave. W. www.risingsunbistro.com. ☎ **406/755-7510.** Main courses $4–$12 breakfast and brunch, $7–$11 lunch, $13–$20 dinner. AE, DISC, MC, V. Tues–Sat 9am–9pm; Sun 9am–2pm.

WHITEFISH ★★

15 miles N of Kalispell

Whitefish has boomed as a resort community, attracting people from all over the country and making it Montana's fastest-growing area. Longtime residents have feared it will become another Aspen or Jackson Hole, but that hasn't quite happened yet. In fact, Whitefish is still relatively sedate.

Whitefish is almost two different towns—the town itself and the Whitefish Mountain ski area. The busy season in town is the summer, and room rates are correspondingly higher there during warm weather. This may seem odd for a ski town, but Glacier National Park attracts about two million visitors a year, while the ski area brings in about 300,000.

Up on the mountain, however, the peak season is winter, especially during Christmas vacation time. So if you don't mind the winding 5-mile drive up (or down) the road to Whitefish Mountain Resort, you can find slightly less expensive accommodations in the appropriate season.

Essentials

GETTING THERE   Whitefish is easier to get to than virtually any other Montana vacation town. From Kalispell, it's a quick drive north on U.S. 93. For the local weather forecast, call ☎ **406/755-4829.**

Glacier Park International Airport (www.iflyglacier.com; ☎ **406/257-5994**) is located north of town at 4170 U.S. 2. **Alaska/Horizon, Allegiant, Delta,** and **United** provide service.

The **Amtrak** (www.amtrak.com; ☎ **800/872-7245**) station on North Central Avenue, with two trains daily—one eastbound and one westbound—is shared with **Burlington Northern** at the edge of downtown in a renovated and charming depot. The bus terminal is also located at the train depot, with daily service to and from Missoula from **Rimrock Stages** (☎ **406/755-4011**).

VISITOR INFORMATION   The **Whitefish Convention and Visitors Bureau** (www.explorewhitefish.com; ☎ **877/862-3548** or 406/862-3501) is located at the chamber downtown, at 307 Spokane Ave., Ste. 103. Here you'll find just about everything you need in the way of brochures, area maps, and travel information. The chamber is open Monday through Friday from 9am to 5pm.

GETTING AROUND   Avis (☎ **800/230-4898**), **Budget** (☎ **800/527-0700**), **Hertz** (☎ **800/654-3131**), and **National/Alamo** (☎ **800/227-7368**) maintain counters at Glacier Park International Airport. Other companies renting cars in Whitefish include **Dollar** (☎ **800/800-3665**) and **Enterprise** (☎ **800/261-7331**). **Flathead Glacier Transportation** can be reached at ☎ **406/892-3390.**

SPECIAL EVENTS   Whitefish is home to the **Winter Carnival ★** (*(C)* **406/862-3501**), a wild and woolly event held annually since 1960. The early February carnival includes a parade, children's events, a dance party, a snow-sculpting competition, and a battle of the bands at local bars. Of special note is the Penguin Plunge, where a group of brave locals take a dip in frigid Whitefish Lake in the name of charity. In summer, Tuesday evenings bring the popular downtown **Whitefish Farmers Market** (www.whitefishfarmersmarket.com), held on the north end of Central Ave. from 5 to 7:30pm, featuring live music, prepared food, and local produce of all kinds.

Getting Outside

Whitefish is truly a paradise for outdoors enthusiasts, with ski slopes, hiking trails, watersports opportunities, and Glacier National Park just down the road. For all kinds of outdoor equipment or apparel, check out **Sportsman & Ski Haus** at the Mountain Mall (*(C)* **406/862-3111**). The **Wave,** 1250 Baker Ave. (www.whitefishwave.com; *(C)* **406/862-2444**), is a first-rate new aquatic and fitness facility, with several pools, weight machines and free weights, massage therapists, and much more.

BIKING

Although there are some road-biking opportunities here, biking in Whitefish really means mountain biking. The same old logging roads that make the hiking only average (see below) make the mountain biking excellent. **Whitefish Mountain Resort** (*(C)* **406/862-2900;** see "Downhill Skiing," below) has 20 miles of single-track bike trails. The trails are free, but the area offers a ride to the top on the chairlift for you and your bike for $15 to $23 for a day pass. There's also a short half-mile trail for beginners and two expert trails of about a mile each. The resort also offers single-ride passes ($9–$13) and bike rentals ($40–$65 per day).

For a less challenging ride, you can make the 20-mile round-trip on paved roads from downtown Whitefish to the head of Whitefish Lake. Most of the route follows East Lakeshore Drive and offers views of the lake. **Glacier Cyclery and Fitness,** 326 2nd St. E. (www.glaciercyclery.com; *(C)* **406/862-6446**), provides excellent service and maintenance, as well as rentals ($19–$39 per day), area maps, and up-to-date information for the serious mountain biker. This outfit has been ranked among the 100 best cycle shops in a pool of 6,800 independent dealers.

BOATING & SWIMMING

The boating is excellent on Whitefish Lake, and the lifeguard-staffed City Beach abuts the west side of town. You can rent water-skiing boats, fishing boats, paddle boats, and personal watercraft from the marina at the **Lodge at Whitefish Lake** (*(C)* **406/863-4000;** see "Where to Stay," later in this section) between mid-May and mid-September. Options range from a canoe or kayak to a water-ski boat. **Sportsman & Ski Haus,** at the Mountain Mall (*(C)* **406/862-3111**) also rents kayaks.

CROSS-COUNTRY SKIING

The **Whitefish Mountain Resort** (see "Downhill Skiing," below) offers 7.5 miles of very challenging cross-country trails. The **Glacier Nordic Club** (www.glaciernordic club.wordpress.com) maintains about 6 miles of trails on the Whitefish Lake Golf Course (see "Golf" below) near the Grouse Mountain Lodge. For more information, contact the **Grouse Mountain Lodge** (*(C)* **406/862-3000**). Another option is **Stillwater Mountain Lodge,** north of town at 750 Beaver Lake Rd. (www.stillwatermtn lodge.com; *(C)* **888/205-7786** or 406/862-7004), with 20 miles of groomed trails (adult day passes are $15) and three guest rooms ($85–$115 per night). The **Flathead**

Convention and Visitor Bureau (☏ 406/756-9091) provides a free outline of trails in or near Whitefish, as well as a list of equipment sales and rental operations.

DOG-SLEDDING

Dog-Sled Adventures (www.dogsledadventuresmontana.com; ☏ 406/881-2275) lets you explore the mountains around Whitefish "at the speed of dog." The guided 12-mile rides in two-person or family-size sleds run through Stillwater State Forest, 2 miles north of Olney. Each trip takes about 1½ hours, and the sleds are equipped with blankets to keep you warm. Many of the dogs pulling the sleds were rescued by the owners from unwanted homes or animal shelters and trained as sled dogs. A sled ride costs $90 per adult, $45 for kids 13 and under, and includes a cup of hot chocolate and homemade cookies at the end of your ride.

DOWNHILL SKIING

Whitefish Mountain Resort ★★ 🎒   Formerly known as Big Mountain, this resort offers lots of powder, lots of skiing in the trees, and plenty of runs for every level of skier. With an average annual snowfall of 300 inches, a vertical drop of 2,353 feet, three terrain parks, and virtually no lines, Whitefish Mountain Resort is one of the best ski areas in the northwestern United States. Three-quarters of the mountain is geared to intermediate (35%) and advanced (40%) skiers, but there is plenty of terrain for experts (10%) and beginners (15%). The expert runs are pretty steep—not as steep as those at Wyoming's Jackson Hole Mountain Resort, but steep enough. There are never any crowds at Whitefish, even in the holiday seasons, so although the prices have gone up a bit over the years, you can still spend your time skiing rather than waiting in lift lines. Perhaps best of all are the **Mountain Ambassadors,** who will take you on a free tour.

Ski school options include 2-hour group lessons for kids 7 to 12 ($60) and half-day private sessions for adults ($285). A 2-day learn-to-ski program is a bargain at $72, rentals included. There's also a full-service ski-rental shop and a kids' center.

For après-ski food and entertainment, Whitefish Mountain Resort holds its own, with a number of restaurants in the village or on the hill. Your choice for food and beverage at the mountain is **Ed & Mully's,** a casual restaurant and bar with a menu chock-full of Memphis-style barbecue. The only mountaintop dining in Montana, **Summit House** is a cafeteria that dishes up burgers and the like during the daytime; dinner is also offered several nights a winter on "Moonlight Dine and Ski" evenings. The **Hellroaring Saloon** serves both lunch and dinners in a typical après-ski atmosphere. The **'Stube** is the mountain's rowdiest watering hole, with good burgers and pizza—hit it on Wednesday at 5:30pm for the raucous Frabert award ceremony for the "clod of the week."

In summer, you can take chairlift rides to the top of the mountain ($8 per person), ride an alpine slide ($24 for four rides) or take one of the best zip line tours in the West ($79 for 3 hr.), or mountain-bike on the trails (bike rentals are available). A new warm-weather diversion is **Walk-in-the-Treetops** ($51 for 3 hr.), a harnessed adventure that goes 70 feet above ground into the forest's canopy. There are also some popular summer concerts and special events.

P.O. Box 1400, Whitefish, MT 59937. www.skiwhitefish.com. ☏ **800/858-3930** or 406/862-2900. Snow reports 406/862-7669. Lift tickets $66 adults, $54 seniors 65–69, $58 ages 13–18, $35 ages 7–12, free for children 6 and under. Beginner and night rates available. AE, DISC, MC, V. Daily early Dec to Apr. 12 miles north of Whitefish on Big Mountain Rd. From Whitefish, head north on Baker Ave. over the viaduct to Wisconsin Ave. for 3 miles until you see the flashing yellow light. Turn right on Big Mountain Rd. and proceed 8 miles to Whitefish Mountain Resort Village.

FISHING

It's not the Madison Valley, but Whitefish does have some hot spots for anglers wanting to try their hand. **Tally Lake** is a deep hole (Montana's deepest lake, actually) located north of Whitefish off U.S. 93. Five miles north of town, turn left onto the Tally Lake Road (signs will direct you). You can expect cutthroat, rainbow, kokanee, brook trout, and whitefish.

In town, across the viaduct toward Whitefish Mountain Resort, lies **Whitefish Lake.** If you can handle the summer bustle, the lake offers some pretty good lake trout. Northern pike can be found here, and rainbow and cutthroat can be nabbed on dry flies in the evening. **Lakestream Outfitters,** 334 Central Ave. (www.lakestream. com; ✆ **406/862-1298**), is the best resource in town for information about fly-fishing the Flathead River and local streams. It's also a great spot for a fly-fisherman to construct a wish list, since the store sells all types of fly-fishing equipment, clothing, books, flies, dust catchers, and memorabilia. The staff here provides full-service fly-fishing, tying, and rod-building services, in addition to clinics and good advice. Guided trips are about $450 a day, $300 for a half-day.

GOLF

The **Whitefish Lake Golf Club ★**, U.S. 93 N. (www.golfwhitefish.com; ✆ **406/862-4000**), is the original 36-hole golf course in the state. Built in the 1930s, the golf club's trees have grown up considerably in the time since.

While not especially long, the course offers a wide variety of shots that will require you to use all the clubs in your bag (and maybe some you forgot). Almost all the fairways are lined with trees. There are few fairway bunkers, but they have strategic placement around the greens. Both 18-hole setups measure a little more than 6,500 yards from the tips. There is also a driving range and putting green. This course may not be as good as Meadow Lake (see the "Golf" section in the Columbia Falls section, later in this chapter), but it is a very fun track. Greens fees are $37 to $56 for 18 holes, $26 to $30 for 9 holes. Carts rent for $34 for 18 holes, $22 for 9.

HIKING

The hiking in the immediate Whitefish area is not great. For the most part, trails either stay in the woods so that you don't see anything except trees, or go along old logging roads—which make for good mountain biking but less interesting hiking. The most popular trail in town is the **Danny On Trail** to the summit of the Big Mountain. Named for a Forest Service ecologist who was killed in a ski accident on the Big Mountain in 1979, it begins in the mountain village and ascends over 2,500 feet up the south face of the mountain on four different paths. There's about a 4-mile trek from the top of the lift along the ridge to Flower Point and back. It takes about 2 hours. The most demanding walk is 5.75 miles from the base of the ski area to the top of the hill and then along the ridge. You can ride the lift back down. Snow can be a problem in late spring and even the early months of summer. The 13-mile **Whitefish Trail** (www.whitefishlegacy.org) connects Whitefish with a network of trails hikers can take into beautiful state forest land.

SNOWBOARDING

Snowboarders will find kindred spirits—as well as an extensive line of boards and apparel—at **Stumptown Snowboards** (www.stumptownsnowboards.com; ✆ **406/862-0955**) at 128 Central Ave. The staff here will fill you in on the local snowboarding scene at Whitefish Mountain Resort (where the shop has a smaller annex) and other spots in the Flathead Valley. Locals love the **White Room Mountain Shop,**

130 Lupfer Ave. (www.whiteroomshop.com; ☎ **406/863-7666**), offering tuning and waxing, gear, and advice.

SNOWMOBILING

Contact the **Flathead Snowmobile Association** (www.flatheadsnowmobiler.com) for current conditions and advice. The **Flathead Convention & Visitors Bureau** (☎ **406/756-9091**) prints a brochure, "Snowmobiling Montana's Flathead Valley," with information on guides, trails, and snowmobile-friendly accommodations. For tours and rentals, contact **J&L Snowmobile Rentals** in Columbia Falls (www.jandlsnowmobilerentals.com; ☎ **406/892-7666**).

Shopping

The main shopping area of Whitefish is on Central Avenue and stretches for 3 blocks. For a ski town, the shopping frenzy is fairly subdued. The largest bookshop in town is **Bookworks,** 244 Spokane Ave. (☎ **406/862-4980**), which stocks the best in nature books, regional writing, and children's literature; it's also the source of current hardcover and paperback bestsellers. **McGough and Company,** 131 Central Ave. (☎ **406/862-9199**), has a large selection of Indian-made jewelry. The **Bear Mountain Mercantile,** 237 Central Ave. (☎ **406/862-8382**), is chock-full of gimcracks, knickknacks, and souvenirs, many with a bear theme. There are a number of art galleries in Whitefish that participate in a "First Thursdays" program on the first Thursday night of each month from July to October. On Tuesday evenings, head to the downtown farmers' market.

For a behind-the-scenes look at some of the local farms and their offerings, contact **FarmHands** (www.whoisyourfarmer.org; ☎ **406/862-7633**) for a free map of Flathead Valley farms that produce everything from goats to garlic and also welcome visitors.

Where to Stay

IN & AROUND TOWN

Whitefish might just have the best range of accommodations in all of Montana, with everything from mom-and-pop motels to graceful inns to slope-side condos. There's a **Super 8,** 800 Spokane Ave. (☎ **800/800-8000** or 406/862-8255), with double rates of about $105 nightly in peak season. The **Pine Lodge,** 920 Spokane Ave. (www.thepinelodge.com; ☎ **800/305-7463** or 406/862-7600), is a good independent option, with doubles and suites for $142 to $225 in summer, less during other times of year.

Best Western Rocky Mountain Lodge ★   Located on the U.S. 93 commercial strip just south of downtown, this is a very nice Best Western, with an emphasis on Western. The rooms are sunny and nicely maintained, with balconies and hot tubs in the higher-priced options. The larger rooms have their own wet bars and fireplaces. This is an especially good option for those passing through on their way to or from Glacier who aren't concerned with proximity to downtown Whitefish or the ski resort. The outdoor year-round pool is a nice perk.

6510 U.S. 93 S., Whitefish, MT 59937. www.rockymtnlodge.com. ☎ **800/862-2569** or 406/862-2569. Fax 406/862-1154. 79 units. $151–$161 double; $202 suite; lower rates fall to spring. Pets accepted on 1st floor ($15–$20 one-time fee). Rates include continental breakfast. AE, DC, DISC, MC, V. **Amenities:** Exercise room; outdoor Jacuzzi; outdoor heated pool. *In room:* A/C, TV, hair dryer, Wi-Fi (free).

The Garden Wall Inn ★★★ 🛏   While it's right on the main Whitefish drag, the Garden Wall Inn is a world of its own. Owners Rhonda Fitzgerald and Chris Schustrom clearly take pride in providing all of the little luxurious extras. The inn is full of country charm—it was built in 1923, and all of the furnishings are period antiques, including claw-foot tubs and Art Deco dressers, depending on your room. Every detail is just about perfect, right down to the towels, which are fluffy and large enough to dry two adults. Since Rhonda and Chris are both trained chefs, breakfast is a gourmet event with an emphasis on local ingredients (the wild huckleberry crepes are a standout), and afternoons end with hors d'oeuvres and beverages. They're also avid outdoorspeople: Ask them for tips before you head out on that excursion to Glacier or Whitefish Mountain Resort.

504 Spokane Ave., Whitefish, MT 59937. www.gardenwallinn.com. © **888/530-1700** or 406/862-3440. 4 units. $155–$195 double; $275 suite. Rates include full breakfast and afternoon refreshments. AE, MC, V. In room: No phone, Wi-Fi (free).

Good Medicine Lodge ★★   The stylish Good Medicine Lodge is an excellent place that is continually improving itself. Two of the best rooms have gas-log stoves and new furnishings. Several second-floor rooms have beautiful views of the Big Mountain, and ground-floor rooms have porches with access to the remarkable backyard, featuring plenty of green grass, a great deck, and all sorts of swings, benches, and chairs. Rooms are large, modern, and clean, and decorated with various themes, including golf, Western, and Native American. One suite has an "outdoor living room" and accepts pets; another features an eight-headed shower. Breakfasts include a delectable smoked trout cake on a savory corn pancake with a poached egg and dill sauce.

537 Wisconsin Ave., Whitefish, MT 59937. www.goodmedicinelodge.com. © **800/860-5488** or 406/862-5488. Fax 406/862-5489. 9 units, including 3 suites. $160–$185 double; $215–$285 suite. Lower rates fall to spring. Rates include full breakfast. AE, DISC, MC, V. Pets accepted in 1 suite. **Amenities:** Outdoor Jacuzzi. In room: A/C, hair dryer, Wi-Fi (free).

Grouse Mountain Lodge ★★   Immediately adjacent to the 18th hole of one of Whitefish Lake's two golf courses, Grouse Mountain Lodge has been one of Montana's premier vacation lodge properties since 1984. The lodge combines luxury accommodations, fine service, and good food to provide a memorable experience. Standard hotel-like rooms are called executive rooms, with vaulted ceilings and a wet bar, and overlook the golf course from the third floor. The loft rooms have a king-size bed, fridge, and microwave downstairs, and a staircase leading to the loft, featuring a TV room and an area with two twin beds. The restaurant has two places to eat: a dining room and a nice patio.

2 Fairway Dr., Whitefish, MT 59937. www.grousemountainlodge.com. © **877/862-1505** or 406/862-3000. 145 units, including 12 lofts. $219–$279 double; $299–$499 loft; lower rates fall to spring. AE, DISC, MC, V. **Amenities:** Restaurant; concierge; golf course; 2 outdoor Jacuzzis; indoor pool; sauna. In room: A/C, TV, Wi-Fi (free).

Haymoon Resort ★   Located 5 miles south of Whitefish, Haymoon Resort consists of several log homes and cabins around a central cattail-fringed lake. Featuring knotty pine, hardwood floors, and exposed log ceilings, the cabins (several of which were built by local Amish craftsmen) sleep 4 to 20 people and are ideal for families and self-sufficient travelers who'd rather have a kitchen than easy access to the restaurants in Whitefish. For those types, however, the resort also has a **hip downtown flat** with a purple-carpeted living room with a foosball table and a massive bar, sleeping up to 10 people in three bedrooms.

1845 Hodgson Rd., Whitefish, MT 59937. www.haymoonresort.com. © **406/862-1471** or 406/270-8771. 7 units. Winter and summer $179–$799 double; lower rates fall and spring. AE, DISC, MC, V. Pets accepted ($150 deposit). **Amenities:** Outdoor Jacuzzi. In room: TV/DVD, kitchen, Wi-Fi (free). Located 5 miles south of Whitefish, east on Hodgson Rd.

Hidden Moose Lodge ★★ 🏢 Striking a nice balance between the service of a B&B and the privacy of a hotel, this small, independent, moose-adorned property is centered on a vaulted, high-ceilinged great room with an impressive river-rock-chimney fireplace. The comfortable rooms are nicely done as well, with a mellow Montana vibe and bathroom mirrors appointed with handmade ironwork. Guests can savor their gourmet breakfast (including some seriously tasty huckleberry waffles and *huevos rancheros*) on their own decks, if they wish. The lodge is located about 1½ miles from town on the road to Whitefish Mountain Resort and has a small trail system on its property that connects with trails into the surrounding mountains.

1735 E. Lakeshore Dr. (on the road to Whitefish Mountain Resort), Whitefish, MT 59937. www.hiddenmooselodge.com. ℂ **888/733-6667** or 406/862-6516. Fax 406/862-6514. 13 units, including 2 suites. $159 double; $209–$249 suite; lower rates fall to spring. Rates include full breakfast. AE, DISC, MC, V. **Amenities:** Outdoor Jacuzzi. *In room:* TV/DVD, movie library, fridge, MP3 docking stations, Wi-Fi (free).

The Lodge at Whitefish Lake ★★ Inspired by the classic lodges in the national parks of the West, this bold building opened in 2005 and keeps getting bigger and better. The latest addition is the Viking Lodge, a 36-room complex overlooking a nature preserve and connected to the main lodge via covered pedestrian bridge. Lodge rooms and suites are attractively decorated, with slate tile floors, rock fireplaces, and private balconies. The preexisting resort condos include a very large tiled kitchen, a dining area, a deck overlooking Whitefish Lake and the marina, and a large loft bedroom, as well as a downstairs bedroom. In summer, there is a full-service marina with boat rentals. The Boat Club restaurant has a popular lakefront deck that attracts a boisterous cocktail crowd for summer sunsets.

1380 Wisconsin Ave., Whitefish, MT 59937. www.lodgeatwhitefishlake.com. ℂ **877/887-4026** or 406/863-4000. Fax 406/863-2750. 121 units, including 18 condos. $249–$395 double; $406–$1,150 suite; $499–$599 condo; lower rates fall to spring. AE, DISC, MC, V. **Amenities:** 2 restaurants; lounge; exercise room; outdoor Jacuzzi; outdoor pool; spa; watersports rentals; Wi-Fi (free). *In room:* A/C, TV, hair dryer, Internet (free), kitchen.

North Forty Resort 🏢 Nestled in the pines along Mont. 40 between Whitefish and Columbia Falls, the North Forty is a great place to stay if you don't like being in town but still want to be close. Even the smaller duplex cabins all have large living areas, fireplaces, kitchens, front porches, and barbecue grills. North Forty is located in a serene and quiet area off the main highway, and there is a hiking/cross-country skiing trail located at the north end of the property.

3765 Mont. 40 W., P.O. Box 4250, Whitefish, MT 59937. www.northfortyresort.com. ℂ **800/775-1740** or 406/862-7740. Fax 406/862-7741. 22 units. Summer $169–$269 double; fall to spring $119–$229 double. AE, DISC, MC, V. Pets accepted ($10 per night). **Amenities:** Outdoor Jacuzzi. *In room:* TV, kitchen, Wi-Fi (free).

AT WHITEFISH MOUNTAIN RESORT

Whitefish Mountain Resort is a full-service ski area, attracting local skiers, Canadian and American vacationers, and families. It provides a wide variety of accommodations to fit almost every pocketbook. Be sure to ask about discounted lift and lodging packages. If you're looking for a house or condo instead of a hotel, inquire at **Whitefish Mountain Resort Lodging** (www.skiwhitefish.com; ℂ **800/858-4152**). Most are available for rent on a nightly basis, although some require longer stays. You can get a low-end condo or house for as little as $150 a night, or a glorious ski home during the holiday season for about $1,250. A video-lending library is available, as is a heated indoor pool for certain condos.

Edelweiss ☺   The Edelweiss has some very nice large rooms, all with kitchens, full bathrooms, and fireplaces, and configurations ranging from basic studios to condo units with lofts and two bathrooms. Many of the rooms have panoramic views of the valley below, and all of them have a small balcony or patio. Convenient to the lifts, the Edelweiss has a large hot tub and a Finnish dry-heat sauna. Residents also have access to an indoor swimming pool.

3840 Big Mountain Rd., Whitefish, MT 59937. www.skiwhitefish.com. 📞 **800/858-5439** or 406/862-5252. Fax 406/862-0586. 50 units. $130–$170 double. AE, MC, V. **Amenities:** Indoor Jacuzzi; sauna. *In room:* TV/VCR, kitchen.

Hibernation House 🔱   This is the least expensive place on the hill, popular with high school and college groups, ski teams, and families on budgets. And if you'll be on the slopes all day and just want a clean bed, this will do just fine. All of the rooms are exactly alike: pretty small with a queen-size bed and a set of bunk beds. Each room has its own television—a relatively recent development—but people still like to congregate in the lobby, where there is a large-screen TV. You can ski right to the back door on a groomed trail, and it is only a short walk to a lift in the morning. Another perk: The complimentary buffet breakfast is quite good.

3812 Big Mountain Rd., Whitefish, MT 59937. www.skiwhitefish.com. 📞 **800/858-5439** or 406/862-1982. Fax 406/862-1956. 42 units. $70–$95 double. Rates include full breakfast. AE, DISC, MC, V. **Amenities:** Outdoor Jacuzzi. *In room:* TV.

Kandahar Lodge ★   Kandahar combines the genteel ambience of a European inn with the requirements of an upscale modern ski hotel. The rooms are large and elegantly appointed, featuring pine walls, leather furnishings, and down comforters. About a third of the units are outfitted with kitchenettes, and the large loft bedrooms have vaulted ceilings. Overall, the lodge is one of the best (and priciest) lodging options at Whitefish Mountain Resort. Likewise, the Cafe Kandahar is the best restaurant on the mountain (see "Where to Eat," below).

3824 Big Mountain Rd., Whitefish, MT 59937. www.kandaharlodge.com. 📞 **800/862-6094** or 406/862-6098. Fax 406/862-6095. 50 units, including 11 suites. $129–$349 double; $279–$659 suite. Rates include continental breakfast. AE, DISC, MC, V. Closed May and Oct–Nov. **Amenities:** Restaurant; lounge; exercise room; outdoor Jacuzzi; spa. *In room:* A/C, TV, fridge, kitchenettes (in some), Wi-Fi (free).

Kintla Lodge ★   A grand native log-and-stone lodge that echoes the architecture in Glacier National Park, Kintla is upscale, with an elevator serving its four floors. All units have wood-clad French doors opening onto a patio, stone flooring in the entry and kitchens, individual ski storage, and tastefully simple pine furnishings. Best of all, Kintla is only 20 feet from Whitefish Mountain Resort's Tenderfoot lift. There is no restaurant on the premises, but the village's tonier shops are located on the ground level outside.

Whitefish Mountain Resort Village, Whitefish, MT 59937. www.skiwhitefish.com. 📞 **800/858-4157** or 406/862-1960. Fax 406/862-2955. 14 units. $150–$450 1- to 3-bedroom unit. AE, DISC, MC, V. **Amenities:** Outdoor Jacuzzi; sauna. *In room:* TV/VCR.

Morning Eagle Lodge ★★   The newest lodging option at Whitefish Mountain Resort, Morning Eagle welcomed its first guests during the 2003–04 ski season and immediately entrenched itself as the most posh address on these slopes. The units range from studios to lavish three-bedroom affairs, all with similar contemporary, mildly Western decor: granite countertops, checkered Berber carpet and slate flooring, large tiled bathrooms, and fully equipped kitchens. The studios here are about 500 square feet, whereas the largest three-bedroom, three-bathroom units are about three times that size. The rooms have great views, pullout sleeper sofas, washer/dryer units, and private balconies. There is a ski room downstairs and a rooftop deck—a great perk, featuring outdoor heaters, a barbecue, and a 10-person hot tub.

Whitefish Mountain Resort Village, Whitefish, MT 59937. www.skiwhitefish.com. ℂ **800/858-4157** or 406/862-1960. Fax 406/862-2955. 49 units. $175–$475 1- to 3-bedroom unit. AE, DISC, MC, V. **Amenities:** Outdoor Jacuzzi; sauna. In room: TV/DVD player, hair dryer, kitchen.

Ptarmigan Village ★ This is an extensive condo setup that is spread over a lower portion of the Whitefish Mountain Resort. The individually owned units are pretty snazzy, featuring vaulted ceilings, fireplaces, fully equipped kitchens, and some unexpected touches: woodstoves, grills, CD players, and spiral staircases. The decks overlook a woody area where signs warn about increased black bear activity in the summer—there's a hiking trail here, too, if the bears don't scare you off. There's also a nice fishing pond where kids can spy out the turtles hiding in the reeds in summer.

3000 Big Mountain Rd., P.O. Box 458, Whitefish, MT 59937. www.ptarmiganvillage.com. ℂ **800/ 552-3952** or 406/862-3594. Fax 406/862-6664. 50 units. $112–$230 condo; $250–$450 private home. AE, DISC, MC, V. **Amenities:** Indoor Jacuzzi; indoor and outdoor pools; sauna; tennis courts. In room: TV/VCR, CD player, kitchen.

CAMPING

Whitefish Lake State Park is tucked on the outskirts of town in a nicely wooded area on Whitefish Lake. A campsite runs $20 to $23 nightly ($15 for Montana residents). Call the **Department of Fish, Wildlife, and Parks** (www.fwp.mt.gov; ℂ **406/862-3991**) for additional information. The **Whitefish KOA Kampground** (www.glacierparkkoa.com; ℂ **800/562-8734** or 406/862-4242) is a comprehensive RV park about 2 miles south of town on U.S. 93 and has RV and tent sites (about $30–$70 each) and cabins ($79–$155).

Where to Eat

A good cup of organic coffee and a selection of baked goods are available at the **Montana Coffee Traders,** located at 110 Central Ave. (ℂ 406/862-7667), which also houses a nifty store (selling kitchen gadgets, food, and gifts) and a nice place to read a book. **Loula's Café,** located downstairs at 300 E. 2nd St. (ℂ **406/862-5614**), serves traditional American breakfasts and salads and sandwiches for lunch in an attractive setting, as well as eclectic dinners Wednesday through Saturday. The **Buffalo Cafe,** 514 3rd St. (ℂ **406/862-2833**), is Whitefish's best breakfast spot—try their legendary bacon-and-egg-filled pies. And for inexpensive but tasty Mexican fare for lunch and dinner, try **La Hacienda,** 130 Central Ave. (ℂ **406/862-6111**), in the Remington Casino. Come late night, the best option is **Second Street Pizza,** 306 2nd St. E. (ℂ **406/862-3620**).

Cafe Kandahar ★★★ FRENCH/NEW AMERICAN Chef Andy Blanton has raised the stakes in the Whitefish culinary scene by reinventing the restaurant at Kandahar Lodge since he took it over with his family in 2006. The appealing room, highlighted by bay windows looking down the mountain and historical photos of the area, is an excellent setting for his handiwork in the kitchen. Patrons can choose off two menus, one that changes nightly, another that lasts a season. Inspired by French and Creole traditions but more than willing to experiment, Blanton uses as much local produce and meats as he can in such creations as seared elk roulade with forest mushrooms, grilled buffalo tenderloin, and beef *tournedos* with oyster mushroom and smoked shallot bordelaise; he also experiments with far-flung influences in a number of creative seafood and pasta dishes. The wine list and the desserts—including a decadently rich molten chocolate soufflé with raspberry-huckleberry *coulis*—are also excellent.

3824 Big Mountain Rd., at Kandahar Lodge, Whitefish Mountain Resort. www.cafekandahar.com. ☏ **406/862-6247.** Reservations recommended. Main courses $20–$60. AE, DISC, MC, V. Daily 5:30–9:30pm. Closed May and Oct–Nov.

Ciao Mambo ITALIAN A dimly lit *ristorante*, Ciao Mambo is otherwise hard to miss. The color scheme and the music are both loud—the bright walls are multicolored and the stereo blasts Sinatra, Louis Prima, and Dean Martin—but it complements the rich Italian fare quite nicely. For an appetizer, you can't miss with the Italian Tootsie Rolls: egg wrappers stuffed with ricotta, mozzarella, and pesto. Cooked in an open central kitchen, main courses range from crackly crust pizza to Papa Biagio's Bolognese (ribbon noodles baked with meat sauce and mozzarella) and Pollo Con Formaggio (two breaded chicken cutlets dripping with four cheeses).

415 2nd St. E. www.ciaomambo.com. ☏ **406/862-5050.** Reservations accepted for parties of 8 or more only. Main courses $11–$27. AE, DISC, MC, V. Mon–Sat 5–10pm; Sun 5–9pm; shorter winter hours.

Green Tea House ★ VEGETARIAN This fresh and airy cafe is one of Montana's few vegetarian-only eateries, using healthy and often local ingredients in a wide range of dishes, including numerous vegan and raw options. Everything is organic and gluten- and dairy-free, from the smoothies and baked goods to the chickpea burgers, wraps, bowls, and salads. Recommended is the chipotle red bean hummus wrap and the pad thai bowl. There are themed dinners on Wednesday and Thursday, and the place has won plenty of local devotees.

415 E. 2nd St. www.thegreenteahouse.net. ☏ **406/863-9600.** Main courses $7–$14. AE, MC, V. Mon–Tues 9am–5pm; Wed–Sat 9am–8:30pm; Sun 10am–5pm; shorter winter hours.

Haskill Station ★ ☺ AMERICAN A kitsch-, ski-sign-, and petroliana-bedecked bar and grill between downtown and Whitefish Mountain Resort, Haskill Station is good for adults and great for kids. Besides the kid-size patio chairs, crayons, and games, the kids' menu ($5–$7) is a cut above, with fresh ingredients and homemade options. The menu for older customers ranges from Mexican (fish tacos and burritos) and American (burgers and salads) to Cajun (cat fish po'boys and muffaleta sandwiches) and Italian (pasta puttanesca), making it hard to leave here unsatisfied.

1705 Wisconsin Ave. ☏ **406/863-5455.** Main courses $9–$14. AE, DISC, MC, V. Daily 5–9:30pm.

Pescado Blanco ★ MEXICAN Located in the pine-clad ground floor of a split-level building in downtown Whitefish, Pescado Blanco puts a creative spin on Mexican food—chef/owner David Lewis dubs this cuisine "Mountain Mexican." Favoring local ingredients and fresh seafood, Lewis plates up such savory and spicy dishes as enchiladas (bison, duck, or seafood), elk chorizo tacos, and tortilla-crusted halibut. The daily seafood specials are standouts, with creative Mexican-inspired preparations like chili-seared ahi with roasted red pepper. The salsa is excellent; beer, wine, and wine-based margaritas are served.

235 1st St. www.pescadoblanco.com. ☏ **406/862-3290.** Main courses $13–$22. DISC, MC, V. Daily 5–10pm (until 9pm fall to spring).

The Tupelo Grille ★★ CONTINENTAL/CAJUN The Tupelo is downtown Whitefish's most reliable restaurant, especially for those with a taste for spicy New Orleans–style food. Creole chicken and dumplings in mustard-sage cream sauce and a Cajun Creole combo (a platter of shrimp Creole, crawfish étouffée, and chicken and sausage jambalaya) are specialties. The rack of lamb is also tough to beat. The atmosphere is pleasant and mildly contemporary, with big, comfortable booths and tables.

17 Central Ave. © **406/862-6136.** Reservations recommended for large parties. Main courses $12–$31. AE, MC, V. Summer daily 5:30–10pm; winter Mon–Sat 5:30–9:30pm.

Wasabi ★★ SUSHI   Few locals thought that a sushi joint in Whitefish would fly, but it turned out to be a match made in heaven. The contemporary space is a real eye-catcher, with purple walls, an orange ceiling, and a large mirror—displaying the chefs hard at work—above checkerboard floors. The menu runs the whole gamut of sushi, from California rolls, to six-fish rainbow rolls, to quinoa-based rolls, and also includes a nice selection of Asian-influenced beef, poultry, and seafood. There's beer, wine, and six varieties of sake, but no liquor. The establishment also encompasses the adjacent **Ginger Grill,** a casual East-meets-West eatery. The desserts, including Key lime pie and huckleberry ice cream, are delectable.

419 E. 2nd St. www.wasabimt.com. © **406/863-9283.** Reservations recommended. Sushi $6–$15 per order; main courses $10–$30. AE, MC, V. Daily 5–9:30pm. Closed Sun fall and spring.

Whitefish Lake Restaurant ★ CONTINENTAL   Located at the public golf course, it is generally considered to be the best restaurant in the Whitefish area. It's housed in a building that was constructed in 1936 as a WPA project. The dining room has an elegant yet rustic atmosphere: dark and quiet, with large log beams and a large stone fireplace providing warmth on chilly evenings. The menu for the evening meal covers the culinary landscape, from vegetable napoleon to 12-ounce prime rib, rack of lamb, and roast duckling; fresh seafood may include lobster, king crab, halibut, or Pacific salmon. The wine list is impressive, as is the bar's martini menu. As formal as a golf club ever gets, it's the only place in Whitefish that approaches dressy, but casual diners will always feel comfortable at the bar.

U.S. 93 N. (at the Whitefish Lake Golf Course). www.whitefishlakerestaurant.com. © **406/862-5285.** Reservations recommended. Lunch $7–$12; dinner $17–$40. AE, DISC, MC, V. Summer daily 11am–3pm and 5:30–10pm; winter Sun–Thurs 5:30–9pm, Fri–Sat 5:30–9:30pm.

 The Yaak

Remote and wild, to say the least, the **Yaak Valley** is nestled in far northwestern Montana on Mont. 308 and is home to the only rainforests in the state. It's extraordinarily beautiful in some places and devastated by clear-cut logging in others. And as a tourist destination, it's certainly not for everyone. I can't recommend any of the few lodging or eating/drinking establishments in the valley—unless you're desperate for a beer or an earful from a gun-toting, anti-government survivalist—but I can recommend some of its campgrounds and hiking trails. I like both the tranquil, two-site Caribou Campground, just

northwest of the town of Yaak on Mont. 308 (no fee), and the Vinal–Mt. Henry–Boulder National Recreational Trail, just west of the campground. Take caution, however: Not only is this wolf and grizzly country, but many of the trails are favored by drug smugglers entering the U.S. from Canada. Contact the **Kootenai National Forest,** 31374 U.S. 2, Libby, MT 59923 (www.fs.usda.gov/kootenai; © **406/293-6211**), for more information. And stock up on groceries and other supplies in Whitefish or Kalispell before you go—the shopping in these parts leaves something to be desired.

Whitefish After Dark

The **Alpine Theatre Project** (www.alpinetheatreproject.org; © **406/862-7469**) and the **Whitefish Theatre Company** (www.whitefishtheatreco.org; © **406/862-5371**) stage musicals and dramas at the O'Shaughnessy Center and Whitefish Performing Arts Center in downtown Whitefish. There's also a pretty good bar scene: Start at the **Black Star Draught House** at the **Great Northern Brewing Company,** 2 Central Ave. (© **406/863-1002**), serving plump sandwiches and beers that are brewed on premise. Then head over to the **Great Northern Bar and Grill,** 27 Central Ave. (© **406/862-2816**), which is jumping on weekend nights. Your final stop: the **Bulldog Saloon,** 144 Central Ave. (© **406/862-5636**). Not just a bar, the Bulldog turns out a pretty mean garlic burger, too.

COLUMBIA FALLS

11 miles N of Kalispell; 9 miles E of Whitefish

Columbia Falls gets a bad rep not only for being the home of the Plum Creek plant, a smoke-billowing institution seen for miles even at night, but also for its not-so-subtle image as a tourist trap. And unlike Great Falls, where the falls are out of town and (gasp!) dammed, Columbia Falls goes one better by not having any falls at all. The redeeming features and equalizers are the town's proximity to Glacier National Park and lodging rates that are relatively inexpensive—it's a good fallback location if you have trouble finding a room in Whitefish. Residents here are real Montanans, something of a rarity in an area being inundated with out-of-staters setting up house.

Essentials

GETTING THERE **Glacier Park International Airport** (www.iflyglacier.com; © **406/257-5994**) is located north of town at 4170 U.S. 2. **Alaska/Horizon, Allegiant, Delta,** and **United** provide service. The closest **Amtrak** station is in Whitefish, 10 miles to the northwest.

VISITOR INFORMATION The **Columbia Falls Area Chamber of Commerce,** P.O. Box 312, Columbia Falls, MT 59912 (www.columbiafallschamber.com; © **406/892-2072**), can provide you with pertinent area information. The chamber and the **U.S. Forest Service** jointly operate an information cabin in Maranette Park on U.S. 2 near the center of town. You can also get Columbia Falls information from the **Glacier Country Regional Tourism Commission** (www.glaciermt.com; © **800/338-5072**).

GETTING AROUND **Dollar,** 5506 U.S. 2 W. (© **406/892-0009**), and **Thrifty,** 4785 U.S. 2 W. (© **406/257-7333**), both have car-rental offices in Columbia Falls.

Getting Outside

Two of the best-kept secrets in this part of the state are the **North** and **South Lion lakes.** To find them, follow the signs to the west side of the Hungry Horse Reservoir. Less than 5 miles after turning off of Mont. 40, you will come to a cutoff to the North Lion Lake and, within a hundred yards, arrive at South Lion Lake. Both are well protected, quiet, and for the most part undiscovered by tourists—excellent for camping, picnicking, fishing, or swimming.

There is a road around **Hungry Horse Reservoir,** a 110-mile round-trip that you can start from the town of Hungry Horse. Hungry Horse is 9 miles south of West

Glacier or 6 miles east of Columbia Falls on U.S. 2. This is an excellent drive for seeing wildlife. You're almost certain to see at least an elk, and maybe a moose or bear. It's also a great place for fishing.

GOLF

Columbia Falls is home to one of Montana's best golf courses, **Meadow Lake** (www. meadowlakegolf.com; ☎ **406/892-2111**) at the Meadow Lake Resort; see "Where to Stay," below. About 6,700 yards from the back tees, the course is very challenging, especially the greens, which are "speed sensitive" and have lots of nearly invisible breaks in them. The fairways are fairly wide but lined with intimidating large trees. Greens fees are $35 to $64 for 18 holes, depending on the time of year and day. Carts rent for $16 per rider.

HIKING

Columbia Mountain, Glacier National Park, and the Jewel Basin are nearby, but the **Great Northern** is the grandpappy of 'em all in these parts. If you want a leisurely stroll with moderate difficulty, stick to the Danny On Trail on the Big Mountain in Whitefish. If you want 8 hours of hardship, then the Great Northern is for you. To get there, take U.S. 2 to Martin City, then turn onto the East Side Reservoir Road for 15 miles. At that point, turn east to Highline Loop Road, and from here you should be able to see the approach route. The hike goes up the 8,705-foot-high Great Northern Mountain in the Great Bear Wilderness. While there's not an official trail, enough people have beaten a path to the summit that one is clear enough to make out. This isn't a leisurely walk, nor is it the most publicized hike in the area, but it is the most rewarding for those willing to make the effort. The views of Glacier and the Hungry Horse Reservoir are remarkable.

Exploring the Town: Kitsch & Camp

Remember when your dad used to drive the family to the ocean or the mountains for the annual family vacation? Whenever you passed the Tent of Miracles or the Cave of 10,000 Rattlesnakes or the Fabulous Mystery House, you'd beg Dad to stop. He always ignored you and drove on as if you hadn't spoken. Columbia Falls offers you the chance to find out what attractions like these are all about.

Montana's largest waterslide park, the **Big Sky Waterpark,** at the junction of U.S. highways 2 and 206 (www.bigskywp.com; ☎ **406/892-5026**), is a good place to cool off. The **Amazing Fun Center,** at U.S. 2 E., Coram (www.amazingfuncenter.com; ☎ **406/387-5902**), offers myriad opportunities to stay dry *and* have some fun. Like rats hunting for an odorless cheese, tourists often enter the Fun Center's maze and emerge hours later. If mazes aren't your bag, the place also has go-carts, mini-golf, and other games. The **House of Mystery,** 7800 U.S. 2 E., Columbia Falls (www. montanavortex.com; ☎ **406/892-1210**), offers a vortex (you'll just have to go in to find out) and other bewilderments.

Where to Stay

Bad Rock Country Bed and Breakfast ★ 🎁 This is a great choice for those who want to use Columbia Falls as a base for visiting both Glacier and Whitefish but want to avoid the hustle and bustle of being right on the highway. Nestled in a beautifully landscaped meadow at the base of the Swan Mountains, this is a very good B&B with three rooms in the main house and five cabin units on the grounds. The cabins are newer, built with square-cut pine logs and furnished with custom lodgepole-pine trappings and fridges, microwaves, and coffeemakers. In the main house, the best room is the Columbia Mountain Suite, with a four-poster queen-size bed, Asian art on its red walls, and a private balcony perfect for watching the sunset. The Bad Rock is known for its lavish breakfasts; you might have bacon-wrapped polenta or Montana potato pie.

480 Bad Rock Dr., Columbia Falls, MT 59912. www.badrock.com. ℂ **888/892-2829** or 406/892-2829. 3 main house units, 5 cabin units. Summer $185–$225 double; fall–spring $145–$150 double. Rates include full breakfast. DISC, MC, V. *In room:* A/C, fridge (in some), hair dryer, microwave (in some), Wi-Fi (free).

Glacier Park Motel and Campground 🏷 This well-maintained, low-cost hostelry offers clean, comfortable accommodations, with prices to match their modesty. Single rooms come with one queen-size bed, and double rooms have two queen-size beds. The accommodations are no better or worse than those found in a typical low-cost national chain. Also available for rent are 13 RV campsites (about $35 each) and four tipis ($75, summer only).

7285 U.S. 2 E. (at U.S. 206), Columbia Falls, MT 59912. www.glacierparkmotelandcampground. com. ℂ **406/892-7686.** Fax 406/892-4575. 25 units, including 4 suites and 3 cabins. $75–$125 double; $55–$75 cabin; $100–$165 suite; lower rates fall to spring. Rates include continental breakfast. AE, DISC, MC, V. **Amenities:** 2 indoor Jacuzzis; outdoor heated pool. *In room:* TV, kitchenettes, Wi-Fi (free).

Meadow Lake Resort ★ Meadow Lake offers a wide variety of excellent accommodations in a modern-resort style. Development focuses on the golf course, which is one of the best in the state. Rooms are stylish in the modern sense, and many of the condo units have jetted tubs. The resort has a recreation center with Nautilus weight machines and aerobic equipment. There are large indoor and outdoor pools and hot tubs. The inn features standard-size hotel rooms with a king-size bed, double sleeper sofa, a large bathroom with double vanity sinks, and a veranda or patio. The condos come in suites (a single room with a partial kitchen, a bathroom, and usually a Jacuzzi), or one- and two-bedroom versions, which all have fireplaces, full kitchens, convenient washer and dryer access, private deck with barbecue, DVD player, and stereo. Even if you haven't come for golf, this is still the best place in town to spend the night.

100 St. Andrews Dr., Columbia Falls, MT 59912. www.meadowlake.com. ℂ **800/321-4653** or 406/892-8700. Fax 406/892-8731. 24 units in inn, plus a wide variety of condos and rental homes. $139–$189 at inn; $139–$620 condo or home. AE, DISC, MC, V. **Amenities:** Restaurant; lounge; children's program; exercise room; 18-hole golf course; Jacuzzi; indoor and outdoor heated pools; sauna; spa. *In room:* A/C, TV/DVD, DVD library, kitchen.

Where to Eat

The Back Room of the Nite Owl 🏷 AMERICAN This old-fashioned roadside eatery is just off the main drag in Columbia Falls. You'll be pleasantly surprised by what the joint has to offer—the roasted chicken, spareribs, and country ribs (small chunks cooked in barbecue sauce) are all delicious and reasonably priced. Fry bread is the house specialty and comes with meals instead of standard bread items. The Sunday pizza, fried chicken, and salad buffet is a bargain for about $12. Up front, the Nite Owl itself is one of the busiest restaurants in the region, serving three hearty American meals daily from 5:30am to 11pm.

U.S. 2 E. (near the intersection with 4th Ave.). www.niteowlbackroom.com. ℂ **406/892-3131.** Most items $9–$19. AE, DISC, MC, V. Daily 4–9pm.

HELENA & SOUTHWESTERN MONTANA

This is where Montana came of age, changing in a few short years from an isolated outback of fur traders and rugged explorers to a series of bustling, boisterous mining camps, where fortunes were made and lost overnight. Butte was once the "Richest Hill on Earth," and gold strikes were also made at Helena's Last Chance Gulch and Virginia City's Alder Gulch. Bannack, another gold-mining boomtown, was the first territorial capital.

The area has calmed down somewhat since then. Butte's Berkeley Pit, full of toxic water, is a Superfund site. The Anaconda copper smelter is shut down, and the Old Works, formerly a Superfund site itself, is now a golf course. Helena is the businesslike state capital, the seat of Montana's politics.

But in the Big Hole Valley, you can still see some ranching and farming done the old-fashioned way. There are plenty of fishing and outdoor opportunities all over the mountains that cloak southwestern Montana.

While signs of modern American life are now rampant, many cross-sections of this region's storied past have been meticulously preserved. The old prison at Deer Lodge can give you an eye-opening perspective on frontier justice, and the preserved mining towns of Nevada City and Virginia City provide a taste of the boomtown, mining-camp life.

SCENIC DRIVES

Two high-speed federal highways—interstates 90 and 15—intersect in the region, but the best roads to take are the well-maintained back roads: state and county highways that follow unlikely and out-of-the-way paths. Traveling from Anaconda to Dillon could be done via the interstate in just over an hour. But a better, less-frequented route through the Big Hole Valley runs east of the Continental Divide and the Anaconda-Pintler Wilderness Area. A good stopping point is Wisdom, which has the dubious distinction of being one of the coldest towns in the Lower 48, and the turnoff for the Big Hole National Battlefield. Driving farther south on Mont. 278 takes you to Jackson, then Bannack State Park, before ending at I-15 south of Dillon. From Dillon, drive north on Mont. 41 to Twin Bridges and the junction with Mont. 287. This road runs south through the Old West towns of Sheridan, Laurin, Alder, Nevada City, and Virginia City before ending in Ennis at the junction with U.S. 287.

Driving Tour 1: The Big Hole Valley

This short loop tour takes you through the Big Hole Valley, nicknamed "Land of 10,000 Haystacks." Begin in Dillon, the largest of the towns in this area, and keep your eye out for white-tailed and mule deer in the morning and early evening. Travel north on I-15 to Divide, then take Mont. 43 southwest to Wisdom. This is a tiny town with little other than its residents and the scenery to recommend it, but the Big Hole National Battlefield (described in detail later in this chapter) is a short drive west on Mont. 43 and is well worth the trip.

Then head back to Wisdom and take Mont. 278 south toward Dillon. Along the way, stop in Jackson for a soak in the hot springs, or tour Montana's territorial capital city, Bannack, in Bannack State Park (see p. 171) just 28 miles farther, off Mont. 278. As you stroll the boardwalks you'll discover the ease with which you can lose yourself in the state's early history—a microcosm that reflects the entire Old West. This drive is great during the summer, when haystacks fill the fields and the Bannack Days celebration re-creates early events in Montana's history. It's not so tame during winter months, though, when roads are icy and caution is required.

Driving Tour 2: The Pintler Scenic Route

This tour is best enjoyed during summer, when area attractions open their doors to visitors and long summer days extend daylight hours.

This scenic route takes you from the mining city of Anaconda on a loop tour with ghost towns, historic buildings, and wildlife. Starting in Anaconda—where you can visit the copper-smelting display at the Copper Village Museum or admire an old Art Deco theater, the **Washoe,** which was ranked fifth in the nation by David Naylor, author of *American Picture Palaces,* for its architectural value—you'll head on little-traveled roads into a mountainous area that rivals any in the state.

Northwest of Anaconda on Mont. 1 lies **Georgetown Lake,** a popular tourist destination in both summer and winter, when anglers and skiers flock to the lake and nearby ski area, **Discovery.** There are dog-sled races here on winter Sundays. Next stop is the charming historic town of **Philipsburg,** a good place for lunch or even an overnight stay. Continue on Mont. 1 to Drummond, known as the "Bull Shipper's Capital of the World."

Heading southeast on I-90 will take you to **Deer Lodge,** home to the state prison, historic **Grant-Kohrs Ranch,** and the **Montana Auto Museum,** which features a slightly depleted collection of 120 antique automobiles—restored, original models from the early 1900s to the 1960s. County Road 273 takes you back to Anaconda.

HELENA ★

64 miles N of Butte; 115 miles SE of Missoula; 89 miles S of Great Falls

Cradled in the foothills of the Montana Rockies, Helena is the focal point of the state's politics. During the week, it's a bustling community of elected officials, lobby-ists, and bureaucrats. On the weekends, however, it seems they all turn into outdoors fanatics, heading to the lakes and mountains. Helena is also a haven for artists and other creative types, evidenced by the galleries that dot the streets once dominated by mining-era saloons and houses of ill repute.

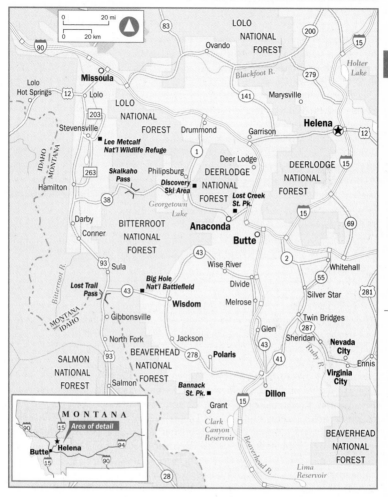

In its early days, Helena was a wild-and-woolly boomtown, built on gold mining. Last Chance Gulch was named when four miners said they had one last chance to hit it big in the West—and they did. The town boomed in the gold rush of 1865. During the height of this prosperity, only Manhattan could boast more millionaires than the small Montana city. And along the way, the town recorded an alarming number of murders and robberies. Then in 1935, earthquakes devastated the town. Beginning October 3, more than 2,000 tremors rocked the city, causing millions of dollars in damage.

After Helena took state capital rights from Virginia City in 1875, Marcus Daly, the Butte copper king with more than just a bystander's interest in the capital's location, decided to steal it away from Helena and move it to Anaconda, 25 miles from Butte.

As we all now know, Daly's efforts proved unsuccessful, but he started a political war that echoes throughout the state even today.

Essentials

GETTING THERE   **Alaskan/Horizon, Delta,** and **United** provide commuter links to larger airports in Montana and other Western states from **Helena Regional Airport** (www.helenaairport.com; © 406/442-2821), northeast of the city on Skyway Drive off U.S. 15.

The **bus depot** is located at 1415 N. Montana Ave. (© 406/442-5860), with service on **Rimrock Stages,** a Trailways affiliate (www.rimrocktrailways.com; © 800/255-7655) that links with Greyhound.

Driving from the east or west, take I-90; turn north on I-15 and head toward Helena. From the north or south, I-15 leads right into town.

VISITOR INFORMATION   A good starting point for local activities and area maps is the **Helena Convention and Visitor's Bureau** at 225 Cruse Ave., Ste. A, Helena, MT 59601 (www.gohelena.com; © 800/743-5362 or 406/447-1530). There is an information office run by the chamber out near the airport at Cedar Street off I-15. Another source is **Gold West Country** (a branch of Travel Montana, the mother lode for brochures and information about the region and the state), 1105 Main St., Deer Lodge, MT 59722 (www.goldwest.visitmt.com; © 800/879-1159).

GETTING AROUND   Car-rental agencies at the airport include **Avis** (© 800/230-4898), **Hertz** (© 800/654-3131), and **National** (© 800/227-7368). **Enterprise** (© 800/261-7331) is in town at 3015 Prospect Ave.

Getting Outside

Just beyond the city limits, the area is chock-full of recreational opportunities, with blue-ribbon trout streams, downhill ski areas, and millions of acres of public land.

FISHING

There are several stretches of prime fishing along the upper stretch of the Missouri River. The section from **Toston Dam** downstream to **Canyon Ferry Lake** offers brown and rainbow trout in the 2- to 10-pound class. Floating with large streamers, wet flies, and lures is the most popular and productive way to catch these fish as they make their way upriver to spawn. The fishing gets progressively better from late spring to fall. The section below **Hauser Dam** to **Beaver Creek** offers a chance for really big trout. Other popular fishing areas include **Park Lake,** 15 miles southwest of Helena; **Lake Helena;** and the **Smith River** to the east of the Big Belt Mountains.

Pro Outfitters, P.O. Box 621, Helena, MT 621 (www.prooutfitters.com; © 800/858-3497 or 406/442-5489), offers customized fly-fishing trips on the Smith River, considered in fishing circles one of the best in the state and the world, and other world-class trout waters. The company offers all-inclusive 3-day trips ($2,080 per person) and 5-day trips ($3,080–$3,950 per person) from mid-May to mid-July, as well as day trips ($475 for one or two anglers) on the Missouri River.

HIKING

Mount Helena City Park covers 628 acres on Mount Helena, a 5,468-foot peak that looks out over the city. Nine trails cover the park, the easiest of which, the **1906 Trail,** follows the base of the limestone cliffs past Devil's Kitchen to the 5,468-foot

HOTELS ■
The Barrister B&B **8**
Best Western Helena
Great Northern **16**
Elkhorn Mountain Inn **23**
Fairfield Inn of Helena **22**
Holiday Inn
Helena Downtown **4**
Jorgensen's Inn & Suites **20**
Red Lion Colonial Hotel **21**
The Sanders B&B **9**

ATTRACTIONS ●
Archie Bray Foundation **1**
Cathedral of St. Helena **10**
Gates of the Mountains **24**
Great Northern Carousel **17**
Holter Museum of Art **14**
Last Chance Tours Train **19**
Montana Historical Society **19**
Montana State Capitol **18**
Myrna Loy Center **7**

RESTAURANTS ◆
Benny's Bistro **12**
Bert & Ernie's **13**
FireTower Coffee House **15**
Lucca's **2**
The Marysville House **25**
On Broadway **6**
Parrot Confectionary **3**
Silver Star Steak Company **16**
Windbag Saloon **5**

SERVICES ●
Helena Convention &
Visitors Center **11**

summit. To reach the 1906 Trail, take West Main south of downtown and turn right on Reeder's Village Drive. Drive up the hill to the dead end, and you're at the trail head. **Hogback Trail** is a rough and rocky hike that leads from the peak to the exposed Hogback Ridge. Contact the Helena Convention and Visitor's Bureau (see above) for information.

There are more than 700 miles of trails in the Helena National Forest. The **Trout Creek Canyon Trail** offers a spectacular view of Hanging Valley. Helena is also the gateway to the **Gates of the Mountains Wilderness.** For a serious hike in the wilderness area, you can go to **Mann Gulch,** the site of a forest fire in August 1949. Sixteen firefighters parachuted into Mann Gulch at about 6pm on August 5. Within 2 hours, all but three had perished. The incident is the subject of Norman Maclean's book *Young Men and Fire.* You can get more information about hiking into Mann Gulch from the Helena Ranger district, with offices in Helena at 2880 Skyway Dr. (www.fs.usda.gov/helena; 🕐 **406/449-5490**).

ROCKHOUNDING

Helena was founded on gold mining, and the area is still rightly famous for its gemstones, particularly Montana sapphires. Sapphires, a variety of the mineral corundum, are harder than any natural stone except a diamond. The Helena area has several commercial areas that allow visitors to dig for sapphires. Diligent treasure seekers can also uncover garnets, moss agates, fossils, and hematite. The **Spokane Bar Sapphire Mine & Gold Fever Rock Shop,** 5360 Castles Rd. (www.sapphire mine.com; 🕐 **406/227-8989**), south of Hauser Lake, lets groups dig buckets for $60. The record sapphire taken from here was 155 carats.

SKIING

Great Divide Ski Area   Great Divide is primarily a local ski hill, not a destination resort, but the resort has added a half-pipe and night lights while expanding to 1,600 acres. With a 1,500-foot vertical drop, it is also pretty tough (15% beginner, 40% intermediate, and 45% advanced), although the Lower Mountain offers wide-open runs that cater to novice and intermediate skiers. There are a total of 139 trails on a trio of mountains served by five double chairs and a surface tow. There is also the Backyard Beginner Slope, with its own tow rope and three terrain parks for snowboarders. Private lessons are also available.

P.O. Box SKI, Marysville, MT 59640. www.skigd.com. 🕐 **406/449-3746.** Snow reports 🕐 406/447-1310. Lift tickets $36 adults, $16 kids grades 1–5 or beginner lift only, $30 middle and high school students, free for preschool children with adult; hourly tickets available for $8. Mid-Nov to early Apr Wed–Fri 10am–4pm, Sat–Sun 9am–4pm, with some Fri and Sat night skiing. Take exit 200 off I-15, then go west on Mont. 279 to Marysville Rd.

SNOWMOBILING

Three major trail systems are within a 30-minute drive of Helena. The Minnehaha-Rimini area grooms 120 miles of trails, and the Marysville and Magpie-Sunshine areas, with views into the Gates of the Mountains Wilderness, each groom 45 miles of trails. For details on these trails, as well as special event information, contact the **Helena Snowdrifters Snowmobile Club** (www.helenasnodrifters.org).

WATERSPORTS

Canyon Ferry Lake Recreation Area, managed by the Bureau of Reclamation (🕐 **406/475-3921**), is a 25-mile-long lake within 20 minutes of Helena. In the spring, summer, and fall, the lake is primarily a rainbow trout fishery, but it does have numerous campgrounds, picnic areas, and boat ramps. The lake is especially popular with water-skiers, jet-skiers, and water-tubers, though you'll see sailboats racing as well. This is also a prime bird-watching area.

Watersports fans also head to two Helena-area state parks that are centered on man-made lakes: **Spring Meadow Lake** (day use only) and **Black Sandy** at Hauser Lake (campsites are $20–$23 for nonresidents). Spring Meadow is a 30-acre, spring-fed lake on Helena's western edge, noted for its clarity and depth. Open to nonmotorized boats only, the lake is popular for swimming and fishing. To reach Spring Meadow Lake, take U.S. 12 west, then head north on Joslyn to Country Club. One of the only public parks on the shores of Hauser Lake, Black Sandy is an extremely popular weekend boating, fishing, and water-skiing takeoff point. To get to Hauser Reservoir, drive 7 miles north of Helena on I-15, then 4 miles east on Route 453, then follow signs 3 miles north on a county road. Information on both is available by calling the regional office (www.fwp.mt.gov; © **406/495-3270**), and each sports a $5 per vehicle day-use fee.

Seeing the Sights

A walking tour of the city will give you a capsule of the history of the Old West. For pointers on where to explore, contact the **Helena Convention and Visitor's Bureau** (© **800/743-5362** or 406/442-1530) and request one of the excellent walking tour brochures by the Montana Historical Society.

Last Chance Gulch was so named because a quartet of gold-seeking prospectors declared the spot to be their "last chance" to strike it rich. It came to be one of the richest gold-producing areas in the world and remains one of Helena's main streets. Located downtown, this historic area combines Helena's colorful past with a contemporary freshness. Architecturally significant buildings, many of which are listed on the National Register of Historic Places, house espresso shops and boutiques, while ultramodern sculptures depict historical events. Interpretive markers are scattered along the pedestrian mall, with historical information relating to period construction.

In Jefferson City, 15 miles south of Helena via I-15, the **Tizer Botanic Gardens & Arboretum,** 38 Tizer Rd. (www.tizergardens.com; © **406/933-8789**), is the only botanic garden in the vicinity, a peaceful display of bulbs, perennials, roses, and other plants crisscrossed by paths. It's open May through September and by appointment other times of year; admission is $6 (free for kids 5 and under).

Archie Bray Foundation   Archie Bray, a Helena resident and enthusiastic supporter of the arts, established this artistic colony for potters in 1951 at the brickyard and kilns of the Western Clay Manufacturing Company. Over the years it has become a premier testing ground for ceramic artists working together to share ideas and techniques. Various playful sculptures dot the lawns. Of special note are several larger, free-standing monuments by Robert Harrison, including *A Potter's Shrine,* dedicated to Bray and incorporating some materials up to 100 years old; *Tile-X,* stacked drain tiles in the shape of a pyramid; and *Aruina,* a monument of brick and tile whose four arches frame the surrounding Helena landscape. Because of the intimate nature of each individual resident's art-making process, visitors are asked to respect their privacy. Ceramic art is also for sale during gallery hours. Allow 1 to 2 hours.

2915 Country Club Ave. www.archiebray.org. © **406/443-3502.** Free admission. Gallery Mon–Sat 10am–5pm; also in summer Sun 1–5pm. Visitors may take a self-guided walking tour of the grounds during daylight hours.

Cathedral of St. Helena   Completed in 1924, the Cathedral of St. Helena was modeled on a church in Vienna, Austria. Its beautiful twin 230-foot spires seem ready to soar heavenward on their own, filigreed and light. The cathedral is decorated with magnificent Bavarian stained-glass windows, hand-carved oak pews, hand-forged bronze light fixtures, and Carrara marble statues. At one time, it was open to all who wandered by, but there are now times when the cathedral is left unattended and the doors are locked. So if you want to see the inside, it is best to call ahead. Masses are held here daily.

530 N. Ewing. www.sthelenas.org. ✆ **406/442-5825.** Open to public; hours vary. Free guided tours available 1–3pm Tues–Thurs Memorial Day to Labor Day and by appointment rest of year.

Gates of the Mountains Boat Tours   Meriwether Lewis coined the name "Gates of the Mountains" while plying this portion of the Missouri with his party. At almost every bend in the waterway, the towering rock formations seemed to block their passage, only to magically open up as they drew closer. Visitors can have an experience similar to Lewis's through a boat tour of this scenic river on the *Pirogue,* the *Sacajawea II,* or the *Hilger Rose.* The 105-minute excursions take you through the mountain "gates," past prehistoric pictographs on the limestone rocks, to a picnic area where wildlife-viewing opportunities abound. You can choose to return on a later boat and take a hike into the nearby Gates of the Mountains Wilderness Area. There are also dinner cruises on many summer Friday nights; call for details.

P.O. Box 478, Helena, MT 59624. www.gatesofthemountains.com. ✆ **406/458-5241.** $14 adults, $12 seniors, $8 children 4–17, free for children 3 and under. Memorial Day to late Sept; call or visit website for cruise schedule departures and returns. From Helena, drive 18 miles north on I-15 to exit 209 (Gates of the Mountains).

Holter Museum of Art ★   Considered one of the premier galleries in the state, the Holter displays artwork in 7,200 square feet and features 10 to 14 different shows each year, all of which include an intriguing diversity of mediums and styles. Specializing in contemporary art of the Northwest region, the museum provides exhibition space for local as well as nationally prominent artists and is definitely worth a couple hours of your time. The museum also runs a summer arts-education program for youngsters and adults and is home to a slick gift shop.

12 E. Lawrence St. www.holtermuseum.org. ✆ **406/442-6400.** Free admission. Tues–Sat 10am–5:30pm; Sun noon–4pm.

Last Chance Tours Train   A train engine on wheels pulls you around Helena on a tour of its historic sites, including the Atlas Block, the Montana Club, and the old governor's mansion. This is an excellent way to get oriented in Helena and learn a few things about the city at the same time. The tours last 1 hour.

Tours leave from the Montana Historical Society Bldg., 225 N. Roberts. www.lctours.com. ✆ **406/442-1023.** Tickets $7.50 adults, $6 children 4–12, free for children 3 and under. Mid-May to mid-Sept; tour times vary seasonally.

The Montana Historical Society Museum ★   The Montana Historical Society maintains a library and archives, as well as a museum. The **Montana Homeland Gallery** displays the history of Montana going back more than 11,000 years. A long-term exhibit, **"Neither Empty nor Unknown,"** covers Lewis and Clark. The **Mackay Gallery of Russell Art** has a permanent display of original Charles Russell masterpieces—from a collection of more than 200 artworks, including oils, watercolors, sculptures, and Russell's famous illustrated letters—that showcase one of the

West's most remarkable artists. The **Northeast and Haynes galleries** house seasonal exhibits. The mounted hide of Big Medicine, a sacred, rare white bison that lived on Montana's National Bison Range from 1933 to 1959, is on display on the second-floor mezzanine.

Guided tours of the original **governor's mansion** ($4 adults, $1 children 5–18, $10 maximum per family; combination museum–mansion tickets available), located at 304 N. Ewing, are also available through the society. This Queen Anne–style mansion with a distinctive checkerboard background was constructed in 1888 for entrepreneur William A. Chessman and his family. The state acquired the mansion in 1913, and governors resided here for half a century, during which time the mansion lost much of its original historical flavor. However, a major restoration of the building was undertaken in 1969, and much of its allure has been recovered. Tours operate on the hour from noon to 4pm Tuesday through Saturday (Oct–Apr Sat only). Allow about 2 hours.

225 N. Roberts St. www.montanahistoricalsociety.org. © **406/444-2694.** $5 adults, $1 children 5–18, free for children 4 and under; $12 maximum per family. Summer Mon–Sat 9am–5pm (Thurs until 8pm). Library and archives Tues–Fri 9am–5pm; Sat 9am–1pm.

Montana State Capitol   Situated on 14 acres, Montana's beautiful state capitol was designed by architects Charles Bell and John Kent in the late 1800s. It's decorated in the French Renaissance style with frescoes, a grand stained-glass dome, and murals. The dome, faced with copper, rises 165 feet. Inside are murals by noted Montana artists Charles Russell, Edgar Paxson, and Ralph DeCamp, including Russell's famed *Lewis and Clark Meeting Indians at Ross' Hole.* The grounds and flower gardens of the state capitol building in Helena are a designated state park, visited by thousands of people each year.

1301 E. 6th Ave. http://visit-the-capitol.mt.gov. © **406/444-4789.** Free admission; no charge for tours. Building Mon–Fri 8am–5pm. Daily tours on the hour May–Sept Mon–Sat 9am–3pm, Sun noon–4pm; rest of year tours on the hour Sat 10am–2pm. Additional spring tours available when the legislature is in session (odd-numbered years).

Shopping

Last Chance Gulch is a 4-block-long pedestrian mall. Though it is not exclusively a shopping area, the office buildings are liberally interspersed with boutiques, restaurants, pubs, and places for the kids to play. Informational kiosks are located in the center of this walking mall and at its north end. The **Atlas Block** is a group of historically significant architectural structures in Last Chance Gulch. As Helena's main areas were leveled several times in the last 125 years or so, once by earthquakes (in 1935) and several times by fire in the 19th century and again in 1928, builders of the Atlas Block carved images of salamanders, which, in medieval European mythology, are impervious to fire.

Lasso the Moon, 25 S. Last Chance Gulch (© **406/442-1594**), is a classic toy shop, featuring rack after rack of unique toys that aren't stocked by the mass-market retailers. Next door at 21 S. Last Chance Gulch, is the longstanding **Ghost Art Gallery** (© **406/443-4536**), which features art on Western and nature themes. Another good gallery is **Upper Missouri Artists,** 7 N. Last Chance Gulch (© **406/457-8240**). For snowboarders who also groove on music and art, stop in at **fourOsix,** 318 N. Last Chance Gulch (www.fourosix.com; © **406/443-4642**), for gear, exhibitions, and live concerts.

The attractive **Great Northern Town Center** is an emerging retail area just west of the intersection of Lyndale Avenue and Last Chance Gulch. Here, **Cobblestone Clothing,** 828 Great Northern Blvd., Ste. 103 (✆ **406/449-8684**), sells upscale women's apparel with a hint of the New West; **Grand Junction Mercantile,** 825 Great Northern Blvd. (✆ **406/442-6210**), is the place for gifts. There is also a new eight-screen movie theater here.

Especially for Kids

Great Northern Carousel ☺ Privately built by the developer of the Great Northern Town Center, this new carousel is an enchanting work of art with a definitive Montana spin—there are hand-carved bison, trout, grizzly bears, dinosaurs, otters, and bighorn sheep alongside the horses, frogs, and pigs. There is also the **Painted Pony Ice Cream Parlor** and a gift shop on-site.

924 Bicentennial Plaza (at the Great Northern Town Center). www.gncarousel.com. ✆ **406/457-5353.** $1.50 per ride. Memorial Day to Labor Day Sun–Thurs 10am–9pm, Fri–Sat 10am–10pm; shorter hours rest of year.

The Parrot Confectionery ☺ Kids and adults alike will love this colorful candy store, established in 1922. The Parrot serves its original cherry phosphates and caramel-cashew sundaes from the soda fountain, beneath its charming collection of ceramic elephants. Family owned, the Parrot has provided gourmet chocolate and candy to Helena for more than 80 years, and loyal customers attest that the place and its products haven't changed a bit over time. In addition to its Helena clientele, the Parrot supplies candy to chocoholics from nearly every state in the union. It's known for its signature parrot confection, chocolate-covered caramels, and many other candies. They also have a "secret recipe" chili for lunch.

42 N. Last Chance Gulch. www.parrotchocolate.com. ✆ **406/442-1470.** Most sundaes and candies $3–$8. AE, DISC, MC, V. Mon–Sat 9am–6pm (soda fountain until 5:30pm).

Where to Stay

There's no shortage of good accommodations in Helena, with a bevy of historic inns and a number of business-oriented hotels and motels that cater to traveling politicos of all stripes. Aside from the options discussed below, you might try the **Holiday Inn Helena Downtown,** 22 N. Last Chance Gulch (✆ **406/443-2200**), a seven-story brick edifice with double rates of $129 to $199. The **Fairfield Inn of Helena,** 2150 11th Ave. (✆ **800/228-2800** or 406/449-9944), is another good option, with doubles for $109 to $129 and an indoor pool. **Elkhorn Mountain Inn,** 1 Jackson Creek Rd., Montana City, at I-15, exit 187 (www.elkhorninn.com; ✆ **866/442-6625** or 406/442-6625), is a top mom-and-pop joint just south of Helena with double rates of $65 to $75.

The Barrister Bed & Breakfast ★ Located directly across the street from the Cathedral of St. Helena, the Barrister is one of many elegant homes near the original governor's mansion. Built in 1874 and listed on the National Register of Historic Places, this Queen Anne–style gem was renovated and converted to a B&B in the early 1990s. The rooms are large and elegantly furnished with antiques. Each has a private bathroom—though some are across the hall. Many rooms have black-and-white photos of local scenes from the 19th century, courtesy of the Montana Historical Society. Guest rooms are elegant and classic, exemplified by the manly Captain's Suite, with a rich red carpet and a nautical theme. The third floor is a two-bedroom apartment that rents for $175 per night but is usually leased on longer term, by the week or the month. The common areas include a parlor, sun porch, den, TV room/ library, laundry room, and office with a guest computer.

416 N. Ewing St., Helena, MT 59601. http://thebarristermt.tripod.com. © **800/823-1148** or 406/443-7330. Fax 406/442-7964. 5 units. $119–$134 double. Rates include full breakfast and evening wine and hors d'oeuvres. AE, DC, DISC, MC, V. Pets accepted. *In room:* A/C, TV w/VCR or DVD player, movie library, hair dryer, Wi-Fi (free).

Best Western Helena Great Northern ★   Helena's newest hotel has rich, somewhat masculine rooms with two queen-size beds or a king-size, high ceilings, railroad-themed art, and a striking red contrast wall. Six of the rooms open up to both the hall and the indoor pool. The hotel is the anchor of the new Great Northern Town Center development and offers a convenient location for visiting the local attractions. It's a bit outside of walking distance to downtown Helena, but worth the short drive because of the rooms' freshness and comfort, which overshadow the downtown Holiday Inn. There's a restaurant attached, the **Silver Star Steak Company** (see "Where to Eat," below), that is under different ownership but will deliver to your room. The entire property is nonsmoking.

835 Great Northern Blvd., Helena, MT 59601. www.gnhotelhelena.com. © **800/829-4047** or 406/457-5500. 101 units. $145–$170 double; $189 suite. AE, DISC, MC, V. **Amenities:** Restaurant; lounge; exercise room; indoor Jacuzzi; indoor pool; room service. *In room:* A/C, TV, fridge, hair dryer, Wi-Fi (free).

Jorgenson's Inn & Suites ✦   Jorgenson's has been a Helena institution since the 1950s, and offers a relative bargain. As you might expect in an older place, the rooms are a little smaller than those in most newer motels, but they have been religiously renovated, modernized, and refurbished throughout the years; some have microwaves and fridges. Guests also have access to the fully equipped fitness center across the street.

1714 11th Ave., Helena, MT 59601. www.jorgensonsinn.com. © **800/272-1770** or 406/442-1770. Fax 406/449-0155. 115 units. $69–$129 double. AE, DC, DISC, MC, V. **Amenities:** Restaurant; lounge/casino; access to nearby fitness center; small indoor pool. *In room:* A/C, TV, Wi-Fi (most rooms, free).

Red Lion Colonial Hotel   This is a fairly upscale property, with a spiral stairway inside that you might expect Scarlett O'Hara to come sweeping down at any moment. The rooms are huge by any standard, and the location right by the interstate is convenient for travelers. Some rooms also offer panoramic views of the valley and mountains beyond. The suites include king-size beds, refrigerators, and microwaves; some have private Jacuzzis.

2301 Colonial Dr. (just off I-15 at U.S. 12), Helena, MT 59601. www.redlion.com/colonial. © **800/733-5466** or 406/443-2100. Fax 406/449-8815. 149 units. $115–$179 double. AE, DC, DISC, MC, V. **Amenities:** Restaurant; lounge; indoor Jacuzzi; indoor and outdoor heated pools; room service. *In room:* A/C, TV, hair dryer, Wi-Fi (free).

The Sanders B&B ★★★   One of the state's oldest and best B&Bs, the Sanders is a lesson in Montana history all on its own. Built and owned by Wilbur Fisk Sanders in 1875, the B&B has been beautifully restored by Bobbi Uecker and Rock Ringling (a fourth-generation descendant of the famous circus family). Sanders was Montana's first U.S. senator and made his reputation by vigorously prosecuting the infamous Plummer gang in Virginia City. Guests sleep on beds from 1875 and look at the same pictures that Sanders did. (One was painted by his wife, an important Western suffragette in her day.) Our favorite accouterment is the elephant "bridle" in the Sanders

Suite, marked with a big round disc reading "The Greatest Show on Earth." Wonder where they got that? Bobbi's enthusiasm shows in every detail, from the savory breakfasts to the advice she can offer on Helena's restaurants and attractions.

328 N. Ewing, Helena, MT 59601. www.sandersbb.com. © **406/442-3309.** Fax 406/443-2361. 7 units. $115–$150 double. Rates include full breakfast and afternoon refreshments. AE, MC, V. *In room:* A/C, TV, hair dryer, Wi-Fi (free).

CAMPING

Twenty miles west of town, **Kim's Marina and RV Resort,** 8015 Canyon Ferry Rd., Helena, MT 59601 (www.kimsmarina.com; © **406/475-3723**), has a complete resort facility that includes comfortable cabins situated on the lakefront. Canoes, deck boats, and paddle boats are for rent on a daily basis. You'll find rental cabins ($90 nightly) along with 50 tent and 60 RV sites ($15–$30), as well as tennis, horseshoes, and boat rentals.

For more primitive sites, the Bureau of Reclamation and Bureau of Land Management jointly run several campgrounds between Townsend in the south and Helena along U.S. 287 at Canyon Ferry Lake. From south to north, they are: **Indian Road Recreation Area** (1 mile north of Townsend on U.S. 287, mile marker 75), **Silos** (7 miles north of Townsend on U.S. 287, mile marker 70), and **White Earth Campground** (13 miles north of Townsend on U.S. 287 to Winston, mile marker 64). The Indian Road Recreation Area offers a fishing pond for children and visitors with disabilities. Call © **406/475-3921** for information on either campground and its facilities.

Where to Eat

FireTower Coffee House, 422 N. Last Chance Gulch (www.firetowercoffee.com; © **406/495-8840**), is a nice place to sit in an overstuffed chair and have a cup of coffee, muffin, or sandwich. Wagon ride dinners are available for $76 per person through **Last Chance Ranch,** 2884 Grizzly Gulch (www.lastchanceranch.biz; © **406/442-2884**).

Benny's Bistro ★★ NEW AMERICAN   This breezy cafe has a jazz theme, with horns and woodwinds on the brick walls and a piano—played during dinner on Fridays—and big windows that face the street. The open kitchen in the back plates up a wide variety of dishes, from Jamaican jerk pork to curry to ravioli. The dinner menu includes "locavore" specialties with pork, chicken, and lamb, as well as excellent steaks (this is Montana, after all). Lunches consist of crepes, gourmet sandwiches on house-baked bread, and big salads. This is the spot to eat downtown if you're looking for casually upscale but not stuffy.

108 E. 6th Ave. www.bennysbistro.com. © **406/443-0105.** Main courses $7–$10 lunch, $18–$26 dinner. AE, MC, V. Mon–Sat 11am–3pm; Wed–Sat 5:30–9pm.

Bert & Ernie's AMERICAN   A stalwart bar and grill in downtown Helena since 1974, Bert & Ernie's has occupied its present Last Chance Gulch location (a former clothing store) since 1990 and remains a good, reliable pick for a casual lunch or dinner. The fun atmosphere with the requisite clutter hanging from the walls (stuffed animals, neon signs, stained glass, and such) is a good match for the menu: a mix of sandwiches, burgers, salads, and dinner entrees such as fajitas, pasta, and steaks. Attached and under the same ownership is the intimate **Sommeliers,** an upscale wine bar that serves appetizers and desserts.

361 N. Last Chance Gulch. www.bertanderniesofhelena.com. © **406/443-5680.** Reservations accepted. Main courses $10–$26. DISC, MC, V. Sun–Thurs 11am–9pm; Fri–Sat 11am–10pm.

Lucca's ★★ ITALIAN   Recently moving to Last Chance Gulch, Lucca's is a swank and dim restaurant specializing in good steaks and good wine. The kitchen also plates up a nice selection of pork, lamb, and pasta dishes, including an excellent sausage-and-mushroom lasagna and a spicy shrimp *fra diavolo* with angel-hair pasta and a red-pepper cream sauce. The dining room is classic but contemporary; it is lined with wine bottles and black-and-white photos of Rome.

56 N. Last Chance Gulch. ✆ **406/457-8311.** Reservations recommended. Main courses $15–$32. AE, DISC, MC, V. Wed–Sun 5pm–close, usually around 9:30pm.

The Marysville House ★ STEAKS/SEAFOOD   Every Rocky Mountain state has a barely surviving ghost town with a still-great steakhouse. Marysville, an 1870 gold-mining town, once boasted a population of 4,000—now it's 70. And the Marysville House is the steakhouse that's still going strong, reportedly selling the most lobster of any eatery in the state. Located in what was once a train depot, the Marysville House serves burgers, steaks, crab legs, and cold, smooth beer in a rustic setting. The no-nonsense meals come with corn on the cob and beans. Guests have their choice of dining inside or out. And how's this for low-key Americana? Meals are served on paper plates, horseshoes and a marshmallow-roasting fire pit can be found outside, and you can eat at a picnic table on the deck.

153 N. Main St., Marysville. www.marysvillemontana.com. ✆ **406/443-6677.** Reservations accepted for groups of 8 or more only. Most dinner main courses $20–$40. MC, V. Wed–Sun 5–9pm (call first, as hours vary with seasons); closed Sun fall to spring. From Helena, take U.S. 15 N. to exit 200, Mont. 279. Go north on Mont. 279 for 23 miles; turn left at the sign for Marysville for 6 miles to find this living ghost town; it's a 45-min. drive from Helena.

On Broadway ★★ ITALIAN   Located in a historic brick building near Last Chance Gulch, On Broadway is a longtime standout in Helena. It's got a warm atmosphere, brick walls contrasting with ferns, two levels of dining, and exceptional food, with artful combinations of meats and vegetables, fresh herbs, and pasta highlighting the menu. A local favorite is the Chicken Broadway, a chicken breast topped with fresh mushrooms and cheese, then baked in a Mornay sauce with mozzarella. The fish menu is the most imaginative, headed up by blackened tuna and oven-roasted salmon.

106 Broadway. www.onbroadwayinhelena.com. ✆ **406/443-1929.** Reservations not accepted. Main courses $16–$26. AE, DISC, MC, V. Mon–Sat 5:30pm–close, usually around 9:30pm.

Silver Star Steak Company ★ STEAKS/SEAFOOD   The culinary anchor of the new Great Northern Town Center development, the Silver Star is an intimate, contemporary space with hints of the new West and a traditional menu. While the menu changes regularly, the food is quite good, with a nice selection of steaks—all USDA-certified Angus beef—and seafood. The latter includes halibut stuffed with brie and crab, and roasted salmon. There is a less expensive menu served in the bar, with burgers and other dishes running $9 to $16. Lunch includes salads, sandwiches, and pasta dishes.

833 Great Northern Blvd. www.silverstarsteakco.com. ✆ **406/495-0677.** Reservations recommended. Lunch $7–$15; dinner $17–$30. AE, DISC, MC, V. Mon–Sat 11:30am–2:30pm; daily 5–10pm. Bar open later.

Windbag Saloon ★ AMERICAN   Helena residents love this restaurant like you'd love an eccentric aunt: She's the most interesting relative you have, and you always have a great time at her place. Who cares if she has a checkered past? This former bordello (it shut down in 1973) continues the location's tradition as a focal part of Helena's nightlife. Try one of a long list of microbrews (including Bag Bitter, brewed exclusively for the saloon by the local Blackfoot River Brewing Company), or order something from the extensive collection of appetizers before moving on to the Little Ida (named for a former madam), 10 ounces of ground sirloin with peppers and onions, and fries so thick you'll barely be able to finish a serving. Seafood is flown in twice weekly, steaks are hand-cut on the premises, and the daily quiches are top of the line.

19 S. Last Chance Gulch. © **406/443-9669.** Lunch $7–$14; dinner $11–$30. AE, DISC, MC, V. Mon–Thurs 11am–2pm and 5:30–9:30pm; Fri 11am–2pm and 5:30–10pm; Sat 2–10pm.

Helena After Dark

Make it a point to visit the state-of-the-art **Myrna Loy Center for the Performing and Media Arts ★**, 15 N. Ewing St. (www.myrnaloycenter.com; © **406/443-0287**). Formerly the county jail, the Myrna Loy (named after the silver-screen legend who was one of Helena's most famous residents) is today a multidisciplinary cultural center. Within its castlelike facade is a 55-seat cinema and a 250-seat performance hall, along with a gallery that focuses on regional art. Other playgoing opportunities include productions by **Grandstreet Theatre,** 325 N. Park Ave. (www.grandstreet. net; © **406/447-1574**), and the **Montana Shakespeare Company** (www.montana shakespeare.org; © **406/431-1154**), which takes to the stage June through August at Tizer Botanic Gardens and Arboretum and other venues.

Of the Queen City's watering holes, we like **Miller's Crossing,** 52 S. Park Ave. (© **406/442-3290**), for the live music, neighborhood atmosphere, and Blackfoot River Brewing suds on tap; and the popular **Brewhouse Pub & Grille,** 939½ Getchell St. (© **406/457-9390**), atop the Lewis & Clark Brewing Company in the Great Northern Town Center area. The bustling **taproom** at Blackfoot River Brewing Company, 66 S. Park Ave. (© **406/449-3005**), is another good option, open daily from 2 to 8pm, with free tasters and a three-beer limit.

BUTTE

64 miles S of Helena; 120 miles SE of Missoula; 82 miles W of Bozeman; 150 miles NW of West Yellowstone

Butte may not be most people's idea of a vacation destination, but in many ways the city is the hidden soul of Montana. Butte's emergence in the 19th century as a hell-raising, wide-open mining town drew a lot of people to the state, including a variety of racial and ethnic groups. Butte has always been a strong union town in a state and region that disdain union activity. This union and socialist tradition from the rip-roaring days has made a lasting contribution to a strong progressive political tradition.

Butte used to be called "the richest hill on earth" for its production of copper, silver, and other precious metals, and during the 1880s, Butte was the world's largest copper producer. In 1955, the world's richest hill became the beginning of one of the world's largest holes, the Berkeley Pit, which provided more cost-efficient open-pit mining of copper. The pit grew and grew and almost swallowed the town. But after the mine closed in the 1980s, groundwater seeped up through the maze of tunnels below, creating a gigantic pollution problem. The town's drinking water—and very survival—is threatened by this toxic sea, but the problem is now being addressed by a $20-million water treatment plant that opened in 2003.

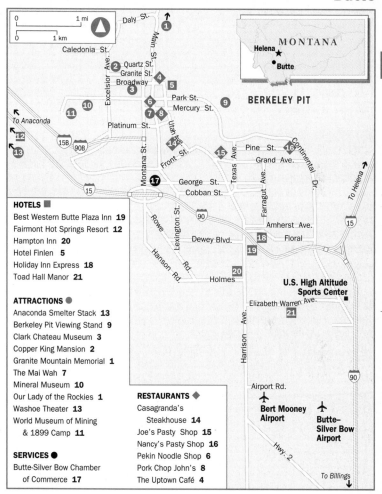

HOTELS ■
Best Western Butte Plaza Inn **19**
Fairmont Hot Springs Resort **12**
Hampton Inn **20**
Hotel Finlen **5**
Holiday Inn Express **18**
Toad Hall Manor **21**

ATTRACTIONS ●
Anaconda Smelter Stack **13**
Berkeley Pit Viewing Stand **9**
Clark Chateau Museum **3**
Copper King Mansion **2**
Granite Mountain Memorial **1**
The Mai Wah **7**
Mineral Museum **10**
Our Lady of the Rockies **1**
Washoe Theater **13**
World Museum of Mining
 & 1899 Camp **11**

SERVICES ●
Butte-Silver Bow Chamber
 of Commerce **17**

RESTAURANTS ◆
Casagranda's
 Steakhouse **14**
Joe's Pasty Shop **15**
Nancy's Pasty Shop **16**
Pekin Noodle Shop **6**
Pork Chop John's **8**
The Uptown Café **4**

If you can look past the signs of decline that remain from the end of the mining era, Butte is full of rich history, colorful citizens, and a sort of blue-collar San Francisco–style charm. Physically, Butte is built along the sides of steep hills, which provides a great vantage point on the valley below. It also boasts Montana Tech, an arm of the University of Montana system and one of the top-rated engineering schools in the country.

Sister city Anaconda was the "company town" formed when copper king Marcus Daly extended his copper empire 24 miles west. The community was spared the name "Copperopolis."

Essentials

GETTING THERE   The **Bert Mooney Airport** (www.butteairport.com; ✆ **406/494-3771**) is served by **Delta/SkyWest.** The **Greyhound** station in Butte is located at 1324 Harrison Ave. (www.greyhound.com; ✆ **406/723-3287**). For current **weather conditions** on the highways, call ✆ **406/721-3939** or 511.

VISITOR INFORMATION   The **Butte Convention and Visitors Bureau Information Center,** 1000 George St., Butte, MT 59701-7901 (www.buttecvb.com; ✆ **800/735-6814** or 406/723-3177), is located off exit 126 near the intersections of I-15 and I-90. The center is a user-friendly facility just off the freeway, close to a wetlands area where you can take a breather from driving and watch wild ducks, geese, and muskrats go about their business. It's also the home of the bronze statue of the locally legendary canine, the Auditor. The Auditor was the mysterious dreadlocked dog that wandered the desolate moonscape around the Berkeley Pit for 17 years until his passing in 2003.

The **Anaconda Chamber of Commerce,** 306 E. Park Ave., Anaconda, MT 59711 (www.anacondamt.org; ✆ **406/563-2400**), can give you information on Butte's sister city. For brochures devoted to area attractions and driving tours, contact **Travel Montana's Gold West Country** (www.goldwest.visitmt.com; ✆ **800/879-1159**).

GETTING AROUND   Car-rental agents at the airport are **Avis** (✆ **800/230-4898**), **Budget** (✆ **800/527-0700**), **Enterprise** (✆ **800/261-7331**), and **Hertz** (✆ **800/654-3131**).

The **Butte–Silver Bow Transit System** city buses run from 6:45am to 6:15pm Monday through Friday and 8:45am to 4:45pm on Saturday; for information on fares and stops, call ✆ **406/497-6515. Mining City Taxi** (✆ **406/723-6511**) provides local transportation 24 hours a day.

SPECIAL EVENTS   Butte's thick Irish heritage from its days as a mining boomtown shines brightly (maybe a bit too brightly) on **St. Patrick's Day ★**, when this mining museum of a town throws a shamrock-tinted bash that is the big event of the year—even the banks shut down. The March 17 celebration is one of the biggest St. Patrick's Day parties outside of New York City, but be forewarned: It tends to be very rowdy and very drunk.

If you want a more family-friendly Irish festival, try **An Rí Rá** (www.mtgaelic.org), an annual 3-day tradition in mid-August. Another fun annual event is **Evel Knievel Days** (www.knieveldays.com), held in late July in honor of the late daredevil and Butte native, featuring motorcycle stunt shows and a parade. Contact the **Butte CVB** (see above) for the dates and times of these activities.

Getting Outside

Lost Creek State Park (www.fwp.mt.gov; ✆ **406/542-5500**), a few miles outside of Anaconda, is a great place to camp, hike, or simply sit and admire the scenery. At the end of the road into the park, a short path will take you to pretty Lost Creek Falls, which tumble over a 50-foot drop. There are also mountain goats and bighorn sheep in residence. Several hiking trails lead off from the road. Among the most interesting things here are the rocks. Exposed on the tops of some cliffs is the 1.3-billion-year-old Newman Formation, a Precambrian rock that's among the oldest exposed rocks in the Lower 48 states. This is a primitive park without services; there is no entrance fee. There are 25 campsites, suitable mostly for tents and car campers ($20–$23 nightly).

From June through September, the **Butte Trolley** tour leaves from the Butte Visitor Center for a 1½-hour tour of the city's key attractions. Driver/tour guides are chosen for their knowledge of the town's history. Fares are $15 for adults, $13 for seniors, $10 for kids 12 to 17, and $6 for kids 4 to 11 (kids under 4 are free). Call 📞 **406/723-3177** for schedules and other information. Year-round **Old Butte Historical Tours** (www.butte tours.info; 📞 **406/498-3424**) offers historic walking tours, covering old speak-easies, brothels, hotels, and more ($15 adults, $8 kids under 12).

To get to the park, drive 1½ miles east of Anaconda on Mont. 1, then 2 miles north on County Road 273, then 6 miles west on Lost Creek Road.

GOLF

The **Old Works ★★**, 1205 Pizzini Way, Anaconda (www.oldworks.org; 📞 **406/563-5989**), is a golf course, a work of landscape art, and a symbol of environmental reclamation. The course is built on a Superfund site that had been a blight on the landscape since 1884, when the upper works began to process 500 tons of copper ore daily under Marcus Daly's voracious eye. By 1887, the lower works were necessary because of the demand. The Old Works closed in 1902, when the new Washoe Smelter—the big tower you can see from anywhere in the valley—took over all the processing. Jack Nicklaus designed the golf course, a tough but fair layout that even eight-handicappers are willing to play from the white tees. The black sand traps, the old processing works, and the vast, forbidding black tailings piles are all worked beautifully into the layout of the course. This is one of the finest courses not just in Montana, but in America. To reach the course, which is open from mid-May to the end of October, take Commercial Street to North Cedar Street, turn north, then east (right) on Pizzini Way. Greens fees are $29 to $62 for 18 holes per person, depending on the day of week and time of year and whether you walk or rent a cart

There's also an 18-hole course ($33–$43) at nearby **Fairmont Hot Springs Resort** (see "Where to Stay," later in this chapter). **Highland View Golf Course** (📞 **406/494-7900**), at Stodden Park in Butte, has two separate 9-hole courses: a par 3 ($15) and a regulation ($18).

ROCK CLIMBING

Spire Rock and the Humbug Spires are the two most popular routes for rock climbers. The **Bureau of Land Management** (📞 **406/533-7600**) can refer guides and provide other climbing information.

ROCKHOUNDING

From the Continental Divide east of Butte through the mountains to the south, diligent rockhounders can find smoky quartz, amethyst, epidote, and tourmaline. Ask the curator at the **Mineral Museum** (see "Seeing the Sights," below) on the Montana Tech campus for leads on local hot spots. The **Butte Mineral and Gem Club,** P. O. Box 4492, Butte, MT 59702, has mining claims on **Crystal Park,** about 70 miles southwest of Butte, that are free and open to the public. From Butte, go south on I-15 and west on Mont. 43; just past Wise River, turn south on the Pioneer Mountains Scenic Byway and drive about 20 miles to Crystal Park.

SKIING

In addition to **Discovery Ski Area,** Butte visitors are within range of **Maverick Mountain** (see "Dillon & the Big Hole," later in this chapter).

Discovery Ski Area   This is another Montana ski resort that falls somewhere in the middle of the pack if you make a list ranking them for nearly any category. With a 2,388-foot vertical drop, the 67 runs on 2,200 patrolled acres here are nicely spread among beginner, intermediate, and expert runs. Three miles of groomed trails will satisfy the Nordic skier, a terrain park offers thrills for snowboarders, or you can blaze your own trail through untracked snow. While the scenery equals or exceeds that of other areas in the state, the real plus here is the proximity to **Fairmont Hot Springs Resort** (see "Where to Stay," below), a four-season facility where soaking and swimming are year-round favorites. Ski rentals and instruction are available (private lessons are $40 per hour), as well as cafeteria-style food. There are no hotels at the ski area; the nearest accommodations are at Fairmont Hot Springs or in Butte and Anaconda.

P.O. Box 221, Anaconda, MT 59711. www.skidiscovery.com. ℂ **406/563-2184.** Full-day lift tickets $38 adults, $19 children 12 and under and seniors; adult half-day tickets $29 beginning at 12:30pm. Late Nov to early Apr 9:30am–4pm. From Anaconda, drive west on Mont. 1 for 20 miles to Georgetown Lake. Turn right (north) at the DISCOVERY SKI AREA sign. Continue north for 4½ miles to the ski area.

SNOWMOBILING

Call the Butte office of the **Beaverhead-Deerlodge National Forest** (www.fs.fed.us/r1/b-d; ℂ **406/494-2147**) for information on nearby trails, most of which explore the Georgetown Lake area. The four major trail systems are Carp Ridge, which terminates at the Anaconda-Pintler Wilderness boundary; Echo Lake, at the midpoint of Georgetown Lake and Discovery Ski Area; Peterson Meadows, a popular spot for cookouts and picnics; and Red Lion Racetrack Lake, with ridge-top views of surrounding peaks.

Seeing the Sights

For information on the **Pintler Scenic Route,** a driving tour that begins in Butte, see p. 134, earlier in this chapter.

The **Berkeley Pit** is rumored to be visible from the moon. It is located just off the Continental Drive in Butte. Starting in 1955, nearly 1.5 billion tons of material were removed from the pit—including more than 290 million tons of copper ore—before mining ceased in 1982. A short walk through a dimly lit tunnel (fully accessible for those with disabilities) takes you to an observation deck where you can view the pit, which is doggedly filling with groundwater. Unfortunately, the water flows through several thousand miles of underground pit tunnels through the mineralized zones and becomes heavily acidic en route to the surface. In 2003, a newly built water treatment plant began processing the polluted water, sidestepping the possibility that the toxic water would seep into the city's drinking water and render the town pretty much uninhabitable. The viewing stand is at the east end of Mercury Street on the fringes of the downtown area and is open to the public ($2 admission for adults, $1 for kids 5–17) during daylight hours May through September. It's free at other times of year, weather permitting. A good online resource is **www.pitwatch.org**. As the Pit is Butte's most-visited attraction, the viewing area underwent a recent face-lift, including a rest area and other new facilities.

Above the pit off N. Main St., the **Granite Mountain Memorial** commemorates a 1917 mining disaster that took the lives of 168 men. A fire sealed the miners to their doom, and it remains hard-rock mining's most deadly accident in history. The view from the memorial is spectacular, encompassing not only the Berkeley Pit but also the city and surrounding mountains.

The 585-foot **Anaconda Smelter Stack,** just off Mont. 1 on the outskirts of Anaconda, is one of the tallest standing brick structures in the world and is designated a Montana State Park, though there is no public access to the structure. Once considered the largest copper-smelting stack in the entire world, all 58 stories of the desolate shaft rise starkly to meet the Montana sky. A few interpretive displays detail the smelter stack's history and construction.

Clark Chateau Museum ★   Built in 1898 for Charles Clark, son of copper king William A. Clark, the Clark Chateau is an impressively restored mansion and art gallery. Stained-glass windows, beveled glass, ornate wrought iron, and intricately detailed woodwork contribute to the mansion's early-20th-century elegance. The home's magnificent staircase leads to a second-story museum, filled with period furniture, and the gallery, which houses traveling displays by Montana artists in a much more modern setting. The two galleries have exhibits that change every 6 weeks. Other highlights include the fourth-floor ballroom, which replicates a grand hunting lodge, and the first-floor gift shop, with hundreds of made-in-Montana items for sale. Under the same umbrella is a coffee shop, the **Venus Rising Espresso House,** 128 W. Granite St. (© **406/723-1150**), with a gallery, an arts store, and regular films and musical entertainment.

321 W. Broadway, Butte. www.bsbarts.org. © **406/723-7600.** $5 adults, $4 seniors, $2 children. Summer daily noon–5pm; winter Tues–Wed 10am–2pm or by appointment. Tours available.

Copper King Mansion   This combination museum and bed-and-breakfast inn is an ideal choice for those who want to savor the historical ambience of one of the most lavish homes of the late 19th century. The huge home was built for mining magnate William A. Clark in 1888 for $260,000. There are 34 rooms on three floors, decorated in a lush "modern Elizabethan" style. The interior features remarkably intricate woodwork and a large number of opulent pieces of period furniture collected by the inn's owners. There are even a few original items from the period of Clark's ownership. In the third-floor ballroom, there's an 814-pipe Estey organ, as well as a private collection of clothing and memorabilia dating from the late 1800s; a small chapel is discreetly located to the side.

   Anaconda Touring Tips

You can take the **Vintage Bus Tour of Historic Anaconda** from the Anaconda Chamber of Commerce, 306 E. Park Ave. (© **406/563-2400**), Monday through Saturday at 10am and 2pm, from mid-May to mid-September. The cost is $8 adults, $4 children 6 and under. The tour includes a stop and inside tour of the fabulous Washoe Theater, which is usually open only at 8pm. The chamber also has a historical walking tour brochure for $2, but you won't see the inside of the Washoe unless you get lucky.

The guest rooms ($75–$125 nightly) are, in general, spacious and furnished with antiques. There are parquet floors downstairs, and the octagon-shaped reception room, the billiards room, and the library all reflect Clark's love of luxury. Antique lamps and chandeliers, ornate frescoed ceilings, and etched amber transoms complement the rooms' original furniture, including two matching African mahogany sleigh beds. If you stay at the B&B, you can sleep in the copper king's room, but you have to get up early and leave when the tours begin at 9am.

219 W. Granite St., Butte, MT 59701. www.thecopperkingmansion.com. ✆ **406/782-7580.** $7.50 adults, $3.50 children. Summer daily 9am–4pm; rest of year by appointment.

The Mai Wah ★   Adjacent to China Alley, the Mai Wah and Wah Chong Tai buildings stand as tributes to Butte's early Chinese population, which numbered 400 in 1890. With a first-floor mercantile and second-floor noodle parlor, the Mai Wah provided a segment of the city's ethnic community with jobs after the mines were exhausted. Today the buildings house exhibits and memorabilia honoring the rich Asian history of the area. The Mai Wah's permanent exhibit, "The Butte Chinese Experience," tells this fascinating story with artifacts, images, and interpretive displays.

17 W. Mercury St., Butte. www.maiwah.org. ✆ **406/723-3231.** $5 adults, $3 children under 13. June–Sept Tues–Sun 10am–4pm.

Mineral Museum   This museum displays only a small percentage of the mineral specimens that belong to Montana Tech's geology department, though that still makes for a pretty impressive mineral display. The explanation of the minerals consists of their identification and place of origin. One display features a comprehensive display of fluorescent minerals, starkly illuminated by ultraviolet lights. One of the area's most exciting discoveries, a 28-ounce gold nugget found in the Highland Mountains south of Butte, is also on display.

Montana Tech Campus. www.mbmg.mtech.edu. ✆ **406/496-4414.** Free admission. Mid-June to mid-Sept daily 9am–5pm; rest of year Mon–Fri 9am–4pm. From the center of Butte, take Park St. west to the Montana Tech Campus and follow the signs to the museum.

Our Lady of the Rockies   When you look up to the eastern heights above Butte, you'll see the large white statue of "Our Lady of the Rockies" in a notch at the top of a hill. The 90-foot statue was built "in the likeness of Mary, Mother of Jesus," and is dedicated to all women, especially mothers. Private cars are not allowed up to the site, but you can get a close-up view of the statue on 2½-hour bus tours. If you don't have time for a tour but are interested in learning more about "Our Lady of the Rockies," visit the information center and gift shop for a look at a panoramic mural of the statue. There is also a 30-minute video detailing the construction: 400 tons of concrete were used just for the statue's base.

Butte Plaza Mall, 3100 Harrison Ave., Butte. www.ourladyoftherockies.net. ✆ **800/800-5239** or 406/782-1221. Free admission to information center and gift shop. June–Sept daily 9am–6pm; winter limited hours. Tours depart Mon–Sat during summer at 10am and 2pm and Sun at 11am. $15 adults, $13 seniors 55 and over, $11 ages 13–17, $7 ages 5–12, $2 ages 4 and under.

Washoe Theater ★   The 1931 Washoe Theater shares the distinction with New York City's Radio City Music Hall of being the last two theaters done in the Art Deco style, and the Washoe is actually the more impressive. The brick exterior is unremarkable, and when you see it, you'll wonder what all the fuss is about. But inside, this is a true movie palace. Considered one of the most architecturally significant theaters in the country, it's a work of art in cerulean, salmon, beige, and yellow, with a fabulous curtain. If you arrive at midday, the theater is usually closed—it's still a working first-run movie theater and doesn't open until evening. But if someone is there, he'll turn on the lights and let you look around. Or you can take a trolley tour through the Anaconda Chamber to get a guaranteed peek.

305 Main St., Anaconda. © **406/563-6161.** Showtimes and ticket prices vary; call for current information.

World Museum of Mining & 1899 Mining Camp ★ This popular museum is a re-creation of the 1899 Hellroarin' Gulch mining town. It's on the site of the Orphan Girl mine, which, though not a blockbuster by Butte standards, managed to produce 7.6 million ounces of silver, along with lead and zinc. The mining town is set up with typical businesses and buildings of the mining era here, with explanations of each of their functions in the community. Underground tours of the first 65 feet of the 2,700-foot-deep Orphan Girl Mine are offered three times daily in summer and less frequently other times of year for an additional fee. There's also a hard-rock mining hall with tools of the trade and examples of types of framing timbers used underground.

155 Museum Way, P.O. Box 33, Butte. www.miningmuseum.org. © **406/723-7211.** Admission $8.50 adults, $7.50 seniors, $6 ages 13–18, $2 ages 5–12, free for ages 4 and under. Underground mine tours $12 adults, $10 seniors and ages 13–18, $5 ages 5–12, not recommended for ages 4 and under. Combination passes available. Apr–Oct daily 9am–6pm, with mine tours at 10:30am, 12:30pm, and 3pm; shorter hours rest of year. From the center of Butte, take Park St. west to the Montana Tech Campus. Continue on Park through the campus and make a left at Museum Way.

Where to Stay

Beyond the options listed below, we recommend the **Holiday Inn Express,** 1 Holiday Park Dr. (© **800/465-4329** or 406/494-6999), with rates of $109 to $119 double and suites for $119 to $139, and the **Hampton Inn,** 3499 Harrison Ave. S. (© **800/426-7866** or 406/494-2250), with double rates of $119 to $179.

Best Western Plus Butte Plaza Inn ★ This property is the best motel in the area because of its facilities, services, and location next to the freeway. Rooms, with modern decor, are small but quiet and clean, all with either king- or queen-size beds. The breakfast buffet, included in the room price, includes scrambled eggs and bacon, fresh fruit, muffins, hot or cold cereals, and juices and coffee. On-site, **Hops** is a pub and casino decorated in the style of an English pub.

2900 Harrison Ave., Butte, MT 59701. www.bestwestern.com/butteplazainn. © **800/543-5814** or 406/494-3500. Fax 406/494-7611. 134 units, including 1 suite. $130–$175 double; $190–$200 suite; lower rates fall to spring. Rates include breakfast buffet. AE, DISC, MC, V. Pets accepted ($50 deposit). **Amenities:** Restaurant; lounge; exercise room; indoor Jacuzzi; indoor pool; room service; sauna. *In room:* A/C, TV, hair dryer, Wi-Fi (free).

Fairmont Hot Springs Resort ★ ☺ This oasis between Butte and Missoula is a great place for families, with a 350-foot water slide and a pair of Olympic-size pools, a small wildlife zoo, and a playground. Parents will enjoy the wide range of activities as well, from golf and tennis to cross-country skiing in the winter—plus, of course, the soothing hot springs (there are two soaking pools) and the fact that Discovery Ski Area is only 30 minutes away. The standard rooms are fairly typical hotel-style accommodations, but they all have balconies, and the suites are as large and snazzy as one could want, sleeping as many as eight guests. Many of the suites also have fully equipped kitchens, and, by resort standards, the cost is modest.

1500 Fairmont Rd., Fairmont, MT 59711. www.fairmontmontana.com. ⓒ **800/332-3272** or 406/797-3241. Fax 406/797-3337. 152 units. Summer $159–$179 double; $279–$405 suite; higher holiday rates and lower rates fall to spring. AE, DC, DISC, MC, V. Exit 211 off I-90. **Amenities:** 2 restaurants; lounge (w/casino); 18-hole golf course; 2 indoor and 2 outdoor hot-springs pools; room service; 2 steam rooms; tennis courts; Wi-Fi (free). *In room:* A/C, TV, hair dryer, kitchen (suites only).

Hotel Finlen   Butte's most historic hotel, the 1924 Finlen was modeled after New York's Astor Hotel after its mining-era predecessor was razed. The lobby is elegant—with soaring copper-accented columns, crystal chandeliers, and marble walls—inside an attractive nine-story brick facade. Some rooms are nicer than others, but they are clean and well maintained, with small bathrooms and a typical motel feel (lacking historical ambience). There is also a motel-style annex with slightly lower rates that represents more than half of the rooms.

100 E. Broadway, Butte, MT 59701. www.finlen.com. ⓒ **800/729-5461** or 406/723-5461. 53 units, including 3 suites. $60–$80 double; $90 suite. AE, DISC, MC, V. **Amenities:** Lounge; Wi-Fi (free). *In room:* A/C, TV.

Toad Hall Manor ★   In 2003, Glenn and Jane Johnson opened their palatial, 11,000-square-foot home on the 16th hole of the Butte Country Club to guests as a splendid B&B. The 1993 home has a more historical feel than you'd think and a quartet of whimsical guest rooms named for characters in the children's classic *The Wind in the Willows*. We like Mr. Mole's Hide-away, with its great mountain views and stately walnut furnishings, but for a splurge, Sir Badger's Suite might be the best room in the city, with two bedrooms, a walk-in closet, and a two-person Jacuzzi, occupying the entire fifth floor. The breakfasts are unique, with such dishes as Toad's Extravagant Omelet and breakfast strudel.

1 Green Lane, Butte, MT 59701. www.toadhallmanor.com. ⓒ **866/443-8623** or 406/494-2625. Fax 406/494-8025. 4 units. $120–$140 double; $175 suite. Rates include full breakfast. AE, DC, DISC, MC, V. *In room:* TV, hair dryer, Wi-Fi (free).

Where to Eat

Butte's ethnic tradition is most evident in its food, with pasties (pronounced *pass*-tees, or *pah*-stees if you're British) ranking high on the list. If you've never tried one of these Cornish meat-filled pastries, you're in for a treat. Try **Joe's Pasty Shop,** 1641 Grand Ave. (ⓒ **406/723-9071**), or **Nancy's Pasty Shop,** 2810 Pine St. (ⓒ **406/782-7410**). Another local delicacy that should not be missed is a $3.25 breaded pork chop sandwich from **Pork Chop John's,** 8 W. Mercury St. (ⓒ **406/782-0812**). This barebones, blue-collar diner is a Butte landmark, and the sandwiches, wrapped in wax paper and topped with pickles, mustard, and onions, are the best deal in town.

Casagranda's Steakhouse ★ STEAKS/ITALIAN   The industrial exterior of this historic warehouse belies an excellent dinner destination, with a menu that runs the gamut from *cioppino* to ribs to duck. Steaks are the house specialty, and the menu includes cuts from 12-ounce filets to 24-ounce T-bones, cooked to order with all sorts of toppers. The menu also features a nice selection of seafood and pasta dishes and a good wine list. The dining room is at once casual and intimate, with many of the old warehouse trappings still in place, and there is also a homey bar.

801 S. Utah Ave., Butte. www.casagrandassteakhouse.webs.com. ⓒ **406/723-4141.** Reservations recommended. Main courses $13–$25. AE, DISC, MC, V. Daily 5–10pm (9pm in winter).

Pekin Noodle Parlor 🍴 CHINESE   Operated by the same family since 1916, the Pekin Noodle Parlor is a time capsule from the days when its neighborhood was a bustling Chinatown. Featuring curtained pink booths that are former brothel stalls (the old opium den is in the basement), the Pekin does a decent job with Chinese standards such as chow mein and chop suey, and also serves a few American standards (burgers, steaks, and egg plates), but the historical ambience outshines the food.

117 S. Main St., Butte. ✆ **406/782-2217.** Reservations accepted for large parties only. Dinner $6–$14. MC, V. Sun–Mon and Wed–Thurs 5–10:30pm; Fri–Sat 5pm–midnight or later. Closed Tues.

The Uptown Café ★★ NEW AMERICAN   The Uptown Café is a white-tablecloth restaurant in a no-tablecloth town. Despite the fact that the restaurant is one of the city's finest, it's also unpretentious, as longtime owners Barb Kornet and Guy Graham present five-course meals built around Montana beef and fresh seafood flown in from the Pacific Northwest. The favorite starter is Clams Maison—succulent clams prepared with white wine, chives, and butter. Other choices include soup—gazpacho, if you're lucky—plus several types of salads, a pasta or vegetable dish, and the main course. We recommend the salmon or halibut, when available, but we wouldn't turn down a steak, either. Every night until 6:30pm, the cafe also serves an early dining special: cheese ravioli with artichokes and roasted red peppers or chicken Dijon, for example, always with a Caesar salad and French bread for only $15. It makes you wonder if this is really Butte.

47 E. Broadway, Butte. www.uptowncafe.com. ✆ **406/723-4735.** Reservations recommended. Lunch $7–$11; dinner $12–$30. AE, DISC, MC, V. Mon–Fri 11am–2pm; Mon–Sat 5–9 or 10pm; Sun 4–8pm.

Butte After Dark

No trip to Butte is complete without a visit to the **M&M Cigar Store,** 9 N. Main St. (✆ **406/530-6020**). The cigar store/saloon/diner/casino that Jack Kerouac said was "the end of my quest for an ideal bar" was continuously open, 24 hours a day, for more than a century after it went into business in 1890, but found itself boarded up

philipsburg: OFF THE BEATEN PATH

Located southwest of Butte on the Pintler Scenic Route (Mont. 1), Philipsburg is one of the best little towns in the state, complete with a vibrant and historic downtown and outdoor recreation in every direction. Many of the historic storefronts are impeccably kept and painted in every color of the rainbow; instead of housing brothels, gambling dens, and saloons, as they did in the mining heyday of "P-burg," they now are more likely occupied by boutiques and galleries. Officially designated a town in 1867, Philipsburg boomed until World War II, at which time the population began to decline. Today the town is livelier than it's been in many decades, as retirees and tourists discover the area. Besides a fair number of B&Bs and other lodgings, there are several restaurants, a theater company, and the **Sweet Palace,** 109 E. Broadway (www.sweetpalace.com; ✆ **406/859-3353**), a confectionery that makes its own fudge, taffy, and caramel on-site. For more information, contact the **Philipsburg Chamber of Commerce** (www.philipsburgmt.com; ✆ **406/859-3388**).

twice in the early 2000s before reopening in 2011. New owner Sam Jankovich said he was "throwing away the keys," and there is no reason to doubt him: The place has a new sports bar in the back room and offers live poker, live keno, and a menu with hearty meals for $5 to $10.

A Side Trip to Deer Lodge

Deer Lodge is home to Montana's state prison, which isn't ordinarily a recommendation for a tourist destination. And we won't recommend any places to stay, because you probably won't want to spend the night. But there is a collection of museums here that makes Deer Lodge worth a morning's stop—especially if you're a car buff or a fan of ranching life.

As you enter Deer Lodge from the west on County Road 275, you'll pass the **Grant-Kohrs Ranch National Historic Site ★** (www.nps.gov/grko; © **406/846-2070**), another of the National Park Service's marvelous facilities. The site preserves the rich history and traditions of ranch life in the West. The ranch itself was founded in the late 1850s when Johnny Grant, a Canadian trader, moved here, eventually building up a herd of several hundred cattle. After a few years, he sold it to legendary cattleman Conrad Kohrs, and the ranch became the headquarters for a vast cattle empire scattered across the open range of Montana, Idaho, and Wyoming. Today the site includes 90 structures, 26,000 artifacts, and a 1,500-acre cultural landscape maintained as a small-scale working ranch. Rangers lead tours of the 1862 Kohrs manor on an hourly basis. Wagon tours are also offered, although on a limited schedule. Admission is free, but donations are appreciated. The site is open to the public daily 9am to 5:30pm in summer (9am–4:30pm winter) except Thanksgiving, Christmas, and New Year's Day.

Gold was discovered near Deer Lodge in 1862. This was an early precursor of the gold rush that reached full bloom with the discoveries at Bannack and Virginia City. One of the consequences of this gold rush is downtown—the castlelike **Old Montana Prison,** at 1106 Main St. (www.pcmaf.org; © **406/846-3111**). Vigilantes initially dealt with the thievery and lawlessness that prevailed during the gold rush, but the need for a real jail was eventually solved by the construction of this prison, which took in its first prisoner in 1871. It was used until 1979, when another facility was built about 5 miles from here. You can take a self-guided tour of the prison. Cellblocks, maximum-security areas, turreted guard towers, and the imposing arches of the "Sally Port" gate are the attractions here, along with a tribute to officers killed in the line of duty at the **Montana Law Enforcement Museum.**

The Old Prison and the Law Enforcement Museum are only two of a collection of museums in Deer Lodge, which are all covered under one admission fee ($8 adults, $4 kids 10–15, and free for kids 9 and under, with lower rates in the winter). The prison complex also houses the **Montana Auto Museum,** the **Powell County Museum,** the **Frontier Montana Museum,** and **Yesterday's Playthings.** The complex is open to the public daily year-round: from Memorial Day to Labor Day 8am to 8pm, and 9am to 5pm or 10am to 4pm the rest of the year; not all of the museums stay open during the off season. Some of the museums have different hours different times of the year; visit www.pcmaf.org or call © **406/846-3111** for current information.

The newest exhibit is **Cottonwood City,** a re-creation of an Old West town, with a blacksmith, cabins, a church, a schoolhouse, and a mortuary (you can get your photo taken in a casket). There's a working blacksmith's shop as well. The **Montana**

Auto Museum houses more than 120 exquisitely restored automobiles—mostly classic Fords and Chevys, but also vintage firetrucks, motor homes, and motorcycles. The **Frontier Montana Museum** has a collection of the tools that were used to win the West. There is a nice exhibit on Colt "peacemakers" and their effect on the keeping of the peace. There are also saddles, spurs, and Desert John's Saloon, with one of the largest bottle and whiskey-memorabilia collections in the country.

The vast weapons collection at the **Powell County Museum,** 1193 Main St., includes long guns and handguns from 1776 to 1956. **Yesterday's Playthings,** 1017 Main St., is a doll and toy museum. The collections of Harriet Free and Pat Campbell are displayed here, with dolls, toys, and antiques of all descriptions: mohair teddy bears, carriages and cradles dating from 1835, clown dolls, and various reproductions.

For additional information on these and other activities in Deer Lodge, contact the **Powell County Chamber of Commerce,** 1109 Main St., Deer Lodge, MT 59722 (www.powellcountymontana.com; ✆ **406/846-2094**), or **Gold West Country,** 1105 Main St., Deer Lodge, MT 59722 (http://goldwest.visitmt.com; ✆ **800/ 879-1159**).

DILLON & THE BIG HOLE

Dillon: 65 miles S of Butte; 141 miles N of Idaho Falls, Idaho

In early Western parlance, a "hole" was a valley surrounded by steep mountains. And Big Hole is, well, a big "hole," in this old sense of a valley. It is a vast expanse of hay meadows, sagebrush flats, and ranch land ringed by towering mountains in the distance. These hay meadows have also given the Big Hole its nickname of the "valley of 10,000 haystacks," which may be a rare case of Rocky Mountain understatement.

While there are plenty of haystacks, there aren't many people. This region is the least densely populated area in western Montana. Beaverhead County, which is as large as Connecticut and Rhode Island combined, has only about 9,000 residents, and most of those live in Dillon, the county's largest town.

Dillon is primarily an agricultural center, still dependent on local farmers and ranchers rather than tourism or industry. The population temporarily jumps from 5,000 to roughly 20,000 people around Labor Day during the event known as **"Montana's Biggest Weekend."** Among the draws are a county fair, which is wrapped around a PRCA Rodeo that draws some of the country's best cowboys, as well as national musical acts. If you plan on attending, book a room at least 3 months in advance.

The scenic loop that takes you around this valley is one of the state's more popular driving tours and is described earlier in this chapter.

Essentials

GETTING THERE   The **Dillon Airport** is located at 2400 Airport Rd. and has paved runways for light planes. See Butte "Essentials," earlier in this chapter, for information on Bert Mooney Airport and the closest airport to the Big Hole Valley, as well as car rentals and train and bus service. Dillon is located on I-15, about 65 miles south of Butte and 78 miles from Anaconda.

This area is also a popular destination for snowmobilers, and visitors are encouraged to call the **avalanche advisory line** (www.mtavalanche.com; ✆ **406/ 587-6981**) before setting out on a snowmobiling excursion. For **current road conditions,** call ✆ **800/226-7623** or 511. For current **weather information,** call ✆ **406/721-3939.**

VISITOR INFORMATION   The **Dillon Visitor Information Center** (operated by the Beaverhead Chamber of Commerce) is located in the Camp Fortunate Interpretive Center at 10 W. Reeder St., Dillon, MT 59725 (www.beaverheadchamber.org; *C* **406/683-5511**).

Getting Outside

Beaverhead County has several natural hot springs, including **Jackson Hot Springs Lodge** (see "Where to Stay," later in this chapter) and **Elkhorn Hot Springs,** which is located about 10 miles off Route 278 on a newly paved road. Go west of Dillon on Route 278 about 30 miles, then turn north toward Polaris at the sign. Follow the road through Polaris to Elkhorn Hot Springs, about 5 miles farther. These waters provide a therapeutic complement to various winter activities, most notably snowmobiling, downhill skiing, and cross-country skiing.

OUTFITTERS & ORGANIZED TRIPS

Montana High Country, 35 miles west of Dillon at 7501 Pioneer Mountain Scenic By-way, Polaris, MT 59746 (www.mhct.com; *C* **406/834-3469**), is operated by sixth-generation Montanan Russ Kipp. The company offers year-round guiding services, including fly-fishing, horseback riding, big-game hunting, and snowmobiling. Whether you're a sportsman looking to bag that elusive elk or a family longing for some quality time together, Kipp has plenty of experience in arranging a unique outdoor adventure. His most popular trips center on southwest Montana's classic trout streams, picturesque limestone canyons, and stunning mountain ranges. Prices range from $900 for a 3-day, 4-night snowmobiling package to $2,550 for a 6-day, 7-night fishing trip; hunting trips are also available. Kipp also operates an Orvis-endorsed guest lodge with rates starting at $150 per person, per night, meals included.

Dan Pence of **Great Divide Wildlands Institute** (www.greatdividetours.com; *C* **406/683-4669**) offers a variety of scenic and historical tours, with a special emphasis on the route of Lewis and Clark and the Nez Perce through the area. Starting at $250 for two people, the packages include day trips to where Lewis first met the Shoshone and other customized historical and scenic tours in the Big Hole.

FISHING

The Big Hole, Beaverhead, and Poindexter rivers are all within easy reach of Dillon, and Jefferson is only half an hour away by car. The fishing season begins early in the year when other streams may still be clearing and extends into October. Big Hole fishermen can find several trout species, including eastern brook, brown, and golden. The **Clark Canyon Reservoir** provides good fishing for rainbow trout. Arctic grayling, ling, and whitefish also populate the waters of the Big Hole Valley. The **Beaverhead-Deerlodge National Forest,** 420 Barrett St., Dillon, MT 59725 (www.fs.fed.us/r1/b-d; *C* **406/683-3900**), can provide you with information on the lakes and streams in the forest.

For guide service, licenses, equipment, and advice on hot fishing spots, check with the locals in Dillon at **Frontier Anglers,** 680 N. Montana St. (www.frontieranglers.com; *C* **800/228-5263**). Guide service costs $425 for a day trip for two people. For similar rates, you can arrange a trip on any of the local rivers with **Tom Smith's Backcountry Angler,** 426 S. Atlantic St., Dillon, MT 59725 (www.backcountryangler.com; *C* **406/683-3462**). Smith has been guiding in Montana since 1983, and he also has a pair of kitchenettes and a private log home on the Beaverhead River available for rent (call for details). In Twin Bridges (just up Mont. 41), your best bet for fishing equipment and outfitting services is the **Four Rivers Fishing Co.,** 205 S. Main St. (www.4riversmontana.com; ✆ **888/474-8377**). Guided day trips are $465 for two people; lodging is $125 nightly. Aficionados of the fishing world should stop at the **R. L. Winston Rod Co.,** also in Twin Bridges, at 500 S. Main St. (www.winstonrods.com; ✆ **406/684-5674**), for a look at some of the finest fly rods in the world. Free tours of the company facility are given each weekday at 11am; a showroom/museum is open weekdays from 8am to 4:30pm.

HIKING

Hike along the **Continental Divide National Scenic Trail** in the **Anaconda-Pintler Wilderness** for interesting geologic discoveries, fabulous scenery, and views of wildlife: Elk, moose, mule deer, antelope, and even black bears are all indigenous to the region. Covering parts of the Bitterroot and Beaverhead-Deerlodge national forests, this 158,500-acre wilderness spans 40 miles along the Continental Divide over four counties. Highways with access to the area are U.S. 93 on the west, Mont. 38 and Mont. 1 from the north, and Mont. 43 from the east and south. The **Wise River Ranger District,** P.O. Box 100, Wise River, MT 59762 (✆ **406/832-3178**), can direct you to the area's most traveled trails. You can also obtain a recreation directory, which describes many of the trails in the forest. The guide is available for free from **Beaverhead-Deerlodge National Forest,** 420 Barrett St., Dillon, MT 59725 (www.fs.fed.us/r1/b-d; ✆ **406/683-3900**).

HORSEBACK RIDING

Diamond Hitch Outfitters, 3405 Ten Mile Rd., Dillon, MT 59725 (www.diamond hitchoutfitters.com; ✆ **406/683-4191** or 683-5494), offers 1½-hour rides, half-day trips, and full-day trips in the Pioneer Mountains. As an alternative, evening horseback rides include a campfire cookout. More adventurous overnight and extended backcountry rides are also available. Rates range from $40 per 1½-hour ride to $1,050 for a 5-day trip.

SKIING

In addition to **Maverick Mountain,** discussed below, Dillon is fairly close to **Lost Trail Powder Mountain** (see "A Side Trip: Skiing & Hot Springs at Lost Trail Pass, p. 97).

Maverick Mountain   Located 35 miles west of Dillon in the Beaverhead National Forest, Maverick Mountain is a small, inexpensive area that attracts mostly local skiers. It remains crowd-free, as it has yet to become a destination ski resort. There are 24 runs on 255 acres with 2,020 vertical feet of skiing. Most of the runs are rated for the intermediate skier. There are some wide-open bowls, meadows, winding runs, and steep chutes. The area gets enough snow—250 inches yearly—to offer some good powder days. Rentals and lessons are available for downhill skis and snowboards. There's a child-care facility, but call ahead to reserve a spot. There are no lodging facilities at the ski area, although there are some nice accommodations nearby. Cafeteria-style meals are available at the base lodge, or you can grab a hot toddy at the Thunder Bar.

Maverick Mountain Rd. (P.O. Box 475), Polaris, MT 59746. www.skimaverick.com. ✆ **406/834-3454.** Full-day lift tickets $32 adults, $20 children and seniors 70 and over. Mid-Dec to mid-Apr Thurs–Sun and holidays 9:30am–4pm. Take Mont. 278 west off U.S. 15 to Polaris Rd. for 13 miles.

SNOWMOBILING

The Wise River trail system features 150 miles of groomed trails in the Big Hole Valley area, including **Anderson Meadows**—which leads to backcountry lakes and a rental cabin—and **Lacy Creek,** with 10 miles of groomed and ungroomed trails to five high-mountain lakes. The Beaverhead-Deerlodge National Forest's **Wise River Ranger District,** P.O. Box 100, Wise River, MT 59762 (© **406/832-3178**), is a good source of information.

Nature Preserves & Wilderness Areas

One of the Bureau of Land Management's Backcountry Byways, the **Big Sheep Creek Canyon** offers the opportunity to observe the majestic bighorn sheep in their spectacular natural habitat. The 50-mile byway begins in Dell, Montana, on I-15, 24 miles north of the Montana–Idaho border, and passes beneath the high rock cliffs of Big Sheep Canyon to the head of Medicine Lodge Creek. From here, it's just a short drive down to the Medicine Lodge Valley to Mont. 324, just west of Clark Canyon Dam.

Clark Canyon Recreation Area, a man-made lake 20 miles south of Dillon on I-15, is a popular spot for water-skiing or trout fishing. Lewis and Clark's Camp Fortunate is located on the northwestern shore of the reservoir, where camping and boat-launching facilities are also available.

Two Dillon-area landmarks are designated state parks because of the historical significance attached to them as a result of the Lewis and Clark expedition. **Clark's Lookout** (www.fwp.mt.gov; © **406/834-3413**) provided the explorers with a vantage point from which to view their route and is reached by taking the Dillon exit from I-15 and then following the signs. **Beaverhead Rock,** 14 miles south of Twin Bridges on Mont. 41 (© **406/834-3413**), was a tribal landmark recognized by expedition scout Sacajawea. Both parks have no admission charge and are day-use only.

Seeing the Sights

Based in Dillon or elsewhere in the valley, you can branch out to see **Big Hole National Battlefield;** see p. 164.

The **Pioneer Mountain Scenic Byway** is a 4-mile drive that begins on Mont. 278 west of Dillon or along Mont. 43, south of the Wise River. Only the northern 28 miles of the road are paved. Driving between the east and west Pioneer Mountain Ranges, you'll experience alpine meadows, jagged peaks, and ghost towns with numerous opportunities to camp, fish, or watch wildlife. Near Coolidge (as you drive south) you'll see the old railroad bed of the Montana Southern Railway. Built to serve the Elkhorn mine, this was the last narrow-gauge railroad built in the U.S.

Beaverhead County Museum The Beaverhead County Museum is located in the center of town. It's housed in the old Union Pacific Railroad Depot, and an 1870s settler's cabin moved to the spot. Inside, there is a little bit of everything from the pioneer era—clothes, tools, cooking utensils, furnishings, and typewriters. Like a lot of small-town museums in the West, though, this one seems more interested in preserving the names of the families that donated items than in telling a coherent historical story.

15 S. Montana St., Dillon. www.beaverheadcountymuseum.com. © **406/683-5027.** $3 adults, $2 seniors, free for children; $6 maximum per family. Mon–Fri 9am–5pm.

University of Montana Western Art Gallery/Museum The most exciting exhibit at this gallery and museum is the Seidensticker Wildlife Collection of big-game trophies, featuring animals from the far-flung locales of Africa and Asia, as well as North American game. The museum also houses a small permanent regional collection and seasonally rotating exhibits, including student artwork.

Main Hall, 710 S. Atlantic St., Dillon. © **406/683-7331.** Free admission. Daily 9am–4pm.

RED ROCK LAKES NATIONAL WILDLIFE REFUGE: a haven for the trumpeter swan

Though well off the beaten path in the Centennial Valley, 28 miles east of Monida (about an hour south of Dillon), the **Red Rock Lakes National Wildlife Refuge** is often called the most beautiful wildlife refuge in the United States. The refuge was established in 1935 to protect the rare trumpeter swan, and it is here that the endangered species has been brought back from near extinction after a century of being hunted for their meat and feathers (quill pens were a hot item in the 1800s). It was feared that these beautiful creatures, which have wingspans of 7 to 8 feet, had been completely wiped out, until biologists discovered several dozen here in 1933. (They're also found along the Pacific coast and in Alaska.)

This is the largest population in the Lower 48 states—300 to 500 of the rare birds winter in the area, with about 100 calling the refuge home. They mate for life and often return to the exact same nest each year to tend their eggs and cygnets. The best place to view the trumpeters is in the open areas near Upper Red Rock Lake, from late April to the end of September.

In addition to the swan population, the 40,000-acre refuge is home to moose, deer, elk, antelope, foxes, great blue herons, sandhill cranes, ducks, and geese; more than 50,000 ducks and geese may be seen during times of migration.

The multiuse refuge is a popular spot for hiking, mountain biking, and canoeing; check with the refuge (http://redrocks.fws.gov; ℭ **406/276-3536**) for regulations concerning these activities within refuge boundaries. To reach the refuge, take I-15 to the town of Monida, then drive east on a gravel-and-dirt road 28 miles to the refuge entrance. If you are coming from West Yellowstone, travel west on U.S. 20 for about 12 miles to Mont. 87. Travel northwest on Mont. 87 for 5 miles and turn south at the Sawtell historical marker. Follow the paved road around the west shore of Henry's Lake for approximately 5 miles and then turn right at Red Rock Pass Road (an improved dirt road), following it west for about 25 miles to the refuge entrance. The refuge is open from 8am to 4:30pm Monday through Friday year-round and is closed on major holidays.

Where to Stay

In addition to the hotels listed below, two other chain options in Dillon are at I-15 exit 63. The **Comfort Inn,** 450 N. Interchange (ℭ 800/442-4667 or 406/683-6831), has double rates from $79 to $139, and the **Super 8 Motel,** 550 N. Montana St. (ℭ **800/800-8000** or 406/683-4288), has double rates from $60 to $80. Of the less expensive independents, I like the **Sundowner Motel,** 500 N. Montana St. (ℭ **800/524-9746** or 406/683-2375), with double rates of $50 to $60.

Best Western Paradise Inn The Paradise Inn is a comfortable two-story facility set back from one of Dillon's busier streets. The standard rooms are cozy and appointed with an eye for efficiency, if a bit dated, but the penthouse suites are well worth the price, with huge bathtubs and large living areas. For families, there is one two-bedroom unit.

650 N. Montana St., Dillon, MT 59725. www.bestwestern.com. ℭ **800/528-1234** or 406/683-4214. Fax 406/683-4216. 65 units. $90–$101 double; $154 suite; lower rates fall to spring. Rates include continental breakfast. AE, DISC, MC, V. **Amenities:** Restaurant; exercise room; indoor Jacuzzi; indoor pool. *In room:* A/C, TV, hair dryer, Wi-Fi (free).

Jackson Hot Springs Lodge ★ 🏕 This establishment effortlessly combines the trappings of a classic mountain lodge with an informal, cowboy-style atmosphere. The accommodations are in a series of attractive cabins, which are large, with pine-framed beds. There's also a tent-only campground on-site ($30 per site, per night). The grounds are landscaped with attractive gardens. On the other hand, you would not be too surprised to see a cowboy ride his horse up to the bar and order a drink—for the horse. The large hot-springs pool—75×30 feet—is free to guests and available to others for a $6 fee. Don't go on Wednesdays, though, because that's when it's emptied and cleaned, and it takes all day to fill up again. There is a small restaurant on the premises, with a menu that changes seasonally. Dinner goes for $9 to $35.

Main St. (P.O. Box 808), Jackson, MT 59736. www.jacksonhotsprings.com. © **888/438-6938** or 406/834-3151. Fax 406/834-3157. 12 cabins. $45 cabin with shared bath; $126–$156 cabin with private bath. AE, MC, V. Pets accepted ($10 per pet, per night). **Amenities:** Restaurant; lounge; outdoor hot-springs pool; massage; Wi-Fi (free). *In room:* No phone.

A FISHING LODGE

Big Hole Lodge ★★ 🏕 This is one of the finest fly-fishing lodges in the West. You can catch every species of trout—rainbow, brown, cutthroat, grayling, and brook. The Big Hole River is the only river in the Lower 48 that still has native grayling in it, and the fine guides here will help you find them; they also take guests to a private spring creek under lease to the operation. The food is excellent, and the accommodations are comfortable, though not luxurious, and well suited for the angler. Deer often loiter in front of the lodge in the evening. The lodge is best for the experienced angler, but the guides are very patient and give beginners casting lessons at the lodge before hitting the streams. Proprietor Craig Fellin is also an avid golfer, and he's installed a 100-yard, par-3 golf hole on the property. You can practice your putting and casting, and then combine a half-day of fishing with a round of golf at the Old Works course in nearby Anaconda (p. 149).

36894 Pioneer Mountains Scenic Byway (P.O. Box 156), Wise River Rd., Wise River, MT 59762. www.flyfishinglodge.com. © **406/832-3252.** 3 cabins. $3,300 per person per 6-night, 5-day package double occupancy; single-occupancy and shorter-stay packages available. Rates include all meals, drinks, fishing guide, and boat. AE, MC, V. **Amenities:** Lounge; activities desk. *In room:* No phone, Wi-Fi (free).

CAMPING

Under new ownership, the year-round **Dillon KOA,** 735 W. Park St., Dillon, MT 59725 (© **406/683-2749**), is right in town. Campers here will find 60 sites for RVs and 35 tent campsites. In addition to the usual bathhouse, there is a seasonal swimming pool, a small grocery store, fishing supplies, propane, and an RV dump station. Rates are $35 to $45 for RV sites and $21 to $28 for tent sites. There are also four camping cabins (which share the campground's bathhouse) at $40 to $50 double.

Where to Eat

Sweetwater Coffee has freshly brewed coffee, some pastries, and light lunch fare. It's located downtown at 26 E. Bannack (© **406/683-4141**). Another recommended option is **Stageline Pizza,** at 531 E. Poindexter St., in the University of Montana–Western student union building (© **406/683-9004**). Order takeout and head down to the riverbank to enjoy a beautiful Montana sunset.

Blacktail Station ★ STEAKS/SEAFOOD Located in the basement below a standout local watering hole called Mac's Last Cast, Blacktail Station used to be the

Mine Shaft, and some of the decorations from its past life still remain—like the trophy heads. But generally, it's a more upscale place than you'd expect in agricultural Dillon; prints by Montana artist Larry Zabel now adorn the walls along with the hard-rock mining detritus. The food is very traditional and very good. The steak almost melts in your mouth, and the twice-baked potato is very popular. For dessert, the chefs crank out a killer bread pudding.

26 S. Montana St., Dillon. www.blacktailstation.com. © **406/683-6611.** Main courses $9–$38. DISC, MC, V. Summer daily 5–10pm; winter Mon–Sat 5–9pm.

The Crossing Bar & Grill ★ ▮AMERICAN Formerly Big Hole Crossing, this neat little restaurant in the dinky town of Wisdom relocated to the historic bar formerly known as Fetty's after the old place across the street burned down. Served in a dining room or woodsy, cattle brand–bedecked bar, the food remains good yet inexpensive and runs toward beef (prime rib on Sat), chicken, seafood, and excellent house-made soups. It's popular with the Forest Service and BLM types for breakfast and lunch, which is usually a good sign, because they tend to work up quite an appetite wrestling mountain lions, corralling grizzly bears, and arguing with ranchers about riparian habitat improvements. The pies, cinnamon rolls, and bagels are all baked in-house and are especially good. While nobody's quite sure what it is, the bumbleberry pie is excellent. (If you'd like to stay the night, ask about the restaurant's rental cabin; a night goes for $70 for two in summer and $110 for two in ski season, lift tickets for Maverick Mountain included.)

327 County Rd., Wisdom. www.thecrossingbarandgrill.com. © **406/689-3260.** Breakfast main courses $4–$11; lunch $5–$11; dinner $9–$28. AE, DISC, MC, V. Summer daily 7am–9pm; winter daily 8am–8pm, Tues–Wed 8am–2pm.

Las Carmelitas MEXICAN Located across the street from the old depot, Las Carmelitas focuses on traditional Mexican cuisine. The menu includes standards like nachos, salads, enchiladas, burritos, and tacos; evening meals include *chiles rellenos*, *mole* chicken or beef, and other south-of-the-border standbys. The atmosphere is very basic, with square tables and metal chairs. Cold beer is available, as are wine-based margaritas, because the establishment's liquor license does not allow for a full bar.

220 S. Montana St., Dillon. © **406/683-9368.** Main courses $7–$13. AE, DISC, MC, V. Mon–Sat 11am–2pm and 4:30–9pm.

Papa T's ☺PIZZA Papa T's is Dillon's version of Chuck E. Cheese's, only better. It's a converted saloon where the kids can run around without getting on anyone's nerves. There are video games lining one wall and a kiddies' carousel for the tykes. The food is basic American: burgers (consisting of local organic beef), chicken, Philly cheese steaks, and pizza. The formula has worked for more than 20 years. The family-owned restaurant is named for founder and patriarch Tom Lohman, whose kids all call him "Papa."

10 N. Montana St., Dillon. © **406/683-6432.** Main courses and pizzas $6–$21. MC, V. Daily 11am–10pm; shorter hours in winter, call for details.

Sparky's Garage AMERICAN/BARBECUE As its name suggests, Sparky's sports a garage theme, with petroliana of all kinds hanging above the red-and-green checkerboard floors. The aroma of gasoline, however, is nowhere to be smelled; instead, the scent of barbecue wafts from the kitchen. The sauce is sweet and slathered all over everything from pork ribs to chicken to pulled pork, with more than respectable results. There are also burgers, steaks, and baskets of fried shrimp and catfish. Beyond dinner, Sparky's is a reliable choice three meals a day near the University of Montana–Western campus and has a full bar. Look for the new location in Uptown Butte, at 222 E. Park St. (© **406/782-2301**).

420 E. Poindexter St., Dillon. © **406/683-2828.** Reservations not accepted. Breakfast $5–$9; lunch and dinner $7–$21. DISC, MC, V. Mon–Thurs 6:30am–9:30pm; Fri 6:30am–10pm; Sat 7am–10pm; Sun 7am–9pm.

Twin Bridges

Twenty-eight miles from Dillon, just up Mont. 41, Twin Bridges is a dinky river town famous for its great fishing. "Floating Flotillas and Fish Fantasies" is the name given to the tiny town's annual summer festival, held in late July or early August, with highlights that include the extremely popular floating parade on the Beaverhead River, dances, and a barbecue. Locals are even given the chance to show their skills at fly-casting, and there's a tug of war over the river. For additional information about the Twin Bridges area and scheduled activities, visit the Greater Ruby Valley Chamber of Commerce's website at **www.rubyvalleychamber.com**.

WHERE TO STAY & EAT

The Old Hotel ★ 🍴 This excellent inn and restaurant is right on the highway in an out-of-the-way spot, serving gourmet meals out of a beautifully restored brick building decorated with a Scottish motif. While the menu changes weekly, you'll always find a creative assortment of main courses, including fresh seafood, vegetarian, and game dishes; past selections have included stuffed quail with ginger-soy sauce and blue crab ravioli with vodka pink sauce. Dinner main courses run about $20 to $30. Sunday brunch is also available, as is Saturday brunch in summer. An excellent wine cellar features French, Italian, Australian, and California labels. The second level has been converted to a two-suite B&B: Accommodations are tailored to the needs of the angler; omelets, oatmeal, and salmon and eggs are among the breakfasts served.

101 E. 5th Ave., Twin Bridges, MT 59754. www.theoldhotel.com. © **406/684-5959.** 2 units. $150 double; lower rates in winter. Rate includes full breakfast. DISC, MC, V. **Amenities:** Restaurant. *In room:* TV, Wi-Fi (free).

BIG HOLE NATIONAL BATTLEFIELD ★★

76 miles W of Dillon; 106 miles S of Missoula

The flight of the Nez Perce across Montana in 1877 is among the most heroic and epic stories of the Indian Wars period. About 800 Nez Perce refused relocation to a reservation and left their homeland in Idaho in June 1877. In an attempt to join Sitting Bull in the relative safety and freedom of Canada, the Nez Perce eluded the pursuing forces of the United States until early October, when they surrendered—not so much from military defeat but from exhaustion and starvation. On October 5, 1877, only 431 remained.

The **Big Hole National Battlefield** commemorates the flight of the Nez Perce over 1,200 miles of some of the roughest land in the Lower 48 states, through Yellowstone National Park, across Montana's high plains, all the while outwitting and outfighting the U.S. Cavalry. There were several battles along the way, but by far the largest skirmish took place here. Between 60 and 90 members of the band were killed. Only 12 of the dead were warriors—the rest were women, children, and seniors. The U.S. military suffered 29 dead and 40 wounded.

The Nez Perce had traditionally lived in eastern Washington, Idaho, and Oregon. They had always maintained good relations with the white explorers, assisting Lewis and Clark in 1805 by caring for the expedition's members when they arrived in their country sick, tired, and low on provisions. They gave them food, two dugout canoes, and guides. The Nez Perce were also the subjects of the first major Protestant mission effort among the Indians, when the stern and domineering Eliza Spaulding—an associate of the later-martyred Marcus Whitman—urged them to give up their traditional ways in return for eternal salvation.

The Nez Perce's problems multiplied in 1860, when gold was discovered. Most were sent to reservations, but Joseph—known as "Young Joseph"—led a nontreaty band to live on his traditional homeland in the Wallowa Valley. Pressure from settlers eventually led to an order forcing Joseph's band onto a reservation.

In the summer of 1877, several Nez Perce braves ignored advice from the tribal elders and attacked and killed four white settlers in Oregon to exact revenge for the earlier murder of the father of one of the braves. This attack raised the ire of settlers, and the cavalry was called in to hunt down the Nez Perce. On June 1, 1877, Joseph's band joined four other Nez Perce groups and crossed the swollen Snake River, fleeing to Canada.

Battles erupted in Idaho before the Nez Perce entered Montana, fleeing from U.S. Army troops under the leadership of Gen. Oliver O. Howard. When the Nez Perce reached the Big Hole Valley, they decided to make camp, thinking all the while that they had left their troubles behind them in Idaho.

However, in addition to Howard's troops behind them, a second group of soldiers, under the command of Col. John Gibbon, was advancing up the Bitterroot Valley toward the unsuspecting tribe. On the morning of August 9, 1877, Gibbon's soldiers, along with a contingent of local volunteers, attacked the sleeping tribe in what is today known as the Battle of the Big Hole. Less than 48 hours after they'd set up camp, the remaining Nez Perce once again found themselves fleeing for their lives and their freedom. They headed toward Canada, but the U.S. Army troops caught up to them at Bear Paw, only 40 miles from the Canadian border. The capture of Joseph's tattered band was the last major military effort of the Indian Wars, period.

The Battle of the Big Hole is somewhat unusual among Indian fights, in that a number of descriptions of the battle exist, many from the Indian point of view. André Garcia, a scout and adventurer, married a Nez Perce woman, In-who-lise, who was wounded in the battle. In his marvelous book *Tough Trip Through Paradise,* he says that he visited the battlefield 2 years later, and human bones and skulls were still scattered everywhere.

Begun as a military reserve in 1883, the area became a national monument in 1910 and was designated a national battlefield in 1963. Today the National Park Service maintains an interpretive center, where rangers help visitors understand the significance of the battle that occurred at Big Hole. Guided tours, a museum, exhibits, a bookstore, movies, and three self-guided walking trails are available.

Trails begin at the lower parking lot and lead to several points of interest. The **Nez Perce Camp,** where soldiers surprised the sleeping tribe, is considered sacred ground. The **Siege Area** marks the place where soldiers were besieged for nearly 24 hours as the Nez Perce fought to save their families from certain death. A fairly steep walk will lead you to the **Howitzer Capture Site,** where soldiers suffered a heavy blow as Nez Perce warriors captured and dismantled the military weapon. This spot affords a spectacular view of the battlefield and surrounding area.

The Big Hole Battlefield represents only a small fraction of the Nez Perce's tragic flight across the West. The 1,200-mile Nez Perce (Nee Me Poo) National Historic Trail follows the entire route of the Nez Perce War, from Wallowa Lake in northwestern Oregon to Bear Paw Battlefield in north-central Montana (see chapter 8). Crossing four states, the trail features several Nez Perce war sites, with interpretive markers telling the story of the tribe's fight for freedom. The trail is administered by the U.S. Forest Service, and the Beaverhead-Deerlodge National Forest (see "Visitor Information," below) can provide you with an excellent map of the four-state area.

GETTING THERE   From Missoula, you can reach the Big Hole National Battlefield by going south on U.S. 93 through the Bitterroot Valley 80 miles to Lost Trail Pass. Then turn east on Mont. 43 and drive 16 miles to the site. From Butte, go south on I-15 20 miles to Mont. 43, go west for 51 miles to Wisdom, then continue west on Mont. 43 for about 10 miles to the site. From Dillon, take Mont. 278 west to Wisdom, then go west on Mont. 43 for 10 miles.

VISITOR INFORMATION   Located 10 miles west of Wisdom on Mont. 43, the **Big Hole National Battlefield Visitor Center,** 16245 Mont. 43 W., P.O. Box 237, Wisdom, MT 59761 (www.nps.gov/biho; ✆ **406/689-3155**), is open daily (except on Thanksgiving, Christmas, and New Year's Day), with summer hours from 9am to 5pm and winter hours from 10am to 5pm. Admission is free. Picnic tables are located at the lower parking lot, though there are no camping or overnight facilities on the premises. Fishing is allowed within the battlefield's boundaries and adjacent national forest, but there are restrictions on the private land adjoining the battle site.

You can obtain a pamphlet with an auto tour of the flight of the Nez Perce through the Big Hole, Horse Prairie, and Lemhi valleys from the **National Park Service, Big Hole National Battlefield** (see above), or the **Beaverhead-Deerlodge National Forest,** 420 Barrett St., Dillon, MT 59725 (✆ **406/683-3900**).

The nearest facilities—restaurants, gas stations, grocery stores, and lodgings—are located in Wisdom, 10 miles to the east.

THE OLD MINING TOWNS: VIRGINIA CITY, NEVADA CITY & BANNACK ★★

Virginia City and Nevada City: 72 miles SE of Butte; 67 miles S of Bozeman; 84 miles NW of West Yellowstone. Bannack: 90 miles SW of Butte, 21 miles SW of Dillon.

Virginia City and nearby Nevada City have both a boisterous and colorful past and present. They are old towns, but Virginia City never turned into a ghost town; in fact, it's one of the oldest continuously occupied towns in the West.

In 1863, a group of miners led by Bill Fairweather took $180 in their first day of gold panning from a creek, which they later named Alder Gulch after the trees growing on the bank. A gold rush soon followed and a mining town grew. The nation was in the midst of the Civil War, and the Southern sympathizers in the crowd wanted to name the new city Varina after Jefferson Davis's wife. But G. G. Bissell, a Northerner and a miners' judge, said, "I'll see you damned first." He wrote "Virginia" on the founding document instead, a sort of compromise, but since Virginia housed the capital of the Confederacy, no one complained.

The restoration of Virginia City began in 1946 when Charles and Sue Bovey began the painstaking task of preserving and restoring many of the structures you see in town today. Most of the buildings were erected during Virginia City's heyday as the state's second territorial capital. In the mid-1950s, Bovey also began to rebuild Nevada City, then a true ghost town, by bringing in buildings he'd acquired from around the West.

In 1991, following the deaths of Sue and Charles, son Fred Bovey determined that he was unable to continue to operate the properties and attractions. He decided to sell the whole kit and caboodle, including millions of dollars of antiques (Sotheby's estimate: $60 million). The state of Montana and Montana Historical Society attempted to have the area designated a national park, but to no avail. Even the National Trust for Historic Preservation got into the act, declaring Virginia City an endangered historic site.

Finally, partly because of a public outcry and due to the efforts of Governor Marc Racicot, the 1997 Montana legislature took dramatic fiscal measures and agreed to fund the $6.5-million purchase (such a bargain), and added $3 million for operational expenses. Today the cities operate under the supervision of the Montana Historical Society and its foundation.

The dusty main drag of Bannack also pays tribute to the mining era. The town grew up quickly after the state's first big gold strike occurred here in 1862, but the vein was a shallow one, and Bannack quickly turned into a ghost town. Despite its short life, Bannack has a colorful history. One writer said, "It is probable that there never was a mining town of the same size that contained more desperadoes and lawless characters than did Bannack during the winter of 1862 to '63."

GETTING THERE   Virginia City and Nevada City are 13 miles west of Ennis on Mont. 287. From Bozeman, take Mont. 84 west to Norris, then go south on U.S. 287 to Ennis, then west on Mont. 287 to the sites. From Butte, take I-90 east to the Whitehall exit (Mont. 55), then go south 27 miles to Twin Bridges. From Twin Bridges, take Mont. 287 east 30 miles to the sites. They are only about a mile apart, with Nevada City being the farther west.

Bannack is reached by driving about 15 miles west of Dillon on Mont. 278, then south on a gravel road at the sign for Bannack State Park.

VISITOR INFORMATION   There are remains of many other Montana ghost towns in this part of the state; it's just that information about them is often hard to find and the towns themselves even harder. Your best bet: Contact the **Virginia City Chamber of Commerce,** P.O. Box 218, Virginia City, MT 59755 (www.virginia citychamber.com; ✆ **800/829-2969**), and **Gold West Country,** 1155 Main St., Deer Lodge, MT 59722 (www.goldwest.visitmt.com; ✆ **800/879-1159**). These two agencies can provide you with free information about the historic ghost towns of Montana. While you're at it, request copies of two brochures that will enhance your visit to the area: *Walking Tour,* a historical, block-by-block guide to Virginia City; and *A Walking Tour of Nevada City, Montana.*

Most attractions in Virginia City (and all of them in Nevada City) are run by the **Montana Heritage Commission,** P.O. Box 338, Virginia City, MT 59755 (www.montanaheritagecommission.com and www.virginiacitymt.com; ✆ **406/843-5247**), and they're open only during the peak summer season, from Memorial Day to Labor Day.

The Old Mining Towns: Virginia City, Nevada City & Bannack

Virginia City

As Virginia City boomed after Bill Fairweather discovered gold, it became the site of a dramatic ordeal of Western lawlessness and revenge that has fueled a thousand cowboy movie plots. Much of Virginia City's history was driven by the vigilante movement, and the town launched the career of Wilbur Fisk Sanders, who eventually went to Washington as Montana's first U.S. senator.

By 1864, when the Montana Territory was created by President Abraham Lincoln, nearly 30,000 people were living along the gulch's 8 miles. Virginia City was named territorial capital in 1865—taking that title from Bannack, virtually a ghost town by then—and held the position until 1875. For many years after its founding, the only currency acceptable to Virginia City merchants was gold dust.

As the town boomed, the incidence of robberies and murders increased. Many of the robberies depended on inside information by people usually called "road agents." The miners' sheriff, Henry Plummer, who had "persuaded" the sheriffs in Bannack, Nevada City, and Virginia City to turn over their duties to him, turned out to be the leader of the road agents. As sheriff, he knew the timing of the gold movements.

No legal relief was possible because the nearest officials to administer an oath were 400 miles away. In 1863, when a popular miner, Dutchman Nicholas Thiebalt, was murdered for $200, the other miners were outraged. The killer, George Ives, was captured and tried by a miners' court, then hanged. The site of his hanging is preserved in Nevada City. The local residents formed "vigilance committees" to capture and bring the road agents to justice. They hanged at least 21 more of the road agents—including Plummer—and some order was restored to the area.

Virginia City is the larger of the two towns; Nevada City is entirely a ghost town, a collection of original and transplanted buildings from the period. A pair of beautifully **restored trains** makes numerous round-trips daily between the two ($6–$15 round-trip, free for children 5 and under).

SEEING THE SIGHTS

Virginia City has a number of operating commercial enterprises interspersed with the historical stuff. Along the main thoroughfare, you'll find the village centerpieces: the **Fairweather Inn,** the **Wells Fargo Overland Company building,** and the **Virginia City Historical Museum.** One of the oldest structures, the **Montana Post Building,** once housed the state's first newspaper; the paper's original press is still used locally for menus, playbills, and placards.

You should start your visit to Virginia City at the **Visitor Center and Museum Store,** at the end of Main Street. The center has photos, a brief explanation of the history of the town, and a friendly staff of volunteers. The government shut down gold mining for good in 1942, and a few years later the Boveys began buying up the property.

The **Virginia City Players** have been an entertainment staple in town since 1949, operating out of the Smith and Boyd Livery Stable (1900). The players are Montana's oldest professional acting company. For information on showtimes, prices, and days for the Virginia City Players, call ✆ **800/829-2969.**

A little farther up the hill is the **Hangman's Building.** On January 4, 1864, the building was still being constructed, and a stout beam was exposed in the unfinished structure. The vigilantes took advantage of this situation to hang four road agents. The history-oriented **J. Spencer Watkins Memorial Museum** (✆ **406/843-5500**), also on the main street, has some photos of the vigilantes on exhibit and a nice collection of period clothing.

Up above the town, looking down over the main street, is **Boot Hill,** the last resting place of several road agents, who required hasty burial after they died with their boots on.

If you *really* want to see the Old West come to life, check out a **Brewery Follies** production. Famous statewide for its funny cabaret-style revues and entertaining period melodramas, the company performs nightly during the summer. The Brewery Follies have a loyal following. For information on showtimes and prices, visit **www.breweryfollies.net** or call ✆ **406/843-5218.**

WHERE TO STAY

Fairweather Inn   This small hotel, located right in the middle of downtown Virginia City, has a great upstairs porch that's a fun place to sit and people-watch. Though most of the rooms are tastefully decorated in an Old West theme, a few of them are distinguished by odd combinations of bright paint and mismatched quilts. Only 6 of the hotel's 14 rooms have private bathrooms; the rest are rooming house style.

305 W. Wallace St. (P.O. Box 205), Virginia City, MT 59755. www.aldergulchaccommodations.com. ✆ **800/829-2969** or 406/843-5377. 14 units, 8 with shared bathroom. $70–$85 double. MC, V. *In room:* No phone.

Gingerbread House   The candied Victorian exterior of this charming B&B has been a landmark on Idaho Street since prominent local citizen C. W. Rank built the two-story house in 1898. There are two rooms in the main house that share a bathroom and a pair of rustic cabin units out back, with private bathrooms. All feature queen-size beds and antique furnishing; the cabins have lofts and one has a full kitchen. The back patio and yard have plenty of space to stretch out and offer terrific mountain views.

201 E. Idaho St., Virginia City, MT 59755. ✆ **877/424-4012** or 406/843-5471. 4 units (2 with shared bathroom), including 2 cabins. $95–$125 double. Rates include full breakfast. AE, DISC, MC, V. *In room:* No phone, Wi-Fi (free).

Stonehouse Inn   Built in 1884 by a local blacksmith/rancher/miner, this Gothic Revival–style B&B is a cozy place to hang your hat while in town for a night. Clad in locally quarried stone, the gray exterior is softened by a few brightly painted accents and a sweeping porch with a rocking chair. Your options range from a masculine room, embellished with antique snowshoes and a NO SPITTING sign, to a romantic upstairs room with stained glass, a private balcony, and lace-laden decor. All of the rooms have brass beds, predominately full-size. While the bathrooms are shared, they are exceptionally spacious and feature antique commodes, showers, and tubs.

306 E. Idaho St., Virginia City, MT 59755. www.stonehouseinnbb.net. ✆ **406/843-5504.** 5 units, none with private bathroom. $85 double. Rates include full breakfast. MC, V. *In room:* No phone.

Camping

The **Alder/Virginia City KOA,** 2280 Mont. 287, Alder, MT 59710 (www.koa.com; ✆ **800/562-1898** or 406/842-5677), has over 100 RV sites and 50 tent sites, and is open from March to November. The campground has a dump station, propane sales, a store, a playground, and a fishing pond. Tent sites are $26, RV sites $38, cabins $60.

WHERE TO EAT

In season, there are a few decent restaurants in Virginia City, including the **Virginia City Café,** 210 Wallace Ave. (✆ **406/843-5311**), serving sandwiches for lunch and Irish fare for dinner.

Nevada City

The distance between Nevada City and Virginia City is only a mile or so, but back in the days before the vigilance committees formed, it was a dangerous mile. Miners dared not go between the two cities after dark. A robber waylaid one miner known as Dutch Fred. When the highwayman found that Fred had only $5 with him—and paper money, not gold dust, at that—the bandit cursed and told him, "If ever you come this way again with only $5, I'll shoot you." The robber shot Dutch Fred anyhow, wounding him in the arm.

Nevada City is the site of the resurgence of law and order in these Montana mining camps. Two thousand people reportedly came to town to watch the trial of George Ives for the murder of Nicholas Thiebalt. Emotions were running high on both sides, and it was in the face of these feelings that Wilbur Fisk Sanders began his place in Montana history by courageously prosecuting Ives before the crowd. The spot where Ives was hanged is marked in town.

Today Nevada City is a tourist attraction—a collection of historic wooden buildings, including an open-air museum depicting the gold-mining and settlement period of the area's turbulent history. Nevada City also exists as the result of Charles Bovey's diligence and dedication to the preservation of history. In the mid-1950s, Bovey began to re-create an authentic Western town with buildings he'd accumulated around the West. The buildings are authentic, though their setting may not be. It looks like a perfect cowboy movie set, though, and has in fact been used for a couple of oaters, including *Missouri Breaks, Little Big Man,* and *Return to Lonesome Dove.*

Weekend admission to the Nevada City site costs $8 adults, $6 for kids 7 to 16, and free for those 6 and under; the site is open Memorial Day to Labor Day daily from 9am to 6pm. For information, call ✆ **800/829-2969** or 406/843-5247.

SEEING THE SIGHTS

With your walking-tour booklet in hand, begin your excursion behind the **Nevada City Hotel,** where you can view the state's only double-decker outhouse, and stroll along the streets to see what a Western mining town might have looked like. Boardwalks pass barbershops, homes, a schoolhouse, and even an Asian section. Some of the buildings are closed, but many include period furnishings and wares.

When you hear a cacophony of horns and whistles, follow the noise to the **Nevada City Music Hall,** located next door to the hotel. There you can see the "famous and obnoxious horn machine from the Bale of Hay Saloon!" A sign on the machine begs visitors not to miss hearing "the machine that has driven 28 change-makers, 72 bartenders, and near a million tourists to the brink of insanity!" The music hall is a fascinating place to spend an hour listening to the many music machines and reading about their history. It's one of the largest collections of its kind on display in the United States today. The building was originally the Canyon Lodge Recreation Hall in Yellowstone.

Across the street is the railroad museum, where you will see **Locomotive No. 12,** which typically ran to and from Virginia City (the railroad depot there is at the west end of town) but was discontinued in 2011. The museum has an observation car once used by Calvin Coolidge and the last "Catholic chapel car" in the world.

Another local attraction is the **Alder Gulch River of Gold Mining Museum,** 1552 Mont. 287 (✆ **406/843-5402**), featuring myriad historic mining tools and vehicles, including the Mount Vernon Dredge (1935), one of the few gold-dredging boats on display anywhere, and gold-panning for visitors. It's open Memorial Day to Labor Day daily 10am to 6pm, and admission is free.

WHERE TO STAY & EAT

You can believe the claim of the **Star Bakery Restaurant and Emporium,** 1585 Mont. 287 (© **406/843-5525**), that it has the best biscuits and gravy in town, because it's also the *only* restaurant in town. Best known for its breakfasts, the cozy country restaurant serves three meals a day. The restaurant dates from 1865 and has an old-fashioned soda fountain and a gift shop. The specialty of the house, believe it or not, is fried pickles. The restaurant is closed Labor Day to Memorial Day.

Just an Experience Bed and Breakfast   If you want something more modern than the Nevada City Hotel and Cabins (see below), this B&B is your only other choice in Nevada City proper (dare we say downtown Nevada City?). Two of the rooms in the house share a bathroom, and one has a private bathroom. The rooms are large, with iron-post beds, but the cabins are larger, with enough room for six people, and include loft bedrooms for the kids, color TVs with VCR/DVD player combos, and full kitchens. The original log house here was built in 1864, but it has been remodeled and incorporated into a modern cedar-sided home. Pets are permitted outdoors only.

1570 Mont. 287, Virginia City, MT 59755. www.justanexperience.com. © **866/664-0424** or 406/843-5402. 3 units, 3 cabins. $95–$130 double. Rates include full breakfast; other meals optional ($10–$25 per person). AE, DISC, MC, V. **Amenities:** Jacuzzi. *In room:* TV/VCR or DVD, movie library, kitchen (cabins only), no phone, Wi-Fi (free).

Nevada City Hotel and Cabins   Entering this hotel is like taking a step back in time. Constructed in the 1860s, it was originally a stage stop near Twin Bridges and still has the cool, musty smell of a mining-camp hotel. Most of the rooms are small and spare, but the upstairs Victorian suites are huge, furnished in rough but exquisite Victorian style, complete with polished burl-wood furniture and private bathrooms. If you rent a cabin, be sure to lock your door—many tourists mistake the cabins for museum exhibits and may come exploring.

Mont. 287 (P.O. Box 205), Virginia City, MT 59755. www.aldergulchaccommodations.com. © **800/ 648-7588** or 406/843-5377. Fax 406/843-5402. 29 units, including 2 suites and 17 cabins. $85 double; $100 suite; $90 double cabin. MC, V. Closed Oct to mid-May. *In room:* No phone.

Bannack

Bannack was the site of the state's first big gold strike in 1862. With more than 60 of the town's original buildings preserved, the tumbledown town is a stark reminder of the heyday of the frontier: vigilantes stalking road agents stalking prospectors, in a place where the rivers yielded gold dust.

Born out of the discovery of placer gold in 1862, Bannack quickly grew to a town of 3,000 people, largely composed of those hoping to strike it rich. Blacksmiths, bakeries, stables, restaurants, hotels, dance halls, and grocery stores rapidly sprang up to complement an expanding mining industry.

Bannack became the first territorial capital and the site of the first territorial legislative session in 1864. But the placer veins in Grasshopper Creek were thin. Only a few years later, it was a ghost town, and the boosters of the capital movement had turned their attention to Virginia City and the richer mines at Alder Creek.

Notorious Henry Plummer killed his first local man in Bannack in Goodrich's saloon. The victim was Jack Cleveland, who had threatened another man about a debt, which the other man had already paid. Cleveland bragged that he wasn't afraid of him. Plummer, apparently a bystander, got to his feet, cursed Cleveland, roared, "I'm tired of this," and commenced shooting. Cleveland got the worst of it, dying 3 hours later.

Plummer was an enigmatic outlaw. He was considered a "gentleman" by the standards of the era. He married a schoolteacher, though she left him after only 10 weeks of wedded bliss. Only a few weeks before he was hanged (see the section on Virginia City, above), Plummer held an elaborate dinner for territorial officials, including the governor and some of the vigilantes, for which he had ordered a $60 turkey from Salt Lake City. His guests apparently saw nothing unusual about enjoying the hospitality of a man they had already decided to hang.

VISITOR INFORMATION Designated a state park in 1954, Bannack is open year-round. Summer hours are daily from 8am to 9pm; winter hours 8am to 5pm. There is a seasonal visitor center, as well as camping and picnic grounds, a group-use area, and hiking trails. Other lodging facilities are available in nearby Dillon (see p. 157). Nonresident day-use fees are $5 per vehicle ($3 for bikes or walk-ins) and $13 for a campsite ($20 in the off season). There are also rental tipis for $25 (available May–Sept).

To get to Bannack from Dillon, drive 3 miles south on I-15 to Mont. 278. Head west 17 miles on Mont. 278, then south 4 miles when you see the sign. For additional information, visit **www.bannack.org** or call ℂ **406/834-3413.**

A SPECIAL EVENT **Bannack Days,** staged annually during the third weekend in July, is a 2-day event commemorating the history and heritage of Montana's early pioneers, with activities centering around frontier crafts, music, pioneer food, and dramas. A black-powder muzzleloader shoot, Sunday church services, and horse-and-buggy rides bring the "toughest town in the West" to life and are fun for the entire family.

THE HI-LINE & NORTH-CENTRAL MISSOURI RIVER COUNTRY

This part of Montana is classic cattle and wheat country, the domain of the authentic American cowboy. The vast northern plains of Montana were once a wilderness of tallgrass, rolling in the wind like the sea, home to millions of pronghorn and buffalo.

Lewis and Clark reported vast herds of the latter, but that wasn't all they saw here. When the adventurers entered Montana in 1805, just past the confluence of the Yellowstone and Missouri rivers, they saw their first grizzly bear rambling on the plains, and Lewis made the first extensive description of the animal for science. Before humans drove them to higher ground, this was prime grizzly habitat. Now only one tiny parcel of prairie is frequented by them, Pine Butte Swamp.

As you travel through this region, you'll likely be closely following the trail of Lewis and Clark to the portage of the Great Falls. In the city of Great Falls, take time to visit the Lewis and Clark National Historic Trail Interpretive Center and experience vicariously one of the great American adventures. This portion of the state is also the landscape that Charles Russell memorialized in his famous Western paintings and bronzes.

But the region isn't all history and vanished mythology. There's plenty of outdoor activity, including fishing and boating on Fort Peck Lake, bird-watching at the Charles M. Russell National Wildlife Refuge, rafting on the wild and scenic Missouri River, and both downhill and cross-country skiing.

SCENIC DRIVES

Driving Tour 1: Kings Hill Scenic Byway

The Kings Hill Scenic Byway is a 71-mile stretch of U.S. 89 through the Little Belt Mountains and the Lewis and Clark National Forest. You pick it up about 22 miles southeast of Great Falls, where U.S. 87 and U.S. 89

divide. Take U.S. 89 south toward the towns of Monarch and Neihart. From the south, take U.S. 89 north from just east of Livingston on I-90. For a leisurely tour, you can watch the wildlife and the scenery, then visit the ghost towns at Castle Town and Hughesville, and the historic mining site at Glory Hole. For a more active trip, go to **Sluice Boxes State Park,** just north of Monarch (http://fwp.mt.gov; ✆ **406/454-5840**), to hike along the abandoned rail line there or fish in Belt Creek. In winter, there is cross-country skiing at the Silver Crest Trail System (just north of Showdown Ski Area; see below) and snowmobiling at Kings Hill. Memorial Falls has a nature trail that is accessible to visitors with disabilities. Primitive backcountry camping sites (free, but you must get a permit and camp a half-mile or more from the trail head) and national forest access points are at numerous spots along the highway.

Driving Tour 2: The Charles M. Russell Trail

The Judith Basin inspired the work of one of the West's seminal artists, Charles M. Russell. This drive on U.S. 87/Mont. 200 between Great Falls and Lewistown provides an intimate glimpse at the unsettled West through Russell's eyes. The drive is lovely in a pastoral way, but it helps to have a copy of the interpretive guide of the trail from Travel Montana's **Russell Country** (www.russell.visitmt.com; ✆ **800/527-5348**) if you want to get the full experience. The guide uses Russell's art to illuminate the history of the basin.

These highways were designated the Russell Trail by the Montana legislature. The scruffy cowhands and toughened Indians that Russell painted have been replaced by carefully tended fields of grain, but with the help of Russell's art and a little imagination, you can put yourself back in the saddle in 1880s Montana.

From Great Falls, you go southeast through the towns of Raynesford, Geyser, and Moccasin, taking in the history of the Blackfeet, the infamous last wolves of the basin in Stanford, and the role of the railroads in Hobson. Spring and fall are the best times to match Russell's color palette with that of the scenery.

There are roadside turnouts along the highway for many of the 25 interpretive sites, including the settings for two of Russell's best-known paintings, *Buffalo in Winter* and *Paying the Fiddler.*

GREAT FALLS

89 miles N of Helena; 219 miles NW of Billings

Great Falls, named for a series of waterfalls on the Missouri River, is a city of about 57,000, making it Montana's third largest (after Billings and Missoula). An important cog in the U.S. military strategy, it is the home of Malmstrom Air Force Base, which several times has been threatened with closure (which would devastate the city), but it has thus far avoided that fate.

But the country around Great Falls looks much as Charles Russell found it and painted it at the end of the 19th century. Russell made Great Falls his home and did much of his painting in his studio there.

Nearly a century before Russell's day, Lewis and Clark came through with the Corps of Discovery in 1805, making an 18-mile portage around the falls. It is a somewhat sad sign of Great Falls's progress that it is now known as "the Electric City," because the falls that Lewis and Clark marveled at have been tamed by a series of dams to provide electric power.

Essentials

GETTING THERE   Great Falls serves as the hub for north-central Montana east of the Rockies. The **Great Falls International Airport** (www.gtfairport.com; © 406/727-3404) has daily service from **Alaska/Horizon, Allegiant, Delta,** and **United.** Shelby, 88 miles northwest, provides the closest **Amtrak** service (www.amtrak.com; © 800/872-7245).

Great Falls is located on I-15, which runs north from Butte, where the highway intersects with I-90, passing through Helena and then Great Falls. From Missoula, you can take Mont. 200 east, or you can take I-90 a little southeast, pick up U.S. 12, and go east to Helena, then north to Great Falls. Mont. 200 is more scenic. From Billings, you can take Mont. 87 north to Lewistown and then west to Great Falls. Or you can go west on I-90 to Livingston, then take Mont. 89, which includes the Kings Hill Scenic Byway (see the driving tour above), northwest to Great Falls. From Bozeman, take U.S. 287 north at Three Forks, then I-15 to Great Falls.

VISITOR INFORMATION   Request tour information from **Russell Country,** P.O. Box 3166, Great Falls, MT 59403 (www.russell.visitmt.com; © 800/527-5348 or 406/761-5036). The **Great Falls Convention and Visitors Bureau** is at 1106 9th St. S., Great Falls, MT 59405 (www.gfcvb.com; © 800/735-8535 or 406/727-8733). There is a visitor center at the Broadwater Overlook at 15 Upper River Rd., right under the tall flagpole.

GETTING AROUND   The best way to explore Great Falls and environs is by car. Most rental franchises operate in town, including **Avis** (© 800/230-4898), **Hertz** (© 800/654-3131), and **National** (© 800/227-7368) at the airport.

Great Falls Transit System (www.gftransit.com; © 406/727-0382) offers bus service Monday through Saturday from early morning to early evening (no service Sun and holidays). Fare is $1 adults, 75¢ students, and 50¢ seniors; kids 5 and under are free.

ORGANIZED TOURS   To see the town, take the 2-hour **Great Falls Historic Trolley** tour (www.greatfallshistorictrolley.com; © 888/707-1100 or 406/771-1100). Tickets are $22 for adults and $5 children 2 to 12, with one stop at the Rainbow Falls. You pick up the tour at the visitor information center at Broadwater Overlook Park. The company also does a Lewis and Clark tour, a parks tour, and custom trips.

A SPECIAL EVENT   Great Falls hosts the **Lewis and Clark Festival** each year in June. Events include history workshops, tours, food booths, and children's activities. For information and tickets, call © 406/452-5661.

Getting Outside
FISHING & BOATING

Great Falls is the unofficial dividing line for cold- and warm-water fish. You can fish for trout from Giant Springs or take one of the many tours available on the Missouri. For half- to 7-day fishing and white-water trips on the Missouri, try **Montana River Outfitters,** 923 10th Ave. N., Great Falls (www.montanariveroutfitters.com; © 800/800-4350 or 406/235-4350).

GOLF

The city offers two public golf courses: **Anaconda Hills,** on Smelter Hill in Black Eagle northeast of town at 2315 E. Smelter Ave. (© 406/761-8459), with greens

8

THE HI-LINE & NORTH-CENTRAL MISSOURI RIVER COUNTRY | Great Falls

HOTELS ■
Best Western Plus
  Heritage Inn **2**
Collins Mansion **3**
Hampton Inn **1**
O'Haire Motor Inn **8**

ATTRACTIONS ●
Benton Lake National
  Wildlife Refuge **12**
Civic Center **4**
C.M Russell Museum
  Complex **10**
Gibson Park **5**
Giant Springs State Park **13**
Lewis & Clark Interpretive
  Center **11**
Malmstrom Air Force Base
Heritage Center & Air Park **13**
Paris Gibson Museum of Art **9**

**RESTAURANTS/
NIGHTLIFE** ◆
Bar S Supper Club **14**
Bert & Ernie's **6**
Sip 'n Dip Lounge **8**

SERVICES ●
Great Falls Convention
  and Visitors Bureau **7**

fees of $24 to $30 for 18 holes and $15 to $18 for 9; and the **Eagle Falls Golf Club,** at 25th Street and River Drive North (✆ **406/761-1078**), with greens fees of $28 to $31 for 18 holes and $17 to $18 for 9. Carts are $13 per person for 18 holes.

HIKING & BIKING

The 40-plus-mile **River's Edge Trail** (www.thetrail.org), along the Missouri River, starts downtown at Oddfellows Park and runs out past Rainbow Dam and Crooked Falls, out to the "Great Falls of the Missouri," below Ryan Dam, and beyond. The trail is ideal for hiking, biking, running, walking, and roller skating. The **Great Falls Convention and Visitors Bureau** (see above) can provide you with information and trail maps.

WINTER SPORTS

Showdown Ski Area   Although relatively undiscovered, this is a full-service ski area, with 34 trails on 640 acres, three chairlifts, a surface lift, and a 1,400-foot vertical drop. The area is perfect for beginning and intermediate skiers (30% beginner, 40% intermediate, 30% expert), with long, uninterrupted runs and lots of dry, light powder. The total average snowfall is 240 inches annually. There are ski rentals and a restaurant and bar. Family-oriented perks include a day-care center and a children's program. Adjacent to Showdown is the **Silver Crest Trail System** for cross-country skiing.

65 miles southeast of Great Falls on U.S. 89, near Neihart. www.showdownmontana.com. ✆ **800/433-0022** or 406/727-5522. For snow conditions, call ✆ 406/771-1300. Full-day lift tickets $38 adults, $28 seniors 70 and over, $33 students, $20 children 6–12, free for 5 and under. Early Dec to early Apr Wed–Sun 9:30am–4pm. Closed Christmas, Martin Luther King, Jr., Day, and Presidents' Day.

Seeing the Sights

Gibson Park, located 1 block north of the Civic Center along Park Drive, is quite nice, with a large pond, playgrounds, flower gardens, and picnic areas. This is a good place to pick up the trail system along the Missouri River. A grizzly bear chased Meriwether Lewis into the Missouri River near here in 1805.

Benton Lake National Wildlife Refuge   Established in 1929 by President Herbert Hoover, the refuge is physically unimpressive, a small lake in a broad, open, treeless plain. But the 12,383 acres are some of the country's most important nesting grounds for waterfowl, especially mallards, pintail, teal, and canvasback. Bird-watching for waterfowl and prairie species is best early in the morning or in the evening. There's a 9-mile auto-tour route that takes about an hour, marked with signs to provide information about what you're seeing, but Mother Nature is constantly changing the refuge attractions.

922 Bootlegger Trail, Great Falls, MT 59404. www.fws.gov/bentonlake. ✆ **406/727-7400.** Free admission. Open daily during daylight hours. Go 1 mile north of Great Falls on Mont. 87, take a left on Bootlegger Trail, then proceed about 9 miles north to well-marked entrance.

C. M. Russell Museum Complex ★★   You can divide the world into two kinds of people—those who like cowboy art and those who don't. It is a measure of Charles Russell's greatness that, although he was a cowboy artist, almost everybody likes his work. This facility, which includes tours of Russell's studio and home, is one of the high points of any trip to Montana, and it's worth going out of your way to see.

Russell and the dime novelists practically invented the West. But the power of his work is that the personality of everyone and everything portrayed—American Indians, cowboys, even the landscape—shines through. Much modern "Western art" concentrates on the scenery and fierce animals without making much of a statement. Conversely, Russell had something to say about a celebrated but passing way of life, and he said it powerfully.

The museum houses the largest collection of Russell's work on the planet, hung in chronological order—starting with a trio of paintings he did when he was 13. From there, visitors get to see an amazing evolution in his vivid, self-taught style, from early watercolors, to statues made of wax and plaster and later bronze, to Christmas cards and sketches, all the way to his final, most renowned oil period before his death in 1926. The studio contains some of Russell's personal belongings, including many of the Indian artifacts he collected to help maintain his art's authenticity. A number of other excellent Western artists are shown to good advantage in the museum; besides the permanent display of works by Russell protégé Olaf Seltzer and another permanent exhibit on bison art, exhibits change several times a year. You can spend an hour or all day here.

400 13th St. N. www.cmrussell.org. © **406/727-8787.** $9 adults, $7 seniors, $4 students (age 6 or older), free for kids 5 and under. May–Sept daily 9am–6pm; Oct–Apr Tues–Sat 10am–5pm. Tours May–Sept Tues–Sat at 2pm. Closed major holidays.

Giant Springs State Park ★ Lewis and Clark came upon and described the Giant Springs, purportedly the largest freshwater spring in the world. The spring now also feeds a fish-breeding facility nearby. It burbles out of the 250-million-year-old Madison Formation, a large water-bearing formation that provides a lot of groundwater throughout the northern West. The springs send out more than 100,000 gallons a minute into the 201-foot-long Roe River, credited as one of the two shortest rivers in the world. The entire park covers 218 acres and has about 2 miles of trails.

The Great Falls that gave Lewis and Clark so much trouble have been dammed, but you can see a few remnants of their former glory from overlooks. In the spring, especially, you can see the power of the river flowing through the spillways at Rainbow Dam, spewing mist hundreds of feet into the air, creating the rainbows in the sunshine that so entranced the explorers. Lewis called Rainbow Falls "one of the most beautiful objects of nature." The Montana Department of Fish, Wildlife, and Parks also operates a fish hatchery and visitor center nearby (Mon–Fri 8am–5pm), where visitors can purchase hunting and fishing licenses.

4600 Giant Springs Rd. www.fwp.mt.gov. © **406/454-5840.** $5 per vehicle ($3 per bicycle or pedestrian). Open daily during daylight hours. Take River Dr. east along the Missouri River to Giant Springs Rd. Turn left and drive about ¼ mile, just past the Lewis & Clark National Historic Trail Interpretive Center.

Lewis & Clark National Historic Trail Interpretive Center ★★ Located on a bluff overlooking the Missouri River, this facility is, hands down, the best Lewis and Clark exhibit between St. Louis and the Pacific Ocean. The facility is cleverly arranged to follow the adventurers' path to each major point along the way. You start at Monticello with Thomas Jefferson's instructions to the Corps of Discovery. Then you go from one high point to the next along the journey. You visit a Mandan earth lodge, see the grizzlies, and feel the voyagers sweat as they pull their 3,000-pound boat along the 18-mile portage of the Great Falls. Of this portage, Clark wrote: "To state the fatigues of this party would take up more of this journal than other notes which I find scarcely time to set down." An excellent facility, it will take several hours to see properly. The docents are wonderfully informed and entertaining. Interpretive programs are held year-round, outdoors at a "River Camp" setting during the summer months.

4201 Giant Springs Rd. © **406/727-8733.** $8 adults, free for children 15 and under. Memorial Day to Sept daily 9am–6pm; Oct to Memorial Day Tues–Sat 9am–5pm, Sun noon–5pm. Closed major holidays.

Malmstrom Air Force Base Heritage Center and Air Park The air park has a number of aircraft from various eras, primarily from the 1950s and 1960s, but the real attractions here are the implements of nuclear weaponry: a Minuteman III ICBM and its transporter erector. Inside, amid scads of military equipment and uniforms and a reconstruction of a World War II–era barracks, is the old command center that once controlled the base's nuclear missiles. Interpretation of the exhibits is minimal, unfortunately.

Malmstrom Air Force Base, east end of 2nd Ave. N. past 57th St. © **406/731-2705.** Free admission; civilian passes are available at the base's visitor center. Air park: Daily during daylight hours. Museum: Mon–Fri 10am–4pm. Closed holidays.

Paris Gibson Square Museum of Art ★ Located in a national historic landmark building that served as Great Falls's first high school, Paris Gibson Square is now the cultural and art center of the city. The changing art shows display the works of artists from around the Northwest, as well as pieces from the permanent collection. The selection includes both contemporary and historical exhibits in a comfortable, beautifully restored space. Among the newest works are Len Steen's "outsider art," stick-figure statues that once graced Montana's roadsides.

1400 1st Ave. N. www.the-square.org. © **406/727-8255.** Free admission. Mon–Fri 10am–5pm (Tues also 7–9pm); Sat noon–5pm.

Shopping

There are at least 19 antiques stores in Great Falls, and the chamber of commerce can give you a map of their locations. The terrific **Dragonfly Dry Goods,** 504 Central Ave. (© **406/454-2263**), specializes in home decor, clothing, gifts, and things Western. **Hoglund's,** 306 1st Ave. S. (© **406/452-6911**), has an awe-inspiring selection of cowboy boots and hats. You can find Montana-made souvenirs or gifts at the **Blue Ribbon of Montana,** 3400 10th St. S. (© **406/761-1233**).

Where to Stay

Aside from the properties listed below, we also recommend the **Hampton Inn,** 2301 14th St. SW (© **406/453-2675**), with rates of $110 to $130 double and $200 for a whirlpool suite.

Best Western Plus Heritage Inn The hotel is located on a sedate street just off the main drag and is the preferred business stop-off in Great Falls, located a little closer to the interstate than downtown. The rooms are comfortable, a notch above your typical chain, and many of them adjoin the central gardened atrium where the pool is located. It has the largest convention center in Great Falls, with a latte bar to boot.

1700 Fox Farm Rd., Great Falls, MT 59404. www.bestwestern.com/heritageinngreatfalls. © **800/548-8256** or 406/761-1900. Fax 406/761-0136. 233 units. $100–$120 double. AE, DC, DISC, MC, V. **Amenities:** Restaurant; lounge/casino; free airport transfers; exercise room; indoor Jacuzzi; indoor pool; sauna. *In room:* A/C, TV, hair dryer, Wi-Fi (free).

Collins Mansion ★★ Built in 1891 and listed on the National Register of Historic Places, this grand Queen Anne–style mansion is today a stylish bed-and-breakfast. At 8,000 square feet, this gleaming white structure stands out (it sits in an otherwise typical neighborhood overlooking the west side of Great Falls) with a wraparound veranda and ornate woodwork. All of the rooms have a private bathroom. The pinnacle is the Black and Gold Room, decorated in its namesake colors and featuring a four-poster king bed and a city view from the bay window. The frilly Lavender Room features canopied beds.

1003 2nd Ave. NW, Great Falls, MT 59404. www.greatfallsbedbreakfast.com. © **866/939-4262** or 406/452-4444. 6 units. $89–$135 double. Rates include full breakfast. AE, MC, V. *In room:* A/C, TV, no phone, Wi-Fi (free).

O'Haire Motor Inn 🗲 A solid independent motel centered on an interior parking lot, this is my lodging of choice in downtown Great Falls, with all of the trappings for a perfect break from the highways en route to Glacier or points beyond. The hotel, built in 1962 and recently updated, is well-kept and clean, a cut above the normal independent. The restaurant, **Clark & Lewie's,** is a more-than-respectable diner with personality and microbrew on tap, serving hearty breakfasts and a pub menu for lunch and dinner. The **Sip 'n Dip Lounge** (see "Great Falls After Dark," below) must be seen to be believed. Besides the usual amenities, rubber duckies come with the rooms.

17 7th St. S. Great Falls, MT 59405. www.ohairemotorinn.com. © **800/332-9819** or 406/454-2141; 800/543-9819 in Canada. Fax 406/454-0211. 69 units. $72–$90 double; $110 suite. AE, DC, DISC, MC, V. **Amenities:** Restaurant; lounge; exercise room; indoor pool. *In room:* A/C, TV, Wi-Fi (free).

Where to Eat

Bar S Supper Club STEAKS/SEAFOOD Authentic cowboy steakhouses have become endangered with the expansion of national chains in recent years, but you'll find the real deal at the Bar S, on the northeast side of Great Falls. The place has a rustic charm, with brands on the walls, lots of red vinyl and wood, and the requisite beer signs. While lunches are primarily burgers and sandwiches, the dinner menu focuses almost exclusively on Montana choice beef, ranging from a 10-ounce tenderloin to a 30-ounce rib-eye, and there is also a fair amount of seafood and a smattering of poultry. Some locals come every Saturday night, and nobody leaves hungry.

5100 N. Star Blvd. © **406/761-9550.** Reservations recommended. Main courses $6–$11 lunch; $20–$50 dinner. AE, DISC, MC, V. Tues–Sat 11am–2pm and 5–10pm; Sun 4–9pm.

Bert & Ernie's AMERICAN This historic redbrick tack store became a restaurant in 1977 (the sister of the eatery of the same name in Helena) and is the most reliable dinner destination in downtown Great Falls. Under a pressed tin ceiling, the busy bar and grill plates up a nice variety of burgers and sandwiches (including a buffalo burger with blackening spice, blue cheese, and bacon); the dinner menu adds steaks, seafood, and barbecued ribs. There is a nice selection of local beers on tap, and a stage is frequented by live acts Thursday through Saturday nights.

300 1st Ave. S. www.bertandernies.com. © **406/453-0601.** Main courses $8–$12 lunch, $8–$24 dinner. AE, DISC, MC, V. Mon–Sat 11am–10pm.

Great Falls After Dark

The bar scene in Great Falls is fairly sedate and typical for a city its size, with one outrageous exception: the **Sip 'n Dip Lounge** at the O'Haire Motor Inn, 17 7th St. S. (© **406/454-2141**), an authentic tiki bar, clad in bamboo and loaded with South Seas paraphernalia of all kinds. The "sip" in the moniker refers to the cocktails served by the bar. The "dip," however, is quite unusual: Windows behind the bar make for a view of a pool where actresses in mermaid garb swim on Wednesday through Saturday nights. Then you've got "Piano Pat" Sponheim tickling the ivories, as she has since

1963, delivering unusual covers of Neil Diamond, Sinatra, and Elvis tunes. This is one of the kitschiest, wackiest, and flat-out coolest nightspots, not just in Montana, but in the entire West.

A Side Trip to Fort Benton

Thirty-six miles north of Great Falls on Mont. 87, you can drop down to the historic town of Fort Benton. The town faces the Missouri River, which formed its destiny. There is a pleasant waterfront park with an interesting series of murals detailing the town's history.

The Lewis and Clark expedition made a critical decision a short distance downstream from Fort Benton, where the Marias River enters the Missouri. The expedition was divided on which was the main branch of the Missouri. The vote was 30-to-2 for the Marias being the main branch. The two who went for the other branch were Lewis and Clark. Had they chosen the Marias branch, there is a good chance that the expedition would have failed, because they would not have been able to get over the Rockies before winter. A statue of the explorers at this decisive point dominates one end of Front Street in Fort Benton. A small visitor center at the Bureau of Land Management (BLM) office on Front Street offers some information about this event.

Next to the Lewis and Clark statue is the **Keelboat Mandan,** a full-scale replica 62 feet long and 13 feet wide built for the movie *The Big Sky.* In the heyday of keelboating, broad-shouldered men could push a boat upstream at a pace of about 2 miles a day. There is also a monument on the riverfront to Shep, a dog whose master died and was sent East by train for burial. After that, Shep met every train in Fort Benton from 1936 until 1942, waiting for his master's return, until—hard of hearing and arthritic—the old dog met his end one wintry morning on the tracks.

The first steamboat reached Fort Benton in 1850, and 600 of them stopped here from 1859 to 1870. Furs, goods, and gold were all shipped through the town. The **Museum of the Northern Great Plains,** 1205 20th St. (www.fortbenton.com/museums; ✆ **406/622-5316** or 622-3201), tells the story of settlement. There is a vast collection of farming equipment here, testifying to the fortitude and ingenuity of the settlers on the Great Plains. The **Museum of the Upper Missouri,** at Old Fort Park and Front Street (www.fortbenton.com/museums; ✆ **406/622-5316** or 406/622-3201), has an excellent historical collection, including the rifle that Nez Perce Chief Joseph surrendered at the Bear Paw battle, and the history and personality of Fort Benton as expressed by the artist Charles Russell, the preacher Brother Van, and the infamous "Madame Mustache," the woman who reputedly introduced Calamity Jane to prostitution. Both museums are open daily late May to late September; call for specific hours. Adult admission is $10 for both museums (which includes access to three other attractions in town), and kids 12 and under are $1.

The BLM manages 149 miles of the Missouri here as a federally designated Wild and Scenic River, and canoeing and keelboating are both good ways to take in the landscape. Contact the **Fort Benton Chamber of Commerce** (www.fortbenton.com; ✆ **406/622-3864**) for a list of river outfitters.

For lodging, you can't beat the **Grand Union Hotel ★★**, 1 Grand Union Sq. (P.O. Box 1119), Fort Benton, MT 59442 (www.grandunionhotel.com; ✆ **888/838-1882** or 406/622-1882), right on the river. Built in 1882 at a cost of $50,000, it was completely restored to its original splendor in 1999. Said to be Montana's oldest operating hotel, the Grand Union has 26 luxurious guest rooms in a range of sizes (with modern conveniences: phones, free Wi-Fi, and TVs), a top-notch restaurant in the **Union Grille** (dinner entrees, such as roasted chicken and grilled beef tenderloin, are $23–$36, with a less expensive bar menu), and a pub. The three suites are largest. During the high summer season, rates start at $120 for a double and go up to $195 for the suites; rates include continental breakfast.

THE ROCKY MOUNTAIN EASTERN FRONT ★

53 miles W of Great Falls

The eastern front of the Rockies is an isolated, sparsely populated section of Montana, but it is no less beautiful than the peaks and valleys to the west. A great paleontological mystery was solved here. Scientists had discovered many dinosaur fossils in the far-eastern part of the state, but no nests or eggs. When fossilized dinosaur eggs turned up along the Rocky Mountain Eastern Front—the shoreline of a shallow sea 65 million years ago—paleontologists learned that the beasts had migrated to this area to lay their eggs.

There are two towns with distinctive personalities on the front: Choteau and Augusta. Choteau bills itself as the gateway to the Rockies. Named for the president of the American Fur Co., who brought the first steamboat up the Missouri, it is one of the oldest towns in Montana.

Tiny Augusta is a cheerful, friendly community. Unlike a lot of small Western towns, it is not hustling to turn itself into something else. It's only about 2 blocks long, with weathered wood exteriors on the buildings. Folks are out and about, and everybody's on a first-name basis with just about everybody else. The pace picks up a bit the last weekend in June, when the rodeo hits town.

Essentials

GETTING THERE   The closest airport is in Great Falls, about 53 miles from Choteau (see the "Great Falls" section, earlier in this chapter, for airport information). From the airport, take I-15 north to the U.S. 89 exit (about 13 miles), then go west on U.S. 89 for 40 miles to Choteau.

To reach the area by car from the northwest, drive on U.S. 2 along the southern border of Glacier National Park. At Browning, go south on Mont. 89 to Choteau. From Choteau, go southwest on U.S. 287. Two miles past the junction of Mont. 21 and U.S. 287, Augusta lies 40 miles due west of Great Falls.

VISITOR INFORMATION   For an information packet, contact the regional tourism office for **Travel Montana's Russell Country,** P.O. Box 3166, Great Falls, MT 59403 (www.russell.visitmt.com; ℂ **800/527-5348**). In Choteau, write to the **Choteau**

    Rental-Car Tip

A reliable four-wheel-drive vehicle is strongly recommended for touring the back roads of the Rocky Mountain Eastern Front. Many are gravel roads that turn into a slippery mush, locally known as "gumbo," during rainy weather. Car-rental companies in Great Falls and other nearby cities keep such vehicles in stock, but requests should be made weeks in advance.

Chamber of Commerce, at 815 Main Ave. N. (P.O. Box 897), Choteau, MT 59422 (www.choteaumontana.com; ℂ **800/823-3866** or 406/466-5316). For hunting and fishing info, contact the **Montana Department of Fish, Wildlife, and Parks** (4600 Giant Springs Rd., Great Falls, MT 59406; www.fwp.mt.gov; ℂ **406/454-5840**).

GETTING AROUND The only way to travel this country is to drive. The closest car-rental agencies are in Great Falls (see earlier in this chapter).

What to Do

See **Pine Butte Guest Ranch** and **JJJ Wilderness Ranch** (see "Where to Stay," below) for learning vacations covering the region's ecology and natural history, backpacking, and horse-packing trips.

Timescale Adventures ☺ Timescale Adventures runs some popular dinosaur field programs, designed for all ages and levels of interest. The 3-hour seminar is a walk along the Rocky Mountain Eastern Front covering identification of dinosaur bones and eggs, and what to do when you find one. The 2-day seminar includes a dig and instruction in fossil-preservation techniques. All of the programs originate from the **Two Medicine Dinosaur Center** in the town of Bynum, 14 miles north of Choteau on U.S. 89. The center, open daily from 9am to 6pm from Memorial Day to Labor Day, with limited hours the rest of the year, houses displays on the various dinosaurs the organization has excavated. Admission is $5 for adults, $4 for seniors, $3 children 3 to 11, and free for kids 2 and under.

P.O. Box 786, Bynum, MT 59419. www.timescale.org. ℂ **800/238-6873** or 406/469-2211. 3-hr. day tour $50 per person; 1-day program $140 per person; longer programs about $125 per person, per day. Advance registration is required; space is limited.

A Scenic Drive

The beautiful **Sun Canyon Drive** on Sun Canyon Road starts out along the plains west of Augusta and then weaves up the canyon past a 1913 Bureau of Reclamation dam. During the time of Lewis and Clark, the Blackfeet called the river that carved the canyon the Medicine River, but it is now known as the Sun River. The canyon, a gray-granite jumble with snowcapped peaks in the distance, is a weekend getaway spot for residents all along the front. There are opportunities for fishing, boating, hiking, and four-wheeling in the area. The road up here is an easily navigable gravel track for the most part, but it can be rugged in portions, especially if they've been trying to fix it. After you get to the national forest, however, the road is paved. Go figure.

Shopping

Latigo and Lace, 124 Main St. in Augusta (ℂ **406/562-3665**), is an eclectic shop overflowing with the work of Montana artists and craftspeople, plus books, cups of cappuccino, and an array of "made in Montana" collectibles.

Where to Stay

The Bunkhouse Inn 🌾 This is the cowboy way. Housed in a building that dates from 1912 and is constantly under renovation, the Bunkhouse is sort of a bed-and-breakfast without the breakfast. The rooms are small and basic; there are no phones or televisions (except for one in the common room), but instead of staring at the idiot box, you can sit out on the second-floor porch watching the slow-paced bustle on Main Street. On Memorial Day weekend, you'll have a front-row seat to Montana's smallest parade as the gray-haired American Legionnaires march to the strains of Sousa marches played on a boombox carried by two of the ladies' auxiliary.

126 Main St. (P.O. Box 294), Augusta, MT 59410. ℂ**800/553-4016** or 406/562-3387. 10 units. $59 double. MC, V. *In room:* No phone, Wi-Fi (free).

JJJ Wilderness Ranch ★   The Triple J is a longstanding guest ranch located in the extraordinary Sun Canyon along the Rocky Mountain Eastern Front. Run by the Barker family for three generations, the ranch offers everything the outdoorsy type could want—horseback riding, hiking, fishing, pack trips into the Bob Marshall Wilderness Area (at an extra charge), and pure and simple relaxation. Nestled in a forest of aspen and spruce, the rustic cabins accommodate a total of 20 guests, so you're never crowded. Though there are few amenities, it's not due to an oversight: Those who come here don't want phones and televisions.

80 Mortimer Rd., P.O. Box 310, Augusta, MT 59410. www.triplejranch.com. ℂ**406/562-3653.** Fax 406/562-3836. 7 cabins. $1,950 per adult, per week, $1,650–$1,800 per child 6–17, per week; 4- and 5-day packages also available. Rates include all meals and ranch activities (except pack trips). AE, DISC, MC, V. Closed Oct–May. **Amenities:** Free transportation from and to the Great Falls airport; children's programs; outdoor Jacuzzi; Wi-Fi (free). *In room:* Fridge, no phone.

Pine Butte Guest Ranch ★ 👪   Located deep in the rugged Sawtooth Range along the Rocky Mountain Eastern Front, Pine Butte Guest Ranch is the property of the Nature Conservancy, a national land-preservation organization. Since a few endangered grizzly bears have made the 15,500-acre Pine Butte Swamp Preserve their home, the Conservancy saw fit to buy it to protect the delicate ecosystem. The preserve is the only place left in the Lower 48 states where grizzlies use both the mountain and prairie ranges as they did before settlement drove them to the remnant habitat in the mountains.

Pine Butte was first homesteaded in the 1930s, but it has always been a guest ranch, not a cattle ranch, which accounts in part for the largely undisturbed habitat. Today the ranch focuses on education, running numerous workshops on topics ranging from grizzly bears to wildflowers. As well as visits to local dinosaur dig sites, guests can also take part in the usual dude-ranch activities—riding, hiking, swimming, and the like. Each of the ranch's handsome, rustic log cabins has a river-rock fireplace and is comfortably equipped with handmade furniture.

351 S. Fork Rd., HC 58, P.O. Box 34C, Choteau, MT 59422. www.nature.org/montana. ℂ**406/466-2158.** Fax 406/466-5462. 10 cabins. Summer $2,200 per adult, per week double; children 13–18 $1,700 per week; children 6–12 $1,500 per week; children 5 and under free. Rates include all meals, riding, and ranch facilities. AE, MC, V. Closed late Sept to late May **Amenities:** Free transportation from and to Great Falls airport, outdoor heated pool, Wi-Fi(free). *In room:* No phone.

Where to Eat

In Choteau, a good pick for takeout or a quick sit-down meal is the **Outpost Deli,** 819 N. Main Ave. (ℂ **406/466-5330**), serving a basic American breakfast menu and burgers and sandwiches for lunch, with an ice cream parlor for the kids.

Buckhorn Bar STEAKS/AMERICAN   The Dellwo family has run this bar in the same location for more than 50 years, serving a selection of steaks, chicken, and burgers. If you've got a serious appetite, your best bet is a charbroiled 16-ounce rib steak with a salad and potato for $19. The portions are remarkably large and moderately priced, the atmosphere classic woody Western, complete with dozens of antler racks overhead, cowboy-hatted patrons, and gaming machines.

Main St., Augusta. ✆ **406/562-3344.** All dishes $2.75–$19. MC, V. Daily 8am–2am. (After 11pm, only pizzas are available.)

Chubby's Diner AMERICAN   Most everyone in town will send you to breakfast at Chubby's, a tiny place with four booths and two tables. You'll get good food at good prices: bacon and eggs, hot cakes, and biscuits and gravy for breakfast; fish and chips and burgers for lunch and dinner. You can also take your pick of ice-cream treats, shakes, and malts. The hours depend on how business is doing.

Main St., Augusta. ✆ **406/562-3408.** All dishes $2–$11. DISC, MC, V. Daily 6am–7pm (until 5pm in winter).

LEWISTOWN

105 miles E of Great Falls; 128 miles N of Billings

The hub of a vast agricultural region, Lewistown is not right on the way to any particular tourist destination, so if you find yourself here, you probably meant to come. The town is blessed with great downtown architecture, stately homes, and modest citizens. And there is some notable recreation here—especially hunting and fishing. Located in the center of the Judith Basin, Lewistown is surrounded by three mountain ranges—the Big and Little Snowies, the Moccasin, and the Judith. While Charles Russell lived in Great Falls later, the Judith Basin is where he worked as a cowboy and where he fell in love with Montana.

Essentials

GETTING THERE   The nearest airports are in Great Falls and Billings. Lewistown is connected to other Montana cities by two-lane U.S. highways that radiate from the town. From Billings, go north 92 miles, then west 31 miles on U.S. 87. From Great Falls, Lewistown is 105 miles east on U.S. 87.

VISITOR INFORMATION   The **Lewistown Chamber of Commerce** has its offices at Symmes Park at 408 NE Main St. (www.lewistownchamber.com and www.destinationlewistownmontana.com; ✆ **866/912-3980** or 406/535-5436). Local maps, and maps from the Bureau of Land Management, the U.S. Forest Service, and the C. M. Russell Wildlife Refuge are all available. Information about Lewistown is also available from **Travel Montana's Russell Country** (www.russell.visitmt.com; ✆ **800/527-5348**).

SPECIAL EVENTS   The **Chokecherry Festival** (www.lewistownchokecherry.com), held on the Saturday following Labor Day, honors that smarter-than-the-average-berry, the chokecherry, one of the few indigenous fruits of the prairie. Generally overlooked by poets and songwriters—no one has ever been the chokecherry of someone's eye, nor has life ever been a bowl of chokecherries—Lewistown attempts to place the chokecherry on its proper pedestal with parades, bake sales, pie cook-offs, and even a pit-spitting contest.

Lewistown's other big annual event is the **Montana Cowboy Poetry Gathering ★** (www.montanacowboypoetrytgathering.com). Each year in mid-August, cowboys, ranchers, large-animal vets, and other swaybacked and bowlegged Montana literati gather to swap lies and poems. Those who may have considered the term "cowboy poetry" an oxymoron are usually pleasantly surprised to find a relentless rhyming vitality to the poetry, along with a lot of humor, and an honest and healthy appreciation of fellow poets. For details on these events, call the **Lewistown Chamber of Commerce** at ✆ **866/912-3980.**

Getting Outside

For information on activities in the national forest lands in this area, contact the **Lewis and Clark National Forest** (✆ **406/791-7700**).

CROSS-COUNTRY SKIING

If you're here in the winter, there is good cross-country skiing in any of the three mountain ranges that ring the valley. There are a number of trails accessible by car in the Judith Mountains north of town, on old logging and mining roads. Head north on U.S. 191 to the Maiden Canyon sign, then take a left and follow the road for 5 miles to the trails.

FISHING

High in the Big Snowy Mountains is **Crystal Lake,** about 35 miles southwest of Lewistown. This is a popular and somewhat remote recreational area that offers good fishing, hiking, and camping. You have to travel about 25 miles on gravel road to get there. Take U.S. 87 west of town for 8 miles, then turn south at the sign for Crystal Lake. After about 16 miles, it runs into Forest Service Road 275, which you should follow for another 9 miles to the lake. Motorized boats are prohibited, but overnight RV and tent camping is available. For good trout fishing closer to town, try **Big Spring Creek,** which begins south of Lewistown and flows north through town to join the Judith River. You can easily access Brewery Flats on Big Spring Creek about 2 miles outside of town on Mont. 238. Flatwillow Creek, in the Forest Grove area of the Little Snowies, provides some rainbow and cutthroat fishing. For **flat-water fishing,** try Upper and Lower Carter's Pond, man-made ponds 6½ miles north of Lewistown on U.S. 191. There are picnic facilities and overnight camping as well. The **James Kipp Recreation Area,** 78 miles north of town on the Missouri River in the Charles M. Russell National Wildlife Refuge, also has fishing, camping, hiking, and a boat ramp. Take U.S. 191 northeast until it intersects with Mont. 19, then go north about 35 miles. Camping is $12 a night. Contact the **Bureau of Land Management** (✆ **406/538-1900** or 406/464-2166) for more information.

GOLF

The 18-hole **Judith Shadows Golf Course,** 464 Rifle Range Rd. (www.judithshadows. com; ✆ **406/538-6062**) is an alternative-spikes-only facility located at the end of Marcella Avenue in the northeast corner of Lewistown. Greens fees are $16 for 9 holes, $30 for 18. Carts are $12 for 9 holes, $24 for 18 holes. **Pine Meadows Golf Course,** on the south side of Lewistown at 320 Country Club Lane (www.pinemeadows lewistown.com; ✆ **406/538-7075**), has 9 holes and charges $17 to $20 in greens fees and $16 for a cart rental.

HIKING

At **Crystal Lake** (see "Fishing," above), there are numerous trails into the Lewis and Clark National Forest, including the Crystal Lake Loop National Recreation Trail. There is also good hiking along the Wild and Scenic Missouri River from the James Kipp Recreation Area. The **Bureau of Land Management** (✆ **406/538-1900**) can give you information on additional hiking trails.

Seeing the Sights

Operated by the local chamber of commerce (and perhaps a little too cutely named), the **Charlie Russell Chew-Choo Dinner Train** (www.montanadinnertrain.com; ℂ **866/912-3980** or 406/535-5436) runs from Lewistown to Denton and back every Saturday from the beginning of June through the end of September, with special holiday trains. On the 56-mile round-trip ride, the train crosses three large trestles and navigates a 2,000-foot tunnel during its 3½-hour run through the Judith Basin. The schedule varies, so call ahead. A regular summer trip with dinner is $90 per adult, $50 for children 12 and under.

The **Central Montana Museum,** next to the Lewistown Chamber of Commerce in Symmes Park at 408 NE Main St. (ℂ **406/535-3642**), displays historical artifacts from the late 1800s to modern day, including a facial reconstruction of Rattlesnake Jake, an outlaw who shot the town up on July 4, 1884, before being gunned down himself. The museum is open daily in summer from 10am to 4pm and by appointment the rest of the year. Admission is free; donations accepted.

Big Spring, located 7 miles south of Lewistown on C.R. 466, is the third-largest freshwater spring in the world. The spring is the water source for the town and is considered one of the purest in the nation. It is bottled by the Big Spring Water Company and sold at stores in the west-central part of the U.S. The spring also feeds the Montana State Fish Hatchery nearby.

Lewistown became a regional commercial center after a ranching and mining boom in the early part of the 20th century. The industry barons built large homes in a range of styles, primarily Gothic and Victorian. The first to build was J. T. Wunderlin, a gold miner and organizer of the Empire Bank & Trust. Others soon followed, creating a neighborhood of elegant homes. They lived in the **Silk Stocking District,** which is just northeast of downtown on Boulevard. (Not the section of Boulevard near Symmes Park; if you're there, you're lost.) The Lewistown Chamber of Commerce (see above) can provide information on self-guided tours. The homes, however, are private residences and not open to the public. At 220 W. Blvd., there is a plaque outside the Symmes-Wicks House describing the area. At the top of the hill overlooking the Silk Stocking District, check out the **Fergus County Courthouse** (7th Ave. and Main St.), a gold-domed, mission-style courthouse built in 1906.

Where to Stay

Calvert Hotel ★★   Dating to 1912, this historic-hotel-turned-apartment-building was reborn as a hotel in 2010 after a four-year restoration. The hard work shows: The tile job in the bathrooms is remarkable, the small central courtyard is capped with an all-season dome, and the onyx bar in the basement is a work of art. The large guest rooms feature king beds, two queens, or two doubles; many have pullout sofas. Nostalgic details like retro reproduction phones and original woodwork balance with modern amenities like flatscreen TVs and Wi-Fi.

216 7th Ave S., Lewistown, MT 59457. www.thecalverthotel.com. ℂ **877/8371-5411** or 406/535-5411. 27 units. $90–$110 double; $120–$140 suite. AE, DISC, MC, V. Pets accepted ($100 deposit). **Amenities:** Restaurants; lounge; indoor Jacuzzi; indoor pool. *In room:* A/C, TV, Wi-Fi (free).

Pheasant Tales Bed-and-Bistro ★   Pheasant Tales is a modern, newly remodeled guesthouse with some unique touches. Proprietors Chris and Rick Taylor are both avid pheasant hunters and anglers. After Chris began preparing gourmet meals with local pheasant, hunters told the couple that if they opened a bed-and-breakfast, they would stay there on hunting trips. Chris instead opened a bed-and-bistro (Pheasant Tales's guests still get breakfast) specializing in eclectically prepared game birds, with impressive results. Spread between two buildings, the inn is done in reddish pine, and the large rooms are comfortably furnished and share a full kitchen. With advance reservations, Chris can often prepare a gourmet dinner in the evening (starting at $35 per person). The Taylors also breed English setters, so there is almost always a brace of puppies providing entertainment. There's an extensive deck, plenty of space, and good fishing nearby as well.

1511 Timberline Rd., Lewistown, MT 59457. www.pheasanttales.biz. ℰ**406/538-2124.** Fax 406/538-6244. 6 units. $95–$125 double; $150 suite. Rates include full breakfast. AE, MC, V. Located 4 miles south of Lewistown. Pets accepted ($10 per night). *In room:* TV, no phone, Wi-Fi (free).

Yogo Inn ★ Once a train depot, the Yogo is now a very good independent hotel and the primary convention center for Montana's midsection, with clean, quiet rooms and a hint of rustic elegance. There is a well-kept interior courtyard that catches the sun and features a stage taken by musicians throughout the summer. The Yogo is popular with business travelers, and everything is functional but not fancy. The indoor pool is next to a marker signifying that the spot is the exact geographic center of the state. It's also the locus of the annual Montana Cowboy Poetry Gathering every August, and it books up pretty quickly for the event.

211 E. Main St., Lewistown, MT 59457. www.yogoinn.com. ℰ**800/860-9646** or 406/535-8271. 123 units. $85–$124 double; lower winter rates. AE, DISC, MC, V. Pets accepted ($10 per night). **Amenities:** Restaurant; lounge/casino; indoor Jacuzzi; indoor pool. *In room:* A/C, TV, Wi-Fi (free).

Where to Eat

Harry's Place ☺ STEAKS/AMERICAN A rock-clad A-frame decorated with memorabilia from the local high school sports teams, Harry's Place is the best place for a good meal in Lewistown. With excellent homemade soups—such as chicken corn chowder—burgers, wraps, and other sandwiches (including six varieties made with prime rib), Harry's is a good bet for lunch and grills the best steaks in town pretty much any day of the week. However, the restaurant truly goes all out on Friday nights, with prime rib, corn fritters, and homemade honey butter. Beer and wine are served, but liquor is not.

631 NE Main St. www.harrysplacemt.com. ℰ**406/708-4331.** Reservations recommended on Fri night. Main courses $6–$10 lunch, $7–$26 dinner. AE, DISC, MC, V. Mon–Thurs 11am–9pm; Fri–Sat 11am–10pm.

THE HI-LINE: U.S. 2

Havre: 115 miles NE of Great Falls; Fort Belknap: 46 miles E of Havre; Glasgow: 279 miles N of Billings

If you're not from Montana and find yourself on the Hi-Line, you're probably on the way to somewhere else. There isn't a great deal of anything up here, except for wheat, birds, lots of ground squirrels, and the occasional pronghorn.

There are a number of National Wildlife Refuges along this drive: the gigantic **Charles M. Russell NWR** and the smaller **Black Coulee, Bowdoin,** and **Medicine Lake**—the latter on the far-eastern border of the state. Like most of the refuges nationwide, they are managed primarily for the benefit of birds, especially migratory waterfowl. This is a good place to bring your field guide: Even if you don't leave your car, you'll be able to identify many species, possibly including the Franklin's gull, with its telltale black wingtips; the melodious western meadowlark; or the marsh hawk (or harrier, not a true hawk). The latter flies low to the ground, flapping its wings more often than the gliding hawks, and is gray when mature, brown when young, with a white bar across its rump.

Caution: The roadsides here are dotted with white crosses—memorials to people who have died in auto accidents. Maintained by friends and family, many are decorated with flowers, flags, and ribbons. There are a lot of them. Don't be fooled by the long, straight stretches of road. Drive carefully.

Call the **Havre Area Chamber of Commerce,** 130 5th Ave., Havre, MT 59501 (www.havremt.com; ☎ **406/265-4383**), for further information about the area.

From Havre to Fort Belknap

Havre probably isn't anyone's idea of a vacation spot, but it has its moments. There are some interesting historic sites, including the nearby **Bear Paw Battlefield** (see "Bear Paw Battlefield: The Nez Perce Surrender," below), the site of the last major battle of the Indian Wars. For both cultural and natural history, the best place to start is the **H. Earl Clack Museum,** 1753 U.S. 2, in the Holiday Village Shopping Center (☎ **406/265-4000**). The museum is open Monday through Saturday from 10am to 5pm and Sunday noon to 5pm from mid-May until Labor Day, with limited winter hours of 1 to 5pm Wednesday through Sunday. Admission is free. Southeast of Havre lies the home of 2,000 Chippewa and Cree Indians on this rather small plot of land at the Western Front of the Bear Paw Mountains. The **Rocky Boy Powwow** is held near Box Elder the first weekend of every August. Call ☎ **406/395-4478** for more information.

Start your driving tour of the region just south of Havre on U.S. 87, coming up from Great Falls. Drive north to Havre until you reach the junction with U.S. 2. Take U.S. 2 east until it converges with Montana's version of Route 66, a state highway running south through the Fort Belknap Indian Reservation. Take 66 through the reservation to the intersection of U.S. 191. Turn left (northeast) and drive about 57 miles until the road joins U.S. 2 again.

SEEING THE SIGHTS

Fort Assinniboine This well-preserved fort was established in 1879, after it was already obsolete. It was intended to protect settlers from Indian attacks, but all the tribes had already been defeated. After the defeat of Chief Joseph in the nearby Bear Paw Battle, the Fort Assinniboine troops didn't have much to worry about. After the fort closed, much of the land around it was turned into the Rocky Boys Reservation. Only guided tours are permitted because the fort is now run by Montana State University as an agricultural research station.

3 miles south of Havre on U.S. 87. ☎ **406/265-4000** or 265-8336. $6 adults, $5 seniors, $3 students, free for children 5 and under. June–Aug guided tours only, originating from the H. Earl Clack Museum in Havre daily at 5pm.

Havre Beneath the Streets ★ This tour of Havre's boisterous history as a railroad and cowboy town provides an interesting look at the past. When a devastating fire in 1904 destroyed Havre's business district, the labyrinth of tunnels and basements under the town served as a subterranean "shopping mall." Many local businesses of the last century were located here. Their products included legal representation, food, and laundry service—not to mention honky-tonk music, gambling, opium, and prostitution. There is also a surface-level railroad museum focusing on the area's rail history.

120 3rd Ave., Havre. ✆ **406/265-8888.** $12 adults, $10 seniors, $8 students, free for children 5 and under. Reservations recommended. Summer daily 9am–5pm, tours 9:30am–3:30pm; winter Mon–Sat 10am–4pm, tours 10:30am–2:30pm.

Wahkpa Chu'gn Bison Kill From a steep cliff above the Milk River called Wahkpa Chu'gn, the Assinniboine drove bison to their deaths to provide food for the tribe. Indians used the jump from 2,000 years ago until the 15th century. The hour-long guided tours are very informative, in part because this is one of the largest and most studied buffalo jumps in existence. Visitors are also given the opportunity to try their skill with an *atl-atl,* or throwing stick.

Behind the Holiday Village Shopping Mall on U.S. 2 W. www.buffalojump.org. ✆ **406/265-6417** or 265-4000. Tour info available at H. Earl Clack Museum. $9 adults, $8 seniors, $5 students, free for children 5 and under. June to Labor Day weekend, tours daily 9am–2pm; tours at other times (including winter) available by reservation, weather permitting.

WHERE TO STAY

El Toro Inn, 521 1st St. (www.eltoroinn.com; ✆ **800/422-5414** or 406/265-5414), is a reliable roadside motel charging $60 to $80 for a double. Rooms are well kept but basic, although they do have refrigerators and microwaves. On U.S. 2 in the eastern part of town, there is a pleasant campground called the **Havre RV Park,** 1415 1st St. (✆ **800/278-8861** or 406/265-8861). There are showers, a saloon, a casino, laundry, and a store. Cost is about $35 for an RV, $20 for a tent.

Best Western Plus Great Northern Inn ★ This is our pick of the Havre lodging scene, and it's a relatively new and upscale place. The rooms have a tad more square footage than your typical Best Western, and they have more extensive facilities than anyplace else in Havre. There is also a bridal suite with an in-room hot tub and a corporate suite. While the hotel lacks a restaurant, you can charge your meal to your room at the restaurant across the street. The 24-hour business center has fax, copying, and computer capabilities, and "business plus" rooms are available, with big desks, ergonomic chairs, and expanded amenities. Single rooms also have microwave ovens and fridges.

1345 1st St., Havre, MT 59501. www.bestwesternmontana.com. ✆ **888/530-4100** or 406/265-4200. Fax 406/265-3656. 75 units. $95–$115 double; $135–$159 suite. Lower rates fall to spring. Rates include continental breakfast. AE, DISC, MC, V. **Amenities:** Lounge/casino; exercise room; indoor Jacuzzi; indoor pool; steam room. *In room:* A/C, TV, fridge (in some), hair dryer, microwave (in some), Wi-Fi (free).

WHERE TO EAT

PJ's AMERICAN You're out on the Hi-Line, driving through Havre, so you might as well eat in a typical Montana place. PJ's is across the street from the railway station; there's a poker game in the corner with the clickety-clack of chips, and the *boop-boop-boop* of the electronic games of chance. The food is pretty good, with a menu of sandwiches for lunch and steaks and seafood for dinner, and you can play keno while you wait.

15 3rd Ave. ✆ **406/265-3211.** Main courses $5–$10 breakfast and lunch; dinner $10–$20. MC, V. Sun–Thurs 7am–9pm; Fri–Sat 7am–10pm.

Wolfer's Diner ☺ AMERICAN Wolfer's is my lunch pick in Havre. The basic dining room sports a 1950s theme, complete with pictures of Elvis, Marilyn, and James Dean hanging alongside a hula hoop and a leather jacket. The kitchen makes

bear paw battlefield: THE NEZ PERCE SURRENDER

One of the most remarkable events of the Indian Wars culminated at the Bear Paw Battlefield (📞 406/357-3130), a unit of the Nez Perce National Historic Park (www.nps.gov/nepe), located 26 miles south of Chinook on C.R. 240.

In 1877, in what is now northeast Oregon, the Army tried to force a band of Nez Perce Indians under the leadership of Chief Joseph onto a reservation far from their native lands. The Nez Perce decided to escape, trying to reach Canada where they hoped to join Sitting Bull's Lakota, who had already found homes there.

Joseph led 800 of his tribal members on a 1,700-mile flight through Yellowstone National Park and eventually north to this site, a mere 45 miles south of the Canadian border and freedom.

The U.S. Army under Gen. Oliver O. Howard pursued the tribe as it fled. A Civil War hero known as "the praying general," Howard, a deeply religious Christian, developed considerable hostility toward some of the Nez Perce leaders because he considered them heathens. Through a series of brilliant maneuvers, Joseph and his band of warriors, women, children, horses, and cattle escaped or defeated the army at every turn. Even Howard was forced to admit in his memoirs about the chase, "The leadership of Chief Joseph was indeed remarkable. No general could have chosen a safer position or one that would be more likely to puzzle and obstruct a pursuing foe."

They fought several battles along the way, but Col. Nelson A. Miles finally caught Joseph and his band in a snowstorm at Bear Paw, a rolling, grassy landscape achingly close to the freedom promised by the Canadian border. After a 6-day fight, Joseph surrendered on October 5, 1877. The chief's rifle is now in the Museum of the Upper Missouri in Fort Benton.

Chief Joseph is believed to have delivered this famous speech, translated by an interpreter:

good sandwiches—I like the Denver, with scrambled eggs, green peppers, ham, and onion on Texas toast (very thick toast)—as well as burgers and shrimp baskets for dinner. Better yet are the hand-dipped shakes, sundaes, freezes, and whips. 126 3rd Ave. 📞 **406/265-2111.** Main courses $6–$10. MC, V. Mon–Sat 11am–8pm.

Fort Belknap Reservation

Established in 1888, the Fort Belknap Reservation is home to the Gros Ventre and Assinniboine tribes. It was named for William W. Belknap, who was Secretary of War under President Ulysses S. Grant. The Gros Ventre call themselves the A'ani, or White Clay People. They had lived in North Dakota's Red River Valley from A.D. 1100 to 1400, gradually being pushed west by competition from other tribes. After coming to the Missouri River country in about 1730, they split into two tribes, and the southern branch became known as the Arapaho.

The Assinniboine split from the Yanktonai Sioux in the early 1600s, supposedly over a squabble. (Two of the first ladies of the tribe fought about a local delicacy, a buffalo heart.) They call themselves the Nakota, the Generous Ones. There is also a branch of the tribe at the Fort Peck Reservation, to the east.

There is a small **museum** and visitor center at the intersection of Mont. 66 and U.S. 2 (www.fortbelknap-nsn.gov; 📞 **406/353-2205** or 353-8473). From here, you

"Tell General Howard I know his heart. What he told me before, I have in my heart. I am tired of fighting. Our chiefs are killed. Looking Glass is dead. Toohoolhootze is dead. The old men are all killed. It is the young men who say yes or no. He who led the young men is dead. It is cold and we have no blankets. The little children are freezing to death. My people, some of them, have run away to the hills, and have no blankets, no food; no one knows where they are—perhaps freezing to death. I want time to look for my children and see how many of them I can find. Maybe I shall find them among the dead. Hear me, my chiefs. I am tired; my heart is sick and sad. From where the sun stands now, I will fight no more forever."

That night, White Bird and 200 of his followers slipped away to Canada. Of the 431 remaining, 21 died by the end of spring. The survivors moved to a reservation in Oklahoma, where another 47 of Joseph's people died and many more became ill. Finally, in 1885, 118 Nez Perce who agreed to convert to Christianity were allowed to relocate to the Lapwai Agency near Lewistown, Idaho. The rest, including Joseph, were settled on the Colville Reservation in Nespelem in northeast Washington State.

Joseph never gave up hope of a return to his homeland in the Wallowa Valley. He met with President William McKinley in 1897, and tried unsuccessfully to purchase the land in 1900. He died at Colville in 1904 at age 64. Even in death, he wasn't returned to the Wallowa Valley, but was buried at Nespelem.

The battlefield is open year-round during daylight hours. For more insight into the flight of Chief Joseph and the Nez Perce, stop at the **Blaine County Museum,** 501 Indiana St., Chinook (✆ **406/357-2590**), and take a look at the interpretive displays and the 20-minute film *Forty Miles from Freedom*. Admission is free.

can arrange a tour of the tribe's herd of more than 800 buffalo and learn a little bit about the tribe's culture (about $50; summer only; reservations recommended).

Nearby Snake Butte was often used as a site of vision quests, where individuals sought supernatural powers or medicine. These powers came with a price. It was said few who had them lived long lives. The Army Corps of Engineers quarried Snake Butte for stone to build the dam at Fort Peck in the 1930s.

If you head south from here to Hays, then turn to the east, you'll come to **St. Paul's Mission,** a solid stone structure established by Jesuit missionaries in 1886. Next to it is a tiny chapel built in 1931 that is dedicated to Our Lady of the Little Rockies. A local devotee has carved a statue practically identical to the supposedly miraculous one at Einsiedeln in Switzerland. To get here, take Mont. 66 south from U.S. 2 at Fort Belknap for about 40 miles to the sign for Hays. Turn left (east). Once you get to Hays, follow the road south after it turns to gravel. The mission is on the left (east) side of the street about a quarter-mile after the road turns south.

Up the road is Mission Canyon, a steep, narrow, cool gash in the otherwise open landscape. Just after entering the canyon, you'll see a natural stone arch. The very brave can climb nearly to the top, and there are several ledges where you can pose for the photographer.

From Glasgow to the Fort Peck Indian Reservation & the C. M. Russell Wildlife Refuge

People moving through the northeast extremes of Montana can find themselves a little disoriented by the sheer vastness of the horizons that stretch unbroken all the way to the Dakotas. Although this is mostly wheat country, it's not totally flat. In fact, it is sharply rolling and canyon-scored country, but it's open to the eye in all directions.

In 1879, Robert Louis Stevenson rode an immigrant train through here and later wrote: "What livelihood can repay a human creature for a life spent in this huge sameness? He is cut off from books, from news, from company, from all that can relieve existence but the prosecution of his affairs. A sky full of stars is the most varied spectacle he can hope. He may walk 5 miles and see nothing; ten, and it is as though he had not moved; twenty, and he is still in the midst of the same great level, and has approached no nearer to the object within view, the flat horizon which keeps pace with his advance."

There is a story, usually attributed to an area just over the border in western North Dakota, but in the same sort of landscape, of a lone Indian who watched patiently as a recently arrived farmer plowed into the virgin earth, turning the soil with its deep and tangled roots to begin the civilization of the already vanishing native prairie. After some time, the Indian came over to the farmer, pointed to the plowed earth, and said, "Wrong side up."

The story is probably another in the long chain of myths on which the West is built in the American imagination. But there are two contrasting sentiments made tangible here that illustrate the conflicting impulses of America: progress and preservation.

The first and easiest to spot is the Fort Peck Dam and Lake. Construction of the dam began in 1933, at the height of the Great Depression, as a way to put men to work and to provide inexpensive water to the growing agricultural area.

The dam is the largest hydraulically earth-filled dam in the world, nearly 5 miles across, backing up a lake that is 134 miles long with 1,600 miles of shoreline—more shoreline, it is said, than the entire coast of California. The dam is one of the many Corps of Engineers projects that have turned the cantankerous Missouri River that Lewis and Clark navigated into a tame and regulated lake from the Mississippi River to the Rockies.

Seven thousand men and women went to work on the dam in 1933, and at the peak of employment, nearly 11,000 were employed here. Locally, the attitude toward the dam was ambivalent, as the residents were losing their homes to the slowly rising water. On the other hand, they could appreciate the need for jobs, for irrigation water, for electric power, even for a large recreational lake. The story of the dam is told at the **Fort Peck Powerhouse Museum** (© **406/526-3493**). The powerhouse looms over the landscape like a chunky Art Deco skyscraper that somehow got lost on its way to Des Moines. Admission is free; it is open daily 9am to 5pm from Memorial Day to Labor Day weekend, and by reservation in winter. Tours of the plant are offered on the hour from 9am to 4pm weekends and at 9 and 11am and 1 and 3pm weekdays. The powerhouse is located on Mont. 24 at Fort Peck Dam. Tours start at the **Fort Peck Interpretive Center and Museum** ★, on Yellowstone Road (www.fortpeckpaleo.com; © **406/526-3493**), which houses a fine collection of dinosaur fossils and displays on the area's history in an impressive new facility that opened in 2005. The big attraction is a frightening, fleshed-out replica of the most complete Tyrannosaurus rex skeleton ever found, unearthed nearby in 1997, but there are also dioramas populated by taxidermy, live fish in aquariums, a look at terrifying aquatic dinosaurs, and the region's human history. It's open year-round Monday to Friday, 9am to 5pm May to September, and varied hours in the off season. Admission is likewise free.

SPECIAL EVENTS **Fort Peck Lake,** backed up by the dam, is the best spot in Montana for walleye fishing. An annual competition, the **Montana Governor's Cup** (www.mtgovcup.com) takes place there each spring. Contact the **Glasgow Area Chamber of Commerce** (www.glasgowmt.net; ✆ **406/228-2222**) for the schedule and details.

SEEING THE SIGHTS

The tiny town of Fort Peck is Montana's only planned community, the result of its heyday as the housing base for the workers at the dam in the 1930s. It started out as a trading post in 1867, then grew with the dam, then faded when construction was finished. It is testimony to the remoteness of this region that in 1934, months after the U.S. Army Corps of Engineers had begun construction of this $100-million project (big money during the Depression), a New York supplier asked the New York army headquarters how to address some equipment it was sending out to Montana. The army solemnly replied that there was no such place as Fort Peck—it had been abandoned in the 1880s.

The **Fort Peck Theatre** (www.fortpecktheatre.org; ✆ **406/526-9943**) is a large former cinema built in the 1930s for the workers. The surprisingly beautiful theater seats 900 people, and its season runs approximately from late June to early September. Tickets run $17 adults and $12 for students.

Surrounding the many miles of shoreline at Fort Peck Lake is the **Charles M. Russell Wildlife Refuge,** named for the famous Western wildlife cowboy artist Charles Russell. Born in 1864 in St. Louis, Russell was a working Montana cowboy at the age of 16 and drew much of his artistic inspiration from those years. He greatly admired the region's American Indians and deplored the plowing of the grasslands. Russell knew that destroying the native grass would destroy the habitat for the animals, the bison would be lost, the Indian conquered. Russell didn't like seeing the West civilized, and he had little use for "settlers."

Turnoffs and campsites are located all along the perimeter of the refuge, as are boat ramps for anglers. Flat Creek, Rock Creek, and Nelson Creek boat ramps are easy to reach, located just off Mont. 24, which skirts the eastern side of the lake. There are 15 campgrounds scattered along the lake margin. The camping varies from rugged to semicivilized. Only two campgrounds—the West End Campground and Downstream Campground—have flush toilets and showers; both are located near the dam. Contact the Corps of Engineers (✆ **406/526-3411**) for information.

The **Fort Peck Indian Reservation** is home to the Assinniboine and the Sioux. The Sioux, who had been on the reservation by themselves, were joined by the Assinniboine nation after smallpox killed more than half of the tribe farther west along the Missouri River and again threatened the tribe after it resettled near Fort Belknap. The escape from the deadly disease brought them to Fort Peck. Now the reservation is home to many non-Indians, with American Indians possessing less than half of the actual reservation.

This has been an extremely important area for the study of dinosaurs. The world's first Tyrannosaurus rex remains were discovered in 1902, just south of where the lake is in Garfield County. The **Garfield County Museum** (✆ **406/557-2517** or 557-2608) in Jordan has replicas of the T. rex skull there, along with a duckbill dinosaur and triceratops. It is open June to September daily from 1 to 5pm; admission is free (donations accepted). Jordan is located at the intersection of Mont. 59 and Mont. 200 in the plains south of Fort Peck Lake. From Miles City, drive north on Mont. 59 for 83 miles. From Glendive, take Mont. 200 west 111 miles. From Fort Peck Dam, take Mont. 24 south 59 miles to Mont. 200, then take Mont. 200 west 36 miles.

WHERE TO STAY

The Cottonwood Inn & Suites   This motel and convention center is far and away the nicest place in Glasgow: modern and clean, if a little small in the lobby. The rooms are conventional motel rooms, with queen- or king-size beds and, for the most part, refrigerators. The restaurant, the **Willows,** is the most popular one in town. It specializes in homemade soups, bread, and pies, all made from scratch. The motel has complimentary wireless Internet access and valet and room service, unusual out here in Hi-Line Country. There's also an adjacent RV park under the same ownership; RV sites are $27 to $30 nightly in summer and lower in winter.

U.S. 2 E. (P.O. Box 1240), Glasgow, MT 59230. www.cottonwoodinn.net. © **800/321-8213** or 406/228-8213. Fax 406/228-8248. 124 units. $83–$95 double. AE, DISC, MC, V. Pets accepted (free). **Amenities:** Restaurant; lounge/casino; exercise room; indoor Jacuzzi; indoor pool; room service. *In room:* A/C, TV, hair dryer, Wi-Fi (free).

Fort Peck Hotel 🛏   A stone's throw from U.S. 2, this registered historic site is an intimate, old-fashioned hotel. Built in 1939—5 years after the completion of the dam—the establishment harks back to a slower way of life in Montana. There are no televisions or telephones in the rooms, a situation that tends to usher people out into the bar in the lobby for (gasp!) conversation. There is a good restaurant that serves three meals a day and summertime dinner buffets that cater to visitors holding tickets to a play at the Fort Peck Theatre. The rooms are small but serviceable, with high ceilings and spare furnishings reminiscent of the 1930s and 1940s.

Missouri Ave. (P.O. Box 168), Fort Peck, MT 59223. © **800/560-4931** or 406/526-3266. Fax 406/526-3472. 33 units. $58 double with shared bathroom; $73 double with private bathroom; $112 for 2 adjoining rooms. Rates include continental breakfast (except summer weekends). DISC, MC, V. Closed Dec–Apr. **Amenities:** Restaurant; lounge; Wi-Fi (free). *In room:* No phone.

BOZEMAN, SOUTH-CENTRAL MONTANA & THE MISSOURI HEADWATERS

Relatively pristine, south-central Montana is a world-class playground for the outdoor recreation enthusiast. Its biggest draws are the mountains that are a haven for hikers and campers, and the fly-fishing waters of the four major rivers that run through its valleys—the Madison, Jefferson, Gallatin, and Yellowstone.

During the winter, downhill skiing takes over at Bridger Bowl, Big Sky, which boasts the largest vertical drop of any hill in the United States (4,350 ft.), and the adjacent Moonlight Basin resort, which combine for the most terrain of any resort in the country. The region is also excellent for cross-country skiing—Lone Mountain Ranch and Bohart Ranch are two of the best Nordic skiing facilities in the state.

Booming Bozeman, home of Montana State University, provides the hip, intellectual charm and culture of a college town—good bookstores and restaurants, charming shops, a lively bar scene—as well as cultural events that appeal to both the cosmopolitan and cowboy cultures. The Livingston Rodeo, one of the best in the region, complements Bozeman's Sweet Pea Festival, a celebration of music and the performing arts.

A few years ago, the area around Bozeman bounded by the Bridger, Gallatin, Madison, and Tobacco ranges seemed like an undiscovered bargain for real estate opportunists. Those times have changed; the communities of Bozeman, Livingston, and Belgrade experienced a boom as newcomers moved in, attracted to the easygoing Montana lifestyle and the wide range of outdoor activities. It's also been discovered by a number of Hollywood types, such as Peter Fonda and Glenn Close, who have purchased real estate in the area. Media mogul Ted Turner is another famous part-time resident.

A SCENIC DRIVE

The Bozeman–Livingston–Three Forks area is one large intersection. **Interstate 90** runs east to west through this region, and from it, three

South-Central Montana

Map of South-Central Montana showing major roads, cities, national forests, and Yellowstone National Park.

**Labels on map:**

15 · Great Falls · Missouri River · LEWIS AND CLARK NAT'L FOREST · Raynesford · 200 · MONTANA · area of detail · 90 · 15 · Helena · 94 · Bozeman · 90 · 90 · Yellowstone Nat'l Park · 15

89 · Stanford · Moccasin · Lewistown · 200 · Neihart · LEWIS AND CLARK · Holter Lake · HELENA NATIONAL FOREST · 191

Helena · 12 · Canyon Ferry Lake · White Sulfur Springs · 12 · Harlowton · Musselshell River · NATIONAL FOREST

Townsend · 265 · HELENA · LEWIS AND CLARK NAT'L FOREST · 191 · 287 · NATIONAL · 89 · GALLATIN NATIONAL FOREST

90 · Three Forks · Belgrade · 86 · Big Timber · FOREST · Yellowstone River · Boulder River · 90 · Columbus

Pony · 84 · Bozeman · Livingston · Norris · Gallatin Gateway · Emigrant · Pray · GALLATIN NATIONAL FOREST · 78

287 · Ennis · 191 · Madison River · Chico Hot Springs · CUSTER NATIONAL FOREST · Red Lodge · Virginia City · Big Sky · GALLATIN NATIONAL FOREST · 89

Cameron · Gardiner · MONTANA · Cooke City · 212 · WYOMING · BEAVERHEAD · Gallatin River · Mammoth Hot Springs · Tower Jct. · NATIONAL · West Yellowstone · Norris Jct. · Canyon Jct. · FOREST · MONTANA · WYOMING · IDAHO · YELLOWSTONE NATIONAL PARK · 20 · 14 · 16 · 20 · Yellowstone Lake

0 20 mi · 0 20 km

Side margin:

9

A Scenic Drive

SOUTH-CENTRAL MONTANA

valley highways extend south or north. The westernmost of these highways, **U.S. 287,** passes through Three Forks and runs 120 miles south along the Madison Valley to the town of Ennis (a fishing mecca) and West Yellowstone, the western gateway to Yellowstone National Park. From Bozeman, **U.S. 191** parallels U.S. 287 down the Gallatin Valley, past the resort community of Big Sky, to West Yellowstone.

The third highway, **U.S. 89,** runs 57 miles south from Livingston through the Paradise Valley to Gardiner and the north entrance of Yellowstone. Though the area is populated primarily by ranchers and there are few developed attractions, it's a beautiful drive, especially through Yankee Jim Canyon.

Red Lodge can be reached a few different ways, but the most scenic is by taking I-90 to exit 408 at Columbus and heading south on Mont. 78 through Absarokee and Roscoe for 48 miles.

The Beartooth Scenic Byway

This loop drive takes you to altitudes of almost 11,000 feet, taking in the sights that led Charles Kuralt to call this the most scenic road in America.

Begin in Livingston. Drive south on U.S. 89, following the Yellowstone River through Paradise Valley, 53 miles to Gardiner, and then into Yellowstone National Park. Once inside the park, you can stop off at Mammoth Hot Springs, a geothermal wonderland just inside the park's northern boundary. Then, take the road from Mammoth Hot Springs east to Tower Junction, continuing east to the park's northeast entrance at Silver Gate to pick up U.S. 212 (this is the Beartooth Byway). From here, the road begins to wind upward along the Montana and Wyoming border for nearly 40 ear-popping miles until it reaches the Beartooth Pass (elevation 10,947 ft.). From that spectacular altitude, you'll see miles and miles of mountains across both Wyoming and Montana. The road then drops for 24 miles as the byway continues on to Red Lodge. From Red Lodge, drive north on Mont. 78 down into the high plains before heading back to the mountains of Bozeman, west on I-90. The entire trip takes between 6 and 8 hours, depending on the time of day you choose to drive it and the condition of the roads. *Note:* The Beartooth Byway is especially subject to the whims of Mother Nature; mudslides have closed the road regularly in recent history. For current information, contact the **Montana Department of Transportation** (www.mdt.mt.gov; ✆ **406/444-6200;** 800/226-7623 or 511 for road conditions).

BOZEMAN ★★

82 miles E of Butte; 142 miles W of Billings; 91 miles N of West Yellowstone

A college town and tourism hot spot with a friendly, semi-bohemian vibe, Bozeman was first settled in the 1860s as a farming hub. Today, its cowboy edge has been mostly chipped away, revealing a sophisticated Western chic in the form of a vibrant downtown strip filled with independent shops and restaurants. The area bustles all year long—whatever the season, the locals are always out and about. The city has also become the unofficial capital of Montana environmental politics, with several nationally important nonprofits based here.

Bozeman has experienced its greatest growth since 1990, and it shows little sign of slacking off. In fact, longtime residents worry that the town may be getting a little too hip. But it's easy to see the city's appeal. The university, Montana State, is a good one, and the downhill skiing at nearby Bridger Bowl is excellent and free of lift lines. The fact that Bozeman is less than 100 miles from Yellowstone certainly doesn't hurt, either.

Essentials

GETTING THERE   Bozeman's **Gallatin Field Airport** (www.bozemanairport.com; ☎ 406/388-8321) serves a wide region in this part of the state. Daily service is available from **Delta, Alaska/Horizon, Frontier, United Express, US Airways,** and **Allegiant.**

Bus service is available through **Greyhound,** with a terminal at 1205 E. Main St. (www.greyhound.com; ☎ **406/587-3110**). **Rimrock Stages** (☎ **800/255-7655**) operates intrastate service.

By car, I-90 handles most of the traffic. It is 140 miles along I-90 from Billings to the east and 202 miles from Missoula to the west. For **statewide road reports,** call ☎ **800/226-7623** or 511.

VISITOR INFORMATION   The **Bozeman Convention and Visitors Bureau** is located at 2000 Commerce Way (www.bozemancvb.com; ☎ **800/228-4224** or 406/586-5421). Information is also available at the **Downtown Bozeman Visitor Center** (www.downtownbozeman.com; ☎ **406/586-4008**) at 224 E. Main St. The state's **Yellowstone Country** publishes an extensive visitors guide, as well as maps detailing the area's farms and historic hot spots. Call ☎ **406/736-5276,** or check out their website at **www.yellowstonecountry.net.**

GETTING AROUND   There are a number of car-rental agencies in Bozeman. Most major chains are at the airport, including **Budget** (☎ 800/527-0700), **Enterprise** (☎ 800/261-7331), **Hertz** (☎ 800/654-3131), and **National** (☎ 800/227-7368). For taxi service, call **Greater Valley Taxi** (☎ 406/388-9999).

With retro designs inspired by vintage Yellowstone buses, the free **Streamline Bus** (www.streamlinebus.com; ☎ 406/587-2434) connects downtown Bozeman with the Montana State campus and points beyond (namely the airport and Belgrade). Buses run from Monday through Saturday from about 7am to 6:30pm, with later service (8:30pm–3am) Thursday through Saturday for the bar crowd.

SPECIAL EVENTS   Held the first full weekend each August, the **Sweet Pea Festival,** at Lindley Park and throughout Bozeman (www.sweetpeafestival.org; ☎ **406/586-4003**), is a music, arts, and sports festival, with a parade, bands from rock to reggae, dance, art, and even a little Shakespeare. Unspooling over 6 days in early October, **Hatch** (www.hatchexperience.com; ☎ **406/600-7642**) is an audiovisual arts festival that has grown to encompass all sorts of other creative areas. The schedule includes film screenings, workshops, Q&As, and live music after dark.

Getting Outside

Many of the outdoor activities discussed in this section take place in the **Gallatin National Forest.** For additional information, including current road and trail conditions, contact the Bozeman Ranger District, 3710 Fallon St., Ste. C, Bozeman, MT 59718 (www.fs.usda.gov/gallatin; ☎ **406/522-2520**).

ORGANIZED ADVENTURES

Yellowstone Safari Company ★★ (www.yellowstonesafari.com; ☎ **866/586-1155** or 406/586-1155) specializes in wildlife-biologist-guided trips in Montana, at Yellowstone and Grand Teton national parks, and along the Lewis and Clark Trail. Founded by biologist Ken Sinay—he's been described as "Vesuvian in his enthusiasm"—the

Bozeman

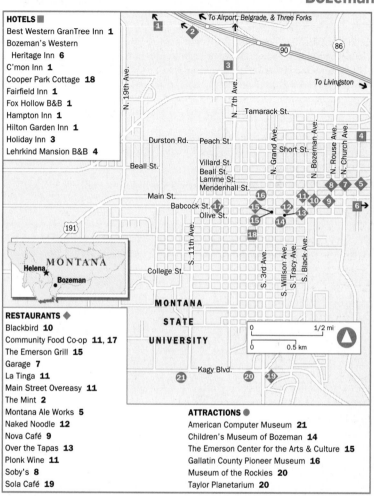

HOTELS ■
Best Western GranTree Inn **1**
Bozeman's Western Heritage Inn **6**
C'mon Inn **1**
Cooper Park Cottage **18**
Fairfield Inn **1**
Fox Hollow B&B **1**
Hampton Inn **1**
Hilton Garden Inn **1**
Holiday Inn **3**
Lehrkind Mansion B&B **4**

RESTAURANTS ◆
Blackbird **10**
Community Food Co-op **11, 17**
The Emerson Grill **15**
Garage **7**
La Tinga **11**
Main Street Overeasy **11**
The Mint **2**
Montana Ale Works **5**
Naked Noodle **12**
Nova Café **9**
Over the Tapas **13**
Plonk Wine **11**
Soby's **8**
Sola Café **19**

ATTRACTIONS ●
American Computer Museum **21**
Children's Museum of Bozeman **14**
The Emerson Center for the Arts & Culture **15**
Gallatin County Pioneer Museum **16**
Museum of the Rockies **20**
Taylor Planetarium **20**

company offers guide services for both individuals and groups. Using specially adapted vehicles and boats, their activities include single- and multiday safari-style expeditions to observe wildlife and explore the natural and cultural history of the area. Full-day trips include guides, transportation, binoculars, spotting scopes, food, and beverages. Rates depend on group size and the kind of tour, with full-day rates varying from $650 for one or two people to about $160 per person for seven people. A half-day safari is $99 per person. Advance reservations are required—the earlier, the better.

Founded by Susan Eckert in 1982 and the first of its kind, **AdventureWomen** ★, 300 Running Horse Trail, Bozeman (www.adventurewomen.com; ℂ **800/804-8686** or 406/587-3883), offers customized trips to just about anywhere in the world for active and adventurous women ages 30 and older. In Montana, the company guides hiking

9

SOUTH-CENTRAL MONTANA | Bozeman

trips as well as skiing and guest-ranch trips. Rates for the weeklong outings start at $2,595 per woman.

In the guiding business since 1985, **Off the Beaten Path ★**, 7 E. Beall St., Bozeman (www.offthebeatenpath.com; ☎ **800/445-2995**), is another top-notch local guiding outfit. The company offers about a dozen trips throughout Wyoming and Montana each year, with an emphasis on Yellowstone and Grand Teton, with expeditions that run the gamut from family outings to wolf-watching. The trips range from 4 to 10 days in length, and prices typically run between $300 and $500 per day.

BIKING

There are plenty of biking opportunities here, mostly off-pavement. Some of the best mountain biking is in the Gallatin National Forest—check with the Bozeman Ranger District office (see "Getting Outside," above) for tips on where to go.

CROSS-COUNTRY SKIING

If you want to explore on your own, many drainages provide excellent skiing around Bozeman. Some local favorites are the 10-mile, moderately difficult **Bozeman Creek to Mystic Lake Trail** that gains 1,300 feet of elevation over its course (go south of S. 3rd St. for 4 miles to Nash Rd., then east on Nash Rd. for a mile to Bozeman Creek Rd., then 1 mile south to the parking area) and the **Hyalite Reservoir Ski Loop,** a 4-mile, relatively flat track around the Hyalite Reservoir, also rated moderately difficult (see the "Hiking" section, below). The road may not be plowed or maintained in winter. Two ski mountaineering routes for the adventurous are the 14-mile **Hyalite Ski Loop** and the 5½-mile **New World Gulch to Mystic Lake Trail.** Check with the Bozeman Ranger District office (see "Getting Outside," above) for directions.

Bohart Ranch, 16621 Bridger Canyon Rd., Bozeman, MT 59715 (www.bohart ranchxcski.com; ☎ **406/586-9070**), next to the Bridger Bowl downhill area, offers 16 miles of groomed and tracked trails for all levels of skiers. There is a biathlon range, a ski school, and ski rentals. Located in Bridger Canyon, 17 miles northeast of Bozeman on U.S. 86, it's open in winter daily from 9am to 4pm and summer daily from dawn to dusk. Cost is $15 for adults, $8 for children 7 to 12, and free for seniors and kids 6 and under.

DOWNHILL SKIING

The nonprofit **Bridger Bowl** is just 16 miles north of town, on Mont. 86 (15795 Bridger Canyon Rd., Bozeman, MT 59715; www.bridgerbowl.com; ☎ **800/223-9609** or 406/587-2111). Although not as steep as Teton Village in Jackson Hole, Bridger Bowl is plenty steep for most of us, and a great hill for good skiers. Among the 71 trails here on 2,000 acres, there is a lot of advanced and extreme terrain (50%), tempered by 50% beginner and intermediate terrain. Full-day lift tickets cost $48 adults, $21 seniors 70 to 79, $16 children 7 to 12, and free for those 6 and under or 80 and over; half-day rates are available. There are five lifts: a fixed-grip quad, three triple chairs, and three doubles. With almost 30 feet of snowfall annually, Bridger sees a lot of powder days. It's usually open from the second Friday in December to early April, daily from 9am to 4pm. There is limited lodging on the mountain; a free shuttle runs from Bozeman. And there are seldom any lift lines. For more downhill skiing in the Bozeman area, see Big Sky and Moonlight Basin in the Gallatin Valley section, later in this chapter.

FISHING

The **River's Edge,** 2012 N. 7th Ave. (www.theriversedge.com; ℂ **406/586-5373**), is a highly professional fly-fishing specialty shop "in the heart of Montana's blue-ribbon trout streams." They offer guided fishing trips year-round—including float fishing and walking or wading trips, plus equipment rental and shuttle service. A full-line Orvis shop, **Montana Troutfitters,** 1716 W. Main St. (www.troutfitters.com; ℂ **800/646-7847** or 406/587-4707), offers guided float, walk and wade, and tube trips to rivers, lakes, and streams, plus 2- and 4-day fly-fishing schools. The Troutfitters are especially good at teaching youngsters the basics of the sport. The **Bozeman Angler,** 23 E. Main St. (www.bozemanangler.com; ℂ **800/886-9111** or 406/587-9111), provides guided trips in the Madison, Gallatin, Yellowstone, Jefferson, and Missouri rivers, plus numerous creeks, reservoirs, and lakes. Anglers can choose float trips in hard-sided drift boats, walk-and-wade trips, or backcountry fishing trips. From all three, full-day guided trips typically run $400 to $500 for two people, a price that includes lunch.

GOLF

Bridger Creek Golf Course, 2710 McIlhattan Rd. (www.bridgercreek.com; ℂ **406/586-2333**), offers a scenic and challenging 18-hole layout, 6,400 yards from the back tees. It costs $33 for 18 holes on the weekend, $31 during the week. Carts are $28 for two people. **Cottonwood Hills Golf Course,** 8955 River Rd. (www.cottonwoodhills.com; ℂ **408/587-1118**), has an 18-hole course and a par-3 executive 9-hole course. Greens fees run $24 to $40 at the former ($28 for carts) and $7 to $10 at the latter ($16 carts).

HIKING

There's a beautiful and popular hiking area near Bozeman, known as the **Hyalite drainage,** in the Gallatin National Forest (see "Getting Outside," above, for contact information). The area includes Hyalite Canyon and reservoir, Palisades Falls Trail, and many trail heads for access to the national forest. A lot of the trails here are steep and difficult, though. An excellent introductory hike to get the lay of the land is the .5-mile **Palisades Falls National Recreation Trail.** From Bozeman, take 19th Avenue south for 7½ miles to the Hyalite Canyon Road, and follow the road to the reservoir. Continue east around the reservoir for 2 miles to the East Fork Road and proceed to the Palisades Falls parking area. The trail gains 540 feet in a little more than .5 mile, which makes it very steep and gives it a rating of "most difficult" for a recreational trail.

Hyalite **Reservoir** itself contains cutthroat and grayling, and there are two campsites here. The **Grotto Falls Trail** is a steep 1.25-mile graveled trail to Grotto Falls, located 13 miles up the West Fork Road in Hyalite Canyon. For a longer hike, go the 7.25 miles up the **Hyalite Peak Trail** to the peak. There is a 3,300-foot elevation gain on this hike.

The Gallatin Valley Land Trust's **"Main Street to the Mountains"** project has connected downtown Bozeman with a 50-mile network that connects with the surrounding communities and mountain ranges. For more information, visit **www.gvlt.org/trails**.

If you're interested in combining a little **bird-watching** with your hiking, try the Kirk Hill nature preserve in the foothills transition zone, where you might spot a colorful western tanager or a great gray owl. From downtown, take South 19th Avenue south for 5 miles until the road curves west. The entrance to the preserve is on the left. There are several miles of steep trails here.

Bozeman

Where to Find Equipment & Supplies

It's easy to find whatever outdoor recreation equipment you need for your particular adventure. Among the rental outlets I recommend are **Panda Sports Rentals,** 621 Bridger Dr. (✆ **406/587-6280**), which rents skis and snowboards; **Chalet Sports,** 108 W. Main St. (✆ **406/587-4595**), a full-line sporting goods store that sells skis, as well as rents bikes, in-line skates, skis, and snowboards; and **Northern Lights Trading Co.,** 1716 W. Babcock (✆ **866/586-2225**), a high-end store selling gear for everything from kayaking to Telemark skiing, and renting canoes, rafts, and kayaks. These stores are also great sources for advice.

WHITE-WATER RAFTING

Montana Whitewater (www.montanawhitewater.com; ✆ **800/799-4465** or 406/763-4465) can get you sprayed in the face by the waters of both the Yellowstone and the Gallatin rivers. You paddle the raft as you fly through the nearly continuous rapids of the Gardiner section of the upper Yellowstone or through the dauntingly named rapids of Snake Bite and Mother Eater on the Gallatin. In addition to the white-water trips, the company offers more sedate scenic trips and "saddle and paddle" outings in which the morning is spent riding and the afternoon rafting. Half-day trips on the Gallatin cost $52 adults, $42 ages 12 and under; on the Yellowstone, it's $39 and $29, respectively. Full-day Gallatin trips cost $86 adults and $70 ages 12 and under, and on the Yellowstone $75 and $55, respectively. "Paddle and saddle" jaunts that mix rafting and horseback riding are $127 per adult per day and $117for kids 10 to 12 (under 10 not recommended). **Wild West Whitewater Rafting** (www.wildwestrafting.com; ✆ **800/862-0557**) offers similar trips on Yellowstone River, including half- and full-day rafting tours ($39–$77 adults; $29–$57 kids 6–12).

Seeing the Sights

American Computer Museum ★ Now located near the MSU campus, this unique museum traces the history of computing technologies from the abacus to the Apple. In an hour or so, you can catch up on more than 4,000 years of computing history and gain a newfound respect for the speed of innovation during the past few decades. Though you won't find any T. rexes here, you can view computing's dinosaurs: slide rules and massive antique computers with a mere fraction of the power of today's superpowered miniatures. There are also special displays on women in science, chipmaking, and video games, along with a rare reproduction of the 2,000-year-old Antikythera, the world's first computer.

2023 Stadium Dr., Unit 1-A. www.compustory.com. ✆ **406/582-1288.** Suggested donation $5 adults, $4 students and seniors 65 and over, free for children 5 and under. June–Aug daily 10am–4pm; Sept–May Tues–Sun noon–4pm. Closed major holidays.

Children's Museum of Bozeman ☺ This converted warehouse space is now the only museum of its kind in the Gallatin Valley. Exhibits include arts-and-crafts tables, a "bubble wall" that allows kids to make a barrier from suds, a 110-gallon aquarium with native Montana fish, and other displays designed to educate and entertain young minds.

202 S. Willson Ave. www.cmbozeman.org. ✆ **406/522-9087.** $5 per person. Mon–Sat 10am–5pm (Fri until 8pm). Closed Sun and major holidays.

The Emerson Center for the Arts & Culture ★ Once a home for schoolchildren, this historic building (ca. 1918) was converted in 1993 into an arts and cultural center. The nonprofit organization hosts a variety of professional and contemporary art exhibits, offers a fine-arts education program, and provides retail and studio space for more than 80 artists in converted schoolrooms. The Emerson also hosts free community events, such as Lunch on the Lawn in summer, with live music and food vendors every Wednesday afternoon; special holiday activities in December; and other concerts, events, and activities year-round. There is also a restaurant (the **Emerson Grill;** see "Where to Eat," below) and a theater and ballroom for a variety of programs.

111 S. Grand Ave. www.theemerson.org. ℰ **406/587-9797.** Free admission. Building daily 8am–10pm; galleries have individual hours.

Gallatin County Pioneer Museum ☺ Located in the old county jail, which was in use until 1982, this museum features county history, focusing in part on law enforcement (as you might expect), the area's military history, and local daily life of the past. There's a display and memorabilia from actor Gary Cooper, known as Frank in the days he grew up in Bozeman and Helena, and the lowdown on town founder John Bozeman. The museum also contains a cell from its days as the jail. There's also a collection of 11,000 historical photos and a research library devoted to Lewis and Clark. Expect to spend about an hour here if you want to dig deep.

317 W. Main St. www.pioneermuseum.org. ℰ **406/522-8122.** $5 adults, free for children 12 and under. Memorial Day to Labor Day Mon–Sat 10am–5pm; rest of year Tues–Sat 11am–4pm.

Museum of the Rockies ★★ This first-class museum explains the history, geology, wildlife, and people of the Rocky Mountains all the way back to the Big Bang. The centerpiece of the museum is the world-class Siebel Dinosaur Complex, which is one of the premier paleontology attractions in the world and home to more T. rex specimens than any other facility (13). The **Hall of Horns and Teeth** is centered on a life-size torosaurus model, next to the actual 9-foot skull (the biggest land-animal noggin ever unearthed) that served as a blueprint; other displays offer an in-depth look into dinosaur biology, ecology, and theoretical behavior. The **Hallway of Growth and Behavior** provides a look beyond the bones, and the **Mesozoic Media Center** allows visitors to get a closer look at dig sites via interactive touch screens. The **Hall of Giants** is populated with lifelike dinosaur models, including a diorama of velociraptor-like deinonychs taking down a much larger sauropod. Visitors can also watch fossil preparers as they clean recently discovered bones.

But that's not all: Young ones can learn about nature and science at the Yellowstone-themed **Children's Discovery Center.** The **Taylor Planetarium** is a state-of-the-art, 40-foot domed multimedia theater, with a computer graphics simulator that provides the illusion of flying through space in three dimensions. There is a collection of regional historical artifacts and traveling exhibits. Outside, the **Living History Farm** is an early-20th-century homestead with costumed interpreters. There's a gift shop on-site, but no dining.

600 W. Kagy Blvd. (on the Montana State University campus). www.museumoftherockies.org. ℰ **406/994-2251.** Admission $13 adults, $12 seniors, $9 children 5–17, free for children 4 and under; admission good for 2 days. Planetarium shows included in admission. Mid-June to early Sept daily 8am–8pm; mid-Sept to early June Mon–Sat 9am–5pm, Sun 12:30–5pm. Living History Farm mid-June to early Sept daily 9:30am–5pm. Closed Thanksgiving, Christmas, and New Year's Day.

Shopping

Main Street offers an Old West feel and New West selection, starting at about 7th Avenue and running out to I-90. Among our favorite stops here are **Vargo's Jazz City and Books,** 6 W. Main St. (℃ 406/587-5383), which sells an eclectic mass of new, used, and out-of-print books, CDs, and LPs (or the elusive, vanishing vinyl); **Schnee's Powder Horn Outfitters,** 35 E. Main St. (℃ 406/587-7373), which sells high-end Western wear and all sorts of outdoor gear; the **Montana Gift Corral,** 237 E. Main St. (℃ 406/585-8625), which offers a wide selection of made-in-Montana gifts, in case you need a moose clock to take home; **Thomas Nygard Gallery,** 135 E. Main St. (℃ 406/586-3636), which specializes in pre-1950 artwork from the Northern Plains; the **Country Bookshelf,** 28 W. Main St. (℃ 406/587-0166), a terrific bookstore; and **Barkenhowell's,** 777 E. Main St. (℃ 406/586-6160), a chic dog boutique. The **Gallatin Valley Mall,** 2825 W. Main St. (℃ 406/586-4565), has department and specialty stores, art galleries, and a food court. The **MSU Bookstore** at the Strand Union on the campus of Montana State University (℃ 406/994-2811) is the place to go for any sort of Bobcats clothing or gear.

Where to Stay

Bozeman has a full complement of chain motels, most just off I-90. In addition to the places listed below, you can stay at the **Best Western GranTree Inn,** 1325 N. 7th Ave. (www.grantreeinn.com; ℃ 800/624-5865 or 406/587-5261); the **Fairfield Inn,** 828 Wheat Dr. (℃ 406/587-2222); and the **Hampton Inn,** 75 Baxter Lane (℃ 406/522-8000). The above are all at I-90 exit 306 and have summer rates for two in the $100-to-$150 range. Newer are the lodgelike **C'mon Inn,** 6139 E. Valley Center Rd. (℃ 866/782-2717 or 406/587-3555), and the **Hilton Garden Inn,** 2023 Commerce Way (℃ 877/782-9444 or 406/582-9900), south of I-90, exit 305, both with double rates in the range of $120 to $180 in peak summer season. The lodge-inspired accommodations feature thoughtful amenities such as in-room exercise kits and a lobby pantry. I also like the independent **Bozeman's Western Heritage Inn,** within walking distance of downtown, 1200 E. Main St. (www.westernheritageinn.com; ℃ 800/877-1094 or 406/586-8534), with double rates of $84 to $140 in summer. Another option is the cozy private 1920s **Cooper Park Cottage,** tucked away in a residential neighborhood at 401 S. 5th Ave. (℃ 406/586-2012), which rents for $100 to $125 double.

Fox Hollow Bed and Breakfast ★   Situated at the end of a road with great views of the Bridger Mountains, Fox Hollow gives you good access to town, as well as the scenery that earned Montana the nickname "Big Sky Country." Rooms are modern and comfortable, with floral and rustic themes. Breakfasts are superlative, including apple-cinnamon French toast, and the inn also offers a "bed and bistro" package that includes dinner for an additional $30 per person.

545 Mary Rd., Bozeman, MT 59718. www.bozeman-mt.com. ℃ **406/642-9545.** 5 units. $139–$169 double; lower winter rates. AE, DISC, MC, V. *In room:* A/C, hair dryer, no phone, Wi-Fi (free).

Holiday Inn   The largest hotel in town, the Holiday Inn opened in 1969 when there was virtually nothing else in the immediate vicinity. It's now surrounded by other chain motels and hotels, but it remains the best. The big, open lobby has a sort of a lodge feel, with a fireplace, contemporary artwork, and two complimentary high-speed Internet terminals in a small business center, and there's a big TV in the adjacent bar that's usually surrounded by a crowd watching a ballgame. The rooms are well kept and nicely furnished, and a few of them have terrific mountain views.

5 Baxter Lane, Bozeman, MT 59715. www.hibozeman.com. © **800/366-5101** or 406/587-4561. Fax 406/587-4413. 179 units, including 1 suite. $99–$179 double; $129–$229 suite. Lower rates fall and winter. AE, DC, DISC, MC, V. From I-90, take exit 306. **Amenities:** Restaurant; lounge/casino; exercise room; high-speed Internet (free); indoor Jacuzzi; indoor pool. *In room:* A/C, TV w/pay movies, hair dryer, Wi-Fi (free).

Lehrkind Mansion Bed & Breakfast ★★★ German-born brewer Julius Lehrkind shunned the tonier neighborhoods on Bozeman's south side and built a stately Queen Anne mansion right next door to his north-side brick brewery in 1897. A century later, former national park rangers Jon Gerster, Jr., and Chris Nixon turned "the house that beer built" into a bed-and-breakfast, with the original woodwork, plumbing, and floor plan intact. Surrounded by vestiges of the neighborhood's beery past, the ornate abode still sticks out in the quasi-industrial but up-and-coming Historic Bozeman Brewery District, looking like something out of a fairy tale inside and out. Everything, from the rare 1897 Regina music box in the parlor, to the many original fixtures in the bathrooms, to the amazingly preserved original carpet in the Audubon Suite, is from Lehrkind's day. A relocated and restored abandoned Victorian farmhouse is also on-site as a five-bedroom counterpart to the four-bedroom mansion.

719 N. Wallace Ave., Bozeman, MT 59715. www.bozemanbedandbreakfast.com. © **800/992-6932** or 406/585-6932. 9 units. $159–$189 double; $189–$229 suite; lower rates in winter. Rates include full breakfast. DISC, MC, V. *In room:* Hair dryer, no phone, Wi-Fi (free).

CAMPING

The **Bozeman KOA** (© **800/562-6036** or 406/587-3030) is the area's largest campground, with sites for 100 RVs and 50 tents. It is adjacent to a natural hot-springs pool (which charges a separate fee), laundry, store, and a variety of other amenities. It is located 7 miles south of Belgrade on U.S. 191, with sites from $30 to $50 and basic cabins for $63 to $73 double. There are also numerous places to camp in the **Gallatin National Forest;** contact the Bozeman Ranger District, 3710 Fallon St., Ste. C, Bozeman, MT 59718 (www.fs.usda.gov/gallatin; © **406/522-2520**), for details.

Where to Eat

Beyond the restaurants that follow, I'm a firm believer in the restorative powers of the breakfast burritos at **Soby's,** in the Bozeman Hotel at 321 E. Main St. (© **406/587-8857**), a favorite student haunt for breakfast and lunch. For a burger (or barbecue) and a beer on an outdoor deck, you can't beat the **Garage,** 451 E. Main St. (© **406/585-8558**). In the winter, the place compensates for the cold weather with the **Soup Shack,** serving seven hot soups and an array of toppings, from a space that houses the ice-cream-oriented **Scoop Shack** in summer. **La Tinga,** 12 E. Main St. (no phone), serves up authentic Mexican burritos, tacos, and tostadas using homemade tortillas and salsa (cash only).

The **Community Food Co-op,** 909 W. Main St. (www.bozo.coop; © **406/587-4039**), is a locally beloved market, with a great deli, salad bar, and seating area upstairs. There is also a new **downtown location** at 44 E. Main St. (© **406/922-2667**), with a more limited grocery selection, a salad bar, and cold and hot meals to take out or eat in.

Blackbird ★★ ITALIAN   Opened in 2009, the casual, hip, and healthy Blackbird has earned a fast local following with its constantly changing menu highlighted by pasta and wood-fired pizzas with toppings like smoked prosciutto and crimini mushrooms. Even the chopped green salad has flair, with fresh ricotta, walnuts, citrus, and herbs. The fare is prepared in a central open kitchen fronted by a stainless-steel bar. The dimly lit space features contemporary art and design and live (but not overbearing) music.

145 E. Main St. www.blackbirdkitchen.com. ✆**406/586-0010.** Reservations accepted for parties of 6 or more only. Main courses $11–$30. DISC, MC, V. Tues–Thurs 5:30–9:30pm; Fri–Sat 5:30–10pm.

The Emerson Grill ★★ ITALIAN   Intimate and artsy, this dinky eatery in the Emerson Center for Arts and Culture has emerged as a local favorite, and it's an equally good bet for a romantic dinner. The kitchen uses locally produced organic ingredients more often than not, creating terrific Italian fare: The menu includes flatbread *pizze*, spaghetti and meatballs, and risotto, as well as grilled bison and Idaho trout. Only beer and wine are available, but the selection is excellent. Next door is the Grill's sister wine bar, the **Emerson Grill North.**

207 W. Olive St., in the Emerson Center for Arts and Culture. www.emersongrill.com. ✆**406/586-5247.** Reservations recommended. Main courses $15–$33. AE, MC, V. Mon–Wed 5–9pm; Thurs–Sat 5–10pm. Emerson Grill North: Thurs–Sat 5–9pm.

Main Street Overeasy AMERICAN   Chef Erik Carr opened this restaurant in 1998, and it has been a local favorite ever since, winning "Bozeman's Best Breakfast" from local weeklies on a near-annual basis The place packs 'em in for breakfast with such dishes as biscuits and gravy, chicken-fried steak, and cinnamon bread pudding with warm vanilla sauce. Or have the "Bobcat Benedict," which is two fried eggs atop chicken-fried steak and biscuits and gravy. Lunches consist of gourmet sandwiches and salads.

9 E. Main St. ✆**406/587-3205.** Breakfast $5–$10; lunch $6–$10. AE, DISC, MC, V. Daily 7am–2pm.

The Mint ★★ 🍴 AMERICAN   Few places meld upscale and cowboy as well as the historic Mint in downtown Belgrade, about 8 miles west of Bozeman. A local landmark since 1904, the interior is lined with black-and-white photos of cowboys, and a stuffed Hereford head guards the entrance, but the blond wood and sleek details make it a tad more formal than your typical Montana roadhouse. The superlative specialties will rouse the carnivore in most anybody: buffalo tenderloin, a 14-ounce New York strip, and half a cast-iron-roasted chicken. There are also daily specials, including a pasta dish and a seafood plate, and a great bar menu running the gastronomic gamut from burgers to crab cakes. The wine list is one of the best within a 100-mile radius.

27 E. Main St., Belgrade. www.themintmt.com. ✆**406/388-1100.** Reservations recommended. Dinner $9–$47. AE, DISC, MC, V. Tues–Sun 4–10pm. Closed Sun in winter. Bar open later.

Montana Ale Works ★ AMERICAN   A casual, social place to see and be seen, Montana Ale Works is a great place to unwind over hearty portions and cold libations or catch a ballgame. I like the Montana Meatloaf, a spicy slab of buffalo, beef, and pork, but other favorites include fish tacos, barbecued ribs, and plenty of steaks. After a long period of dormancy, the former railroad warehouse became a restaurant in 2000. The place hangs on to a bit of its past in the form of industrial chic decor, with brick walls and an exposed ceiling framing a vast room with plenty of nooks and crannies to find a seat. There are also pool tables, but no cigarette smoke. In the center of it all is a full bar with plenty of seating and, of course, plenty of ale: Of the 40 beers on tap, about half are brewed in Montana.

611 E. Main St. www.montanaaleworks.com. ✆ **406/587-7700.** Reservations accepted. Main courses $9–$30. AE, DISC, MC, V. Sun–Thurs 4–10pm; Fri–Sat 4–11pm. Bar open 1 hr. later.

Naked Noodle 🍜 NOODLES If you like to sample from several cuisines, or everybody in your group wants something different, this is the perfect choice. At this casual eatery in a brick-and-funky-art-clad space just off Main Street, you can get noodles of all kinds, from soba noodles in Thai green chile curry, to Italian fettuccine Alfredo, to good old American mac and cheese, with four varieties of the latter. The signature dish is the Gaucho: cavatappi pasta topped with chipotle cream sauce, black beans, and tortilla chips. Also on the menu are a number of filling salads with the same international variety, as well as gluten-free and kids' options.

27 S. Willson Ave. www.nakednoodle.com. ✆ **406/505-4501.** Most items $6–$14. AE, MC, V. Mon–Sat 11am–9pm; Sun 11–8pm.

Nova Cafe ★ AMERICAN A colorful diner with blue tabletops, vintage concert posters, and a health-oriented menu, the Nova is a great breakfast spot. The menu includes dozens of scrambles, omelets, Benedict variations (like Eggs Argyle with salmon standing in for the bacon), and other egg dishes, as well as turkey hash, pancakes, sausages du jour, and no less than six daily specials. Breakfast is served whenever the place is open; lunchtime also brings a selection of creative salads and sandwiches. There's a kids' menu; vegetarian, vegan, and gluten-free options; and espresso and smoothies.

312 E. Main St. www.thenovacafe.com. ✆ **406/587-3973.** Reservations accepted for parties of 6 or more only. Main courses $6–$12 breakfast and lunch. AE, DISC, MC, V. Daily 7am–2pm.

Over the Tapas ★ TAPAS/MEDITERRANEAN A favorite since opening in 2007, the basic room of black tables and booths is one of the few midprice options downtown, and the long lines on weekend nights reflect that. The small plates are excellent, ranging from meatless cheese and olive samplers to grilled lamb chops. Most of the items are Spanish standards, like paella and spinach croquettes. Beer and wine (mostly Spanish and South American) are available, but liquor is not.

19 S. Willson Ave. www.bozemantapas.com. ✆ **406/556-8282.** Most tapas $3–$14 lunch and dinner. AE, DISC, MC, V. Mon–Sat 11am–9:30pm.

Plonk Wine ★★★ CONTEMPORARY/WINE BAR A dimly lit hot spot that feels more San Francisco than Bozeman, Plonk (Euro-slang for ordinary table wine) took over the space that housed the Stockman's Bar from 1921 to 1971 and molded it into an eatery that oozes with a hip, urban atmosphere. The menus (there are six in all) change on a regular basis, but you can count on Bozeman's best selection of wine, cheese, and decadent desserts. The dinner menu focuses on local sustainably raised meat; standbys include steaks and bison, as well as an excellent chicken and pear salad. Across from the well-stocked shelves of vino, there is a full bar, above which hangs a restored brand-laden mural that dates from Plonk's Stockman's Bar era. There is a full bar with house-infused liquors; DJs entertain the crowd on Friday nights.

29 E. Main St. www.plonkwine.com. ✆ **406/587-2170.** Reservations accepted for parties of 6 or more only. Main courses $8–$10 lunch; $15–$25 dinner. AE, DISC, MC, V. Daily 11:30am–10:30pm (from 4pm Sun and Mon in winter). Bar open later (usually until 2am).

Sola Café ★ NEW AMERICAN This funky, labyrinthine restaurant near the Montana State University campus serves some of the best and healthiest food in town. Breakfast and lunch bring sandwiches (with contents ranging from eggs to peanut butter to steak); there are also entree salads and grass-fed beef burgers. Dinner features entrees like Vietnamese banh mi pork, Moroccan curry, and stuffed portobello mushrooms. There is beer and wine, an espresso bar, and ready-to-go takeout.

290 W. Kagy Blvd. www.solacafe.com. ✆ **406/922-7652.** Main courses $5–$12 breakfast and lunch, $7–$14 dinner. AE, DISC, MC, V. Mon–Sat 6am–9pm; Sun 6am–8pm.

Bozeman After Dark

Bozeman is a college town, so there are lots of places to get a casual drink accompanied by loud music. Popular watering holes include the Irish-themed **Pub 317,** 321 E. Main St. (✆ **406/582-8898**); the vintage **Crystal Bar,** 123 E. Main St. (✆ **406/587-2888**); and the **Zebra,** 321 E. Main St., in the old Bozeman Hotel (✆ **406/585-8851**), ground zero for the local live music scene. Another fun option (with a limit of 48 oz. per customer per day) is the **Bozeman Brewing Company's** bustling taproom, 504 N. Broadway (www.bozemanbrewing.com; ✆ **406/585-9142**). It's open Monday through Saturday from 4 to 8pm, pouring the brewery's popular Bozone-brand beers.

Bozeman is also home to coffee shops galore, including the **Leaf and Bean,** 35 W. Main St. (✆ 406/587-1580); **HomePage Internet Cafe,** 242 E. Main St. (✆ 406/582-9388); **Wild Joe's Coffee,** 18 W. Main St. (✆ 406/586-1212); and, near the MSU campus, **Daily Coffee Bar & Bakery,** 1013 W. College St. (✆ 406/585-8612). **Lindley Perk** (✆ 406/582-9800) is a coffee shop in the beloved new library at 626 E. Main St.

Montana Shakespeare in the Parks (www.montana.edu/shakespeare; ✆ **406/994-3901**) is a professional touring company that was formed in 1973. Based in Bozeman, the troupe of 10 to 12 actors produces more than 60 performances during the summer at communities throughout Montana, Wyoming, and Idaho—often in a different town each day. Some summer weekends find them at their Bozeman stage—located on the MSU campus on 11th Avenue near the corner of Grant Street—for "Shakespeare Under the Stars." Parking is available just north of the MSU field house. Call for the schedule. Performances are always free.

For edgy and experimental fare, one-act-play festivals, and the stylings of a local comedy troupe, head to the **Equinox Theatre,** 2304 N. 7th Ave. (www.equinoxtheatre.com; ✆ **406/587-0737**).

THE MADISON RIVER VALLEY: THREE FORKS & ENNIS ★★

Ennis: 54 miles SW of Bozeman; 71 miles N of West Yellowstone

The Madison Valley is an almost mythical place surrounded by spectacular mountain scenery where anglers from all over gather to fish. The main attraction is the Madison River, which flows through the valley at the base of the Madison Range, a stretch of peaks that runs toward Yellowstone Park.

Besides the phenomenal fishing, the Madison Valley has tourist-worthy historical sites. The **Missouri Headwaters State Park** is at the confluence of the Jefferson, Madison, and Gallatin rivers, where Lewis and Clark paused to take shelter; **Lewis and Clark Caverns State Park,** with its spectacular underground peaks, is just up the road; and **Madison Buffalo Jump State Park** is nearby.

Essentials

GETTING THERE   The Bozeman airport, **Gallatin Field** (discussed earlier in this chapter), is the closest airport to the valley.

Greyhound stops in Three Forks at 2 Main St. (✆ **406/285-6870**).

Three Forks is located on I-90, 30 miles from Bozeman, 170 miles from Billings, and 173 miles from Missoula. Three Forks is 66 miles from the capital, Helena. Ennis is 45 miles south of Three Forks on U.S. 287.

VISITOR INFORMATION   Contact the **Three Forks Chamber of Commerce,** P.O. Box 1103, Three Forks, MT 59752 (www.threeforksmontana.com; © **406/285-4753**), or the **Ennis Chamber of Commerce,** P.O. Box 291, Ennis, MT 59729 (www.ennischamber.com; © **406/682-4388**). **Yellowstone Country** (www.yellowstone country.net; © **800/736-5276**) is the Travel Montana tourism office for the region.

GETTING AROUND   If you're flying into Bozeman, pick up a car at the airport (see "Getting Around," earlier in this chapter, for more information). For **statewide road reports,** call © **800/226-7623** or 511 on your mobile phone.

Getting Outside

There is plenty of fishing water along the road from Three Forks to Quake and Hebgen lakes along U.S. 287. The first fishing access is **Cobblestone,** just a few miles south of Three Forks on the right side of U.S. 287. If you plan to base yourself in Ennis, the **Valley Garden, Ennis Bridge, Burnt Tree,** and **Varney Bridge** fishing accesses are within minutes of town along U.S. 287. Between Ennis and Quake Lake, the accesses begin popping up frequently. **McAtee Bridge, Wolf Creek, West Fork,** and **Reynolds Pass** are all accessible from the roadside. Hebgen Lake, just south of the dam, and Quake Lake are also great fishing spots.

On Ennis's Main Street, it seems that every second door houses a fly-fishing outfitter. The **Madison River Fishing Company,** 109 Main St. (www.mrfc.com; © **800/227-7127** or 406/682-4293), has a good stock of fishing supplies and a guide service. Guided trips, for one or two people, cost $325 for a half-day and $425 for a full day; full-day trips include lunch. They also offer a free brochure that contains a map of fishing spots and various facilities along the way. Other guide services, with similar rates, include **Clark's Guide Service** (© **406/682-7474**); **Howard Outfitters** (© **406/682-4834**); and the **Tackle Shop Outfitters,** 127 Main St. (www.thetackleshop.com; © **800/808-2832** or 406/682-4263).

In Ennis proper, kids will love **Lions Club Park,** on the banks of the Madison River on the east side of town, featuring trails, a playground, and a stocked fishing pond with some monster trout that's free and open to kids under 13 only.

Seeing the Sights

Lewis & Clark Caverns State Park ★   These lovely limestone caverns are named for the famous explorers, but there is no evidence that their party ever saw or visited them. Discovered in the late 19th century, these caverns are a succession of vaulted chambers and passageways, thickly decorated with stalactites and stalagmites, as well as other underground formations such as massive, gleaming organ pipes; silky, delicate soda straws; intricate filigrees; and weirdly hung draperies. Plan at least 2 hours for the 2-mile guided tour through the caverns; aboveground, there are hiking trails, several picnic areas, and a large campground (see "Camping," below). A Christmas candlelight tour is held on two weekends in December. Reservations should be made in early December for one of the 200 or so spots available. There is a campground, as well as three cabins on the premises with electric heat; rates are $55 for nonresidents in summer.

Located 19 miles west of Three Forks (midway btw. Butte and Bozeman) on Mont. 2. www.fwp. mt.gov. © **406/287-3541.** Entrance fee $5 per car. Cave tours $10 adults, $5 children 6–11; no children 5 and under allowed. Park and campground open daily year-round. Guided cave tours May to mid-June and mid-Aug to Sept daily 9am–4:30pm; mid-June to mid-Aug daily 9am–6:30pm. Tours leave as required by demand. Closed Oct–Apr (except for Christmas event).

Madison Buffalo Jump State Park This is one of a few buffalo jumps, or *pishkun*, that have been excavated. Prior to the advent of the horse, the Northern Shoshone and the Bannock drove the bison off this steep cliff to their death on the rocks below. Long rows of rocks funneled the animals to the cliff. There is a well-worn trail up to the base of the cliff, making for a short but steep hike.

Located 23 miles west of Bozeman, off I-90 exit 283. www.fwp.mt.gov. ©**406/994-4042.** Entrance $5 per car. Daily 24 hr. From the Logan exit off I-90, 7 miles south on Buffalo Jump Rd.

Missouri Headwaters State Park ★★ You can easily spend an hour just exploring the interpretive signage at this historic state park. Begin by following the Missouri River out from Three Forks. The headwaters themselves are no great shakes—just another river—but the sunsets from the bank of the river are breathtaking. From the headwaters, drive back toward Three Forks where, on the opposite side of the road, you'll see a parking area with interpretive markers. Allow plenty of time to read about Lewis and Clark and Sacajawea, the young Shoshone guide, as well as early American Indians, trappers, traders, and settlers. Camping and RV sites are available, along with access to hiking, boating, and fishing.

Located 4 miles northeast of Three Forks. www.fwp.mt.gov. © **406/994-4042.** Entrance $5 per car. Daily 24 hr. Drive east on C.R. 205, then north on C.R. 286; follow signs.

National Fish Hatchery The Ennis National Fish Hatchery, constructed in 1931, is probably the only place in America where you can observe two genetic mutants of ordinary rainbow trout: albino and blue. (These fish are not released into the wild trout population.) Some of the trout in the hatchery ponds weigh more than 20 pounds and are more than 5 years old. The hatchery cultivates seven different strains of rainbow trout. You can learn about the operation in the small exhibit area and tour the facility. When some of those huge adults are past their use as brood stock, they too are released into lakes and streams to test fishermen.

180 Fish Hatchery Rd., Ennis. www.fws.gov/ennis. © **406/682-4847.** Free admission. Daily 7:30am–5pm. The hatchery is 12 miles southwest of Ennis. Take U.S. 287 south from town to R.R. 249 and go west to Call Rd. Turn left (south), then left (east) on Fish Hatchery Rd. after ½ mile.

Norris Hot Springs ★ ♙ You'll be hard-pressed to find a more scenic spot for a soak, or a better soaking pool with live music, or a better place to work away the aches and pains induced by outdoor recreation than Norris Hot Springs, about a 45-minute drive west of Bozeman. The year-round hot springs–fed pool, which is lined with wood, sits adjacent to an eatery that grows a good portion of what it serves and a geodesic dome that provides musicians with shelter. Suit and towel rentals are available ($1 each).

Mont. 84, Norris, 16 miles north of Ennis and 34 miles west of Bozeman. www.norrishotsprings. com. © **406/685-3303.** Admission $5 adults, $3 kids under 12. Year-round Wed–Fri 4–10pm; Sat–Sun noon–10pm.

Quake Lake Just before midnight on August 17, 1959, a massive earthquake measuring 7.5 on the Richter scale jolted Yellowstone and the Madison River canyon, sending large chunks of mountain into the river. A campsite just below the mountain was covered with rubble, and 19 people were buried alive. The rubble that collapsed into the river created a dam and the aptly named Quake Lake. The ghostly fingers of trees that died when they were swamped still poke skyward from the lake. The visitor center on the north side of the highway offers exhibits, a video every half-hour, and an observation area from which you can see the massive slides. The area around Yellowstone and Quake Lake is still very seismically active, and southwest Montana is second only to California in terms of earthquake frequency. The visitor center has a great deal of information about the area's seismic activity and hypotheses of how it got this way.

Off U.S. 287, 27 miles northwest of West Yellowstone and 43 miles south of Ennis. ☏ **406/682-7620** or 823-6961. Visitor center $3 per car; $1 per person on motorcycle or bicycle. Memorial Day to Labor Day daily 8:30am–6pm. **Note:** The visitor center will close in early July 2012 for a renovation and reopen Memorial Day 2013.

Where to Stay

In addition to the properties discussed below, the **Rainbow Valley Motel,** 1 mile south of Ennis on U.S. 287 (P.O. Box 26), Ennis, MT 59729 (www.rainbowvalley. com; ☏ **800/452-8254** or 406/682-4264), offers large, well-maintained cabin-style rooms, with rates for two people of $88 to $125. There are also a couple of large cabin homes for $165 to $185 a night. In town, I like the **Riverside Motel,** 346 E. Main St. (www.riversidemotel-outfitters.com; ☏ **406/682-4240**), with duplex cabin units as well as two-bedroom units and kitchens, with rates of $80 to $140.

El Western Cabins & Lodges ★★ It's a little hard to categorize this place, which has some inexpensive log duplex-style cabins, as well as large, expensive two- and three-bedroom lodges and uniformly well-maintained rooms. The original portion, built in 1948, is done with knotty-pine interiors and built-in wooden cabinets. The newest lodge is the Eagle's Loft, a three-bedroom, three-bathroom, two-story cabin with a vaulted ceiling and rock fireplace, plus a whirlpool tub and washer and dryer. Every unit enjoys spectacular views of the Madison Range, including Fan Mountain and the Spanish Peaks. You can't go wrong here, and the overnight cabins are as affordable as anything in the valley. There's no restaurant or lounge associated with the property, but a new conference center with a large, inviting deck and picture windows serves both business and family groups.

4787 U.S. 287 N., P.O. Box 487, Ennis, MT 59729. www.elwestern.com. ☏ **800/831-2773** or 406/682-4217. Fax 406/682-5207. 29 units. $80–$105 double; $120–$165 creek-side kitchen cabin; $180–$285 deluxe mountainside kitchen cabin; $275–$475 lodge. Lower rates fall to spring. AE, DISC, MC, V. From the town of Ennis, drive south 1 mile on U.S. 287. Closed mid-Dec to May except lodges. In room: TV, hair dryer, kitchen, Wi-Fi (free).

Sacajawea Hotel ★★ Originally opened in 1910 and extensively renovated a century later, the Sacajawea Hotel is a gleaming hotel with unexpectedly luxurious trappings. Rooms are decorated with a sleek take on classic styles, and the picture-perfect porch is lined with comfortable chairs. Rooms have one full-size bed or a king or queen; a few have two full beds or queens. There is a restaurant, **Pompey's Grill,** a woodsy bar, and the **Madison House Spa** on-site.

5 N. Main St. (P.O. Box 648), Three Forks, MT 59752. www.sacajaweahotel.com. ☏ **406/285-6515.** Fax 406/285-4210. 29 units. $109–$199 double; $219 suite; lower rates fall to spring. AE, DISC, MC, V. Pets accepted ($25 per night). **Amenities:** Restaurant; lounge; spa. In room: A/C, TV, Wi-Fi (free).

Wade Lake Cabins 🏕 This secluded cabin resort, which consists of five cabins, is located in a picture-perfect forested canyon on Wade Lake. The cabins are basic but tidy, with only a refrigerator, running water, heat, a gas stove, and a gas barbecue grill. A shared modern bathhouse is out back. Bring food to cook because the nearest restaurant is 11 miles back up the road. The area is very beautiful, though—Wade has been designated a Montana Wildlife Viewing Site. A hiking and mountain-biking mecca in summer and a cross-country skiing destination in winter (guests ski in 6 miles, and a snowmobile takes their luggage), the area is rich in wildlife, with eagles and osprey nesting on the lake, and moose, elk, bear, and other locals dropping in occasionally. It also helps you remember what real quiet and real darkness are like.

P.O. Box 107, Cameron, MT 59720. www.wadelake.com. ✆ **406/682-7560.** 5 cabins. Summer $85–$110 double; winter $125 double, 3-night minimum. No credit cards. Drive 40 miles south of Ennis to the Wade Lake turnoff, marked by a sign. Turn west on the bumpy, gravel Wade Lake Rd. and follow the signs about 6 miles to Wade Lake. Closed fall and spring. **Amenities:** Watersports rentals. *In room:* Kitchen, no phone, Wi-Fi (free, most rooms).

CAMPING

Lewis & Clark Caverns State Park (see "Seeing the Sights," above; ✆ 406/287-3541) has 40 campsites ($20–$23 for nonresidents), showers, a dump station, and fishing access on a river, plus hiking trails and interpretive programs. **Missouri Headwaters State Park** (see "Seeing the Sights," above; ✆ 406/994-4042) has a year-round campground ($20–$23) with 20 sites and basic cabins ($35) scattered along the river, plus numerous hiking trails and plenty of fishing access. Maximum trailer length is 25 feet; there's a boat ramp and dump station. Those wanting RV hookups and the usual commercial campground amenities should head to **Camp Three Forks,** on U.S. 287, 1 mile south of I-90 exit 274 (www.campthreeforks.com; ✆ 406/285-3611), which has a pastoral setting as well as a clean bathhouse, swimming pool, rec room, and playground. It's open May through September, with sites for both tents and RVs at rates of $20 to $36, and basic cabins for $45 to $50. In Ennis, the **Riverside Motel,** 346 Main St. (www.riversidemotel-outfitters.com; ✆ 406/682-4240), has RV spots for $28; tents are not permitted

Where to Eat

NEAR THREE FORKS

Wheat Montana Bakery and Deli, I-90 and U.S. 287 (✆ 406/285-3614), is a popular breakfast and lunch spot where Montana-grown wheat is turned into bread, and just the smell of bread baking makes it worth the stop. In the Ennis Pharmacy, at 124 Main St., **Yesterday's Restaurant and Soda Fountain** (✆ 406/682-4246) serves hearty American breakfasts and lunch every day of the week.

Willow Creek Café and Saloon ★ ⋔AMERICAN   This place is a find, if you can find it—it's located 7 miles southwest of Three Forks on the Old Yellowstone Trail. It's worth the search, though, because Willow Creek is the best restaurant in the area (don't let the bullet holes in the ceiling scare you off). It began as the Babcock Saloon around 1916, and continues as a remarkable reflection of what's best in Montana: hearty meals and friendly people. The ever-popular baby back pork ribs draw repeat customers from around the country, but the local cowboys know that the beef is tops here, so the hand-pounded chicken-fried sirloin steak is their recommendation. The pasta dishes are very good, and the homemade soups really taste homemade. The weekend-only lunches are also recommended.

21 Main St., Willow Creek. ✆ **406/285-3698.** Dinner reservations recommended in summer. Lunch $4–$10; dinner $10–$30. AE, DISC, MC, V. Tues–Fri 4–10pm; Sat–Sun 11am–10pm. Shorter hours in winter.

ENNIS

Continental Divide ★★ NEW AMERICAN   The effortlessly elegant Continental Divide has been the culinary pacesetter in Ennis since it opened in 1982. Featuring creative continental fare with an emphasis on game, steaks, and seafood, chef Eric Trapp changes the menu on a seasonal basis but often includes specialties like lobster cannellini, filet mignon, and slow-roasted duck. The wine list is excellent, but liquor is not served.

47 Geyser St. ✆ **406/682-7600.** Main courses $18–$40 dinner. AE, DISC, MC, V. Summer daily 5–9:30pm (limited hours early and late season); closed in winter.

Gravel Bar ★ AMERICAN/MEXICAN   This horseshoe-lined, thoroughly Western bar and grill has two restaurants in summer: **Banditos** (formerly a Virginia City mainstay) serves Mexican, and the namesake **Gravel Bar** serves sandwiches of all kinds, including pulled pork, pastrami, and kitchen. In winter, Banditos closes down, but the bar serves food and drink year-round. There is a dining room adjacent to the copper-topped bar, and a social atmosphere.

305 E. Main St. ✆ **406/682-5553.** Main courses $8–$13 lunch and dinner. DISC, MC, V. Daily 11am–9pm. Bar open later.

THE GALLATIN VALLEY ★★

Big Sky: 53 miles S of Bozeman; 48 miles N of West Yellowstone

According to legend, the Sioux and Nez Perce once engaged in a bloody battle in the lower Gallatin Valley. On the third day of the fighting, the sun was blotted out and a booming voice told the warriors to forget old wrongs and stop fighting because they were in the Valley of Peace and Flowers.

These days, the sun mostly shines around here, and the only booming voices heard are those calling you for your tee time or your dinner reservation. The transition of Big Sky from peace and flowers to year-round resort was not entirely without dissension, however. When legendary NBC newsman Chet Huntley—a Montana native—proposed the Big Sky ski resort, there was an outcry from the budding environmental movement. But Huntley's dream was realized in 1973, and the resort has blossomed into a world-class facility, with a second ski area—Moonlight Basin—opening in 2003.

The valley is a narrow, shining slice of Montana edged by the Absaroka and Gallatin ranges to the east and the Madison Range on the west. The Big Sky Resort covers two of the western peaks—Lone Mountain, elevation 11,186 feet, and Andesite Mountain, 8,800 feet. Moonlight Basin's runs are also on Lone Mountain and connect with those of Big Sky.

There are several distinct "villages" in Big Sky. The **canyon area** along U.S. 191 has a haphazard collection of motels, taverns, restaurants, gas stations, and whatnot. The **Meadow Village,** 2 miles west of the highway, includes a community of condos, a few overnight lodging places, and the golf course. The main base area for the ski resort is at the **Mountain Village,** 8 miles west of the highway, with condos, restaurants, and hotels. The Moonlight Basin development is just above Mountain Village.

The valley's summers bring excellent fly-fishing, horseback riding, and white-water rafting. This beautiful scenery may seem familiar—the Gallatin River was the setting for the film *A River Runs Through It.*

Essentials

GETTING THERE   Big Sky is about 53 miles south of Bozeman's **Gallatin Field Airport** on U.S. 191. From the airport, you can ride to the ski area with **Karst Stage** (www.karststage.com; ✆ **800/845-2778** or 406/556-3500), a company that has a transportation fleet of sturdy four-wheel-drive vehicles. The ride is about $80 round-trip per adult and $40 per child 3 to 12 in winter. Or you can take a van or town car provided by **Shuttle to Big Sky** (www.bigskytaxi.com; ✆ **406/995-4895**) for about $150 one-way.

GETTING AROUND   A car gives you the greatest flexibility in getting around this area. For service between condominiums, hotels, restaurants, and activities within the ski area, take Big Sky's free local shuttle-bus system, which operates daily during the ski season.

Getting Outside

BIKING

Big Sky Resort rents mountain bikes and offers bike rental/lift ticket combos. Call ✆ **406/995-5840** for details.

CROSS-COUNTRY SKIING

Big Sky Resort (see below) offers some groomed trails for cross-country skiing. But for the real deal, go to **Lone Mountain Ranch ★★★** (P.O. Box 160069, Big Sky, MT 59716; www.lonemountain.com; ✆ **800/514-4644** or 406/995-4644), which has 50 miles of cross-country trails over terrain that will challenge every level of skier. Near the ranch headquarters, in the meadows, lies some flat terrain that beginners might appreciate. There's also a steeper portion to practice your Telemark technique and 18 miles of snowshoe trails. Intermediate trails with more hills make up about 60% of the area, and expert trails provide plenty of challenging downhill runs. Lessons, guided tours, and ski and snowshoe rentals are also available; there is also a tasty trailside buffet. Full-day trail passes cost $18 for adults, $9 for seniors 60 to 69, and free for kids 12 and under and seniors 70 and over. The entrance to Lone Mountain Ranch is off Lone Mountain Trail (the main road to the Big Sky Resort), about 4 miles west of its intersection with U.S. 191 and 2 miles east of the Meadow Village.

DOWNHILL SKIING

In 2005, Big Sky and Moonlight Basin connected their trail systems, making for a combined 5,532 acres of terrain—the largest ski area in the country. Skiers and snowboarders can buy the **"Biggest Skiing in America" ticket** for a day of unlimited access to both resorts' runs for $98 adults, $88 seniors 70 and over and college students, and $78 for juniors 11 to 17 (free for kids 10 and under).

Big Sky Resort ★★   Tennis, golf, and rock climbing are all very nice, but the real reason to come to Big Sky is to ski. It's a huge hill, with more than 3,832 acres of terrain and 85 miles of trails. You can ski for nearly a vertical mile from the top of the tram, at 11,166 feet elevation, to the bottom of the Lone Moose lift, at 6,800 feet, the third-longest vertical drop of any U.S. resort. There is terrain here for everybody, with 60% for advanced and expert skiers, 26% for intermediate, and 14% beginner. Big Sky gets 400 inches of snowfall, offering plenty of powder days. There's an ambitious children's program, offering lessons for kids as young as 3, and day care for kids who don't want to ski. Full ski-rental packages are available. New in the winter is a zipline operated by the ski school.

SOUTH-CENTRAL MONTANA | The Gallatin Valley

P.O. Box 160001, Big Sky, MT 59716. www.bigskyresort.com. ☎ **800/548-4486** or 406/995-5000; 406/995-5900 for snow conditions; 406/995-5743 for ski school. Peak-season lift ticket $84 adults, $74 seniors (70 and over), $64 college students with ID and juniors 11–17, and free for children 10 and under. Late Nov to mid-Apr daily 9am–4pm.

Moonlight Basin ★ The first new destination ski resort in the U.S. in more than 20 years, Moonlight Basin opened in 2003 to rave reviews from hard-core skiers, but its long, steep runs may be a bit challenging for neophytes. (This makes the "Biggest Skiing in America" ticket, above, a safe bet if you're on the fence about your abilities.) Seven lifts (a high-speed six-passenger lift, three quads, one triple, one double, and a conveyor) serve 1,900 acres of terrain crisscrossed by about 90 trails—with a precipitous 4,150-foot drop. Most of the terrain is for the advanced skier, but there are some easier runs. Like Big Sky, the resort gets more than 400 inches of snow a year. It also features a spa, a snow sports school, kids' programs, and other outdoor activities. But the folks behind this infant of a resort look like they're just getting started. A private Jack Nicklaus–designed golf course opened in 2010.

P.O. Box 160040, Big Sky, MT 59716. www.moonlightbasin.com. ☎ **877/822-0430** or 406/993-6000; 406/993-6666 for snow conditions. Lift ticket $64 adults; $55 seniors (70 and over), college students with ID and juniors 11–17; free for children 10 and under. Late Nov to mid-Apr daily 9am–4pm.

FISHING

According to an Indian legend, folks who drink the water of the Gallatin River will return to the valley before they die, but of course, you should no longer drink untreated water out of even high mountain streams because of the possibility of giardia, an intestinal microbe that you don't want traveling back home with you. We're not sure if eating the fish that live in the water counts toward the legend, but it's worth a try. Several guides offer trips for prices ranging from about $250 to $300 for a half-day for two, to $350 to $500 for a full day. For details, contact **Lone Mountain Ranch** (☎ **406/995-4644**), **Gallatin Riverguides** (www.montanaflyfishing.com; ☎ **406/995-2290**), or **East Slope Anglers** (www.eastslopeoutdoors.com; ☎ **406/995-4369**).

GOLF

Big Sky Golf Course, Meadow Village (☎ **406/995-5780**), is a striking Arnold Palmer design that is fairly short, fairly open, and harder than it looks on the card. A few of the holes wander next to the West Fork of the Gallatin River, which runs through the property. Cost, which includes the cart fee, is about $40 to $70 for 18 holes, $30 to $50 for 9. Tee times can be reserved up to a week in advance.

HIKING

As you might expect in an area surrounded by three mountain ranges and two national forests, there is an abundance of hiking opportunities not far from Big Sky. An easy, 4-mile hike to **Porcupine Creek** is accessible nearby. Go south 2¾ miles on U.S. 191 from the intersection with the mountain village road. Turn left at the sign that announces Porcupine Creek, and go about a half-mile to the trail head. The first mile of the hike wanders along Porcupine Creek and then offers a choice of either a north or a south fork. The left (north) fork goes up into the foothills, offering a view of the creek below.

If you want more of a workout, try the **Lava Lake** trail, which begins about 13 miles north of the intersection of the mountain village road and U.S. 191 on the highway. Take the Lava Lake turn. The trail climbs steeply, without much relief, for 3 miles to an alpine lake in the shelter of three mountains.

SOUTH-CENTRAL MONTANA

The Gallatin Valley

The entrance to **Yellowstone National Park** is only about 40 miles south of Big Sky, and you can hike there for a lifetime and still not cover every trail.

Where to Stay

Big Sky Resort, P.O. Box 160001, Big Sky, MT 59716 (www.bigskyresort.com; ✆ **800/548-4486** or 406/995-5000), handles a wide variety of lodgings—from economy to full-fledged luxury, scattered among nearly 70 properties. The three-story **Huntley Lodge,** with 205 units, was the beginning of late NBC newsman Chet Huntley's original vision for Big Sky. It offers rooms that can sleep up to four and several loft rooms that can accommodate six. The 97-unit **Shoshone Condominium Hotel** combines the living quarters of a condo with the amenities and services of a hotel; units sleep four to six. Weight-training centers, saunas, an outdoor pool, gift shops, and ski storage are included at both places. The **Summit at Big Sky ★**, with 213 luxury condominiums, offers European sophistication in a Western style. All three properties are slopeside and offer ski-in/ski-out convenience. Winter rates start around $180 a night double and top out at more than $1,000.

Moonlight Basin, P.O. Box 160040, Big Sky, MT 59716 (www.moonlightbasin. com; ✆ **877/822-0430** or 406/993-6000), offers properties ranging from condos to private residences, to luxurious penthouses. The **Moonlight Lodge and Spa ★★** (✆ **800/845-4428**) is a magnificent mountain lodge offering luxurious penthouse suites and secluded mid-mountain cabins, plus a sophisticated yet down-home restaurant, a relaxed-atmosphere bar, and a deli. There's also a full-service spa with treatment rooms, complete fitness center, steam rooms, heated pool, and a cascading waterfall hot tub; a concierge ready and able to organize everything from fly-fishing trips, to backcountry skiing, to dog-sled adventures; and even an ice-skating rink just outside in winter. Winter rates start at about $225 a night double during the ski season and top out at well over $1,000.

In the Big Sky area, rates vary with the season and within the ski season. The highest rates are during Christmas vacation, the lowest in the spring and fall "shoulder" seasons.

Buck's T-4 Lodge ★   Begun in 1946 as a hunting camp, Buck's T-4 came to the valley before electricity did. It has grown quite a bit over the years. Buck's still offers a woody, Western ambience on the highway about 10 miles away from the ski resort lodgings, with large, comfortable rooms in a wide variety of floor plans, all with nice views and tasteful decor. The current lodge is modern, including two hot tubs large enough for the kids to swim in, a game room, and all of the other amenities you want in ski- and Yellowstone-area accommodations. The best thing about the place, though, is the restaurant, reviewed below. Standard rooms, suites, and suites with kitchenettes are available. Ask about ski packages and vacations when making reservations.

P.O. Box 160279, U.S. 191, Big Sky, MT 59716. www.buckst4.com. ✆ **800/822-4484** or 406/995-4111. Fax 406/995-2191. 72 units, including 3 suites. $129–$159 double; $199–$309 suite. Lower rates spring and fall. Rates include hot buffet breakfast. AE, DC, DISC, MC, V. About ½-mile south of the intersection of U.S. 191 and Lone Mountain Trail. Pets accepted ($10). **Amenities:** Restaurant; lounge; 2 outdoor Jacuzzis. *In room:* TV, fridge, hair dryer, kitchenette (suite only), MP3 player docking stations, Wi-Fi (free).

Gallatin Gateway Inn ★   Located about midway between Bozeman and Big Sky, the Gallatin Gateway Inn is a model of historical elegance from the days of luxury railroad travel. The hotel opened in the summer of 1927, as visitors were beginning to come to Yellowstone in large numbers. With lavish appointments that include

Polynesian mahogany woodwork, decoratively carved beams, and high arched windows, the Spanish-style building recalls pre–World War II elegance, and you almost expect to see Teddy Roosevelt and Buffalo Bill Cody relaxing side by side on the porch. The spacious guest rooms provide a tastefully understated balance to the regal lobby. They maintain the refined historical feel but have been updated with light colors, providing a more open and airy feeling than you usually find in hotels of this vintage. Serving dinner only, the **Porter House** restaurant's seasonally changing menu includes regional specialties showcasing ingredients from local growers; combinations are imaginative and portions generous.

76405 Gallatin Rd. (U.S. 191), P.O. Box 376, Gallatin Gateway, MT 59730. www.gallatingatewayinn. com. © **800/676-3522** or 406/763-4672. Fax 406/763-4777. 33 units, including 6 suites. $149 double; $199–$249 suite. Lower rates in winter. Rates include continental breakfast. AE, DISC, MC, V. 28 miles north of Big Sky on U.S. 191. **Amenities:** Restaurant; lounge; outdoor Jacuzzi; outdoor pool. *In room:* A/C, TV, Wi-Fi (free).

Lone Mountain Ranch ★★★ ☺ Before there was even a community of Big Sky, there was Lone Mountain Ranch. Started in 1915 as a working cattle ranch, Lone Mountain rapidly blossomed into a year-round destination as a guest ranch and cross-country ski area. In the summer, the ranch blends traditional guest-ranch activities—riding, hiking, fishing, and eating—with naturalist programs that will improve your understanding of Yellowstone. Lone Mountain prides itself on a family atmosphere and has separate activities for children, including animal tracking and campouts. In winter, the ranch is a cross-country skiing and snowshoeing destination, with 50 miles of trails, and offers a wide range of activities, from Yellowstone tours to sleigh rides to winter fly-fishing. Accommodations here vary from small, woodsy cabins to the large, modern Ridgetop Lodge, which can host an entire family reunion. Some of the cabins are historic—from the original ranch—while the new lodge was built more recently. All are spacious, with private bathrooms and attractive pine interiors.

P.O. Box 160069, Big Sky, MT 59716. www.lonemountainranch.com. © **800/514-4644** or 406/995-4644. Fax 406/995-4670. 23 cabins, 1 house, 6 rooms in Ridgetop Lodge. Winter: Cabin or lodge room $2,562–$3,528 1st person, $1,605 each additional person; Douglas Fir House $5,005 1st person, $1,605 each additional person. Lower rates for children 12 and under. Rates include 7 nights' lodging, 3 meals daily, an 8-day trail pass with unlimited access to the ranch's trail system, evening entertainment, a sleigh-ride dinner, and a trail buffet lunch. Summer rates are slightly higher. DISC, MC, V. From Bozeman, head south on U.S. 191 about 45 miles. **Amenities:** Restaurant; lounge; children's program; outdoor Jacuzzi. *In room:* Hair dryer, no phone, Wi-Fi (free).

320 Guest Ranch ☺ Bordered by the Gallatin River, the 320 Guest Ranch dates from 1898 and is one of the few cowboy-oriented accommodations in Montana that takes guests by the night (and not the week) year-round. With a full slate of activities—horseback riding, fishing in the river or a trout pond on-site, hayrides, and plenty more in the winter—the ranch is self-contained but also offers a good base for skiing Big Sky's slopes or Yellowstone's wildlands. Accommodations come in the form of seven lodge rooms and 52 cabins and log homes on the extensive grounds (320 acres, thus the name) that range from small and fairly basic, to two-bedroom log cabins on the river, to even larger guest homes. The furnishings are unremarkable but fitting, and the campfire out front roars every night for marshmallows and cowboy poetry.

205 Buffalo Horn Creek, Gallatin Gateway, MT 59730. www.320ranch.com. © **800/243-0320** or 406/995-4283. Fax 406/993-4694. 59 units, including 52 cabins and log homes. $148–$398 double; lower rates in winter. AE, DISC, MC, V. 15 miles south of the turnoff to Big Sky Resort on U.S. 191. **Amenities:** Restaurant; lounge. *In room:* TV, kitchen, Wi-Fi (free).

Where to Eat

There are almost two dozen eateries at Big Sky, so you know you won't go hungry. But the closer you are to the slopes, the more expensive the food is; on-mountain is naturally most expensive. Restaurants range from simple snack bars to the upscale **Huntley Lodge Dining Room** (℃ **406/995-5783**), which has a good breakfast buffet in the morning and fine dining in the evening. Big Sky also has more than a dozen nightspots.

In the **Meadow Village** area, there are about a dozen restaurants, including the **Blue Moon Bakery** (℃ **406/995-2305**), which is open for all three meals and has good sandwiches and fresh-baked pastries, along with salads, soups, and pizza, and free delivery after 5pm. The locals' favorite is the **Corral Bar and Steakhouse,** 42895 U.S. 191, about 5 miles south of the turnoff to Big Sky (℃ **406/995-4249**), serving primarily steaks—including buffalo T-bone—and seafood. Main courses run $10 to $35 at dinner.

The restaurant at **Lone Mountain Ranch** (see "Where to Stay") is excellent, and in the winter, there is a sleigh ride and dinner at the ranch's North Fork cabin. There is a buffet breakfast and lunch each day. Call ℃ **406/995-2782** after 3pm for dinner reservations.

Buck's T-4 Restaurant ★★ NEW AMERICAN   Buck's offers an adventurous menu of "Montana cuisine," with about a half-dozen wild game dishes, including pan-seared elk chops (a bone-in pork chop, chargrilled and served with raspberry-chipotle sauce), pan-roasted pheasant breast, and the New Zealand red deer sirloin. Our choice here, though, is any of the chargrilled steaks, served with hand-smashed potatoes and a daily vegetable. Of special note is the old bar, part of the original building here and still sporting the same well-worn bar and Technicolor vinyl-tile flooring.

U.S. 191, Big Sky. www.buckst4.com. ℃ **406/993-5222.** Reservations recommended. Entrees $24–$32. AE, DC, DISC, MC, V. About ½-mile south of its intersection with Lone Mountain Trail. Daily 6–9:30pm. Closed mid-Apr to mid-June and early Oct to late Nov.

LIVINGSTON & THE PARADISE VALLEY ★★

Livingston: 26 miles E of Bozeman; 110 miles W of Billings; 58 miles N of Mammoth Hot Springs in Yellowstone National Park

Livingston is caught between very cowboy and very hip. As the largest community in the Paradise Valley, it has been discovered by the Hollywood set who want to get away from it all, but unfortunately still bring some of it with them. Peter Fonda has a ranch here, and you might see Dennis Quaid, Robert Redford, or Anthony Bourdain.

The Paradise Valley is the product of the Yellowstone River, the largest undammed river in the Lower 48. Along with the two valleys paralleling it to the west—the Gallatin and Madison—this portion of Montana is a fly-fishing paradise. There are lots of fishing guides and tackle shops, and millions of acres to wander in and wonder at.

Essentials

GETTING THERE   The nearest airport is Bozeman's **Gallatin Field,** 26 miles west along I-90. It's also possible to fly into Billings's **Logan Airport,** 116 miles east along I-90.

The Gardiner entrance to Yellowstone National Park is 53 miles south on U.S. 89. For **statewide road reports,** call ℂ **800/226-7623** or 511. Greyhound and Rimrock Stages provide bus service. The bus depot is at 1404 E. Park St. (ℂ **406/222-2231**).

VISITOR INFORMATION   The **Livingston Area Chamber of Commerce** is located at 303 E. Park St. (www.livingston-chamber.com; ℂ **406/222-0850**). For information on **Yellowstone Country,** call ℂ **800/736-5276** or 406/556-8680 (www.yellowstonecountry.net).

GETTING AROUND   Car rentals are available at Gallatin Field Airport in Bozeman.

Getting Outside

Much of the outdoor recreation in this area takes place in the **Gallatin National Forest.** Check with the Yellowstone-Livingston Ranger District, 5242 U.S. 89 S., Livingston, MT 59047 (www.fs.usda.gov/gallatin; ℂ **406/222-1892**). Another good source of information on hiking, mountain biking, cross-country skiing, and snow-shoeing, as well as equipment rentals and sales, is **Timber Trails Outdoors Co.,** 309 W. Park St. (ℂ **406/222-9550**).

CROSS-COUNTRY SKIING & SNOWSHOEING

The most popular spots are in the national forest. For specific locations and current conditions, check with the Livingston Ranger District or Timber Trails Outdoors Co. (see above).

DOGSLEDDING

Absaroka Dogsled Treks (www.extrememontana.com; ℂ **406/222-4645**), based in Chico Hot Springs Resort (p. 223), offers a variety of dogsled treks on trails in the Mill Creek Canyon and the Absaroka Mountain range. Established in 1990, this is the oldest dogsled tour operator in Montana. Guests can choose to mush (drive the sled) or ride in the wooden sleds and simply enjoy the untouched scenery. Tours range from half-day to full-day, and cost from $120 to $320 per person.

FISHING

Montana has the best trout fishing in the country, and the area around here is the best trout fishing in Montana. Livingston is the gateway to classic Montana fly-fish-ing in the blue-ribbon Madison River, the Paradise Valley, and the Yellowstone River. **Dan Bailey's Fly Shop,** 209 W. Park St. (www.dan-bailey.com; ℂ **800/356-4052**), in business since 1938, offers all manner of fishing tackle for sale or rent. Bailey's can give you some tips on where to fish on your own, or provide a guide for about $400 a day for one angler or $425 for two. **Hatch Finders Fly Shop,** 113 W. Park St., No. 3 (www.hatchfinders.com; ℂ **406/222-0989**), can tie your custom flies and also provide outfitters almost anywhere in the state. A full-day guided trip in the Yellowstone River area is $450 for two anglers (plus Montana fishing licenses), or $475 in Yellowstone proper. About a quarter-mile south of town, at 5256 U.S. 89 S., **George Anderson's Yellowstone Angler** (www.yellowstoneangler.com; ℂ **406/222-7130**) is another fully equipped equipment store and guide service ($450 a day for two). Anderson also offers a fly-fishing school. About 20 miles south of Livingston in the town of Pray is **Knoll's Yellowstone Tackle and Fly Shop,** 104 Chicory Rd. (www.knolls.us; ℂ **406/333-4848**). Here you can learn how to cast and how

SOUTH-CENTRAL MONTANA

Livingston & the Paradise Valley

feathers mysteriously become fishing flies, or purchase a handcrafted rod or reel. Take U.S. 89 south to Emigrant, then east and northeast on C.R. 540 to Pray.

Early-season fishing before runoff starts—in late April and early May—offers excellent dry fly-fishing. In late May and June, the water on most of the rivers is running high and muddy, but the Firehole River in Yellowstone National Park has a heavy early hatch, and the fishing is good. All fishing in the park is catch and release. The rivers drop in July and August, and there are hatches daily for good fishing.

HIKING & BIKING

This area is nearly surrounded by the **Gallatin National Forest,** which has several thousand miles of hiking and biking trails, including more than 800 miles of hiking trails in two designated wilderness areas—the Lee Metcalf and Absaroka-Beartooth. Popular trails that are relatively easily accessible include **Pine Creek Falls,** south of town off the East River Road. The falls themselves are a short walk from the campground at the end of the access road, and Pine Creek Lake is about 4 miles farther along. **Livingston Peak** (or Mount Baldy Trail) is east of town off Swingley Road, and the **Big Timber Canyon Trail** is north of the town of Big Timber. The Livingston Ranger District of the U.S. Forest Service and Timber Trails Outdoors Co. (see "Getting Outside," above) can provide information about trails and access routes to them. Timber Trails also rents mountain bikes starting at about $25 per day.

HORSEBACK RIDING

Chico Hot Springs (✆ 406/333-4933), about 22 miles south of Livingston off U.S. 89 to the east, also offers horseback riding. **Wilderness Pack Trips,** 209 K St. (www.wildernesspacktrips.com; ✆ 406/848-9953), offers 4- to 10-day horse-packing trips into Yellowstone National Park. Rates are about $1,500 to $3,000. Call or check their website for their current schedule and availability.

RAFTING

Both scenic and white-water rafting and kayaking are available on the Yellowstone River throughout the Paradise Valley. **Rubber Ducky River Rentals,** 4 Mount Baldy Dr. (www.riverservices.com; ✆ 406/222-3746), provides guided trips June through September, or will rent boats and equipment and provide river shuttles. Call for current schedules and rates.

Seeing the Sights

The main attractions in downtown Livingston are its two museums, both of which contain gift shops.

Livingston Depot Center ★ This is a beautifully restored 1902 Northern Pacific railway depot, built in handsome Italianate style, that is one of the most stunning railroad stations I've ever seen (it was designed by the same architects who designed Grand Central Station in New York City). The depot houses a museum with exhibits that concentrate on the history of the railroad and how it contributed to the development of the area. There are videos and interactive displays in this thoroughly modern look at the olden days, and the museum also hosts changing exhibits on some aspect of local history, such as explorers Lewis and Clark (the depot is a designated stop on the Lewis and Clark Trail) or the story of Montana's railroads.

200 W. Park St. www.livingstonmuseums.org. ✆ *406/222-2300.* Free admission. June–Sept Mon–Sat 9am–5pm; Sun 1–5pm. Closed Oct–May.

Yellowstone Gateway Museum of Park County Located in a historic school, this museum offers artifacts from Livingston's early days—including an 1889 train caboose and a Yellowstone National Park stagecoach—and exhibits of the pre-historic people who lived in this area some 10,000 years ago.

118 W. Chinook St. www.livingstonmuseums.org. ✆ **406/222-4184.** $4 adults, $3.50 seniors, $3 children 6–12, free for kids 5 and under. May–Aug daily 10am–5pm; Mar–Apr and Sept–Dec Thurs–Sat 10am–5pm.

Art Galleries

Livingston is a center of Western art and artists, and there are about a dozen galleries in town. For Western wildlife and fly-fishing art, try the **Visions West Gallery,** at 108 S. Main St. (www.visionswestgallery.com; ✆ **406/222-0337**), with woodcarvings, bronzes, and original oils. You'll find the work of Russell Chatham, a Livingston artist known for his oils and lithographs of Western landscapes, at the **Chatham Fine Art Gallery,** 120 N. Main St. (www.russellchatham.com; ✆ **406/222-1566**). The **Danforth Gallery,** 106 N. Main St. (www.pcfadanforth.org; ✆ **406/222-6510**), is a nonprofit gallery of contemporary Western art that changes its exhibits every month in the summer.

Where to Stay

Right across from Livingston's downtown depot, the **Murray Hotel,** 201 W. Park St. (www.murrayhotel.com; ✆ **406/222-1350**), opened in 1904 and has since put up everyone from director Sam Peckinpah to the queen of Denmark. Off the lobby, there's a good restaurant and a classic Western bar. Double rates are $79 to $98; suites are $139 to $339 for a two-bedroom, two-bath unit with a kitchen. Among the chains in town are **Rodeway Inn,** 102 Rogers Lane (✆ **406/222-6320**), a woodsy motel with a candy shop on-site and double rates of $69 to $149, and the **Best Western Yellowstone Inn and Conference Center,** 1515 W. Park St. (www.theyellowstoneinn.com; ✆ **800/770-1874** or 406/222-6110), with a long list of facilities and amenities and rooms for $89 to $135 double.

Chico Hot Springs Resort ★★ Rambling over 150 magnificent acres in the Paradise Valley, just 30 miles north of Yellowstone National Park, Chico offers a taste of gentility, cowboy style. The hot springs were discovered in 1876. The lodge opened in June 1900 and has been going strong ever since. There's a bewildering variety of lodgings, from small rooms that share a bathroom to newer deluxe rooms, plus rustic log cabins, a standalone caboose-turned-lodging, and a five-bedroom, two-bathroom private house. The three-story original Main Lodge is furnished mostly with antiques and houses the casually elegant restaurant (p. 224). Two open-air mineral hot-springs pools are just outside and are open daily from 6am to midnight year-round. Most rooms have high-speed Internet access. In the film *Rancho Deluxe*—screenplay by local resident Tom McGuane—Sam Waterston and Jeff Bridges soak in Chico's hot pool in their cowboy hats.

1 Chico Rd., Pray, MT 59065. www.chicohotsprings.com. ✆ **800/468-9232** or 406/333-4933. Fax 406/333-4964. 110 units. $124–$129 double; $55–$93 double with shared bathroom; $179–$225 suite; $79–$225 cabin; $169–$355 private house. AE, DISC, MC, V. Pets accepted ($20 per pet, per stay). **Amenities:** 2 restaurants (see "Where to Eat," below); saloon; 2 outdoor hot-springs pools; Wi-Fi (free). *In room:* Kitchen (in some), no phone.

Mountain Sky Guest Ranch ★★ ☺ This guest ranch sits among 5,000 acres and is just 30 miles from the north entrance of Yellowstone and about an hour's drive from Bozeman. Weeklong stays focus on outdoor activities such as white-water rafting, riding, and hiking. Summers are popular with families (couples would do better coming in fall or spring), and the kids' camp program keeps the young ones busy. Individual log cabins come in various one-, two-, or three-bedroom configurations; the two-bed/two-bathroom Granite is popular, as is P3, with its big living room, three bedrooms, and view over the property. Yoga and massage are offered, but keep in mind that the latter fills up quickly, so sign up for your time slots when you check in. Dining is community style, so if you don't know anyone at the start of your trip, you'll be sure to leave with at least a few new friends.

P.O. Box 1219, Emigrant, MT 59027. www.mtnsky.com. ℭ **800/548-3392** or 406/333-4911. 32 cabins. Weekly rates mid-June to late Aug adults $3,460–$5,000, ages 7–12 $2,930–$4,310, ages 18 months–6 $2,275–$3,460, and ages 17 months and under $725; early May to mid-June and late Aug to mid-Oct adults only $335–$365 double. Rates include all meals, beverages, gratuities, and on-ranch activities, such as hiking, horseback riding, and pond fishing. MC, V. Closed mid-Oct to late Apr or early May. From Bozeman, take I-90 east, then U.S. 89 south; ranch is 7 miles past Emigrant. **Amenities:** Restaurant; bar; children's programs; fitness center; outdoor Jacuzzi; heated outdoor pool; sauna; outdoor tennis court; Wi-Fi (free). *In room:* A/C, hair dryer, no phone.

CAMPING

There are plenty of camping opportunities in the Gallatin National Forest, including **Pine Creek** and **West Boulder** campgrounds to the south of town toward Yellowstone National Park. For information, contact the Yellowstone-Livingston Ranger District, 5242 U.S. 89 S., Livingston (www.fs.usda.gov/gallatin; ℭ **406/222-1892**).

Nine miles south of Livingston is the **Livingston/Paradise Valley KOA,** 163 Pine Creek Rd. (ℭ **800/562-2805** or 406/222-0992). Open from May to mid-October, the facility boasts an indoor heated pool, a snack bar, liquefied petroleum (LP) gas sales, and a bathhouse. The campground is situated along the Yellowstone River, with shady sites that cost $25 to $30 for tents and $20 to $41 for RVs. Cabins range from $65 to $150 a night. **Yellowstone's Edge,** 3502 U.S. 89 S., Livingston (www.mtrv.com; ℭ **800/865-7322** or 406/333-4036), is located on a bluff overlooking the Yellowstone River. Open from May to mid-October, it has both pull-through sites and back-in sites along the river for RVs, plus grassy tent sites and a lodge with a store, game room, laundry room, and bathhouse. There's also a dump station and LP gas available. RV sites cost $44 to $49. A fully furnished cabin, the River Suite, rents for $160 for the first night and $125 each additional night.

Where to Eat

The Sport Bar & Grill, 114 S. Main St., Livingston (www.thesportbarandgrill.com; ℭ **406/222-3800**) is a great casual spot for a beer and a burger; they serve up beer exclusively from the local Neptune Brewery.

The Chico Dining Room ★★★ CONTINENTAL The Chico Hot Springs Resort is 30 miles north of Gardiner, but if you're in the area, stop here for some of the best food in the Greater Yellowstone Ecosystem and a soak in this resort's hot springs. The carnivorous traveler will enjoy the selection of locally sourced top-drawer beef, the pine nut–crusted Alaskan halibut is a seafood aficionado's dream, and wine lovers won't be disappointed one bit by the award-winning list. Many of the incredibly fresh veggies originate in the resort's garden and greenhouse, and the menu always includes a vegetarian selection. You'll want to linger over the food, so consider a night's stay.

Old Chico Rd., Pray. www.chicohotsprings.com. ✆ **406/333-4933.** Reservations recommended. Main courses $25–$40. AE, DISC, MC, V. Summer daily 5:30–10pm; winter Sun–Thurs 5:30–9pm, Fri–Sat 5:30–10pm; Sun brunch 8:30–11:30am.

Grand Hotel ★ LAMB/SEAFOOD   This beautiful restaurant is located in downtown Big Timber, about 30 miles east of Livingston, in an 1890 hotel that has been beautifully restored. The ingenious menu lists starters such as elk *rellenos* and calamari tempura, before giving way to main dishes such as herb-roasted racks of lamb, "butterknife" filets, and mountain morel-crusted chicken breasts. The restaurant has won the *Wine Spectator* award of excellence numerous times for its all-American wine list.

139 McLeod St., Big Timber. www.thegrand-hotel.com. ✆ **406/932-4459.** Lunch and brunch $5–$12; dinner $17–$35. DISC, MC, V. Sun–Fri 11am–2pm; daily 5–9pm.

Second Street Bistro ★★ FRENCH/AMERICAN   This slick, stylish eatery, in the lobby of the Murray Hotel, is the cream of the Livingston culinary crop, serving a creative, simple menu of French-inspired plates with an emphasis on local ingredients. Appetizers include escargot, fried brie, and of course French fries, while main courses include individual gourmet pizzas and hearty American standards (meatloaf and pork chops) as well as steaks, pastas, and salads. There is a voluminous wine list, as well as a full bar.

123 N. 2nd St., in the Murray Hotel, Livingston. www.secondstreetbistro.com. ✆ **406/222-9463.** Reservations recommended. Main courses and pizzas $12–$29. AE, DISC, MC, V. Daily 5–9pm. Closed Mon in winter.

RED LODGE & THE ABSAROKA-BEARTOOTH WILDERNESS

60 miles SW of Billings; 62 miles NW of Cody, Wyoming

Nestled in a steep valley at the edge of the Absaroka-Beartooth Wilderness and surrounded by the spectacular Beartooth Mountains, the community of Red Lodge is not quite a tourist town, not quite a destination ski resort, but still not the sleepy little town it once was, either. It has elements of all three, giving it a homey and still busy feel. While it is slowly losing its small-town identity in favor of a resort persona, this hasn't happened completely.

Founded as a coal-mining community in the late 1880s, it did fairly well until the mines closed in the 1930s. Today it's the beautiful scenery and outdoor activities around Red Lodge that attract us. It doesn't hurt that the town sits at the northern end of the Beartooth National Scenic Byway, which the late Charles Kuralt called the most beautiful road in America.

Essentials

GETTING THERE   To reach Red Lodge, you'll have to fly into Billings's **Logan International Airport** (www.flybillings.com; ✆ 406/247-8609). From Billings, take I-94 west to Laurel, about 16 miles, then go south on U.S. 212/310. The route diverges after about 12 miles at the small town of Rockvale. Follow U.S. 212 southwest 44 miles to Red Lodge. Rental cars are plentiful at Billings's airport (see p. 232). For **road conditions** concerning the Red Lodge area and closures of the Beartooth National Scenic Byway, call ✆ **800/226-7623** or 511 on your mobile phone.

VISITOR INFORMATION   Contact the **Red Lodge Area Chamber of Commerce,** 601 N. Broadway, P.O. Box 988, Red Lodge, MT 59068 (www.redlodge chamber.com; ✆ **888/281-0625** or 406/446-1718).

Getting Outside

Many of the outdoor activities in these parts take place in Custer National Forest. For information, contact the **Beartooth Ranger District Office** of Custer National Forest, at the south end of town along U.S. 212 (HC 49, P.O. Box 3420, Red Lodge, MT 59068; www.fs.fed.us/r1/custer; ✆ **406/446-2103**). The office is open daily from 8am to 5pm in summer, and Monday through Friday 8am to 4:30pm in winter.

BIKING

The area around Red Lodge offers wonderful trails for biking. **Beartooth Bike Tours** (www.beartoothbiketours.com; ✆ **406/426/0787**), offers a variety of tours, taking riders to the top of the Beartooth National Scenic Byway (in a bus), then letting riders cycle downhill on the scenic road; bike tours cost $45–$50 per person.

CROSS-COUNTRY SKIING

Cross-country skiing is available at the **Red Lodge Nordic Center** (www.beartooth trails.org/nordic-center), just a few miles northwest of the town of Red Lodge. There are about 10 miles of groomed trails here; the fee is $5 per person. Equipment can be rented from the **Sylvan Peak Mountain Shop** (✆ **406/446-1770**) in Red Lodge.

DOWNHILL SKIING

Red Lodge Mountain Resort (P.O. Box 750, Red Lodge, MT 59068; www.red lodgemountain.com; ✆ **800/444-8977** or 406/446-2610) is a relatively small, family-oriented ski area. But it's growing: The skiable terrain includes 1,600 acres of mountain, with a vertical drop of 2,400 feet. There are about 70 trails, with 17% of the terrain for beginners, 45% intermediate, and 38% advanced and expert. Of the eight lifts, two are high-speed quads. An average of 250 inches of snow falls each year, plus Red Lodge has one of the largest snowmaking operations in the Rockies. Lift

AND THEY'RE OFF . . . TO THE pig RACES?

Bored with the rodeo? Horse racing seems ho-hum? Just head down to the **Bear Creek Saloon & Steakhouse** (www.redlodge.com/bearcreek; ✆ **406/446-3481**); behind the bar is Bearcreek Downs, site of the famed local pig races.

After the famous fires in Yellowstone in 1988 created a slow tourist season, the Bear Creek Saloon & Steakhouse owners decided that a **pig race** might generate some visitor interest. There was some question over whether the races were legal, but the Montana legislature stepped in and said pig races were okay by them, provided the proceeds went to

charity. So Bearcreek Downs porkers are sending Carbon County students to college—more than $75,000 has gone for scholarships so far. Pig races are held Thursday through Sunday at 7pm, from Memorial Day to Labor Day.

Even if you don't come for the races, the Bear Creek Saloon & Steakhouse is a great place to eat. It's an authentic Western tavern, and the grub is mostly beef. Prices range from $7.50 to $28, and food is served Thursday through Sunday from 5 to 10pm. The saloon is 7 miles east of Red Lodge on County Road 308.

tickets cost $49 for adults, $41 for seniors 65 to 69, $42 for juniors 13 to 18, and $19 for children 6 to 12 (free for kids 5 and under and seniors 70 and over); half-day tickets are also available. The season usually runs from late November to early April, with hours of 9am to 4pm.

GOLF

The **Red Lodge Mountain Golf Course** (© **406/446-3344**) is notorious for swallowing golf balls. Water comes into play on 13 of the 18 holes. The signature hole is the 238-yard, par-3 no. 15, where you hit to an island green from an elevated tee about 80 feet above the hole. Adult greens fees are $43 to $56 for 18 holes, cart included.

HIKING

There are some popular and challenging day hikes not far from Red Lodge. Drive south on Route 212 about 10 miles to County Road 2346, then 2 miles down that road to the **Lake Fork of Rock Creek.** From here, you can do a full loop of 19 miles to the West Fork of Rock Creek trail head (or do it as an overnight backpacking trip), or just walk up a few miles to some great fishing in the streams and lakes along the way and return.

Other popular hikes leave from the trail head at the **West Fork of Rock Creek.** Head west on Red Lodge Mountain Resort's access road, known locally as Ski Run Road. When the road forks, stay left and continue for several miles past a number of campgrounds. The road turns to gravel and ends at the West Fork trail head. The hike from here to Timberline Lakes is a moderate 9 miles round-trip. If you're not feeling that energetic, you can hike for about a mile to a picturesque waterfall. The fishing in Lake Mary near the trail is very good.

The **Absaroka-Beartooth Wilderness area** is a 950,000-acre wilderness that extends from the boundary of Yellowstone through two national forests. It's some of the most spectacular country in the Lower 48 states. Because of its proximity to the park, it is heavily used. There are lots of great hikes, incredible vistas, and pristine lakes with excellent trout fishing. **Granite Peak,** at 12,807 feet, is the tallest mountain in Montana, but it's only one of the 28 mountains topping 12,000 feet in the Absaroka-Beartooth.

For information about the above trails, contact the **Beartooth Ranger District Office** (see "Getting Outside," above).

Seeing the Sights

When it's open, the **Beartooth National Scenic Byway,** a 64-mile stretch of U.S. 212 from Red Lodge to Cooke City, is an incredible road that takes you to almost 11,000 feet elevation. Make sure a camera is handy when Pilot Peak comes into view, just outside Cooke City.

Beartooth Nature Center The Beartooth Nature Center is the only nature center in Montana that provides a home exclusively for animals that have been injured, orphaned, or too accustomed to humans to be returned to the wild. Residents, about 60 at a recent count, include mountain lions, wolves, coyotes, black bears, bison, eagles, and other animals native to Montana.

615 2nd Ave. E., Red Lodge. www.beartoothnaturecenter.org. © **406/446-1133.** $7 adults, $6 seniors 55 and older, $3 children 5–15, free for children 4 and under. May–Sept daily 10am–5pm; Oct–Apr daily 10am–2pm.

Carbon County Historical Society Museum Highlights of this well-run and interesting museum include a simulated coal mine that recalls Red Lodge's underground past, and the Greenough Collection of cowboy and rodeo gear. There's also a Crow Indian tipi, a mountain man camp, and pioneer displays. This is the place to find out more about "Liver Eatin'" Johnston, who got his name because . . . no, it's too repulsive. You'll have to find out for yourself.

224 N. Broadway at 8th Ave., Red Lodge. www.carboncountyhistory.org. ℂ **406/446-3667.** $5 adults, $3 students, free for children 5 and under. Memorial Day to Labor Day Mon–Sat 10am–6pm, Sun 11am–3pm; rest of year Thurs–Fri 10am–5pm, Sat 11am–3pm.

Where to Stay

In addition to the properties discussed below, I recommend the **Comfort Inn of Red Lodge,** 612 N. Broadway, Red Lodge, MT 59068 (ℂ **406/446-4469**), which charges $140 to $160 double in peak season.

Chateau Rouge The Chateau Rouge offers excellent accommodations at a very reasonable price, especially for families. Though run like a motel, the Chateau Rouge is actually a collection of privately owned condominiums. Most are two-story, two-bedroom affairs with a living room (with a fireplace) and kitchen on the first floor and the sleeping rooms upstairs. The two-story condos have large, fully appointed kitchens, while the studios have small but complete kitchens. All are attractively decorated and maintained. The only drawback—a minor one, in our opinion—is that they are not air-conditioned, which can be uncomfortable on those rare summer days when the mountain temperatures reach the 90s (30s Celsius).

1505 S. Broadway, Red Lodge, MT 59068. www.chateaurouge.com. ℂ **800/926-1601** or 406/446-1601. Fax 406/446-1602. 24 units. $89–$119 double studio; $125–$149 double 2-bedroom condo. Lower rates in spring and fall. AE, DC, DISC, MC, V. **Amenities:** Indoor Jacuzzi; indoor pool. In room: TV, kitchen/kitchenette, Wi-Fi (free).

The Pollard ★★ Built in 1893 by the Rocky Fork Coal Company at an initial cost of $20,000, the Pollard has undergone a magnificent restoration a century later, integrating modern conveniences with historical character and elegance. It has been a stopover for a number of Old West celebrities, including Buffalo Bill Cody, Calamity Jane, and Jeremiah "Liver Eatin'" Johnston. The Pollard has a three-story gallery with a wood-burning fireplace. No two rooms are exactly alike, but most are large, done with manly oak furniture and ladylike flower-print comforters. Six have balconies overlooking the lobby; many have Jacuzzi tubs. The entire operation is first class. For fine dining, the **Vintage One Bistro** opened in 2011 (see p. 230).

2 N. Broadway, Red Lodge, MT 59068. www.thepollard.com. ℂ **800/765-5273** or 406/446-0001. Fax 406/446-0002. 38 units. $95–$200 double; $270–$295 suite. Lower rates spring and fall. Rates include full breakfast. AE, DISC, MC, V. **Amenities:** 2 restaurants; lounge; health club; indoor Jacuzzi; room service; sauna. In room: A/C, TV/VCR, hair dryer, Wi-Fi (free).

Rock Creek Resort ★★ This property was built in 1963 as a dormitory for members of an international ski-racing camp founded by owner Pepi Gramshammer. Rock Creek retains much of the ski atmosphere that produced it, although the ski hill is a good 5 miles away, plus it's got all sorts of warm-weather recreation (a stocked trout pond, horseshoe pits, and a soccer field). The cedar-sided Beartooth Lodge, the main building, boasts a huge fireplace made of river rock and windows that offer mountain views. A wide variety of accommodations decorated in a Western theme are available, from mountain lodge–style units with lots of wood, to luxurious

Red Lodge & the Absaroka-Beartooth Wilderness

SOUTH-CENTRAL MONTANA

condominiums and three-bedroom town houses. Many units have wood-burning stoves or fireplaces, patios or balconies, or a private hot tub. It would be hard to find a room here without a wonderful view.

6380 U.S. 212 S., Red Lodge, MT 59068. www.rockcreekresort.com. ⓒ**800/667-1119** or 406/446-1111. Fax 406/237-9851. 87 units. $140–$375 double. AE, DC, DISC, MC, V. From Red Lodge, drive 5 miles south on U.S. 212. **Amenities:** 2 restaurants; 2 lounges; bike rental; weight room; Jacuzzi; indoor pool; sauna; 4 tennis courts; volleyball court. *In room:* TV, hair dryer, kitchenette, Wi-Fi (free).

CAMPING

There are 16 Forest Service campgrounds available in the Red Lodge area, with sites for more than 700 campers. Many of the larger campgrounds accept reservations through the **National Recreation Reservation Service** (www.recreation.gov; ⓒ 877/444-6777), and the rest are first come, first served. For information, contact the **Beartooth Ranger District Office** of Custer National Forest, at the south end of town along U.S. 212 (ⓒ **406/446-2103**).

Those seeking commercial campgrounds, with all the usual RV hookups and other amenities, can head to the **Red Lodge KOA,** 7464 U.S. 212 (ⓒ **800/562-7540** or 406/446-2364). It has grassy and shady sites, a heated outdoor pool, and a convenience store, and charges $27 to $34 for tents, $35 to $45 for RVs, and $55 to $60 for basic cabins. It's typically open from mid-May through September.

Where to Eat

In addition to the restaurants discussed below, see the box "And They're Off . . . to the Pig Races?" above for information on the **Bear Creek Saloon & Steakhouse.** **Bogart's,** 11 S. Broadway (ⓒ 406/446-1784), offers pizza, sandwiches, and Mexican fare. A good bet for a burger, a bowl of chili, a beer, or a ballgame (or any combination thereof) is **Foster and Logan's Pub and Grill,** 17 S. Broadway (ⓒ 406/446-9080). The **Red Lodge Ales Brewery,** 1445 N. Broadway (www.redlodgeales.com; ⓒ 406/446-0243), offers up a variety of sandwiches and salads, along with their home-brewed beers. **Café Regis** (www.caferegis.com; ⓒ **406/446-1941**) is a great spot for breakfast and lunch, with hearty local, organic fare.

Bridge Creek Backcountry Kitchen and Wine Bar ★★ NEW AMERICAN Bridge Creek is a local favorite, with a widely varied, moderately priced menu. Lunches include wraps, salads, sandwiches on fresh-baked breads, and homemade soups, including an excellent clam chowder. At dinner, you'll find creative seafood, chicken, beef, and pasta dishes, as well as hand-tossed gourmet pizzas. The house salad with huckleberry-balsamic vinaigrette is a must. The wine bar is a small, bright room with an extensive wine list that for several years has received the *Wine Spectator* Award of Excellence. The atmosphere is casual, sort of California cafe with a Western flavor. Open at 11am daily, a Starbucks coffee bar here serves a wide selection of espresso, cappuccino, latte, mocha, and iced drinks, plus freshly baked pastries, and offers free Wi-Fi. There is also a wine shop and specialty market up front.

116 S. Broadway Ave. www.eatfooddrinkwine.com. ⓒ **406/446-9900.** Lunch main courses $9–$23; dinner $10–$33. DISC, MC, V. Sun–Thurs 11am–9pm; Fri–Sat 11am–10pm. Closed Sun–Mon fall to spring.

Old Piney Dell ★★ 🏠 SWISS/AMERICAN Located in a 1920s homesteader's cabin on the banks of Rock Creek, this is where locals come for a special evening. If you like Wiener schnitzel, this place is for you—the veal is lightly breaded and delicately pan-fried to perfection. The steaks and pretzel-crusted pork chops are other specialties, and chicken and lamb are also on the menu. Ask about the nightly specials.

In Rock Creek Resort. www.rockcreekresort.com. ✆ **406/446-1196.** Reservations recommended. Dinner main courses $14–$30. AE, DISC, MC, V. Mon–Thurs 5:30–9pm; Fri–Sat 5:30–10pm; Sun 9am–1pm. Closed Sun–Wed Nov–May. From Red Lodge, drive 5 miles south on U.S. 212.

Vintage One Bistro ★★ AMERICAN   Located inside the Pollard hotel, this elegant fine dining option is a member of the Western Sustainability Exchange, serving locally-sourced organic food. Start with the antipasto platter which features local specialties, like homemade wild game charcuterie from the nearby 4th Avenue Meat Market, house-made pickles, and smoked trout spread with crostini and cheese. Excellent main dishes include a heaping portion of succulent prime rib of beef, slow-roasted duck leg confit, and salmon wellington. There are several vegetarian options on the menu, like wild mushroom risotto and quinoa-stuffed squash. Complement your meal with a glass of wine from the expansive wine list or a vintage cocktail from the bar, like a Pimm's Cup or a Sazerac. The restaurant is also open for breakfast daily.

In the Pollard. www.thepollard.com. ✆ **406/446-0001.** Reservations recommended. Dinner main courses $16–$32. AE, MC, V. Fri–Tues 7–11am and 5:30–9pm; Wed–Thurs 7–11am.

BILLINGS & EASTERN MONTANA

The plains of eastern Montana offer a more subtle beauty than the rugged mountains to the west. A land of rolling hills, dusty bluffs and badlands, and the occasional rock-walled canyon, this is classic cattle and wheat country, with grass thick and green in spring, brown and dry by fall, and blanketed by snow in winter. Temperatures can be extreme: hot in the summer under a blazing sun, and bitter cold in the winter, dipping below zero for long stretches.

Eastern Montana's history is rich: Lewis and Clark trekked along the Missouri River, and one of the most famous battles of the American West, the Battle of the Little Bighorn, was fought here.

In the old days, travel in eastern Montana was defined by the railroads. Virtually every town with 300 people and a tavern could be reached by either the main line or a spur. But the romantic days of rail travel have been replaced by the automobile, and interstates have triumphed over the rails. I-94 sweeps across the state west to east, I-15 cuts through the Rockies from Idaho to the Canadian border, and I-90 dips south from near Billings to the Crow Reservation in Sheridan, Wyoming.

BILLINGS

104 miles W of Cody, Wyoming; 123 miles N of Sheridan, Wyoming; 142 miles E of Bozeman; 339 miles E of Missoula

The most populous city in Montana with about 105,000 residents, Billings might well be the most urban place in Montana or Wyoming. You'll find real shopping malls here, along with the occasional five o'clock traffic jam and the tallest free-standing brick building in the world (the 23-story Crowne Plaza). Since its 1880s development by Frederick Billings as a railroad town, the city has evolved into the economic and industrial hub for the entire region.

Once a booming oil town, as well as a crossroads for the railroads, Billings has now positioned itself as the progressive medical center for all of eastern Montana, the Dakotas, and Wyoming. The economy is still centered on energy and agriculture, but downtown Billings boasts new banks and contemporary business centers, with many historic buildings enjoying restorations since the turn of the 21st century. Billings also has its share of scenic splendor: From the rimrocks surrounding the city, you can see the Pryor Mountains, the Bighorns, and the majestic Beartooths to the west.

Essentials

GETTING THERE   Billings's **Logan International Airport** (www.flybillings.com; *☎* **406/247-8609**) is the state's busiest, located about 2 miles north of downtown. Service is provided by **Alaska/Horizon, Allegiant, Delta/SkyWest, Frontier, Northwest,** and **United.** Also here is **Gulfstream International Airlines** (www. flygia.com; *☎* **800/499-7450**), flying in eastern Montana to such cities as Glendive, Havre, and Wolf Point.

If you're traveling by car, I-90 connects Billings to Bozeman, Butte, and Missoula in the west before crossing into Idaho; I-90 east heads southeast into Wyoming. I-94 branches off I-90 10 miles east of town and runs northeast through Miles City and Glendive before reaching North Dakota. U.S. 87 heads north out of Billings to Roundup, and U.S. 310 goes south to Lovell, Wyoming.

VISITOR INFORMATION   The **Billings Chamber of Commerce & Convention and Visitors Bureau,** 815 S. 27th St. (P.O. Box 31177), Billings, MT 59107 (www.visitbillings.com; *☎* **406/245-4111**), has brochures, maps, and area information. Travel Montana's **Custer Country** (www.custercountry.com; *☎* **800/346-1876**) is another information source.

GETTING AROUND   Billings's downtown street system might be a bit confusing at first but can be mastered if you remember that Montana Avenue is the dividing line between north and south. Numbered avenues run parallel to Montana, starting with 1st Avenue North and 1st Avenue South, which are located 1 block away on each side of it, and increasing from there. The numbered streets run perpendicular to Montana, their names changing from North to South as they cross it, and increase numerically from east to west. The heart of downtown lies north of Montana and is relatively compact. Its boundaries are North 27th and North 29th streets and 1st and 6th avenues North.

To access downtown from I-90, which skims the southern edge of the city, take exit 450 and go north on 27th Street; the Business Loop follows Montana Avenue between exits 446 and 452. Coming from the north, from Roundup, U.S. 87 turns into a four-lane road before heading west into the Heights, the northeastern part of the city. Follow this road into downtown, or turn right on Airport Road to reach Logan International Airport.

The best way to see Billings is to drive. Car-rental companies at the airport include **Alamo/National** (*☎* **800/227-7368**), **Enterprise** (*☎* **800/261-7331**), **Hertz** (*☎* **800/654-3131**), and **Thrifty/Dollar** (*☎* **800/847-4389**).

The city bus service is **MET Transit** (*☎* **406/657-8218**), with buses running from 5:50am to 6:40pm weekdays and 8:10am to 5:45pm Saturday. Fare is $1.25. Taxi service is available from **City Cab** (*☎* **406/252-8700**), **Yellow Cab** (*☎* **406/245-3033**), and **Montana Custom Tours** (www.montanacustomtours. com; *☎* **406/860-7439**).

Getting Outside

Montana Fun Adventures Tours (www.montanafunadventures.com; *☎* **888/618-4386** or 406/254-7180) offers historical tours of Billings and vicinity, as well as

Black Otter Trail Scenic Drive

The Black Otter Trail Scenic Drive, following about 3 miles along the edge of the sheer rimrock overlooking Billings, affords a spectacular view of the city and the three mountain ranges in the distance. To get there, take Montana Avenue east to U.S. 87 and turn left (north). After you pass the MetraPark arena complex on your right, turn left onto Airport Road and, shortly thereafter, left again onto Black Otter Trail. Boot Hill Cemetery is at this end of the road and contains 40 of the unlucky residents of the town of Coulson, most of whom "died with their boots on." It's also the final resting place of the famous scout Yellowstone Kelly, who asked to be buried here above the land he scouted.

2-day packages into Yellowstone National Park. **Total Transportation** (www.mttotal transportation.com; ✆ **800/698-1778** or 406/252-1778) offers trolley, carriage, and bus tours.

FISHING

Though the Yellowstone River runs through the city, it is wide, busy, and often muddy. The best nearby fishing is in the **Bighorn Canyon National Recreation Area** (see p. 242, later in this chapter), 83 miles southeast of town. Fishing guides come and go pretty often in the Billings area; to find a local one, the best bet is to ask at the **Base Camp,** 1730 Grand Ave. (www.thebasecamp.com; ✆ **406/248-4555**).

GOLF

Lake Hills Golf Club (www.lakehillsgolf.com; ✆ **406/252-9244**), **EagleRock Golf Course** (www.eaglerockgolfcourse.com; ✆ **406/655-4445**), and the **Peter Yegen, Jr., Golf Club** (www.yegengolfclub.com; ✆ **406/656-8099**) are the three 18-hole public golf courses in Billings, with greens fees of $25 to $43, cart included. The par-3, 9-hole **Exchange City Golf Course** (✆ **406/652-2553**) has greens fees of $12.

NEARBY PARKS & NATURE PRESERVES

In town, there is a good **multiuse trail system** popular with joggers, walkers, and bikers. Contact **Billings Parks & Public Lands** (www.prpl.info; ✆ **406/657-8371**) for information.

An unusual side trip is to **Pictograph Cave State Park** (www.pictographcave. org; ✆ **406/247-7342**), where you can see cave paintings made by prehistoric people more than 4,500 years ago. There are more than 100 pictographs, in red and black pigments made from ashes, clay, and animal fat. The meaning of the designs is continually debated—were they ceremonial, or perhaps celebrations of a successful hunt or battle? (There are many images of shield-bearing warriors.) A short but fairly steep interpretive trail leads up to the caves, which are more like large stone alcoves than caves in the usual sense. They lie in a classic, sheer, broad sandstone canyon inhabited by rabbits and an occasional rattlesnake—so stay on the trail. From Billings, take I-90 east to exit 452 and follow the signs for 6 miles. The park is open May 1 to September 30 daily from 9am to 7pm, with shorter hours the rest of the year and an entrance fee of $5 per vehicle ($3 daily for walk- or bike-in visitors).

Billings

MONTANA

Helena ★

Billings

HOTELS
C'mon Inn **2**
Crowne Plaza Hotel Billings **8**
Dude Rancher Lodge **12**
Holiday Inn Grand Montana **3**
Josephine B&B **13**

ATTRACTIONS
Moss Mansion **6**
Peter Yegen, Jr. Yellowstone County Museum **5**
Pictograph State Park **19**
Western Heritage Center **9**
Yellowstone Art Museum **11**
ZooMontana **1**

RESTAURANTS
Bistro Enzo **4**
Juliano's **14**
King's Hat Drive-In **7**
McCormick Café **16**
Montana Brewing Company **15**
Q **17**
The Soup Place **10**
Walkers Grill **15**

SERVICES
Billings Chamber of Commerce & Visitors Bureau **18**

Locals go to nearby **Lake Elmo State Park,** 10 miles north of Billings on U.S. 87 (www.fwp.mt.gov; ✆ **406/247-2955**), for picnicking, swimming, windsurfing, fishing, and volleyball. Boat rentals and windsurfing lessons are available in the summer; gas-powered boats are prohibited. There is also a dog park. Entrance fee is also $5 per vehicle ($3 daily for walk- or bike-in visitors).

Seeing the Sights

To view some modern artists' contributions to decorating the West, drive the **Avenue of the Sculptures** along 27th Street (from I-90, take exit 450 to the airport) for an outdoor art show. The first work, *The Cattle Drive Monument,* is right outside the chamber of commerce's visitor center. *The Sheriff Webb Memorial Marker* is on the courthouse lawn, and finally, in front of the airport is the *Range Rider of the Yellowstone,* posed for by silent-screen cowboy actor William Hart. Also around downtown, visitors will spot more public art in the form of a number of colorful equines from 2002's "The Horse, Of Course!" fundraiser for the Billings Depot restoration.

Kids will enjoy **Geyser Park,** 4910 Southgate Dr. (www.geyserpark.net; ✆ **406/254-2510**), featuring video games, a climbing wall, a laser tag arena, and a pizzeria.

Moss Mansion ★   This massive red-sandstone mansion, built in 1901 for Billings banker Preston B. Moss, was designed by prominent New York architect Henry Janeway Hardenbergh. It has many European influences, including a Moorish entry, a Shakespearean library, and a French Louis XVI parlor. Oak and mahogany millwork gives an elegant feel to the upstairs bedrooms. The mansion, listed on the National Register of Historic Places, has been used in various TV miniseries and Hollywood films, and was featured on A&E's *America's Castles* in 1997. Visitors view a short video about Moss and early Billings before taking the 1-hour guided tour of the home. The Moss Mansion also hosts various events during the spring and summer months, and is elaborately decorated for Christmas.

914 Division St. www.mossmansion.com. ✆ **406/256-5100.** $7 adults, $5 seniors and students with ID, $3 children 6–12, free for children 5 and under. Summer guided tour every hour on the hour Mon–Sat 9am–4pm, Sun 1–3pm; winter daily 1–3pm, with expanded holiday hours from mid-Nov to Dec. Closed Thanksgiving, Christmas, and New Year's Day.

Peter Yegen, Jr., Yellowstone County Museum   Located next to the airport, this collection is housed in a century-old cabin, which has had such eminent visitors as Teddy Roosevelt and Buffalo Bill Cody. Rotating exhibits describe the history and diverse cultures of Montana and the Yellowstone River Basin, from prehistory through the 1950s. Changing exhibits of contemporary local and national artists are in the Landmarks Gallery. Also on the grounds: a vintage steam engine and a stuffed two-headed calf. The view of Billings and the surrounding countryside from the museum's deck is terrific.

1950 Terminal Circle, adjacent to Logan International Airport. www.yellowstonecountymuseum. org. ✆ **406/256-6811.** Free admission. Mon–Sat 10:30am–5:30pm; shorter winter hours. Closed Sun and national holidays.

Western Heritage Center   A lot of Western museums are just vast collections of dusty reminders of bygone eras. But this facility, an affiliate of the Smithsonian Institution, has done an excellent job of interpreting and editing its extensive collection, making the panoramic history of Western settlement accessible to casual visitors. In addition to the usual exhibits of the area's settlement by white people, the Heritage Center includes sensitive displays on the Crow tribe and on Japanese and

The only wildlife and botanical park within 500 miles of Billings, **ZooMontana** concentrates on northern plains wildlife, some of which you may see on your trip through the state. There are nature trails meandering among the natural habitats of red pandas, eastern gray wolves, Manchurian sika deer, bald eagles, great horned owls, and the North American river otter; there's a petting zoo in a farm and ranch setting.

Managed by the Beartooth Nature Center near Red Lodge, the zoo is also home to 2 of the 300 Siberian tigers remaining in the world, as well as to the retirees from a captive breeding program for black-footed ferrets, North America's rarest mammal. A state-of-the-art grizzly bear habitat opened in 2008.

Take exit 443 north off I-90, head northwest on King Avenue to Shiloh Road, and then go south (www.zoomontana.org; ℂ **406/652-8100**). Admission is $6.25 adults, $3.25 children 3 to 15, and $4.25 seniors 65 and over. May through late September, the zoo is open daily 10am to 5pm; late September through April daily 10am to 3pm.

---

other minority settlers. Interactive presentations include videos and recorded memories of three Yellowstone County homesteaders.

2822 Montana Ave. www.ywhc.org. ℂ **406/256-6809.** $5 adults, $3 students and seniors, $1 children 11 and under. Tues–Sat 10am–5pm.

Yellowstone Art Museum ★★　Montana art aficionados are justifiably proud of the Yellowstone Art Museum, a leader in the contemporary Western art movement. The museum showcases the best the new West has to offer, from Deborah Butterfield's ranch sculptures, to Russell Chatham's gauzy landscapes, to Rudy Autio's colorful, erotic ceramics. Additionally, the museum's permanent collection—more than 3,000 pieces— includes the largest public gathering of the drawings, paintings, books, and memorabilia of cowboy illustrator Will James, plus paintings and drawings by other historic regional artists such as J. H. Sharp and Charles M. Russell. Changing exhibitions have recently spotlighted Pulitzer Prize–winning photographs and contemporary Native American beadwork by Montana artist Molly Murphy. Expect to spend up to 2 hours.

401 N. 27th St. www.artmuseum.org. ℂ **406/256-6804.** $6 adults, $3 students and children 6–18, free for children 5 and under, $10 family. Tues–Sat 10am–5pm (Thurs–Fri until 8pm); Sun 11am–4pm.

Shopping

In the downtown area, the shopping district covers about 4 blocks on North 29th Street, Broadway, and 1st and 2nd avenues North. The area is heavy in the antiques line, but it also has a few boutiques and independent bookshops. For contemporary art, try the **Toucan Gallery,** 2505 Montana Ave. (ℂ 406/252-0122), in the city's historic district, offering prints, oils, handmade furniture, and ceramics. Open since 1919, the classic Western department store, where lots of real cowboys get their gear, is **Lou Taubert Ranch Outfitters** (ℂ 406/245-2248), at 123 Broadway. Another Western standby, carrying everything from feed to fine art, is **Shipton's Big R,** with locations at 216 N. 14th St. (ℂ 406/252-0503) and 2600 Gabel Rd. (ℂ 406/652-9118). If you're in the market for a top-of-the-line custom cowboy hat, call **Rand's Custom Hats,** 2205 1st Ave. N. (www.randhats.com; ℂ 800/346-9815). For outdoor clothing and equipment, check out **Base Camp** (ℂ 406/248-4555) at 1730

Grand Ave. The primary mall is **Rimrock Mall,** 300 S. 24th St. W. (www.rimrock mall.com; ☎ 406/656-3206), with Dillard's, a movie theater, and a wide range of national and local stores.

Where to Stay

In addition to the properties discussed below, you might consider the **Holiday Inn Grand Montana,** 5500 Midland Rd. (I-90 exit 446; ☎ **406/248-7701**), with double rates of $129 to $159; or the **C'mon Inn,** 2020 Overland Ave. (I-90 exit 446; ☎ **406/655-1100**), with double rates of $100 to $150.

Crowne Plaza Hotel Billings ★★ Declared the world's tallest free-standing brick building by the Brick Institute of America, this 23-story tower is like a beacon in the heart of downtown—you can see it from just about everywhere. The rooms are stylish and chic, with comfortable beds, plush chairs, and the best views around, and the list of amenities is comprehensive. The hotel caters to the business traveler—there's a 24-hour business center, rates are lowest on weekends, and the desks are huge—but it fits the bill for anyone who wants quick access to downtown. The restaurant on the 20th floor, **Montana Sky,** has great steaks and the best views in town. There is also a **Starbucks** off the lobby.

27 N. 27th St., Billings, MT 59101. www.crowneplaza.com. ☎ **800/588-7666** or 406/252-7400. Fax 406/252-2401. 289 units, including 3 suites. $149–$169 double; $500 suite; lower weekend rates. AE, DISC, MC, V. **Amenities:** Restaurant; lounge; concierge; exercise room; room service; 2 saunas. *In room:* A/C, TV, hair dryer, Wi-Fi (free).

Dude Rancher Lodge ⚑ Now on the National Register of Historic Places, the Dude Rancher has been offering real Western hospitality since it opened in 1949. Inside the weeping mortar walls, the rooms (which in turn surround an inner courtyard parking lot) are comfortable and quiet, with ranch oak furniture, cattle-brand carpeting, and king- and queen-size beds, or two doubles. Many have fridges and microwaves, so request one if you are in need. The motel's downtown location puts you within easy walking distance of numerous restaurants, shopping, banks, the library, and the Alberta Bair Theatre.

415 N. 29th St., Billings, MT 59101. www.duderancherlodge.com. ☎ **800/221-3302** or 406/259-5561. 57 units. $65–$110 double. AE, DISC, MC, V. **Amenities:** Restaurant; room service. *In room:* A/C, TV, fridge (in some), hair dryer, microwave (in some), Wi-Fi (free).

The Josephine Bed & Breakfast ★ The Josephine is housed in a 1912 Victorian built by a wealthy rancher to give his children access to schools in Billings. Named for a steamboat that once plied the waters of the Yellowstone River, the inn is located within walking distance of downtown, offering a quiet retreat amid Billings's urban bustle. Owners Bobbi and Harvey Bybee have installed high-speed Internet access, and there's a modern whirlpool tub in one room, but most rooms feature the classic claw-foot tubs familiar to Western movie buffs. The Captain's Room offers a masculine feel, from the pipes on the night table (but don't light one up; the entire inn is nonsmoking) to the four-poster bed. The other rooms have more feminine touches. There is a library, parlor, and dining room for breakfast, and a wraparound porch outside. Breakfasts are memorable: Harvey makes a terrific caramel-pecan French toast, and his sourdough pancakes aren't bad at all.

514 N. 29th St., Billings, MT 59101. www.thejosephine.com. ☎ **800/552-5898** or 406/248-5898. 5 units. $95–$170 double. AE, DISC, MC, V. *In room:* A/C, TV, Wi-Fi (free).

Where to Eat

For breakfast and lunch, we like the **McCormick Café,** 2419 Montana Ave. (⟨ **406/255-9555**⟩), and its offerings of eggs, crepes, sandwiches, pizza, and numerous vegetarian dishes. A classic drive-in known for its pork chop sandwiches and trademark UFO-shaped "flying burgers," **King's Hat Drive-In,** 105 S. 37th St. (⟨ **406/259-4746**⟩), is open Tuesday through Saturday; credit cards are not accepted. New to downtown is the **Soup Place,** 106 N. Broadway (⟨ **406/294-7687**⟩), which makes homemade soup (as well as sandwiches and soup-and-sandwich combos), with gumbo, Brunswick stew, and Cincinnati-style chili on the dinner menu.

Bistro Enzo ★ MEDITERRANEAN   The diverse and creative menu at this high-ceilinged restaurant on Billings's west side melds influences from not only the Mediterranean, but Asia and the Rockies as well: Entrees include Kobe burgers, Moroccan couscous, and Asian vegetarian pasta, as well as a rib-eye and good old macaroni and cream-Parmesan cheese. There is a seating area with booths and a bar on the main floor and a quieter upstairs loft. Homemade desserts include crème brûlée and a decadent chocolate popover with caramelized bananas and cappuccino cream. Beer and wine are available, but liquor is not.

1502 Rehberg Lane. www.bistroenzobillings.com. ⟨ **406/651-0999.** Main courses $12–$28. AE, DISC, MC, V. Tues–Sun 5–9pm.

Café de Camp ★★ AMERICAN   Once you get past the somewhat dodgy industrial setting and step inside Café de Camp, you'll find a small but homey dining room that's filled with intentionally mismatched chairs and quirky furnishings. A member of Montana's Western Sustainability Exchange, Café de Camp serves organic, locally-sourced food. The menu changes seasonally, but might include a variety of sweet and savory crepes (such as an Emu Carbonara crepe), sandwiches (like Strawberry Rhubarb Smoked Turkey Ciabatta), burgers (like the Real Montana Lamburger and the Local Bison Burger), and fish and meat entrees. For dessert, try the one-of-a-kind Pine Needle Marshmallow S'mores crepe, with home-made marshmallows, whiskey, Mexican Cacao truffles, and burnt graham cracker crumbs. The restaurant is planning to move to a new and much larger space on 2905 Montana Avenue in late-2012.

1404 6th Ave N. www.cafedecamp.com. ⟨ **406/256-7285.** Reservations not accepted. Main courses $9–$21. AE, MC, V. Tues–Sat 11am–2pm and 5:30–9pm. Closed Sun–Mon.

Juliano's ★★ NEW AMERICAN   One of the best restaurants in Montana, Juliano's serves excellent, original food in a casually elegant atmosphere. It's a little hard to categorize the food here. Chef Carl Kurokawa is a native of Hilo, Hawaii, and his menu is a fitting intersection between East and West. The menu changes monthly, but you can depend on it having the fresh Hawaiian fish that Kurokawa insists on flying in. For dinner, you might get locally raised lamb or Rocky Mountain elk, or maybe a beer-battered calamari steak. At lunch, there are salads—if you're feeling adventurous, try the crispy chicken and grapefruit salad—plus sandwiches and pasta dishes. The building was originally the stable of the sandstone "castle" next door, built in 1902. A pressed-tin ceiling with Bacchus hoisting a glass covers one of the dining rooms, and there is an outdoor patio for nice days. There is an extensive wine list—call for the dates of special wine dinners.

2912 7th Ave. N. ⟨ **406/248-6400.** Reservations recommended. Lunch $8–$11; dinner main courses $23–$30. AE, DISC, MC, V. Mon–Fri 11:30am–2pm; Wed–Sat 5:30–9pm. Closed Mon Jan–Feb.

10

BILLINGS & EASTERN MONTANA

Billings

Montana Brewing Company ★ ☺ MICROBREWERY A bustling bar and grill, Billings's downtown microbrewery has won a number of medals at the Great American Beer Fest, and it's easy to taste why. Their beers, brewed in vats behind the dining room, include Fat Belly Amber Ale, Whitetail Wheat, and several seasonal beers; nine are always available on draft. The food is pretty good, too, including pizza, fish and chips, enchiladas, and a gamut of burgers and sandwiches—including bison burgers and a burger served on a pretzel bun. Despite the noisy bar area and adjacent casino, this is a pretty good place for families, and there's a kids' menu to boot.

113 N. Broadway. www.montanabrewing.com. ✆ **406/252-9200.** Reservations accepted for large parties only. Main courses $7–$10. AE, DISC, MC, V. Daily 11am–11pm. Bar open later.

Q ★★ MEDITERRANEAN/CONTEMPORARY An anchor in the ongoing revitalization of Historic Montana Avenue, Q is sleek and hip, and feels more California than Montana. The room combines historic details—an original pressed-tin ceiling, for one—with contemporary design—suede wall panels, custom veneers, and striking yellow lamps. The menu meshes Mediterranean and Asian influences with a contemporary American slant: Entrees include pastas, steaks, salmon, and a few vegetarian dishes. The restaurant is attached to the **Carlin Martini Bar and Nightclub,** equally hip and serving a mean kamikaze martini.

2503 Montana Ave. www.qcuisine.com. ✆ **406/245-2503.** Reservations recommended. Main courses $10–$28. AE, DISC, MC, V. Mon–Sat 4:30–10pm.

Walkers Grill ★★ AMERICAN BISTRO Longtime Billings stalwart Walkers moved into posh new digs in 2004, taking over the first floor of a new brick loft building in the heart of downtown. Featuring the work of 26 different artists, the space itself is a masterwork of contemporary Western design, marked by barbed-wire chandeliers, wheat-field-inspired carpeting, a host stand made from a hitching post, and a bar made from a cattle guard. The food is also excellent: The menu, which changes several times a year, offers a bit of the exotic (such as house-made salmon pastrami) along with plenty of creative interpretations of local standards. You might find buffalo osso bucco, an herb-crusted veal chop, or Thai peanut spaghetti. A tapas menu of gourmet pizzas, appetizers, and small versions of main courses is also served. The wine list is extensive, including many French wines—often difficult or impossible to find on the plains.

2700 1st Ave. N. www.walkersgrill.com. ✆ **406/245-9291.** Reservations recommended. Main courses $16–$34; tapas $7–$14. AE, DISC, MC, V. Daily 5–10pm. Tapas bar Mon–Fri 4–11pm; Sat–Sun 5–11pm.

Billings After Dark

Playing host to productions and live music of all kinds, the **Alberta Bair Theater,** Broadway and 3rd. Ave. (www.albertabairtheater.org; ✆ 877/321-2074 or 406/256-6052), is the prime performing arts venue in Billings, recently hosting Don McLean and a touring production of *Young Frankenstein.* The **Rainbow Bar,** 2403 Montana Ave. (✆ 406/259-0047), has a reputation for stiff drinks; other diversions include shuffleboard and live music. **Hooligan's,** 109 N. Broadway (✆ 406/294-3495), is a good sports bar with an Irish theme. Beyond the **Montana Brewing Company** (see "Where to Eat," above), there are three breweries with tasting rooms—**Carter's Brewery,** 2526 Montana Ave., unit B (www.cartersbrewing.com; ✆ 406/252-0663); **Yellowstone Valley Brewing Company,** 2123-B 1st Ave. N., unit B (www.yellowstonevalleybrew.com; ✆ 406/245-0918); and **Angry Hank's,** 2405 1st Ave. N. (✆ 406/252-3370)—within easy walking distance of one another. Nearby is **Bones Brewing,** with a pub and restaurant at 1425 Broadwater (www.bonesbrewing.com; © 406/839-9231).

A Side Trip to Pompeys Pillar National Monument

A 150-foot-high sandstone butte 29 miles east of Billings holds the only concrete evidence left along the way of the famous journey of Lewis and Clark through the Louisiana Purchase. On July 25, 1806, Capt. William Clark carved his name and the date on the side of the rock. He noted in his famous journals for that day, "The nativs [sic] have ingraved [sic] on the face of this rock figures of animals & near which I marked my name and the day of the month and year." Clark then walked to the top and described the panoramic view of the river and plains that can be captured from that vantage. Clark had to scramble up through the yucca and sagebrush, but visitors now are aided by stairways and enthusiastic and informative volunteer guides who will point out the historic sites and wildlife—from ant lions to eagles' nests.

Halfway up a 120-foot stairway, Clark's name is now locked under a protective glass cabinet, but many others have added their names. The pillar was originally called Pompy's Tower by Clark, using the nickname he'd given the youngest member of their expedition, little Baptiste Charbonneau, the son of Sacajawea and Touissaint Charbonneau, the expedition guides. The boy traveled in Clark's dugout, and the captain called him "my boy Pomp." Continue up to the top of the stairway for incredible views and photo opportunities.

The monument, operated by the Bureau of Land Management, is open from Memorial Day to Labor Day, daily from 8am to 8pm; then into late September (and sometimes later, weather permitting) from 9am to 4pm; after that, you have to park a half-mile away and walk in. The fee is $7 per carload during the season, free at other times. The interactive multimedia exhibits at the modern visitor center are worth an hour of your time. There is also a film on Lewis and Clark regularly playing in the visitor center's theater. For more information, call the visitor center (© **406/875-2400**), or visit **www.pompeyspillar.org**. To get there, go 29 miles east of Billings to I-94 exit 23. The signage is somewhat confusing: Don't turn right to go to the town of Pompeys Pillar; go straight over the bridge to Pompeys Pillar National Monument.

THE CROW RESERVATION

54 miles E of Billings

The beautiful Crow Reservation—the Crow People call themselves the Apsáalooke, "Children of the Large-Beaked Bird"—encompasses over 9 million acres in southeastern Montana. It consists of seven main communities, of which Crow Agency, on I-90, is the hub of tribal management and government.

One of the main Indian Nation events of the summer-long powwow trail is **Crow Fair,** held here the third week in August. Powwows are social gatherings featuring traditional food, dress, and dances. Visitors are welcome at powwows, but flash photography is not allowed during contests, and you should always ask dancers for permission before taking their photographs. For more information, contact the **Tribal Headquarters,** P.O. Box 159, Crow Agency, MT 59022 (© **406/638-3700**), or visit **www.crow-fair.com**.

The most famous historic site here is the **Little Bighorn Battlefield National Monument** (see p. 244), a somewhat ironic inclusion on this reservation. The Crow scouted for Custer, and the Little Bighorn is the site of the cavalry's most infamous defeat at the hands of the Indians.

A good place to learn about the Crow culture is at **Chief Plenty Coups State Park** (www.fwp.mt.gov; ✆ **406/252-1289**). The tribe's last traditional chief, Chief Plenty Coups, deeded his home and lands as a memorial to the Crow Nation, and the interpretive center houses many of the Crow leader's personal items, plus interpretive displays about the Crow people. From Billings, drive about 25 miles south on Montana highways 416 and 418 to Pryor; then go a mile west, following signs. There are picnic facilities but no overnight camping. The grounds are open May through September daily from 8am to 8pm, and the visitor center is open from 10am to 5pm (by appointment in the off season). Admission is $5 per vehicle, $3 if you are walking or on a bicycle.

BIGHORN CANYON NATIONAL RECREATION AREA

Fort Smith: 83 miles SE of Billings

Over eons, the Bighorn River carved a steep, sheer canyon out of the rolling plains of present-day southeastern Montana and into northwestern Wyoming. The construction of the Yellowtail Dam—named for Crow chairman Robert Yellowtail—near Fort Smith on the Crow Reservation, provides not only power and irrigation, but also marvelous recreational opportunities on and around 71-mile-long Bighorn Lake. Established on October 15, 1966, the Bighorn Canyon National Recreation Area encompasses more than 120,000 acres and straddles the Montana–Wyoming border.

The lake and recreation area are remote and not easy to get to, requiring long drives on winding roads through small towns. The Wyoming and Montana portions of the recreation area are not connected by a road, although a boater can cruise easily up and down the reservoir. But it's worth the effort to get here: Steep walls soar above the deep waters, and there's superb water fun, some hiking, and tremendous photo opportunities.

Essentials

ACCESS POINTS There are two portions of the recreation area and two different access points. On the **Montana** side, from Billings, exit I-90 at Hardin and follow Route 313 south to Fort Smith and Yellowtail Dam.

The **Wyoming** section is accessed about 3 miles east of Lovell. From I-90 north of Sheridan, head west on U.S. 14 and turn north on Wyo. 37. The route is well marked.

FEES The daily entrance fee is $5 per vehicle.

VISITOR INFORMATION Contact **Bighorn Canyon National Recreation Area,** P.O. Box 7458, Fort Smith, MT 59035 (www.nps.gov/bica; ✆ **406/666-2412**).

Bighorn Canyon has visitor centers with exhibits and a descriptive film in each of its sections. Near Lovell, Wyoming, the **Cal S. Taggart Bighorn Canyon Visitors Center,** 20 Hwy. 14A E., Lovell, WY 82431 (✆ **307/548-5406**), is open daily from 8am to 6pm in the summer and from 8:30am to 4:30pm Thursday through Monday in the winter. The **Yellowtail Dam Visitor Center** (✆ **406/666-3218**) in Montana is open 9am to 5pm daily from Memorial Day to Labor Day, as well as Saturday through Wednesday in early May and late September.

For additional information on the area, contact the **Lovell Area Chamber of Commerce,** 287 E. Main St., Lovell, WY 82431 (www.lovellchamber.com; ✆ **307/548-7552**).

REGULATIONS & WARNINGS   The park has a number of black bears, which are not generally as dangerous to people as grizzlies but can cause problems when they learn that humans carry food. Therefore, *never* feed the bears, not only for your safety, but for theirs as well.

Getting Outside

Bighorn Canyon is primarily a flat-water recreation area with excellent boating and fishing, plus swimming, water-skiing, and scuba diving. There are limited hiking trails and scenic drives.

Fishing regulations are tricky in these parts since the Crow Reservation encompasses nearly all of the Montana portion of the canyon. A state fishing license from whichever state you'll be fishing in is needed, and unless you are certain which it will be, it's best to get both. The visitor center has information on limits, regulations, and fishing conditions.

ON THE MONTANA SIDE

A park ranger can help you find the **Om-Ne-A Trail,** which stretches for 3 steep miles one-way along the canyon rim. The **Beaver Pond Trail** is a short trip from the visitor center along Lime Kiln Creek.

ON THE WYOMING SIDE

The south side of the park offers some of the more sensational canyon views and is a prime viewing spot of some of the last wild horses to run free in North America. The **Horseshoe Bend** area, on Wyo. 37, has a full-service marina (✆ **307/548-7230**), typically open from Memorial Day to Labor Day.

Leaving Horseshoe Bend, you'll pass burgundy-colored hills and enter the **Pryor Mountain National Wild Horse Range,** which has been home to wild mustangs—the virtual emblem of the West, along with the buffalo—for more than a century. Sometimes you can catch a glimpse of a few from the road. If you want more information, there is a new **Pryor Mountain Wild Mustang Center** (www.pryor mustangs.org; ✆ **307/548-9453**) in Lovell. Just across the Montana border is the **Devil Canyon Overlook,** offering a view of the river as it winds through a steep canyon of gray limestone and orange shale.

At the end of the highway is **Barry's Landing,** with a boat ramp and fishing access, and the focus for most of the recreational opportunities in the southern part of the park.

The self-guided **Canyon Creek Nature Trail** (.5 mile), which starts at Loop C of the campground at Horseshoe Bend, and the trail from **Barry's Landing** to the campground at Medicine Creek (2 miles) are the only hikes on this side of the park.

Where to Stay

There are five park-service campgrounds in the recreation area; sites are free and first come, first served. Accommodations on the south side of the park are available in **Lovell,** 3 miles west of the intersection of Wyo. 37 and U.S. 14A (Alt. 14).

10

BILLINGS & EASTERN MONTANA

Bighorn Canyon

Forrester's Bighorn River Resort ★ (www.forrester-travel.com; ✆ **800/665-3799** or 406/666-9199) is an outfitting company owned and run by former wildlife biologist Nick Forrester and his wife, Francine, a Manhattan-trained chef. There are seven rustic but very comfortable private cabins and a lodge with a massive river-rock fireplace in the living room, cigar loft, pro shop, and dining room where Francine serves meals to soothe weary fishermen. Located about a half-mile north of Fort Smith, the cabins sit on a bluff overlooking the Bighorn River. The Forresters offer hunting and fishing packages that include all meals and lodging, starting at about $600 per person, per day.

LITTLE BIGHORN BATTLEFIELD NATIONAL MONUMENT

56 miles E of Billings

Perhaps there is no phrase in the English language that serves as a better metaphor for an untimely demise than "Custer's Last Stand." It was on this battlefield, on the dry, sloping prairies of southeastern Montana, that George Armstrong Custer met his end. Though the details of the actual battle that took place on June 25, 1876, are sketchy at best, much remains for the visitor to explore and ponder in this mysterious place. The **Little Bighorn Battlefield National Monument** chronicles the history of this world-famous engagement, offering a coherent look at how the battle developed, where the members of Custer's contingent died, and how it might have looked to the swarming warriors.

Essentials

GETTING THERE The monument is located 56 miles east of Billings. Take I-94 east to I-90 south; just past Crow Agency, take exit 510 for U.S. 212. The battlefield is located a few hundred yards east.

ADMISSION & HOURS The park and visitor center are open daily 8am to 9pm from Memorial Day through July, 8am to 8pm from August through Labor Day, 8am to 6pm in spring and fall, and 8am to 4:30pm in winter. The visitor center is closed on Christmas, New Year's Day, and Thanksgiving. Admission costs $10 per vehicle or $5 for those on foot or motorcycle.

VISITOR INFORMATION At the **visitor center** just inside the park entrance, you'll see actual uniforms worn by Custer, read about his life, and view an eerie reenactment of the battles on a small-scale replica of the battlefield. For advance information, contact the Superintendent, Little Bighorn Battlefield National Monument, P.O. Box 39, Crow Agency, MT 59022-0039 (www.nps.gov/libi; ✆ **406/638-2621**).

TOURING THE MONUMENT It's possible to view the site in less than a half-hour, but you'll shortchange yourself with that approach. Instead, plan to spend enough time to explore the visitor center, listen to interpretive historical talks presented by rangers there, and then tour the site. You'll leave with a greater appreciation for the monument and an understanding of the history that led up to the battle.

After stopping at the **visitor center,** drive 4½ miles to the **Reno–Benteen Monument Entrenchment Trail,** at the end of the monument road, and double back. Interpretive signs at the top of this bluff show the route followed by the companies under Custer, Benteen, and Reno as they approached the area from the south, and the positions from which they defended themselves from their Indian foes.

As you proceed north along the ridge, you'll pass **Custer's Lookout,** the spot from which the general first viewed the Indian village. This was the spot where Custer sent for reinforcements, though he continued marching north.

Capt. Thomas Weir led his troops to **Weir Point** in hopes of assisting Custer but was immediately discovered by the Indian warriors and forced to retreat to the spot held by Reno.

The **Medicine Trail Ford,** on the ridge, overlooks a spot well below the bluffs in the Medicine Trail Coulee on the Little Bighorn River, where hundreds of warriors who had been sent from the Reno battle pushed across the river in pursuit of Custer and his army.

Farther north, the Cheyenne warrior Lame White Man led an attack up **Calhoun Ridge** against a company of the Seventh Cavalry that had charged downhill into the coulee. When Indian resistance overwhelmed the army, troops retreated back up the hill, where they were killed.

As you proceed to the north, you will find detailed descriptions of the events that occurred on the northernmost edges of the ridge, as well as white markers that indicate the places where army troops fell in battle. The bodies of Custer, his brothers Tom and Boston, and his nephew Autie Reed were found on Custer Hill.

Indian casualties during the rout are estimated at 60 to 100 warriors. Following the battle, which some say began early in the morning and ended within 2 hours, the Indians broke camp in haste and scattered to the north and south. Within a few short years, they were all confined to reservations.

The survivors of the Reno–Benteen armies buried the bodies of Custer and his slain army where they fell. In 1881, the graves that could be located were reopened, and the bones reinterred at the base of a memorial shaft found overlooking the battlefield. Custer's remains were eventually reburied at the U.S. Military Academy at West Point in 1877.

The adjacent **National Cemetery,** established in 1879, incorporates a self-guided tour to some of the more significant figures buried there. In 2003, there was a dedication for a new Indian memorial, a sculpture garden dubbed "Peace Through Unity." There are also three **walking trails** within the monument for visitors wishing to explore the battle in greater depth.

A SPECIAL EVENT   The **Hardin Area Chamber of Commerce,** 10 E. Railway (www.thehardinchamber.org; 𝄞 **406/665-1672**), sponsors **Little Bighorn Days** around June 25 each year (in town, not at the monument). The events include a reenactment of Custer's Last Stand, parade, symposiums, and, of course, food. For information, visit **www.custerslaststand.org**.

MILES CITY ★

145 miles E of Billings; 70 miles SW of Glendive

Miles City gets its name from Col. Nelson A. Miles—the commander of the Fifth Cavalry who was ordered to return bands of Indians to reservations in the summer of 1876. As the world moves on around it, Miles City has retained its Western flair for more than a century. In the early days, as portrayed in Larry McMurtry's novel *Lonesome Dove,*

Miles City was a cowboy town on the verge of becoming a leading cattle market; the market came with the arrival of the Northern Pacific Railroad in 1881.

Today, Miles City maintains its cowboy traditions with its annual Bucking Horse Sale—which attracts rodeo stock contractors from all over the country—and the Range Riders Museum, a thorough collection of photographs and firearms from the old days. It's where remote ranchers come when they need barbed wire or tractor axles, and still boasts a traditional Main Street with a saloon and lunch counter. Residents take an active pride in the town's lack of parking meters—a vestige of its civility and small population.

Essentials

GETTING THERE   It's an easy 145-mile drive on I-94 from Billings. Miles City's **Frank Wiley Field** (✆ **406/234-1296**) is serviced by **Gulfstream International Airlines** (www.flygia.com; ✆ **800/499-7450**), with connecting flights to Billings.

VISITOR INFORMATION   The **Miles City Area Chamber of Commerce,** at 511 Pleasant St., Miles City, MT 59301 (www.milescitychamber.com; ✆ **406/234-2890**), provides maps and guides to the town. Or get an area vacation guide from **Custer Country** (www.custercountry.com; ✆ **800/346-1876**).

Getting Outside

There's an attractive municipal swimming facility at the west end of Main Street.

FISHING & BOATING

Miles City isn't classic Montana fishing country, but there is plenty of access to the Yellowstone and Tongue rivers for walleye, sauger, catfish, crappie, and, occasionally, the unusual paddlefish (see "Paddlefishing," later in this chapter). Fishing throughout the area is best in late spring and early fall. **Twelve-Mile Dam,** 11 miles south of Miles City on Mont. 59, then 1 mile south on Tongue River Road, has camping facilities, a boat launch, and a handicapped-accessible fishing platform.

Luring in floaters with Yellowstone River access, **Pirogue Island State Park** (www.fwp.mt.gov; ✆ **406/234-0926**) is just north of Miles City. Go 1 mile north on Mont. 59, then 2 miles east on Kinsey Highway, then 2 miles south on an unnamed

THE WORLD-FAMOUS MILES CITY bucking horse SALE

Since 1914, rodeo contractors—the men who supply the animals for the West's rodeos—have been meeting in Miles City and lining up their stock. This gathering, which began as an informal event, has now become the "World-Famous Miles City Bucking Horse Sale," held every third weekend in May. More than 200 horses are sold at auction, from untried stock to spoiled saddle horses. There are pari-mutuel horse races, a parade, a trade show, and rodeos, as well as wild-horse racing. The downtown area is virtually closed down at night, bands play on the streets, and beer is swilled and spilled while the city's open-container ordinances are suspended inside the "people corral." Tickets cost $12 to $17. For the current schedule, call the **Miles City Area Chamber of Commerce** (✆ **406/234-2890**), or visit www.buckinghorsesale.com.

county road (look for a sign for the park). Stop by **Red Rock Sporting Goods,** 700 S. Haynes Ave. (✆ **406/232-2716**), for gear and information.

GOLF

Miles City has the 9-hole **Town and Country Club golf course** (www.milescity tcc.com; ✆ **406/234-1500**) running along the banks of the Tongue River southeast of town. It's relatively short—3,280 yards. Greens fees are $16 to $21 for 9 holes; carts are $7 per rider.

Seeing the Sights

Custer County Art and Heritage Center ★★ ☺   The old city water plant, built between 1910 and 1924, has been reincarnated as an art-and-history museum, with one-time water tanks now filled with art. There are changing exhibits of tradi- tional and contemporary art from the museum's permanent collection, plus national and regional touring exhibits. Listed on the National Register of Historic Places, the museum building is actually an attraction itself. In 1979, it was awarded the gover- nor's trophy for best adaptation of a historic structure. The art center hosts an annual "Quick Draw" event on the third weekend in May and an art auction each year in late September.

Waterplant Rd. off W. Main St. (just west of town). www.ccac.milescity.org. ✆ **406/234-0635.** Free admission. May–Sept Tues–Sun 9am–5pm; rest of year Tues–Sun 1–5pm.

Range Riders Museum ★   The amazing thing about this collection is its size— the Western memorabilia collection fills 11 buildings and includes a frontier town, an art gallery that includes the work of Charles Russell, and a gun collection of more than 400 firearms, including an elephant gun, all on the site once occupied by Fort Keogh. Items on display also include American-Indian artifacts and French sabers. There are 500 photos of local celebrities in the Wilson Photo Gallery, and a replica of Old Milestown—as the town was originally called—of 1877. Of particular interest are the excellent photos of Cheyenne tribal members taken in the 1890s.

U.S. 12 (on Main St., just west of town at I-94 exit 135). www.rangeridersmuseum.org. ✆ **406/232- 6146.** $5 adults, $4 seniors, $1 high school and college students, 50¢ elementary and middle school students, free for children 5 and under. Apr–Oct daily 8am–5pm. Closed Nov–Mar.

Where to Stay & Eat

There are several properties at I-94 exit 138 in Miles City. The **Holiday Inn Express,** 1720 S. Haynes Ave. (✆ **888/700-0402** or 406/234-1000), is a well- maintained facility with 52 units. There's a pool and whirlpool; rooms have wireless Internet access, irons and boards, hair dryers, and coffeemakers. Rates are $99 to $139 double and include an expanded continental breakfast. The **Best Western War Bonnet Inn,** 1015 S. Haynes Ave. (✆ **800/528-1234** or 406/234-4560), has 54 units, including three suites with microwaves and refrigerators, plus there's an indoor pool, hot tub, and sauna. Rates are $80 to $150 double. Open mid-April through October, the **Miles City KOA Campground,** 1 Palmer St., Miles City, MT 56301 (✆ **800/562-3909** or 406/232-3991), is shaded by more than 70 cotton- woods and has full RV hookups, tent sites, a pool, and a store. Campsite rates range from $22 to $39; basic cabins are $50.

For a small Montana town, Miles City offers several pretty good restaurants. The **Stagecoach Station,** 3020 Stower St. (✆ **406/234-2288**), offers steak, seafood, great barbecue, and pasta (dinner items are in the $10–$20 range) with Old West hospitality and atmosphere to match—from the boot upholstery to "old Gabby" greeting you at the door. It's open daily from 6:30am to 10pm (Fri–Sat until 11pm). For fine dining, visit **Club 519,** 519 Main St., on the second floor of the Professional Building (© **406/232-5133**), a softly lit, quiet, comfortable restaurant serving very good steaks and seafood, with dinner prices in the $10-to-$30 range. It's open daily from 5 to 10pm. For a vintage Montana diner and corresponding grub, look no farther than the **600 Cafe,** 600 Main St. (© **406/234-3860**), with hearty American standards for breakfast and lunch, a well-worn breakfast counter, and maroon booths. Menu items are $3 to $9.

Miles City After Dark

The cowboys in their dress hats come out after dark in Miles City, mostly in the bars. The historic **Montana Bar ★**, 612 Main St. (© **406/234-5809**), has a Montana map for a sign, with Miles City marked by a check. Built in 1893, this is where stockmen gathered. It was enlarged and received a new facade in 1914, but has changed little since and is known as one of the most authentic Western bars in the state. It has a multicolored tile floor, an antique back bar, a pressed-tin ceiling, and a bullet hole in one leaded-glass panel. Patrons used to have to stand up to the bar and "drink like a man," but bar stools have been added for the modern tippler.

10 GLENDIVE

222 miles E of Billings; 196 miles W of Bismarck, North Dakota

A cattle town in the 1880s, Glendive has gradually become a farming community, producing mostly sugar beets and wheat. The city's most curious attraction is paddle-fishing—dropping a line in the Yellowstone River in hopes of hooking a prehistoric monster (the state record is 142 lb.).

GETTING THERE   It's a 222-mile drive on I-94 from Billings, or you can fly **Gulfstream International Airlines** (www.flygia.com; © **800/499-7450**) to **Dawson Community Airport** (www.glendiveairport.com; © **406/687-3372**).

VISITOR INFORMATION   The **Glendive Area Chamber of Commerce and Agriculture,** 808 N. Merrill Ave., Glendive, MT 59330 (www.glendivechamber.com; © **406/377-5601**), provides brochures and maps.

Paddlefishing

Thousands of anglers come every year to try to snag one of these prehistoric spoonbill sturgeons from the bottom of the Yellowstone River. The season is from May 15 to whenever the annual quota is met or June 30, whichever comes first, and the best fishing spot is at the intake diversion dam on the Yellowstone, 17 miles northeast of town on Mont. 16. Thought to be extinct until an angler snagged one here in 1962, these monsters (adults generally weigh 60–120 lb.) are "snagged"—caught on treble hooks dragged along the bottom of the river—and the limit is one fish per fisherman. Interestingly, local nonprofits accept paddlefish roe as a donation, and they sell the caviar to raise funds. You'll need both a Montana fishing license and a special tag, which several places in town sell; a concessionaire rents poles and lures. Call the chamber (© **406/377-5601**) for additional information.

Makoshika State Park

Montana's largest state park, at 11,531 acres, **Makoshika State Park ★★** (www. fwp.mt.gov; ℂ **406/377-6256**) is a few blocks from town via the railroad underpass. The name is Lakota and means "bad earth" or "bad land." Erosion has done wonders with the park's upper and most malleable layer, forming magnificent spires in some places and coulees that cut deep into the multicolored valleys in others. Ponderosa pine trees are scattered over much of the park. The amazing thing about this state park is not necessarily the uncanny resemblance to Badlands National Park in South Dakota, but the abundance of dinosaur bones that have been removed from under the loess. Among the exhibits in the visitor center is the actual skull—not a replica or cast—from a young triceratops uncovered in the park. For more on the region's pre-history, pay a visit to the **Makoshika Dinosaur Museum,** 111 W. Bell St. in down-town Glendive (www.makoshika.com; ℂ **406/377-1637**). Admission is $5 adults, $3 students and seniors, and free for kids 5 and under.

A paved road—steep and narrow even by Montana mountain standards—winds about 4 miles to an overlook that provides a wonderful view of the badlands. From there, the road becomes gravel and continues for another 3½ miles before mainte-nance ends. There are also 5 miles of hiking trails (with 10 more to come at some point), along with a number of off-trail backpacking routes. The visitor center (daily 10am–6pm Memorial Day to Labor Day; Mon–Sat 9am–5pm the rest of the year) has a fine display of the history, prehistory, and geology of the park. There is also a "folf," or Frisbee golf, course and several hiking trails. The day-use fee is $5 per vehicle; campsites are $20 to $23 for nonresidents.

Where to Stay & Eat

Lodging here includes the historic **Glendive Inn,** 222 N. Kendrick Ave. (ℂ **406/377-5555**), with rates of $88 to $95 double; and **Super 8,** 1904 N. Merrill Ave. (ℂ **406/365-5671**), which charges $40 to $60 double. For lunch or dinner, we like the family-friendly beer-and-pizza joint, the **Gust Hauf,** 300 W. Bell St. (ℂ **406/365-4451**), featuring a video arcade and casino and a big kitschy beer stein out front.

Charley Montana Bed & Breakfast ★★ An impeccable restoration of a majestic neoclassical mansion, Charley Montana is a top-flight B&B in what was once the palatial, 26-room abode of rancher Charles Krug. Built in 1906, the house has been restored to its original condition, with impeccable attention to the wood-work inside and out. The five guest rooms include the Charles Room, the old master bedroom with the leather-bound encyclopedia from the Krug family library, as well as the Annie Suite, named for Krug's wife, with an impressive wardrobe and separate sitting area with heirloom armchairs. The 8,000-square-foot inn is located on the outskirts of downtown Glendive, cater-cornered to an old silo and a stone's throw from the old Bell Street Bridge across the Yellowstone River, now reserved for pedes-trians and bicyclists.

103 N. Douglas St. (P.O. Box 1192), Glendive, MT 59930. www.charley-montana.com. ℂ **888/395-3207** or 406/365-3207. 5 units. $105–$120 double; $145 suite. Rates include full breakfast. AE, DISC, MC, V. *In room:* A/C, TV, hair dryer, Wi-Fi (free).

A Side Trip to Fort Union

Strictly speaking, the **Fort Union Trading Post National Historic Site** is in North Dakota. The Montana–North Dakota border bisects the parking lot, and the fort itself is a few paces east. But Fort Union was so important to Montana's development that it should be part of any trip through the eastern part of the state.

For 30 years after 1828, Fort Union was the edge of the frontier—the most important trading post in John Jacob Astor's beaver-pelt-and-buffalo-robe empire in the Northern Plains. This National Park Service site has been spectacularly reconstructed from pictures and descriptions. The main gate of the glistening, white-washed wooden stockade overlooks the wide Missouri, and two tall stone bastions stand sentinel over the river at the fort's corners.

Lewis and Clark camped near here on their trip to the Pacific, on April 25 and 26, 1805. Lewis commented in his journals on the "wide and fertile vallies" and how ideal the site would be for a fort. The Bourgeois House has been converted into a modern visitor center and contains excellent exhibits detailing the life and times of the fur traders. Artist George Catlin visited in 1832, as did Karl Bodmer in 1833 and John James Audubon in 1843. In 1867, the U.S. Army acquired the fort, and its lumber was used to expand nearby Fort Buford and fuel steamboats.

GETTING THERE & VISITOR INFORMATION From I-94 exit 213 at Glendive, take Mont. 16 northeast to the North Dakota border, then North Dakota 58 north to the fort (it's about 75 miles). Contact **Fort Union Trading Post National Historic Site,** 15550 N. Dak. 1804, Williston, ND 58801 (www.nps.gov/fous; ✆ **701/572-9083** or 701/572-7622). Admission is free, and the park is open daily from 8am to 8pm during the summer and 9am to 5:30pm in winter. While the site is located in two time zones, it observes Central Standard Time, running an hour later than Montana.

YELLOWSTONE NATIONAL PARK

America's first national park is just as alluring as it was when John Colter of the Lewis and Clark expedition first spied it in 1807. Colter's descriptions of spewing hot springs and boiling mud were unlike anything the public had ever heard of, and modern visitors still have the same reaction to Yellowstone's incredible geography. Once inside Yellowstone, most travelers see Old Faithful and the Grand Canyon but never venture far enough to see its geyser basins up close. It's an otherworldly journey worth making.

Active Pursuits Thermal features steam, bubble, boil, and hiss throughout Yellowstone National Park. See these curiosities and others on **day hikes** such as **Geyser Hill Loop** and **Fountain Paint Pot Trail.** The popular **Lonestar Geyser Trail** accommodates hikers and cyclists, follows the Firehole River, and doubles as a **cross-country ski trail** in winter. **Fish** for cutthroat and other trout species on the Yellowstone River just below Yellowstone's Grand Canyon, a 1,000-foot-deep, 24-mile-long gorge carved in yellows and reds.

Flora & Fauna For many, the primary reason for visiting Yellowstone is its wildlife: **bear, bighorn sheep, bison, elk, river otters**, and **moose** all wander, often within roadside view of travelers. One of the park's largest **elk** herds grazes near Mammoth Hot Springs, while **bighorn sheep** maneuver over rocky precipices near Mount Washburn. North America's largest free-roaming **bison** herd grazes near the Firehole River and in the Hayden Valley, an area also known for its **grizzly** and **black bears.**

Where to Stay & Eat The best hotels in the park are the **Old Faithful Inn** and the **Lake Yellowstone Hotel.** Some of the finest food from the park includes **bison prime rib** and **stuffed trout.** The beauty of the famous **Old Faithful Inn's** log construction, its elk antler chandeliers, and proximity to Old Faithful make this restaurant a good choice. **Camping and cooking supplies** are readily available in Mammoth Hot Springs, Canyon Village, Grant Village, Old Faithful, and Yellowstone Lake.

THE GATEWAY TOWNS: WEST YELLOWSTONE, GARDINER & COOKE CITY

West Yellowstone: 91 miles SW of Bozeman; 30 miles W of Old Faithful; 320 miles NE of Salt Lake City. Gardiner: 79 miles SE of Bozeman; 163 miles SW of Billings. Cooke City: 127 miles SW of Billings

West Yellowstone

By making itself the headquarters for snowmobilers who want to travel the park's roads in winter, **West Yellowstone**—just outside the park's west gate—has created a year-round tourist economy and attracted an ever-growing number of big hotel chains. The quiet fly-fishing town that once was is no more: The shops are chock-full of curios, and the streets are clogged with tour buses and, in the winter, rumbling snow machines.

One could argue that West Yellowstone made its Faustian bargain with tourism long ago, when the Oregon Short Line's *Yellowstone Special* train first arrived in 1909. Originally called Riverside, then Yellowstone, the town was grudgingly renamed West Yellowstone in 1920 when Gardiner residents complained that tourists would mistakenly believe the town was the park. Name aside, this place is more about shopping than about nature, and its biggest attraction is the zoolike Grizzly & Wolf Discovery Center.

ESSENTIALS

GETTING THERE   The **West Yellowstone Regional Airport** (www.yellowstone airport.org; © 406/646-7631) is in Montana, where the airport sits just 1 mile north of town (and the west entrance) on U.S. Hwy. 191. The airport has commercial air service seasonally, June through the end of September only, on **Delta Connection/SkyWest,** connecting through Salt Lake City. If you're driving the 91 miles from Bozeman to West Yellowstone, take U.S. 191 south (a pretty journey along the Gallatin River) to its junction with U.S. 287 and head straight into town. From Idaho Falls, take I-15 north to U.S. 20, which takes you directly into West Yellowstone, a 53-mile drive.

VISITOR INFORMATION   Contact the **West Yellowstone Chamber of Commerce,** 30 Yellowstone Ave., P.O. Box 458, West Yellowstone, MT 59758 (www.westyellowstonechamber.com; © 406/646-7701).

GETTING AROUND   At the West Yellowstone Airport, **Avis** (www.avis.com; © 800/230-4898 or 406/646-7635) and **Budget** (www.budget.com; © 800/527-0700 or 406/646-7882) offer car rentals. **Yellowstone Taxi** (www.yellowstonetaxi.com; © 406/646-1118) provides local service.

GETTING OUTSIDE

Most people arrive here on their way to the park, but there is no fence along the park's boundary, so some of the best wild country is actually to the west. If you like fishing, the rivers—the Gallatin and the Madison, particularly—are among the best in the country. The following tackle shops offer the full gamut of guided fishing trips and instruction: **Arrick's Fly Shop,** 37 Canyon St. (© 406/646-7290); **Bud Lilly's Trout Shop,** 39 Madison Ave. (© 406/646-7801); **Jacklin's,** 105 Yellowstone Ave. (© 406/646-7336); and **Madison River Outfitters,** 117 Canyon St. (© 406/646-9644).

Come winter, **cross-country skiers** hit the trails (see p. 283, "Winter Sports & Activities"). Ski rentals are available in West Yellowstone at **FreeHeel and Wheel,**

FROMMER'S favorite YELLOWSTONE EXPERIENCES

Witness the World's Most Famous Geologic Alarm Clock. Old Faithful is known for its reliability, but it's slowing down a little with age. Still, about once every 90 minutes, give or take, you can watch her blow, making her the most predictable geyser on the planet. While you're there, get a good look at the beautiful and historic Old Faithful Inn.

Escape to the Backcountry. If the packed benches at Old Faithful give you the impression that Yellowstone is overrun, venture into the backcountry for a dose of true wilderness. It will restore your spirits and perhaps your belief in national parks. Get advice from a ranger on how to travel safely in bear country, and then have it mostly to yourself—most of the three million annual park visitors rarely leave the roadways.

Get Hooked on Yellowstone Trout. There is some fine fly-fishing water in and near the park. Try the Madison, the Gibbon, and the Firehole rivers, or troll the lakes for cutthroat, brown, rainbow, and brook trout. When a big trout slaps the twilight surface of the Yellowstone River, Izaak Walton smiles in fly-fishing heaven.

Have a Howling Good Time at Lamar. Since wolves were reintroduced in Yellowstone in 1995, they have surprised biologists by making frequent morning and late-afternoon appearances along Slough Creek and in other parts of Lamar Valley. This especially untamed area in the northeast corner of Yellowstone is loaded with wildlife: bison, elk, coyotes, and grizzly bears.

Make Like Teddy and Be a Rough Rider. At Roosevelt Lodge, visitors relive the Old West by taking organized rides on horseback, stagecoach, or wagon. A more adventurous alternative is the Old West cookout; you will arrive by either horseback or wagon for hearty meat-and-potatoes grub.

Learn Something at the Yellowstone Association Institute. You can take classes on everything from bears to butterflies at the Yellowstone Association Institute, which inhabits the old Lamar Buffalo Ranch in the park's northeast corner. It's a friendly, communal way to get a more intimate knowledge of the ecosystem.

Sleep on a Historic Pillow in the Park. Old Faithful Inn, dating from 1904, is a log cathedral within view of the geyser. Relax with a drink on the second-floor terrace, or climb the timber lattice that holds up the great roof. Original rooms may not all have private bathrooms, but it's still the nicest place to stay in the park. Ask for suite no. 3014 or room no. 229 to watch the geyser erupt from your room.

40 Yellowstone Ave. (© **406/646-7744**), or **Bud Lilly's,** 39 Madison Ave. (© **406/ 646-7801**).

Despite a quota system in the park, **snowmobiling** is a huge draw in West Yellowstone, where sleds are more common than cars on snowpacked winter streets. In addition to driving the machines on the snowpacked roads of Yellowstone—where speed limits are strictly enforced—you can take the trails in surrounding national forests with fewer restrictions. There are tricks to riding on backcountry snow, so if you're inexperienced, rent a guide as well as a machine. All the major hotels and motels in West Yellowstone arrange snowmobile rentals that include gear, and there are numerous independent operations offering rentals and guides, including **Yellowstone Arctic/Yamaha,** 208 Electric St. (© **406/646-9636**), and **Yellowstone Adventures,** 131 Dunraven Ave. (© **406/646-7735**).

Expect to pay $250 to $300 per day per snowmobile, plus about $225 for a guide (required), and unless you have a helmet and winter gear to protect you from subzero wind chill, plan on spending another $25 for clothing. Also popular are **snowcoach tours,** offered in vans equipped with tanklike treads to travel on snow. Check with **Yellowstone Alpen Guides Co.,** 535 Yellowstone Ave. (© **800/858-3502**), or with snowmobile outfitters, who often offer snowcoach rides as well.

SEEING THE SIGHTS

Beyond the attractions below, families interested in firefighting will want to drop into the **National Smokejumper Center,** just east of the chamber (www.smokejumper center.org; © **406/646-7557**). In a cluster of relocated historic log structures, kids can take part in a Junior Smokejumper Program at 9am in summer to learn about smokejumpers' tools, tricks, and training to fight fires in inaccessible corners of the wilderness.

Grizzly and Wolf Discovery Center Those who haven't the patience to search out and observe the free-ranging wildlife of Yellowstone might want to try this not-for-profit educational center. The interpretive center gives a detailed explanation of the history of wolves and grizzlies in this country, along with the difficult and controversial efforts to revive them in the wild. This is a closer look than you'll likely get with animals in the park, but did you really come to Yellowstone to look at grizzlies imported from Alaska in an enclosure?

201 S. Canyon St. in Grizzly Park. www.grizzlydiscoveryctr.org. © **800/257-2570** or 406/646-7001. $11 adults, $9.75 seniors, $5.50 children 5–12, free for children 4 and under. Summer daily 8:30am–8:30pm; shorter hours in winter.

Yellowstone Historic Center ★ Located in the historic 1909 Union Pacific depot, this is the only museum that focuses on Yellowstone's cultural history, providing an interesting look into the ways of the park's first tourists, with scads of memorabilia, postcards, and concessionaire ephemera. There are also displays on the historic Yellowstone railroad and other transportation, covering epochal events such as the 1959 earthquake that created Quake Lake and the 1988 fires, along with a mounted grizzly bear known in his animate days as "Old Snaggletooth."

At Yellowstone Ave. and Canyon St. www.yellowstonehistoriccenter.org. © **406/646-1100.** $5 adults, $4 seniors, $3 children and students, free for children 2 and under. Mid-May to late May and early Sept to mid-Oct daily 9am–6pm; late May to early Sept daily 9am–9pm. Closed rest of year.

Yellowstone IMAX Theater This theater is next door to the **Grizzly and Wolf Discovery Center,** and together they form the centerpieces of a real-estate development on the edge of the park, which includes several new hotels. Regardless, the IMAX concept works pretty well here—there are things an airborne camera can show you on a six-story-tall screen that you'll never see on your own two feet. A film called *Yellowstone* plays fairly often, with swooping views of the canyon, falls, and other sights.

101 S. Canyon St. www.yellowstoneimax.com. © **888/854-5862** or 406/646-4100. $9 adults, $8.50 seniors, $6.50 children 3–12, free for children 2 and under. Summer 8:30am–9pm, shorter hours in winter. Call or check the website for exact show times.

WHERE TO STAY

Make your reservations early if you want to visit in July or August, or if you're going to spend Christmas or New Year's here. If you're smart, you'll come in the fall, when there are plenty of empty rooms and better rates, and spend your days fishing the Henry's Fork or one of the other great streams in the vicinity. Rates for rooms often reflect the seasonal traffic, and prices fluctuate. Unless noted, all these establishments are open year-round.

You'll find chains like **Comfort Inn,** 638 Madison Ave. (www.comfortinn.com; ✆ **406/646-4212**), with summertime doubles for $129 to $229; and **Days Inn** (www.daysinn.com; ✆ **800/548-9551** or 406/646-7656), at 301 Madison Ave., with summer rates of $119 to $189 for a double. There are three **Best Western** affiliates, ranging from about $160 to $220 a night for a double during the summer. Call ✆ **800/528-1234** or go online to www.bestwestern.com for information and reservations. The **One Horse Motel,** at 216 N. Dunraven St. (www.onehorsemotel.com; ✆ **800/488-2750** or 406/646-7677), is a top-notch independent across the street from City Park, with doubles for $79 to $129 a night. Another good inexpensive option (with more character than the chains, to boot), the 1912 **Madison Hotel,** 139 Yellowstone Ave. (www.madisonhotelmotel.com; ✆ **800/838-7745** or 406/646-7745), has historic rooms for $59 to $99 for a double or $33 for a bunk in a dormitory, and newer motel doubles for $79 to $139. Another option with historic cachet—and a one-time favorite of broadcasting legend Charles Kuralt—is the **Parade Rest Guest Ranch,** 10 miles north of West Yellowstone at 1279 Grayling Rd. (www.paraderestranch.com; ✆ **800/753-5934** or 406/646-7217), in a serene setting near Hebgen Lake. Rates are about $190 per day for adults and $70 to $150 for kids, all meals and horseback riding included; lodging runs only $160 double per cabin.

Bar N Ranch ★★ One of the oldest brands in Montana, the Bar N is an excellent lodging option in West Yellowstone. Located on 200 acres of unsullied ranchland with 2 miles of the Madison River and a fishing pond, the lodge is an image of the New West, with a great river-rock fireplace and a knotty pine banister leading up to the rooms upstairs. The lodge rooms mix equal parts Ralph Lauren and Old West, exuding a simple but rich style with antler lamps, hardwood floors, and jetted tubs. The cabins are one- and two-bedroom units arranged in a half-circle around the lodge, with decor that echoes that of the lodge; all of them have fireplaces and private outdoor hot tubs.

890 Buttermilk Creek Rd. (P.O. Box 250), West Yellowstone, MT 59758. www.bar-n-ranch.com. ✆ **406/646-0300.** Fax 406/646-0301. 15 units, including 8 cabins. Lodge rooms $235–$250 double; cabins $290–$365 double; 4-bedroom cabin $465; lower rates late Oct and early May. AE, DC, DISC, MC, V. **Amenities:** Restaurant; Jacuzzi; small outdoor pool; Wi-Fi (free). *In room:* TV/DVD, fridge, no phone.

Holiday Inn West Yellowstone ★ This is the town's best modern hotel. The rooms are sizable and comfortable, well maintained, and regularly updated. At the tour desk, you can arrange fishing and rafting trips, bike and ATV rentals, and chuck-wagon cookouts. The Iron Horse Saloon serves regional microbrews, and the Oregon Short Line Restaurant serves Western cuisine, including game and seafood dishes. At the center of the restaurant sits the restored railroad club car that brought Victorian gents to Yellowstone a century ago.

315 Yellowstone Ave. (P.O. Box 470), West Yellowstone, MT 59758. www.doyellowstone.com. ✆ **800/646-7365** or 406/646-7365. 123 units. $199–$249 double; $279–$319 suite. Lower rates fall to spring. AE, DISC, MC, V. **Amenities:** Restaurant; lounge; bikes; children's program; health club; Jacuzzi; large indoor pool; sauna. *In room:* A/C, TV, fridge, hair dryer, Wi-Fi (free).

Moose Creek Cabins ★ 🎒 A 1950s motel complex that got a slick revamp in 2004, Moose Creek Cabins offers comfortable and stylish rooms and cabins in the heart of West Yellowstone. The one-time Ranger Motel—which spent 2 decades as employee housing before becoming Moose Creek—is a good value and one of the better-maintained properties in town. There are stand-alone kitchenette cabins (good for families) and cabin-style motel rooms with queen beds; both are laden with pine and charming individual themes. The proprietors also own a good motel, the Moose Creek Inn, a few blocks away, with double rooms for $100 to $110 and suites for $180 in summer.

220 Firehole Ave., West Yellowstone, MT 59758. www.moosecreek-cabins.com. (℗ **406/646-9546.** 13 units and cabins. $100–$120 double; $190–$200 cabin. Lower rates fall to spring. DISC, MC, V. *In room:* TV, kitchenette, no phone, Wi-Fi (free).

Three Bear Lodge ★ ☺ Rebuilt from the ground up after a 2008 fire, this woodsy, family-friendly inn is located less than 3 blocks from the park entrance. Those familiar with the old Three Bear will be hard pressed to recognize the slick new incarnation, featuring recycled wood, a striking lobby with a monolithic stone fireplace and scads of taxidermy, and stylish guest rooms. Some rooms are family suites that sleep up to eight people. About half of the rooms survived the fire but were updated as the main lodge was rebuilt. The Three Bear offers snowmobile and snowcoach tours in the winter, as well as van tours in the summer.

217 Yellowstone Ave. (P.O. Box 1590), West Yellowstone, MT 59758. www.threebearlodge.com. (℗ **800/646-7353** or 406/646-7353. Fax 406/646-4567. 72 units, including 8 family suites. $159–$219 double. Lower rates fall to spring. AE, DISC, MC, V. **Amenities:** Restaurant; lounge; exercise room; indoor Jacuzzi; outdoor heated pool (seasonal); sauna. *In room:* TV, hair dryer, Wi-Fi (free).

WHERE TO EAT

West Yellowstone is a good place to stop for a quick bite on your way into the park. For coffee and baked goods, visit the espresso bar at the excellent **Book Peddler** in Canyon Square (℗ **406/646-9358**). **Morning Glory Coffee & Tea,** 129 Dunraven St. (℗ **406/646-7061**), roasts its own beans on-site and offers a low-key atmosphere for getting going.

Beartooth Barbecue ★ BARBECUE   A bustling and funky space that plates up some mean barbecue, this is my pick for a casual meal in West Yellowstone. At the bar or a table in the bric-a-brac-laden room (hanging from the walls are sleds, ristas, a traffic light, and sports memorabilia), order a plate of St. Louis–cut spareribs or beef brisket for lunch or dinner (or a sandwich with brisket, sausage, or chicken) and plenty of tangy sauce. The bar has Montana microbeer on draft and serves wine by the glass, but no liquor is served.

111 Canyon St. (℗ **406/646-0227.** Lunch and dinner $10–$27. MC, V. Daily noon–10pm. Closed Oct–Apr.

The Canyon Street Grill AMERICAN   It's hard not to like an establishment whose slogan is "We are not a fast-food restaurant. We are a cafe reminiscent of a bygone era when the quality of the food meant more than how fast it could be served." With checkerboard floors and shiny red booths, this delightful 1950s-style spot serves hearty food for breakfast, lunch, and dinner. Hamburgers and chicken sandwiches are popular, accompanied by milkshakes made with hard ice cream or a famous root beer float.

22 Canyon St. www.canyonstreetgrill.com. (℗ **406/646-7548.** Main courses $5–$12. DISC, MC, V. May–Nov Mon–Sat 11am–10pm; shorter hours rest of year. Closed Apr to mid-May.

Eino's Tavern AMERICAN   Locals snowmobile out from West Yellowstone to Eino's (there's a trail that follows U.S. Hwy. 191) to become their own chefs at the grill here. It's a novel concept, and it keeps patrons coming back to this casual restaurant with a fine view of Hebgen Lake time and time again. There's usually a line out the door, but it's fun to peruse the walls, plastered with dollar bills and other currency, as well as bras and funny photos, while you wait. After placing your order for a steak, teriyaki chicken, hamburger, or hot dog, keep a straight face when you're handed an uncooked piece of meat. Go to the grill, slap it on, and stand around, drink in hand, shooting the breeze with other patrons until your food is exactly the way you like it. Steaks and chicken come with your choice of a salad (or the place's trademark "hot potatoes" in winter), and hamburgers come with chips.

155 Eino's Loop (9 miles north of West Yellowstone on U.S. Hwy. 191). ℂ **406/646-9344.** Main courses $5.50–$25. No credit cards; ATM on premises. Winter daily 9am–9pm; rest of year Mon–Fri 4–9pm, Sat–Sun noon–9pm. Closed Thanksgiving to mid-Dec.

The Outpost Restaurant ☺ AMERICAN   Tucked away in a downtown mall, this rustic restaurant laden with Western bric-a-brac serves old-fashioned home-style fare, such as its hearty beef stew, with fork-size chunks of carrots and potatoes. There's also salmon, steak, trout, liver, and an excellent salad bar. For breakfast, if you're really hungry, you can't beat the Campfire Omelet, smothered in homemade chili, cheese, and onions. There's no video poker, beer, wine, liquor, or smoking, making for a relatively quiet, family-friendly atmosphere. The desserts include pie and a wild huckleberry sundae.

115 Yellowstone Ave. (in the Montana Outpost Mall). ℂ **406/646-7303.** Breakfast $5–$16; lunch $6–$14; dinner $9–$25. AE, DISC, MC, V. Daily 6:30am–10:30pm. Closed mid-Oct to mid-Apr.

Sydney's Mountain Bistro ★★ NEW AMERICAN   The most upscale option in a meat-and-potatoes town, Sydney's offers an intimate setting, an excellent wine list, and a menu that balances seafood and vegetarian fare with beef, poultry, and pork. With interesting preparations—such as flash-fried calamari for starters and entrees including sweet-chile salmon and butternut squash ravioli—and a breezy patio complementing the upscale atmosphere inside, this is my pick for a special meal in West Yellowstone.

38 Canyon St. www.sydneysbistro.com. ℂ **406/646-7660.** Dinner $15–$38. MC, V. Daily 5–10pm.

Gardiner

Of all the towns that stand sentry on the roads into Yellowstone, Gardiner is the prototype gateway community. This is partly due to the historic stone Roosevelt Arch that marks the entrance through which the earliest visitors passed into the park. This is the only park entrance that's open to auto traffic year-round, in order to keep a connection open to Cooke City, which in winter can be reached only through the north entrance.

Gardiner sits at the junction of the Gardner and Yellowstone rivers (the town's eight-letter name has been attributed to a 19th-c. spelling error), still looking like the gritty little mining town it once was. Nobody puts on airs in the coffee shops and bars, and nobody raises an eyebrow when a bison or deer wanders through town.

GETTING THERE   From Bozeman (the nearest jet-service airport), take I-90 26 miles east to Livingston, then take U.S. 89 south 53 miles to Gardiner.

VISITOR INFORMATION   Contact the **Gardiner Chamber of Commerce,** 222 Park St., P.O. Box 81, Gardiner, MT 59030 (www.gardinerchamber.com; ℂ **406/848-7971**). Across from the landmark Roosevelt Arch is the slick new headquarters of the **Yellowstone Association** (www.yellowstoneassociation.org; ℂ **406/ 848-2400**), a restored historic building by renowned architect Robert Reamer, complete with a terrific store and visitor center. Up the hill from town is the Yellowstone Association Institute's new **Overlook Field Campus,** featuring cabins with superlative views and open to participants in seminars and tours.

GETTING OUTSIDE

Gardiner is the spot to go for white-water rafting on the Yellowstone River. Several outfitters take guests on half- and full-day trips on routes skirting the park's northern boundary; the best of the bunch is the **Yellowstone Raft Company,** U.S. Hwy. 89 (www.yellowstoneraft.com; © **800/858-7781** or 406/848-7777), with half-day trips for $37 and full days for $80; children get on the boat for $27 half-day or $60 full day. While this is not a **snowmobiling** hub on the magnitude of West Yellowstone, a few motels here rent snow machines or offer snowcoach tours. And **hiking** and **fishing** opportunities are bountiful in every direction from town.

WHERE TO STAY

Dinky, personable, and a bit eccentric, Gardiner has long had ultra-friendly lodging—thin-walled motels where, if you show up late, they've gone to bed and left a key in the door. These days it also has some newer, chain-affiliated properties, built to accommodate the ever-increasing traffic to the park. As with all the gateway towns, make your reservations early if you're coming during the peak season. The steep off-season decline in traffic results in discounts that can be considerably less expensive than the high-season rates quoted below, so be sure to ask.

Inexpensive chains motels fill up during the summer months: the **Yellowstone Park Travelodge,** 109 Hellroaring Rd. (© **406/848-7520**), and **Super 8,** 702 U.S. Hwy. 89 (www.super8.com; © **800/800-8000** or 406/848-7401), are open year-round with rates during the summer high season between $120 and $160 for a double. The **Best Western by Mammoth Hot Springs,** on U.S. Hwy. 89 (www.bestwestern.com; © **800/828-9080** or 406/848-7311), is another option, with doubles for $149 to $189 in summer.

Of the independents, I like **Yellowstone River Motel,** 14 E. Park St. (www.yellowstonerivermotel.com; © **406/848-7303**) with doubles for $80 to $110 in peak season. Fans of vintage roadside motels and their indelible neon signage might also take a look at the bare-bones cabins at **Jim Bridger Motor Court,** 901 Scott St. (© **406/848-7371**), built in the 1930s around a shady green courtyard. Cabins come with one or two queen beds and range from $50 to $199 nightly.

WHERE TO EAT

An indication that Gardiner has kept in touch with its mining-town roots is the relative dearth of fancy restaurants—you'll find mostly steakhouse fare, hearty breakfasts, and travelers' food. A few upscale eateries have come and gone in recent years, but the dish-clattering local color of the park-side coffee shops is hard to beat.

The Corral Drive-In AMERICAN   Since 1960, this place's reputation has rested on burgers that are nothing short of colossal. With a half-pound of meat (beef, elk, or buffalo), several slices of American cheese, bacon, and all the usual veggies, these burgers have been known to measure a full 7 inches from bun to bun. The monstrous things garnered the nickname "Helen's Hateful Hamburgers" after a dissatisfied customer wrote a letter to the local paper dubbing them just that. Corral founder Helen Gould ran with it, using the intended insult as a sarcastic slogan in promotions and on T-shirts. Ice cream, chicken and fish sandwiches, and an assortment of fried goods round out the menu.

U.S. Hwy. 89 at Yellowstone St. © *406/848-7627.* Reservations not accepted. Menu items $4–$16. MC, V. May–Sept daily 11am–11pm. Closed mid-Oct to Apr.

Sawtooth Deli ★ DELI/AMERICAN   This stalwart eatery on Park Street is a reliable spot for hearty American breakfasts and plump subs. I like the breakfast burritos in the morning (especially before a big hike) and the Philly cheese steaks and veggie subs for lunch (especially after a big hike). With a basic main room and a breezy patio, there is both wait service and a to-go counter. Dinner features the lunch menu plus nightly specials like pasta and ribs. Beer and wine are served, but not liquor.

222 W. Park St. ✆ **406/848-7600.** Main courses $5–$8 breakfast and lunch; $5–$16 dinner. MC, V. Summer Tues–Sat 8am–4pm and 5–9pm; shorter hours rest of year.

Cooke City

If little ol' Gardiner seems just a little too connected to the civilized world, you ought to spend a winter in tiny Cooke City or even tinier Silver Gate, just outside Yellowstone National Park's northeast entrance. In the winter, when the cloud-scraping Beartooth Pass closes to the north, supplies for these towns have to come through the park. Better to visit in the summer and take the breathtaking drive north over the pass (U.S. 212 toward Red Lodge) or south along the scenic Chief Joseph Highway (Wyo. 296). For 100 years, the lifeblood of this town was mining gold, platinum, and other precious metals, but now there is only park tourism, which seems a little anemic by comparison. Fewer than 100 residents live year-round in the town today, and Silver Gate, right next to the park entrance, has perhaps a dozen hardy year-round residents. Contact the **Colter Pass/Cooke City/Silver Gate Chamber of Commerce** at P.O. Box 1071, Cooke City, MT 59020 (www.cookecitychamber.org; ✆ **406/838-2495**), for information. The chamber operates a visitor center at 206 W. Main St. that is open daily in summer.

GETTING THERE From Billings, Montana, drive west on I-90 to Laurel, then south on U.S. 212 to Red Lodge, a total distance of 60 miles; then continue another 67 miles south over spectacular Beartooth Pass, dipping into Wyoming and back up into Montana at Cooke City.

WHERE TO STAY & EAT A room for the night will be less expensive than in other gateway towns, typically from $60 to $120 a night. The **Soda Butte Lodge,** 209 Main St. (www.cookecity.com; ✆ **406/838-2251**), is the biggest motel in Cooke City, with doubles for $80 to $90 and suites for $120, and it includes the **Prospector Restaurant** and a small casino; or you can go to the **Alpine Motel,** 105 Main St. (www.cookecityalpine.com; ✆ **888/838-1190** for reservations, or 406/838-2262), with doubles for $78 to $85 and suites for $120. The newest property is a woodsy **Super 8,** 303 Main St. (www.cookecitysuper8.com; ✆ **877/338-2070** or 406/838-2070), with doubles for about $100. For a bite to eat and a great selection of beers, try the funky **Beartooth Cafe** (✆ **406/838-2475**), also on Main Street. I also like the sandwiches and barbecue plates at **Buns 'N' Beds,** 201 Main St. (✆ **406/838-2030**). In Silver Gate, the **Log Cabin Café and B&B** (✆ **406/838-2367**) is a rustic-meets-refined eatery specializing in trout dinners.

JUST THE FACTS

Before You Go

To obtain maps and information about the park prior to arrival, contact **Yellowstone National Park,** Yellowstone National Park, WY 82190 (www.nps.gov/yell; ✆ **307/344-7381**). Information regarding lodging, some campgrounds, tours, boating, and horseback riding in Yellowstone is available from **Yellowstone National Park Lodges,** operated by Xanterra Parks & Resorts, P.O. Box 165, Yellowstone National Park, WY 82190 (www.yellowstonenationalparklodges.com; ✆ **866/439-7375** or

307/344-7311). For information regarding educational programs at the **Yellowstone Association Institute,** contact **Yellowstone Association,** P.O. Box 117, Yellowstone National Park, WY 82190 (www.yellowstoneassociation.org; ☏ **406/848-2400**). The association operates bookstores in park visitor centers, museums, and information stations, and the old Lamar Buffalo Ranch in the park's northeast corner is the Institute's primary campus. They also have a catalog of publications you can download from the website or order by mail.

Getting There

If interstate highways and international airports are the measure of accessibility, then Yellowstone is as remote as Alaska's Denali National Park or the Serengeti Plains of Africa. But three million people make it here every year, on tour buses, in family vans, on bicycles, and astride snowmobiles, even from the other side of the world.

The closest airport to Yellowstone is in **West Yellowstone,** Montana, which sits just outside the park's west entrance. For information on flying into West Yellowstone, see p. 254.

Visitors can reach the park from the south by flying into **Jackson,** Wyoming (only 14 miles from the southern entrance to Grand Teton), then driving 56 miles through Grand Teton to the southern entrance of Yellowstone. **American Airlines, Delta/SkyWest, Frontier,** and **United** all have flights to and from **Jackson Hole Airport** (www.jacksonholeairport.com; ☏ **307/733-7682**).

To the north, **Bozeman,** Montana, is 87 miles from the West Yellowstone entrance on U.S. Hwy. 191. Or you can drive east from Bozeman to Livingston, a 20-mile journey on I-90, and then south 53 miles on U.S. Hwy. 89 to the northern entrance at Gardiner. Bozeman's airport, **Gallatin Field** (www.gallatinfield.com; ☏ **406/388-8321**), provides daily service via **Alaska, Allegiant, Delta, US Airways,** and **United,** as well as **Horizon** and **Frontier.**

Also to the north, **Billings,** Montana, is 129 miles from the Cooke City entrance. Billings is home to Montana's busiest airport, **Logan International** (www.flybillings.com; ☏ **406/247-8609**), which is 2 miles north of downtown. Daily service is provided by **Allegiant, Delta, Frontier, Horizon,** and **United.** From Billings, it's a 65-mile drive south on U.S. Hwy. 212 to Red Lodge and then 30 miles on the Beartooth Highway to the northeast entrance to the park.

From **Cody,** Wyoming, it's a gorgeous 53-mile drive west along U.S. Hwy. 14/16/20 to the east entrance of the park. Cody's **Yellowstone Regional Airport** (www.flyyra.com; ☏ **307/587-5096**) serves the Bighorn Basin, as well as the east and northeast entrances of Yellowstone National Park, with year-round commercial flights via **Delta/SkyWest** and **United.**

Airfares to the small airports surrounding the parks can be pricey, so if you like to drive, consider flying in to **Salt Lake City,** Utah, and driving about 300 miles to Grand Teton National Park, a drive that has some nice scenic stretches. Even **Denver,** a drive of roughly 500 miles, is an alternative, although the route is not nearly as scenic. Most of the major auto-rental agencies have operations in the gateway cities.

Access/Entry Points

Yellowstone has five entrances. The **north entrance,** near Mammoth Hot Springs, is located just south of Gardiner, Montana, and U.S. 89. In the winter, this is the only access to Yellowstone by car.

The **west entrance,** just outside the town of West Yellowstone on U.S. 20, is the closest entry to Old Faithful. Inside the park, turn south to see Old Faithful or north to the Norris Geyser Basin. This entrance is open to wheeled vehicles April through November, and during the winter to snowmobiles and snowcoaches.

The **south entrance,** on U.S. 89/191/287, brings visitors into the park from neighboring Grand Teton National Park and the Jackson area. As you drive north from Jackson, you'll get a panoramic view of the Grand Tetons. Once in the park, the road winds along the Lewis River to the south end of Yellowstone Lake, at West Thumb and Grant Village. It is open to cars May through November and to snowmobiles and snowcoaches December through March.

The **east entrance,** on U.S. 14/16/20, is 52 miles west of Cody, Wyoming, and is open to cars May through September and to snowmobiles and snowcoaches December through March. The drive up the Wapiti Valley and over Sylvan Pass is especially beautiful.

The **northeast entrance,** at Cooke City, Montana, is closest to the Tower-Roosevelt area, 29 miles to the west. This entrance is open to cars year-round, but beginning on October 15, when the Beartooth Highway closes, until around Memorial Day, the only route to Cooke City is from Gardiner through Mammoth Hot Springs. When it's open, the drive from Red Lodge to Cooke City is a grand climb into the clouds.

Regardless of which entrance you choose, when you enter the park, you'll be given a good map and up-to-date information on facilities, services, programs, fishing, camping, and more.

Note: Check **road conditions** before entering the park by calling for a road report (✆ **307/344-7381**). There always seems to be major road construction in one part of the park or another, so be forewarned.

Visitor Centers & Information

There are five major visitor and information centers in the park, and each has something different to offer. Unless otherwise indicated, summer hours are daily from 8am to 7pm.

The **Albright Visitor Center** (✆ **307/344-2263**), at Mammoth Hot Springs, is the largest and is open daily, year-round. It provides visitor information and publications about the park, has exhibits depicting park history from prehistory through the creation of the National Park Service, and also houses displays on wildlife.

The **Canyon Visitor Education Center** (✆ **307/344-2550**), in Canyon Village, completed in 2007, is the place to go for books and an informative display about the park's geology, with a focus on the underlying volcanism. It's staffed with friendly rangers used to dealing with crowds and open 8am to 8pm daily in summer.

The state-of-the-art **Old Faithful Visitor Education Center** (✆ **307/344-2751**) opened in 2010, showing a film on Yellowstone's thermal features throughout the day and featuring exhibits focusing on the park's geysers and other thermal features. You'll also find projected geyser-eruption times here, making it a good first stop for those looking to see Old Faithful do its thing. It's open in summer 8am to 8pm.

The **Fishing Bridge Visitor Center** (✆ **307/344-2450**), near Fishing Bridge on the north shore of Yellowstone Lake, has an excellent display that focuses on the park's bird life. You can get information and publications here as well.

The **Grant Visitor Center** (✆ **307/344-2650**) has information, publications, a video program, and a fascinating exhibit that examines the role of fire in Yellowstone.

Park literature and helpful staff are also found at several small information stations: the **Madison Information Station** (✆ 307/344-2876; summer daily 9am–6pm), home of the **Junior Ranger Station;** the **Museum of the National Park Ranger** (no phone; summer daily 9am–5pm) and the **Norris Geyser Basin Museum and Information Station** (☎ 307/344-2812; summer daily 9am–6pm), both at Norris; the **West Thumb Information Station** (☎ 307/344-2650; summer daily 9am–5pm); and the West Yellowstone **Visitor Information Center,** 100 Yellowstone Ave. (☎ 307/344-2876; summer daily 8am–8pm, limited hours the rest of the year). In Gardiner (but also within Yellowstone boundaries) is the **Yellowstone Heritage and Research Center** (☎ 307/344-2664), housing a library, archives, and other resources available to the public. It is open 9am to 4pm year-round but is not equipped to handle standard visitor inquiries.

Fees & Permits

Entrance for up to 7 days costs $25 per vehicle and covers both Yellowstone and Grand Teton national parks. A snowmobile or motorcycle pays $20 for 7 days, and visitors on bicycles, on skis, or on foot pay $12. You can buy an **annual permit** for $40, but the various national park passes are the best deal (p. 47).

BACKCOUNTRY PERMITS   Backcountry permits are free, but you have to have one for any overnight trip, on foot, on horseback, or by boat. Camping is allowed only in designated campsites, many of which are equipped with food-storage poles to keep wildlife away. These sites are primitive and well situated, and you won't feel at all like you're in a campground. If designated campsites in a particular area have already been reserved, you're out of luck. So while you can make a reservation as few as 48 hours before beginning a trip, you would be wise during peak season to make a reservation well in advance (you can contact the park for reservations for the upcoming year beginning Apr 1), although it costs $20. The **Yellowstone Backcountry Office** (P.O. Box 168, Yellowstone National Park, WY 82190) will send you the useful "Backcountry Trip Planner" brochure with a detailed map showing where the campsites are; it is also available online as a PDF (see www.nps.gov/yell/planyourvisit/backcountry tripplanner.htm). Call the office for more information at ☎ **307/344-2160.**

Pick up your permit in the park within 48 hours of your departure, at one of the following visitor ranger stations any day of the week during the summer: Bechler, Canyon, Mammoth, Old Faithful, Tower, West Entrance, Grant Village, Lake, South Entrance, and Bridge Bay. Boating permits for motorized craft can be obtained at only the last four ranger stations.

BOATING PERMITS   Any vessels used on park waters must have a permit. For motorized craft, the cost is $20 for annual permits and $10 for a 7-day pass. Fees for nonmotorized boats are $10 for annual permits and $5 for 7-day permits. Rivers and streams are closed to boats of any kind, except for the stretch of the Lewis River between Lewis and Shoshone lakes, which is restricted to hand-propelled craft. Coast Guard–approved personal flotation devices are required for each person boating.

FISHING PERMITS   Permits are required for anglers 16 and over; the permit costs $15 for 3 days, $20 for 7 days, and $35 for the season. Youths 12 to 15 years of age also must have a permit, but it's free. Children 11 and under may fish without a permit. Permits are available at any ranger station, visitor center, and Yellowstone General Store, along with most fishing shops in the gateways. The season usually begins on the Saturday of Memorial Day weekend and continues through the first Sunday in November. Exceptions to this rule are Yellowstone Lake, its tributaries, and sections of the Yellowstone River. In the search for ecological equilibrium, the regulations have two key wrinkles: Any nonnative lake trout caught within the park must not be released alive, and cutthroat trout are catch-and-release only.

Regulations

You can get more detailed information about these rules from a park ranger, at a park visitor center, or at the park's website (www.nps.gov/yell).

BICYCLES Bicycles are not allowed on the vast majority of the park's trails or any of the boardwalks, but the park is a popular destination for pavement cyclists. Because of the narrowness of park roads and the presence of large recreational vehicles with poor visibility, it's recommended that you wear helmets and bright clothing. There are some designated off-pavement bicycling areas; contact the park for more information.

CAMPING In any given year, a person may camp for no more than 30 days in the park, and only 14 days during the summer season. Food, garbage, and utensils must be stored in a vehicle or container made of solid material and suspended at least 10 feet above the ground when not in use.

CLIMBING Because of the loose, crumbly rock in Yellowstone, climbing is discouraged throughout the park and prohibited in the Grand Canyon of the Yellowstone.

DEFACING PARK FEATURES It's illegal to pick wildflowers or collect natural or archaeological objects. Only dead-and-down wood can be collected for backcountry campfires.

FIREARMS Firearms are allowed in Yellowstone National Park. Those in possession of a firearm must have a legal license, and they are prohibited in marked facilities.

LITTERING Littering in the national parks is strictly prohibited—remember, if you pack it in, you have to pack it out. Throwing coins or other objects into thermal features is illegal.

MOTORCYCLES Motorcycles, motor scooters, and motorbikes are allowed only on park roads. No off-road or trail riding is allowed. Operator licenses and license plates are required.

PETS Pets must be leashed and are prohibited in the backcountry, on trails, on boardwalks, and in thermal areas. If you tie up a pet and leave it, you're breaking the law.

SMOKING There is no smoking in thermal areas, visitor centers, ranger stations, or any other posted public areas.

SNOWMOBILING Yellowstone's latest winter use plan limits snowmobiles entering the park to 318 a day and requires a licensed guide for all trips. Snowmobilers must have a valid driver's license, stay on the designated unplowed roadways, and obey posted speed limits.

SWIMMING Swimming or wading is prohibited in thermal features or in streams whose waters flow from thermal features in Yellowstone. (Two exceptions: Boiling River near Mammoth, where visitors can take a warm soak between daybreak and dusk except during spring runoff, and the swimming hole in Firehole Canyon.) Swimming in Yellowstone Lake is discouraged because of the low water temperature and unpredictable weather. Bathing suits are required.

WILDLIFE It is unlawful to approach within 300 feet of a bear or within 75 feet of other wildlife. Feeding any wildlife is illegal. Wildlife calls such as elk bugles or other artificial attractants are forbidden.

When to Go

During the quiet "shoulder" seasons of spring and fall, there are more bison and elk around than autos and RVs. Before the second week in June, you'll be rewarded by the explosion of wildflowers as they begin to bloom, filling the meadows and hillsides with vast arrays of colors and shapes. After that, roads become progressively busier. Traveling before peak season has economic advantages as well, since rates at gateway-city motels are lower, as are the costs of meals. After Labor Day weekend, crowds begin to thin again and the roads become less traveled. In addition to improved wildlife and fishing conditions in some areas, the fall foliage transforms the area to a calendar-quality image.

In the winter, Yellowstone has a storybook beauty, as snow and ice soften the edges of the landscape and shroud the lumbering bison. Geyser basins appear even more dramatic, the frigid air temperature in stark contrast to the steaming, gurgling waters. Nearby trees are transformed into eerie "snow ghosts" by frozen thermal vapors. Wildlife clusters at the thermal areas to take advantage of the softer ground and more accessible vegeta-

> ## Impressions
>
> *[W]e beheld one of the grandest displays of the kind we had ever beheld—a perfect geyser—an immediate volume of clear, hot water projected into the air one-hundred and fifty vertical feet, attended with dense volumes of steam rising upward for many hundred feet, and floating away in clouds . . .*
> —Edwin Stanley, from
> *Rambles in Wonderland*, 1878

tion. Lake Yellowstone's surface freezes to an average thickness of 3 feet, creating a vast ice sheet that sings and moans as the huge plates of ice shift.

The other winter sound is made by the herds of snowmobiles that roam the roads and are at the center of a contentious issue of late. (For more information on the snowmobile issue, see the box "Snowmobiling: To Ban or Not to Ban," on p. 284, and the section "Snowmobiling," above.)

You can also enter the park in snowcoaches, the tracked vehicles that deliver visitors to the beautifully rebuilt Old Faithful Snow Lodge and tour the park. From the lodge or Mammoth—which also stays open to cars during the winter—you can ski, snowmobile (assuming regulations still permit it), or visit the thermal areas. The only road within the park open for automobile traffic is the road between Mammoth Hot Springs and Cooke City through the Lamar Valley.

SEASONS

Natives of the region describe weather in the Yellowstone ecosystem as predictably unpredictable. Because of the region's high elevations and changing weather systems, the park is characterized by long, cold winters and short, though usually warm, summers.

The first sticking snows typically fall by November 1, and cold and snow may linger into April and May (and even June), though temperatures generally warm up by then. The average daytime readings during spring are 40°F to 50°F (4°C–10°C), gradually increasing to 60°F to 70°F (16°C–21°C) by early June. Yellowstone is never balmy, but temperatures during the middle of the summer are typically 75°F to 85°F (24°C–30°C) in the lower elevations, and are especially comfortable because of the lack of humidity. Even during the summer months, nights will be cool, with temperatures dropping into the low 40s (4°C–7°C). No matter how warm you expect it to be, it's a good idea to bring a warm jacket, rain gear, and water-resistant walking shoes. And because this is high altitude, bring plenty of sunscreen and a wide-brimmed hat to protect yourself in the thin atmosphere. As summer thunderstorms are common, a tarp and an umbrella are also recommended.

During winter months, temperatures hover in the single digits, and subzero overnight temperatures are common. You should bring long underwear, heavy shirts (fast-drying synthetic fabrics, not cotton), vests and coats, warm gloves and hats, and warm, wicking socks. The lowest temperature recorded at Yellowstone was a dangerously chilly –66°F (–54°C) in 1933.

AVOIDING THE CROWDS

One of the things you'll discover when you venture down a trail is that the majority of Yellowstone's three million annual visitors aren't going to follow you. (Only about 10% of visitors wander beyond the trail heads.) Some are afraid of grizzly bears, some are in a hurry, and others just don't want the exercise. Regardless, Yellowstone rewards those who expend a bit of shoe leather: A mere half-mile from the traffic jams, you'll find few people and much better opportunities to smell the wildflowers.

If you really want a Yellowstone experience that's all your own, head for the backcountry. This is some of the deepest, most exquisite wilderness in the country, and you definitely won't be fighting a mob. While visitation at Yellowstone increases yearly, backcountry permits do not—they've actually declined a bit in the last 30 years. My favorite areas are the Thorofare region, in the park's southeast corner at the headwaters of the Yellowstone River, and the shores of Shoshone Lake, the largest backcountry body of water in the Lower 48, but there's so much wilderness here that it's hard not to find views of your own.

Educational Programs

Yellowstone offers free **ranger-led educational programs** ★★ that will significantly enhance a visitor's understanding of the area's history, geology, and wildlife. Most programs run from early June through late September. Detailed information on location and times is listed in the park newsletter, which is distributed at the entrance gates. On a more informal basis, you'll run into ranger-naturalists roaming the geyser basins and along the rim of the Grand Canyon of the Yellowstone, and in areas where wildlife gather in both parks, leading informative walks and answering the questions of inquisitive visitors.

Evening campfire programs are presented nightly in the summer at Mammoth, Norris, Madison, Bridge Bay, Grant, and Canyon. Many of these activities are accessible to those with disabilities. It's a good idea to bring a flashlight, warm clothing, and rain gear. Rangers also conduct walking, talking, and hiking programs throughout the park, including half-day "Adventure Hikes" that are free but require reservations that can be made at each visitor center.

As one would expect, there are quite a few programs in the **Old Faithful** area. The topics of the guided walks, which can run as long as 1½ hours, usually focus on the geysers, their fragile plumbing, and their role in the Yellowstone ecosystem. There is an outdoor talk in the visitor center's amphitheater in the evening.

Beginning in June, daily hikes in the **Canyon** area skirt along the rim of the Grand Canyon; a ranger talk on the art inspired by the falls is held several times a day at the lower platform of Artist Point. An explanation of the origins of the hot pools and mud pots is conducted twice daily beginning in June as part of a walk of the Lakeshore area of the **West Thumb Geyser Basin.** The **Lake Village/Fishing Bridge** agenda includes walking tours of the Mud Volcano area and the shores of Yellowstone Lake. There is an afternoon "Featured Creature" talk at the Fishing Bridge Visitor Center about such wildlife as grizzlies and wolves, and a discussion concerning the native cutthroat is held on the west end of the Fishing Bridge.

Mammoth Hot Springs is host to several interesting ranger-led programs, including talks on the park's natural and cultural wonders and a historical tour of the original site of Fort Yellowstone, established more than 100 years ago. There is also a guided tour of the hot springs terraces. The hottest, most dynamic, and oldest geyser basin in the park is at **Norris,** where a popular 1½-hour tour begins at the Norris museum on a daily basis, in season.

Many changes are made annually in these presentations; consult the park newsletter that is distributed at the entrance gates for the current calendar.

Astronomers from the **Museum of the Rockies** in Bozeman, Montana, often bring their telescopes and stories to a series of stargazing sessions throughout the park—contact the museum at ℂ **406/994-3466** for a schedule.

The **Yellowstone Association Institute** ★★★ (www.yellowstoneassociation. org/institute; ℂ **406/848-2400**) offers a slew of guided classes, from daylong hikes to multiday backcountry adventures, often with a historical or scientific bent. Participants can bunk in cabins at the historic buffalo ranch in Lamar Valley or above Gardiner at the new Overlook Field Campus, featuring cabins with shared kitchens and a commanding view. The Institute has teamed with Yellowstone National Park Lodges to offer visitors days spent exploring trails with guides and nights at the comfortable lodgings throughout the park. These **Lodging & Learning** packages are excellent options for those who want to delve into the park without too much of the traditional "roughing it." Rates are about $250 per person per day and include box lunches, breakfast, and in-park transportation. Contact **Xanterra Parks & Resorts** (www.yellowstonenationalparklodges.com; ℂ **866/439-7375**).

In September, the Institute takes over **Roosevelt Lodge** with the **Roosevelt Rendezvous,** a series of 4-day educational experiences with a daily menu of different field trips led by park experts. There are also evening programs. Rates start at $729 per person, which includes tuition, a cabin, and three meals a day.

Services & Supplies

Independent of Xanterra, Yellowstone General Stores is the concessionaire behind the bulk of the park's retail operations. The company operates **stores** throughout the park, including Old Faithful, Mammoth Hot Springs, Lake, Fishing Bridge, and Grant Village, which feature gift shops, grocery supplies, and soda fountains. Depending upon the location, you may find a limited supply of fresh veggies and canned goods (as at the Canyon store), plus fishing supplies, souvenirs, and, of course, ice cream. **Service stations** are located at major visitor areas: Old Faithful, Canyon, Mammoth Hot Springs, and Grant Village. Exact locations of all services and stores are listed in the park newspaper you receive at the entrance gates.

If you have medical problems while visiting the park, Yellowstone Park Medical Services provides help at the **Lake Hospital** (ℂ **307/242-7241**), an acute-care facility; the **Old Faithful Clinic** (☎ **307/344-7325**); and the **Mammoth Clinic** (☎ **307/344-7965**), the only year-round facility of the three.

Organized Tours & Activities

A number of tour companies offer bus and van tours of the park originating in gateway communities: **Yellowstone Alpen Guides** (www.yellowstoneguides.com; ☎ **800/858-3502**) takes travelers around the park from West Yellowstone; rates run about $50 per person for a 4-hour tour. Salt Lake City–based **AdventureBus** (www.adventurebus.com; ☎ **888/737-5263**) takes groups to Yellowstone and Grand Teton between June and August; weeklong tours run about $1,000 per person. I highly recommend **Escape Adventures** (www.escapeadventures.com; ☎ **800/596-2953**), which offers supported 6-day road-biking tours of Yellowstone and Grand Teton for about $1,500 if you camp or $2,300 if you stay in the park's accommodations. If you are looking for specialized guided trips—such as photo safaris—contact the chambers of commerce in the gateway community where you want to begin.

Within the park, the hotel concessionaire, **Yellowstone National Park Lodges** (www.yellowstonenationalparklodges.com; ☎ **866/439-7375**), has a variety of general and specialized tours. Five different motorcoach tours are available from all of Yellowstone's villages. For $66 adult ($33 kids 3–11), you can explore the **Circle of Fire** (Old Faithful, Yellowstone Lake, the Hayden Valley), or you can do the **Yellowstone in a Day** tour. These are full-day tours, with stops at all the sights and informative talks by the guides. Eight restored **Old Yellow Buses** that roamed the Yellowstone roads here in the first half of the 20th century are today back in service for Xanterra. Tours in the buses range from 1 to 5 hours ($26–$85). Other specialty trips include custom van tours, photo safaris, wildlife trips up the Lamar Valley, and Yellowstone Lake sunset tours.

At Bridge Bay Marina, 1-hour "**Scenicruises**" (☎ **877/439-7375**) depart throughout the day from June to the end of September for a trip around the northern end of giant Yellowstone Lake. You view the Lake Yellowstone Hotel from the water and visit Stevenson Island while a guide fills you in on the history, geology, and biology. Fares are $15 for adults and $9 for children ages 2 to 11. Guided fishing trips on 22-foot and 34-foot cabin cruisers are also available at Bridge Bay ($160 and $200 for 2 hr., respectively), and you can rent smaller outboards and rowboats.

Buses are replaced in the winter by **snowcoach tours.** These are closer in size to a van than a bus, mounted on tank treads with skis in front for steering. The snowcoach can pick you up at the south or west entrances, or at Mammoth, and take you all over the park. You can spend a night at Old Faithful and then snowcoach up to Mammoth the next night, or do round-trip tours from the gates or wherever you're staying in the park. One-way and wildlife-watching trips are $57 to $70 for adults and $29 to $35 for kids 3 to 11. **Yellowstone Alpen Guides** (www.yellowstoneguides.com; ☎ **800/858-3502**) offers snowcoach trips and tours from West Yellowstone for $115 per person and up.

Guided horseback trail rides lasting from 1 to 2 hours are available at Roosevelt Lodge and Canyon Village. Children must be at least 8 years old and 48 inches tall; adults cannot exceed 240 pounds. Tour prices are $38 for a 1-hour ride and $58 for a 2-hour ride (no discount for children). Check any activity desk for times and dates. Reservations are recommended and can be made at **Xanterra Parks & Resorts** activity centers in the hotels, although not before you leave home.

For Travelers with Disabilities

In recent years, both parks have become increasingly user-friendly for travelers with disabilities. People who are blind or who have permanent disabilities can obtain an **Interagency Access Pass,** which costs nothing and allows lifetime access to all national parks and other federal fee areas. All passes are available at any entrance point to Yellowstone or Grand Teton. The Interagency Access passes must be obtained in person.

Wheelchair-accessible accommodations are located in the Dunraven and Cascade lodges and Western cabins at Canyon Village; in Grant Village; in the Old Faithful Inn and Snow Lodge and Cabins; and in the Lake Yellowstone Hotel. For a free *Visitors Guide to Accessible Features in Yellowstone National Park,* write to the **Park Accessibility Coordinator** (www.nps.gov/yell; ✆ **307/344-2314**), P.O. Box 168, Yellowstone National Park, WY 82190, or pick up the guide at the gates or visitor centers. There are wheelchair-accessible campsites at Fishing Bridge, Bridge Bay, Madison, Canyon, and Grant campgrounds, which you can reserve by calling ✆ **307/344-7311.**

Wheelchair-accessible restrooms with sinks and flush toilets are located at all developed areas except West Thumb and Norris. Wheelchair-accessible vault toilets are found at West Thumb and Norris, as well as in most scenic areas and picnic areas.

Many of Yellowstone's roadside attractions, including the south rim of the Grand Canyon of the Yellowstone, West Thumb Geyser Basin, much of the Norris and Upper Geyser basins, and parts of the Mud Volcano and Fountain Paint Pot areas, are negotiable by wheelchair.

Visitor centers at Old Faithful, Grant Village, and Canyon are wheelchair-accessible, as are the Norris Museum and the Fishing Bridge Visitor Center. The Albright Visitor Center at Mammoth is also accessible via a rear entrance.

Wheelchair-accessible parking is available at Old Faithful, Fishing Bridge, Canyon, Norris, and Grant Village, although you'll have to look for it; at some locations, it is near a Yellowstone General Store.

A PARK PRIMER

A Brief History

A trip to Yellowstone has changed considerably since the days of George Cowan: When he visited the park in 1877, he set a new standard for "roughing it." Cowan was kidnapped from his horse-packing camp and shot by the Nez Perce Indians, then subsisted on roots and coffee grounds as he dragged his paralyzed body for days through the wilderness.

Let's just say the United States government had a bit to learn about how to run the world's first national park. It still does, but it's getting better all the time. For more than 125 years, the National Park Service has been directing traffic at this complex intersection of wilderness and tourism, juggling the protection of powerful natural wonders while allowing for civilized comforts. And if anyone complains that the roads are potholed or the coffee is cold . . . well, George Cowan would not be sympathetic.

Yellowstone was never known as a hospitable place. Nomadic Indian bands crossed the plateau but never settled there, except for a small group of Shoshone known as "Sheep Eaters." The first white explorer to lay eyes on Yellowstone's geothermal wonders was probably John Colter, an explorer who broke away from the Lewis and Clark

expedition in 1806 and soon found himself wandering through a surreal landscape of mud pots and geysers. When he described his discovery on his return to St. Louis, no one believed him, and he settled down to life as a farmer. Later, miners and fur trappers followed in his footsteps, occasionally making curious reports of a sulfurous world still sometimes called "Colter's Hell."

The first significant exploration of what would become the park took place in 1869, when a band of Montanans led by David Folsom completed a 36-day expedition. Folsom and his group traveled up the Missouri River, then into the heart of the park, where they laid eyes on the falls of the Yellowstone, mud pots, Yellowstone Lake, and the Fountain Geyser. But it was an 1871 expedition led by U.S. Geological Survey Director Ferdinand Hayden that brought back astonishing photographs of Yellowstone's wonders by William Henry Jackson.

Crude health spas and thin-walled "hotels" went up near the hot springs. A debate soon followed over the potential for commercial development and exploitation of the region. Many people take credit for the idea of creating the national park—members of the Folsom party later told a story about thinking it up around a campfire in the Upper Geyser Basin. In any case, the idea caught on as Yellowstone explorers hit the lecture circuit back East. In March 1872, President Ulysses S. Grant signed legislation declaring Yellowstone a national park.

No one had any experience in managing a wilderness park, and many mistakes were made: Superintendents granted favorable leases to friends with commercial interests in the tourism industry; poachers ran amok, decimating the wildlife population; a laundry business near Mammoth cleaned linens in the hot pool.

By 1886, things were so bad that the army took control of the park; its firm-fisted management practices resulted in new order and protected the park from those intent upon exploiting it, although the military participated in the eradication of the plateau's wolf population. By 1916, efforts to make the park more visitor-friendly began to bear fruit: Construction of the first roads had been completed and guest housing was available in the area. Stewardship of the park was then transferred to the newly created National Park Service.

The Park Today

It has long been difficult for park managers to both provide the public with a good vacation and protect the natural wonders of the parks. One challenge is to make the parks accessible to three million annual visitors, many with different, even contradictory, expectations of a wilderness excursion. This brings about the construction of new facilities and ongoing road maintenance and repair. At the same time, the parks are wild preserves, and the National Park Service must cope with the impact of six million feet on the forests, meadows, and thermal areas, as well as on the day-to-day lives of the millions of animals that inhabit the area.

It's a tough balancing act. Some of the pivotal issues in the parks today include the impact of snowmobiles; the reintroduced wolves and the resulting livestock losses of ranchers in and around the parks; the inadequacy of the park's infrastructure to cope with three million annual human visitors; invasive nonnative species, such as lake trout and zebra mussels; and the reduction of habitat surrounding the parks, coupled with a growing population of elk and bison seeking forage beyond park boundaries and possibly infecting domestic animals with a disease called brucellosis. And that's the short list.

Possible solutions are often "too little, too late," layering complex management strategies on an ecosystem that might do better if it were simply allowed to work things out naturally. The problem is, Grand Teton and Yellowstone have already been altered significantly by humans, so "natural" becomes a relative concept.

A good example is the reintroduction of a natural predator of the overpopulated elk: gray wolves, which were eliminated in the 1920s. These days, ranchland surrounds the

wildlife & WHERE TO SPOT IT

Biologists consider Yellowstone one of the most important wildlife habitats in the world. You'll find all sorts of creatures here, from the dramatic bald eagle to the less-publicized reptiles of the thermal areas. What particularly distinguishes this collection of wildlife is that the elk, bison, and all their brethren are free-roaming.

Bison (buffalo) are right at home here, wandering along the main thoroughfares without much regard for their human spectators. They are easy to view in the summer months, often seen munching grass, wallowing in dust pits, and even wrestling sumo-style for mates in the Lamar, Hayden, and Pelican valleys; the Bechler River area; and in the geyser areas near the Firehole River. **Caution:** They have poor eyesight and cranky dispositions, and, like moose, they can move with sudden speed (up to 35 mph) to batter anyone who invades their personal space.

Biologists have trouble agreeing on how many **bears** there are in Yellowstone, but most will acknowledge that their numbers are on the rise. (However, car–bear accidents are on the rise as well.) Their food supplies seem to have stabilized a bit with the wolf reintroduction (more carcasses) and pro-cutthroat fishing regulations. In the Greater Yellowstone Ecosystem, there are probably about 1,000 black bears and 600 grizzlies, but estimates vary. Grizzlies were delisted as an endangered species in 2007, but conservationists argued the move was premature, and they were relisted in 2010.

Decades ago, bears foraged in open-pit garbage dumps near the lodges, or tourists hand-fed bears who begged along the park roads. When the dumps were closed in the 1970s and bear feeding was prohibited, the population of bears plummeted. Diminishing habitat around the park also had an impact. However, bears are creative omnivores; they tend to gravitate toward elk and bison (either the very young or the very old) and wolf kills, but their diet has been assessed as being about three-quarters vegetarian.

Black bears are most commonly sighted in the spring, sometimes with cubs, in the Canyon, Tower, Madison, and Old Faithful areas, where they feed on green grass and herbs, berries, ants, and carrion. The more aggressive grizzly's unpredictable behavior makes them the likely suspect in the rare instances of bear attacks on humans, but blacks have demonstrated that they also are capable in this regard.

Odds of seeing a grizzly are best during May and June, in the Lamar and Hayden valleys, before they retreat into the backwoods for the summer. Backcountry travelers often see bears in the remote Thorofare Country on the park's southeast border, where bears (and avid anglers) journey to the Yellowstone River headwaters for the spawning cutthroat trout in the spring.

It is estimated that over 30,000 **elk** (wapiti) populate the entire ecosystem, although numbers have been on the decline in park boundaries in recent

parks, so the Defenders of Wildlife set up a trust to pay anyone who loses a calf to a wolf—and ranchers do because wolves haven't read the management plan. And wolves from Yellowstone have migrated south into Grand Teton and beyond; besides the packs that den in and around the Gros Ventre area, a lone wolf was spotted at the Wyoming–Colorado border, and two others turned up dead in Colorado in 2004 and 2009.

years, in large part because of predation by wolves. You should have no problem telling elk from deer or antelope by their size (typically 900 lb.); the males have large antler racks, chestnut-brown heads and necks, and a distinctive tan patch on their rumps. One herd can usually be located around **Mammoth Hot Springs;** others are often seen in the meadows between Old Faithful and Madison Junction.

During winter months, the northern Yellowstone herd heads to a winter grazing area near Gardiner as the southern herd descends to the National Elk Refuge near Jackson. Listen in the fall for the distinctive bugling of the males, a throaty gargle that slips into a piercing, high whistle.

Moose are grumpy loners and not very patient with the tourists. They usually appear in alder thickets and marshes around streams, particularly around Canyon and near Shoshone Lake in the backcountry. They are recognizable by their dark coats, massive antlers, and the fleshy dewlap that hangs beneath their necks like a bell. A moose is capable of traveling at 30 mph; cows will charge any perceived threat to a calf, and bulls become particularly ornery in the fall. Give them a wide berth.

The **pronghorn,** usually labeled antelope (though unrelated to the true African antelope), is often sighted grazing near the northern entrance to Yellowstone. These fleet and flighty animals have excellent vision, and they'll take off at 45 mph when photographers try to

get near. However, the park's population of pronghorn has plummeted in recent years. The pronghorn is identified by its short black horns, tan-and-white body, and black accent stripes.

For a long time, the **coyote** has been the predator most often spotted by park visitors, but the arrival of wolves has taken its toll on the smaller canine. Coyotes may be seen alone or in small packs—they're particularly visible in winter—with brown to gray coats that grow silvery after the snow falls. They prey on small animals like squirrels and rabbits, or larger ungulates like elk and deer that have grown old or ill. They'll also scavenge the leftovers of other predators. Biologists estimate there are around 500 coyotes in the park. You'll see them out in the open meadows of the Hayden Valley, and you might get lucky and see the interaction between wolves and coyotes in places like Slough Creek.

Gray wolves from Canada were reintroduced to the park in 1995. There are more than 1,500 wolves in the Northern Rockies today, but the number in the park dropped from about 175 to under 100 in 2011 due to a bout with distemper. The Lamar Valley is where they were first released, and patient observers at dawn and dusk can sometimes see them in the Lamar Valley. Look for park wolf guru Rick McIntyre—he's there most of the summer—or one of the many dedicated wolf trackers on hand in springtime, and ask for advice, or check at the northeast gate or Mammoth Visitor Center for the best sighting opportunities.

Yellowstone's artificial boundaries also cause problems for bison. The state of Montana now allows hunters to shoot bison when they stray outside the park. Ranchers fear bison because of brucellosis, a disease that, when transmitted to cattle, causes cows to abort fetuses. A full 1,400 animals were killed when they left the park for low country in Montana in 2008 (and several hundred animals in subsequent years), although so far there are almost no documented cases of bison infecting livestock.

As the park attracts more visitors (2010 and 2011 were record-setting years), there are more opportunities for human–animal interactions. 2011 proved to be a bad year, with two fatal grizzly attacks, the first such incidents in a quarter-century. And grizzlies are killed on a near-annual basis in car accidents, and park officials have euthanized numerous problem animals as well.

As for the proliferation of snowmobiles and cars, most agree that there must be changes as visitation continues to grow. Currently, snowmobilers flock to the park as soon as the snow starts falling and remain until late February. While the popularity of the sport has had a positive effect on the tourism industry in the gateways of West Yellowstone, Jackson, and Gardiner, park officials are studying the long-term environmental impact of the machines. In their opinion, the snowmobiles create their own types of problems. The machines are noisy, and engine emissions create air pollution, which some say presents a health hazard. While better technology has reined in the noise and smog to a large degree, the snowmobiles still share narrow trails with wildlife during months when the animals' energy levels are depleted by bad weather and a lack of food. As a consequence, a 3-year phase-out of snowmobiles was agreed upon in 2000, but it was overturned before park policy could be changed. The compromise resulted in a quota system that limits the number of snowmobiles in the park to 318 per day and requires guides and best-available technology.

Then there's the traffic issue. Park roads are narrow and twisty, so the intrusion of 30-foot-long motor homes and pickup trucks towing trailers creates congestion, especially during the peak summer months. There have been studies of transportation alternatives to unclog park roadways, even a costly monorail that would wind through Yellowstone, but no decisive action has been taken.

Recently, park scientists have battled to protect the native cutthroat trout in Yellowstone Lake from the impact of lake trout introduced by man. They have also recognized the enormous value of the microbes evolving in Yellowstone's super-hot thermal areas, and scientists are using them in new technologies ranging from nanocircuitry to industrial bleaching products. As the world awakens to the accelerating loss of vital species in shrinking wild habitat, it becomes ever more imperative to find ways in which to preserve the relatively unspoiled ecosystems, like that of Greater Yellowstone.

Plant Life of the Park

The large mammals may be the stars of Yellowstone National Park, but flower lovers will find plenty to enjoy here among the park's 1,200 native plants. Flowers and shrubs broadcast bright shades of blues, purples, yellows, and oranges throughout the park, providing a colorful accent to the forests and meadows.

The plateau's volcanoes, fires, and glaciers have created a series of tumultuous changes that have had an enormous impact on plant life. At one site in the Lamar Valley, the inspection of petrified tree stumps exhumed by erosion resulted in the identification of 27 distinct layers of forests, one atop the other.

The plants have evolved with the ever-changing Yellowstone environment. Forests once populated with hardwoods, such as maple, magnolia, and sycamore, are now filled with conifers, the most common of which are pine, spruce, and fir. A smattering of cottonwood and aspen thrive in the cool park temperatures.

Vegetation zones tend to reflect altitude: Lower-elevation valleys tend to be dry and grassy, with sagebrush and few trees; forests of fir dominate between about 6,000 and 7,500 feet, followed by lodgepole pine stands and then spruce and more fir up to the timberline, with open meadows where wildflowers explode in the spring. At high elevations, shrubs and carpetlike vegetation take over, and you have to lean over to examine the tiny blossoms.

Attempts by park officials to manage the ecosystem have had an impact, too. Climax forests—a plant succession leading to conifers that create a shady canopy and block the growth of seedlings—had a prolonged reign in Yellowstone because of fire suppression, which contributed to the ferocity of fires in the dry summer of 1988. However, once the fires were allowed to burn, it became clear that fire was crucial in the life cycle of lodgepole pine. Since its cones release seeds only after a burn, many of the areas that were "ravaged" in 1988 are now carpeted by dense juvenile forests.

SEEING THE HIGHLIGHTS

This is a wonderland you can return to again and again, sampling a different pleasure each time. All the sites mentioned here are easily accessible along the loop tours detailed in "Driving the Park," p. 279. The farther you get from the pavement, and the farther from July and August you schedule your visit, the more private your experience will be.

I've organized this list geographically, following the roadways that form a figure eight at the heart of the park. We'll begin in the north, then move south, first along the east side, then the west. Get out the oversize map you receive at the gate or by mail, and follow along.

Mammoth Hot Springs

At the park's north entrance, 5 miles south of Gardiner, Mammoth Hot Springs is home to spectacular limestone terraces, historic park buildings, and the Mammoth Hot Springs Hotel. It's one of the older park settlements, with stone buildings dating from the late 19th century, when the army was stationed here at Fort Yellowstone.

There are no geysers at **Mammoth Hot Springs Terraces ★★**, but this cascading staircase of hillside hot pools, among the oldest in the park, offers a boardwalk tour of gorgeous pastels in shades of white, yellow, orange, and green, the unintentionally artistic work of microscopic bacteria in the sediments. The mineral-rich springs constantly bubble to the surface, depositing travertine as the water cools in contact with the air. It's a vivid illustration of the park's unusual geological situation: a rare geologic hot spot of seismic activity in the middle of the continent, where molten rock nearly makes it to the earth's surface.

Whether or not you spend the night at the **Mammoth Hot Springs Hotel**—not the most distinguished lodging in the park, but it has historic character—you should drop by the **Albright Visitor Center.** This building once housed Fort Yellowstone's bachelor officers, but you won't find a pool table here today; rather, you'll find displays on park history, wildlife and photography exhibits, helpful rangers dispensing advice, and numerous park publications and maps. For more information, call ✆ **307/344-2263.**

Once upon a time, travelers in Yellowstone bathed, cooked, and laundered their clothes in the hot springs, but such activities are illegal nowadays. There is one spot on the east side of the road to the north entrance, however, where the public is allowed to take a dip. Called **Boiling River ★★**, the hot springs here run into the Gardner River and create a series of temperature-graded (around 100°F/38°C) pools. This was once a late-night skinny-dipping secret, but you can't do that anymore: There's a parking lot, gate, and posted hours (daybreak to dusk, closed during times of high runoff). Regardless, this is just about the best possible way to cap off a day of touring and hiking: sitting in Mother Nature's hot tub, surrounded by beautiful scenery.

Tower-Roosevelt Area

East of Mammoth Hot Springs, you enter a delicious mix of high plains, deep forest, and twisting rivers. Toward the northeast corner lies one of the most beautifully serene valleys in the Rockies, the **Lamar Valley ★★★**. This glacier-carved swath of grassy bottom and forested flanks sits apart from the vehicular chaos at the center of the park—a good thing, because the traffic here is not automobiles, but the bison, bears, wolves, and elk whose presence has earned the valley the nickname "The Serengeti of the United States." If you continue east and leave Yellowstone via the park's northeast entrance, you'll be heading up to the spectacular views of the **Beartooth Highway.**

The area around the Tower-Roosevelt Junction was once a favorite spot of U.S. President Theodore Roosevelt. At **Roosevelt Lodge,** visitors can enjoy the kind of simple accommodations that fit the tastes of the Bull Moose himself: those with the rustic flavor of the Old West. This is the most relaxed of the park's villages and a great place to take a break from the more crowded attractions. Get into the cowboy spirit by taking a **guided trail ride,** a **stagecoach ride,** or a **wagon ride.** You can skip the dining room and ride out for an **Old West cookout,** served from a chuckwagon to patrons who arrive by either horseback or wagon. The nearby 132-foot **Tower Falls ★** is named for the looming volcanic pinnacles at its brink and provides an excellent photo opportunity. While in the area, take time to view the petrified forests on **Specimen Ridge,** where a wide variety of fossilized plants and trees date back millions of years. All things considered, Roosevelt is a great place to escape the hordes.

Farther south, **Pelican and Hayden valleys** are the two most prominent remnants of large, ancient lakebeds in the park. They are now vast, subalpine meadows, thriving with plant life that provides feed for sizable bison and elk populations. You might see a bear here, too.

The Grand Canyon of the Yellowstone River

Hayden Valley flanks the featured attraction of the park's center: the **Grand Canyon of the Yellowstone River ★★★**, a colorful, 1,000-foot-deep, 24-mile-long gorge that some can't resist comparing to its larger counterpart in Arizona. Okay, then: This canyon is greener, the water clearer, the air cooler, and it has two dramatic waterfalls, the big one taller than Niagara. As it drops through this gorge, the Yellowstone River in some places moves at 64,000 cubic feet of water per second.

Volcanic explosions and glaciers surging and receding shaped the canyon. The geological story is told in the canyon itself, where hard lava flows formed the lip of the falls next to softer quartz-rich rock that gave way, allowing the river to cut deeply through the layers of red, orange, tan, and brown hue. Plumes of steam pinpoint vents along the canyon's rock spires, where viewing opportunities are extensive and varied. There are many hikes along and down into the canyon, which is 24 miles long and up to 1,200 feet deep, and you'll be surprised at how few people you encounter away from the parking areas. Many do trek down to a view of the Lower Falls on **Uncle Tom's Trail ★★** (which is actually a 328-step staircase bolted to the canyon wall) from the South Rim, and a short path from a parking area for Upper Falls View also offers breathtaking views. Two other favorite trails are **Inspiration Point** and **Artist Point;** both are wheelchair accessible.

Canyon Village has a sprawling 1950s look, which puts off some visitors, but the architecture is starting to come back in vogue. It's usually crowded, but you can find many useful services there, and some of the newer lodging is an improvement.

Norris Geyser Basin

If you travel south from Mammoth on the west side of the park, you pass some interesting rock formations, **Obsidian Cliff** and **Roaring Mountain,** before coming to **Norris Geyser Basin ★★.** Norris is not nearly as famous as the Mammoth terraces or the crowd of geysers around Old Faithful, but there's a lot going on here, from the steaming pools of the **Porcelain Basin** to the eruptions of **Echinus Geyser.** If you're the patient type, you can sit by the blowhole of **Steamboat Geyser** and hope that this, the largest of park geysers with a maximum height of 400 feet, will erupt. But be prepared to wait: It erupted eight times between 2000 and late 2009, but blew its top only twice during the preceding 12 years and not at all between 1911 and 1961. This is one of the hottest, most active thermal areas on the plateau, at the intersection of three faults in the earth's crust; when they shift, new geysers pop up and old ones disappear. The **Norris Geyser Basin Museum** explains geothermal features, and the nearby **Museum of the National Park Ranger** tracks the history of the park's stewards.

Old Faithful

About a quarter of the world's geysers are crowded into hills, valleys, and riverbanks around **Old Faithful ★★,** where the hot pools and spouts are divided into three

 ## petrified WOOD

With so many hot pots, mountain peaks, geysers, and bison to gawk at, it's not surprising that many visitors to Yellowstone miss some of the finest examples of petrified forest found anywhere. The trees were preserved, scientists believe, when their organic matter was replaced by volcanic material during one of the many eruptions on the plateau. Some of the tree trunks still stand, particularly in the Specimen Ridge area in the northeast area of the park, and they are a monument to the region's warmer, swampier past: Sycamore, magnolias, and dogwoods are all preserved in stone. Check at the Tower Ranger Station for maps showing you where to find petrified wood. This is not a renewable resource: Don't touch or take.

areas: the **Lower, Midway,** and **Upper geyser basins.** Here you'll find burbling mud pots, radiant pools like **Chromatic Spring,** and geysers with a variety of tricks, from the angled shots of **Daisy Geyser** to the witches' cauldron of **Crested Pool.**

But the grand old dame of geysers, the star of the show, is **Old Faithful.** Over the past 100 years, its eruptions have been remarkably consistent, blowing 15 to 23 times daily, with a column averaging about 134 feet and a duration of about 40 seconds. Recent seismic activity has elongated the intervals (to about 92 min.) between eruptions a tad, but it's still the most predictable geyser in the world. Estimates posted at the visitor centers are give-or-take 10 minutes; if the last eruption was a long one, you might have to wait 2 hours for the next burst. (No big deal—there's plenty else to see here.)

The new state-of-the-art **Old Faithful Visitor Education Center** (© **307/344-2751**) opened in 2010, showing a film on Yellowstone's thermal features throughout the day and featuring exhibits focusing on the park's geysers and other thermal features. You'll also find projected geyser-eruption times here, making it a good first stop for those looking to see Old Faithful do its thing. It's open in summer 8am to 8pm.

A National Historic Landmark, the shingled, steep-roofed **Old Faithful Inn** was built of local stone and hand-hewn timber, including a pair of interior balconies above the lobby floor.

Yellowstone Lake

West of Old Faithful, over Craig Pass, or south of Canyon, through the wildlife-rich **Hayden Valley,** is gigantic **Yellowstone Lake ★★**, another natural wonder unique to Yellowstone. At 20 miles long, 14 miles wide, and more than 300 feet deep in places, it's the largest lake on the continent above 7,000 feet in elevation. If you took a dip in the frigid water (not recommended), you could hardly guess that the caldera underneath the lake is filling with hot liquid magma, actually tilting the lake northward at a measurable pace. The caldera is the sunken remainder of a huge volcanic blast 600,000 years ago, and another about 700,000 years before that. Experts believe it's due to blow again some time in the next 100,000 years—any day now, at least in geologic time. Volcanic underpinnings aside, grizzlies work the tributary streams in the spring when fish spawn (some campgrounds are closed), and lots of other wildlife congregate here, including moose and osprey.

The lake has long been a favorite fishing spot, but recent regulations have made cutthroat trout a catch-and-release species park-wide. This is part of a desperate attempt by park biologists to help the cutthroat come back against the planted Mackinaw or lake trout, which dine on small cutthroat and therefore are not to be released alive. You'll see some big sailboats braving the quirky winds of the lake, and experienced paddlers may want to **kayak** or **canoe** into the south and southeast arms of the lake, which are closed to motorboats. These deep bays are true wilderness and great areas to fish and view wildlife. When you pick up a boating permit, you'll also get a stern warning from rangers to watch out for the changeable weather if you get out on the lake's open water. They're right to urge caution; even the best paddlers risk their lives in a sudden afternoon storm.

Lake Village, on the north shore of the lake, offers a large range of amenities, including fine restaurants at either the rustic cabins at **Lake Lodge** or the Victorian majesty of **Lake Yellowstone Hotel.** This historic lodging has Greek columns and a spacious solarium overlooking the lake, the best place for a cocktail or a romantic dinner within park boundaries. It's very different from the Old Faithful Inn, but a rival for its beauty and history. Just south of Lake Village is **Bridge Bay Marina,** the park's water-activity center. Here you can obtain guided fishing trips, small-boat rentals, and dock rentals; there's also a store and tackle shop.

West Thumb & Grant Village

On the south end of the lake, at **West Thumb,** the boiling thermal features extend out into the lake. You can see steaming cones and churning water created by the action of the underwater hot springs. **Fishing Cone** is rumored to be the place where fishermen once used the "hook and cook" method, immediately tossing their catch into a hot pot for instant meal preparation. Don't try it—it's illegal to drop anything into a thermal feature, and the geyser water has traces of mercury and arsenic. You can walk among the lakeshore pools at the **Central Basin** and look at the colorful, thick fudge of the **Thumb Paint Pots.**

Grant Village, named for President Ulysses S. Grant, was completed in 1984 and is the newest of Yellowstone's villages. It has some of the most modern facilities in the park, but it's also the least inspired. On the plus side, this area is a great vantage point for watching sunrises and afternoon squalls move across the lake, and you may see **river otters** and **cutthroat trout** in the old marina's waters. (Come wintertime, the otters like to use holes melted by the underwater thermal features as base camps for ice-fishing escapades.) The **Grant Visitor Center** plays a video that explores the role of fire in the Yellowstone ecosystem.

DRIVING THE PARK

Yellowstone has approximately 370 miles of paved roads, and they are in a perpetual state of maintenance during the summer, with crews filling potholes, widening shoulders, and redoing some roads completely. The wear and tear of heavy RVs and trailers undoes the work as quickly as it's done, and since road construction is limited to the warm months of summer, drivers often encounter delays along the park's roads. If you travel in July or August, you'll share these frustrations with a lot of other drivers. But you can see a surprising number of interesting sights along the figure-eight roadways at the heart of the park. You can take in both north and south loops—together known as the **Grand Loop**—in 1 day if a quick blink at each stop is enough for you. Better, though, to take your time, or explore different areas on different trips.

 WINTER road conditions

Be cautious if you're planning a winter road trip to Yellowstone. Icy roads and blinding snowstorms take their toll every year. The park itself is largely closed to automobiles in the winter—only the northern entrance is open to wheeled vehicles. The road through Lamar Valley to the northeast gate is kept open to get essential supplies to Cooke City, but from there you can go no farther north into Montana because the Beartooth Highway is closed in winter. The rest of the park's primary roads are open during the snowy months to snowcoaches and snowmobiles, along with bison, which find the packed roads convenient and think nothing of lolling along with a line of frustrated snowmobilers waiting for a chance to pass. For up-to-the-minute information on weather and road conditions, call ☎ **307/344-7381.**

The Upper Loop

At 70 miles, the Upper Loop, which begins at the north entrance, is the shorter of the two loop drives. If you start by going east from **Mammoth Hot Springs** and the park headquarters, orient yourself at the **Albright Visitor Center**, then take in the **Blacktail Plateau** or rustic **Roosevelt Lodge** (a good place for lunch). If you'd prefer, take a side trip up the pretty **Lamar Valley ★★★** for wildlife viewing at least as far as Slough Creek—checking out the views of **Tower Falls** and **Mount Washburn** (the highest point in the park)—and up **Dunraven Pass** to look out over the Mirror Plateau. Then head west from Canyon Junction to Norris Junction and north to the **Norris Geyser Basin ★★**, with pastel pools and a few burbles and spouts, and its fine museum. You'll continue north past **Roaring Mountain** (a travertine cascade by the road; get out only if you have some extra time) and **Obsidian Cliff** (same advice), and then have dinner in the dining room at the historic **Mammoth Hot Springs Hotel** or the **Park Street Grill** in **Gardiner,** 5 miles north.

If you're doing only the Upper Loop on this trip, you should include the **Grand Canyon of the Yellowstone ★★★** on your tour—it's a short way south of Canyon Village, where the loop runs west to Norris.

The Lower Loop

The longer **Lower Loop** covers some of the more famous park landmarks in its 96-mile circuit. Beginning at the south entrance, you would join the loop at the **West Thumb** of Yellowstone Lake, an otherworldly shoreline of hot springs and mud pots. If you go east, the loop skirts the west shore of **Yellowstone Lake** to the handsome **Lake Hotel** at the north end, where the Yellowstone River outlet is spanned by **Fishing Bridge.** The route then encompasses the **Grand Canyon of the Yellowstone, Madison Junction,** the **Firehole Canyon Drive,** the **Lower Geyser Basin** and the **Fountain Paintpots,** the **Midway Geyser Basin,** and the **Upper Geyser Basin** and stalwart **Old Faithful,** where you can top off the day with a meal at historic **Old Faithful Inn** or the relatively new **Old Faithful Snow Lodge.** Then head east over **Craig Pass** to the lake again.

Put the two loops together, and you've done the Grand Loop of approximately 166 miles. At its conclusion, you will have seen most of the major attractions in the park.

Out of the Loops: Entrances & Other Detours

Rapturous descriptions of the **Lamar Valley ★★★** elsewhere in this guide should encourage you to take a run out of the park's northeast entrance. The valley is wide and beautiful and alive, with elk and bison grazing by the river, and coyotes, wolves, and grizzly bears making guest appearances. Beyond the park gate, you'll find Cooke City, a friendly little town, and then a switchback climb north on the Beartooth Highway, with its spectacular views.

Roads to the other entrances also have allure. If you head east along the north shore of Yellowstone Lake, you'll begin climbing into **Sylvan Pass,** the 8,530-foot exit route that will take you through the east gate into the beautiful Wapiti Valley and eventually to the town of Cody (see chapter 13, "Cody & North-Central Wyoming"). The north and east shores of the lake have beaches where you can sun, swim, or begin a paddling journey to the remote southern corners of the lake. The **south entrance road** skirts **Lewis Lake** and follows **Lewis River,** where you'll often see the graceful parabolas of fly-fishing lines at work. You'll also see some of the stark handiwork of the 1988 fires. Similarly, areas along the **west entrance road** are still marked by the burned husks of trees; there are also peaceful views of the **Madison River** along this road.

There are also some trips off the main roads that are worth taking. Try the short **Firehole Canyon Drive** (just south of Madison Junction, head west on the one-way loop) for a look at Firehole Falls and a dip in the idyllic spring-warmed swimming hole a bit farther down the road. For a chance at sighting wolves, drive into **Slough Creek** in the Lamar Valley in the early morning or late afternoon. Drive across the Yellowstone River just south of Canyon Village and hike from majestic overlook to majestic overlook along the **South Rim.** Drive to the **Mount Washburn** picnic area off Dunraven Pass (elev. 8,859 ft.), and if you want to see a panorama of the entire caldera, hike 3 miles to the top of the 10,243-foot peak.

SUMMER SPORTS & ACTIVITIES

Bicycling

Considering the vast expanse of real estate the park covers, the challenging terrain, and the miles of paved roads and trails, a cyclist could conclude that the park is a prime area for biking, on or off the roads.

It looks good on paper, but the reality borders on harrowing. The narrow and twisty roads have no bike lanes, so bikers continually fight for elbowroom with wide-bodied RVs and trailers. Off-road opportunities are limited because bikes are allowed on only a small number of trails.

Nevertheless, plenty of bicyclists take the challenge. The following trails are available to bikers, but know that you will share the roads with hikers. The **Mount Washburn Trail,** leaving from the Old Chittenden Road, is a strenuous trail that climbs 1,400 feet. The **Lonestar Geyser Trail,** accessed at Kepler Cascade near Old Faithful, is an easy 1-hour ride on a user-friendly road. Near Mammoth Hot Springs, **Bunsen Peak Road** and **Osprey Falls Trails** present a combination ride/hike: The first 6 miles travel around Bunsen Peak; getting to the top requires a fairly short (but fairly steep) hike. A round-trip hike down to Osprey Falls adds another 3 miles—and a steep climb back up—to the journey.

Bike rentals are available in West Yellowstone at **FreeHeel and Wheel** (𝄐 406/646-7744), and in Jackson at **Hoback Sports** (𝄐 307/733-5335).

Boating

The best place to enjoy boating in Yellowstone is on **Yellowstone Lake,** which has easy access and panoramic views. The lake is one of the few areas where powerboats are allowed; you can rent rowboats and outboard motorboats at **Bridge Bay Marina** (𝄐 866/439-7375). Motorboats, canoes, and kayaks can be used on Lewis Lake (about 15 miles north of the south entrance).

Fishing

There are two primary types of anglers in Yellowstone. First are the fly casters, purists more interested in the artistry and seduction of fly-fishing than in keeping what they catch. There are stretches of the Yellowstone and Madison rivers where the anglers are packed tippet to tippet and the trout must be punch drunk from catch-and-release.

Then there are the powerboat fishermen who troll the deep waters of **Yellowstone Lake.** Seven varieties of game fish live in the parks: five trout species (cutthroat, rainbow, brown, brook, and lake), grayling, and mountain whitefish. Of the trout, only the cutthroat are native, and they are being pressured in the big lake by the larger lake trout. As a result, you can't keep any pink-meat cutthroat caught in Yellowstone Lake, and you must keep any lake trout. These policies have diminished the number of fishing boats on Yellowstone Lake in recent years, but they're necessary.

The Yellowstone fishing season typically opens on the Saturday of Memorial Day weekend and ends on the first Sunday in November, except for Yellowstone Lake, which has a slightly shorter season, and the lake's tributaries, which are closed until July 15 to avoid conflicts between humans and grizzly bears, both of which are attracted to spawning trout.

The **required Yellowstone fishing permit** is available at any ranger station, visitor center, or Yellowstone General Store in the park. Anyone 16 and older needs a fishing permit, which costs $15 for 3 days, $20 for 7 days, and $35 for the season. Fishers ages 12 to 15 also need a permit, but it's free. Casters under 12 can fish without a permit when supervised by an adult.

In June, one of the best fishing spots is on the **Yellowstone River** downstream from Yellowstone Lake, where the cutthroat trout spawn; anglers head to **Madison River** near the west entrance in July and then again in late fall for rainbow and some brown trout; in late summer, the **Lamar River** and **Soda Butte Creek** in the park's beautiful northeast corner are popular spots to hook cutthroats in September. You'll find more isolation at **Trout Lake,** a small backcountry lake about 10 miles west of the northeast entrance.

You can fish the **Yellowstone River** below the Grand Canyon by hiking down into **Seven Mile Hole,** a great place to cast (thanks to the dearth of vegetation to snag on) for cutthroat trout from July to September, with the best luck around Sulphur Creek.

Other good fishing stretches include the **Gibbon and Firehole rivers,** which merge from the Madison River on the park's west side, and the 3-mile **Lewis River Channel** between the Shoshone and Lewis lakes during the fall spawning run of brown trout.

There is an access for anglers with disabilities at the **Madison River,** 3½ miles west of Madison Junction at the Haynes Overlook. Here you'll find a fishing platform overhanging the river's edge for 70 feet.

Horseback Riding

People who want to pack their gear on a horse, llama, or mule must either get permits to enter the Yellowstone backcountry or hire an outfitter with a permit (see below). Other visitors who want to get in the saddle but not disappear in the wilderness can put themselves in the hands of the concessionaire, **Yellowstone National Park Lodges** (www.yellowstonenationalparklodges.com; © **866/439-7375**). Stables are located at Canyon Village and Roosevelt Lodge. Choices are 1- and 2-hour guided trail rides (the prices are $38 and $58, respectively) aboard well-broken, tame animals. Wranglers refer to these as "nose-and-tail" tours, and an experienced rider is likely to find them awfully tame.

If you're looking for a longer, overnight horse-packing experience, contact the park and request a list of approved concessionaires who lead backcountry expeditions. Most offer customized, guided trips, with meals, horses, and camping and riding gear provided. Costs run from $250 to $500 per day, per person, depending on the length of the trip and number of people. One good outfitter is **Rockin' HK Outfitters** (www.rockinhk.com; ℂ **307/333-4505**), offering 3- to 10-day trips for about $450 per person, per day. Out of Bozeman, **Greater Yellowstone Flyfishers** (www.gyflyfishers.com; ℂ **406/585-5321**) offers custom 3-day/2-night fly-fishing pack trips in the park.

WINTER SPORTS & ACTIVITIES

Yellowstone's average snowfall of more than 10 feet every year—and 30 feet of the white stuff at higher elevations—provides the perfect backdrop for a multitude of winter activities. The north entrance remains open, so you can drive in from Gardiner for a day and drive back out. You can travel throughout the park by snowmobile or snowcoach and spend the night either at Mammoth or at the handsomely rebuilt Old Faithful Snow Lodge. For additional information on all of the following winter activities and accommodations, as well as snowcoach transportation and equipment rentals, contact **Yellowstone National Park Lodges** (www.gyflyfishers.com; ℂ **866/439-7375**). There are also many activities, outfitters, and rental shops in the park's gateway towns.

Cross-Country Skiing

The best cross-country trails in Yellowstone are the Howard Eaton Trail to **Lonestar Geyser,** a fairly level 8-mile round-trip through a remote setting, starting at the Old Faithful Snow Lodge, and the **Fern Cascades Trail,** which begins in the Old Faithful housing area on the south side of the road and winds for 3 miles through a rolling wooded landscape. Energetic skiers can tackle the 12-mile **Mallard Lake Trail,** though it may take them all day—it departs north of the Old Faithful Lodge area along the north side of the Upper Geyser Basin, then loops north and east to Mallard Lake and back to Old Faithful.

Equipment rentals (about $20 per day), ski instruction, ski shuttles to various locations, and guided ski tours are all available at the **Old Faithful Snow Lodge** and the **Mammoth Hot Springs Hotel,** the park's two winter lodging options. Discounts are available for multiday rentals of skis or snowshoes. Ski instruction costs around $30 per person for a 1-hour private lesson; a full-day guided excursion costs $140 per person (lunch may or may not be included). Guided snowshoe trips are also available.

The **Yellowstone Association Institute ★★★** (ℂ **406/848-2400**) offers winter courses throughout the park. Past offerings have included 3-day classes devoted to wintertime photography, cross-country skiing, and the ecology of wolf reintroduction. The institute's faculty and staff are a knowledgeable and friendly bunch, and a class is one of the best ways to acquaint yourself with the park in any season.

Ice-Skating

The **Mammoth Hot Springs ice rink** is located behind the Mammoth Hot Springs Recreation Center. On a crisp winter's night, you can rent a pair of skates (free) and glide across the ice while seasonal melodies are broadcast over the PA system. It's cold out there, but there's a warming fire at the rink's edge. There is also an Old Faithful rink; rentals are likewise free. Call ℂ **866/439-7375** for more information.

Snowcoach Tours

It is possible to enjoy the sights and sounds of Yellowstone without raising a finger—except to write a check or sign a credit card voucher—by taking one of the scenic snowcoach tours that originate at the south and west entrances, as well as at

11 | snowmobiling: **TO BAN OR NOT TO BAN?**

During his final days in office, President Bill Clinton approved a ban on snowmobiles in Yellowstone and Grand Teton national parks. In December 2003, a judge ruled that the ban would become effective in December 2004. It was a win for environmentalists, who argued that snowmobilers brought pollution, noise, and the destruction of natural habitat to the national parks. But hold on: In February 2004, that ban was overturned and another study commissioned, leaving the fate of snowmobiling in Yellowstone up in the air until the National Park Service announced a final winter use plan. New regulations have reduced the snowmobile quota from 720 per day to 318 per day. Additionally, over-snow travel on the Continental Divide Snowmobile Trail has been discontinued in Grand Teton National Park and the John D. Rockefeller, Jr., Memorial Parkway.

Snowmobilers have been allowed access to only certain roads, must be accompanied by a licensed guide, and must have a valid driver's license. In addition, snowmobilers must travel in groups of 11 or fewer, including the licensed guide. There are also BAT (best available technology) requirements for most snowmobiles. Snowmobiles and cars are prohibited from 9pm to 7am. Road closings begin on March 7 and typically continue into April, when the winter season officially comes to an end.

Mammoth and Old Faithful. One-way and wildlife-watching trips range from about $30 to $70, while round-trips cost $120 to $140.

If you've never seen a snowcoach, you're in for a treat. Don't be fooled into thinking that this distinctively Yellowstone mode of transportation is merely a fancy name for a bus that provides tours during winter. Imagine instead an Econoline van with tank treads for tires and water skis extending from its front, and you won't be surprised when you see this unusual-looking vehicle. The interiors are toasty warm, with seating for a large group, and they usually allow each passenger two bags. They aren't the fastest, smoothest, or most comfortable form of transportation, but they do allow large groups to travel together, and they're cheaper and warmer than snowmobiles. They're also available for hire by groups at many snowmobile locations. Guides provide interesting and entertaining facts and stories of the areas as you cruise the park trails, and they give you opportunities to photograph scenery and wildlife.

For snowcoach information, contact **Yellowstone National Park Lodges** (www.yellowstonenationalparklodges.com; ✆ **866/439-7375** or 307/344-7311). Out of West Yellowstone, **Yellowstone Vacations** (www.snowcoachyellowstone.com; ✆ **800/426-7669** or 406/646-9564) and **Yellowstone Alpen Guides** (www.yellowstoneguides.com; ✆ **800/858-3502** or 406/646-9591) provide service as well.

Snowmobiling

Roads that are jammed with cars during the summer fill up with snowmobiles and bison during the winter. In deference to the shaggier road warriors, moderate speed limits are strictly enforced, but this is still an excellent way to sightsee at your own pace. A driver's license and guide are required for rental at **Mammoth Hot Springs Hotel** or **Old Faithful Snow Lodge.** Day tours from **Xanterra** (✆ **866/439-7375**) cost about $275 for a single rider or $300 double; custom tours are also available but considerably more costly. A helmet is included with the snowmobile, and you can rent a clothing package for protection against the bitter cold. **Warming huts** are located at Mammoth, Indian Creek, Canyon, Madison, West Thumb, and Fishing Bridge. They offer snacks, a hot cup of coffee or chocolate, and an excellent opportunity to recover from a chill.

Snowmobile rentals are also available in the **gateway communities** of Gardiner and West Yellowstone, Montana, and south of Grand Teton in Jackson, Wyoming. Most rental shops accept reservations weeks in advance, so reserving at least 2 weeks ahead of time is a good idea. Plan on making reservations for the week between Christmas and New Year's at least 6 months in advance.

HIKING

Getting your car snarled in one "wildlife jam" after another in pursuit of a glimpse of one of the park's four-legged denizens is one way to enjoy the outdoors. Another is taking a hike, even a short one, because you'll see a whole new side of the park. There are gentle hikes where you never lose sight of the road, moderate hikes where you might spend an afternoon penetrating the forest to visit a spot of secluded beauty, and overnight trips where you can hike and camp for days without seeing anyone but the people who embarked on the journey with you.

Part of the reason so few people hike and camp in the Yellowstone wilderness is fear of bears. Bear attacks are extremely rare and usually involve a sow protecting her cubs, but you should carry pepper spray, just in case; when you camp, secure your food and cooking gear in a tree well away from tents. Park rangers can advise you on current bear activity and safe practices. This is true wilderness, but if you equip yourself properly and learn proper techniques, you'll be safer than you are on a city street. If you go into the backcountry, you need a permit (see "Where to Go & How to Reserve a Spot," later), which also ensures that someone knows where you are.

For those who would rather sleep in a bed, there are still excellent day hikes that allow you to escape the crowd and view wildlife in its own habitat, take in the scenery, or climb a peak. Rangers at visitor centers can advise you on a hike to match your interests and abilities, and provide maps of the extensive trail system in the park. Besides a good map, always bring a good supply of water (and, if you can, a purifier or iodine pills) and rain gear.

Here is a small selection of good hikes, long and short. In addition to these individual hikes, the **Continental Divide Trail (CDT)** ★★★ links many of them together as part of a continuous trail from Mexico to Canada, roughly following the spine of the continent. The Yellowstone Backcountry Office maintains a guide to CDT trails. The Howard Eaton Trail system once went all through the park but was supplanted by the Grand Loop Road. Sections of the old trail are still maintained and will be found in trail guides, though some of them closely parallel park roads. For a more extensive list of trails and details than what follows here, pick up longtime ranger Mark C. Marschall's excellent *Yellowstone Trails* (Yellowstone Association, $9.95) or the maps provided by the park.

Hikes Around Mammoth

The **Beaver Ponds Loop Trail** starts in Mammoth at Clematis Gulch (btw. Liberty Cap and an old stone Park Service residence) and makes a 5-mile loop to a series of beaver ponds, where your best chances of seeing the big-tailed beasts are early morning or afternoon. There are some good views coming and going, including Mount

Everts. More ambitious hikers can link up with the **Sepulcher Mountain Trail,** which features hot springs, gardens of oddly shaped limestone boulders, and scenic views from the ridges of the Mammoth area. Be in shape for this one and bring a good map of the crisscrossing trail system, because you'll cover at least 6 miles, depending on your route.

Nearby is the **Bunsen Peak Trail ★★**, a short but steep trip to the summit of this volcanic remnant, with a 1,300-foot gain in elevation. Make the hike early, and you can watch the morning sun strike Electric Peak, which glows with a golden hue. The 2.1-mile trail passes through mosaic burns from the 1988 fires, and when you get to the top, you'll have a view from 3,000 feet above the Yellowstone Valley. After topping the peak, you can take an alternative route down Bunsen's east side and come back along the Old Bunsen Peak Road Trail for a 6-mile round-trip. If you're looking for more, hike the **Osprey Falls Trail ★** and add 3 miles down a series of switchbacks for a great view of a 150-foot waterfall to the trek.

Hikes in the Tower-Canyon Area

The **Tower Falls** overlook is easy to get to; it's only 300 feet from the Tower Falls parking area. Walk .5 mile more along some steep switchbacks, and you'll be at the less crowded base of the falls for a stunning view. You can also hike 3.5 miles to the falls from Roosevelt Lodge, a good car-free choice if you happen to be staying there. Begin on the **Lost Lake Trail** and take a left when the trail forks .5 mile from the lodge.

Just south of Canyon Village, the **Chittenden Bridge** crosses from the Loop Road to the South Rim Road near the top of the Grand Canyon of the Yellowstone. You can park and hike either the **South Rim** or **North Rim trail,** with spurs that drop steeply (but briefly) down to viewing platforms at the Upper and Lower falls. If you want a more complete and less crowded view of this deep gorge, take the **7-Mile Hole Trail** (which is actually 5.5 miles long) along the north canyon rim. You'll see the Silver Cord Cascade from the rim and then drop down to the river after a couple of miles in an area where the canyon widens enough for trees. There are some active hot springs along this hike. This is quite a drop (1,400 ft.), and hikers should be prepared for a fairly demanding climb out.

Across the road from Uncle Tom's Trail parking area (the first parking area to the left after crossing the bridge to the South Rim) is the trail head for the **Clear Lake/ Ribbon Lake Loop Trail ★**. The hike to Clear Lake is 1.5 miles, a gradual climb across a high plateau, and Ribbon Lake lies less than 2 miles beyond it. Bears are often active in this area early in the year, so check with rangers for current conditions before heading out. Views of the plateau improve with each footstep, until you find yourself surrounded by a panoramic view of the mountains surrounding the canyon area. During early and late spring, it's a bit more difficult because snow runoff and rain can make trails wet and muddy, but that shouldn't be an impediment to anyone interested in the spectacular views. Clear Lake itself is intimately small and gives you the opportunity to see subsurface activity of the thermal areas below the lake. On a circumnavigation of the lake along a trail, you will see and smell venting activity making its way to the surface; in some spots, the lake looks like a boiling pot. This trail also connects to the **Howard Eaton Trail,** an arduous 14-mile trail to Fishing Bridge and Yellowstone Lake.

The **Mount Washburn Trail ★★★** falls into the "if you can only do one hike, do this one" category. It's a short hike to panoramic views, with wildflowers decorating

AN OLD FAITHFUL secret

For a spectacular view of Old Faithful from above, take the **Observation Point Trail ★**, a 2-mile jaunt (beginning at the Old Faithful Visitor Center) that will take you by numerous thermal features on the other side of the Firehole River. Follow the Geyser Hill Trail across the river and then climb the switchbacks to the observation point to watch Old Faithful burst in relative solitude.

the way and nonchalant bighorn sheep often browsing nearby. Trail heads are located at the summit at Dunraven Pass (elev. 8,859 ft.) and on Old Chittenden Road, where there's more parking available. Either hike is 6 miles round-trip, with an increase in elevation of 1,400 feet; however, the climbs are fairly gradual and interspersed with long, level stretches. From the summit, the park will lie before you like a map on a table: You'll see the Absaroka Mountains to the east, Yellowstone Lake to the south, and the Gallatin Mountains to the west and north. In addition to sheep, you may see marmots and red fox; bears have also made use of the area in recent years. You'll be climbing a summit that's 10,243 feet, so pace yourself, and bring warm clothing to fend off the storms that often buffet the top. The hike to the summit is an easy 90-minute walk at a steady pace, which can stretch to 2 hours if you take time for breaks. There's a day-use shelter in the base of the ranger lookout, with viewing telescopes and restrooms.

Hikes near Old Faithful

The popular trail to **Lonestar Geyser** covers a little more than 2 miles of mostly level terrain to the geyser, which rewards visitors with eruptions up to 50 feet tall every 3 hours. The trail follows the Firehole River from the Kepler Cascades parking area, with a forest canopy to keep it cool in the summer, widening now and then into broad riverbank meadows. The geyser erupts from a brown cone about 12 feet high and is surrounded by a meadow pocked by steam vents and thermal features. The path begins from a parking lot on the Old Faithful–West Thumb road just south of the Kepler Cascades. It's partially paved to the geyser and open to bicyclists. If you want to try a less busy (and less scenic) route, take the **Howard Eaton Trail** just east of the Old Faithful overpass, 3 miles to the geyser. From the geyser, you can continue on—bicycles can't—over Grants Pass to join the Bechler River Trail to Shoshone Lake.

From the Biscuit Basin parking lot, you can take a fine 3-mile round-trip hike to **Mystic Falls,** which fall 100 feet to the Firehole River. Continue up switchbacks to the top of the falls and beyond, and you'll link up with the **Little Firehole Meadows Trail** to return to Biscuit Basin, with more views on the way. You can make this trip in less than 2 hours, with only a 460-foot elevation gain.

Fairy Falls plummets a more impressive 200 feet and can be reached by hiking 2.5 miles on the Fairy Falls Trail, which begins from the Old Faithful–Madison road just south of the Midway Geyser Basin parking area. Hikers who don't mind a slightly longer haul (about 8 miles round-trip) will be rewarded with better wildlife-viewing opportunities by starting from the **Imperial Meadows** trail head a mile south of the Firehole River bridge on Fountain Flat Drive. The hike winds through an area populated by elk along Fairy Creek, then past the Imperial Geyser, where it joins the Fairy Creek Trail and travels east to the base of the falls. The total gain in elevation is only 100 feet. If you turn west instead, you'll find an unmarked trail north to the Imperial Geyser.

Hikes near Yellowstone Lake

At the north end of the lake, the **Pelican Valley Trail** takes a loop north of the lake around an area loaded with elk, bison, sandhill cranes, trout, eagles, grizzlies, and the new kids on the block, wolves. You can take hikes of different lengths, up to a 16-mile loop, but a lot of folks, having had their fill of wildflowers and beasts, go no farther than Pelican Creek Bridge, a 7-mile round-trip. If you continue on, you'll pass through forest and "bear meadows." This is a daytime-only hiking area (9am–7pm), and it's closed in the early summer until July 4 because of bear activity.

The **Elephant Back Loop Trail ★** is an opportunity to get a bird's-eye view of the island-dotted expanse of Yellowstone Lake, the Absaroka Mountains, and the Pelican Valley—and maybe a moose. It's a great photo opportunity and a fairly

 WILDERNESS U.: guided backpacking

The Yellowstone Association Institute (YAI) uses the park's backcountry as a 2.2-million-acre classroom for many of its 400 annual classes. In fact, a number of courses are guided backpacking trips into the Yellowstone wilderness.

I went on a YAI expedition with about 10 other customers in August 2004, following the same route the Nez Perce Indians took through Yellowstone in summer 1877 while evading the U.S. Army. Our 4-day adventure—which was preceded by a day in an indoor classroom in Gardiner—traversed 40 miles under the leadership of experienced backcountry guide and park historian Lee Whittlesey, whose wry humor nicely complemented his historical insight.

We learned about the obstacles the Nez Perce faced en route to their ultimate surrender in Montana. Led by Chief Joseph, 600 to 800 people, including a good number of children and seniors, evaded capture from June into October, cutting through a slice of the fledgling national park known as Yellowstone. We also learned about the rugged terrain the Nez Perce crossed and about differing accounts of their exact path through the park. We learned about wolf tracks, as

well as about the "Leave No Trace" etiquette upheld by backcountry enthusiasts. Most important, we learned that the flight of the Nez Perce has been the key event in the tribe's history since 1877. The 5-month ordeal haunts many of its members to this day. The contemporary Nez Perce are a nostalgic tribe, still focused on the events of summer 1877, and thus—for better or for worse—they are quite different from the typically modern people of the United States.

The "Flight of the Nez Perce" backcountry course has become a staple in the YAI catalog, along with guided backpacking classes about wolves, grizzly bears, waterfalls, photography, and the microbes that inhabit the park's thermal features. Taking a course is a great way to educate yourself and to learn the ins and outs of backpacking—plus, you meet a bunch of like-minded Yellowstone lovers in the process. Trips typically last 3 days to a week and cost $700 to $1,000 per person. You need to bring food and most of your own gear. Call 406/848-2400 or visit **www.yellowstoneassociation.org/institute** for a course catalog and other information.

BLACK BEAR OR grizzly?

Because a black bear can be black, brown, or cinnamon, here are some identifiers. The grizzly is the larger of the two, typically 3½ feet at the shoulder, with a dish-face profile and a pronounced hump between the shoulders. The black's ears are rounder, just like those you see on stuffed animals. The grizzly's color is typically more yellowish-brown, but the coat is sometimes recognized by its cinnamon color, often highlighted by silver tips. In terms of tracks, the black bear's toes follow an arc around the footpad, while the grizzly's toes are arranged in a nearly straight line. The grizzly's claws are also considerably longer.

Caution: Park rangers attempt to keep track of grizzlies to avoid human/bear incidents. However, it is best to assume that they are always around; make noise when traveling in isolated spots.

easy 3.6-mile loop, beginning a mile south of Fishing Bridge Junction off the road to Lake Village.

You can walk along the north shore of Yellowstone Lake on the **Storm Point Trail ★**, but be aware that it's occasionally closed due to grizzly bear activity. This easy, level 2-miler terminates at a point jutting into the lake where you'll find lovely panoramic views. It begins in the Indian Pond area, 3½ miles east of Fishing Bridge directly across from the Pelican Valley trail head.

Hikes to Remote Areas & Overnight Backcountry Trips

The **Bechler Meadows Trail** enters the southwest corner of the park, an area rich in waterfalls, cascades, and thermal features rarely seen by human eyes. The access is by Idaho 47 from Ashton, Idaho, which will take you to the Bechler Ranger Station in the southwest corner of the park. About 5 miles into the hike, the trail makes several fords of the river as it enters Bechler Canyon, passing Collonade Falls and Iris Falls. There are places on this trail where you can view the Grand Tetons in the distance, and some thermal features bubble and churn on the Bechler River's banks. This is a camping trip—you can cover nearly 30 miles if you hike all the way into the Old Faithful area—best made late in the summer to avoid high water during creek crossings. You'll need a backcountry permit for overnight stays (see "Camping," below).

The **Slough Creek Trail,** which begins in the Lamar Valley of the park's northeast corner, takes hikers through some of the best wildlife habitat in the park. You can see elk, bison, trumpeter swans, the occasional grizzly bear, and the wolves that have quite happily taken up residence among abundant prey. The presence of wolves has made this area more popular, and the trail is also used by horse-packers. The trail starts from the road to Slough Creek campground, following the creek's valley north, then crossing a ridge to a second valley. You can hike a few miles, or take your camping gear and head for the park boundary, 11 miles to the north.

The **Thorofare Trail** follows the eastern shore of Yellowstone Lake and then skirts the Yellowstone River up into some of the most remote and beautiful backcountry in the Rockies. It's a long, steep trail, but you'll be rewarded with views of the Upper Yellowstone Valley, Two Oceans Plateau, and abundant wildlife. Eventually you'll reach a gorgeous alpine valley just outside the park's boundary, with a ranger station known as Hawk's Rest. Fishermen love this area, as do grizzly bears, especially during the cutthroat trout spawning season. This is the most remote roadless area in the Lower 48, a good 30 miles from the trail head at the lake, and even the most capable hikers should consider riding with an outfitter. You can cut 9 miles off the trip by getting a boat shuttle (about $300 round-trip, with a maximum capacity of six people) to the mouth of the lake's southeast arm (call the **backcountry shuttle office** at ℂ **307/242-3893**), or you can come in through the Bridger-Teton National Forest to the south (check with the forest's Blackrock Ranger Station in Moran, Wyoming; ℂ **307/543-2386**).

CAMPING
Where to Go & How to Reserve a Spot

The National Park Service has shifted management of five major campgrounds to Yellowstone National Park Lodges, the park concessionaire, which means, predict-ably, higher fees, but also allows you to make reservations ahead of arrival. The other seven campgrounds still managed by the park are available only on a first-come, first-served basis. These lower-cost campgrounds ($12–$14 per night) are located at Indian Creek, Lewis Lake, Mammoth, Norris, Pebble Creek, Slough Creek, and Tower Fall. We like Lewis Lake and Indian Creek, which tend to be available when others are full. Check with rangers about campsite availability when you enter the park; some campgrounds fill up as early as 8am.

Yellowstone National Park Lodges operates the large campgrounds at Bridge Bay, Canyon, Grant Village, Madison, and Fishing Bridge, where the fees are $20 per night. The **Fishing Bridge RV Park** is the only campground equipped with water, sewer, and electrical hookups for RVs and trailers, though it accepts hard-sided vehicles only (no tents or tent trailers), and the fees are $35 per night. The **Madison campground** is the first to open in early May, while **Grant Village** is closed until mid-June to avoid bear conflicts during trout-spawning season. These campgrounds are usually busier, and some, like Bridge Bay, are rather barren of trees unless you get a site on the fringes. Most campgrounds close in September, but Madison is open until mid-October, and Mammoth is open year-round. If you plan to travel in July or August, make your reservations 6 months ahead of time by calling ℂ **866/439-7375** or 307/344-7311, or by writing **Yellowstone National Park Lodges,** P.O. Box 165, Yellowstone National Park, WY 82190.

Camping is allowed only in designated areas, and visitors are limited to 14 days between June 15 and Labor Day, and to 30 days the rest of the year, except at Fishing Bridge, where there is no limit. Checkout time for all campgrounds is 10am. Quiet hours are strictly enforced between 8pm and 8am.

There are plenty of opportunities for backcountry camping as well. Some areas in the Yellowstone backcountry include delicate habitat—the southeast arm of Yellow-stone Lake is an example—and visitors must camp in designated areas for a limited time only. Check with the **Yellowstone Backcountry office** (www.nps.gov/yell; ℂ **307/344-2160**) for rules, reservations, and advice.

What to Expect

Remember, these are campgrounds, not motels, so the amenities are spare. But some have showers and bathrooms and potable water. Check the chart below to determine the level of comfort at each campground. Showers and laundry facilities are available

Amenities for Each Campground in Yellowstone National Park
(Where Flush Toilets Are Not Available, Vault Toilets Are Provided)

CAMPGROUND	# SITES	FEE	SHOWERS/ LAUNDRY	FLUSH TOILETS	DISPOSAL STATIONS	GENERATORS PERMITTED
Bridge Bay*	425	$20	No	Yes	Yes	Yes
Canyon*	272	$20	Yes	Yes	Yes	Yes
Fishing Bridge*	346	$28–$37	Yes	Yes	Yes	Yes
Grant Village*	425	$20	Yes	Yes	Yes	Yes
Indian Creek	75	$12	No	No	No	No
Lewis Lake	85	$12	No	No	No	No
Madison*	275	$20	No	No	Yes	Yes
Mammoth	85	$14	No	No	Yes	No
Norris	100	$14	No	No	Yes	No
Pebble Creek	30	$12	No	No	No	No
Slough Creek	28	$12	No	No	No	No
Tower Fall	31	$12	No	No	No	No

*Reserve through Yellowstone National Park Lodges; **www.yellowstonenationalpark lodges.com**; ℂ **866/439-7375** or 307/344-7311.

at Canyon, Fishing Bridge, and Grant Village campgrounds. In addition, campers may use the shower and laundry facilities at Lake Lodge and Old Faithful Lodge.

In the northeast area of the park, the **Tower Fall campground** is near a convenience store, restaurant, and gas station at Tower Lodge, 19 miles north of Canyon Village and 18 miles east of Mammoth. **Mammoth campground** is just below the hot springs and the hotel at Mammoth Hot Springs, and the only year-round campground in the park. **Slough Creek campground** ★ is located in a remote section of the Lamar Valley near the northeast entrance. The good news is there are fewer people, good fishing, and the possibility of wolf sightings; the bad news is that restroom facilities are pit toilets. **Canyon campground** is the busiest in the park. Sites are in a heavily wooded area; the store, restaurants, visitor center, and laundry at Canyon Center are nearby. Because it's in an area of spring bear activity, attempts have been made over the years to close the RV park at **Fishing Bridge.** It's still open, but only hard-sided camping vehicles are allowed here. **Bridge Bay** is located near the shores of Yellowstone Lake, so you get tremendous views, especially at sunrise and sunset. Unfortunately, though surrounded by the forest, much of the area has been clear-cut, so there's not a whole lot of privacy. It's close to boat-launching facilities and the boat-rental operation. **Madison** ★ and **Norris campgrounds** are attractive, wooded locations in the heart of the park, close to wildlife activity, hiking trails, and rivers. These camp areas seem less like outdoor motels than the big campgrounds on the park's east side.

WHERE TO STAY IN THE PARK

For listings of accommodations just outside the park, see "The Gateway Towns: West Yellowstone, Gardiner & Cooke City," at the beginning of this chapter.

The first thing you should know: no televisions. Private bathrooms have arrived and phones are in place, but televisions are in only two rooms in the entire park (the suites at Mammoth).

Yellowstone accommodations are nor-mally open from May to mid-October. Rooms are typically fully booked during the peak season in July and August, so reservations should be made up to a few months in advance. For information or reservations at any of the locations within the park, contact **Yellowstone National Park Lodges** at P.O. Box 165, Yellow-stone National Park, WY 82190 (www.yellowstonenationalparklodges.com; ℭ **866/439-7375** or 307/344-7311).

Railroad companies built most of the park's hotels and lodges around the start of the 20th century, and they would offer their primped Victorian guests a package tour that delivered them by train and stagecoach to luxurious resorts with rocking chairs on the verandas and gourmet food. A good deal of that old-style ambience has been thankfully retained at Yellowstone. Many of the newer facilities erected by the park concessionaire (in particular, the Old Faithful Snow Lodge and the new lodges at Canyon) are suitably matched to older buildings, at least on the exterior. However, the push for more features may come in the near future, and during recent upgrades at the Lake Hotel, the wiring was installed for televisions—just in case. Many of the hotels provide beautiful examples of architecture and craftsmanship, but they're not perfect: The plaster walls transmit some sound and the bathrooms tend to be small-ish. However, even the most budget-conscious traveler will find a room in the park that fits the pocketbook. Look over the descriptions below carefully, though, because some of the cheaper lodgings are primitive indeed.

Canyon Lodge and Cabins   This complex is one of the newer facilities in the park (both Cascade and Dunraven lodges were completed here in the 1990s), but it can't escape the bustle of Canyon Village. However, the lodges are located a mere half-mile from the Grand Canyon of the Yellowstone and Inspiration Point, one of the most photographed spots in the park. Cascade Lodge offers simple rooms appointed with tasteful log furnishings in the three-story building; the newer Dunraven is simi-lar, although it is more modern (with an elevator); both are located adjacent to a woodland setting. The cabins are single-story duplex and fourplex structures with private bathrooms that are among the largest in the park. They're a bit weathered but generally acceptable, but given the sheer number of units involved (over 600), this isn't the place to "get away from it all."

In Canyon Village, P.O. Box 165, Yellowstone National Park, WY 82190. www.yellowstonenational parklodges.com. ℭ **866/439-7375** or 307/344-7311. Fax 307/344-7456. 605 units. $170 double; $96–$179 cabin. AE, DISC, MC, V. Closed late Sept to early June. **Amenities:** Restaurant; lounge. In room: No phone.

Grant Village   The southernmost of the major overnight accommodations in the park, Grant Village was completed in 1984 and is one of the more contemporary choices in Yellowstone. It's not as architecturally distinctive as the Old Faithful options, consisting of six condo-style units (with motel-style rooms), but it's also less touristy and more isolated. Rooms are tastefully furnished, most outfitted with light wood furniture, track lighting, electric heat, and laminate counters. Nicer and more expensive rooms affording lake views have mullioned windows, one queen or one or two double beds, and full bathrooms.

On the West Thumb of Yellowstone Lake, P.O. Box 165, Yellowstone National Park, WY 82190. www.yellowstonenationalparklodges.com. © **866/439-7375** or 307/344-7311. Fax 307/344-7456. 300 units. $152 double. AE, DISC, MC, V. Closed early Oct to late May. **Amenities:** Restaurant; lounge.

Lake Lodge Cabins ★ These cabins surrounding Lake Lodge stand a little ways from the lake in a relatively quiet, traffic-free area. The old Western lodge's most attractive feature is a large porch with wicker rockers that invite visitors to sit and gaze out across the waters. The accommodations are in well-preserved, clean, freestanding cabins near a trout stream that threads through a wooded area. (Access is usually restricted when grizzlies emerge from hibernation.) The cabins come in three grades: Motel-style **Western** cabins provide electric heat, paneled walls, two double beds (and, in some cases, an extra twin), and combination bathrooms, while historic **Frontier** and **Pioneer** cabins are smaller and sparsely furnished, with one or two double beds each and small shower-only bathrooms—but the former have been modernized. Because the dining room here is a tad short on atmosphere, you might want to make the short trek to the Lake Yellowstone Hotel for a more sumptuous meal in a more appetizing setting.

On Yellowstone Lake, P.O. Box 165, Yellowstone National Park, WY 82190. www.yellowstonenational parklodges.com. © **866/439-7375** or 307/344-7311. Fax 307/344-7456. 186 cabins. $69 Pioneer cabin; $106 Frontier cabin; $179 Western cabin. AE, DISC, MC, V. Closed mid-Sept to early June. **Amenities:** Restaurant; lounge. *In room:* No phone.

Lake Yellowstone Hotel and Cabins ★★ The Ionic columns, dormer windows, and deep porticos on this classic yellow building faithfully recall the year it was built: 1891. It's an entirely different world from the rustic Western style of other park lodgings. The facility was restored in the early 1990s, and its better rooms are the most comfortable and roomy in the park, with soul-stirring views of the massive lake. The three- and four-story wings house the hotel rooms, and there's also a motel-style annex and an assortment of cabins. The upper-end rooms here are especially lavish for Yellowstone, with stenciled walls and traditional spreads on one queen or two double beds. Smaller rooms in the annex are fitted with two double beds and bring to mind a typical motel chain. The freestanding yellow-clad cabins here are passable, decorated with knotty pine paneling and furnished with double beds and a writing table.

On the north side of the lake, P.O. Box 165, Yellowstone National Park, WY 82190. www.yellowstone nationalparklodges.com. © **866/439-7375** or 307/344-7311. Fax 307/344-7456. 300 units, including 1 suite. $149–$223 double; $130 cabin; $549 suite. AE, DISC, MC, V. Closed late Sept to mid-May. **Amenities:** 2 restaurants; lounge. *In room:* No phone (cabins).

Mammoth Hot Springs Hotel and Cabins ★ Below the steaming terraces of Mammoth Hot Springs, this is one of two Yellowstone hotels open during both summer and winter seasons. (The other is the Old Faithful Snow Lodge.) Established in 1911, the hotel itself is less distinguished than the Lake Yellowstone Hotel or the Old Faithful Inn, but it manages to blend a wide range of rooms into a satisfying whole. The only truly high-end accommodations are the suites. Standard rooms and cabins offer minimal amenities but make up for it with charm. Some have tubs only, some have showers only, and some share a bathroom down the hall. The cottage-style cabins are clustered in rings adjacent to the hotel and vary in quality, but are generally good picks for families and those who want a little more elbowroom. Make sure you drift into the **Map Room** (named for the massive inlaid map of the United States on one of the walls), a great place to spend an evening reading or listening to a pianist.

At Mammoth Hot Springs, P.O. Box 165, Yellowstone National Park, WY 82190. www.yellowstone nationalparklodges.com. © **866/439-7375** or 307/344-7311. Fax 307/344-7456. 212 units, including 2 suites. $87–$120 double; $81–$112 cabin; $217 hot tub cabin; $439–$449 suite. AE, DISC, MC, V. Closed Oct to mid-Dec and early Mar to early May. **Amenities:** 2 restaurants; lounge. *In room:* No phone (cabins).

Old Faithful Inn ★★★   There are three hotels within viewing distance of the geyser, but this is undoubtedly the crown jewel of Yellowstone's man-made wonders. Seven stories tall, with dormers peaking from a shingled, steep-sloping roof, it's an architectural marvel designed by Robert Reamer to blend into the natural environment, first welcoming guests in 1904.

The cavernous, log-laden lobby is striking, with an ambience that is half elegant palace and half rugged wilderness lodge. You can climb the stairs to its internal balconies, but seismic activity eventually closed the crow's nest, where a chamber orchestra once performed for the well-dressed guests below. Within 40 miles of the west and south entrances, this is the first stop for many visitors, so make reservations well in advance.

Guest rooms are basic, appointed with conservative fabrics and park-theme art, and they don't all have private bathrooms; the wing rooms offer better facilities and more privacy.

At Old Faithful, P.O. Box 165, Yellowstone National Park, WY 82190. www.yellowstonenationalpark lodges.com. © **866/439-7375** or 307/344-7311. Fax 307/344-7456. 327 units, including 6 suites. $126–$236 double with private bathroom; $96–$183 double with shared bathroom; $399–$499 suite. AE, DISC, MC, V. Closed early Oct to early May. **Amenities:** 2 restaurants; lounge. *In room:* No phone.

Old Faithful Lodge Cabins 🔥   These are the leftovers from the days when crude cabins littered the landscape around the world's most famous geyser. The ones closest to the geyser were hauled away years ago, but you still get a sense of what tourism was like in the park's early days, especially if you rent one of the **budget cabins,** which are only slightly less flimsy than tents and have basic beds and sinks, no more. Showers and restrooms are a short walk away. **Frontier cabins** are the better units, adding a private bathtub to other amenities. If amenities are irrelevant, these rustic, thin-walled cabins are an economical way to put a roof over your head in the park. The lodge itself is perhaps the busiest spot in the geyser area, featuring several snack shops and a huge cafeteria dishing up varied fast-food items.

At Old Faithful, P.O. Box 165, Yellowstone National Park, WY 82190. www.yellowstonenationalpark lodges.com. © **866/439-7375** or 307/344-7311. Fax 307/344-7456. 96 cabins, some with shared bathroom. $67–$110 double. AE, DISC, MC, V. Closed late Sept to mid-May. **Amenities:** 2 restaurants. *In room:* No phone.

Old Faithful Snow Lodge and Cabins ★★   This is the newest and most modern property in Yellowstone. The dormitory-style lodge was torn down in 1998, replaced the next year by this new, award-winning structure. Its contemporary big-beam construction and high ceiling in the lobby echo the Old Faithful Inn, and a copper-lined balcony curves above the common area, where guests can relax in wicker furniture. Public areas have a contemporary (but appropriate) style, some of the lodge's wood was recycled from the same mill that provided the lumber for the Old Faithful Inn in 1904, and wrought-iron bears abound on everything from lamps to fireplace grates. The modern rooms are spacious and comfortable, second only to the upper-end accommodations at the Lake Yellowstone Hotel. There's also a few surrounding cabins with motel-style furnishings, many of which were built after the 1988 fires.

At Old Faithful, P.O. Box 165, Yellowstone National Park, WY 82190. www.yellowstonenationalpark lodges.com. ℂ 866/439-7375 or 307/344-7311. Fax 307/344-7456. 134 units. $197–$206 double; $96–$149 cabin. AE, DISC, MC, V. Closed late Oct to mid-Dec and early Mar to late Apr. **Amenities:** Restaurant; lounge. *In room:* No phone (cabins).

Roosevelt Lodge Cabins ★ ☺ This is considered the park's family hideaway, a low-key operation with dinky, primitive cabins; stables; and a lodge restaurant that feels like a big ranch house. The bare-bones cabins are called **Roughriders,** and they're furnished with two simple beds, clean linens, a writing table, and a wood stove. A step up, the **Frontier** cabins have their own bathrooms and showers. The lodge is a rugged-but-charming stone edifice; its large, inviting porch is outfitted with rockers so guests can sit back and watch the world go by. Stagecoach rides, horseback trips, and Western trail cookouts give this place a cowboy flavor, and it's a less hectic scene than the other park villages—and it's also the one with the best access to the Lamar Valley and its incomparable wildlife.

At Tower Junction, P.O. Box 165, Yellowstone National Park, WY 82190. (At junction of Mammoth-Tower Rd. and Tower-Canyon Rd.) www.yellowstonenationalparklodges.com. ℂ **866/439-7375** or 307/344-7311. Fax 307/344-7456. 80 cabins, 14 with private bathroom. $65–$110 cabin. AE, DISC, MC, V. Closed early Sept to early June. **Amenities:** Restaurant; lounge. *In room:* No phone.

WHERE TO EAT IN THE PARK

While they're not world-class establishments, Yellowstone's restaurants are well suited to their location and the appetites of their patrons: The portions definitely won't leave anyone going hungry. Most of the menus include a selection of unadventurous, all-American meat-and-potatoes grub alongside several more creative entrees. Consistency can be a problem because the volume is high and the kitchen staffs are seasonal.

If you're not up for restaurant dining, but you don't want to cook over your camp stove the entire time, there is counter-style fast-food service at the **Yellowstone General Stores,** as well as snack shops and cafeterias at Canyon, Mammoth, Grant Village, Lake Lodge, and Old Faithful. Try the new **Geyser Grill** at the Old Faithful Snow Lodge, or the old lunch-counter scene at the **Fishing Bridge Yellowstone General Store.** The **Glacier Pit Snack Bar** is a nostalgic breakfast counter at the Yellowstone General Store in the Canyon Lodge area, open from mid-May to late September.

Canyon Lodge Dining Room ☺ STEAKS/SEAFOOD This is a spacious dining area—a tad sterile, perhaps—and when it fills up, it's noisy. The salad bar is long and loaded, but otherwise the dinner fare is largely geared toward the carnivore, with a wide selection of steaks alongside some seafood and pasta selections. The breakfast buffet is a good way to start your day, with all the standard American fixings. The crowds can be large at Canyon Village, but there is a relaxed and unhurried feel to this place that you don't find at some of the park's other busy points. Families, in particular, might appreciate the ability to take their time with their meals.

At Canyon Lodge. www.yellowstonenationalparklodges.com. ℂ **307/344-7311.** Reservations not accepted. Breakfast $5–$12; lunch $7–$10; dinner $12–$26. AE, DISC, MC, V. Early June to late Sept daily 7–10am, 11:30am–2:30pm, and 5–10pm.

Grant Village Dining Room ★ AMERICAN   Breakfast and lunch at the Grant Village restaurant are much like those at the other restaurants in the park, although the chef often surprises diners with interesting dinner items that stray from the norm. Lunch includes pan-fried trout covered with toasted pecans and lemon butter, huge burgers, and Monte Cristo sandwiches. The dinner menu ranges from herb-roasted chicken, to penne with balsamic-roasted veggies, to prime rib, but the specialty is trout, pan-fried with pecans. Quality and ambience here are comparable to those of the better dining rooms at the major park hotels.

At Grant Village. www.yellowstonenationalparklodges.com. ℂ **866/439-7375.** Dinner reservations required. Breakfast $5–$12 lunch $8–$11; dinner $10–$27. AE, DISC, MC, V. June–Sept daily 6:30–10am, 11:30am–2:30pm, and 5:30–10pm.

Lake Yellowstone Hotel Dining Room ★★ CONTINENTAL   This represents the finest dining Yellowstone has to offer, with a view of the lake stretching south from a vast dining room that doesn't feel crowded even when it's full. One of the best ways to start your day is with a generous breakfast buffet, but the polenta corn cakes with hazelnut-huckleberry butter are also quite good. Lunch entrees are gourmet sandwiches and burgers. The dinner menu is the most adventurous in the park. Appetizers include velvet corn soup and lobster ravioli, while entrees include vegetable paella, bison tenderloin, and blackened salmon.

On the north side of the lake. www.yellowstonenationalparklodges.com. ℂ **307/344-7311.** Dinner reservations recommended. Breakfast $6–$14; lunch $8–$14; dinner $13–$30. AE, DISC, MC, V. Mid-May to early Oct daily 6:30–10am, 11:30am–2:30pm, and 5–10pm.

Mammoth Hotel Dining Room ★ STEAKS/SEAFOOD   At Mammoth, there's a good balance between casual and formal because the dining room is reminiscent of an above-average neighborhood restaurant: comfortable and pleasant, without too much of the hotel's Victorian past. The view of the Old Fort Yellowstone buildings and surrounding slopes is also quite enjoyable. The breakfast buffet is essentially identical to what you'll find here at other locations, featuring eggs, French toast, and the like. The lunch menu focuses on an array of sandwiches, including smoked turkey on Parmesan-crusted sourdough, trout tacos, and smoked salmon club. The dinner menu includes bison top sirloin, Idaho trout, and tasty pork chops, and the vegetarian entrees are creatively inspired and surprisingly good.

At Mammoth Hot Springs. www.yellowstonenationalparklodges.com. ℂ **307/344-7311.** Reservations recommended in winter. Breakfast $4–$12; lunch $8–$16; dinner $11–$25. AE, DISC, MC, V. Closed early Oct to late Dec and early Mar to mid-May. Mid-May–early Oct daily 6:30–10am, 11:30am–2:30pm, and 5–10pm; late Dec–early Mar daily 6:30–10am, 11:30am–2:30pm, and 5:30–8pm.

Obsidian Dining Room ★ STEAKS/SEAFOOD   In the snazzy new Snow Lodge, a spacious restaurant provides a comparatively contemporary alternative to the dining room at the Old Faithful Inn. It's a little quieter, a little less expensive, and a little less formal. It still has some flash on the menu—braised bison short ribs shank and linguine with shrimp or chicken, for instance. For breakfast, try the vegan breakfast burrito.

At the Old Faithful Snow Lodge. www.yellowstonenationalparklodges.com. ℂ **307/344-7311.** Reservations not accepted in summer. Breakfast $5–$12; lunch $7–$20; dinner $10–$30. AE, DISC, MC, V. Early May to mid-Oct daily 6:30–10:30am and 5–10:30pm; mid-Dec to mid-Mar daily 6:30–10am, 11:30am–3pm, and 5–9:30pm.

Old Faithful Inn Dining Room ★ STEAKS/SEAFOOD   The food notwithstanding, the true highlight is the gnarled log architecture of this distinguished historic inn. Breakfast is buffet or a la carte, and there's a lot to choose from. There's another buffet at lunchtime (headlined by pan-fried trout and barbecue chicken), as well as a generous assortment of salads and sandwiches. Dinnertime brings yet another buffet (prime rib being the headliner), along with menu entrees like steaks, fish, and a vegetarian dish. The fare has gotten more distinguished in recent years, with such creative options as bison ravioli and pan-seared elk medallions making regular appearances on the menu.

At the Old Faithful Inn. www.yellowstonenationalparklodges.com. ✆ **307/344-7311.** Dinner reservations required. Breakfast and lunch $5–$15; dinner $15–$26. AE, DISC, MC, V. Early May to early Oct daily 6:30–10:30am, 11:30am–2:30pm, and 5–10pm. Closed in winter.

Roosevelt Lodge Dining Room STEAKS/SEAFOOD   This is supposed to be the cowboy alternative to the fancier cuisine served at the bigger Yellowstone hotels, but the menu is unadventurous. For breakfast, it's eggs and flapjacks; lunch is burgers and sandwiches. Come suppertime, the menu is dominated by barbecue and steaks. A better idea: Join Roosevelt's Old West Dinner Cookout, and ride by horse or wagon through the Pleasant Valley to a chuckwagon dinner that includes cornbread, steak, watermelon, those famous beans, and apple crisp. It's a daily summer event (reservations required) that costs $68 to $84 for an adult, depending on the route of your horseback ride, or $57 if you go by wagon. Children pay about $10 less.

At Tower Junction. www.yellowstonenationalparklodges.com. ✆ **307/344-7311.** Reservations not accepted, except for Old West cookouts. Breakfast $5–$10; lunch $7–$11; dinner $9–$25. AE, DISC, MC, V. Mid-June to early Sept daily 7–10am, 11:30am–3pm, and 4:30–9pm.

JACKSON HOLE & GRAND TETON NATIONAL PARK

Grand Teton compares to Yellowstone somewhat the way a Generation X snowboarder compares to an old ski patrol graybeard: It's younger, flashier, and closer to the bars. The Tetons are a young mountain range in geologic time, and Grand Teton is a young national park, on the rolls in its present form since 1950. (Yellowstone, by comparison, dates from 1872.) And whereas the geysers of Yellowstone are a pretty long drive from anywhere, you can come off a climb at Grand Teton and be in a posh eatery 20 minutes after you hit the floor of the idyllic valley known as **Jackson Hole,** home to the resort town of the same name.

Jackson is a spiffy resort town with a little cowboy still in it. There are million-dollar homes all over the valley, but there is still open space, which allows visitors to imagine what it was like early in the 19th century, when fur trappers first camped here. They were followed by ranchers, who soon became *dude* ranchers. Today the community holds an interesting mixture of the wealthy jet set crowd, ski bums, outdoorsy types, and even a few old-time cowboys. The cosmopolitans of this motley crew came not just with a hunger for scenery, but also with a taste for music, art, and good restaurants, and the selection here is unrivaled in Wyoming. The big ski hill lures a younger crowd, with the final ingredient for resort status—celebrities—supplied by transplants like Harrison Ford.

JACKSON HOLE ★★

57 miles S of Yellowstone National Park; 432 miles NW of Cheyenne; 275 miles NE of Salt Lake City; 177 miles SW of Cody

Of the few Rocky Mountain communities that successfully toe the line between resort and indigenous town, Jackson is a standout. Located 60 miles south of Yellowstone, Jackson Hole's million-dollar homes sprout all over the valley (formerly called a "hole"), but there is still open space, a respect for cowboys, and resistance to too much glitz. Modern Jackson Hole has become a mix of ski bums, blue bloods, nouveau riche, avid outdoor types, and a few real, live cowboys.

JACKSON OR JACKSON HOLE—what's the difference?

You'll likely see every kind of merchandise imaginable fashioned with an image of the Tetons and the words "Jackson Hole, Wyoming" scrawled over it. You may notice that on the map, the town just south of Grand Teton National Park is called Jackson. But your plane ticket says Jackson Hole. But wait a minute—the postmark just says Jackson. What gives?

The mystery of the town's name is actually pretty simple. Three mountain men ran a fur-trapping company in these parts in the 1800s: one named David

Jackson, another named Jedediah Smith, and a third named William Sublette. Mountain men in those days referred to a valley as a hole. As the story goes, Sublette called the valley Jackson's Hole because Jackson spent a great deal of time in it. That name was shortened, and when the town materialized, it was also named for David Jackson. So the city itself is Jackson, Wyoming, and it lies in the great valley that runs the length of the Tetons' east side, Jackson Hole.

Skiing   Knee-deep powder and a backdrop of the soaring Grand Tetons greets skiers at **Jackson Hole Mountain Resort.** Steep slopes and challenging drop-offs are the norm at this resort, a favorite among enthusiasts. Gentler inclines occupy skiers at **Grand Targhee Resort.** With over 500 inches of fresh, dry powder each winter, snow lovers can count on Alpine and Nordic nirvana during the day, and romantic, starlit sleigh rides after dark.

Things to Do   **Grand Teton National Park** has always been a prime draw for visitors to Jackson Hole. Footpaths meander throughout this mountainous park, under whispering aspens, alongside crystal-clear Jenny Lake and beneath the jagged, lavender peaks of the Teton Range. Jackson Hole's **Snake River** hosts rafting trips until the snow flies. The upper Snake takes boaters past grazing moose and elk; the lower Snake is a wild, whitewater nail-biter. Soar above it all on the tram at the **Jackson Hole Mountain Resort** for unparalleled views year-round.

Eating & Drinking   Because of its cosmopolitan devotees, Jackson offers the best selection of restaurants in Wyoming, running the gamut of cuisine and price. Local fish and game fill menus at Jackson Hole restaurants, from the traditional to the contemporary. Try pan-seared elk chops, lean buffalo burgers, or freshly caught, pecan-crusted salmon. If you're looking to drink with the cowboys, head to the famous **Silver Dollar Bar** or the very famous **Million Dollar Cowboy Bar.**

Nature   When the autumn chill sets in, Jackson Hole's resident bull elks fill the air with their shrill bugle calls. By December, a herd of thousands fills the **National Elk Refuge,** their imposing antlers held impossibly high. Visitors see the herd up close on **horse-drawn sleigh rides** through March. Nearby, Wyoming celebrates the animal kingdom at the **National Museum of Wildlife Art.** Bronze sculptures, pottery, oil paintings, and photographs depict bison, bears, and birds from 2500 B.C. to the present.

Essentials

GETTING THERE The **Jackson Airport** (www.jacksonholeairport.com; *©* 307/733-7682) is located north of town at the southern end of Grand Teton

Jackson

HOTELS ■
The Alpenhof **4**
Alpine House **20**
Amangani **12**
Anvil Motel **22**
A Teton Treehouse **7**
Buckrail Lodge **37**
Days Inn **9**
Four Seasons Resort
Jackson Hole **4**
The Hostel **4**
Hotel Terra **4**
Inn on the Creek **15**
Lexington at Jackson Hole **19**
Motel 6 **11**
Rustic Inn **16**
Rusty Parrot Lodge
and Spa **14**
Snake River Lodge
and Spa **4**
Spring Creek Ranch **12**
Super 8 **11**
Wildflower Inn **2**
Woods Hotel **25**
Wort Hotel **28**

RESTAURANTS ◆
Betty Rock Cafe **35**
The Blue Lion **26**
The Cadillac Grille/Billy's
Giant Hamburgers **27**
D.O.G./Everest
Momo Shack **33**
Il Villaggio Osteria **3**
The Kitchen **24**
Koshu Wine Bar **34**
Mangy Moose **3**

Nani's Genuine
Pasta House **21**
Nora's Fish Creek Inn **8**
North Grille **13**
Q Roadhouse **6**
Rendezvous Bistro **10**
Shades Café **31**
Snake River Brewing Co. **36**

Snake River Grill **30**
Stiegler's **1**
Sweetwater
Restaurant **32**
Trio **33**

ATTRACTIONS ●
Grand Targhee Resort **17**
Jackson Hole Aerial Tram **5**
Jackson Hole Mountain
Resort **5**
Jackson Hole Historical
Society Museum **23**
National Elk Refuge **18**
National Museum of
Wildlife Art **17**
Snow King Resort **38**
Town Square **29**

National Park. **American Airlines** flies in from Chicago, and regular service is provided from Denver and Salt Lake City by **Delta, Frontier,** and **United.**

If you're getting here on your own wheels, come north from I-80 at Rock Springs on U.S. 189/191, or come east from I-15 at Idaho Falls on U.S. 26 and either come through Snake River Canyon on that highway or veer north over Teton Pass on Wyo. 32. If you are coming south from Yellowstone National Park, you can stay on U.S. 89, which runs north and south through both parks and into town. For up-to-date weather information and local road conditions, contact the Jackson Hole Chamber of Commerce (see below).

VISITOR INFORMATION The **Jackson Hole Chamber of Commerce** is a source of information concerning just about everything in and around Jackson. Along with the Bridger-Teton, Yellowstone, and Grand Teton rangers, chamber representatives can be found at the **Jackson Hole and Greater Yellowstone Visitor Center** (no phone), 532 N. Cache St., open daily from 8am to 7pm in summer and 9am to 5pm in winter. For information on lodging, events, and activities, contact the chamber at P.O. Box 550, Jackson, WY 83001 (www.jacksonholechamber.com; ✆ 307/733-3316). For lodging information and reservations, call **Jackson Hole Central Reservations** (www.jacksonholewy.com; ✆ 888/838-6606).

GETTING AROUND Once you're on the ground, major car-rental operations serving the airport include **Alamo/National** (✆ 800/227-7368), **Avis** (✆ 800/230-4898), and **Hertz** (✆ 800/654-3131). Also providing rentals in the area are **Dollar** (✆ 800/800-3665) and **Thrifty** (✆ 800/847-4389).

Taxi service is available from **Buckboard Cab** (✆ 307/733-1112) and **Cowboy Cab** (✆ 307/413-1000). **Alltrans** (www.jacksonholealltrans.com; ✆ 800/443-6133 or 307/733-3135) offers shuttle service from the airport and national park tours. Many of the hotels and car-rental agencies in the Jackson area offer free shuttle service to and from the airport.

The **Southern Teton Area Rapid Transit (START)** offers bus transport from Teton Village to Jackson daily for $3 (half-price for seniors 60 and over and students; children 8 and under ride free). Service includes about 70 trips a day between downtown and Teton Village in the winter, and 15 in the summer; it shuts down around midnight year-round. For specific schedule information, contact START at ✆ 307/733-4521 or browse **www.startbus.com**.

SPECIAL EVENTS Held annually in late May, **Old West Days** is a 4-day event dedicated to Jackson's frontier past, with a shootout, cowboy poetry readings, a parade, and a rodeo. The other big annual event is the **Jackson Hole Fall Arts Festival,** a 10-day extravaganza in September with special events every day. Contact the Jackson Hole Chamber of Commerce (see above) for further information on either.

Getting Outside
BIKING
You can rent a bike and pick up maps at several of the shops listed on p. 309, or take a guided trip in Yellowstone, Grand Teton, or the national forest with **Teton Mountain Bike Tours** (www.tetonmtbike.com; ✆ 800/733-0788) or Hoback Sports's **Fat Tire Tours** (✆ 307/733-5335), which places bikes in the Snow King chairlift for an easy ride up the mountain.

CLIMBING

The sight of the 13,770-foot Grand Teton towering above the valley has been setting hearts pumping for generations. A century ago, no one had reached the top; now, thousands have, often carefully roped and cared for by professional guides. Experienced guides and established routes ensure a modicum of safety, but climbing accidents and deaths still occur. Overnight climbers must pick up a free permit. The American Alpine Club provides inexpensive dormitory beds ($14 nightly for AAC members, $22 for nonmembers) for climbers at the **Grand Teton Climbers' Ranch** (www.american alpineclub.org; ✆ **307/733-7271**). A pair of long-standing operations offers classes and guided climbs of Grand Teton: **Jackson Hole Mountain Guides** in Jackson (www. jhmg.com; ✆ **800/239-7642** or 307/733-4979) and **Exum Mountain Guides ★** in Moose (www.exumguides.com; ✆ **307/733-2297**). Expect to pay $700 to $1,000 for a guided 2-day climb of Grand Teton or $150 to $200 for a class.

The **Jenny Lake Ranger Station** (✆ **307/733-3392**), which is open only in summer, is the center for climbing information; climbers are encouraged to stop in and obtain information on routes, conditions, and regulations.

CROSS-COUNTRY SKIING

With five Nordic centers and a couple of national parks at your feet, plus the 3.5-million-acre Bridger-Teton National Forest, cross-country skiers have plenty of choices. If you're new to cross-country skiing on any level, you might choose to start on the groomed, level trails at one of the Nordic centers. If, however, you have experience in the steep, deep powder of untracked wilderness, visit or call the National Park Service in **Grand Teton National Park** (www.nps.gov/grte; ✆ **307/739-3300**) or the **Bridger-Teton National Forest** in downtown Jackson at 340 N. Cache St. (www.fs.fed.us/r4/btnf; ✆ **307/739-5500**), and check in before you go.

The local ski shops are excellent sources of unofficial advice about the area's backcountry. Keep in mind that many of the trails used by cross-country skiers are also used by snowmobiles. For those seeking instruction, lessons are available at the Nordic centers, or you can check the schedule of **Teton Parks and Recreation** (www.tetonwyo.org/parks; ✆ **307/733-5056**), which takes visitors on various cross-country ski outings from mid-December to mid-March, weather permitting.

The **Jackson Hole Nordic Center,** 7658 Teewinot St., Teton Village (www. jacksonhole.com; ✆ **307/733-2292**), on the flats just east of Teton Village, is a small part of the giant facility that includes some of the best downhill skiing around (see below). Trail passes ($14) allow access to 11 miles of groomed trails. **Teton Pines Cross Country Skiing Center** (www.tetonpines.com; ✆ **800/238-2223** or 307/733-1005) has 7.5 miles of groomed trails that wind over the resort's golf course. At **Grand Targhee** (www.grandtarghee.com; ✆ **800/827-4433** or 307/353-2300), you can rent or buy anything you need in the way of equipment and take off on the resort's 9.3 miles of groomed trails.

DOG SLEDDING

If your idea of mushing is not oatmeal but a pack of yipping dogs, you might want to try your hand at dog sledding, an enjoyable open-air way to tour the high country during the winter. **Jackson Hole Iditarod** (www.jhsleddog.com; ✆ **800/554-7388**), associated with Iditarod racer Frank Teasley, offers both half- and full-day trips in five-person sleds (the fifth companion is your guide), and you can take a turn in the driver's stand. The half-day ride costs around $245 per person, gives the dogs an 11-mile workout, and includes a light lunch before you head back to the kennels. For about $300 a head, you can take the full-day excursion out to Granite Hot Springs, a 22-mile trip total. You get a hot lunch, with your choice of trout or steak.

DOWNHILL SKIING

Low temperatures, black-diamond runs, remote location, and an intimidating vertical drop haven't scared skiers away from Jackson Hole—this is what *attracts* them. The two largest ski resorts in the area have been expanding, putting in faster chairs, and eliminating long waits in lift lines. The quality of snow on the mountain can vary, but skiers who seek challenges will not be disappointed. All resorts are open daily.

Jackson Hole Mountain Resort ★★   This resort is booming, with scads of new hotels and timeshares going up at the mountain's foot in recent years, more than doubling the guest capacity in just a few short years. There is special grandeur to this ski resort, from its spectacular mountaintop views, to its daring black-diamond runs, to its 400 annual inches of powder. Head to the top of **Rendezvous Mountain** and plunge down Tensleep Bowl if you want to get a taste of skiing on the edge. You'll find an inexhaustible supply of steep runs that require skiing expertise: The terrain is rated 10% beginner, 40% intermediate, and 50% expert. There are lesser runs to the north, including gentler journeys down the sides of **Apres Vous Mountain** that will better suit an intermediate skier. There is a fairly new $25-million, 100-passenger tram, which opened in time for the 2008–09 season.

Crowded days have been few in recent years—lucky for skiers, if not the owners. With 2,500 acres of skiable terrain and 4,139 feet of vertical drop, there's plenty of room. Ten lifts, a gondola, and an aerial tram are available from early December to the beginning of April. (The resort turns into a mountain-biking playground come summer.) For an orientation, join the Mountain Hosts, who gather groups at the top of the Rendezvous lift to escort newcomers on a 2-hour tour.

The competition among ski resorts compels growth—not just on the slopes, but also in the resort villages below. A variety of restaurants, lodging, a medical clinic, shops, and entertainment—from sleigh-ride dinners to a skating rink—make it unnecessary to leave the complex during a ski vacation.

If you've never skied in powder up to your kneecaps, make an early-morning trip to the **Hoback Zone,** just under Cheyenne Bowl. The ski patrol closes it off as soon as the snow gets tracked out.

3395 W. Village Dr. (P.O. Box 290), Teton Village, WY 83025. www.jacksonhole.com. © **888/333-7766** or 307/733-2292; 307/733-2291 for snow conditions; 888/838-6606 for central reservations. Full-day lift tickets $64–$99 adults, $48–$74 seniors 63 and over, $38–$59 children 14 and under. Late Nov to early Apr daily 9am–4pm. From Jackson, take Wyo. 22 west to Wyo. 390 and go north to Teton Village, about 5 miles.

Grand Targhee Resort ★   The Grand Targhee resort has struggled at times, changing ownership, wheeling and dealing with federal land managers, and sparring with local conservationists over expansion plans and real-estate development. None of that affects the snow, however, which is terrific—or the deep, forgiving powder from November through spring (more than 500 in. annually), and a more peaceful, less-crowded village that provides a worthy alternative to Teton Village. Many skiers break up a Jackson ski trip by driving over Teton Pass for a day or two on these slopes.

This may also be a better place for less aggressive skiers. There is a beginner's powder area and hundreds of acres of wide-open powder slopes for intermediates and other cruisers. You can take a high-speed quad to the adjacent Peaked Mountain and ski in thigh-deep, untracked snow. A problem you might encounter is, oddly enough, fog. Now and then the mountain gets socked in with gray moisture, forcing skiers to ski below the thick blanket. The **Lost Groomer Chute,** a run that takes full advantage of the weather moving west to east, will provide the most insatiable powder hound with enough dust.

Here are a few of the other treats at Targhee: You can ride a sleigh on a starlit evening to a round-table dinner in a snow-buried yurt; your kids can enroll in the Powder Scouts program, which gives kids ages 6 to 12 a full day of instruction, food, and skiing for $131, rental included; and a spa offers everything from massage to an herbal body wrap, along with hot tubs, sauna, exercise room, and heated outdoor pool. Lodging is available at several slopeside hostelries; double rooms start at $149 during regular ski season.

3300 E. Ski Hill Rd., Box SKI, Alta, WY 83422. www.grandtarghee.com. ⓒ **800/827-4433** or 307/353-2300. Full-day lift tickets $69 adults, $44 seniors 65 and older, $29 children 6–12, free for children 5 and under. Mid-Nov to Apr daily 9am–4pm. From Jackson, take Wyo. 22 over Teton Pass into Idaho, then Idaho 33 north to Driggs, then follow the signs west (back into WY) to Targhee Resort, about 38 miles.

Snow King Resort If you enter Jackson from the north on a winter night, the lit slopes of Snow King are an appealing sight. Snow King offers a variety of recreation, including a tubing hill, ice rink, and snowboard park. Plus, it's conveniently located near the heart of town. It's the oldest ski hill in Wyoming, operating since 1939, and the hotel has moderately priced rooms. The only problem is the skiing itself: A limited number of fairly steep runs don't offer much variety. The beginner's slope is small and amounts to only 15% of the terrain, the snow is notoriously icy, and there's not enough intermediate snow to satisfy all levels of ability. The two other area resorts are much bigger, with more and longer runs and a greater variety of challenges. "Town Hill," as it's known, has 400 acres of skiable terrain, a triple chair, two double chairs, and two surface tows (one for tubing). *Note:* At press time, the resort was struggling financially and for sale.

400 E. Snow King, Jackson, WY 83001. www.snowking.com. ⓒ **800/522-5464** or 307/733-5200; 307/734-2020 for snow conditions. Lift tickets $42 adults, $36 seniors 60 and older and children 13 and under. Late Nov to late Mar Tues–Sat 10am–7pm, Sun–Mon 10am–4pm. Take Cache St. south to Snow King Ave. Turn left and follow the signs to the resort.

FISHING

Yellowstone and Grand Teton national parks are home to some fabled fishing spots (see the park sections for details), but some of the best angling in the region is found outside the park boundaries.

The **Snake River** emerges from Jackson Lake Dam as a broad, strong river, with decent fishing from its banks in certain spots—like right below the dam—and better fishing if you float the river. Fly-fishermen should ask for advice at local stores on recent insect hatches and good stretches of river, or hire a guide to keep them company. **High Country Flies ★**, 185 N. Center St. (www.highcountryflies.com; ⓒ **866/733-7210** or 307/733-7210), has a vast selection of high-quality fishing gear, flies, and fly-tying supplies, along with lessons and guided trips, as well as free advice if you just want to gab about where to cast. If you'd like a guide who knows the holes, try **Jack Dennis Fishing Trips** (www.jackdennisfishingtrips.com; ⓒ **307/690-0910**), **Triangle X Float Trips** (www.trianglex.com; ⓒ **307/733-5500**), or **Westbank Anglers** (www.westbank.com; ⓒ **800/922-3474** or 307/733-6483). The going rate for guided fishing is about $450 for a full day for two people.

GOLF

More than one American president has played a round of golf in Jackson, which, despite its short putting season, has some world-class links. The semiprivate Robert Trent Jones, Jr.–designed **Jackson Hole Golf and Tennis Club** (www.jhgtc.com; ✆ **307/733-3111**), north of Jackson off U.S. Hwy. 89, has an 18-hole course that's one of the best in the country—and it's also home to a good restaurant, the **North Grille** (see "Where to Eat," later in this chapter). Seasonal greens fees range from $70 to $145 for 18 holes, cart included. The **Teton Pines Resort,** 3450 N. Clubhouse Dr. (www.tetonpines.com; ✆ **800/238-2223** or 307/733-1005), designed by Arnold Palmer and Ed Seay, is a challenging course; greens fees range from $65 to $160, cart included, depending on the season. Both courses are open to the public.

HIKING

One benefit of having so many mountain ranges converging around Jackson is that you have choices—especially when it comes to hiking. The most popular place to go for a stroll in the vicinity of Jackson is **Grand Teton National Park,** which shows off some glorious aspen colors in the fall. Less traveled are the forests that abut the park, particularly **Bridger-Teton National Forest** just east of Jackson. Bridger-Teton and its eastside counterpart, **Shoshone National Forest,** encompass a huge piece of mountain real estate, including glaciers, 13,000-foot peaks, and some of the best alpine fishing lakes in the world. Among the mountain ranges included in these forests are the **Absarokas,** the **Gros Ventre,** the **Wyoming,** and the **Wind River Range,** or "Winds," as they're called by locals, which stretch about 120 miles from just southeast of Jackson near Pinedale to the South Pass area and the Red Desert. The **Jackson Hole and Greater Yellowstone Visitor Center,** 532 N. Cache St., in downtown Jackson, provides all of the hiking and access information you'll need for the national forest, as well as for the Gros Ventre and Teton wilderness areas. Call the **Forest Service** (www.fs.fed.us/r4/btnf; ✆ **307/739-5500**) for additional information. For those who would like a hiking/backpacking (or snowshoeing/cross-country skiing) guide—for about $120 a day per adult—contact **The Hole Hiking Experience** (www.holehike.com; ✆ **866/733-4453** or 307/690-4453).

HORSEBACK RIDING

Some hotels, including those in Grand Teton National Park, have stables and operate trail rides for their guests. For details, contact **Jackson Hole Outfitters** (www.jacksonholetrailrides.com; ✆ **307/654-7008**), **Spring Creek Ranch Riding Stables** (www.springcreekranch.com; ✆ **800/443-6139** or 307/733-8833), or the **Mill Iron Ranch** (www.millironranch.net; ✆ **888/808-6390** or 307/733-6390). Rides typically cost around $50 for 2 hours or $150 for a day.

KAYAKING, CANOEING & SAILING

With the Snake and Hoback rivers and the lakes of Grand Teton National Park, it's no surprise to see all kinds of watercraft towed or tied to the roofs of SUVs in Jackson. Canoeists and kayakers enjoy the upper Snake River, from Jackson Lake Dam down to Moose, and expert kayakers are attracted to the ride through Snake River Canyon and Hoback white water. Beginners should be wary of the upper Snake—snags and spring currents have claimed lives, so a guide is advisable. Canoeists paddle Jenny Lake and, with a small portage or two, String and Leigh lakes. The big lake, **Jackson,** attracts sailboats and sea kayaks, but beware of the sudden afternoon eruptions of gusty wind and thunderstorms.

Several operators in Jackson run schools and guide paddlers of all skill levels. The two major outfits are the **Snake River Kayak and Canoe School,** 260 N. Cache St. (www.snakeriverkayak.com; ℭ **800/529-2501** or 307/733-9999), and **Rendezvous River Sports,** 945 W. Broadway (www.jacksonholekayak.com; ℭ **307/733-2471**).

RAFTING

The most popular way to experience the Snake River is white-water rafting; these are wet, wild, white-knuckle tours. Several companies offer adrenaline-pumping day trips down the Snake, but don't plan on being just a passenger—this is a participatory sport. Contact **Barker-Ewing** (www.barker-ewing.com; ℭ **800/448-4202**), **Sands Wildwater** (www.sandswhitewater.com; ℭ **800/358-8184** or 307/733-4410), **Dave Hansen Whitewater** (www.davehansenwhitewater.com; ℭ **800/732-6295** or 307/733-6295), or **Mad River Boat Trips** (www.mad-river.com; ℭ **800/458-7238**). Generally, a full-day trip runs $80 to $100, lunch included, and a half-day trip costs about $50 to $70.

SNOWMOBILING

Although West Yellowstone is the most popular base for snowmobiling in the Yellowstone area, Jackson has a growing contingent of snowmobile aficionados and outfitters. The operators who rent snowmobiles (including the necessary clothing and helmets) also have guides to take you on 1-day and multiday tours of Jackson Hole and the surrounding area. **High Country Snowmobile Tours, Wyoming Adventures,** and **Rocky Mountain Snowmobile Tours** share a website and reservation service (www.snowmobiletours.net; ℭ **800/647-2561**), offering guided trips in Jackson Hole, Yellowstone, and the surrounding wildlands. **Jackson Hole Snowmobile Tours,** 515 N. Cache St. (www.jacksonholesnowmobile.com; ℭ **800/633-1733** or 307/733-6850), offers 1-day trips in Yellowstone and multiday trips along the Continental Divide. A typical guided, full-day outing costs from $250 to $300 for a single rider, with pickup and drop-off service, equipment, fuel, a continental

---

offbeat BUT MEMORABLE WAYS TO SEE THE TETONS

Aerial Touring: For a much quicker climb to the mountaintops, call **Teton Aviation** (www.tetonaviation. com; ℭ 208/354-3100), in Driggs, Idaho. You'll actually be looking down at the summits that climbers strain to top, and you'll get a new perspective on the immensity of the Grand Teton (although you won't get too close—the park has some air-space restrictions). Teton has 1-hour flights in planes and gliders (starting at $250 per flight) that take you to 11,800 feet on the west side of the Grand.

Ballooning: The folks at the **Wyoming Balloon Company** ★ (www.wyomingballoon.com; ℭ 307/739-0900) like to fire up early, in the still air that cloaks the Teton Valley around 6am. Their "float trips" stay aloft for a little more than an hour, cruising over a 3,000-acre ranch with a full-frontal view of the Tetons. The journey concludes with a champagne toast at the landing site. Prices are $325 adults and $285 for children ages 6 to 12 (no kids under 6 allowed).

breakfast, and lunch at Old Faithful included. Also in Jackson, snowmobiles and relevant gear can be rented at **Leisure Sports,** 1075 S. U.S. Hwy. 89 (www.leisure sportsadventure.com; © **307/733-3040**).

Exploring the Area

Jackson Hole Aerial Tram ★ After the resort's legendary tram shut down in 2006, a new tram nicknamed "Big Red" opened for the 2008–09 ski season. From the top, you can see the Tetons from an elevation above 10,000 feet, but don't expect a private tour. During busy summer days, the tram carries 45 passengers, packed in like the skiers that take the lift in the winter. You can hike down, take the tram, or even paraglide. The top of Rendezvous Mountain offers an incredible view, but it can get pretty chilly, even in the middle of summer, so bring a light coat. Atop the tram, **Corbet's Cabin** offers a place to eat before you head back down.

At Jackson Hole Mountain Resort, 7658 Teewinot St., Teton Village. www.jacksonhole.com. © **307/739-2753.** Tickets $19–$29 adults and seniors, $10–$20 children 6–17, free for children under 6. Early Sept to early Oct and late May to mid-June daily 9am–5pm; mid-June to early Sept daily 9am–6pm. Tram runs approximately every half-hour.

Jackson Hole Historical Society Museum Reopened in a new facility in 2011, the Jackson Hole Historical Society Museum nicely covers the lore and legends of Jackson Hole in its inaugural exhibit, "Playing Hard: Labor and Leisure in Jackson Hole." On display are exhibits covering everything from skiing and snowplanes to gambling, painting, and rodeo in the valley. There are Western getups for kids to try on, as well as a special display dedicated to such movies shot on location here, including *Shane, Dances With Wolves,* and *Rocky IV.* There is also a good gift shop here.

225 N. Cache St. (at the corner of Deloney St.). www.jacksonholehistory.org. © **307/733-2414.** Admission $6 adults, $5 seniors, $4 students and children. Mon–Sat 10am–6pm; Sun noon–5pm. Shorter hours fall to spring.

National Museum of Wildlife Art ★★ If you don't spot this museum on your way into Jackson from the north, consider that a triumph of design: Its jagged, red-sandstone facade is meant to blend into the steep hillside facing the elk refuge. Within this 50,000-square-foot castle is some of the best wildlife art in the country. There are 12 exhibit galleries that display traveling shows and collections dating from 2000 B.C. to the present, including a gallery devoted to the American bison, as well as a showcase for local great Carl Rungius. Younger visitors will be entertained by the many interactive exhibits and a "Kid's Kit" loaner to tote around the museum. The facility also houses a repository of internationally acclaimed wildlife films, and there's a good little cafe, too.

2820 Rungius Rd. (3 miles north of town on U.S. Hwy. 89, across from the National Elk Refuge). www.wildlifeart.org. © **800/313-9553** or 307/733-5771. Admission $12 adults, $10 seniors, $6 children 5 to 18, free for children 4 and under. Daily 9am–5pm (fall to spring Sun 11am–5pm).

Wildlife-Watching

National Elk Refuge ★ It's not exactly nature's way, but the U.S. Fish and Wildlife Service makes sure that the elk in this area eat well during the winter by feeding them alfalfa pellets. It keeps them out of the haystacks of area ranchers and creates a beautiful tableau on the flats along the Gros Ventre River: thousands of elk, some with huge antler racks, dot the snow for miles. Drivers along U.S. Hwy. 89 might also see trumpeter swans, coyotes, moose, bighorn sheep, and, lately, wolves. As autumn begins

Especially for Kids

Snow King may not have the best skiing in the valley, but it caters to kids and families. In the summer, kids can frolic on the **Snow King's Alpine Miniature Golf Course and Alpine Slide** (📞 **307/ 733-5200**). A round of 18 holes is $8 for adults, $7 for seniors, $6 for kids 6 to 13, and $3 for kids 5 and under. The **Alpine Slide** is the golf course's untamed neighbor. It's a wild ride down the 2,500-foot ophidian highway running from the top of the blue-and-yellow chairlift to the bottom of Snow King Mountain; it's like a water slide without the water. A trip down the slide is $15 per person.

In the winter, there are ski schools for kids, with day-care options at all the ski resorts. Once again, Snow King has a few extras: a tubing hill ($21 for 2 hr. adults, $18 kids 13 and under) and an ice-skating rink, which opens in October and features skating ($6 adults, $4 kids 13 and under; skate rentals $3) and hockey until spring. For more information, call 📞 **307/733-3000.**

to chill the air in September, you'll hear the shrill whistles of the bull elk in the mountains; as snow begins to stick on the ground, about 5,000 animals make their way down to the refuge—the world's largest winter concentration of elk. Although the cultivated meadows and pellets help the elk survive the winter, some biologists say this approach results in overpopulation and the spread of diseases such as brucellosis.

Regardless, this is a great opportunity to see these magnificent wapiti up close. Each winter from mid-December to March, the Fish and Wildlife Service offers **horse-drawn sleigh rides** that weave among the refuge elk. Riders early in the winter will find young, energetic bulls playing and banging heads, while late-winter visitors (when the Fish and Wildlife Service begins feeding the animals) wander through a more placid scene. Rides embark from the Jackson Hole and Greater Yellowstone Visitor Center (532 N. Cache St.) daily between 10am and 4pm on a first-come, first-served basis. Tickets for the 45-minute rides cost $18 for adults and $14 for children 5 to 12.

Located 3 miles north of Jackson on U.S. Hwy. 26/89. http://nationalelkrefuge.fws.gov. 📞 **307/733-9212.** Free admission. Visitor center: summer daily 8am–7pm; winter daily 9am–5pm.

Shopping

In recent years, big national chains have opened factory-outlet stores in Jackson, and among the ever-changing array of shops (rents are high; so is turnover) you can find everything from American-Indian crafts to cowboy boots to Oriental rugs. But these are what you'll find in most resort towns. The areas where Jackson excels are its art galleries and outdoor-wear shops.

ARTS & ANTIQUES

Collectors, tired of bighorn sheep on the crags and weather-beaten cowboys on their horses, often dismiss Western art. But while Jackson has plenty of that genre in stock, some of its two dozen galleries are more adventurous and sophisticated. **Cayuse Western Americana,** 255 N. Glenwood St. (www.cayusewa.com; 📞 **800/405-4096** or 307/739-1940), focuses on antiques of all kinds, from beadwork to spurs to belt buckles to paintings. **Tayloe Piggott Gallery,** 745 W. Broadway (www.tayloepiggottgallery.com; 📞 **307/733-0555**), showcases contemporary paintings and other edgy work. A mile north of town, at 1975 U.S. Hwy. 89 (toward the park), is the

Wilcox Gallery (www.wilcoxgallery.com; ℂ 307/733-6450), which showcases more than 20 painters and sculptors from across the nation. The **Jackson Hole Galleries Association** (www.jacksonholegalleries.com) is a great resource.

SPORTING GOODS & EQUIPMENT RENTALS

Serious climbers with serious wallets will appreciate the gear at **Teton Mountaineering ★**, at 170 N. Cache St. (www.tetonmtn.com; ℂ 800/850-3595 or 307/733-3595), a block from the square, where you can get killer Nordic skis and high-grade fleece jackets. This is a great spot for climbing, camping, and winter gear. **Adventure Sports,** at Dornan's in the town of Moose (ℂ 307/733-3307), has a small selection of mountain bike, kayak, and canoe rentals, and advice on where to go with the gear. When snowboards are put away for the summer, the **Boardroom** switches to BMX bikes and skateboards, at 225 W. Broadway (www.boardroomjacksonhole.com; ℂ 307/733-8327). **Hoback Sports,** 520 W. Broadway (www.hobacksports.com; ℂ 307/733-5335), has a large selection of skis, boards, and summer mountain bikes for rent and sale. **Skinny Skis,** at 65 W. Deloney Ave. off Town Square (www.skinny skis.com; ℂ 888/733-7205 or 307/733-6094), is a year-round specialty sports shop and has an excellent selection of equipment and clothing. For serviceable factory seconds at steeply discounted prices, head north to the little town of Moose, near the entrance to Grand Teton National Park, and shop **Moosely Seconds ★** (ℂ 307/739-1801), where you'll find surprisingly deep discounts on quality outdoor wear.

Where to Stay

The thin-walled, dimly lit motels of the past are just memories now—Jackson lodgings these days come with palatial trappings and, in some cases, prices that start at $500 a night. Prices are generally discounted in off season (spring/fall), but not during ski season.

Clustered together near the junction west of downtown where Wyo. 22 leaves U.S. Hwy. 26/89 and heads north to Teton Village is a colony of chain franchises: a surprisingly chic **Motel 6,** 600 S. U.S. Hwy. 89 (ℂ 307/733-1620); **Super 8,** 750 S. U.S. Hwy. 89 (www.super8.com; ℂ 307/733-6833); and the more upscale and expensive **Days Inn,** 350 S. U.S. Hwy. 89 (www.daysinn.com; ℂ 307/733-0033), with private hot tubs and fireplaces in suites. High-season prices for these chain motels range from $150 to $200 per double. North of Town Square, the **Lexington at Jackson Hole** (formerly the Trapper Inn), 285 N. Cache St. (www.lexjh.com; ℂ 888/771-2648 or 307/733-2648), is a solid pick, with doubles for $229 and suites for $299 in summer.

On the inexpensive end of the scale, the **Anvil Motel,** 215 N. Cache St. (www.anvilmotel.com; ℂ 800/234-4507 or 307/733-3668), offers double rooms for $110 to $148 in summer. I also like the summer-only **Buckrail Lodge,** at the base of Snow King Mountain, at 110 E. Karns Ave. (www.buckraillodge.com; ℂ 307/733-2079), a comfortable independent that's been nicely maintained since it opened in the 1960s. Doubles are $91 to $143.

IN JACKSON

Alpine House ★★   Stylish, environmentally conscious, and melding the best of the B&B and hotel worlds, Alpine House began as a six-room operation in 1996 and expanded nearly fourfold in 2000, when it also opened a spa. Modeled after Scandinavian lodging, the rooms are woodsy and Western but modern and functional, with one king, one queen, or two queen beds and nice views. Some have lofts with additional beds; all have a shared or private balcony, a fireplace, and a soaking tub. The public areas, indoors and out, are quiet and serene. There are five spacious creekside cottages a block away from the main building. Owners Hans and Nancy Johnstone are former Olympians and great resources for planning outdoor adventures in Jackson Hole.

285 N. Glenwood St. (P.O. Box 1126), Jackson, WY 83001. www.alpinehouse.com. ⓒ **800/753-1421** or 307/739-1570. Fax 307/734-2850. 27 units, including 2 suites and 5 cottages. $185–$275 double; $295 suite; $325–$400 cottage. Lower rates Oct–May. Rates include full breakfast (inn, not cottages). AE, MC, V. **Amenities:** Lounge; sauna; spa. *In room:* A/C, TV (except original 6 rooms), kitchenette, MP3 docking station, Wi-Fi (free).

Inn on the Creek ★   Tucked into a quiet corner of Jackson, this bed-and-breakfast has an enviable location away from the bustle but within easy walking distance of it. The rooms, many of which feature a great view of Flat Creek lolling along behind the inn, are adorned with nature and wildlife art and nicely balance charm and comfort. The suite features a working gas fireplace and full kitchen; many rooms have jetted tubs. This is a perfect spot for couples looking for both privacy and access to the town's dining and nightlife.

295 N. Millward St. (P.O. Box 445), Jackson, WY 83001. www.innonthecreek.com. ⓒ **800/669-9534** or 307/739-1565. Fax 307/734-9116. 9 units, including 1 suite. $179–$425 double; $599 suite. Lower rates spring to fall. Rates include continental breakfast. AE, DISC, MC, V. *In room:* A/C, TV, Wi-Fi (free).

Rustic Inn ★★ ☺   Opened in 2008 on the creekside former home of the Wagon Wheel Motel, the Rustic Inn is a standout property with something for everybody, especially families. The rooms come in a wide variety of layouts and sizes, from nicely redone historic motel rooms dating back to the Wagon Wheel days, to shiny new standalone cabins and four-plexes on Flat Creek. All of the units are decorated in a tasteful "New West" style, featuring antler chandeliers and dual-head showers in the bath. There is plenty of space here—7 acres in all—and one of the few swimming pools at a lodging in Jackson proper.

475 N. Cache St. (P.O. Box 14250), Jackson, WY 83002. www.rusticinnatjh.com. ⓒ **800/323-9279** or 307/733-357. Fax 307/733-0568. 152 units. $229–$529 double. Lower rates spring to fall. Rates include full breakfast. AE, DISC, MC, V. **Amenities:** Restaurant; lounge; exercise room; outdoor year-round pool; sauna; spa. *In room:* A/C, TV, hair dryer, Wi-Fi (free).

Rusty Parrot Lodge and Spa ★★   The name sounds like an out-of-tune jungle bird, but the Rusty Parrot demonstrates excellent pitch, cultivating a country lodge and spa right in the heart of busy Jackson. Located across from Miller Park, the Parrot is decorated in the nouveau Western style of peeled log, with an interior appointed with elegant furnishings and river-rock fireplaces. One very attractive lure is the Body Sage Spa, where you can get yourself treated to all sorts of scrubs, wraps, massages, and facials. Another is the excellent restaurant, the Wild Sage. Rooms are large, and several have private balconies.

175 N. Jackson St. (P.O. Box 1657), Jackson, WY 83001. www.rustyparrot.com. ⓒ **800/458-2004** or 307/733-2000. 30 units, including 1 suite. $360–$425 double; $625–$750 suite. Lower rates spring and fall. Rates include full breakfast. AE, DISC, MC, V. **Amenities:** Restaurant; lounge; outdoor Jacuzzi; spa. *In room:* A/C, TV, Wi-Fi (free).

Woods Hotel ★ 🏠   Originally opening in 1950, the Woods Hotel was collecting cobwebs from 1998 to 2006 until new ownership reinvented the place as a boutique lodging in 2007. The brick exterior (and vintage sign) belies the innlike rooms, featuring spare Western-chic style: leather headboards, warm earth tones, and a few rugged touches. The standard rooms are small and lack air-conditioning, but the brick structure stays surprisingly cool, and the suites and one family room (with bunk beds) give guests more space to stretch out, plus microwaves and minifridges.

120 N. Glenwood St. (P.O. Box 266), Jackson, WY 83001. www.thewoodshotel.com. © **800/963-2200** or 307/733-2200. 11 units, including 4 suites. $129–$149 double; $159–$189 suite. AE, MC, V. Closed Oct–May. *In room:* TV, no phone, Wi-Fi (free).

Wort Hotel ★★   Located on Broadway just off the Town Square, the Wort stands like a charming old tree. Opened in the early 1940s by the sons of Charles Wort, an early-20th-century homesteader, the Tudor-style two-story building was largely rebuilt after a 1980 fire. Nowadays, it has an old-fashioned style, both in the relaxed **Silver Dollar Bar** (distinctively graced with 2,032 silver dollars) and in the quiet, formal dining room. In the manner of an old cattle-baron hotel, the lobby is graced by a warm, romantic fireplace; another fireplace and a huge, hand-carved mural accents a mezzanine sitting area, providing a second hideaway. The inciting rooms aren't Tudor at all—the Wort labels them "New West." Brass number plates and doorknobs welcome you into comfortable, air-conditioned guest rooms with modern decor, thick carpeting, and armoires. The Silver Dollar Suite features a wet bar inlaid with silver dollars, as in the bar below.

50 N. Glenwood St. (at Broadway), Jackson, WY 83001. www.worthotel.com. © **800/322-2727** or 307/733-2190. 59 units, including 5 suites. $359 double; $659–$799 suite. Lower rates fall to spring. Valet parking $10 daily. AE, DISC, MC, V. **Amenities:** Restaurant; lounge; exercise room; indoor Jacuzzi. *In room:* A/C, TV, CD player, MP3 docking station, Wi-Fi (free).

NEAR JACKSON

Amangani ★★★   Cut into the side of East Gros Ventre Butte, Amangani's rough rock exterior blends incredibly well so that the lights from its windows and pool appear at night to glow from within the mountain. Understated and rustic, all details are done with high contemporary style. From the high-ceilinged corridors to the idyllic outdoor pool, this place is all about class and privacy, not to mention superlative views. Hotelier Adrian Zecha has resorts like this around the world, from Bali to Bhutan, and while the designs are tailored to the landscape, the approach is the same: personal service, luxury, and little touches like iPod cradles in every bedroom, plush throws on the daybeds, and stunning slate and redwood interiors.

1535 NE Butte Rd., Jackson, WY 83002 (on top of East Gros Ventre Butte). www.amanresorts.com. © **877/734-7333** or 307/734-7333. 44 units, including 4 private houses. $725–$1,700 double; $3,400–$7,500 private house. AE, DISC, MC, V. **Amenities:** Restaurant; lounge; health club; Jacuzzi; year-round outdoor pool; spa. *In room:* A/C, TV/DVD, hair dryer, MP3 docking station, Wi-Fi (free).

Spring Creek Ranch ★★   Perched atop East Gros Ventre Butte, 1,000 feet above the Snake River and minutes from both the airport and downtown Jackson, this resort commands a panoramic view of the Grand Tetons and 1,000 acres of land populated by deer, moose, and the horses at its riding facility in the valley below. Views aside, Spring Creek has much going for it: The rooms, divided among nine buildings with cabinlike exteriors, all have wood-burning fireplaces, Native American floor and wall coverings, and private decks and balconies. Most rooms have a king- or two queen-size beds, and the studio units boast kitchenettes. The resort can also arrange accommodations in the privately owned condominiums and vacation homes that dot the butte—large, lavishly furnished, and featuring full kitchens. The resort also staffs in-house naturalists who lead guests on "Wildlife Safaris" into the parks.

1800 Spirit Dance Rd. (on top of the East Gros Ventre Butte; P.O. Box 4780), Jackson, WY 83001. www.springcreekranch.com. © **800/443-6139** or 307/733-8833. 126 units. $340–$500 double; $375–$2,200 condo or home. Lower rates in spring and fall. AE, MC, V. **Amenities:** Restaurant; concierge; Jacuzzi; outdoor pool; room service; spa; tennis court (outdoor). *In room:* A/C, TV/VCR, kitchenette, Wi-Fi (free).

A Teton Tree House ★ 🛏️   This B&B is an architectural marvel "and a quiet port in the storm" of bustling Jackson Hole, says innkeeper, builder, and longtime Jackson adventurer Denny Becker. Under construction for 40-some years on a forested hillside above Wilson where flying squirrels glide amid the sunset canopy, the labyrinthine inn is located 95 steps up from the parking lot and is full of books, staircases, and all sorts of funky nooks and crannies. Nearly every room has a private deck with a splendid view of the valley; the Downy Woodpecker room has a king bed and an outdoor swing, and adjoins with the Clark's Nuthatch room, with two queens, for larger parties. Denny and his wife, Sally, eat heart-healthy breakfast (meaning no eggs or meat) with their guests; Denny is known for his breakfast banana splits (with light yogurt), Sally for her baking, and both have plenty of good advice.

6175 Heck of a Hill Rd. (P.O. Box 550), Wilson, WY 83014. www.atetontreehouse-jacksonhole.com. © **307/733-3233.** 6 units. $225–$285 double; 3-night minimum. Rates include breakfast. No children under 5. DISC, MC, V. 8 miles west of Jackson. Closed mid-Oct to mid-May. *In room:* No phone, Wi-Fi (free).

Wildflower Inn ★★   A terrific B&B on 3 lush and secluded acres near Teton Village, the Wildflower Inn is the brainchild of jack-of-all-trades Ken Jern, a log-home builder and climbing guide, and his wife, Sherrie, a former ski instructor who now runs the inn full-time. Besides being founts of local information, the Jerns are remarkable hosts who pride themselves on both the big picture and the little details. Rooms, named after local wildflowers, are comfortable and luxurious, with private decks, exposed logs, and a remarkable sense of privacy for an inn. Guests also get access to house bikes, rain gear, and trekking poles—not to mention hammocks. Breakfasts are excellent, including veggie frittatas, sour cream coffeecake, and yeast-raised waffles.

3725 Teton Village Rd. (P.O. Box 11000), Jackson, WY 83002. www.jacksonholewildflower.com. © **307/733-4710.** Fax 307/739-0914. 5 units, including 1 suite. $320–$350 double; $400 suite. MC, V. **Amenities:** Bikes (free); indoor Jacuzzi. *In room:* TV, hair dryer, no phone, Wi-Fi (free).

IN TETON VILLAGE

Teton Village is gradually becoming the self-contained resort town now typical of better ski resorts—it has everything you need, from food to powder to a massage, a short limp from the chairlifts. The village is located on the west side of the Snake River, surrounded by ranchlands that have been protected from development. While lodging in the town of Jackson tends to be a little cheaper in the winter than the summer, the ratio is reversed at Teton Village—rooms by the ski hill get more expensive after the snow falls. For a wide range of basic condos and deluxe vacation homes, contact **Jackson Hole Resort Lodging** (www.jhrl.com; © **800/443-8613** or 307/733-3990). All establishments are open year-round unless otherwise indicated.

Very Expensive

Four Seasons Resort Jackson Hole ★★★   The most deluxe lodging option in Teton Village, the ultrastylish Four Seasons sets a high bar for ski-in, ski-out luxury. From a year-round pool landscaped to resemble a mountain creek to the cowboy-hatted doorman to the rooms—stately, luxurious, and definitively Western—this is one of the top slopeside properties in the country. The range of rooms starts at the high end and goes up from there, but even the standard kings are large and plush, and most units have a balcony or a fireplace. One especially notable perk: the hotel's "Base Camp," a full-service outdoor-activity concierge who can arrange mountain-biking, hiking, fishing, and ballooning excursions, and who will outfit you in style. In winter, the service transforms into a first-rate ski concierge, and s'mores and hot chocolate are served poolside. The eating and drinking facilities are also a cut above and range from casually hip to elegant.

7680 Granite Loop (P.O. Box 544), Teton Village, WY 83025. www.fourseasons.com/jacksonhole. ✆ **307/732-5000.** Fax 307/732-5001. 156 units, including 18 suites and 32 condos. $400–$750 double; $700–$4,000 condo or suite. Lower rates spring and fall. Valet parking $24 daily. AE, DISC, MC, V. **Amenities:** 2 restaurants; lounge; concierge; health club; 3 Jacuzzis; year-round outdoor pool; room service; sauna; spa. *In room:* A/C, TV/DVD, hair dryer, kitchen, Wi-Fi ($10 per day).

Hotel Terra ★★ The newest—and greenest—property in Teton Village, Hotel Terra combines sustainable design and contemporary Western style, with satisfying results. The LEED-certified hotel incorporates granite stonework and understated decor into inviting and sleek spaces. The rooms, which range from studios to three-bedroom suites with full kitchens, demonstrate superior attention to detail; there are organic cotton sheets and towels, rain shower heads, fair trade coffee, and touch-screen telephones. The hotel's facilities are uniformly excellent, including the terrific CHILL Spa and an excellent restaurant, **Il Villaggio Osteria** (see "Where to Eat," later in this chapter).

3355 W. Village Dr. (P.O. Box 558), Teton Village, WY 83025. www.hotelterrajacksonhole.com. ✆ **800/631-6281** or 307/739-4000. 132 rooms, including 39 suites. $359–$499 double; $499–$1,700 suite. Lower rates spring and fall. Underground valet parking $15 per day. AE, DISC, MC, V. **Amenities:** 2 restaurants (cafe/Italian, see listing for Il Villaggio Osteria); lounge; concierge; outdoor Jacuzzi; outdoor year-round pool; spa. *In room:* A/C, TV/DVD, hair dryer, kitchen, MP3 docking station, Wi-Fi (free).

Snake River Lodge and Spa ★★ Under the management of RockResorts, this is one of the slickest spots to hang your hat in Teton Village. Lodgepole beams, wooden floors, and stone fireplaces accent the main reception area. The main lodge provides accommodations where classy overshadows rustic, with exposed wooden-beam ceilings, billowy comforters, and luxurious furnishings. There are three levels of suites, from oversize versions of the standard rooms to three-bedroom versions with top-of-the-line kitchen. The 17,000-square-foot spa is Wyoming's largest, featuring everything from massage to hydrotherapy to free weights. Winter visitors can ski directly to a ski valet and drop their skis off for an overnight tune-up.

7710 Granite Loop Rd. (P.O. Box 348), Teton Village, WY 83025. snakeriverlodge.rockresorts.com. ✆ **307/732-6000.** 130 units. $250–$499 double; $699–$2,000 suite. Lower rates in spring and fall. AE, MC, V. **Amenities:** Restaurant; lounge; children's program; concierge; health club; Jacuzzi; indoor/outdoor pool; room service; spa. *In room:* TV, hair dryer, kitchenette, Wi-Fi (free).

Expensive

The Alpenhof ★★ No other spot in the village has quite the Swiss-chalet flavor of this long-standing hostelry, which has a prize location only 50 yards from the ski-resort tram. Four stories tall, with a pitched roof and flower boxes on the balconies, it offers a little old-world atmosphere, as well as excellent comforts and service. The rooms feature brightly colored alpine fabrics, handcrafted Bavarian furnishings, and tiled bathrooms with big, soft towels. You can choose from two junior suites with wet bars and five rooms with fireplaces, and many rooms have balconies or decks.

Economy rooms offer two doubles or one queen-size bed, while deluxe units are larger. The resident **Alpenrose** restaurant specializes in fondue.

3255 W. Village Dr. (P.O. Box 288), Teton Village, WY 83025. www.alpenhoflodge.com. ℭ **800/732-3244** or 307/733-3242. Fax 307/739-1516. 42 units, including 1 suite. $189–$379 double; $479–$539 suite. Lower rates in spring and fall. AE, DISC, MC, V. Closed Nov. **Amenities:** 2 restaurants; lounge; Jacuzzi; outdoor pool; sauna. *In room:* A/C, TV, hair dryer, Wi-Fi (free).

Inexpensive

The Hostel ★ 🏄 If you came to Wyoming to ski, not to lie in the lap of luxury, get yourself a room at the Hostel and hit the slopes. Open since 1967 and fortuitously spared the wrecking ball—and known as Hostel X until 2008—it's a great bargain for those who don't need the trimmings. And it's not just dormitory bunks, either—the comfortable but simple private rooms (slickly renovated in 2011) hold up to four people; they have either one king bed or four twins. There's also a good place to prep your skis; a library; and a common room with chessboards, a Ping-Pong table, a fireplace, Internet access, and a pair of TVs. You can walk to the Mangy Moose and other fun spots, and nobody will be able to tell you apart from the skiers staying at the Four Seasons.

3315 W. Village Dr. (P.O. Box 583), Teton Village, WY 83025. www.thehostel.us. ℭ **307/733-3415.** 55 rooms, 20 dormitory-style bunks. $79–$89 double; $18–$32 bunk. AE, DISC, MC, V. *In room:* No phone, Wi-Fi ($5 one-time fee).

NEARBY GUEST RANCHES

Though there have been ranches in the valley for more than a century, many of Jackson Hole's residents have always made part of their living hosting visitors from Europe and the eastern U.S. who came to hunt, see the sights, and enjoy the outdoors. Somewhere around 1900, the term "dude ranching" came into discourse, and Jackson joined Sheridan and Cody as popular Wyoming destinations for folks who wanted a cowboy experience. You can come out to work hard on horseback, move cattle, eat wranglers' grub, and pay dearly for it; but many of the dude ranches offer a more relaxed vacation, with riding, river floating, fine food, and plenty of boots-up porch time.

Flying A Ranch ★★ Nestled at 8,300 feet between the Gros Ventre and Wind River ranges of Wyoming, the Flying A stuns its visitors with panoramic views. Quaking aspen, stream-fed ponds, and curious antelope are hardly disturbed by this exclusive operation, which hosts only 14 guests at a time. Built in the 1930s, the ranch cabins have been carefully restored, with evocative touches that include wood-burning stoves, handmade pine furniture, and regional artwork. Typical of a dude ranch, everything is included: unlimited horseback riding, fly-fishing (with lessons, if you wish), mountain biking, guided hikes, gourmet meals, and unlimited hot-tub time. The cabins are rustic on the outside but have complete bathrooms and fireplaces, porches, and views. The quiet intimacy of this small operation is underlined by an adult-oriented operation—while children are welcome, there are no specific children's activities. It's a 50-mile drive from the ranch to Jackson for shopping and sightseeing excursions.

771 Flying A Ranch Rd., Pinedale, WY 82941 (50 miles southeast of Jackson on U.S. 191). www.flyinga.com. ℭ **888/833-3348** or 307/367-2385. 7 cabins. $1,500–$1,950 per person, per week. Rates include all meals and ranch activities. No credit cards. Closed mid-Sept to mid-June. **Amenities:** Restaurant; outdoor Jacuzzi. *In room:* Hair dryer, kitchenette, no phone, Wi-Fi (free).

Heart 6 Ranch ★ ☺ Slightly more than an hour's drive north of Jackson, just east of the Moran Junction, is the Heart 6, a fistful of fun for families. The Heart 6 isn't the fanciest of the guest ranches in and around Jackson Hole, but it's certainly not short on entertainment. Fishing, horseback riding, hiking, or just enjoying the fantastic views lead the long list of outdoor activities. A naturalist from the Park Service is also on hand to educate guests on the local wildflowers. The ranch offers Wednesday trips to the rodeo in Jackson, Yellowstone tours on Friday, and extensive children's programs for tykes 3 and over; babysitting service is also available with prior notice.

16985 Buffalo Valley Rd. (35 miles north of Jackson and 5 miles east of Grand Teton National Park on U.S. 26/287), Moran, WY 83013. www.heartsix.com. (C) **888/543-2477** or 307/543-2477. 15 cabins. $2,599 per adult, per 6-night stay June–Aug; $1,095–$2,199 for children 3–12; free for children 2 and under; $89–$259 double Sept–May. Summer rates include all meals; 4-day packages also available. AE, DISC, MC, V. **Amenities:** Restaurant; babysitting; children's programs; outdoor Jacuzzi; outdoor heated pool; Wi-Fi (free). *In room:* No phone.

Lost Creek Ranch & Spa ★★★   Located in Grand Teton National Park, the Lost Creek is beloved by guests, most of whom return for another stay after their first visit. Reservations are at a premium, with a short season and a maximum capacity of about 50 guests. If you manage to wrangle a reservation, this ultraplush ranch offers a wide range of outdoor activities, crowned by gourmet meals. After all that activity, you can pamper yourself in the spa (not included in the rates): Get a massage, a sea-salt body scrub, or a facial, or take a yoga class. If you want to get away from the kids, there's a lounge with billiards and cards and a skeet-shooting range. Duplex cabins, representing the height of rustic elegance, can be rented or subdivided; each section is outfitted with queen-size and twin beds and a private bathroom. There's also a two-bedroom cabin with a fireplace that sleeps six.

P.O. Box 95, Old Ranch Rd., Moose, WY 83012. www.lostcreek.com. (C) **307/733-3435.** Fax 307/733-1954. 10 cabins. $5,250–$13,500 per cabin, per week. Rates include all meals, float trips, horseback riding, and many other activities. Call for discounted off-season rates. MC, V. Closed mid-Sept to May. Off U.S. 89, 20 miles north of Jackson. **Amenities:** Children's programs; health club; outdoor Jacuzzi; outdoor heated pool; sauna; spa; tennis courts. *In room:* Fridge, hair dryer, no phone, Wi-Fi (free).

Red Rock Ranch ★ ☺   This working cattle ranch makes room for families amid the peaceful wilderness of the Gros Ventre Mountains east of the park. With excellent catch-and-release fly-fishing on a private stretch of Crystal Creek, horseback riding in the mountains, and activities that include cookout rides for the kids and weekly country dances, this guest ranch northeast of Jackson is a great spot to bring the entire bunch. The one- and two-bedroom log cabins were built in the 1950s, each furnished with Western trappings and a woodstove. The kids will have a blast here. The **Children's Riding Program** (for those 6 and older) takes kids all over the ranch by horseback, but the cookout is the real Western treat. After a horseback ride, the kids cook supper over an open fire with the help of a couple of wranglers. Back at the ranch, meanwhile, parents are served a gourmet dinner with wine pairings.

P.O. Box 38, Kelly, WY 83011. www.theredrockranch.com. (C) **307/733-6288.** Fax 307/733-6287. 10 cabins. $1,925 per adult, per week; $390–$1,425 per child 12 and under, per week. Rates include all meals and horseback riding. Minimum 6-day stay (Sun–Sat). No credit cards. Closed mid-Sept to May. 30 miles northeast of Jackson on U.S. 26/287. **Amenities:** Restaurant; lounge; children's programs; outdoor Jacuzzi; outdoor heated pool; Wi-Fi (free). *In room:* Fridge, no phone.

CAMPING

There aren't a lot of campsites for trailers close to this resort town anymore because property values attract more upscale investments. The standby is the **Snake River Park KOA Campground,** on U.S. 89, 10 miles south of town (www.srpkoa.com; (C) **800/562-1878** or 307/733-7078). Campsites are $43 to $79 a night. If you're looking to set up a tent when the parks are full, **Curtis Canyon Campground**

(📞 **307/739-5500**) is a great campground behind the elk refuge in Bridger-Teton National Forest. It's open from early June through mid-September, and a site here costs only $12 a night.

See also "Grand Teton National Park," p. 320, for details on camping in Grand Teton National Park.

Where to Eat

Jackson has more dining options than all the other towns in this book combined, running the gamut of cuisine and price. You'll find the predictable steak/seafood/pasta menus—usually injected with a few de rigueur wild-game dishes, too—but you'll also find more unusual options. For a morning jump-start, head to **Shades Cafe,** 82 S. King St. (📞 **307/733-2015**), which serves good coffee, sandwiches, and other breakfast and lunch entrees. Another a.m. stalwart, the **Betty Rock Cafe,** 325 W. Pearl Ave. (📞 **307/733-0747**), serves creative breakfasts and plenty of espresso. **D.O.G.,** Glenwood Street and Broadway (📞 **307/733-4422**), serves coffee, burgers, and superlative breakfast burritos for breakfast and lunch, and transforms into **Everest Momo Shack** Thursday through Monday evenings to plate up Nepalese cuisine.

EXPENSIVE

The Blue Lion ★★ NEW AMERICAN   In the fast-moving, high-rent world of Jackson dining, the Blue Lion stays in the forefront by staying the same. Owned and operated by Ned Brown since 1978, the restaurant is located in a two-story blue clapboard building that looks like a comfy family home. Inside, in intimate rooms accented with soft lighting, or outside on a picture-perfect patio, diners enjoy slow-paced and elegant meals. The menu features rack of lamb and wild-game specialties, such as grilled elk loin in a peppercorn sauce. Fresh fish is flown in daily for dishes such as the nori-crusted ahi.

160 N. Millward St. www.bluelionrestaurant.com. 📞 **307/733-3912.** Reservations recommended. Main courses $15–$45. AE, DC, DISC, MC, V. Summer daily 5:30–10pm; winter daily 6–9pm

The Cadillac Grille ★ NEW AMERICAN   The nostalgic neon and hip American cuisine gives this restaurant a trendy air that attracts see-and-be-seen visitors as well as locals. The chefs work hard on presentation, but they also know how to prepare a wide-ranging variety of dishes, from fire-roasted game dishes to fresh wild salmon. A *Wine Spectator* favorite, the wine list is equally long and varied. The Grille's upscale dining room is one of three options at this address; you can also eat at the posh bar or the '50s-themed confines of **Billy's Giant Hamburgers,** where a great burger runs about $7. For the best of both worlds, order a burger at the bar.

55 N. Cache St. 📞 **307/733-3279.** Reservations recommended. Lunch $5–$18; dinner $12–$35. AE, MC, V. Daily 11:30am–3pm and 5:30–10pm.

Il Villaggio Osteria ★★ ITALIAN   The swankiest restaurant in Teton Village, Il Villaggio Osteria features tables as well as a 12-seat wine bar and 8-seat salumi bar where imported meats and cheeses are sliced to order. The menu includes gourmet wood-fired pizzas with such exotic toppings as figs, arugula, and hummus, as well as creative dishes with Mediterranean influences: wild mushroom risotto, braised pork with polenta, and housemade wild boar ragu. The tantalizing dessert list includes a delectable tiramisu. The lunch menu (offered Dec–Apr) focuses on salads, pizzas, paninis, and lighter versions of the dinner entrees.

In the Hotel Terra, 3335 W. Village Dr., Teton Village. ℭ **307/739-4100.** Reservations recommended. Lunch $10–$19; dinner $15–$27. AE, DISC, MC, V. Summer daily 5:30–10pm; winter daily 11am–10pm.

Snake River Grill ★★★ NEW AMERICAN   This is a popular drop-in spot for locals, including some of the glitterati who spend time in the valley. The front-room dining area overlooks the busy Town Square, and there's also a more private, romantic room in the back. It's an award-winning restaurant for both its wine list and its menu, which features regular fresh-fish dishes (ahi tuna is a favorite), crispy pork shank, and some game-meat entrees such as venison chops and buffalo sirloin. The pizzas—cooked in a wood-burning oven—are topped with exotic ingredients such as venison pepperoni or steak tartare.

84 E. Broadway, on the Town Square. www.snakerivergrill.com. ℭ **307/733-0557.** Reservations recommended. Main courses $19–$52. AE, MC, V. Summer daily 5:30–10pm; winter daily 6–10pm. Closed Nov and Apr.

Stiegler's ★ 🍴AUSTRIAN   Austrian cuisine isn't exactly lurking beyond every street corner, waiting to be summoned with a Julie Andrews yodel, so the discerning Austrian will certainly appreciate Stiegler's. Since 1983—aside for a year-long respite in 2010—Stiegler's has been confusing, astonishing, and delighting customers with such favorites as elk Försterin, bratwurst, and schnitzel, as well as less recognizable (and not as heavy as Austrian food's reputation might suggest) delicacies. Each plate is served with at least three veggies for a terrific presentation and variety of tastes. The desserts are more familiar: apple strudel and crepes. Peter Stiegler, the Austrian chef, invites you to "find a little *Gemütlichkeit*"—the feeling you get when you're surrounded by good friends, good food, and, of course, good beer. The inviting copper bar has its own menu ($10–$20, with great burgers), and there are intimate tables and booths inside and a poolside patio outside.

3535 Moose-Wilson Rd. at the Aspens. ℭ **307/733-1071.** Reservations recommended. Main courses $18–$44. AE, MC, V. Tues–Sun 5:30–9:30pm. Closed Mon and mid-Apr to mid-May.

MODERATE

The Kitchen ★★ NEW AMERICAN   With a picture-perfect outdoor deck and plenty of creative flair, the Kitchen is the latest eatery from Gavin Fine, proprietor of Rendezvous Bistro, Q Roadhouse, and Il Villaggio Osteria (see separate listings). As usual, Fine doesn't disappoint: Featuring fresh seafood from its crudo bar, starters like braised pork nachos and truffle fries, and constantly changing main courses from superlative burgers (with provolone, bacon, and chipotle aioli) to cornmeal-dusted trout and seared red deer, the Kitchen showcases a wide range of culinary influences and inclinations. The restaurant also makes inspired cocktails and has a terrific wine list.

155 N. Glenwood St. www.thekitchenjacksonhole.com. ℭ **307/734-1633.** Reservations recommended. Main courses $16–$28. AE, DISC, MC, V. Daily 5:30–10pm.

Koshu Wine Bar ★★ 🍴ASIAN FUSION   Housed in the back half of the Jackson Hole Wine Company, this small, sleek dining room serves ingenious, addictive, Asian-inspired creations. The Far East is just a starting point, with offerings that meld dozens of influences into dishes such as buttermilk-battered softshell crab and pork ribs; the menu changes on a regular basis. Thanks to its location in a wine store, patrons can choose from 800 varieties of wine at retail price (plus a nominal corking fee).

200 W. Broadway in the back of the Jackson Hole Wine Company. ℭ **307/733-5283.** Reservations recommended. Main courses $15–$30. AE, MC, V. Daily 5:30–10:30pm. Bar open till 2am, depending on crowd.

Mangy Moose ☺ AMERICAN Coming off the slopes at the end of a hard day of skiing or snowboarding, you can slide right to the porch of this Teton Village institution. Good luck getting a seat inside, but if you like a lot of noise and laughter, a beer or a glass of wine, and tasty food, you'll be patient—it beats getting into your car and driving into town. The decor matches the pandemonium: It looks like an upscale junk shop, with bicycles, old signs, and, naturally, a moose head or two hanging from the walls and rafters. The food is customary Wyoming fare (steak, seafood, and pasta)—I'm a big fan of the buffalo meatloaf and the fresh Idaho trout. There is often live music in the saloon, which serves both lunch and dinner. An affiliated cafe, the RMO Cafe, serves breakfast, lunch, and pizza in a separate room downstairs.

1 W. Village Dr., Teton Village. www.mangymoose.net. ✆ **307/733-4913.** Reservations recommended for larger parties. Main courses $12–$29 in the dining room; $4–$13 in the bar and cafe. AE, MC, V. Daily 5:30–10pm (dining room), 7am–10pm (cafe), and 11:30am–10pm (bar). Saloon open later.

Nani's Genuine Pasta House ★★★ 🕎 ITALIAN In a warmly appointed dining room with a slick wine bar, Nani's serves extraordinary food. The menu features pasta favorites such as *amatriciana* (tomato, onion, guanciale, and freshly ground black pepper) and fresh mussels in wine broth, as well as a list of specialties from a different featured region of Italy. Depending on when you visit, it might be Sicily, where executive chef Camille Parker's family has its roots, or Emilia-Romagna, where prosciutto, Parmesan, and balsamic vinegar are culinary staples. Parker ventures to Italy annually for research, and you can literally taste her passion. Your only problem with her restaurant might be finding it—it's tucked away behind a little relic of a motel, but it is definitely worth seeking out.

242 N. Glenwood St. www.nanis.com. ✆ **307/733-3888.** Reservations recommended. Main courses $13–$34. AE, MC, V. Daily 5–10pm. Bar open most nights till 11pm.

North Grille ★ NEW AMERICAN The resident eatery at the Jackson Hole Golf and Tennis Club, the North Grille is located at the LEED-certified clubhouse, a slick and stylish building with incredible views of the Tetons. For sunset watching, I recommend the outdoor patio, but the dining room, clad in dark wood and bookcases, is a cozy setting for the winter months. The menu is neatly organized into categories by price point: $14 nets you a garlic-roasted chicken breast or steamed clams; $20 brings halibut medallions on biscuits with lobster gravy or a spicy pork filet; and $28 allows for rack of lamb or chargrilled king salmon. Lunch brings similar but lighter fare.

5000 Spring Gulch Rd. www.jhgtc.com. ✆ **307/733-7788.** Reservations recommended. Lunch $8–$12; dinner $14–$28. AE, DISC, MC, V. Daily 11:30am–2:30pm and Wed–Sat 5:30–9pm.

Q Roadhouse ★ AMERICAN This bustling joint on the road to Teton Village offers a casual eatery on one side and a bar favored by locals on the other. There are brick walls, complimentary peanuts (toss your shells on the floor), and a laid-back vibe. The Southern-accented menu ranges from barbecued baby back ribs, to veggie enchiladas, to blackened catfish. Burgers and sandwiches are also available.

2550 Moose-Wilson Rd. ✆ **307/739-0700.** Reservations recommended. Main courses $10–$27. AE, DISC, MC, V. Daily 5–10pm. Bar open later.

Rendezvous Bistro ★★ AMERICAN/SEAFOOD The Rendezvous opened in 2001 and garnered a fast local following. It's easy to see why: The place is contemporary yet casual, the food is affordable but very good, and the service is excellent. Climb into one of the intimate booths and order a dozen oysters on the half shell and slurp away, but save some room for a main course, ranging from steak frites, to spicy chipotle trout, to grilled chile-rubbed pork chops. It might sound formal, but it's really not—the beauty is that the food is the best upscale value in town, while the atmosphere is very laid back.

380 S. Broadway. © **307/739-1100.** Reservations recommended. Main courses $15–$25. AE, DISC, MC, V. Daily 5:30–10pm.

Sweetwater Restaurant ★★ AMERICAN   Although this little log restaurant serves American fare, it does so in a decidedly offbeat way. The eclectic menu includes, for example, a Greek salad, a Baja chicken salad, and a cowboy-grilled roast-beef sandwich. During the summer, there's outside dining. The dinner menu is just as quirky and livened by nightly specials; try the blue cheese fondue or fried green tomatoes before diving into a blackened catfish filet topped with crab, or a delectable chipotle-tomato buffalo skirt steak with boursin cheese. Vegetarians will want to sample the spinach and feta soufflé.

85 King St. www.sweetwaterjackson.com. © **307/733-3553.** Reservations recommended. Lunch $10–$13; dinner $22–$30. AE, DISC, MC, V. Summer daily 11:30am–3pm and 5:30–10pm; winter daily 11:30am–2:30pm and 5:30–9:30pm.

Trio ★★ NEW AMERICAN   Opened in 2005 by a trio (thus the name) of owner/chefs who formerly worked at the Snake River Grill, this instant local favorite offers an inviting atmosphere and remarkable food. Served in a dimly lit, social room with a fossil-rock bar and semi-open kitchen, the seasonal menu might include appetizers such as heirloom tomato and ricotta bruschetta and house-cured salmon, and entrees like Dungeness crab pasta or a killer Idaho rainbow trout on a bed of blackened corn and avocado. Everything is uniformly mouthwatering, and the portions are perfectly sized and impeccably presented and served. The restaurant is perhaps best known for its killer fries—served with scallions, black pepper, and an addictive blue cheese fondue.

45 S. Glenwood St. www.bistrotrio.com. © **307/734-8038.** Reservations recommended. Main courses $15–$44 dinner. AE, MC, V. Mon–Fri 11am–2pm; daily 5:30pm–close, usually 9–10pm.

INEXPENSIVE

Nora's Fish Creek Inn ★ 📖 AMERICAN   If you like to eat among locals, and if you like to eat a lot, Nora's is the place to hang out in Wilson, 6 miles northwest of Jackson—just look for the 15-foot trout on the roof. At once rough and cozy, it's an institution, and if you come here often, you'll start to recognize the regulars, who grumble over their coffee and gossip about doings in the valley. Breakfast is especially good, when there are pancakes and *huevos rancheros* that barely fit on the huge plates. Trout and eggs is another specialty. Prices are inexpensive compared to those at any of the other restaurants in town. Dinner is burgers, barbecue, and smoked trout.

5600 W. Wyo. 22, Wilson. © **307/733-8288.** Reservations accepted for dinner. Breakfast and lunch $5–$13; dinner $10–$37. AE, DISC, MC, V. Mon–Fri 6:30am–2pm; Sat–Sun 6:30am–1:30pm; daily 5:30–9pm. Call for winter hours.

Snake River Brewing Co. ★ 🍺 MICROBREWERY   One of the West's best (and busiest) microbreweries, the industrial-meets-contemporary-looking establishment offers a menu of pasta, applewood-fired pizzas and paninis, and salads, plus a few entrees like "Slash and Burn Trout," served with fennel relish. The real standouts are the beers, especially Custer's Last Ale and Zonker Stout, regular winners at the Great American Beer Fest and other competitions. This place is a local favorite and a great lunch spot, with daily $7 specials like turkey-and-brie wraps and chipotle BBQ sandwiches.

265 S. Millward St. www.snakeriverbrewing.com. ☏ **307/739-2337.** Most dishes $8–$14. AE, DISC, MC, V. Daily 11:30am–11pm. Bar open till midnight.

Jackson After Dark

Talented musicians from well-known orchestras participate in the **Grand Teton Music Festival ★** (www.gtmf.org; ☏ **307/733-3050** or 307/733-1128 for the box office), held in summer in the amphitheater next to the tram lift. Tickets, typically $55 or less, are usually available on short notice, especially for the weeknight chamber music performances, which are often terrific.

Wyoming's only year-round professional theatrical group, the **Off Square Theatre Company,** performs classic and contemporary comedies and dramas at the Center for the Arts, 265 S. Cache St. (www.offsquare.org; ☏ **307/733-3021**). Tickets (typically $15–$25) for all shows should be reserved.

Those less impressed with dramaturgy should head down to the **Silver Dollar Bar,** at 50 N. Glenwood St. in the Wort Hotel (☏ **307/733-2190**), for a drink with one of the real or wannabe cowpokes at the bar. And, yes, those 2,032 silver dollars are authentic. At the very famous **Million Dollar Cowboy Bar** on the Town Square, at 25 N. Cache St. (www.milliondollarcowboybar.com; ☏ **307/733-2207**), you can dance the two-step to live bands or just mill around and check out the unique details: knobby pine, saddle barstools, and plenty of taxidermy. For live music and DJs, the young, restless, and intoxicated congregate at **43° North,** 645 S. Cache St. (☏ **307/733-0043**), near the base of Snow King. For sports nuts, **Sidewinders Tavern,** 945 W. Broadway (☏ **307/734-5766**), offers a slew of flatscreen TVs and a casual atmosphere. If you want some high-octane dancing fun led by some talented local hoofers, head west to Wilson and the **Stagecoach Bar** (☏ **307/733-4407**) on Wyo. 22 on a Sunday night. It's the only night there's regularly scheduled live music in this classic Western joint, and the place is jammed wall to wall.

GRAND TETON NATIONAL PARK ★★★

12 miles N of Jackson

Grand Teton National Park sits just south of its larger, better-known neighbor, Yellowstone, but the Tetons offer around 310,000 acres of beauty all their own. The purplish-gray, jagged peaks of the Teton Range jut into the sky above the flat Snake River valley called Jackson Hole. Mountain trails lead hikers and horseback riders through a forest of rustling aspens and past glassy Jenny Lake. In higher elevations, bighorn sheep clatter over the rocks, while down below, elk graze alongside the road.

Active Pursuits   Delve deep into the wilderness, hiking **Inspiration Point Trail** alongside **Jenny Lake** and past the splash of Hidden Falls. Mountaineers relish the vertical challenge of **climbing** the rocky faces of the Tetons. Take a **horseback-riding** trip through aspen forest at Colter Bay and Jenny Lake Lodge. **River-rafting** companies escort adventure enthusiasts down the sometimes smooth but always brisk Snake River. In winter, the park becomes a hotspot for cross-country **skiing, snowshoeing,** and **snowmobiling.**

Flora & Fauna   Animals seldom seen outside the zoo frequent the roadsides, mountain trails, and riverbanks in the Teton Range. The largest **elk** herd in North America grazes just outside Jackson Hole, while the only population of **grizzlies** south of

Canada feeds in remote forest areas. Large **moose cows** nurse their calves in open meadows and alongside alpine lakes. If you're lucky, you may spot the elusive, regal-looking **bighorn sheep** skitter over rocky precipices toward the top of the Tetons.

Relaxation Silvery cutthroat trout, lake trout, and whitefish draw **anglers** to the park's crystal-clear rivers and lakes. The **Teton Range** towers over Jackson Hole and is reflected in the smooth surface of Jenny Lake—the serene scene of a thousand postcards. Campers know that the stars shine a little brighter and coyotes are a little easier to hear on an overnight stay in the heart of the forest. A favorite campground is **Signal Mountain,** with its Jackson Lake beach access.

A Brief History

Your first look at the Tetons, rising like spears from the Snake River plain, will take your breath away. Geologists say these mountains are still growing along a crack in the earth's crust that thrusts the range upward from the west as the valley sinks to the east. The lake-bed sediments of the valley floor are actually "younger" than the pre-Cambrian rock of the peaks. Recent earthquakes in the area indicate the fault is still active. Like much of the Rocky Mountains, this range has been sculpted by glaciers, which gouged out the deep U-shaped valleys between the peaks. When the ice sheet that covered Jackson Hole melted for the last time, 15,000 years ago, it left a depression and a big mound of debris—called a terminal moraine—that formed a natural dam at the end of Jackson Lake.

The receding layers of ice created beautiful glacial lakes such as Phelps, Taggart, Bradley, Jenny, String, and Leigh; polished the sides of Cascade Canyon; and honed the peaks to their present jagged state. The glaciers live on, the most prominent being the five that have survived on Mount Moran.

The first human inhabitants of the region appeared about 12,000 years ago. Among the tribes that hunted here were the Blackfeet, Crow, Gros Ventre, and Shoshone. Summers were spent here hunting and raising crops; winters meant migration to warmer climes. The trappers and explorers who followed the tribes into the valley were equally distressed by the harsh winters and short growing season, which made Jackson Hole marginal ranchland at best. These early homesteaders quickly realized that their best hope was to market the beauty of the area, which they began doing in earnest as early as a century ago.

The danger of haphazard development soon became apparent. There was a dance hall at Jenny Lake, hot-dog stands and piles of debris along the roads, and vacation homes going up on prime wildlife habitat. In the 1920s, Yellowstone park officials and conservationists met to discuss how the Grand Teton area might be protected, and eventually they enlisted philanthropist John D. Rockefeller, Jr., to acquire lands for a future park. In 1929, a park was established to protect the mountains, while Rockefeller continued buying up ranches at the base of the Tetons, using a dummy corporation to hide his involvement. Wyoming's congressional delegation fought hard against park designation in the valley as Jackson Hole public opinion swayed like a pendulum, so President Franklin D. Roosevelt created the Jackson Hole National Monument in the 1940s. In 1950, the park was expanded to its present form.

Just the Facts

ACCESS/ENTRY POINTS

Like the range of mountains it protects, Grand Teton National Park is a strip of real estate centered on a north–south axis. Teton Park Road, the primary thoroughfare,

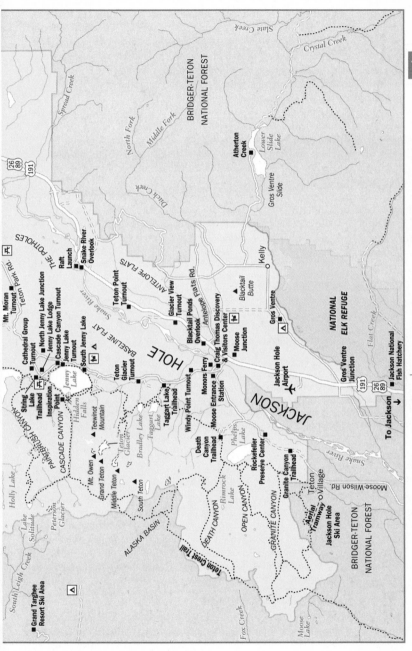

State Creek

Crystal Creek

BRIDGER-TETON
NATIONAL FOREST

Spread Creek

North Fork

Middle Fork

Atherton
Creek

Lower
Slide
Lake

Gros Ventre
Slide

26
89

191

Ditch Creek

THE POTHOLES

Mt. Moran
Turnout
Teton Park Rd.

Raft
Launch

Snake River
Overlook

Teton Point
Turnout

Glacier View
Turnout

Kelly

Cathedral Group
Turnout

North Jenny Lake Junction

Jenny Lake Lodge

Cascade Canyon Turnout

Jenny Lake
Turnout

South Jenny Lake

Snake River

ANTELOPE FLATS

Antelope Flats Rd.

Blacktail Ponds
Overlook

Blacktail
Butte

Craig Thomas Discovery
& Visitors Center

Gros Ventre

BASELINE FLAT

HOLE

Moose
Junction

NATIONAL
ELK REFUGE

String
Lake
Trailhead

Inspiration
Point

Jenny
Lake

Hidden
Falls

Teton
Glacier
Turnout

Teewinot
Mountain

Menors Ferry

Moose Entrance
Station

Windy Point Turnout

Taggart Lake
Trailhead

Jackson Hole
Airport

Gros Ventre
Junction

26
89

191

To Jackson

Jackson National
Fish Hatchery

Flat Creek

CASCADE CANYON

PAINTBRUSH CN

Mt. Owen

Grand Teton

Middle Teton

South Teton

Taggart Lake

Bradley Lake

Death
Canyon
Trailhead

Phelps
Lake

Rockefeller
Preserve Center

JACKSON

Snake River

Moose-Wilson Rd.

Holly Lake

South Leigh Creek

Lake
Solitude

Peterson
Glacier

Teton
Glacier

Rimrock
Lake

DEATH CANYON

OPEN CANYON

GRANITE CANYON

Granite Canyon
Trailhead

Aerial
Tramway

Teton
Village

Jackson Hole
Ski Area

BRIDGER-TETON
NATIONAL FOREST

Grand Targhee
Resort Ski Area

ALASKA BASIN

Teton Crest Trail

Fox Creek

Moose
Lake

Moose Creek

skirts along the lakes that pool at the mountains' base. From the **north,** you can enter the park from Yellowstone National Park, which is connected to Grand Teton by a wilderness corridor called the **John D. Rockefeller, Jr. Memorial Parkway,** through which U.S. 89/191/287 runs for 8 miles, where you may see wildlife through the trees, some of which are bare and blackened from the 1988 fires. When you come this way, you will already have paid your entrance to both parks, so there is no entrance station, but you can stop at **Flagg Ranch,** approximately 5 miles north of the park boundary, and get park information. December through March, Yellowstone's south entrance is open only to snowmobiles and snowcoaches.

You can also approach the park from the **east,** via U.S. 26/287. This route comes from Dubois, 55 miles east on the other side of the Absaroka and Wind River Mountains, and crosses **Togwotee Pass,** where you'll get your first—and one of the best—views of the Tetons towering above the valley. Travelers who come this way can continue south on U.S. 26/89/191 to Jackson without paying an entrance fee, though they are within the park boundaries.

Finally, you can enter Grand Teton from Jackson in the **south,** driving about 13 miles north on U.S. 26/89/191 to the Moose turnoff and the park's south entrance. Here you'll find the park headquarters, a visitor center, and a small community that includes dining, rental cabins, and shops.

For details on how to fly into the region, see "Getting There" in "Jackson Hole," p. 299.

VISITOR INFORMATION

There are three visitor centers in Grand Teton National Park. Opened in 2007, the dazzling **Craig Thomas Discovery and Visitor Center** (✆ 307/739-3399) is a half-mile west of Moose Junction at the southern end of the park. Featuring exhibits on alpinism, geology, and wildlife; an art gallery; a "video river" and other multimedia installations; and a theater, it's open daily 8am to 7pm from June to Labor Day, 8am to 5pm after Labor Day through October, and 9am to 5pm the rest of the year. The **Colter Bay Visitor Center** (✆ 307/739-3594), the northernmost of the park's visitor centers, is open daily 8am to 7pm from early June to Labor Day, and 8am to 5pm after Labor Day through early October. There is also **Jenny Lake Visitor Center** (✆ 307/739-3343), open daily 8am to 7pm from early June to Labor Day, and daily 8am to 5pm after Labor Day through late September. Maps and ranger assistance are available at all three centers, and there are bookstores and exhibits at Moose and Colter Bay. On the Moose-Wilson Road, you'll find the **Laurance S. Rockefeller Preserve Center** (✆ 307/739-3654), open early June to Labor Day from 8am to 6pm, and late May to early June and Labor Day through late September from 9am to 6pm. Finally, there is an information station at the **Flagg Ranch** complex (✆ 307/543-2372), which is located approximately 5 miles north of the park's northern boundary, open 9am to 3:30pm from early June through early September, although it may be closed for lunch.

To obtain park maps before your arrival, contact **Grand Teton National Park,** P.O. Drawer 170, Moose, WY 83012-0170 (www.nps.gov/grte; ✆ 307/739-3300).

FEES & BACKCOUNTRY PERMITS

There are no park gates on U.S. Hwy. 26/89/191, so you can get a free ride through the park on that route; to get off the highway and explore, you'll pay $25 per automobile for a 7-day pass (admission is good for Yellowstone or Grand Teton). The winter day-use fee is $5. If you expect to visit the parks more than once in a year, buy an annual pass for $50, but I consider the various interagency passes, which are also honored here, to be a better deal (see chapter 16). For information on camping fees at Grand Teton National Park, see "Camping," later in this chapter.

Backcountry permits are required from the Park Service for overnight use of backcountry campsites. The permits are free, but they can be reserved only from January 1 to May 15 (and the reservation itself costs $25); thereafter, all backcountry permits are issued on a first-come, first-served basis up to 24 hours before your first night out. Permits are issued at the Moose and Colter Bay visitor centers and the Jenny Lake ranger station. Reservations may be made by writing the **Permits Office,** Grand Teton National Park, P.O. Drawer 170, Moose, WY 83012, or faxing 307/739-3438. Reservations can also be made online at **www.nps.gov/grte**. Phone reservations are not accepted, but information is available by calling © **307/739-3602.**

Boating permits are required if you bring your own boat (for motorized craft, $40 for an annual permit and $20 for a 7-day permit; for human-powered vessels, $20 for an annual permit and $10 for a 7-day permit). You can get permits at the visitor centers at Moose or Colter Bay; the cost is included in the price of a boat rental. Motorized boats are permitted on Jenny, Jackson, and Phelps lakes; sailboats, windsurfers, and jet skis are allowed on Jackson. Boats paddled by humans are permitted on most park lakes and the Snake River.

State of Wyoming **fishing licenses** are required for fishers 13 years of age and over. An adult nonresident license runs $14 for 1 day, $92 for the season; $3 per day, $15 per season for youngsters 14 to 18; no license is required for kids 13 and under. A $13 Conservation Stamp is also required for all licenses except the 1-day variety. (A Wyoming resident pays $24 for a season permit.) You can buy licenses at sporting-goods stores or park visitor centers. The entirety of the Snake River is open for fishing from April through October, but Jackson Lake is closed all of October. Because the Snake River flows into and exits Jackson Lake, different regulations apply to various sections of the river, and several are closed; the prudent angler will become knowledgeable of these laws to avoid a hefty fine.

REGULATIONS

The rules here are similar to those in most national parks. It is illegal to damage or collect natural, archaeological, or historical objects, and even picking wildflowers is prohibited. Pets must be leashed and are not allowed more than 50 feet from roadways; on trails, boats, or boardwalks; or in the backcountry. They are allowed in campgrounds but must be restrained at all times. Licensed guns are permitted.

SEASONS

Spring is an excellent time to visit the park—but remember that spring starts later in Wyoming than in most other parts of the country. In **May** and **June,** mild days and cool nights intersperse with occasional rain and snow. The snow typically doesn't melt in the mountains above the valley until mid-June. Wildflowers are in bloom, and, on a clear day, the snow-covered Tetons stand out boldly against a crisp blue sky. Better yet, trails are virtually devoid of hikers, though at higher elevations, snow might still block the paths; check in at one of the ranger stations for trail conditions.

Summer is the most intense season at Grand Teton, with flowers blooming, fish and wildlife feeding, and all sorts of activity crammed into a few months of warm weather, from July to early September.

Those who are only passing by and never plan to get far from their cars can see the full spectacle of these mountains without paying a park entry fee. If you come from the east, you will pass no tollbooths on your way south on U.S. 26/89/191, but there are frequent pullouts on the west side of the road that give you a panoramic overview of the Snake River and the Tetons. For that matter, you get a more distant, but equally grand, view of the mountains coming over **Togwotee Pass** on U.S. 26/287.

In **September,** sunny days and cooler nights alternate with rain and occasional snowstorms, and by the middle of the month, fall colors begin to make their way across the landscape.

The first big snow usually arrives by the beginning of **November** (though it's not unheard of in July!). In winter months, temperatures stick in the single digits, with subzero overnight temperatures common.

AVOIDING THE CROWDS

Summer is the busy time here, but crowds thin in the park after Labor Day, and you can enjoy sunny days and brilliant aspen yellows well into October. When there are crowds, you can avoid them by staying away from the centers of activity, which are Colter Bay, Jenny Lake, and Moose. Check out the overlooks, photograph the sites, and take in a few educational exhibits; then abandon the paved areas for unpaved trails.

TIPS FOR TRAVELERS WITH DISABILITIES

Visitor centers at Moose, Colter Bay, Jenny Lake, and Flagg Ranch provide interpretive programs, displays, and visitor information in several formats, including visual, audible, and tactile. Large-print scripts, Braille brochures, and narrative audiotapes are available at Moose and Colter Bay.

Wheelchair-accessible parking spaces are located close to all visitor center entrances; curb cuts are provided, as are accessible restroom facilities.

Campsites at Colter Bay, Jenny Lake, and Gros Ventre campgrounds are on relatively level terrain; Lizard Creek and Signal Mountain are hilly and less accessible. Picnic areas at String Lake and Cottonwood Creek are both accessible, though the toilet at Cottonwood is not.

Wheelchair-accessible dining facilities are located at Flagg Ranch, Leeks Marina, Jackson Lake Lodge, and Jenny Lake Lodge.

More information is available by contacting **Grand Teton National Park,** P.O. Drawer 170, Moose, WY 83012 (www.nps.gov/grte; ✆ **307/739-3600**).

Viewing the Peaks

Grand Teton National Park is famous for its mountains, and rightly so. The Cathedral Group is composed of **Grand Teton** (elev. 13,775 ft.), **Teewinot** (elev. 12,325 ft.), and **Mount Owen** (elev. 12,928 ft.). Nearby, almost as impressive, are **South Teton** (elev. 12,514 ft.) and **Middle Teton** (elev. 12,804 ft.).

If you come from the north and Yellowstone National Park, you will have paid a park-entry fee and be entitled to explore along **Teton Park Road,** west of the Snake.

You'll be looking at mountains as you drive the eastern shore of Jackson Lake, and you'll find plenty of opportunities to pull over and snap your shutter. Four miles south of Colter Bay, you can take an unpaved 1-mile road heading east from the highway to the **Grand View Overlook.** A large, flat area at the end of the road offers a commanding view of the Grand Tetons, and an excellent picnic spot. This road is great for autos, hikers, and bicycles, but not for large RVs.

You'll also get excellent views of the Cathedral Group on the trails and roads that ring **Jenny Lake** (see "Seeing the Highlights," below).

Signal Mountain, southeast of Jackson Lake, may not rank up there with the other Tetons, but you can drive right up to an excellent lookout spot. Navigating the twisting, narrow road pays off at the summit, where you can gaze out over the valley, Cascade Canyon, Jackson Lake, and the Tetons.

Slightly north of Jenny Lake is the underrated yet astoundingly humbling **Mount Moran** (elev. 12,605 ft.), the fourth-largest peak in the range; its curiously flattened, sheared-off summit is the result of erosion back in geologically volatile times.

Seeing the Highlights
JACKSON LAKE & THE NORTH END OF THE PARK

A great many people enter Grand Teton National Park from the north end, emerging from Yellowstone's south entrance with a 7-day park pass that gets them into Grand Teton as well. Yellowstone is connected to Grand Teton by a wilderness corridor called the **John D. Rockefeller, Jr. Memorial Parkway** where the highway runs for 8 miles. Along it, you'll see an interesting area of meadows sometimes dotted with elk, the Snake River as it runs into Jackson Lake, and forests that in some places still show the impact of the 1988 fires. Some people complain about the sight of blackened tree trunks, but others are heartened to see the mosaic shapes of natural burn and the soft green of new trees sprouting.

Along the parkway, not far from Yellowstone, you'll pass your first lodging option, **Flagg Ranch** (see "Where to Stay in the Park," later in this chapter), with gas, restaurants, and other services. In the winter, this is a busy staging area for the snowcoach and snowmobile crowds, but the new snowmobile quotas led the place to close its rental cabins in the winter in recent years.

JACKSON LAKE The north end of the park is dominated by giant **Jackson Lake,** a huge expanse of water that fills a deep gorge left 10,000 years ago by retreating glaciers. Though it empties east into the Snake River, curving around in the languid **Oxbow Bend**—a favorite wildlife-viewing float for canoeists—the water from Jackson Lake eventually turns south, then west through Snake River Canyon and into Idaho. In 1911, potato farmers downstream were instrumental in getting Congress to fund Jackson Lake Dam, which raised the lake about 40 feet and waterlogged the forest around the shoreline. Stream flow is now regulated at the dam for both farmers and rafters in the canyon, and, for better or worse, we have an irrigation dam in a national park. The dead trees have long since been cleared out, and the dam was rebuilt with an eye for aesthetics in 1989. In general, the lake looks quite natural, except when water level plummets in the fall.

LEEKS MARINA As the road follows the east shore of the lake from the north, the first development travelers encounter is **Leeks Marina,** where boats can launch, gas up, and moor from mid-May to mid-September. A casual restaurant serves light fare and pizza during the summer. But drivers also have the option of stopping at numerous picnic pullouts along the lake.

COLTER BAY Just south of Leeks is **Colter Bay,** a busy outpost of park services where you can get groceries, postcards and stamps, T-shirts, and advice. If this is your first stop in the park, get maps and information at the **Colter Bay Visitor Center.** Here you can view park and wildlife videotapes and attend a park-orientation slide program throughout the day. Ranger-led activities include museum tours, park-orientation talks, natural history hikes, and evening amphitheater programs. Colter Bay has lots of overnight options, from its cabins, to its old-fashioned tent camps, to its trailer park and campground. There is also a general store and do-it-yourself laundry, two restaurants, a boat launch and boat rentals, and tours. You can take pleasant short hikes in this area, including a walk around the bay or out to **Hermitage Point** (see "Hiking," below).

The **Indian Arts Museum ★** (© **307/739-3594**) at the Colter Bay Visitor Center is worth a visit, though it is not strictly about the Native-American cultures of this area. The artifacts are mostly from Plains Indian tribes, but there are also some Navajo items from the Southwest. The collection was assembled by David T. Vernon and includes pipes, shields, dolls, and war clubs sometimes called "skull crackers." Visiting Indian artists work in the museum all summer long and sell their wares on-site. Admission is free.

JACKSON LAKE JUNCTION From Colter Bay, the road veers east and then south again past **Jackson Lake Lodge** (see "Where to Stay in the Park," later in this chapter), a slick, 1950s-style resort with a magnificent view of the Tetons and brushy flats in the foreground where moose often roam. Numerous trails originate here (see "Hiking," below), heading both to **Jackson Lake** and east to **Emma Matilda Lake.** The road then becomes **Jackson Lake Junction,** where you can either continue west along the lakeshore or go east to the park's **Moran Entrance Station.** Here the park's odd entrance configuration comes into play: If you go out through the Moran entrance, you are still in the park, and may turn south on U.S. 26/89/191 and drive along the Snake River to Jackson, making most of your journey within the park's borders, though you might not know it.

SIGNAL MOUNTAIN If you're here to enjoy the park, you'd probably turn west on **Teton Park Road** at Jackson Lake Junction, and arrive after only 5 miles at **Signal Mountain.** Like its counterpart at Colter Bay, this developed recreation area, on Jackson Lake's southeast shore, offers camping sites, accommodations in cabins and multiplex units, two restaurants, and a lounge with one of the few live televisions in the park. This is also the place to fill up on gasoline and provisions from the small convenience store. Boat rentals and scenic cruises of the lake also originate here.

If you turn east instead of west off Teton Park Road at Signal Mountain, you can drive up a narrow, twisting road to the top of the mountain, 700 feet above the valley, where you'll have a fine view of the ring of mountains—Absarokas, Gros Ventres, Tetons, and Yellowstone Plateau—that create Jackson "Hole." Note also the potholes created in the valley's hilly moraines left by retreating glaciers. Below the summit, about 3 miles from the base of the hill, is **Jackson Point Overlook,** a paved path 300 feet long leading to the spot where the Hayden Expedition's photographer, William Henry Jackson, shot his famous wet-plate photographs of Jackson Lake and the Tetons more than a century ago—proof to the world that such spectacular places really existed in the Rockies.

JENNY LAKE & THE SOUTH END OF THE PARK

JENNY LAKE   Continuing south along Teton Park Road, you move into the park's southern half, where the tallest peaks rise abruptly above a string of smaller lakes strung together in the foothills—**Leigh Lake, String Lake,** and **Jenny Lake,** which is the favorite of many park visitors. At North Jenny Lake Junction, you can take a turnoff west to **Jenny Lake Lodge** (see "Where to Stay in the Park," later in this chapter)—the road then continues as a one-way scenic loop along the lakeshore before rejoining Teton Park Road about 4 miles later.

Beautiful **Jenny Lake** gets a lot of traffic throughout the summer, both from hikers who circumnavigate the lake on a 6-mile trail and from more sedentary folks who pay for a boat ride across the lake to Hidden Falls and the short, steep climb to **Inspiration Point** (see "Hiking," below). The parking lot at **South Jenny Lake** is often jammed, and there can be a long wait for the boat ride, so you might want to get there early in the day. There is also a tents-only campground, a visitor center, and a general store stocked with a modest supply of prepackaged foods and even less fresh produce and vegetables. You can take a fairly level and easy hike around the south end of the lake to Hidden Falls or grab a ride with the **Jenny Lake Boating Company** (www. jennylakeboating.com; ✆ **307/734-9227**); round-trips cost $10 for adults and $5 for children 5 to 12.

SOUTH OF JENNY LAKE   South of the lake, Teton Park Road crosses open sagebrush plains with never-ending views of the mountains. You'll pass the **Climbers' Ranch** (see "Climbing," later in this chapter)—an inexpensive dorm-lodging alternative for climbers—and some trail heads for enjoyable hikes to **Taggart Lake** and elsewhere. Look closely in the sagebrush for the shy pronghorn, more commonly (and incorrectly) labeled antelope. This handsome animal, with tan cheeks and black accent stripes, can spring up to 60 mph. Badgers also roam the brush here; you might encounter one of the shy but ornery creatures in the morning or at twilight.

The **Teton Glacier Turnout** presents a view of a glacier that grew for several hundred years until, within the past century, it reversed direction, pressured by hotter summer temperatures, and began retreating.

MOOSE   The road arrives at the park's south entrance here (well within the park's boundaries) and the **Craig Thomas Discovery and Visitor Center,** as well as park headquarters in the old visitor center across the street. If you are approaching the

---

 Insider Tips

Some of the best spots aren't highlighted on the map. On the west side of the road from Signal Mountain to the Jenny Lake cutoff, a little over a mile north of the Spring Lake–Jenny Lake scenic drive cutoff, is an unmarked, unpaved road that leads to **Spalding Bay.** You'll travel through bumpy moose habitat before curling down a steep hill to a back bay of the lake, where you'll find a small campsite, a boat launch with parking for trucks and boat trailers, and a primitive restroom. Use of the campsite requires a park permit, but we think this site provides an excellent opportunity to find seclusion with excellent views of the lake and mountains. The road is easily negotiable by an automobile or sport-utility vehicle; we would not recommend an RV or towed trailer.

park from the south rather than the north, this is where you can find maps, advice, and some interpretive displays.

Just behind the visitor center is **Menor's Ferry.** Bill Menor had a country store and operated a ferry across the Snake River at Moose back in the late 1800s. The ferry and store have been reconstructed, and you can buy items similar to the ones Menor used to sell here. Nearby is a historic cabin where a group of locals met in 1923 and planted the seed for the protection of the natural and scenic quality of the area, an idea that eventually led to the creation of the national park.

Also in this area is the **Chapel of the Transfiguration.** In 1925, this chapel was built in Moose so that settlers wouldn't have to make a long buckboard ride into Jackson. It's still in use for Episcopal services spring through fall and is a popular spot for weddings, with a view of the Tetons through a window behind the altar.

DORNAN'S This is a small village area just south of the visitor center on a private holding of land owned by one of the area's earliest homesteading families. There are a few shops and a good grocery store, a post office, rental cabins, a bar with occasional live music, and, surprisingly, a first-rate wine shop.

Other Park Highlights

The highway route through the park on the east side of the Snake has several turnouts for shutterbugs (better have a wide-angle lens!). Among the stops you can make are the **Glacier View Turnout** (where you can view an area that was filled with a 4,000-ft.-thick glacier 150,000 years ago) and the **Blacktail Ponds Overlook** (a beaver-dam subdivision). Gazing out across **Snake River Overlook** at the plateaus that roll from riverbed to valley floor lends vivid insight into the power of the glaciers and ice floes that sculpted this landscape. If you want to go a way off-road and down to the river, you can try the dirt **Schwabacher Road** or the newly repaved **Deadman's Bar Road.**

Only 5 miles north of Jackson on U.S. 26/89/191, you can turn east on the **Gros Ventre River Road** and follow the river east into its steep canyon; a few miles past the little town of Kelly, you'll leave the park and enter the **Bridger-Teton National Forest.** In 1925, a huge slab of mountain broke off the north end of the Gros Ventre Range on the east side of Jackson Hole, a reminder that nature still has an unpredictable and violent side. The slide left a gaping open gash in the side of Sheep Mountain, sloughing off nearly 150 million cubic feet of rock and forming a natural dam across the Gros Ventre River half a mile wide. Two years later, the dam broke, and a cascade of water rushed down the canyon and through the little town of Kelly, taking several lives. The town of **Kelly** is a quaintly unconventional community with a large number of yurts.

Up in the canyon formed by the Gros Ventre River, there is a roadside display with photographs of the slide area and a short nature walk from the road down to the residue of the slide and **Lower Slide Lake,** with signs identifying the trees and plants that survived or grew in the slide's aftermath.

Ranger-Led Activities

It's got to be the best bargain in the world: National parks offer all sorts of free presentations and guided hikes throughout the summer days, and the rangers are generally personable and knowledgeable. At Grand Teton, these range from a ranger-led 3-mile hike from the Colter Bay Visitor Center to Swan Lake, as well as a relaxed evening chatting with a ranger on the deck of the Jackson Lake Lodge while you watch for moose and birds through a spotting scope. There are numerous events during the summer at Colter Bay, South Jenny Lake, and the Craig Thomas Discovery and Visitor Center at Moose. Check the daily schedules in the park's newspaper, the *Teewinot,* which is available at any visitor center.

From Moose, rangers lead visitors out to the "lek"—the mating ground of the strutting grouse, whose males' displays are dramatic, to say the least, during the springtime mating season. In winter, **guided snowshoe hikes** begin at the visitor center in Moose.

There are guided morning hikes to Phelps Lake (at the Laurance S. Rockefeller Preserve) and Hidden Falls from Jenny Lake (you take the boat across the lake), among other activities.

Youngsters 8 to 12 can join **Young Naturalist programs** at Colter Bay or Jenny Lake and learn about the natural world for 2 hours while hiking with a ranger. Signups are at the visitor centers (the fee is a mere $1), and the kids will need basic hiking gear.

There are also evening campfire gatherings at most of the campground amphitheaters on a variety of park-related topics.

Other Organized Tours & Activities

The **Grand Teton Lodge Company** (www.gtlc.com; ✆ **800/628-9988** or 307/543-2811) runs half- and full-day bus tours of Grand Teton ($36 adults, $18 children 3–11) and Yellowstone ($66 adults, $41 children 3–11) from late May to early October, weather permitting.

The **Teton Science Schools ★★**, 700 Coyote Canyon Rd., Jackson, WY 83001 (www.tetonscience.org; ✆ **307/733-1313**), have an excellent curriculum for students of all ages, from integrated science programs for junior-high kids to adult seminars covering everything from botany to astronomy. Classes take place at campuses in Jackson and Kelly, and other locations in Jackson Hole. The school's **Wildlife Expeditions** (✆ **877/404-6626**) offers tours that bring visitors closer to the park's wildlife. These trips range from a half-day to a week, covering everything from bighorn sheep to the wolves of Yellowstone.

Scenic Safaris (www.scenic-safaris.com; ✆ **888/734-8898**) offers tours of Grand Teton and Yellowstone out of Jackson in comfortable luxury vans. Often centering on a hike in the park, the tours are half- and full-day affairs that range from $125 to $205 per adult and $85 to $125 for kids under 13. In the winter, the company offers snowcoach and snowmobile tours of both parks for $189 to $299; additional snowmobile riders cost $99 to $149.

Hiking
DAY HIKES

Many people cross Jenny Lake, either by boat or on foot around the south end, to hike up into **Cascade Canyon ★★**, a steep but popular journey that takes you first to **Hidden Falls** (less than 1 mile of hiking if you take the boat; 5 miles if you walk around) or another .5 mile to **Inspiration Point.** Skip the boat shuttle to avoid the crowds; the easy hike around the south end of the lake is refreshing, uncrowded, and a good prelude to heading up the canyon. Most people go no farther than Inspiration Point, but if you're physically up to it, you really should go on. It's a steep climb to the entrance of the canyon, followed by a gentle ascent though a glacially sculpted canyon. At a fork in the trail around 4 miles from Inspiration Point, you can follow either the north fork of Cascade Creek to Lake Solitude (3 miles) or the south fork to Hurricane Pass (5 miles). Try the north fork for a more relaxed day hike. Wildflowers carpet the area, ducks nest along Cascade Creek, and moose and bear may be spotted. The round-trip up into the canyon is about 9 miles.

A less taxing alternative to the Cascade Canyon trip is a detour to **Moose Ponds,** which begins on the Inspiration Point trail. The ponds, located 2 miles from the trail head, are alive with birds. The area near the base of Teewinot Mountain is populated with elk, mule deer, black bears, and moose. The trail is flat (at lake level), short, and easy to negotiate in 1 to 1½ hours. The best times to venture forth are in early morning and evening.

Just down the road from South Jenny Lake is the trail head to **Taggart Lake,** a particularly interesting hike that winds through a recovering burn area to a glacial lake. The hike from the parking lot to the lake (a decent fishing spot) is only 1.5 miles along the eastern route, and rarely crowded. After reaching the lake, you can return by the same trail or continue the loop on the **Taggart Lake Trail,** which leads around one end of the pond and loops back to the trail head through a more heavily forested area. This route adds almost a mile to the round-trip, and the elevation gain is 467 feet. At its highest point, the trail overlooks all of Taggart Lake and the stream that flows from it.

Upon reaching Taggart Lake, a second alternative is to continue north .9 mile to **Bradley Lake,** the smaller of the two, and then return to the Taggart Lake trail head. Like others in Grand Teton, this hike is best made during the early morning or early evening hours, when it is cooler and there is less traffic.

Yet another hike in this busy area begins at the **Leigh Lake trail head,** next to String Lake at the String Lake Picnic Area. This trail head is between Leigh Lake and Jenny Lake (String Lake is a smaller body of water between the two). The Leigh Lake trail is well marked and relatively flat, and goes through a forested area that is always within sight of the lake. Picnickers willing to hike roughly .4 mile from the String Lake Picnic Area to the edge of the lake will find themselves eating in a less congested area that provides spectacular views of the Tetons. The trail continues along the shore of Leigh Lake but is rather uninteresting; a better option, if time allows, is to return to the picnic area, cross the String Lake inlet, and explore the western edge of Jenny Lake.

Just footsteps from the entrance to the Signal Mountain Lodge is a sign marking the trail head for the 4-mile **Signal Mountain Summit Trail ★**, which is not generally described in commercial trail books. Though it's well marked, it's not well traveled, since most visitors drive their automobiles in this area. The trail begins steeply and subsequently opens onto a broad plateau covered with lodgepole pines, grassy areas, and wildflowers. Cross the paved road, and you'll arrive at a large, lily-covered pond at the opening of a meadow, home to frogs and waterfowl. The trail then winds along the south and east perimeter of the pond before turning east and heading toward the summit, a climb that will take up to 2 hours. Shortly after passing the pond, you'll come to a fork in the road that converts the trip into a loop trail. Take the northern route, and you'll travel the rim of the mountain, meandering to the summit through a forest of sagebrush and pine trees. On the return, the southern trail skirts large alpine ponds where you'll find waterfowl, moose—and perhaps black bears.

The day hikes at the north end of the park are less crowded. The easy but lengthy trip to **Two Ocean Lake** begins off the Pacific Creek Road north of Moran Junction and eventually circumnavigates the lake, with much of the mostly level walk through cool conifer forest. Or, located near Colter Bay Visitor Center, the **Hermitage Point trail head** branches out into trips ranging in distance from 1 to 9 miles, mostly in lodgepole pine, with recurring views of the lake and the peaks on the other side. With careful planning, you can start the day with a hike from Colter Bay that leads past **Cygnet Pond** across **Willow Flats** to Jackson Lake Lodge (for lunch). Then take the same path back to Colter Bay in time for the evening outdoor barbecue—all told, that's 10 miles round-trip.

Among the loops you can take from the Hermitage Point trail head are trails to **Swan Lake** and **Heron Pond** (which share the same point of origin), the kind of country where wildflowers, Canada geese, moose, beaver, and bears all thrive. The two most prominent flowers here are heart-leaf arnicas and Indian paintbrush. Don't be put off by the fact that the first 600 feet of the Swan Lake/Heron Pond trails are steep; after reaching the top of a rise, the terrain levels out and has only moderate elevation gains from that point on. Within minutes, this trail opens to a broad meadow covered with sagebrush and, later in the summer, blooming wildflowers. Here you'll find one of the most spectacular views of Mount Moran, and the peaks reflect on the surfaces of the water.

Finding swans at Swan Lake requires a trip to the south end, where a small island affords isolation and shelter for nests. There are also osprey, kingfishers, and white pelicans in this neck of the woods. The distance from Swan Lake, through a densely forested area, to the Heron Pond intersection is .3 mile; Hermitage Point is 3 miles from this junction, along a gentle path that winds through a wooded area popular with bears. Circumnavigation from the Colter area is doable in 2 hours.

A shorter hike in the Colter area, the **Lakeshore Trail** is a wide, shady thoroughfare that skirts the bay, leading to gravelly beaches that present views across Jackson Lake of the entire Teton Range. The views leap out at you when you arrive at the end of the trail; water gently laps at the shore, and, thankfully, you're out of the dense roadside traffic. This 2-mile loop can be completed in about 1 hour of brisk walking.

LONGER HIKES

If you decide a day hike isn't enough, you must get an overnight permit and camp in one of the various camping zones reserved through the visitor centers. Much longer trips can be strung together into the mountainous backcountry, crossing the mountains' spine to **Teton Canyon** on the Idaho side, or, at the north end of the park, exploring deep into the **Jedediah Smith Wilderness.**

Within the park, you can go far beyond the day hikes described above—extending a Cascade Canyon hike, for instance, by going north to Lake Solitude, then coming down into **Paintbrush Canyon** (where you can camp, with a permit) and out at String Lake. You can also take the tram to the top of the ski area in Teton Village and follow the **Teton Crest Trail** north into the park, eventually dropping down through **Death Canyon** (another camping area) to **Phelps Lake** (also a camping zone, the closest one to civilization). A trip like this is more than 20 miles and will take several days.

The Park Service has a helpful brochure that delineates the 20 or so backcountry camping zones and lakeshore sites. You'll need to reserve sites, and rangers can brief you on the quality of different routes, the areas where you're likely to encounter bears, and "leave no trace" camping techniques.

Other Sports & Outdoor Activities

For lovers of outdoor recreation, Grand Teton National Park offers one of the most accessible playlands of rock and water in the Lower 48. In addition to hiking, mountaineers and technical climbers can attack the highest hills; paddlers glide across the smooth waters of the lakes or splash along the livelier flow of the Snake River; and boaters find waters open to motorized vessels and sailboats.

BIKING   The roads in Grand Teton were not built with bicyclists in mind, though the flats of the valley seem perfect for pedaling. The problem is safety—there are huge RVs careening about, and some roads have only narrow shoulders. Teton Park Road has been widened somewhat, but traffic is heavy. Debuting in 2009, there is a popular 8-mile multiuse trail between Jenny Lake and Moose. Road bikers should also try **Antelope Flats Road,** beginning at a trail head 1 mile north of Moose Junction and going east. Sometimes called **Mormon Row,** this paved route crosses the flats below the Gros Ventre Mountains, past old ranch homesteads and the small town of Kelly. It connects to the unpaved **Shadow Mountain Road,** which actually goes outside the park into national forest, climbing through the trees to the summit. Total distance is 7 miles and the elevation gain is 1,370 feet, and you'll be looking at Mount Moran and the Tetons across the valley.

Mountain bikers have a few more options, but keep in mind that bikes are prohibited on the park's backcountry trails and boardwalks. Try **Two-Ocean Lake Road** (reached from the Pacific Creek Rd. just north of Moran Junction) or the **River Road,** a 15-mile dirt path that parallels the Snake River's western bank. Ambitious mountain bikers may want to load their overnight gear and take the **Grassy Lake Road,** once used by Indians, west from Flagg Ranch 50 miles to Ashton, Idaho. Books and maps with biking routes are available at **Adventure Sports** (© 307/733-3307) in Moose, where you can also rent mountain bikes ($36–$48 for a full day), as well as road and performance bikes for a few dollars more. Children's bikes are also available.

BOATING   Boaters have quite a few opportunities here. Motorboats are permitted on Jenny, Jackson, and Phelps lakes. Rafts, canoes, dories, and kayaks are allowed on the Snake River within the park. No boats are allowed on Pacific Creek or the Gros Ventre River. Bigger boats find room on Jackson Lake, where powerboats pull skiers, sailboats move noiselessly in summer breezes, and fishermen ply the waters in search of wily trout. Those who venture on the big lake need to be aware that the weather can change suddenly, and late-afternoon lightning is not uncommon; sailors should be particularly wary of the swirling winds that accompany thunderstorms. **Scenic cruises ★** of Jackson Lake are conducted daily by the **Grand Teton Lodge Company** (© 307/543-2811), and breakfast and dinner cruises run twice weekly, both leaving from the **Colter Bay Marina** from May through September. See "Fees & Backcountry Permits," earlier in this chapter, for information on boat permits. Boat and canoe rentals, tackle, and fishing licenses are available at **Colter** and **Signal Mountain.** Shuttles to the west side of Jenny Lake, as well as cruises, are conducted by **Jenny Lake Boating Company** (© 307/733-9227). Additionally, you can rent kayaks and canoes at **Adventure Sports,** at Dornan's, in the town of Moose (© 307/733-3307), which is in the boundaries of Grand Teton National Park.

CLIMBING   Every year there are rescues of climbers who get trapped on Teton rock faces, and many years there are fatalities. Yet the peaks have a strong allure for climbers, even inexperienced ones, perhaps because you can reach the top of even the biggest ones in a single day. But it isn't easy. The terrain is mixed, with snow and ice year-round—knowing how to self-arrest with an ice axe is a must—and the weather can change suddenly. The key is to get good advice, know your limitations, and if you're not already skilled, take some lessons at the local climbing schools.

Climbers who go out for a day do not have to register or report to park officials, so they should be sure to tell friends where they're going and when they'll be back. Overnight climbers must pick up a free permit. Climbing rangers who can lead rescue efforts are on duty at the **Jenny Lake Ranger Station** at South Jenny Lake from June until the middle of September. The American Alpine Club provides inexpensive dormitory beds ($14 nightly for AAC members, $22 for nonmembers) for climbers at the **Grand Teton Climbers' Ranch** (www.americanalpineclub.org; ℂ **307/733-7271**). A pair of long-standing operations offers classes and guided climbs of Grand Teton: **Jackson Hole Mountain Guides** in Jackson (www.jhmg.com; ℂ **800/239-7642** or 307/733-4979) and **Exum Mountain Guides** ★ in Moose (www.exumguides.com; ℂ **307/733-2297**). Expect to pay $700 to $1,000 for a guided 2-day climb of Grand Teton, or $150 to $200 for a class.

CROSS-COUNTRY SKIING   You can ski flat or steep in Grand Teton; the two things to watch out for are hypothermia and avalanches. As with climbing, know your limitations, and make sure you're properly equipped. Check with local rangers and guides for trails that match your ability. Among your options is the relatively easy **Jenny Lake Trail,** starting at the Taggart Lake Parking Area, about 8 miles of flat and scenic trail that follows Cottonwood Creek. A more difficult ski is the **Taggart Lake–Beaver Creek Loop,** a 3.1-mile route that has some steep and icy pitches coming back. About 4 miles of the **Moose-Wilson Road**—the back way to Teton Village from Moose—is unplowed in the winter and is an easy trip through the woods. You can climb the windy, unplowed road to the top of **Signal Mountain**—you might encounter snowmobiles—and have some fun skiing down. There is an easy ski trail from the Colter Bay Ranger Station area to **Heron Pond**—about 2.5 miles, with a great view of the Tetons and Jackson Lake. Get a ski trail map from the visitor centers.

FISHING   The lakes and streams of Grand Teton are popular fishing destinations, loaded with lively cutthroat trout, whitefish, and Mackinaw (lake) trout in Jackson, Jenny, and Phelps lakes. You'll most likely catch fish under 20 inches, fishing deep with trolling gear from a boat during hot summer months. The Snake River runs for about 27 miles in the park and has cutthroat and whitefish up to about 18 inches. It's a popular drift-boat river for fly-fishing. If you'd like a guide who knows the holes, try **Jack Dennis Fishing Trips** (www.jackdennisfishingtrips.com ℂ **307/690-0910**), **Triangle X Float Trips** (www.trianglex.com; ℂ **307/733-5500**), or **Westbank Anglers** (www.westbank.com; ℂ **800/922-3474** or 307/733-6483). The going rate is $425 to $475 for a full day for two people. **Signal Mountain Lodge** (www.signalmtnlodge.com; ℂ **307/543-2831**) offers guided half-day trips on motorized craft in **Jackson Lake** for one or two people for $280. As an alternative, stake out a position on the banks below the dam at **Jackson Lake,** where you'll have plenty of company and just may snag something. You'll need a Wyoming state fishing license (see "Fishing" in the Jackson section, earlier in this chapter).

RAFTING & FLOATING TRIPS   The upper end of the Snake River in the park can be deceptive—its smooth surface runs fast during the spring, and there are deadly snags of fallen trees and other debris. Check with rangers before putting your boat in—they'll discourage you if they think your skills may not match the river—and proceed with caution. It's a wonderful river for wildlife, too, with moose, eagles, and other animals coming, like you, to the water's edge. There are many commercial float operators in the park who will allow you to relax more and look around. They run mostly from mid-May to mid-September (depending on weather and river-flow conditions). These companies offer 5- to 10-mile scenic floats, some with early-morning and evening wildlife trips. Try **Solitude Float Trips** (www.grand-teton-scenic-floats.com; ✆ **888/704-2800**), **Barker-Ewing Float Trips** (www.barkerewing.com; ✆ **800/365-1800** or 307/733-1800), **Grand Teton Lodge Company** (www.gtlc.com; ✆ **307/543-2811**), or **Signal Mountain Lodge** (www.signalmtnlodge.com; ✆ **307/543-2831**). Scenic float trips cost about $50 to $70 for adults, with discounts for children under 12.

Camping

Since Grand Teton is so much smaller than its counterpart to the north, the mileage between campgrounds is much shorter. As a consequence, selecting a site in one of the five National Park Service campgrounds within the park becomes a matter of preference (rather than geography) and availability. Fees in all campgrounds are $15 per night, and all have modern comfort stations. Campgrounds operate on a first-come, first-served basis, but reservations are available to groups of 10 or more by contacting the **Grand Teton Lodge Co.,** P.O. Box 250, Moran, WY 83013 (www. gtlc.com; ✆ **800/628-9988** or 307/543-2811). You can get recorded information on site availability by calling ✆ **307/739-3603.** Reservations for **trailer sites** at Colter Bay campground may also be made by contacting the **Grand Teton Lodge Co.** Additionally, there is a concessionaire-operated campground located in the Flagg Ranch complex on the John D. Rockefeller, Jr. Memorial Parkway. The area has 97 sites with utility hookups, 74 tent sites, showers, and a launderette. For reservations, contact **Flagg Ranch,** P.O. Box 187, Moran, WY 83013 (✆ **800/443-2311**).

All the campgrounds but Jenny Lake can accommodate tents, RVs, and trailers, but there are no utility hookups at any of them. **Jenny Lake Campground ★★**, a tents-only area with 51 sites, is situated in a quiet, wooded area near the lake. You have to be here first thing in the morning to get a site.

The largest campground, **Gros Ventre,** is the last to fill, if it fills at all—probably because it's located on the east side of the park, a few miles from Kelly on the Gros Ventre River Road. It has 350 sites, a trailer dump station, a tents-only section, and no showers. If you arrive late in the day and you have no place to stay, go here first.

Signal Mountain Campground ★, with views of the lake and access to the beach, is another popular spot that fills first thing in the morning. It has 81 sites overlooking Jackson Lake and Mount Moran, as well as a pleasant picnic area and boat launch. It has no showers or laundry, but there's a store and service station nearby.

Colter Bay Campground and Trailer Village has 350 sites (some with RV hookups), a general store, showers, and a laundry. The area has access to the lake but is far enough from the hubbub of the village to offer a modicum of solitude; spaces are usually gone by noon.

Lizard Creek Campground, at the north end of Grand Teton National Park near Jackson Lake, offers an aesthetically pleasing wooded area near the lake with views of the Tetons, bird-watching, and fishing (not to mention the mosquitoes: bring your repellent). It's only 8 miles from facilities at Colter Bay and has 60 sites that usually fill by 2pm.

Amenities for Each Campground in Grand Teton National Park

CAMPGROUND	# SITES	FEE	SHOWERS	LAUNDRY	FLUSH TOILETS	DISPOSAL
Colter Bay	350	$20	Yes	Yes	Yes	Yes
Colter Bay Trailer Village	112	$56	Yes	Yes	Yes	Yes
Gros Ventre	350	$20	No	No	Yes	Yes
Jenny Lake*	51	$20	No	No	Yes	No
Lizard Creek	60	$21	No	No	Yes	No
Signal Mountain	81	$21	No	No	Yes	Yes

Tents only

Where to Stay in the Park

If you plan to visit Grand Teton during a "fringe" season—usually the best, least-crowded time to go, in the fall or spring—you'd better check first to see if an inn is open. Three different companies run the lodgings in the park, and they all run on different schedules. In early May, you'll find padlocks on the doors everywhere but at Flagg Ranch, which technically isn't in Grand Teton anyway, but in the limbo of the John D. Rockefeller, Jr. Memorial Parkway. Likewise in late fall: By mid-October, there are hardly any beds available in the park, and you'll be bunking in Jackson.

You can get information about or make reservations for Jackson Lake Lodge, Jenny Lake Lodge, Colter Bay Village, and Flagg Ranch through the **Grand Teton Lodge Company,** P.O. Box 250, Moran, WY 83013 (www.gtlc.com; ✆ **800/628-9988** or 307/543-2811). For **Signal Mountain Lodge,** contact P.O. Box 50, Moran, WY 83013 (www.signalmountainlodge.com; ✆ **307/543-2831**). Reservations at **Headwaters Lodge and Cabins at Flagg Ranch** can be made by contacting P.O. Box 187, Moran, WY 83013 (www.flaggranch.com; ✆ **800/443-2311**).

Rooms in Grand Teton National Park properties have telephones but no televisions or air-conditioning. You'll find televisions in the lounge areas at the Jackson Lodge, Signal Mountain Resort, and Flagg Ranch.

EXPENSIVE

Jackson Lake Lodge ★★   Much the way that Old Faithful Inn or the Lake Yellowstone Hotel captures historic eras of Yellowstone tourism, Jackson Lake Lodge epitomizes the architectural milieu of the period when Grand Teton became a park. That era was the 1950s, an age of right angles, flat roofs, and big windows. While not as distinctive as Yellowstone's standouts, the lodge is more functional and comfortable than its northern counterparts. The setting is sublime, overlooking Willow Flats with the lake in the distance, and, towering over it without so much as a stick in the way, the Tetons and Mount Moran. You don't even have to go outside to see this impressive view—the lobby has 60-foot-wide windows showcasing the panorama. A few guest rooms are in the three-story main lodge, but most are in cottages scattered about the property, some of which have large balconies and mountain views. Remodeled in 2009, rooms are spacious and cheery, and most offer double beds, electric heat, and newly tiled bathrooms. For a premium, the view rooms provide guests with a private picture window facing the Tetons.

P.O. Box 250, Moran, WY 83013. www.gtlc.com. ℂ **800/628-9988** or 307/543-2811. 385 units. $229–$319 double; $625–$750 suite. MC, V. Closed mid-Oct to mid-May. **Amenities:** 2 restaurants; lounge; heated outdoor pool; Wi-Fi (free). *In room:* Hair dryer.

Jenny Lake Lodge ★★★   My favorite property in any national park, this lodge justifiably prides itself on seclusion, award-winning food, and the individual attention that comes with a cabin resort kept intentionally small. Catering to an older, affluent, and exceedingly loyal clientele, the style here blends peaceful rusticity with occasional reminders of class and formality. The property is a hybrid of mountain-lake resort and dude ranch, with various extras included in its prices, such as horseback rides, meals, and cool cruiser bicycles. The cabins, each named for a resident flower, are rustic on the outside and luxurious within—decorated with bright braided rugs, dark wood floors, beamed ceilings, cushy plaid armchairs, and tiled bathrooms. Rooms have one queen-size, one king-size, or two double beds. Some were old dude-ranch cabins from the 1920s, and some were built on the property in the 1990s; the latter have larger baths and more modernity, but less character.

P.O. Box 250, Moran, WY 83013. www.gtlc.com. ℂ **800/628-9988** or 307/543-2811. 37 units. $620 double; $800–$885 suite. Extra person $150 a night. Rates include MAP (modified American plan), horseback riding, and use of bicycles. AE, MC, V. Closed mid-Oct to May. **Amenities:** Restaurant; lounge; Wi-Fi (free). *In room:* Fridge.

MODERATE

Colter Bay Village ★ ☺   You might call this the people's resort of Grand Teton, with simpler lodgings, lower prices, and a lively, friendlier atmosphere that seems particularly suited to families. Situated on the eastern shore of Jackson Lake, Colter Bay Village is a full-fledged recreation center. Guest accommodations are in rough log cabins perched on a wooded hillside; they are clean and simply furnished with area rugs on tile floors and reproductions of pioneer furnishings—chests, oval mirrors, and extra-long bedsteads with painted headboards. If you want to take a trip back to the early days of American auto travel, when car camping involved unwieldy canvas tents on slabs by the roadside, you can spend an inexpensive night in tent cabins. The shower and bathroom are communal. Overall, the village provides an excellent base of operations for visitors because it has the most facilities of any area in the park.

P.O. Box 250, Moran, WY 83013. www.gtlc.com. ℂ **800/628-9988** or 307/543-2811. 166 units. $65 log cabin w/shared bath; $165–$219 log cabin w/private bath; $52 tent cabin. MC, V. Closed late Sept to late May. **Amenities:** 2 restaurants; Wi-Fi (free). *In room:* No phone.

Dornan's Spur Ranch Cabins ★   An outfitter's camp since the 1940s, Dornan's is now a collection of year-round cabins built in the 1990s and nicely renovated in 2010. Located at a family-owned operation in Moose that also includes a market, a wine shop, an outdoors store, guide services, and dining, the dozen cabins here are a good option for families and larger groups. All the units have tub/shower combinations, fitting lodgepole-pine furnishings, and fully equipped kitchens. Two of the cabins are right on the Snake River, but they're often booked a year in advance during peak season.

P.O. Box 39, Moose, WY 83012. www.dornans.com. ℂ **307/733-2522.** 12 units. $175–$250 for up to 6 people. Lower rates fall through spring. AE, DISC, MC, V. **Amenities:** 2 restaurants; lounge. *In room:* Kitchen.

Headwaters Lodge and Cabins at Flagg Ranch   At this resort on the Snake River with log-and-luxury ambience, accommodations are duplex and fourplex log cabins that were constructed in the 1990s. The rooms feature patios with rocking chairs, king- and queen-size beds, spacious sitting areas with writing desks and chests of drawers, and bathrooms with tub/shower combinations and separate vanities. There are float trips, horseback rides, and excellent fishing in Polecat Creek or the Snake River. The lodge is a locus of activity, with its double-sided fireplace, fancy dining room, gift shop, espresso bar and pub with large-screen television, convenience store, and gas station. A campground is situated on the grounds amid a stand of pine trees.

P.O. Box 187, Moran, WY 83013. www.flaggranch.com. ℰ **800/443-2311** or 307/543-2861. Fax 307/543-2356. 92 cabins, 171 campsites. $180–$250 cabin double; $64 RV site; $35 tent site. AE, DISC, MC, V. Closed mid-Oct to mid-May. **Amenities:** Restaurant; lounge.

Signal Mountain Lodge ★ 🏠   Signal Mountain has a different feel—and different owners—from the other lodgings in Grand Teton, adding to the sense that any place you choose to stay in this park is going to give you a fairly unique atmosphere. What they all have in common is the Teton view, and this lodge, located right on the banks of Jackson Lake, might have the best. To top it off, it's got lakefront retreats, which you can really inhabit, with stoves and refrigerators and foldout sofa beds for the kids. Other accommodations, mostly rustic log cabins, come in a variety of flavors, from motel-style rooms in four-unit buildings set amid the trees to beachfront family bungalows. These carpeted units feature handmade pine furniture, electric heat, covered porches, and tiled bathrooms; some have fireplaces, and all are non-smoking. Recreational options include rafting and fishing, and sailboat tours on the lake. A convenience store and gas station are on the property.

P.O. Box 50, Moran, WY 83013. www.signalmountainlodge.com. ℰ **307/543-2831.** 80 units. $131–$300 double. Pets accepted ($15 per night). AE, DISC, MC, V. Closed late Oct to early May. **Amenities:** 2 restaurants; lounge; Wi-Fi (free). *In room:* Kitchenette.

INEXPENSIVE

Moulton Ranch Cabins 🍴   A century-old homestead now offers an off-the-beaten-track alternative to the bustling developments on Jackson and Jenny lakes. The small but comfortable cabins here are a few miles west of Moose Junction, scattered around a verdant, private acre entirely surrounded by the park. The cabins, built in stages from the 1930s to 2004, range from dinky to family-size, and packages are available to those who require numerous cabins. The Granary, Grand, and Bunkhouse are larger, with kitchenettes and space for six to sleep.

Mormon Row, Kelly, WY 83011. www.moultonranchcabins.com. ℰ **307/733-3749.** 5 units. $95–$249 double. MC, V. Closed Oct–Apr. No pets. *In room:* Kitchenette, no phone.

Where to Eat

Also at the Headwaters Lodge and Cabins at Flagg Ranch, on the John D. Rockefeller, Jr. Memorial Parkway, **The Steakhouse** (ℰ **800/443-2311**) is open for breakfast lunch, and dinner. In addition to Flagg Ranch, tasty gourmet pizzas are available at **Leeks Marina** (ℰ **307/543-2494**), which is located inside the park, a few miles north of Colter Bay. In Moose, chuckwagon fare (three meals a day) and pasta dishes and pizzas (lunch and dinner) are available at two separate facilities at **Dornan's** (ℰ **307/733-2415**). The outdoor **bar** here is a great place to watch the sun set and enjoy a cocktail.

Grand Teton National Park

Colter Bay Village AMERICAN Here you'll find two sit-down restaurants (although there's also a snack shop in the grocery store). Three meals are served daily during the summer months. **John Colter Café Court** serves sandwiches, burgers, and pretty good Mexican fare. Breakfasts at the new **Ranch House** are hearty; lunch is a soup-and-salad bar and hot sandwiches; dinner is more of an event but nonetheless family friendly. Among the dinner entrees are trout, pasta, and beef and buffalo steaks. The bar is worth a look, emblazoned with the brands of a number of Jackson Hole–area ranches.

Across from the visitor center and marina in Colter Bay Village. ✆ **307/543-2811.** Reservations accepted for parties of 8 or more at Ranch House only. Breakfast and lunch $5–$13; dinner $6–$25. MC, V. John Colter Café Court: Daily 11am–10pm. Ranch House: Daily 6:30–10:30am, 11:30am–1:30pm, and 5:30–9pm. Closed early Sept to May.

Jenny Lake Lodge Dining Room ★★★ CONTINENTAL The finest meals in either park (or, for that matter, in *any* park) are served here, where a talented chef creates culinary delights for guests and, occasionally, a president of the United States. Breakfast, lunch, and dinner are served here, and all are spectacular. (Nonguests should have lunch here if they can.) The five-course dinner is the bell-ringer, though. Guests choose from appetizers that might include elk carpaccio; salads with organic greens, pecans, and dried cherries; and entrees such as buffalo short ribs, braised rabbit leg, or a venison strip loin. Desserts are equally creative and tantalizing. Price is no object, at least for guests, because meals are included in the room charge; nonguests should expect a hefty bill. Casual dress is discouraged, with jackets requested for dinner.

At Jenny Lake Lodge. ✆ **307/733-4647.** Reservations required. Prix-fixe breakfast $23; lunch main courses $9–$14; prix-fixe dinner $78, not including alcoholic beverages. AE, MC, V. Summer daily 7:30–9am, noon–1:30pm, and 6–8:45pm.

The Mural Room ★★ BEEF/WILD GAME Jackson Lake's main dining room is quiet and fairly formal, catering to a more sedate crowd; it's also more expensive than other park restaurants. The floor-to-ceiling windows provide stellar views across a meadow that is moose habitat to the lake and the Cathedral Group. (The staff applauds sunset every night.) Walls inside are adorned with hand-painted Western murals created by Carl Roters. The food is the perfect complement to the view and markedly superior to most of what you'll find in Yellowstone. Three meals are served daily in summer. Breakfast items include a "healthy start" breakfast, organic granola, and fruit smoothie, as well as a breakfast buffet. Dinner might be a grand five-course event that includes buffalo carpaccio, lobster and brie bisque, and house salad, followed by an entree of Idaho trout, slow-roasted prime rib, vegetable Wellington, or molasses-spiced elk loin. Dessert includes delicious homemade ice cream and a rich fudge cake. Aside from the dining room at Jenny Lake Lodge and Lake Yellowstone Hotel, this is the most romantic and upscale eatery in either park.

At Jackson Lake Lodge. ✆ **800/628-9988** or 307/543-2811. Reservations recommended. Breakfast $6–$15; lunch $9–$17; dinner $18–$38. MC, V. Summer daily 7–9:30am, 11:30am–1:30pm, and 5:30–9pm.

Pioneer Grill ☺ AMERICAN Bedecked with regional homesteading antiques and photos, this 1950s-style luncheonette, with its curving counter and old-fashioned soda fountain, offers hearty meals and a casual, friendly atmosphere. Breakfasts are basic but ideal for hiking appetites—bagels, eggs, flapjacks, and the like. For lunch, try one of the Grill's ever-popular buffalo burgers or a plump turkey sandwich. Dinner is similarly laid-back and traditional—you can't miss with the pan-fried rainbow trout. (And don't miss the huckleberry milkshakes for dessert.) When a tour bus stops at the lodge, the restaurant is often overrun with business, so you might want to head next door to The Mural Room if you're looking for peace or romance. If you're looking for convenience, good service, and a relatively quick meal, though, this spot is hard to beat.

At Jackson Lake Lodge. © **800/628-9988** or 307/543-2811. Reservations not accepted. Breakfast $4–$9; lunch $7–$10; dinner $9–$18. MC, V. Summer daily 6am–10pm.

Signal Mountain Lodge ⚓ MEXICAN/AMERICAN   There are actually two restaurants here, serving delicious food in the friendliest style in the park. The fine dining room and lounge are called **Peaks** and **Deadman's Bar,** respectively, and the **Trapper Grill** supplements the continental fare with Mexican entrees, pizzas, and plump sandwiches. You eat up the scenery, too, with a view of Jackson Lake and Mount Moran.

Bargain hunters flock to the bar for the decadent nachos supreme: a foot-tall mountain of chips, cheese, chicken, beef, beans, and peppers that runs a mere $15. You'll easily fill four people for that price, leaving you plenty of change for the bar's signature blackberry margaritas. Because the bar has one of three televisions in the park and is equipped with cable for sports nuts, the crowd tends to be young and noisy. Full meals are served in the proper dining room, with an emphasis on sustainable cuisine. Entrees include free-range chicken with organic black beans and rice, vegetarian lasagna, and filet mignon served on a potato cake with sautéed spinach, the most expensive entree.

At Signal Mountain Resort. © **307/543-2831.** Reservations required for breakfast and dinner. Breakfast $7–$10; lunch $8–$16; dinner $19–$35. AE, DISC, MC, V. Summer daily 7–10am and 11:30am–10pm.

A SIDE TRIP TO DUBOIS & THE WIND RIVER RANGE

86 miles NE of Jackson

For years, Dubois was a kind of a doppelgänger to Jackson, a blue-collar logging town with some quietly wealthy folks living on nice ranches up the nearby draws. Now the sawmill is closed, and wealthy folks who want to stay ahead of the latest real estate fashion are wandering over Togwotee Pass and buying up the beautiful Upper Wind River Valley. That means Dubois is poised for some serious development, but it hasn't quite happened yet, which dismays some residents and pleases others. Lying as it does along one of the Yellowstone access roads, Dubois is just far enough from the park entrances to be spared the West Yellowstone gateway syndrome, and if locals keep their heads, they'll protect the great trout streams, uncluttered wilderness, and small-town ambience from uncontrolled growth. So far, so good. It's a fun town, often with several bands playing in the bars on weekends. To get there from Jackson, go north on U.S. 26/89/191 to Moran Junction, then east over Togwotee Pass on U.S. 26/287.

In the lake-dotted Whiskey Basin, just south of town, one of the largest extant herds of bighorn sheep migrates down in the winter to get away from the deep snows, and so there is a **National Bighorn Sheep Interpretive Center,** 907 W. Ramshorn (www.bighorn.org; © **888/209-2795** or 307/455-3429), located just off the highway in the center of town. Just across the park at the **Dubois Museum,** 909 W. Ramshorn (www.duboismuseum.org; © **307/455-2284**), is a look at the past of the town, the Sheepeater Indians, and other interesting artifacts with local flavor. The museum is open from 9am to 6pm daily mid-May through mid-September and 10am to 4pm Tuesday to Saturday the rest of the year. Contact the **Dubois Chamber of Commerce,** P.O. Box 632Y, Dubois, WY 85213 (www.duboiswyoming.org; © **888/518-0502**), for additional information on the community.

Where to Stay

Brooks Lake Lodge & Spa ★★ This remote and historic mountain lodge sits above the shores of Brooks Lake, a prize fishing lake surrounded by soaring pinnacles. This is the entry point to some of the most remote and challenging wilderness in the Rockies, packed with elk, trout, and grizzly bears. Yet the handsome lodge, with its hand-stripped timbers and deep porch overlooking the lake, is as cozy and comforting as anyone could ask. You can lounge or take advantage of the riding stock, guided up steep trails to incredible views. Accommodations are seven guest rooms in the lodge (one room is a suite with a Jacuzzi and a fireplace) and eight cabins along the tree line. The cabins, each decorated with a distinct frontier motif, are comfortable, spacious affairs that have Western pine furniture, woodstoves, and large decks or porches with views of the lake. Snowmobile rentals are available in winter.

458 Brooks Lake Rd., Dubois, WY 82513. www.brookslake.com. © **307/455-2121.** 12 units, 3 family cabins. Summer $340–$440 per person, per night; winter $250–$300 per person, per night. Rates include all meals and activities. AE, MC, V. Closed Apr–May and Oct–Nov. **Amenities:** Restaurant; exercise room; outdoor Jacuzzi; sauna; spa. *In room:* Hair dryer, no phone, Wi-Fi (free).

Where to Eat

For dinner, the **Rustic Pine Steakhouse,** 123 E. Ramshorn (© **307/455-2772**), does a good job with beef, seafood, and pasta. The **Village Cafe,** 515 W. Ramshorn (© **307/455-2122**), serves three hearty American meals a day and also houses a Daylight Donuts franchise.

CODY & NORTH-CENTRAL WYOMING

D eep, broad valleys, cupped by daunting mountain ranges, provide some of the most livable pockets of the Rocky Mountain West. Not only do the mountains provide some protection from howling storms, but their snowmelt keeps streams running through the summer and their beauty supplies a spectacular backdrop for the communities nestled below.

Such a valley runs down the center of Wyoming, cradled by the Bighorn Mountains in the east and the Absarokas and Yellowstone Plateau in the West. Though the area around the town of Cody gets only about 10 inches of moisture annually, founder William "Buffalo Bill" Cody recognized a century ago that with a few dams and ditches in the right places, the mountains' snowpack could supply water year-round. His legacy continues to shape the basin's economy today: A great summer scene of cowboy fun attracts hordes of visitors, and green fields of sugar beets and grains stretch for miles from the mouth of the Wapiti Valley.

While Cody was staking claims to water rights along the Shoshone River in the early 20th century, the U.S. Bureau of Reclamation was storing that water behind the Buffalo Bill Dam, the world's tallest when it was completed in 1910. The reservoir today irrigates about 100,000 acres in central Wyoming, and the swift winds that skim the lake's surface attract the bravest of windsurfers.

In the post–"Buffalo Bill" era, the charms of north-central Wyoming have taken many a visitor by surprise on their journey to and from Wyoming's famous national parks. And quite a few travelers find reason to linger longer in the nearby valleys, exploring a wealth of American-Indian and Wild West history, geology, mountain scenery, outdoor recreation, and small-town charm. Highlights include fun-loving Cody, the Bighorn Canyon National Recreation Area, the gushing hot springs of Thermopolis, and the forests and rivers of Shoshone National Forest and other public lands.

The combination of stunning scenery and historic cattle operations makes the Cody area a natural center for dude ranches, where visitors can saddle up and swing a lariat. Or you can mount a more stationary seat in the stands at one of the summer rodeos. Cody's rodeo grounds light up every night in the summer, and nearly every town in the basin has its special rodeo weekend. On the Wind River Indian Reservation, the evening outdoor entertainment is often a powwow, featuring drum groups, colorful garb, and traditional dancing, with visitors welcome and food stands offering Indian tacos and other treats.

SCENIC DRIVES

The two-lane roads of north-central Wyoming follow the contours of a craggy landscape, tracking the twists and turns of the river and switchbacking over the mountain passes; the roads are narrow but generally not too crowded, except for the constant stream of traffic to Yellowstone's east entrance. **U.S. 14/16/20,** the east entrance road (also called the Yellowstone Hwy.), is the major east–west route through this region. The breathtaking views as it snakes through the Wapiti Valley and up over Sylvan Pass into Yellowstone make the traffic and seemingly interminable road repairs worthwhile. West of Cody, almost any road you take will reward you with a canyon or a climb, but many of them narrow into rough dirt byways as they delve deeper into the forest. **Wyo. 291** does that as it follows the **South Fork of the Shoshone River** upstream toward the white-capped peaks of Yellowstone's Thorofare country. Along the way are prominent volcanic rock formations like Castle Rock, a succession of picturesque ranches, and sometimes a lucky glimpse of bighorn sheep, before the road finally dead-ends on the fringes of the Absaroka Range.

Cody is also an alternative starting point for the **Chief Joseph Scenic Highway,** which links up to the Beartooth Scenic Byway into Montana (see p. 199).

Note: Most of the sights mentioned in the following driving tours are discussed in greater detail later in this chapter.

Driving Tour 1: Bighorn Mountain Loop

This moderately easy day trip will open your eyes to an extraordinary mountain range, on a route that encompasses the towns of **Powell** and **Lovell,** as well as the scenic **Shell Canyon** area. Begin in Cody by taking U.S. 14A northeast to Lovell and the **Bighorn Canyon National Recreation Area** (see p. 242). A side trip north along Wyo. 37 provides views of the wild horses of the Pryor Mountain National Wild Horse Range and Bighorn Lake from the Devil Canyon Overlook.

After crossing the Bighorn River, U.S. 14A rises through the foothills and up the steep flanks of the Bighorns, not far from the footpaths of prehistoric travelers who built the **Medicine Wheel,** a 74-foot stone circle with 28 spokes. Like other mysterious wheel designs in the Rockies, it may have served ancient peoples as an astronomical key or a long-distance travel marker. To get here, turn off U.S. 14A at the Medicine Wheel sign and hike 1.5 miles from the parking area to the site. American-Indian spiritual leaders still conduct ceremonies here. Visitors are asked not to remove offerings or disturb American Indians using the site for prayer or fasting. For more information, contact the **Medicine Wheel Ranger District of the Bighorn National Forest** in Lovell (*©* **307/548-6541**).

Once you have crested the divide of the Bighorn Mountains, take U.S. 14 southwest at Burgess Junction toward Shell Canyon and the towns of Shell and Greybull. The road drops sharply through steeply cut canyons, and you can stop at the **Shell Falls Interpretive Center** and follow a paved path to a close-up view of the creek, tumbling and twisting amid tall granite slabs. As the road flattens out near the town of Shell, you're surrounded by the deep red sandstones of the **Chugwater Formation,** set off by the rich greens of cultivated fields. This area enfolds some well-packed dinosaur fossil beds. U.S. 14/16/20 takes you back to Cody, toward the embrace of the Absaroka Mountains and Yellowstone. This driving tour can be enjoyed year-round, though winter drivers should proceed cautiously on the steep grades around Burgess Junction.

Driving Tour 2: Bighorn Basin Loop

This all-day trip keeps to the Bighorn River Basin, navigating rolling sagebrush hills, cultivated farmlands, hot-spring terraces, and one-pump (formerly one-horse) Western towns.

Depart from Cody and travel south along Wyo. 120 to the tiny burg of **Meeteetse** on the banks of the Greybull River. From here, continue on Wyo. 120 to **Thermopolis,** self-proclaimed home of the world's largest free-flowing hot springs (New Zealand does not agree). After a relaxing soak and a brief drive east for a glimpse of the bison herd that roams **Hot Springs State Park,** travel northeast on U.S. 16/20 to **Worland,** an important agricultural center. Then drive east along U.S. 16 to **Ten Sleep,** which lies at the base of another steep-sided canyon cutting down through the Bighorn Mountains. You may want to hike and cast a line in Ten Sleep Creek.

Here, take the Norwood Road north, which joins Wyo. 31, to Manderson and follows the base of the Bighorns. From Manderson, follow U.S. 16/20 north to Basin, take Wyo. 30 west to the junction of Wyo. 120, and continue north to Cody. Along the way, you'll enjoy views of the Bighorn River and the Greybull River Valley. Winter isn't too harsh on this loop, which could include a detour south of Meeteetse on Wyo. 290 to the **Wood River Valley Cross-Country Ski Park** (© **307/868-2603**). If it's summer, rangers at Hot Springs State Park have a map and key to Legend Rock petroglyph sites north of Thermopolis, where you can hike around the cliffs.

CODY ★

52 miles E of the east entrance of Yellowstone; 177 miles NE of Jackson; 214 miles NW of Casper

The legendary scout and entertainer William F. "Buffalo Bill" Cody really knew how to put on a show, and he also knew where to put a town. Cody, founded by its namesake in 1887, is beautifully situated near the juncture of rivers that pour from the rugged Absaroka Range. Every summer, the town of Cody stages a cow-town circus that would do the founder proud, entertaining throngs of visitors on their way to and from Yellowstone 52 miles west. And the drive to the park is sublime: Theodore Roosevelt called the Wapiti Valley "the most scenic 50 miles in the world."

Stop by Cody before the mid-May opening of Yellowstone's east entrance, and it's rather lifeless. For 3 months every summer, though, the town parades its Western charm for masses of travelers. When the sun goes down, the lights come on at the rodeo grounds, and the broncos do a little busting of their own. A world-class museum, a reassembled Old West town, and retail shops all attract the crowds.

THE mystery OF BUFFALO BILL'S GRAVE

Buffalo Bill's legend looms large over Cody, but some locals believe that it's more than his spirit looking down from the surrounding peaks. Rumor has it that Buffalo Bill is buried not atop Lookout Mountain in Golden, Colorado, but on Cedar Mountain, just outside of Cody. After the legendary showman's 1917 demise, the mayor of Denver and the *Denver Post* arranged to buy his body as the centerpiece to a tourist attraction. As the story goes, a trio of Cody residents took it upon themselves to see to it that Cody be laid to rest outside the town that bears his name. They swapped Buffalo Bill's body (which sat on ice for 6 months in Denver before the funeral) with that of an anonymous old cowboy who died in Cody without any kin. While there's more than one story floating around regarding the true whereabouts of Cody's grave, longtime Cody residents (including some of Buffalo Bill's descendants) swear that a nameless cowboy is buried on Lookout Mountain in Colorado and that William F. Cody's final resting place is where he wanted it—in Cody, Wyoming.

Though lacking the resort density and sophistication of Jackson, Cody's Western charm feels more authentic.

Essentials

GETTING THERE   Cody's **Yellowstone Regional Airport** (www.flyyra.com; © **307/587-5096**) serves the Bighorn Basin, as well as the east and northeast entrances of Yellowstone National Park, with year-round commercial flights via **Delta** and **United** through Salt Lake City and Denver.

If you're driving from **Cheyenne,** travel north on I-25 to Casper, then west on U.S. 20/26 to Shoshoni, where U.S. 20 turns north to Thermopolis. From there, it's another 84 miles to Cody on Wyo. 120. From **Jackson,** take U.S. 191 to the West Thumb Junction in Yellowstone, drive east along the northern boundary of Yellowstone Lake, and continue on U.S. 14/16/20 to Cody. Coming from the southwest, drive north from Rock Springs on U.S. 191 to Farson, Wyo. 28 to Lander, Wyo. 789 to Thermopolis, and Wyo. 120 to Cody.

VISITOR INFORMATION   For printed information on this area of Wyoming, contact the **Buffalo Bill's Cody/Yellowstone Country,** 836 Sheridan Ave. (P.O. Box 2454), Cody, WY 82414 (www.yellowstonecountry.org; © **307/587-2297**), or the **Wyoming Travel & Tourism,** 1520 Etchepare Circle, Cheyenne, WY 82007 (www.wyomingtourism.org; © **800/225-5996** or 307/777-7777).

GETTING AROUND   If you haven't come by car, you'll probably need to rent one; there's little public transportation. **Budget** (© **800/527-0700**), **Hertz** (© **800/654-3131**), and **Thrifty** (© **800/847-4389**) maintain desks at Yellowstone Regional Airport.

SPECIAL EVENTS   In mid-June, the **Plains Indian Museum Powwow** brings alive the Robbie Powwow Garden on the south end of the Buffalo Bill Historical Center parking lot with whirling color. Traditional dance competitions are coupled with craft shows and American-Indian food, and non-Indians are welcomed into round dances. Call the Buffalo Bill Historical Center (© **307/587-4771**) for information. Every July 1 to July 4, during the **Cody Stampede,** the streets are filled with parades, fireworks, street dances, barbecues, and entertainment, capped by a top-notch rodeo. Call © **800/207-0744** or 307/587-5155 for tickets (see **www.cody stampederodeo.com** for more information). In mid-August, the Buffalo Bill Historical Center (© **307/587-4771**) stages the **Buffalo Bill Invitational Shootout,** where celebrities and local shooters test their skills in trap, skeet, sporting clays, and five-stand shooting.

Getting Outside

If you'd rather not be a driver in the park's heavy summer traffic, guided Yellowstone National Park tours are available locally through **Grub Steak Expeditions,** P.O. Box 1013, Cody, WY 82414 (www.grubsteaktours.com; © **800/527-6316** or 307/527-6316). Bob Richard, Grub Steak's proprietor (and one of the most knowledgeable guides you'll find), is a third-generation Cody resident and former Yellowstone ranger. Full-day tours run about $500 for two people and $140 for additional adults, $75 for additional kids 15 and under.

Cody has fewer organized recreation options than Jackson does, but there is no shortage of places to go outdoors. **Buffalo Bill State Park,** located along the canyon and reservoir 6 miles west of Cody, is a hot spot for outdoors buffs, with opportunities for hiking, fishing, and a variety of watersports, particularly windsurfing. The park also has facilities for camping and picnicking.

BIKING

If you want to explore the area on two wheels, bike rentals and advice are available from **Absaroka Bikes,** 2201 17th St. (*C* **307/527-5566**) for $45 a day. Although there isn't a marked network of bike paths in the Cody area, you can ride on the Forest Service trails west of town off U.S. Hwy. 14/16/20 in the Shoshone National Forest. For specific trail information, call the **Forest Service** (www.fs.usda.gov/shoshone; *C* **307/527-6241**).

CROSS-COUNTRY SKIING

If you favor a groomed course for cross-country skiing, try the **North Fork Nordic Trails** in Shoshone National Forest, near the east entrance to the park off U.S. Hwy. 14/16/20. You can circuit 16 miles of trails adjacent to the Pahaska Tepee Resort.

DOWNHILL SKIING

After slumbering for several years, **Sleeping Giant Ski Area,** U.S. 40 (P.O. Box 400), Cody, WY 82414 (www.skisg.com; *C* **307/527-8988**) reopened for the 2009–10 winter. With two lifts, 150 skiable acres, and 500 feet of vertical drop, this is a dinky, family-oriented ski area with a mix of beginner, intermediate, and expert runs. Full-day lift tickets run $29 for adults, $24 for seniors and students 13 to 17, $12 for children 6 to 12, and free for kids 5 and under.

FISHING

Yellowstone's legendary fly-fishing waters are a short drive away, though you should try the smaller but excellent angling streams west of Cody: **Clark's Fork of the Yellowstone,** the **North and South Forks of the Shoshone,** and **Sunlight Creek.** To the east, the warmer and slower **Big Horn River** and **Big Horn Lake** nurture catfish, walleye, and ling for boat fishers. For advice on the trout streams near Cody, ask at **Tim Wade's North Fork Anglers,** 1107 Sheridan Ave. (www.northforkanglers.com; *C* **307/527-7274**), which stocks gear and clothing and also guides day trips for $375 to $425 for two people. If you like to troll or cast from a boat, try **Buffalo Bill Reservoir,** which has produced some big mackinaw, as well as rainbow, brown, and cutthroat trout.

GOLF

Greens fees at the 18-hole **Olive Glenn Golf and Country Club,** 802 Meadow Lane (www.oliveglenngolf.com; *C* **307/587-5551**), are $40 for 9 holes and $70 for 18, cart included.

RAFTING

There aren't lots of class IV, serious white-water rapids on the rivers around Cody, but the upper stretches of the North Fork of the Shoshone River run pretty fast in the spring. Contact **Wyoming River Trips,** 233 Yellowstone Ave. (www.wyomingrivertrips.com; *C* **800/586-6661** or 307/587-6661). Prices run from about $25 to $70, depending on the length and difficulty of the trip.

SNOWMOBILING

The most popular Cody snowmobiling trails originate from nearby **Pahaska Tepee Resort,** located 51 miles from Cody on U.S. Hwy. 14/16/20 (see "Where to Stay," later in this chapter). Don't take the Pahaska Tepee Trail over 8,541-foot Sylvan Pass if you're afraid of heights; but if you're not, go for it: You'll connect with the Yellowstone National Park trails (guides are required within the park) and the lengthy Continental Divide Snowmobile Trail, and have some breathtaking views, including of Avalanche Peak (10,566 ft.) and Cody Peak (10,267 ft.). The **Sunlight trail system** is located 36 miles north of Cody and winds through the wilds to a stunning view of the Beartooth Mountains. Sledders start from a parking area at the junction of Wyo. 296 and U.S. Hwy. 212 and follow the Beartooth Scenic Byway east for 16 miles to a warming hut. To the east, there are 70 miles of snowmobile routes in the Bighorn Mountains. Snowmobiles can be rented in Cody from **Mountain Valley Engine Service,** 422 W. Yellowstone Ave. (www.mountainvalleyengine.com; ✆ **307/ 587-6218**) for about $225 a day.

WINDSURFING

The 8-mile-long, 4-mile-wide **Buffalo Bill Reservoir,** which receives wind from three mountain gorges, is one of the top windsurfing destinations in the continental United States. It's best experienced in the warmer months of June to September. There is a boat ramp near the campground on the north side of the reservoir, just off U.S. Hwy. 14/16/20. There are no places to rent a windsurf board in the vicinity.

Seeing the Sights

Those with a special interest in antique firearms will also want to check out the one-of-a-kind **Cody Dug Up Gun Museum,** upstairs at 1020 12th St. (www.cody dugupgunmuseum.com; ✆ **307/587-3344**), showcasing over 750 guns excavated from all over the world, including three from Custer's Last Stand and one that a tree slowly engulfed. The museum is open from 9am to 9pm daily from May to September, and admission is by donation.

Buffalo Bill Historical Center ★★★ Nicknamed the "Smithsonian of the West," this vast museum is top-drawer, casting a scholarly eye on the relics of the West's young history while offering some flash and entertainment for the easily distracted. From its beginnings in a rustic log building, it's grown into a thoroughly impressive modern edifice that now houses five different museums in all.

The **Buffalo Bill Museum** is a monument to one of the earliest manifestations of America's celebrity culture, displaying the wares that turned a frontier scout and buffalo hunter into a renowned showman. Posters trumpet his world-famous Wild West shows featuring "Custer's Last Rally" and "Cossack of the Caucasus," and there are some grainy film clips of the show itself. The newly renovated **Whitney Gallery of Western Art** showcases work by the adventurous artists who carried their palettes to the frontier to record firsthand the wilderness beauty, the proud Indian cultures, and the lives of trappers and cowboys in the 19th century. Bygone Western artists such as Frederic Remington, Charlie Russell, Albert Bierstadt, and Gutzon Borglum share exhibition space with contemporary practitioners. The **Plains Indian Museum** is devoted to the history of Plains tribes, including the Blackfeet, Cheyenne, Crow, Gros Ventre, Shoshone, and Sioux. Interactive exhibits explain the migrations and customs of the tribes and display art and artifacts, including cradleboards, ceremonial dresses and robes, pipes, and beadwork. Situated in an eye-catching rotunda populated by dozens of engaging exhibits, the **Draper Museum of Natural History** focuses on man's scientific exploration of nature over time, with specific attention on the Greater Yellowstone Ecosystem (there's a regional map composed of 27,000 tiles) and many interactive displays. The **Cody Firearms Museum** displays weaponry dating back to 16th-century Europe in its collection of more than 5,000 pieces.

The center also features rotating special exhibitions, and its research library is an unparalleled resource for all things Western. Additionally, numerous educational programs are held throughout the year. Expect to spend anywhere from 2 hours to 2 days exploring the center, depending on your level of interest.

720 Sheridan Ave. www.bbhc.org. © **307/587-4771.** Admission $18 adults, $16 seniors, $13 students 13–17 or with valid college ID, $10 children 5–12, free for children under 5; maximum $45 per family. Admission is good for 2 consecutive days. Group tour rates available by request. Nov–Mar Thurs–Sun 10am–5pm; Apr daily 10am–5pm; May to mid-Sept daily 8am–6pm; mid-Sept to Oct daily 8am–5pm.

Buffalo Bill Reservoir The **Buffalo Bill Dam** drops like a slim concrete knife 325 feet into the gorge carved by the Shoshone River west of Cody, and you can walk out atop the dam and look down the steep canyon or back across the deep blue water of the reservoir. Several workers died building it, and when it was completed in 1910, it was the tallest dam in the world. The lake behind it serves anglers, boaters, and windsurfers, while providing irrigation water to farmers downstream. An octagonal visitor center perched next to the dam provides exhibits on the reservoir, wildlife, and area recreation. There is a boat launch along the north lakeshore off U.S. Hwy. 14/16/20 and a clean, spacious campground that lacks much in the way of shade.

6 miles west of Cody on U.S. Hwy. 14/16/20 at the top of Shoshone Canyon. www.bbdvc.org. © **307/527-6076** for visitor center. Free admission. May and Sept Mon–Fri 8am–6pm, Sat–Sun 9am–5pm; June–Aug Mon 8am–7pm, Tues–Fri 8am–7:30pm, Sat–Sun 9am–5pm. Visitor center closed Oct–Apr.

Cody Nite Rodeo ★★ ☺ If you want to see an authentic Wyoming rodeo, Cody (aka "The Rodeo Capital of the World") offers a sure thing: a nightly tussle between bulls, broncos, and cowboys, as well as roping, cutting, and kids' events such as the "calf scramble"—about 100 young patrons chasing a bewildered young calf. Pay an extra $2, and you get a seat just above the chutes in the Buzzard's Roost. The 6,000-seat stadium sits out on an open terrace above the Shoshone River west of town—not a bad place to be on a cool Wyoming evening beneath the stars. Once a year, some of the nation's top rodeo competitors show up for the Fourth of July Cody Stampede (see "Special Events," above). Before the rodeo, there's a kiddie event with various activities.

Stampede Park (on U.S. Hwy. 14/16/20 west of town, toward the Wapiti Valley). www.codystampede rodeo.com. © **800/207-0744** or 307/587-5155. Admission $18 adults, $8 children 7–12, free for children under 7. June–Aug nightly at 8pm; gates open at 7pm.

Cody Trolley Tours ★ An informative, witty look back at Cody's colorful past, with a focus on the town's founding father himself, Buffalo Bill, this hour-long tour in a restored trolley takes visitors on a loop that includes historic homes, public art, and the Buffalo Bill Reservoir. The owner/operators, Mike and Margie Johnson, deliver a running commentary augmented by visual aids and recorded snippets that will keep the kids interested. While the couple's narration occasionally comes off as an economic-development pitch for Cody, it also packs a dense serving of fun facts and trivia into the 60-minute drive.

1192 Sheridan Ave. (tours begin and end on the front porch of the Irma Hotel). www.codytrolley tours.com. © **307/527-7043.** Admission $24 adults, $22 seniors, $12 children 6–17, free for children under 6. Ask about a combination ticket for the Buffalo Bill Historical Center. Tours offered early June to late Sept daily at 11am and 3pm.

Museum of the Old West at Old Trail Town ☺   Walking the authentically creaky boardwalks here, you'll pass by gray storefronts and clapboard cabins gathered from ghost towns around the region and assembled on the original town site of Cody City, a short jog from the rodeo grounds. The curators haven't wasted any paint on these relics, which include an 1883 cabin from Kaycee, Wyoming, where Butch Cassidy and the Sundance Kid once conspired; a saloon decorated with bullet holes; and what must be the largest collection of worn-out buckboard carriages in the U.S. Also on-site: the relocated graves of a number of Western notables, including John "Liver-eatin'" Johnston, the model for Robert Redford's *Jeremiah Johnson*.

1831 DeMaris Dr. www.museumoftheoldwest.org. © **307/587-5302.** Admission $8 adults, $7 seniors, $4 children 6–12, free for children under 6. Mid-May to Sept daily 8am–7pm.

Tecumseh's Old West Miniature Village and Museum ☺   You have to pass through a trading post of Western tourist plunder and hand-crafted beadwork to get to this finely detailed miniature diorama of Wyoming and Montana history. Described by creator Jerry Fick as his "lifetime work," the room-size landscape depicts everything from fur trappers floating the rivers to Custer's last moments at Little Big Horn. There is also a sizable collection of Indian and pioneer artifacts and taxidermy.

142 W. Yellowstone Ave. www.tecumsehs.com. © **307/587-5362.** Free admission. Mid-May to mid-Sept daily 9am–7pm; early May and late Sept daily 9am–5pm. Call for hours in winter.

Where to Stay

If you want to book lodging before you arrive, a good accommodations resource is **Cody Lodging Company,** 1302 Beck Ave. (www.codylodgingcompany.com; © **800/587-6560**), which manages numerous properties, from Victorian B&Bs to three-bedroom houses. Rates range from about $100 to $500 a night in the summer season.

Buffalo Bill Village Resort: Comfort Inn, Holiday Inn, and Buffalo Bill Village Historic Cabins ★   Consisting of three distinct lodging options at the same convenient location, Buffalo Bill Village has something for everybody. The Holiday and Comfort inns are similar to their chain brethren elsewhere, while the village of historic cabins offers a rustic exterior and a more Western feel, with modern conveniences inside. The former two are priced nearly identically and have similar amenities. The one- and two-bedroom cabins at Buffalo Bill Village are simply equipped and surrounded by plenty of room for the kids to roam. The cabins themselves first housed the contractors who built the city around 1920. Also on-site: an Old West-style boardwalk where you can shop for curios or sign up for tours and river trips, an outdoor heated pool, and several restaurants.

17th St. and Sheridan Ave., Cody, WY 82414. www.blairhotels.com. © **800/527-5544.** Fax 307/587-2795. Comfort Inn: 75 units. $89–$169 double. Holiday Inn: 189 units. $89–$169 double. Buffalo Bill Village Historic Cabins: 83 units. $79–$159 double. AE, DC, DISC, MC, V. Historic Cabins closed Oct–Apr. **Amenities:** Restaurant; lounge; exercise room; outdoor pool (summer only). *In room:* A/C, TV, hair dryer, Wi-Fi (free).

The Chamberlin Inn ★★   A boardinghouse opened here in 1904, and the property evolved and devolved over the course of the next century until Ev and Susan Diehl took over the property in 2005 and completely restored it—and then some. Centered on a serene and green courtyard, the Chamberlin Inn is now Cody's best lodging option, just a block from the center of town and featuring charming historic rooms and apartment units. Of special note are the Hemingway Suite—"Papa" stayed here in 1932—with an angling motif and a small Hemingway library; and the lavish Courthouse unit, the original town courthouse reimagined as a luxury apartment.

1032 12th St., Cody, WY 82414. www.chamberlininn.com. ✆ **888/587-0202** or 307/587-0202. 21 units, including 10 suites and apartments. $165–$185 double; $235–$650 suite or apt. AE, DISC, MC, V. *In room:* A/C, TV, kitchen, Wi-Fi (free).

The Cody ★★   The Cody immediately became the top modern hotel in the town of its name when it opened in May 2008. Located on the west end of town near the rodeo grounds, the hotel has a colorful, thoroughly Western-chic design in both the common areas and the spacious guest rooms, which have one king bed or two queens, warm earth tones, and a Native American motif. Some have sleeper sofas; those on the west side have balconies with terrific views of Shoshone River Canyon. The facilities are also excellent, including the exercise room and indoor pool, and there are a number of special packages catering to anglers, rodeo-goers, and Yellowstone visitors.

232 W. Yellowstone Ave., Cody, WY 82414. www.thecody.com. ✆ **307/587-5915.** 75 units. Summer $209–$249 double; off-season $99–$169 double. Additional person $15. Rates include hot breakfast buffet. AE, DISC, MC, V. Pets accepted. **Amenities:** Exercise room; indoor Jacuzzi; small indoor pool. *In room:* A/C, TV/DVD, fridge, hair dryer, MP3 docking station, Wi-Fi (free).

Cody Cowboy Village ★   This is a couples-oriented resort in a family-oriented town. The "village," consisting of a cluster of cabin units near the rodeo grounds, is a world away from the bustling boardwalks of downtown Cody. The log cabins meld contemporary and cowboy in their decor. All have a deck in front; suites feature microwaves and fridges. Most units have one king bed, but six have two queens.

203 W. Yellowstone Ave., Cody, WY 82414. www.codycowboyvillage.com. ✆ **307/587-7555.** 50 units, including 10 suites. $79–$159 double; $109–$199 suite. Rates include continental breakfast. AE, MC, V. Closed Nov–Mar. **Amenities:** Small outdoor Jacuzzi. *In room:* TV, hair dryer, Wi-Fi (free).

The Irma Hotel ★   Buffalo Bill's entrepreneurial gusto ultimately left him penniless, but it also left us this century-old hotel (named for his daughter). Cody hoped to corral visitors who got off the train on their way to Yellowstone, and one of his lures was an elaborate cherrywood bar, a gift from straight-laced Queen Victoria. You can still hoist a jar on Her Royal Majesty's slab in the Silver Saddle Saloon, or spend the night in a renovated room that might have once housed a president or prince.

Suites are named after local characters from the town's early days: The Irma Suite, on the corner of the building, has a queen-size bed, a small sitting area, and an old-fashioned bathroom. While the Irma's aura will surely please history buffs, those acclimated to ultramodern convenience will probably want to look elsewhere. But the hotel's location in the middle of town helps compensate.

1192 Sheridan Ave., Cody, WY 82414. www.irmahotel.com. ✆ **800/745-4762** or 307/587-4221. Fax 307/587-1775. 73 units, including 15 restored suites. $112 double; $162 suite. Lower rates fall to spring. AE, DISC, MC, V. **Amenities:** Restaurant; lounge. *In room:* A/C, TV, hair dryer, Wi-Fi (free).

The Mayor's Inn ★★   This two-story A-frame, built in 1905 for Mayor Frank Houx, found itself in the path of a wrecking ball in 1997. However, new owners moved it on a truck to its current location, just a few blocks away. It's now one of Cody's best B&Bs, with rooms such as the Yellowstone, featuring a lodgepole-pine bed frame and black-and-white photos of the park's early years, and the Hart Mountain Suite, with romance and floral decor in spades. There's also a carriage house (breakfast not included) with a well-equipped kitchen. The breakfasts here are a hearty treat, featuring sourdough flapjacks and buffalo sausage, and innkeepers Bill and Dale Delph also run a gem of a dinner house here Thursday through Saturday nights in the summer (see "Where to Eat," later in this chapter).

1413 Rumsey Ave., Cody, WY 82414. www.mayorsinn.com. ✆ **888/217-3001** or 307/587-0887. 5 units, including 1 suite. $125–$160 double; $215 suite. Rates include full breakfast. AE, DISC, MC, V. **Amenities:** Restaurant. *In room:* A/C, TV, hair dryer, no phone, Wi-Fi (free).

GUEST RANCHES & RESORTS

Pahaska Tepee Resort ★   Buffalo Bill's hunting lodge, only 2 miles from the east entrance to Yellowstone, was dubbed with his Lakota name, *Pahaska* (Longhair), when he opened the lodge to park visitors in 1905. Near the top of the beautiful Wapiti Valley along U.S. Hwy. 14/16/20, Pahaska is a popular stop for people visiting the Yellowstone area. The cabins are scattered on the hill behind the historic (and colorfully decorated) lodge. Accommodations have limited amenities and might best be described as "minimotels" with two to five rooms, each with a private entrance. Some bathrooms have only showers, some have tubs—it's best to ask in advance. The resort also has a gift shop, a restaurant, and trail-ride stables.

183 Yellowstone Hwy., Cody, WY 82414. www.pahaska.com. ✆ **800/628-7791** or 307/527-7701. Fax 307/527-4019. 47 units. June–Aug $115–$175 double, $575 condo, $1,095 lodge; May and Sept to mid-Oct $70–$140 double, $450–$495 condo, $895–$995 lodge. DISC, MC, V. Closed mid-Oct to Apr. **Amenities:** Restaurant; lounge; Wi-Fi (free). *In room:* Kitchen.

Rimrock Ranch ★   Tucked along Canyon Creek at 6,300 feet above sea level, Rimrock Ranch has an intimate feel not found on larger dude ranches that's been honed since it opened in 1956. With a top capacity of three dozen guests, the cabins nestled alongside the creek are fairly modern and definitely a cut above some of the more "rustic" cabins in the area. The weekly package includes backcountry rides, rodeo trips, fishing, cookouts, and river floats. A small outdoor pool perches next to the lodge, with a view down the canyon. In summer, horse-packing trips are available.

2728 North Fork Rte., Cody, WY 82414. www.rimrockranch.com. ✆ **307/587-3970.** Fax 307/527-5014. 8 cabins. Mid-May to mid-Sept $1,650–$1,850 per adult, per week; $1,450 per child 6–18, per week; $400 per child 3–5, per week. Rates include all meals. DISC, MC, V (for deposits). Closed mid-Sept to mid-May. Drive 25 miles west of Cody on U.S. 16/20/14 (Yellowstone Hwy.); ranch is on the south side of highway. **Amenities:** Outdoor Jacuzzi; outdoor heated pool; Wi-Fi (free). *In room:* No phone.

7D Ranch ★★ ☺   Beautiful Sunlight Creek runs through this venerable ranch, which has a homey, lived-in quality missing in slicker operations. The Dominick family has owned the ranch for 50 years, and they know the nooks and crannies of the Sunlight Basin and the Beartooth Mountains, which guests explore on daylong rides, hikes, and fishing expeditions. Riding and casting lessons, skeet shooting, hiking, trips to Yellowstone, weekly dances, a weekly sweat lodge, and bonfires are all part of the package. And the cabins, cheerfully decorated with heaps of frontier charm and names like Big Buffalo, Racquet Club, and Waldorf have personality to spare. September is adults only, but the rest of the season the ranch is family-friendly, with numerous children's activities.

Sunlight Basin, P.O. Box 100, Cody, WY 82414. www.7dranch.com. ✆ **888/587-9885** or 307/587-9885. 10 cabins. Mid-May to mid-Sept $1,610–$1,875 per adult, per week; $1,050–$1,545 per child 3–12, per week. Rates include all meals, activities, and gratuities. MC, V. Closed mid-Sept to mid-May. Drive north from Cody on Wyo. 120 to Wyo. 296, then head west. Ranch is 50 miles from Cody via Sunlight Rd. **Amenities:** Children's programs; Wi-Fi (free). *In room:* No phone.

Where to Eat

For its size, Cody may have more good restaurants than you'd expect. If you need something less than a formal meal, such as a plateful of fuel food or a jolt of caffeine for a busy day, Cody has a good supply of familiar fast-food joints and a few informal, inexpensive places. **Peter's Cafe Bakery,** at 1219 Sheridan Ave. (www.peters-cafe. com; ℂ **307/527-5040**), across the street from the Irma, serves breakfast (freshly baked bagels, pastries, and espresso), plus subs and burgers for lunch and dinner. One of the best places day or night to get a steak or a beer and a burger (or Rocky Mountain oysters!) is the thoroughly Western **Proud Cut Saloon,** 1227 Sheridan Ave. (ℂ **307/527-6905**), where lots of rodeo riders keep a running tab.

Cassie's Supper Club ★★★ WESTERN Cassie's is the sort of classic road-house you might expect and look for in the West: big platters of beef, four bars serving drinks, and ornery roadhouse decor with taxidermy, antelope skulls, and assorted cowboy ephemera. This place has the routine down, having been in business since 1922. Located along the highway west of town in what was once a "house of ill fame," Cassie's is now very respectable and quite good. Besides the requisite steaks—grilled to perfection—there's seafood (including a great walleye dinner), pasta, and chicken, plus a full menu of specialty drinks. In the Buffalo Bar, a 20-foot mural depicts horses, cowboys, and shootouts. The dance floor bustles to the twang of live country music every night in summer.

214 Yellowstone Ave. www.cassies.com. ℂ **307/527-5500.** Reservations recommended. Lunch and Sun brunch $7–$25; dinner $12–$40. AE, DISC, MC, V. Daily 11am–10pm.

The Mayor's Inn Dining Room ★★ AMERICAN The Mayor's Inn is one of the very few establishments in Cody where you can get a room, a meal, and a drink. The restaurant is a great pick for a leisurely dinner: Innkeepers Dale and Bill Delph focus on just one seating an evening. The antiques-laden dining room has a nice air to it, and Bill showcases his culinary chops with steaks, seared elk medallions, buffalo meatloaf, and a regularly changing menu of flavorful preparations he dubs "regional fusion."

1413 Rumsey Ave. ℂ **307/587-0887.** Reservations recommended. Dinner main courses $17–$25. AE, DISC, MC, V. Summer Thurs–Sat 6–9pm.

Shiki ★★ SUSHI An anomalous standout in meat-and-potatoes Cody, Shiki is a superlative sushi bar. With spare Asian decor—consisting primarily of artfully hung cloth and an attractive water feature—matches the top-notch sushi rolls and tempura, teriyaki, and curry entrees. The sushi includes rolls like spicy tuna and eel, as well as a few regional variations—like the Heart Mountain, with crab, cucumber, avocado, and crunchy tempura flakes. Don't be alarmed by the lack of an ocean nearby: Fresh fish is flown in two to three times a week from both coasts.

1420 Sheridan Ave. ℂ **307/527-7116.** Reservations not accepted. Sushi rolls $5–$15; main courses $15–$26. AE, DISC, MC, V. Mon–Fri 11am–2pm and 4–9pm; Sat 11:30am–9pm; Sun 4–9pm.

Wyoming's Rib & Chop House ★★ STEAKS One of an upscale regional chain with locations in Billings and Livingston, Montana, among others, this is the place to head for everything from chicken-fried steaks to buffalo rib-eyes. Chicken and seafood round out the menu, but vegetarians will have difficulty finding a meatless main course. Desserts like "Pecan Meltaway"—a chocolate crust filled with ice cream, pecans, and more chocolate—provide decadent finales. A new bar opened in 2011.

1367 Sheridan Ave. www.ribandchophouse.com. ℂ **307/587-4917.** Lunch $6–$10; dinner $10–$33. AE, DISC, MC, V. Daily 11am–10:30pm. Shorter winter hours.

Cody After Dark

Cody has a lively nightlife, headed by **Cassie's,** 214 Yellowstone Ave. (© **307/527-5500**), with a dance floor laden with real and wannabe cowboys and cowgirls. Downtown, the historic **Silver Dollar Bar,** at 1313 Sheridan Ave. (© **307/527-7666**), has tasty burgers, live music, pool tables, and numerous TV screens. The two bars at the **Irma Hotel,** 1192 Sheridan Ave. (© **307/587-4221**), have historic character and plenty of local color. **Dan Miller's Music Revue,** 1549 Sheridan Ave. (www.cowboymusicrevue.com; © **307/272-7855**), offers a cowboy-style musical variety show Monday through Saturday at 8pm May through September. Tickets are $14.

A SIDE TRIP AROUND THE BIGHORN BASIN

Greybull: 40 miles E of Cody; 60 miles W of Sheridan

The prehistoric past of this region is written in the rock, and nowhere in Wyoming is that more true than in **Greybull,** named for a legendary albino bison sacred to American Indians. The town lies amid red-rock formations rich in fossils and archaeological treasures. The **Greybull Museum,** 325 Greybull Ave. (© **307/765-2444**), houses one of the largest fossil ammonites in the world, as well as petrified wood, agates, and American-Indian artifacts. This fine museum is open Monday through Saturday, 10am to 8pm from June to Labor Day, and more restricted hours in the winter, with free admission. Just north of town, you'll find a spectacular 15-mile-long, 2,000-foot-high natural fortress named **Sheep Mountain,** a textbook example of a "doubly plunging anticline," geo lingo for a natural arch folded into layered rock.

Greybull is a gateway town to the Bighorn Mountains on scenic U.S. 14 up Shell Canyon. Just 7 miles outside of town heading east is the **Stone Schoolhouse,** listed on the National Register of Historic Places. The one-room schoolhouse was built in 1903 of locally quarried sandstone and, in recent years, was converted to a bookstore/gallery, though its hours are unpredictable. Less than a mile farther along the highway, turn south on Red Gulch Road and drive 5 miles to a signed parking area where you can view dinosaur tracks. Driving east from Greybull, U.S. 14 climbs through steep and beautiful **Shell Canyon.**

Fifty miles south of Greybull and east through little Hyattville brings you to the **Medicine Lodge State Archaeological Site** (http://wyoparks.state.wy.us; © **307/469-2234**), where prehistoric peoples decorated the sandstone cliffs along Medicine Lodge Creek with carved petroglyphs and painted pictographs of hunting scenes. You can fish the small stream for brown trout. There is a shady, inexpensive, 26-site campground here, open May through October, with no RV hookups. To reach the site and campground, take Wyo. 789/U.S. 16/20 for 20 miles from Greybull to Manderson, and then drive 22 miles along Wyo. 31 to Hyattville. In Hyattville, drive north and turn right onto Cold Springs Road. Follow the signs 5 miles to the site. There is no day-use fee; campsites are $11 for nonresidents.

THERMOPOLIS

84 miles S of Cody; 130 miles NW of Casper; 218 miles E of Jackson

Steaming water cascades over pastel-colored terraces and down to the Bighorn River at Hot Springs State Park, one of the undiscovered treasures of Wyoming. Trumpeted as the largest hot springs in the world (it's not quite: New Zealand's Whakarewarewa rightfully claims that honor), the 134°F (57°C) water from the Big Spring supplies two indoor/outdoor pool facilities, two hotels, and a state-run soaking spa. The town of Thermopolis grew up around the hot springs after it was sold to the U.S. government by the tribes of the Wind River Indian Reservation in 1896. Developers dreamed of a health spa to rival Saratoga, but it never quite happened. What did happen is a small, peaceful town with a great place to soak or slide, a nearby canyon of exciting white water, and surrounding hills holding a trove of dinosaur bones and prehistoric petroglyphs.

Essentials

GETTING THERE   The closest airports are the **Riverton Regional Airport,** 55 miles south of Thermopolis, off U.S. 26 West at 4700 Airport Rd. (www.flyriverton.com; ☏ 307/856-1307), and Cody's **Yellowstone Regional Airport,** 84 miles northeast, at Duggleby Drive (www.flyyra.com; ☏ 307/587-5096). There is a small airport in Thermopolis used by private fliers.

United and **Frontier** fly into Riverton. Cody service is provided by **United** and **Delta.**

To reach Thermopolis from Cody, drive 84 miles southeast on Wyo. 120. From Cheyenne, drive north on I-25 to Casper (178 miles), west on U.S. 20/26 to Shoshoni (98 miles), and north on U.S. 20 to Thermopolis. From Rock Springs, take U.S. 191 to Farson, Wyo. 28 to Lander, and Wyo. 789 through Riverton and Shoshoni to Thermopolis.

VISITOR INFORMATION   The **Thermopolis Chamber of Commerce,** 220 Park St., Thermopolis, WY 82443 (www.thermopolis.com; ☏ 877/864-3192), sends out packets of information about local attractions.

GETTING AROUND   If you've arrived by plane at one of the area airports, you'll need to rent a car to get around. **Hertz** (☏ 800/654-3131) maintains counters at both the Riverton and Cody airports.

Getting Outside

Hot Springs State Park (see the detailed listing below) offers a variety of outdoor activities, from splashing in mineral water to picnicking on the lawn. South and upstream on the Bighorn River is twisting **Wind River Canyon,** a tricky but bountiful fishing and floating section (you'll need permits from the Wind River Indian Reservation), topped by 19,000-acre **Boysen Reservoir,** about 20 minutes from Thermopolis on U.S. 20. The campgrounds ($17 a site, which includes the requisite $6 day-use fee for nonresidents) on the largely treeless shore of this state park can be a bit buggy and hot in August, but the water attracts boaters to sail, fish, and water-ski. There are three small public beach areas on the reservoir's northeastern and western shores. For more information on the park, contact **Boysen State Park,** Boysen Route, Shoshoni, WY 82649 (http://wyoparks.state.wy.us; ☏ 307/876-2796), or call Wyoming State Parks and Historic Sites headquarters in Cheyenne at ☏ 307/777-6323.

FISHING

Whether you like fishing lakes or streams, this area has trophy-size opportunities— Boysen grows record-setting walleye, as well as trout and perch, while the Bighorn River grows some fat brown and cutthroat trout. Check locally to be sure you've got the right fishing license: The canyon requires a tribal permit; the reservoir and other stretches of river require a state license—both available at local sporting-goods stores. If you have your own boat, or hire an outfitter, you can float and fish from the bottom of the canyon at the Wedding of the Waters (where there's a wheelchair-accessible boat ramp) to Thermopolis. During the warmest part of summer, algae can darken the river and hamper fishing, but spring and fall are anglers' dreams.

GOLF

The **Legion Town and Country Golf Course** is a 9-hole course that overlooks the city from Airport Hill. Call ℂ **307/864-5294** to book a tee time at affordable prices—9 holes for $20 or less, depending on the time of year. The pro shop offers cart rentals, a driving range, and lessons.

HIKING

A boardwalk allows you to explore the bulbous travertine terraces without scalding your soles in the hot-spring water that flows over them. The paths extend to a suspended footbridge across the Bighorn River and a riverside walkway below. For more earnest hikers, there is the approximately 6-mile **Volksmarch Trail,** one of several around the state that are marked with a trademark brown-and-yellow insignia. This one loops through the park and downtown Thermopolis. Just north of town off U.S. 20, you can hike **T Hill** for a bird's-eye view of Thermopolis, the Wind River Canyon, and the Owl Creek Mountains. The 2-mile round-trip up **Roundtop Mountain** is another rewarding hike, culminating in spectacular views of the Hot Springs and Thermopolis, with the trail head beginning near the Monument Hill Cemetery on Airport Road.

WHITE-WATER RAFTING ★★

The tribes of the **Wind River Indian Reservation** virtually gave away the hot springs, but not the canyon upstream, through which the Wind River tumbles and twists (for reasons no one can explain, the Wind River becomes the Bighorn River as it leaves the canyon). A Shoshone-owned company now takes rafters through rapids named after historic tribal figures like Chief Washakie and Sharp Nose. "Sphincter Rapid" is not an Indian name, but it descriptively tells you that there are some Class III to IV white-water thrills ahead. You can run half the canyon or the entire thing, take a more leisurely fishing trip, or camp overnight with **Wind River Canyon Whitewater,** 210 U.S. 20 S., Ste. 5, Thermopolis (www.windrivercanyonraft.com; ℂ **888/246-9343** or 307/864-9343 in season, 307/486-2253 during off season). White-water trips run $30 to $45 for a half-day or $90 for a full day.

Hot Springs State Park ★★

Few state parks in Wyoming are as nice as **Hot Springs** (http://wyoparks.state.wy.us; ℂ **307/864-2176**), with its shady trees, striking flower gardens, and a stretch of the Bighorn River running through it, as well as a roaming buffalo herd and the main event: the magnificent hot springs, with some of its water funneled into swimming pools and slides. It's located at the north side of town off U.S. 20, and admission is free. The park's only shortcoming is that you can't camp overnight, which must please nearby private campgrounds and lodgings. As a Wyoming tourist attraction, the hot springs places a distant third to Yellowstone and Grand Teton national parks, but the sparse crowds allow Thermopolis to retain its small-town style.

At the north end of the park, you can climb a few stairs to look down into the bottomless blue-green depths of the Big Spring—the placid surface belies the fact that the spring pumps out around 15 million gallons a day.

An annual production, the pageant reenacts the sale of the hot springs and surrounding lands by the Shoshone and Arapaho peoples to the federal government in 1896. The pageant portrays the sale as an act of peace and neighborly brotherhood. In fact, the tribes were starving and desperate. Indians from Wind River play some of the roles in the pageant. The pageant is performed annually during the first weekend in August, along with a powwow. Contact the **Thermopolis Chamber of Commerce** (✆ **877/864-3192**) for information.

SOAKING IN THE BATHS

You can't just plop yourself down in this 134°F (57°C) water, but there are three bathing facilities in the park. To get to them, take the loop road; at the north end are the bathing areas. First, and simplest, is the **State Bath House ★** (✆ **307/864-2176**), a small spa open to the public free of charge, thanks to famed Shoshone Chief Washakie. When the tribes sold the federal government the hot springs in 1896—it would later become state property—Washakie noted that the springs had always been a place of peace and neutrality among tribes and should therefore always be free to all people. The small, clean indoor and outdoor pools aren't for frolicking or swimming laps—just soaking, wading, and perhaps conversing with some of the old-timers who come here. Soaks are limited to 20 minutes per session. You can rent a towel, locker, and bathing suit for about a dollar each, and it's open Monday through Saturday from 8am to 5:30pm, Sunday from noon to 5:30pm. On either side of this peaceful place are the more raucous commercial pools.

STAR PLUNGE The big lure at **Star Plunge** (www.starplunge.com; ✆ **307/864-3771**) is its three big slides—the kids' favorite "Little Dipper," the outdoor "Super Star," and the enclosed "Blue Thunder," the latter a 300-foot spin around a 60-foot tower that will thrill you to your claustrophobic, free-falling toes. Indoor and outdoor pools, hot tubs, Jacuzzis, a snack bar, and an arcade make this the favorite of the young set. On a crowded summer afternoon, there are lines at the slides, splashing all around, and a teenage volume level, but you can still find stillness in the "vapor cave." Admission is $10 for children 5 and over and adults, $5 for children 4 and under, $8 for seniors. It's open daily from 9am to 9pm year-round.

HELLIE'S TEPEE POOLS Hellie's Teepee Pools (www.tepeepools.com; ✆ **307/864-9250**) is a little more peaceful under its big dome than its neighbor to the east, but it has its share of lively teens and a contingent of young families. The slides are not as big here, but you can hear yelps of delight as bodies zip down the twisting indoor open tube. There is a fast-moving open slide outdoors, too, and often a wet basketball game in the roomy outdoor pool. Soaking pools, a steam room, a sauna, and a game room complete the scene. Admission is $10 for ages 6 to 61, $5 for ages 5 and under, and $8 for 62 and over. Open daily from 9am to 9pm.

Seeing the Sights

Hot Springs County Historical Museum and Cultural Center The original cherrywood bar from the Hole-in-the-Wall Saloon—Butch Cassidy's hangout—is the biggest draw at this local museum, which has some gems among the musty clutter of historical artifacts. Alongside a trove of Native-American weaponry and art, various modes of transportation are represented, including a caboose and a stagecoach used to tour Yellowstone. Other exhibits trace the local economic threads, primarily coal mining, petroleum extraction, and agriculture. On the lower level are a fully outfitted print shop, general store, and dentist's office. The museum's cultural center features local artwork and crafts on a rotating basis. Expect to spend an hour.

700 Broadway. www.hschistory.org. © **307/864-5183.** Admission $4 adults, $2 seniors 60 and over and children 6–12, free for children 5 and under. Memorial Day to Labor Day Mon–Sat 9am–5pm; rest of year Tues–Sat 9am–4pm.

Legend Rock Petroglyph Site ★ 📷

Petroglyphs—prehistoric drawings inscribed in rock—are scattered throughout the foothills of Wyoming's mountains. Legend Rock is one of the richest petroglyph sites in the Rockies, and it is managed—rather informally—by state agents at Hot Springs State Park (© **307/864-2176**). Visitors can pick up a gate key at the State Bath House and then drive up Wyo. 120 to the Hamilton Dome turnoff, then continue 8 miles west, partly on a dirt road, to the site. There you can hike up and down Cottonwood Creek to find pecked representations of turtle-like creatures, birds, hunters, and musicians. To get a good view of some of the panels, you need to scramble up on ledges. Weather has taken its toll on this soft sandstone, and so have souvenir hunters—hands off, please! Be sure to ask for a map to the site when you pick up the key; the route is not well marked. You can drive down by the creek, but you're better off, particularly when it's wet and muddy, parking up by the gate and taking the short hike down.

Near Hamilton Dome, 27 miles northwest of Thermopolis. For information, contact Hot Springs State Park (© **307/864-2176**) or the Thermopolis Chamber of Commerce (© **307/864-3192**). Free admission. Pick up key at park or Chamber of Commerce Mon–Fri 8am–5pm, or at the park only Sat 8am–5pm, Sun noon–5pm.

Outlaw Trail Ride

Butch Cassidy was a well-known character around Thermopolis, although not by any means the only outlaw who favored this rugged country. Visitors who want to relive a Wild West getaway can join the annual Outlaw Trail Ride in August and journey 100 miles up through the dry, hidden canyons of Hole-in-the-Wall country. Only about 25 riders can participate in the weeklong event, and it's popular, so book well in advance. You must BYO horse and sleep on the ground.

Outlaw Trail, Inc., P.O. Box 1046, Thermopolis, WY 82443. www.rideoutlawtrail.com. © **307/330-4350.** $1,200 per rider. The ride occurs annually in early Aug.

Wyoming Dinosaur Center & Dig Sites ★ ☺

This dinosaur museum is located right at the site where modern-day paleontologists have unearthed dinosaur bones from the Jurassic period. There are 20 full skeletons on display at the center, as well as eggs, shells, and other remnants from around the world. Except in winter, visitors can take guided tours of dig sites and then watch workers clean and prepare bones in the laboratory at the center. Visitors can also get dirty with the center's Dig for a Day program ($150 per adult, $80 per child 4–13); reservations are required.

110 Carter Ranch Rd., Thermopolis, WY 82443. www.wyodino.org. © **800/455-3466** or 307/864-2997. Museum: $10 adults, $5.50 children 4–13 and seniors 60 and over, free for children 3 and under. Dig site: $13 adults, $8.75 children 4–13 and seniors 60 and over, free for children 3 and under. Combination museum and dig site tour: $19 adults, $12 children 4–13 and seniors 60 and over, free for children 3 and under. Summer daily 8am–6pm; museum winter daily 10am–5pm. Closed major holidays. Dig site closed in winter.

Where to Stay

Thermopolis has a number of motels and campgrounds with a little age on them, so if you're arriving in the busy summer season you should have a reservation, or risk landing in a room with the amenities of a closet. Recently, chain affiliates have taken a new interest in lodgings here, so the choices are growing.

Best Western Plus–The Plaza Hotel ★ If you'd rather not have a wildebeest staring at you on your way to breakfast (see Days Inn Hot Springs Convention Center, below), but still want to be in the park (and just an easy walk from the pools), try this alternative, a funky old brick place that once operated as a hostel but now has been nicely fixed up. Centered on a pleasant inner courtyard, the 1918 structure is on the National Register of Historic Places, and the aura is more urban inn than chain motel. Several of the rooms and suites still have working fireplaces.

116 E. Park St. (P.O. Box 866), in Hot Springs State Park, Thermopolis, WY 82443. www.bestwestern wyoming.com. © **800/528-1234** or 307/864-2939. 36 units. $110–$150 double; $145–$165 suite. Reduced rates in winter. Rates include continental breakfast. AE, DC, DISC, MC, V. **Amenities:** Outdoor Jacuzzi; outdoor pool. *In room:* A/C, TV, hair dryer, Wi-Fi (free).

Days Inn Hot Springs Convention Center ★ ☺ Formerly the Holiday Inn of the Waters, this is no cookie-cutter Days Inn—it's a hot-springs resort along the Bighorn River within Hot Springs State Park. The huge volume of superheated water that surges from the upturned sandstones is piped into the outdoor Jacuzzi next to the big pool. If lolling under the stars doesn't soften you up, take a turn in the health club and submit to the ministrations of a licensed masseuse. Unique to this property as a Days Inn are its location in the park, several "classic" 1970s-style rooms, and frequent promotions (like the Hot Water Holiday Package: 2 nights, dinner, and champagne for two for $209–$220 from Sept–May). Certainly, no other Days Inn has a restaurant like the Safari Room, arrayed with enough big-game trophies from around the world to make Ernest Hemingway blush and vegetarians gag.

115 E. Park St. (P.O. Box 1323), in Hot Springs State Park, Thermopolis, WY 82443. www.thermopolis daysinn.com. © **800/329-7466** or 307/864-3131. 80 units. $90–$150 double. Rates include complimentary continental breakfast. AE, DC, DISC, MC, V. **Amenities:** Restaurant; lounge; health club; outdoor Jacuzzi; outdoor pool; sauna. *In room:* A/C, TV, hair dryer, Wi-Fi (free).

Super 8 Thermopolis ☺ The tile-roofed Southwest style of architecture distinguishes this new motel from other Super 8's and from the many older, somewhat drab lodgings in Thermopolis. Inside, the decor is fairly typical, but there is a big indoor pool, a pleasant lobby and eating area for the full breakfast, and a honeymoon suite with a marble Jacuzzi. And it's a good bet for kids, offering eight family rooms, each with a bunk bed, two queen-size beds, a VCR, and a Nintendo for only $15 extra.

Lane 5 S., Hwy. 20, Thermopolis, WY 82443. www.super8.com. © **800/800-8000** or 307/864-5515. Fax 307/864-5447. 52 units, including 1 suite. Summer $89–$129 double, $189–$229 suite; winter $65–$99 double, $189–$229 suite. Rates include full breakfast. AE, DISC, MC, V. **Amenities:** Indoor Jacuzzi; indoor heated pool. *In room:* A/C, TV/VCR (in some), hair dryer, Wi-Fi (free).

CAMPING

The **Fountain of Youth RV Park** (www.fountainofyouthrvpark.com; © **307/864-3265**) has tent and RV sites available year-round and is located 1½ miles north of town by the river on U.S. 20. The campground features a large hot mineral spring pool, barbecue grills, showers, laundry room, dump station, and camp store. RV sites cost $33 to $35 for two people (tent sites are $30 for two). When things are busy in the summer, you may find yourself overhearing the unmuffled conversation of the Harley riders parked in the next slot. Open April through October, the **Eagle RV Park** (www.eaglervpark.com; ✆ **888/865-5707** or 307/864-5262) offers RV sites for about $32, tent sites for $20, and log cabins for $40 to $70—and peace and quiet. It's located at 204 S. U.S. 20, just south of Thermopolis.

Where to Eat

The **Safari Room** at the Days Inn (see "Where to Stay") is your best bet for a nice dinner in Thermopolis.

Pumpernick's 🍴 AMERICAN   The three rooms where meals are served at Pumpernick's clearly weren't designed as a restaurant, but the bric-a-brac-bedecked quarters add a friendly intimacy to good food. In the summer, you can escape the elbows by eating outside in the roomy adjacent arbor. Pumpernick's serves burgers, salads, and plump specialty sandwiches for lunch. Dinner features steaks and seafood, including salmon and shrimp scampi. The place bakes its own breads, which it uses for sandwiches and dinner rolls. Try the brownie sundae for a melt-in-your-mouth chocolate treat.

512 Broadway. ✆ **307/864-5151.** Main courses $6–$9 lunch; $11–$18 dinner. AE, DISC, MC, V. Mon–Sat 11am–9pm.

WIND RIVER VALLEY

Riverton: 164 miles E of Jackson; 140 miles N of Rock Springs; 140 miles S of Cody

The deep curve of the Wind River Valley is shaped by the snowcapped Wind River Range to the West and the Absaroka and Owl Creek ranges on the east, forming a cottonwood-lined bottom that many consider one of the most beautiful areas in Wyoming. A sizable portion of the valley belongs to the Eastern Shoshone and Northern Arapaho tribes of the **Wind River Indian Reservation,** where there is considerable poverty but also productive ranches and spectacular wilderness reaching up to the Continental Divide. The largest towns are Riverton and Lander, but there are smaller communities like Dubois, Shoshoni, Fort Washakie, and the historic gold-mining town of Atlantic City.

Riverton

Notched in a big bend of the Wind River is **Riverton,** a settlement that was carved out when the federal government opened the northern portion of the reservation to non-Indian people a century ago. Riverton has established itself as a retail commercial center for west-central Wyoming. Contact the **Riverton Area Chamber of Commerce,** 213 W. Main St., Riverton, WY 82501 (www.rivertonchamber.org; ✆ **307/856-4801**), for information, including useful suggestions for day trips in the area and a list of events. That calendar includes a summer **Riverton Rendezvous and Balloon Rally,** held during the second and third weeks in July, when colorful balloons from all over the Rockies rise against the majestic backdrop of the Wind River Range, and the town puts on arts and crafts fairs, a demolition derby, a family dinner with live entertainment, and even a treasure hunt. Also in July, there is the nostalgic **1838 Rendezvous** (www.1838rendezvous.com), staged at the junction of the Wind River and the Little Wind River, with black-powder shooting, Indian dancing, tomahawk throws, and bead trading. Come wintertime, the February **Wild West**

Winter Carnival has drag races, ice sculpting, and fishing derbies on the frozen surface of Boysen Reservoir.

GETTING THERE The **Riverton Regional Airport,** 4700 Airport Rd. (www.fly riverton.com; ✆ **307/856-1307**), is served by **United** and **Frontier.** By car, from Thermopolis, take U.S. 20 south through scenic Wind River Canyon to Shoshoni, then U.S. 26 south to Riverton.

WHERE TO STAY If you plan to stay overnight in Riverton, your best bet is the **Holiday Inn** (✆ **877/857-4834** or 307/856-8100). Located at 900 E. Sunset Dr., it has 122 rooms that rent for $109 to $159 double. Or you could head 24 miles farther west on Wyo. 789 to **Lander** (see below).

Lander

If you head 24 miles farther west of Riverton on Wyo. 789, you hit **Lander,** tucked snugly into the foothills of the Wind River Range where the three fingers of the Popo Agie River draw together. When railroads were the nation's primary mode of travel, Lander was "where the rails end and the trails begin": the takeoff point for backcountry trips to hunt, fish, or explore the lake-dotted wilderness that climbs to the Continental Divide. The trains are gone, but this is still where you put on your hiking or riding boots. For more information, contact the **Lander Area Chamber of Commerce,** 160 N. 1st St., Lander, WY 82520 (www.landerchamber.org; ✆ **800/433-0662** or 307/332-3892).

Just west of town on Wyo. 131 is **Sinks Canyon State Park** (http://wyoparks.state.wy.us; ✆ **307/332-3077** or 332-6333), where the Middle Fork of the Popo Agie disappears into a limestone cave and reappears farther down the canyon at a pool with an overlook where you can feed kibble to giant trout (no hooks allowed!). Day use is $6. The park has a nature trail, a visitor center with naturalist displays, a campground ($17 a night, includes day-use fee), and tumbling waterfalls for those willing to hike some switchbacks. For a different kind of experience, drive south 37 miles on U.S. 287 to the **South Pass City Historical Site** (http://wyoparks.state.wy.us; ✆ **307/332-3684**), which re-creates a gold-mining town from the 1860s and where Esther Hobart Morris became the nation's first female justice of the peace. There is a $6 day-use fee.

Lander has a justly famous **Fourth of July parade and Pioneer Days Rodeo,** and later in July it hosts the **International Climber's Festival** (www.climbersfestival.org). Slide shows by climbing greats, clinics, an equipment show, and climbers testing their mettle on the walls of Sinks Canyon and Wild Iris draw hundreds of serious climbers to the event. Some of the climbers are residents here, partly thanks to the **National Outdoor Leadership School ★**, which has been teaching outdoor types responsible ways of enjoying the wilds since 1965 and now has branches all over the world. For course offerings from India to the Rocky Mountains, write the school's Lander headquarters at 284 Lincoln St., Lander, WY 82520 (www.nols.edu; ✆ **800/710-6657** or 307/332-5300).

If you want an exotic element to your trail adventure, try the **Lander Llama Company,** 2024 Mortimore Lane, Lander, WY 82520 (www.landerllama.com; ✆ **307/332-5624**). Their naturalist-led Red Desert trip is as enlightening as it is enjoyable, incorporating ancient American-Indian history and fossil viewing with stunning Wyoming scenery. Three-day trips start at $750 per adult and $705 per child 12 and under. If you'd prefer to horse around, check out **Allen's Diamond Four**

Ranch, P.O. Box 243, Lander, WY 82520 (www.diamond4ranch.com; ✆ **307/332-2995**), for guided horseback tours in the Popo Agie Wilderness and Wind River Range. The ranch's overnight accommodations are barebones—woodstoves, propane lights, bring your own bedding—but the emphasis is on riding, fishing, and seeing the high country. Trips are about $350 per person, per day on the trail; $300 per person, per day for groups of four or more. There are special programs for kids.

Winter transforms this country into a snowmobiler's playground, with 250 miles of the **Continental Divide Trail** from Lander to Yellowstone. Call the **Wind River Visitors Council** (www.wind-river.org; ✆ **800/645-6233**) or the Lander Area Chamber of Commerce (see above) for information on this and other trails.

WHERE TO STAY & EAT

As far as lodging and grub go, there are quite a few options in Lander, from pizzerias and roadside motels to supper clubs and historic B&Bs. The **Pronghorn Rodeway Inn,** 150 E. Main St. (www.pronghornlodge.com; ✆ **800/424-6423** or 307/332-3940), is a reliable choice, with frontier-style trappings and a riverfront setting. Standard doubles run $70 to $130. The Lander Llama Company (see above) rents the **Bunk House,** a stylishly rustic cabin (with a kitchenette) on the Popo Agie River, for $115 a night or $575 a week in high season ($60 a night in winter), with a five-guest limit. If you *really* want to get away from it all, head to **Louis Lake Lodge,** about 30 miles down the highway and 9 miles down a dirt road from Lander, at 1811 Louis Lake Rd. (www.louislake.com; ✆ **307/330-7571**), where there is no electricity and most cellphones don't work. Cabins are a reasonable $80 to $200 a night, and lodge rooms go for $100 to $140 nightly; there are discounts for longer stays. For dining, try the **Gannett Grill,** 126 Main St. (www.landerbar.com; ✆ **307/332-2228**), with a more-interesting-than-it-sounds menu of thick burgers, sandwiches, pizzas, and salads. Under the same ownership next door is **Cowfish,** 128 Main St. (www.landerbar.com; ✆ **307/332-8227**), which specializes in beef and seafood and has an organic garden on-site. There is a jointly managed microbrewery here as well.

Wind River Indian Reservation

The starting point for a tour of the Wind River Indian Reservation is Fort Washakie, located 14 miles north of Lander on U.S. 287, or 146 miles from Jackson (U.S. 26/89/191 to Moran Junction, then U.S. 287 over Togwotee Pass to Dubois and then on to the reservation).

More than 2 million acres of the **Wind River Indian Reservation** surround the town of Riverton, encompassing an area that stretches 70 miles east to west and 55 miles north to south. Wyoming's sole reservation is home to more than 2,500 Eastern Shoshone and 5,000 Northern Arapaho tribal members, governed by a council made up of representatives from both tribes.

The Shoshone were given a huge reservation to buffer westward travelers from more hostile tribes to the north, such as the Sioux and Blackfeet. A reservation that once included parts of Wyoming, Utah, and Colorado was reduced greatly when non-Indians discovered gold, grazing land, and water on tribal lands. Today, the Wind River Indian Reservation is a still-sizable 2.2 million acres, including oil and gas fields, several small communities, and some of the most pristine wilderness—and best fishing—in the United States.

The Northern Arapaho came to Wind River in the late 1870s for what they thought was a temporary placement before moving to their own reservation farther east.

However, government promises were forgotten or ignored, and the Arapaho settled in to stay. The two tribes have unrelated languages and a history of warfare, but their relationship has gradually improved.

There is poverty and high unemployment on the reservation, but there is pride, too, quite evident at the powwows. Outsiders are welcome at these dances, which are held May through September at various sites (the Wind River Visitors Council can provide a schedule; www.wind-river.org; 𝄞 800/645-6233), where you'll see a more open, friendly side of the Arapaho and Shoshone, as long as you are respectful. Sun dances are more spiritual affairs, and while visitors are not banned, these moving ceremonies are not for tourists, and no photographs or videos are allowed.

Services for visitors are not well developed on the reservation, but you can learn more about the Shoshone tribe at the **Eastern Shoshone Tribal Cultural Center** (𝄞 307/332-9106) in Fort Washakie, and about the Arapaho tribe at the **St. Stephen's Mission** (𝄞 307/856-7806).

Sacajawea, the famed Shoshone scout for the Lewis and Clark expedition, is supposedly buried on a reservation that bears her name, west of Fort Washakie. There is some debate about whether she is buried there, but it's a beautiful cemetery on a hill and worth a visit (ask for directions in Fort Washakie). You might also stop by nearby **Roberts Mission**—John Roberts was an Episcopal minister who lived most of his life on the reservation and had a tremendous influence on the tribes, founding a school and recording useful historical and anthropological information about the tribes. Chief Washakie, the venerated Shoshone chief, is buried in a cemetery along the Little Wind River on the north side of Fort Washakie. He lived to be more than 100 years old and was buried with full honors by the U.S. Army—the only Indian chief to be so honored.

In late June, **Eastern Shoshone Powwow and Indian Days** is one of the West's largest powwows and all–American Indian rodeos, including thrilling bareback relay horse races.

There are hundreds of lakes in the reservation's high country, and in the summer they come alive with trout—browns, cutthroats, brook, and golden. You can purchase a reservation fishing permit at local sporting-goods stores and find your way with maps to Bull and Moccasin lakes by car, or pick up USGS topographical maps and head for the high country on foot. Check with the fly-tying experts at **Rocky Mountain Dubbing Company,** 115 Poppy St. (www.rmdstore.com; 𝄞 800/866-4094 or 307/332-2989), off U.S. 287 just south of Lander, for permits, maps, equipment, and advice.

SHERIDAN & EASTERN WYOMING

A s you enter Wyoming from the east, the plains begin to roll like ocean swells, rising and falling until they break against the Rockies. As the elevation rises, the grass grows shorter. Rains taper from dependable downpours to sporadic cloudbursts. The wind races across the surface, combing down the grass and sculpting the snow.

Bison once roamed these prairies in enormous herds, and people were few. But the modern era brought rapid change. In the 18th century, Indian bands mounted horses that had escaped from Spanish conquistadors and enjoyed a brief era of prosperity on the plains, hunting buffalo with great skill. Then the white people arrived: trappers searching for beaver pelts, and pioneers who wanted to either settle here or just pass through on their way to Utah, California, or Oregon. But it was the Texas trail drives, moving north, not west, that most shaped the history and culture of eastern Wyoming.

The landscape hasn't changed much since then. There are still widely scattered settlements; a few small, irrigated fields; and lots of grass and cattle. The billboards announce WELCOME TO THE COWBOY STATE, but these days, it's more often the coal and oil and gas beneath the prairies that subsidize the human population in these wide-open spaces. But the cowboy life is still vibrant and friendly to visitors: You can see rodeos or join a cattle drive, or just buy a hat and pair of boots and pretend. You can explore the mostly unchanged landscapes where cattle barons and their hired guns battled homesteaders in the Johnson County War, where outlaw Butch Cassidy and the Hole-in-the-Wall gang did their "work," and Indian chiefs Crazy Horse and Red Cloud clashed with the cavalry.

Adventurers come to climb **Devils Tower,** a natural skyscraper of volcanic rock that suddenly rises more than 1,000 feet from the flatlands of eastern Wyoming. Visitors also come to hike and fish in the Bighorn Mountains, a handsome range somewhat overshadowed by the peaks of the Continental Divide farther west.

You can explore this region by interstate—I-25 runs north–south, while I-90 dips down from Montana and then east to Gillette and Devils Tower—or take small highways like U.S. 18 and Wyo. 59 to reach smaller towns and more remote country. But since Sheridan is often the target of travelers to the area, this chapter begins there, exploring south to Buffalo and then east to Gillette and Devils Tower before backtracking to Casper, Wyoming's second-largest city.

SHERIDAN

144 miles N of Casper; 130 miles S of Billings; 156 miles E of Cody

Sheridan looks right at home where the Rockies meet the plains, its deep roots evident in its well-preserved historic downtown. The Bighorn Mountains cast afternoon shadows in this direction, across the ranches in the foothills where dude ranching was defined and perfected. One of the largest of Wyoming's small towns, with about 16,000 residents, Sheridan, named after Civil War general Philip Sheridan, retains its small-town charm with century-old buildings along Main Street and the mansions of cattle barons.

The source of prosperity in more recent times lies in the massive coal deposits to the north and east. After decades of production, the big strip mines are in a slow decline, and tourism is on the rise, with an influx of adventurous mountain bikers, rock climbers, paragliders, snowmobilers, and cross-country skiers who are lured by the Bighorns. Ranching these days is less about beef and more about providing saddle time for vacation dudes and retreats for wealthy corporate kings. Or queens—Queen Elizabeth of England, who has distant relations here, stopped by in the 1980s, and like any sensible horsewoman would, she dropped by **King's Saddlery,** known worldwide for hand-tooled tack and ropes.

Essentials

GETTING THERE   The **Sheridan County Airport** (www.sheridancountyairport. com; © 307/674-4222), just southwest of town on Airport Road (take exit 25 off I-90), has daily service from Denver on United affiliate **Great Lakes Airlines,** as well as **Frontier.**

If you drive from Billings, take I-90 south 130 miles to Sheridan. From Sheridan, you can continue south on I-90 and then I-25, sliding along the eastern side of the Bighorn Mountains, 147 miles to Casper, or drive the full 325 miles to Cheyenne. From Yellowstone and Cody, follow U.S. 14 across the basin and over the Bighorns, and drop into Ranchester, where you'll take I-25 15 miles south to Sheridan.

VISITOR INFORMATION   **Sheridan Travel and Tourism,** P.O. Box 7155, Sheridan, WY 82801 (www.sheridanwyoming.org; © 888/596-6787 or 307/673-7120), is located at the State Information Center, off I-90 at exit 23. Across 5th Street is the **Wyoming Game and Fish Visitors Center** (© 307/672-7418), with information on wildlife habitats, fishing, hunting regulations, and the best places to spot wildlife.

GETTING AROUND   You can rent a car from **Avis** (© 800/230-4898) or **Budget** (© 800/527-0700) at Sheridan's airport. In summer, there is a trolley that runs from the visitor center to downtown and other destinations; fare is $1. Or call **Sheridan Taxi Service** (© 307/674-6814).

SPECIAL EVENTS   Held every Labor Day Weekend, **Don King Days** attracts about 1,500 people to the Big Horn Equestrian Center. Named for late, great local saddle-maker Don King, the event is a rodeo with few fences—spectators get a great view of the action. Call **Sheridan Travel and Tourism** (see above) for additional information.

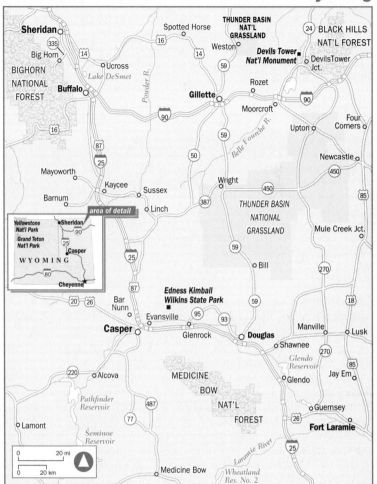

Getting Outside

The **Bighorn National Forest** offers some of the best outdoor recreation in the country, with hundreds of miles of marked trails for hiking, mountain biking, cross-country skiing, snowshoeing, and snowmobiling; plus campgrounds, fishing streams, and fantastic wildlife-viewing opportunities. For maps and advice, contact the forest headquarters and Tongue Ranger District office, 2013 Eastside 2nd St. (www.fs.usda.gov/bighorn; ☎ **307/674-2600**).

In town, there is an excellent trail network dubbed **community walkways.** Pick up a map at the visitor center at I-90, exit 23.

BC Bike and Mountain Works, 330 N. Main St. (℡ 307/672-2453), is a full-service mountain-bike facility with sales, repairs, and rentals, as well as a nice assortment of backpacking and camping gear.

Ron Spahn of **Spahn's Big Horn Mountain Bed and Breakfast** (℡ 307/674-8150) offers daylong tours of the area, with a focus on the off-the-beaten-path sites that are representative of the "real West," looking at Indian history and modern social problems, mining and environmental issues, outlaw hideouts, wildlife, and the wild horses of the Pryor Mountains. Ron drives customers in a four-wheel-drive vehicle and offers a field lunch and an engaging, educated perspective. His tours run $95 per person, with a $325 minimum.

The scenic drive, the **Bighorn Mountain Loop** (p. 345), can easily be undertaken with Sheridan as the starting or ending point, or as both.

EQUESTRIAN EVENTS

Polo? In Wyoming? Well, they ride horses, don't they? Introduced by early English cattle barons, the tradition continues with matches every summer Sunday at the **Big Horn Equestrian Center,** south of Sheridan near the town of Big Horn on Bird Farm Rd. (www.thebighornpoloclub.com; ℡ 307/674-4928), and Thursday and Saturday at the **Flying H Polo Club,** just west on Bird Farm Rd. (www.flyinghpolo. com; ℡ 307/674-9447). Admission is free (unless a benefit match is scheduled).

FLY-FISHING

The Tongue River is the Bighorns' blue-ribbon stream. There are browns, rainbows, and brook trout up to 20 inches. Inquire at the **Wyoming Game and Fish Visitors Center,** 700 Valley View Dr. (℡ 307/672-7418), for local catch limits and licenses. For equipment needs, advice, and guided trips, contact the **Fly Shop of the Big Horns,** 227 N. Main St. (www.troutangler.com; ℡ 800/253-5866).

GOLF

Dubbing itself the Golf Capital of Wyoming, Sheridan offers several excellent courses with views of the Bighorn Mountains, including one of the state's best, the **Powder Horn ★★**, 6 miles south of Sheridan in Big Horn (www.thepowderhorn.com; ℡ 307/672-5323). The semiprivate course includes 27 beautiful holes that mix Scottish-style golf with plenty of wide-open fairways and target golf. Greens fees for 18 holes run $65 to $84, plus $15 per seat for a cart. There is also the 18-hole **Sheridan Country Club,** west of Sheridan at 1992 W. 5th St. (www.sheridancountryclub. com; ℡ 307/674-8135), with greens fees of $45, plus $16 per seat for carts; and the 18-hole **Kendrick Golf Club** on Big Goose Road (℡ 307/674-8148), charging $20 to $29 for 18 holes, plus $13 per seat for carts. In Buffalo, the **Buffalo Golf Club,** 550 W. Hart (www.buffalowygolf.com; ℡ 307/684-5266), is a hilly 18-hole public course with greens fees of $32 for 18 holes, $24 for a cart.

HANG GLIDING

Sand Turn, in the Bighorn Mountains west of Sheridan, is a hang-gliding mecca in the summer. There are fly-ins in late May and over Labor Day weekend; spectators are welcome. Call **Sheridan Travel and Tourism** (℡ 888/596-6787) for additional information.

WINTER SPORTS

In the winter, snowmobiling, cross-country skiing, and snowshoeing are all popular activities in the Sheridan area. The 218-mile **Bighorn Mountains Trail System** is a perpetually top-rated snowmobiling area, with the nearest trail head just 15 miles southwest of Sheridan. Call **Sheridan Travel and Tourism** (✆ **888/596-6787**) for additional information.

Seeing the Sights

Ask at the State Information Center at I-90, exit 23, for the excellent "Historic Downtown Walking Tour" leaflet, which has summaries on 31 notable structures and a handy foldout map. Another good guide to pick up is the "Art on Display" brochure, detailing temporary and permanent installations of public art around town.

Bradford Brinton Memorial Ranch ★   From a distance, surrounded by cottonwoods and dwarfed by the hills and horizon, the Brinton ranch house doesn't look much different from most other two-story, white wood-frame homes. But the house, dating from the late 1800s, is not the real reason to visit. Yes, this 20-room residence offers a fine example of how a "gentleman rancher" lived in the early 1900s—the tables are set with china and the shelves filled with gold- and leather-bound volumes—but on the walls hangs a first-class art collection. Here you'll see *Fight on the Little Bighorn,* by Frederic Remington, and *When Ropes Go Wrong,* by Charles Russell. Will James, John Audubon, and a host of other notable artists show up in one of the best but least-known Western art collections in the Rockies.

239 Brinton Rd., Big Horn (10 miles south of Sheridan on U.S. 87). www.bradfordbrintonmemorial. com. ✆ **307/672-3173.** $4 adults, $3 children 13–18 and seniors 62 and over, free for children 12 and under. Memorial Day to Labor Day Mon–Sat 10am–4pm, Sun noon–4pm; limited hours fall to spring, depending on exhibition; call or check website for details.

King's Saddlery and Don King Museum ★   Founded by the late saddle-making legend Don King, this Main Street emporium is a cowboy's candy store, with an extensive collection of Western tack and any size, length, and lay of ropes. Wander the shop to see the tools of the modern cowboy, and watch the King brothers hand-tool leather. Then step back in time to their museum, housing one of the largest collections in the world of Indian artifacts and cowboy trappings—including high-back saddles, chaps, Spanish bits, silver spurs, and quirts.

184 N. Main St. www.kingropes.com. ✆ **800/443-8919** or 307/672-2702. Free admission; donations accepted. Mon–Sat 8am–5pm.

Sheridan County Museum   Located in a former barbecue restaurant near I-25, the Sheridan County Museum offers an interesting glimpse into Sheridan's rich history. The stories of mining and logging are told through intricate dioramas, and works by local artist Bernard Thomas and local photographer Elsa Spear Byron are spotlighted, alongside historic ranching artifacts and other displays.

850 Sibley Circle. www.sheridancountyhistory.org. ✆ **307/675-1150.** $4 adults, $3 seniors, $2 students, free for children 11 and under. May and Sept to mid-Dec daily 1–5pm; June–Aug daily 10am–6pm. Closed mid-Dec to Apr.

Sheridan Inn   The majestic Sheridan Inn was hailed as the finest hotel between Chicago and San Francisco when it opened in 1893, and visitors today can step back to that time as they explore the restored first floor. Modeled after Scottish hunting lodges, the hotel has dormer windows for each of the 62 rooms and three impressive river-rock fireplaces. The back bar was imported from England, and the building boasted the town's first electric lights, running water, and telephone. The Sheridan Inn has hosted a variety of visiting celebrities and dignitaries, including Buffalo Bill

Cody, Calamity Jane, Theodore Roosevelt, Will Rogers, and Ernest Hemingway. Although it hasn't operated as a hotel since 1965, the Sheridan houses a restaurant, **1893 Grille & Spirits** (© 307/673-2777)—and the handsome and historic bar still serves drinks. A complete restoration of 22 rooms will allow overnight stays, but the project has been slow to come to fruition.

856 N. Broadway. www.sheridaninn.com. © **307/674-2178.** $2 self-guided tour of the 1st floor and museum. Mon Fri 10am–3pm. Call for appointment.

Trail End State Historic Site   The Kendrick Mansion, the only example of Flemish Revival architecture in Wyoming, sits on 3¾ acres of manicured grounds. John Kendrick, orphaned in Texas, arrived in Wyoming in 1879 at age 22 on a cattle drive. By 1912, he'd built a 200,000-acre cattle ranch and amassed a net worth of $1 million. The next year, he completed construction on a home so large, it took a ton of coal each day to warm its 20 rooms. He later became Wyoming's governor, then U.S. senator. Visitors today can marvel at materials not common in pioneer Wyoming: silk, mahogany, Italian marble, Georgia pine beams, and a maple floor in the ballroom. Also on the grounds is a carriage house, which serves as a community theater.

400 Clarendon Ave. www.trailend.org. © **307/674-4589.** $4 adults 18 and over, free for children under 18. June–Aug daily 9am–6pm; Mar–May and Sept to mid-Dec daily 1–4pm. Closed mid-Dec to Feb.

The Ucross Foundation   Retreats for writers, artists, and musicians are not all that common in the West, but Ucross has gained an international reputation by providing a quiet, beautiful setting for seclusion and creativity. This ranchland, 27 miles east of Sheridan, was once the headquarters of the Pratt and Ferris Cattle Company, established in 1879. Now over half of the 22,000-acre ranch is protected with a conservation easement with the Nature Conservancy. You don't need an artist's residency to stop in and visit **Big Red,** a magnificently restored structure that once served as the main ranch house but today is a showcase of antique furniture; and the **Big Red Gallery,** which every year mounts four exhibits. If you're in the area on the Fourth of July, this is the place to be; several thousand people show up for the fireworks.

30 Big Red Lane, Clearmont. www.ucrossfoundation.org. © **307/737-2291.** Free admission. Mon–Fri 8:30am–4pm. From Sheridan, drive 27 miles east on U.S. 14 to junction with U.S. 16.

Where to Stay

The Sheridan area has a great range of lodging establishments, running the gamut from modern hotels, to Victorian B&Bs, to authentic dude ranches. The two best chain properties are the **Best Western Sheridan Center,** 612 N. Main St. (© **866/430-902** or 307/674-7421), with double rates of $110 to $130 in the summer, $69 to $99 in the winter; and the **Holiday Inn,** 1809 Sugarland Dr. (© **307/672-8931**), with rates of $109 to $159 double. The **Wingate Inn,** 1950 E. 5th St. (© **307/675-1101**), is another solid option, with double rates of $119 summer, $89 winter.

Mill Inn   From 1921 to 1972, the Sheridan Flouring Mills served as, yes, a flour mill, but a maverick businessman soon turned the place into a motel with office suites. It's since been upgraded; the very nice rooms have a mild Western motif (historical photos, cowboy-speckled bedspreads), with the trademark concrete grain elevator still in place. The only downside is traffic noise, as the inn is close to both the interstate and the main drag through town.

2161 Coffeen Ave. (at I-90, exit 25), Sheridan, WY 82801. www.sheridanmillinn.com. © **307/672-6401.** 44 units. $65–$135 double. Rates include continental breakfast. AE, DISC, MC, V. *In room:* A/C, TV, hair dryer, Wi-Fi (free).

Sheridan Cottages ★   Located 2 miles from downtown, these colorful metal-sided cottages meld quaintness and modernity in their exterior and feature comfortable and stylish "New West" interiors. Great for couples or families, all of the cabins have maple hardwood floors and kitchens with granite counters; some feature a den area. There is a shared laundry room and nicely landscaped yard area out front. The location, between a commercial district and a residential neighborhood, is unremarkable but quiet and convenient to the interstate.

1185 Sugarview Dr., Sheridan, WY 82801. www.sheridancottages.com. © **307/751-0793.** 5 units. $135–$165 double, with a 3-night minimum stay. Discounts available for longer stays. AE, DISC, MC, V. *In room:* TV, kitchens, Wi-Fi (free).

Spahn's Big Horn Mountain Bed and Breakfast ★★   Spahn's Big Horn Mountain B&B prides itself on being the oldest B&B in Wyoming, and it's certainly one of the best. Picture this: a four-story log cabin; a common room with a crackling fire, shelves of books, and a piano; and, outside, a deck with a 100-mile view of prairie stretching to the east. The rooms glow with varnished peeled logs and have such country comforts as patchwork quilts and claw-foot tubs. Ron Spahn (he's run the place for more than 20 years with his wife, Bobbie) leads evening wildlife safaris in search of moose, elk, and deer on Monday and Thursday; he also takes customers on daylong tours of the area (see "Getting Outside," earlier in this chapter).

P.O. Box 579, Big Horn, WY 82833. www.bighorn-wyoming.com. © **307/674-8150.** 3 units. $100–$175 double. Rates include full breakfast. MC, V for reservation deposit only; payment by cash or check. Closed Oct–Apr. 15 miles southwest of Sheridan via U.S. 87 and Wyo. 335. *In room:* No phone, Wi-Fi (free).

GUEST RANCHES

Eatons' Ranch ★★ ☺   This is the country's oldest guest ranch and one of the best. Founded by Howard Eaton (the namesake of the Howard Eaton Trail in Yellowstone), the ranch got its start in North Dakota in 1882 before relocating in 1904 to remote and rugged Wolf Creek Canyon, about 20 miles west of Sheridan and a picture-perfect spot for a guest ranch. The third through fifth generations of Eatons now run the ranch, which has repeat guests year after year thanks to a first-rate horseback-riding operation, hearty meals, and terrific rustic cabins that range from truly historic to modern, with big river-rock fireplaces, elk trophies, and a rich dose of Western ambience. Other diversions include fishing in a stocked pond, pack trips (for an additional charge), movie nights, barbecue dinners and dances on Sunday nights, and Wednesday afternoon softball games (guests versus staff).

270 Eatons Ranch Rd., Wolf, WY 82844. www.eatonsranch.com. © **800/210-1049** or 307/655-9285. Reservations required at least 2 months in advance. 51 cabins. $190–$245 per adult, per day; $140–$185 per child 17 and under. 3-day minimum stay required. Rates include all meals and ranch activities. AE, DISC, MC, V. Closed late Sept to May. About 18 miles northwest of Sheridan via Wyo. 331. **Amenities:** Dining room; children's programs; outdoor Jacuzzi; outdoor heated pool; Wi-Fi (free). *In room:* Hair dryer, no phone.

HF Bar Ranch ★ ☺   With reasonable rates and plenty of activities for children, the HF Bar Ranch really caters to families—nannies are encouraged to come along at half-price. This hospitable ranch is a real working ranch and a hoedown of old-fashioned fun, with weekly hayrides and dances. Ice and wood are delivered daily to each of the cabin's front porches, and hearty family-style meals are served in the main lodge. Guests can take daily trail rides or arrange a pack trip to the remote and rustic "mountain camp" 15 miles into the Bighorns. For an additional fee, the sports enthusiasts of the group can fish the miles of stream banks, shoot on one of the six sporting-clay courses, or hunt pheasant and chukar on a private bird reserve.

1301 Rock Creek Rd., Saddlestring, WY 82840. www.hfbar.com. © **307/684-2487.** Reservations required at least 6 months in advance. 30 cabins. $295 per person, per day; free for children under 5. Rates include all meals and most ranch activities. DISC, MC, V. Closed mid-Sept to Apr. Take I-90 35 miles south of Sheridan to exit 47. Drive west on Shell Creek Rd. and Rock Creek Rd. for 12 miles to ranch. **Amenities:** Dining room; babysitting; children's program; outdoor heated pool; Wi-Fi (free). *In room:* No phone.

CAMPING

The **Sheridan/Bighorn Mountain KOA Campground,** 63 Decker Rd. (© **800/ 562-7621** for reservations, or 307/674-8766), a half-mile north of Sheridan at the Port of Entry exit, offers quiet and shady tent and RV sites, plus all the usual commercial campground amenities, including an outdoor swimming pool and miniature golf. The campground is open year-round, with rates from $27 to $44 and cabins for $62 to $72. Another option is **Peter D's RV Park,** 1105 Joe St. (www.wyoming rvpark.com; © **888/673-0597** or 307/674-4613), with rates of $25 to $30 for a site. The **Bighorn National Forest** has several campgrounds in the area, with sites costing $12 to $15 per night. Contact the **Bighorn National Forest office** (© **307/ 674-2600**) for further information.

Where to Eat

LuLu's Cafe ★★ 🍴 AMERICAN   With old rock-'n-roll LP covers laminated as placemats and mix-and-match furniture, this fun and funky place a block off the main drag makes healthy taste good. The morning menu includes burritos with or without eggs and creative spins on French toast, oatmeal, and breakfast sandwiches. (The LU-Zekiel Madness is a standout, with fresh fruit and nuts on toast, topped with yogurt, peanut butter, and local honey.) Lunch brings salads, sandwiches, and wraps. Service is friendly; there is a patio out front.

118 N. Brooks St. www.luluscafewyo.com. © **307/674-5858.** Main courses $7–$12 breakfast and lunch. AE, DISC, MC, V. Tues–Fri 7am–2pm; Sat–Sun 8am–2pm. Closed Mon.

Oliva's Kitchen MEXICAN/ITALIAN   Beginning as a dinky takeout counter down the street, Oliva's is a colorful restaurant on Main Street that has quickly emerged as a local favorite. Serving Mexican standards like burritos, *chile verde,* and enchiladas, the eatery also plates up some more-than-respectable pasta dishes (I favor the spicy shrimp), burgers, and steaks. The breakfast burritos are also hard to beat, but there are also tostadas and steak and eggs. The basic restaurant has tables and a counter (as well as a full bar) and great service.

437 N. Main St. © **307/673-0986.** Main courses breakfast $6–$11, lunch and dinner $8–$23. AE, DISC, MC, V. Mon–Thurs 6am–9pm; Fri–Sat 6am–10pm. Closed Sun.

Oliver's ★★ CONTEMPORARY AMERICAN   Oliver's brings some big-city flair to the cowboy environs of Sheridan. Opened in 2002 by Matt Wallop, the son of former U.S. Senator Malcolm Wallop, the monthly changing menu has some Western touches among its wide range of influences. You might get pheasant ravioli; a filet of locally raised beef tenderloin, with applewood-smoked bacon, caramelized onions, and Gorgonzola; or maybe macaroni and cheese made with Gouda, white cheddar, and

Parmesan. Like the menu, the space itself is contemporary, with a San Francisco–inspired design that melds elegant and industrial with a hint of the West. There is also a nice inventory of wines and such tantalizing desserts as espresso crème brûlée.

55 N. Main St. © **307/672-2838.** Reservations recommended. Main courses $7–$20 brunch and lunch, $7–$39 dinner. AE, DISC, MC, V. Mon–Fri 11am–2pm; Mon–Sat 5–10pm; Sun 11am–2:30pm and 4:30–9pm. Bar open later.

Sanford's Grub & Pub CAJUN   The maze of rooms at Sanford's, located in a 1907 historic building, is decorated like the dorm room of a junkman's son: Televisions, beer signs, and license plates are crammed to the rafters. You might even say the same about the dinner menu, which leans toward Cajun dishes, with really good jambalaya and Cajun-flavored burgers and steaks—try the New York strip Cajun style. But the restaurant also has a whole lot of other things, including some items, such as fried okra, that you wouldn't expect to see above the Mason-Dixon line. Sanford's is a good spot for beer drinkers, with a large selection of bottled beers, plus the restaurant's own on draft.

1 E. Alger St. (at N. Main St.). © **307/674-1722.** Main courses $8–$21. AE, DC, DISC, MC, V. Daily 11am–10pm (9pm in winter).

Sheridan After Dark

The doors of the legendary **Mint Bar,** 151 N. Main St. (© **307/674-9696**), first swung open in 1907. The place operated as a speak-easy until Prohibition ended, then evolved into the prototypical Western bar; "Meet me at the Mint" became a catchphrase in these parts. It's still decorated just as it was in the 1940s, with all sorts of taxidermy and historical photos. There's an 8-foot Texas rattlesnake skin (said to have formerly sheathed an 80-pounder) above the bar and plenty of local color seated in front of it. For the beer aficionado, there's the bar at the slick **Black Tooth Brewing Company,** 312 Broadway (www.blacktoothbrewingcompany.com; © **307/675-2337**).

Built in 1912, the **WYO Theater,** 42 N. Main St. (www.wyotheater.com; © **307/672-9084**), is a model for other old theaters in the West. It was a broken-down movie palace facing the wrecking ball in the early 1980s when locals stepped in and saved it, restoring the proscenium and reviving live entertainment in Sheridan. Classical music, local choral groups, touring dance companies, and popular performers like Leon Russell and the Craft Brothers fill the house. Tickets are usually between $10 and $30.

BUFFALO ★

35 miles S of Sheridan; 182 miles E of Cody

Though Sheridan remains the busy hub of this Wyoming region, it is surrounded by interesting little towns like Dayton, Story, and Ranchester, plus one big enough to deserve its own slot: Buffalo. A short drive south of Sheridan on I-90, this old ranching town is near the site of the infamous Johnson County War (a battle among settlers over the use of rangeland) and not far from the Hole-in-the-Wall country favored by Butch, Sundance, and other outlaws.

Though this was a favorite area of Indian bison hunters, it was not named for a shaggy beast: The original settlers drew names from a hat, and the winner had written his New York hometown.

The historic downtown area is compact enough to explore on foot. Follow the **Clear Creek Centennial Trail** on a wheelchair-accessible path from downtown to a pleasant grassy area where it joins a 3-mile unsurfaced road to the base of the Bighorn Mountains. Maps are available from the **Buffalo Chamber of Commerce,** 55 N. Main St., Buffalo, WY 82834 (www.buffalowyo.com; ✆ **800/227-5122** or 307/684-5544). You'll see the old **Occidental Hotel** at 10 N. Main (see "Where to Stay," below). At the excellent **Jim Gatchell Memorial Museum,** 100 Fort St. (www.jimgatchell.com; ✆ **307/684-9331**), you'll find American-Indian artifacts like arrowheads and medicine rattles, as well as cavalry items and the bridle Tom Horn braided while awaiting execution. The museum is open May through early October and closed the rest of the year ($5 adults, $3 children ages 6–17, free for kids 5 and under).

Buffalo lies on the route of the Bozeman Trail, a 19th-century shortcut to the gold country of Montana that cut right through the hunting grounds of several resentful tribes. The U.S. Army built forts to protect travelers and engaged in skirmishes with the resident Sioux, Cheyenne, and Arapaho. The largest fort was **Fort Phil Kearny,** exit 44 off I-90 (www.philkearny.vcn.com; ✆ **307/684-7629**), where soldiers endured repeated raids by hostile Indians. Though the original fort is gone, the site today is a national historic site with a visitor center and tours of two major battlefields nearby: the 1866 Fetterman Massacre, in which Crazy Horse and his band overwhelmed a small army contingent, and the Wagon Box Fight, which went the other way. The visitor center is open daily 8am to 6pm from mid-May to September, and Wednesday through Sunday noon to 4pm the rest of the year; admission is $4 for nonresidents, while kids under 17 are free.

Robert LeRoy Parker (Butch Cassidy) and his partner, Harry Longabaugh (Sundance Kid), assembled their infamous group of bandits known as the Wild Bunch to rob trains and banks and steal herds of horses and cattle. One of their favorite places to hide was the **Hole-in-the-Wall,** a red-rock canyon area above the Middle Fork of the Powder River. The Hole-in-the-Wall is located about 45 miles south of Buffalo near the town of Kaycee. Take I-25 south from Kaycee to the Triple T Road exit, continue south 14 miles to County Road 111, go west 18 miles to County Road 105, then go north 8 miles to the U.S. Bureau of Land Management directional sign for Hole-in-the-Wall. It's a 3-mile hike into the actual site. The Hole itself is no more than a notch in a butte, disappointing to folks used to Disney-like re-creations of outlaw hideouts. But for the intrepid on horse or in four-wheel-drive vehicles, you can explore the spacious **Outlaw Cave.** There are tipi rings in the surrounding area and large pictographs and stenciled handprints under a rock overhang.

Note: Most of this area is private land. Be sure to check with the U.S. Bureau of Land Management office in Buffalo (✆ **307/684-1100**) before exploring on your own.

Just a few miles northwest of Buffalo along I-90 is **Lake DeSmet,** an excellent fishing and boating destination, with opportunities for picnicking and camping.

Where to Stay

The Occidental Hotel ★★ The Occidental started as a tent in 1878 and evolved into a hotel that was demolished and rebuilt in 1900. It was lost in a poker game in 1919 to the Smith family, ranchers who ran it as a hotel for more than 50 years. It closed in 1980, and the dust and cobwebs took over for 20 years. But new owners John and Dawn Wexo reopened the historic hotel in 2002. The rooms—often fashioned out of two or three of the old rooms—are decorated with original furnishings and reproduction wallpaper, as well as vintage radios that pick up old radio programs from an in-hotel transmitter. We like the masculine Teddy Roosevelt Suite, with an original sink and tub. Visit the historic saloon downstairs, with its woodwork pocked with bullet holes from Buffalo's Wild West past, and great bluegrass jams on Thursday nights.

10 N. Main St., Buffalo, WY 82834. www.occidentalwyoming.com. © **307/684-0451.** 14 units (2 with shared bathroom). Summer $75–$210 double, $260–$285 suite; winter $50–$125 double, $140–$210 suite. AE, DISC, MC, V. Pets accepted (fenced yard outside). **Amenities:** 2 restaurants; lounge. *In room:* A/C, TV, no phone, Wi-Fi (free).

Paradise Guest Ranch ★ Aptly named, this guest ranch 45 miles south of Sheridan adds modern conveniences to the ambience and activities you expect on a ranch. The log cabins not only have decks with views of the surrounding valley, mountains, or streams, but also come equipped with their own washers and dryers. As with most resort ranches in the West, several trail rides depart daily for guests of all levels of ability. And if you're riding all day, you can get a chuckwagon dinner. There are ample after-dark activities for the entire family, with evening entertainment in the ranch's saloon and recreation center.

Box 790, Buffalo, WY 82834. www.paradiseranch.com. © **307/684-7876.** 18 cabins. $1,400–$2,0 per adult per week; $550–$1,850 per child 12 and under per week. Rates include all meals a ranch activities. AE, DISC, MC, V. Closed Oct to mid-May. From Buffalo, drive 13 miles west on U 16, then turn right at Hunter Creek Rd. to the road leading to the ranch. **Amenities:** Dining roo lounge; Wi-Fi (free). *In room:* Kitchenette, no phone.

GILLETTE

103 miles E of Sheridan; 243 miles E of Billings

Gillette is now "Energy Capital of the Nation" and boasts the local convention visitors' bureau, but just a century ago it was a huge sea of open range. Where the were once herds of cattle, you can now see several massive surface coal mines s as the RAG Coal West–Eagle Butte Mine. The mine, which opened in 1978, con ues to produce more than 40 million tons of coal a year. The huge coal mines, a with recently discovered coal-bed methane gas, have made Gillette a booming munity of about 25,000 residents, which means that this is a pleasant enough to live, with a variety of modern facilities, including a first-class swimming poo water park. There is still plenty of undeveloped plains habitat, too, particularly 1.8-million-acre **Thunder Basin National Grassland.** Anyone who likes geol wonders, and anyone who enjoyed *Close Encounters of the Third Kind,* will w visit the nearby **Devils Tower National Monument.**

Essentials

GETTING THERE Great Lakes Airlines/Frontier (www.greatlakes © **800/554-5111**), **Delta, United,** and **Great Lakes** fly into the **Gillette-C bell County Airport** (www.iflygillette.com; © **307/686-1042**), off U.S. 14/
   By road, Gillette is 103 miles east of Sheridan via I-90 and 61 miles south Devils Tower National Monument.

VISITOR INFORMATION Contact the **Campbell County Chamber o merce,** 314 S. Gillette Ave., Gillette, WY 82716 (www.gillettechamber.com; **682-3673**).

GETTING AROUND   You can rent cars from **Avis** (✆ 800/230-4898) or **Hertz** (✆ 800/654-3131) at the airport or in town, or get a taxi from **City Cab** (✆ 307/685-1000).

Getting Outside

Golf addicts can get their fix at either the **Gillette Golf Club,** 1800 Country Club Rd. (✆ 307/682-4774), or the **Bell Nob Golf Course,** 1316 Overdale (✆ 307/686-7069). The former is a 9-hole course; Bell Nob has 18.

Bird-watchers will enjoy the waterfowl of **McManamen Park,** near the corner of Gurley Street and Warlow Drive. **Hunters** are drawn here to bag elk, mule deer, pronghorn, and upland birds. Numerous hunting guides operate in the Gillette area; contact the Campbell County Chamber of Commerce (see above) for assistance in finding one.

Seeing the Sights

If you are impressed by big holes and big machinery, you've come to the right place. The RAG Coal West–Eagle Butte Mine has an impressive overlook near mile marker 100 on U.S. 14/16, about 1 mile north of Gillette's airport. The mine company and the Gillette Convention and Visitors Bureau jointly sponsor **free summer tours** to the mine site, where you can see the massive equipment used to extract the coal. Reservations should be made by calling ✆ 307/686-0040.

The **Campbell County Rockpile Museum ★**, 900 W. 2nd St. (www.rockpile museum.com; ✆ 307/682-5723), is the place to learn something about the history of this area. Displays include artifacts of the area's past, such as saddles, rifles, arrowheads, and the like, but I prefer the big stuff—antique vehicles, including several Ford Model Ts, and a wagon collection that includes a horse-drawn hearse and an old sheep wagon. Kids like the vintage tractors they can climb on, as well as the other hands-on displays, including one that helps children identify the area's animals. There's also a "Grandma's Attic" section, where kids can dress up in historical (and funny-looking) fashions from days gone by. Adjacent to the museum building is a historic schoolhouse and a homesteader's cabin from the early 1900s. Both of these buildings were relocated to the museum grounds from other parts of the county. Finally, for those who like firecrackers—we mean really, really big firecrackers—don't miss the 10-minute big-screen video on coal mining that shows what dynamite can really do. Admission to the museum is free. It's open year-round Monday through Saturday from 9am to 5pm.

The **CAM-PLEX** (www.cam-plex.com; ✆ 307/682-0552), a massive event pavilion, has been the host in recent years of the National High School Rodeo Finals, as well as an array of other exciting events. Call or visit the website to find out what's scheduled.

Where to Stay & Eat

Lodging rates in Gillette are highest in summer, and sometimes as much as a third less at other times; the rates below are peak rates. The largest lodging property in town is the **Best Western Tower West Lodge,** 109 N. U.S. 14/16 (✆ 307/686-2210), which charges $89 to $179 double or $189 to $229 for a suite. The **Comfort Inn & Suites,** 1607 W. 2nd Ave. (✆ 307/685-2223), charges $89 to $159 for two people; and the **Holiday Inn Express,** 1908 Cliff Davis Dr. (✆ 307/686-9576), charges $149 to $189 double.

The restaurant I like in Gillette is the **Prime Rib Restaurant & Wine Cellar,** 1205 S. Douglas Hwy. (www.primeribgillette.com; ℂ **307/682-2944**), an upscale steak and seafood place where you can get tender, slow-roasted prime rib, charbroiled filets, sautéed halibut, and shrimp scampi, among other items, as well as a wine list that's garnered acclaim from *Wine Spectator.* Lunch prices are in the $7-to-$15 range, and most dinner entrees cost $10 to $35. The restaurant is open Monday through Friday from 11am to 10pm, Saturday from 4 to 10:30pm, and Sunday from 4 to 9:30pm.

DEVILS TOWER NATIONAL MONUMENT ★

62 miles NE of Gillette; 230 miles SE of Billings; 110 miles W of Rapid City, South Dakota

Once upon a time, so the Kiowa legend goes, seven sisters were playing with their brother when he suddenly turned into a bear. Fleeing, the girls scrambled onto a small rock and prayed. The rock started to grow, pushing them into the sky. While the bear clawed at the rock's sides, trying to get at the girls, the rock thrust them so high that they became the points of the Big Dipper. Rising 1,267 feet above the Belle Fourche River below, the formation became named Mato Tipila, or "Bear Lodge." The site is sacred to the Lakota and other tribes native to the northern plains.

Col. Richard Irving Dodge, who commanded a military escort to a U.S. Geological Survey party that visited the Black Hills in 1875, is credited with giving the formation its current name. In his book *The Black Hills,* written the year after his journey, Dodge described Devils Tower as "one of the most remarkable peaks in this or any other country."

As a battle to preserve the monument from commercial encroachment was being waged in 1893, two local ranchers decided it was time someone made the first recorded climb to its summit.

William Rogers and Willard Ripley planned for months before making their first attempt on the southeast face on July 4, 1893. As the date approached, the pair began distributing handbills offering such amenities as ample food and drink, daily and nightly dancing, and plenty of grain for horses. The flyers also touted the feat as the "rarest sight of a lifetime."

Rogers and Ripley used a wooden stake ladder for the first 350 feet of the climb. As more than 1,000 spectators watched, the pair made the harrowing climb in about an hour, raised Old Glory, then sold pieces of it as mementos of the occasion. Thereafter, the tower became a popular place for Independence Day family gatherings. At the annual affair in 1895, Mrs. Rogers used her husband's ladder to become the first woman to reach the summit.

In 1906, Congress declared it the nation's first national monument. The tower was further popularized in the 1977 movie *Close Encounters of the Third Kind.*

While the 50-million-year-old tower itself is composed of hard igneous rock, much of the remaining exposed rock within the 1,347-acre monument is composed of soft sediments from the warm, shallow seas of the Mesozoic era. These colorful bands of rock encircling the igneous core include layers of sandstone, shale, mudstone, siltstone, gypsum, and limestone.

Any visitor will understand immediately the allure of this striated column of volcanic rock. It's especially evocative in the evening—as darkness shrouds the surrounding hills, Devils Tower stands above the horizon, glowing amber.

Essentials

GETTING THERE   From Gillette, take I-90 east to Moorcroft (exit 154) and follow signs to Devils Tower; from Jackson, take U.S. 26/287 to Riverton, then U.S. 26 to Casper, then I-90 through Gillette to Moorcroft; from Sheridan, take I-90 to Gillette, then see above.

VISITOR INFORMATION   Contact **Devils Tower National Monument,** P.O. Box 10, Devils Tower, WY 82714-0010 (www.nps.gov/deto; ✆ **307/467-5283**). The **Devils Tower Natural History Association,** P.O. Box 37, Devils Tower, WY 87214-0037 (✆ **307/467-5283,** ext. 631), operates a bookstore at the monument's visitor center and offers a variety of publications.

VISITOR CENTER   Open from early April to late November only, the visitor center is located 3 miles from the monument's entrance, with exhibits about the tower's history and geology.

FEES & REGULATIONS   The entrance fee is $10 per vehicle (motorcycles included) or $5 per person on foot or bike. Disturbing any wildlife or gathering items such as rocks or flowers is prohibited. Especially do not feed, chase, or disturb prairie dogs; they bite and may carry diseases. Abandoned prairie-dog holes are often homes to black widow spiders and rattlesnakes.

Seeing the Monument

It's easy to experience much of what Devils Tower has to offer in less than a day. Rangers recommend that you allow 2 to 4 hours to walk a trail, stop at the visitor center, and view the prairie dogs.

Surrounded by ponderosa pines and bathed in blue sky, the towering rock obelisk is visible for miles, and it's easy to imagine the reaction of the first lonely American-Indian scouts and French fur trappers who stumbled upon this stunning geologic anomaly a few centuries ago. The paved 1.3-mile round-trip **Tower Trail,** rated easy, goes all the way around the formation, offering close-up views of the tower on fairly level ground. Wayside exhibits tell the Devils Tower story. It connects to the 1.5-mile **Joyner Ridge Trail,** which has some wide-open grassland that makes for a sublime view of the tower.

Home to the feisty black-tailed **prairie dog,** the grounds of Devils Tower National Monument are perfect for picnicking and viewing wildlife. You can watch the

AT day's end

Visitors to Devils Tower should take the time to stay a night, if only to watch the drama that unfolds at dusk. Head to Joyner Ridge via Joyner Ridge Rd., about 2.5 miles up the main road from the park entrance, with a picnic dinner on a nice night, and just gaze at the tower and watch the moon rise. It also offers a tremendous vantage point to photograph the tower. There are also occasional guided full-moon hikes here in the summer; contact the park for details.

sociable prairie dogs in their colony, or "town," just inside the park's east entrance station. The critters excavate elaborate networks of underground passageways, then guard their burrows with warning "barks" when predators such as hawks, eagles, bullsnakes, coyote, red fox, and mink come too close. Walk the leisurely .6-mile round-trip **Valley View Trail** to see a prairie-dog town, or savor a picnic lunch among the wildflowers at the monument's picnic area on the banks of the sleepy Belle Fourche River.

Climbing the Tower

Climbers have been wedging their fingers in the tower's cracks for more than a century, at a rate in recent years of about 5,000 climbers annually. (About one-third actually make it to the summit.) Climbers must register with a ranger before starting and upon their return; otherwise, there are no permits or requirements for climbing the tower. Be prepared for sudden storms; carry rain gear and a flashlight. Rockfall is common, so helmets are advised. Ask a ranger for additional safety and climbing information; the visitor center has a list of the guides permitted to lead climbs up the tower. We recommend Frank Sanders's **Above All Climbing Guides and Instruction** (www.devilstowerclimbing.com; ℭ **888/314-5267**), which specializes in working with novice climbers and has rates starting at $300 per day for one person. Above All has a climbing gym on the monument boundary where its introductory packages begin and always has at least one guide for every two customers. *Note:* A voluntary climbing ban is observed each June out of respect for American-Indian religious ceremonies that are held on Devils Tower at that time.

Where to Stay

Immediately outside of the monument's boundaries, climbing guru Frank Sanders runs the **Devils Tower Lodge,** P.O. Box 66, Devils Tower, WY 82714 (www.devilstowerlodge.com; ℭ **888/314-5267** or 307/467-5267), an eclectic four-room bed-and-breakfast in the former superintendent's residence. The rooms all have private bathrooms; the facilities are geared toward climbers, and the communal mood makes guests feel as if they're staying in a home instead of an inn. Rooms are $125 to $200 a night ($250 for the cottage), full breakfast included. MasterCard and Visa are accepted. In Hulett, try the **Hulett Motel,** 202 Main St., Hulett, WY 82720 (www.hulettmotel.com; ℭ **307/467-5220**). Double rates are $65 to $95 year-round; Discover, MasterCard and Visa are accepted. Rooms are clean and well maintained, and there's also a row of trim and tidy cabins on the Belle Fourche River.

CAMPING   Located a mile from the monument's headquarters, **Belle Fourche Campground** is open April through October and rarely fills up except for Sturgis

(South Dakota) Motorcycle Rally time in August. Its 30 sites accommodate RVs (up to 35 ft. long) and tents on a first-come, first-served basis. Each campsite has a cooking grill, a table, and nearby drinking water. There are no showers, RV hookups, or dump stations. Sites cost $12 per night, and there are three group sites, which cost $2 per person per night, with a six-person minimum. The adjacent Valley View Trail skirts a giant prairie-dog town, and the campground's amphitheater offers excellent ranger programs.

Those looking for a commercial campground with RV hookups and hot showers will find the **Devils Tower KOA,** P.O. Box 100, Devils Tower, WY 82714 (www.devilstowerkoa.com; ✆ **800/562-5785** or 307/467-5395), just outside the monument entrance. Open from May through September, it offers 56 RV sites, 100 tent sites, 11 camping cabins (which share two bathhouses and other campground facilities), and a camping lodge. Rates for two adults are $25 to $80 in hookup sites, $20 to $60 for tents, $75 to $300 for the camping lodge, and $45 to $80 for cabins. Amenities include a heated outdoor pool, self-service laundry, free Wi-Fi, game room, cafe, two gift shops (featuring homemade fudge), horseback rides, hayrides, propane sales, and a nightly showing of *Close Encounters of the Third Kind* Memorial Day to Labor Day.

CASPER

153 miles S of Sheridan; 178 miles NW of Cheyenne; 300 miles S of Billings; 240 miles NW of Denver

Casper is a pleasant little city between the Great Plains and Rocky Mountains that owes much of its success to the oil and gas industry. Its first oil refinery was built in 1895, and although, like most boom towns, Casper has had its share of ups and downs, the petroleum industry continues to help the economy keep rolling along. But what keeps many residents here, and what makes the community of interest to many visitors, is not what's under the ground, but what is on the ground.

Casper has a small but fun ski area, and there is a lot of wildlife in the vicinity, including more than 75% of the world's pronghorn. Also look for mule and white-tailed deer, fox, and a variety of birds. The North Platte River, which meanders through the city, is a premier year-round trout fishery.

This is also an ideal spot to see the real history of the West. Casper stands at the crossroads of westward expansion and in the ruts of the Oregon, Mormon, California, and Pony Express trails. Fur traders stopped here in 1812 on their way back East, building a hovel from rocks and buffalo hides, perhaps the first building constructed by non-Indians in Wyoming. Later, pioneers and Mormons crossed the North Platte River here. Then came the oil miners, and Casper boomed.

Today, Casper is the second-largest city in the state, with about 50,000 residents. It is also the hometown of former U.S. Vice President Dick Cheney.

Essentials

GETTING THERE Casper's **Natrona County International Airport,** 8500 Airport Pkwy. (www.iflycasper.com; ✆ **307/472-6688**), 12 miles northwest of Casper on U.S. 20/26, has daily flights from **Allegiant, Delta,** and **United.**

To reach Casper from **Sheridan,** drive 153 miles south on I-25. From **Cheyenne,** take I-25 north for 178 miles. From **Jackson,** take U.S. 191 to the Moran Junction, then drive 255 miles east on U.S. 26/287.

VISITOR INFORMATION Visit the **Casper Area Convention and Visitors Bureau,** 992 N. Poplar St., Casper, WY 82601 (www.casperwyoming.info; ✆ **800/852-1889** or 307/234-5362).

GETTING AROUND Rent a car with **Avis** (✆ 800/331-1212), **Budget** (✆ **800/527-0700**), or **Hertz** (✆ **800/654-3131**) at the airport. Need a cab? Call **RC Cab** (✆ **307/235-5203**).

SPECIAL EVENTS Casper draws its largest crowds during the 5-day **Central Wyoming Fair and Rodeo** (www.centralwyomingfair.com; ✆ **307/235-5775**), which takes place each summer in early to mid-July. Call for details. In early August, the **Beartrap Summer Festival** (www.beartrapsummerfestival.com; ✆ **307/266-5252**) celebrates bluegrass and other music on top of Casper Mountain.

Getting Outside

To escape the heat of the summer or ski a few runs in the winter, head up **Casper Mountain,** being sure to stop at the pullouts to take in the view of the plains stretching north toward the Bighorn Mountains. The mountain rises 8,000 feet above sea level, and there are campgrounds, hiking trails (try Garden Creek Falls), ski tracks, groomed snowmobile tracks, and mountain-biking trails. Another popular destination for outdoor recreation is **Muddy Mountain.** Much of the public land here is under the jurisdiction of the **Bureau of Land Management,** 2987 Prospector Dr. (✆ **307/261-7600**). The office has maps and other information available. At **Mountain Sports,** 543 S. Center St. (✆ **800/426-1136** or 307/266-1136), you'll find winter and summer outdoor equipment, plus rentals. The **Ugly Bug Fly Shop,** 240 S. Center St. (www.crazyrainbow.net; ✆ **307/234-6905**), is a great angler's resource, with advice, gear, and guides ($285–$395 per day, per boat).

There are some great hiking opportunities on Casper Mountain, including the **Lee McCune Braille Trail,** which enables visually impaired visitors to enjoy the beauty of Beartrap Meadow, with interpretive Braille markers describing the area's ecology. The Casper Area Convention and Visitors Bureau (see above) can provide you with maps detailing this and other hiking trails.

Edness Kimball Wilkins State Park (http://wyoparks.state.wy.us; ✆ **307/577-5150**) is a pleasant day-use park just 6 miles east of Casper off I-25, where you'll find huge old cottonwoods over the North Platte River. The park has hard-surfaced walking paths, a canoe- and raft-launch ramp, a swimming area, picnic tables, and a playground. There is also an accessible fishing pier and excellent bird-watching opportunities for species including cormorants, yellow-billed cuckoos, golden and bald eagles, and numerous ducks. The park is open daily from 7am to 10pm; admission costs $6 per vehicle.

SKIING

A cheerful little ski area is a big plus in an area of sometimes howling winters, and Casper has a good one in the municipal **Hogadon Ski Area** ★ (www.hogadon.net; ✆ **307/235-8499** or 307/235-8369 for the snow report), situated atop Casper Mountain (drive south on Wyo. 258 from I-25 to Casper Mountain Rd.). It has a 600-foot vertical rise to a top elevation of 8,000 feet. Two double chairs and a Poma lift cover its 60 acres of groomed trails, and there are also on-site equipment rentals, a snack bar, and a ski and snowboarding school. Nearby, a county-owned cross-country ski area is groomed for skating and track skiing. The ski area generally opens around early December and closes sometime in April. Lift tickets are $40 for adults,

$35 for students 13 to 18, and $25 for children 5 to 12. During ski season, Hogadon is open Wednesday through Sunday, plus holidays (except Christmas Day), from 9am to 4pm.

Seeing the Sights

Casper Planetarium This planetarium offers a multimedia jaunt into space, with changing programs ranging from a basic exploration of the night sky to trips through the solar system. There are also other astronomy-related programs, such as one on the possibility of life beyond earth, plus special kids' shows. The planetarium also offers telescope-user workshops, instruction on how to build your own rocket, and lectures. There are hands-on science displays and exhibits of meteorites and tektites, plus a gift shop.

904 N. Poplar Ave. www.casperplanetarium.com. ✆ **307/577-0310.** $2.50–$5 per person, per program. June–Aug showings daily at 4, 7, and 8pm; Sept–May Tues–Thurs 4pm and Sat 7 or 8pm. Call for additional holiday programs.

Fort Caspar Museum and Historic Site Come to Fort Caspar for a look at what the "good old days" in these parts were really like. The first occupation of this site was in 1847, when Brigham Young and the Mormon Pioneer party constructed a ferry to cross the North Platte River. The post also served as a relay station for the Pony Express, and the transcontinental telegraph crossed the river here. The U.S. Army occupied the site in 1862, naming the post Platte Bridge Station. While attempting to reach an army supply train on July 26, 1865, members of the Sioux and Cheyenne tribes attacked Lt. Caspar W. Collins and troops from the fort. Collins and 26 other soldiers were killed during battles that day, and the fort was later renamed Fort Caspar to honor the lieutenant.

Today the site includes the reconstructed fort buildings furnished as they would have appeared in 1865—the mess hall, telegraph hall, officers' quarters, store, blacksmith shop, stables, commissary, and the like. Expanded in 2007, the museum features exhibits on the social and natural history of central Wyoming. During the summer, there are living-history programs and lectures. Allow 1 or 2 hours.

4001 Fort Caspar Rd. www.fortcasparwyoming.com. ✆ **307/235-8462.** $3 adults, $2 for students 13–18, free for children 12 and under. June–Aug daily 8am–7pm; May and Sept Tues–Sat 8am–5pm. The museum is open year-round, but the fort buildings are open May–Sept only.

National Historic Trails Interpretive Center ★★ This excellent facility opened in Casper in 2002, using state-of-the-art exhibits to give modern travelers an idea of what life on the "road" was like to the emigrants who passed through here in the mid-1800s on the Oregon, Mormon, California, and Pony Express trails. A number of engaging multimedia exhibits cover the pioneer story, from the packing of the wagons to the ferrying of the rivers—the latter is demonstrated by a faux wagon that visitors ride across the Platte River, simulated with motors and a movie. Be sure to take in the informative 18-minute film that tells the trails' history with real-life accounts of pioneers' journeys before the railroad rendered the trails obsolete. The final "exhibit" is the trails themselves, leaving from this spot and marked by BLM markers, for those that want to see a landscape that's changed little in the past 200 years. Allow 2 hours.

1501 N. Poplar St. www.blm.gov/wy/st/en/NHTIC.html. ✆ **307/261-7700.** $6 adults, $5 seniors 60 and over, $4 students 16 and over with valid student ID, free for children 15 and under. May–Aug daily 8am–5pm; Sept–Apr Tues–Sat 9am–4:30pm.

Time Travel

Historic Trails West, P.O. Box 428, Mills, WY 82644 (www.historictrailswest.com; ✆ **307/266-4868**), organizes trips that take you back in time as you rattle in a wagon or sway in the saddle along the Oregon, California, Pony Express, and Mormon trails. Trips range in length from 2 hours ($85 adults, $65 children 10 and under) to all day ($215 adults, $185 children 10 and under), which includes lunch. Prices are slightly higher for those who opt to ride horses instead of sitting in the wagons. There are also overnight and multiday wagon-train trips, with 5-day trips priced at $995 adults, $795 children 10 and under. Trips are scheduled May through October.

Nicolaysen Art Museum and Discovery Center   This attractive facility presents changing exhibitions of works by national and regional artists, with an emphasis on art by Western artists or with a Rocky Mountain West theme. There are one large and six small galleries, and three exhibitions take place simultaneously, for a total of a dozen different shows each year. Works range from traditional Western to contemporary. The Discovery Center is a hands-on self-guided studio with about a dozen stations, some often related to the current exhibits, where participants of all ages can create their own art. Allow 1 or 2 hours.

400 E. Collins Dr. www.thenic.org. ✆ **307/235-5247.** $5 adults, $3 children 5–17, free for children 4 and under. Tues–Sat 10am–5pm; Sun noon–4pm.

Tate Geological Museum   You like rocks? If so, this is the place to come. You can see a vast collection of Wyoming jade, a variety of minerals, and meteorites here. The Tate also has a section on dinosaur excavations from the Natrona County area, including a T. rex skull and the leg and skull of a brontosaurus, as well as the nearly intact skeleton of "Dee the Mammoth." There's also an interactive computerized weather station, plus "please touch" exhibits of fossils and minerals.

125 College Dr. www.caspercollege.edu/tate. ✆ **307/268-2447.** Free admission. Mon–Fri 9am–5pm; Sat 10am–4pm.

Where to Stay

In addition to the lodging properties discussed below, reliable chains in Casper include the **Days Inn,** 301 E. E St.(✆ **800/329-7666** or 307/234-1159), with double rates of $89 to $169; and the attractive **Best Western Ramkota,** 800 N. Poplar St. (✆ **307/266-6000**), with double rates of $89 to $129.

C'mon Inn ★   This impressive new hotel on the south side of town is my pick for a night in Casper. Resembling the grand national park lodges, the C'mon Inn looks like no other chain property in town and has a slick Western interior that nicely matches the wood exterior. The rooms have lots of exposed wood, river rock, and Western art, and are available in a number of different options, from basic doubles to grand suites. There is also a pair of kitchenettes. The best thing about the hotel is the central Jacuzzi Courtyard, with a pool, a baby pool, five hot tubs, and a waterfall.

301 E. Lathrop Rd., Evansville, WY 82636. www.cmoninn.com. ✆ **866/782-2690** or 307/472-6300. 125 units, including 3 suites. $119–$149 double; $189–$249 suite. AE, DISC, MC, V. **Amenities:** Exercise room; 5 indoor Jacuzzis; indoor heated pool. *In room:* A/C, TV, Wi-Fi (free).

14

SHERIDAN & EASTERN WYOMING

Casper

Hotel Higgins ★   Built by area oil tycoon John Higgins in 1916, the Hotel Higgins is a small historic hotel—listed on the National Register of Historic Places—that is plain on the outside but beautiful within, and a wonderful place to soak up the post-Victorian ambience of the early-20th-century American West. It has mahogany and oak woodwork, with distinctive decorative touches that include alabaster chandeliers, beveled glass doors, and terrazzo tile floors. Standard rooms are somewhat small by today's standards (as is the case in most historic hotels), decorated with antiques, including some original pieces from the hotel. The brass, iron, or massive wooden beds have attractive quilted bedspreads, and dressers are oak or walnut.

416 W. Birch St. (P.O. Box 577), Glenrock, WY 82637. www.higginshotel.com. © **800/458-0144** or 307/436-9212. 9 units. $70–$80 double; $85–$95 suite. AE, DISC, MC, V. From Casper, take I-25 south for 20 miles to the 1st Glenrock exit. **Amenities:** Restaurant; lounge. *In room:* TV, no phone, Wi-Fi (free).

Where to Eat

In addition to the restaurants discussed below, you can get a good burger or traditional American breakfast at a reasonable price at **Johnny J's,** 1705 E. 2nd St. (© **307/234-4204**), a '50s-style diner open for three meals daily.

Gegi's Bistro ★★ NEW AMERICAN   Located in the historic Tate Pumphouse on the North Platte River, Gegi's is a great dinner destination in Casper. Its constantly changing menu showcases what is fresh and in season, with namesake chef Gegi Scott showcasing a wide range of culinary influences on the ever-changing menu. You might get paella, smoked gouda chicken, and stuffed pork loin; there is also fresh seafood. Lunch includes sandwiches (including bratwurst and a signature reuben), as well as seafood and pasta.

1775 W. 1st St. at the Tate Pumphouse. www.gegis.com. © **307/234-9796.** Reservations recommended. Lunch $11–$12; dinner $18–$38. AE, DISC, MC, V. Tues–Fri 11am–2pm and Tues–Sat 5–9pm.

The Paisley Shawl ★ CONTINENTAL   This is the area's best fine-dining establishment. Located inside the historic Hotel Higgins, 20 miles east of Casper, the Paisley Shawl is the dining complement to a very good guest inn/restaurant combination. Specialties include filet mignon, roast duckling, jumbo shrimp done in a variety of preparations, and an apple-marinated pork tenderloin. Set inside the hotel's former ballroom—next to a fun little bar—the restaurant is expansive, with seating for 60.

In the Hotel Higgins, Glenrock. www.higginshotel.com. © **800/458-0144** or 307/436-9212. Reservations recommended on weekends. Lunch $7–$10; dinner $20–$26. AE, DISC, MC, V. Tues–Sat 11am–2pm and 6–9pm. From Casper, take I-25 south for 20 miles to the 1st Glenrock exit.

Wonder Bar AMERICAN   A Casper stalwart where drinkers once rode their horse to the bar, the Wonder Bar has reinvented itself as a slick, smoke-free microbrewery in recent years. Served under an amazing tin ceiling and inside walls clad with Western bric-a-brac, the menu includes half-pound burgers with all sorts of toppings, as well as salads, sandwiches, pasta, and a smattering of seafood. Skip the W.B.B.F.B.—a 5-pound burger that costs $22—in favor of some tasty fish tacos. The brewery makes five beers, including a stout and a wheat.

256 S. Center St. www.thewonderbar.net. © **307/234-4110.** Reservations accepted. Main courses $7–$15. AE, DISC, MC, V. Mon–Sat 11am–10pm. Bar open later (usually until midnight on weekdays and 2am on weekends).

DOUGLAS: "THE jackalope CAPITAL OF THE WORLD"

Douglas, about 50 miles east of Casper via I-25 S., is the self-proclaimed "jackalope capital of the world." For the uninitiated, the mythical jackalope is a jack rabbit with a full rack of antlers growing between its ears, measuring about 4 feet at the shoulder. The city honors the beast with an 8-foot statue at the aptly named Jackalope Square (3rd and Center sts.) and an annual festival in June. Jackalope hunting licenses are even available from the **Douglas Area** **Chamber of Commerce,** but the season is limited to only 2 hours each year. For more information, contact the chamber at 121 Brownfield Rd., Douglas, WY 82633 (www.jackalope.org; ✆ **307/358-2950**). While legend holds that pioneers first spotted jackalopes in the sagebrush around Douglas in the 1800s, others point to a pair of local sons, the Herrick brothers, who might just have had the ingenuity to attach a rack of pronghorn antlers to a stuffed rabbit in the 1930s.

FORT LARAMIE NATIONAL HISTORIC SITE

125 miles SE of Casper

On a hot day in 1834, mountain man William Sublette stopped his pack train laden with goods for the Green River rendezvous. Looking at the confluence of the Laramie and Platte rivers, then to the east, across the dusty plains, and then to the west, toward the mountains, he decided that this was a good place for a trading post. Over the next 15 years, the fort served as a hub of the buffalo trade, then as a way station for weary travelers who needed a break on their way to the Pacific.

In 1849—the year of the California gold rush—the U.S. Army bought the fort to "defend" the rising tide of immigrants from the "savages." The Indian Wars hadn't really started yet, not until 1854, when a lame Mormon-owned cow wandered off and was eaten by a starving Miniconjou. A young lieutenant marched into the tribe's camp and demanded that the cow-eater be turned over for swift justice; soon his troops opened fire on the village, and the wars had begun. Many battles later, the Indian tribes gathered here to negotiate the Treaty of 1868, which gave the Sioux and their allies the Powder River country and the Black Hills for "as long as the grass shall grow and the buffalo shall roam."

Soon thereafter, gold was discovered in the Black Hills, and the promise was broken. The army corralled the Indians onto reservations, the railroad replaced the wagon trails, and the beaver and the buffalo were exterminated; the fort closed down in 1890. It wasn't until 1938 that Franklin Roosevelt designated Fort Laramie a national historic site. In its time, travelers from Jim Bridger to Mark Twain stopped at the fort; today tourists ramble through many of the site's 22 original structures.

For an in-depth look at life at the fort, stop by the **visitor center** and watch the 18-minute video about the fort and its role in the settlement of the West. You'll see historical photos there, and a gift shop sells a wide selection of Western-themed books and gift items. Pick up a paper copy of the self-guided tour of the fort's historic buildings, or for $3, rent the audio tour, which not only tells the history of the fort, but also brings it alive with the voices and sounds of the past.

Fort Laramie National Historic Site

Some of the more notable (and restored) buildings you'll see are the **cavalry barracks,** where dozens of soldiers slept, crowded into a single room; **Old Bedlam,** the post's headquarters, which later served as housing for officers, bachelors, and married couples; the **guardhouse,** a stone structure that housed the fort's prisoners; and the **bakery.** Living-history programs are conducted every summer, from June to mid-August, when rangers dress in period costumes, give talks, and answer visitors' questions.

Before leaving the fort, consider driving to the **Old Bedlam Ruts** (ask for a map from the visitor center), 2 miles northwest of the fort. The bumpy gravel road allows you to view the rutted trail marks left by the wagon trains of early Western settlers. Look for Laramie Peak and the grave of Mary Homsley, one of the many who died along the trail.

The grounds and buildings are open daily from sunrise to sunset. From mid-May to mid-September, the visitor center is open daily from 8am to 7pm, and daily from 8am to 4:30pm the rest of the year. Admission costs $3 for adults, free for those 15 and under. To get to the fort from Casper, take I-25 east past Douglas to U.S. 26 (exit 92) and head east to Wyo. 160, which you take southwest 3 miles to Fort Laramie. For more information, contact **Fort Laramie National Historic Site,** National Park Service, 965 Gray Rocks Rd., Fort Laramie, WY 82212 (www.nps.gov/fola; *℃* **307/837-2221**).

SOUTHERN WYOMING

S outhern Wyoming has long been less a destination than a land passed through. All of the famous transcontinental trails—the Bozeman, the California, the Emigrant, the Mormon, the Overland, and the Pony Express—lead somewhere else.

Even today, if you stand on a hill just outside the state capital of Cheyenne, where two major interstates intersect, you'll see a cluster of mega-gas stations crowded with RVs, autos, and big-rig trucks, fueling up before speeding east or west.

In the middle of the 19th century, nearly a half-million people passed through Wyoming on the Oregon Trail. They paused at Independence Rock only long enough to rest and to carve their names in the stone (it's still there—west of Casper on Wyo. 220). This cross-state journey, which can now be done in less than a day, took a month in the 1840s. Along this route, travelers left wagon tracks, cast-iron stoves, worn-out boots, crippled livestock, and their dead. It was no easy passage: On average, they dug 10 graves for every mile of trail.

By 1868, the railroad had forged across the plains, following the more southerly route of the Overland Stages. The arrival of the railroad brought shantytowns of gambling tents, saloons, and brothels, known as "Hell on Wheels." Left behind as the rails moved on, the makeshift towns collapsed, and a cycle of booms and busts began. New discoveries of coal, oil, gold, or uranium would spur a revival, followed by another bust.

Today that legacy colors the character of towns along I-80, which follows the same path used by the first transcontinental railroad. A new generation of miners dig coal and trona (a mineral used in cleaning agents) and keep the oil and natural gas flowing. Mineral money builds sparkling new schools and government buildings, but there is still a rough-and-ready quality to the downtown districts.

But unlike the old days, the communities now have a better grip on the landscape. **Cheyenne** is the state capital, home to thousands of government workers. The holdovers from the ranching families that once dominated the area come out in force every year for **Frontier Days,** a rodeo extravaganza known the world over. West over the pass in **Laramie,** the University of Wyoming is the state's cultural and intellectual nexus. From Laramie west, I-80 climbs around Elk Mountain and races across the high desert—an expansive (some might say bleak) view from behind the windshield, and a sometimes-harrowing drive during winter blizzards.

Cross-country travelers often miss the unexpected beauty in this land because they steadfastly stick to the interstate instead of the two-lane roads that lead to chalk buttes and rust-colored mesas. Take an off-ramp and head north among the stirring buttes of the Red Desert, read the ancient archaeological record at Fossil Butte, hike the mountain cirque of the Snowy Range, or dip in the clear waters of Flaming Gorge. On summer afternoons, the dry air turns humid, the sky blackens, and lightning dances on the red rims. When the sun breaks again, the cliffs burn copper.

SCENIC DRIVES

I-80 runs the length of southern Wyoming along the same path followed by the first transcontinental railroad: straight, fast, convenient, but not often scenic. To the curious eye, though, there are interesting sights along the way.

Geology buffs will be interested in the road cuts made by the interstate—eons of geologic history are revealed. Historians will appreciate the remnants left more than a century ago: Take exit 272, 41 miles west of Laramie, and visit **Little Arlington,** where you'll find what's left of an old stage station and a log cabin, back in the trees. Here along the interstate you'll also see one of Wyoming's latest contributions to the nation's energy pool: a wind farm of spinning propellers lining the ridges like an infantry on stilts.

But to break the monotony of the long drive across southern Wyoming, you need to take a loop off the interstate. There's plenty of great scenery out there, including the landscapes you'll see on the following trips. Many of the sights mentioned here are discussed in further detail later in this chapter.

Driving Tour 1: The Snowy Range Scenic Byway: Laramie to Saratoga

The **Snowy Range Road** (Wyo. 130), designated the nation's second scenic byway, twists up and over the Medicine Bow Mountains south of I-80 and west of Laramie, through corridors of pines and between snow banks (even in midsummer), and tops Snowy Range Pass at 10,847 feet. During the winter, heavy snows close the pass, but you can reach a ski area (both Alpine and Nordic) on the Laramie side, 6 miles past Centennial.

To reach the Snowy Range Scenic Byway from Laramie, take exit 311 off I-80 and head west along Snowy Range Road. Once past the little town of Centennial, the road switchbacks uphill at a steep grade. As you top the pass, you'll see sharp granite peaks to the north, often skirted by snow, bordering a group of snowmelt-fed lakes. This is the top of the range, with elevations more than 12,000 feet above sea level. On a summer day, you'll have plenty of company at the turnouts—people stopping to look, to fish, to hike a nature trail, to picnic. Half a day of vigorous hiking (if you're adjusted to the altitude) will get you atop Medicine Bow Peak, the highest summit in the range. The road then descends the east side of the range, following French Creek to the **Upper North Platte River** (known as the Miracle Mile), which is popular with anglers. When you come to a T in the road, turn right on Wyo. 130 and drive 8 miles north to **Saratoga,** a friendly little town where many boats are launched to fish the excellent waters of the Platte. Continue north from here to rejoin I-80 at Walcott.

FINISH THE LOOP: A DIFFERENT WAY BACK TO LARAMIE You can return on I-80 to Laramie, or take a more adventurous route by going north from

15

SOUTHERN WYOMING | Scenic Drives

Walcott on U.S. 30/287 toward Medicine Bow. This road follows the rail line and, as such, bypasses the mountains—in the winter, it's often a better route than the interstate. The landscape is sagebrush plains and hills, where antelope roam. Every 20 miles or so, you'll hit a crumbling town. One community with a little life still left in it is **Medicine Bow,** location of the Virginian Hotel (another model for Owen Wister's *The Virginian*) and of a watering hole with character, the Diplodocus Bar. Take a look at the bar itself—a solid slab of Wyoming jade, 40 feet long. Some of the great historic dinosaur discoveries were made in this area, at nearby Como Bluff. Continue east to finish the loop in Laramie.

Driving Tour 2: The Rivers Road & Highway 70: Laramie to Baggs

This scenic drive goes from Laramie to the town of Baggs along Wyo. 230 and a recently completed stretch of Wyo. 70. **Wyo. 230** (also known as "the Rivers Rd.") winds its way southwest from Laramie along the Laramie River to the town of **Mountain Home,** where the road dips south into Colorado. Here it makes a loop along Colo. 127/125 for 18 miles and reenters the state of Wyoming on the other side of the Medicine Bow Mountains. The route then continues northwest along Wyo. 230 to the old logging town of Encampment. This last portion offers beautiful river scenery with aspen and lodgepole pines, and opportunities for trout fishing. From Encampment, take Wyo. 70 west to Baggs across 58 miles of Carbon County land in the Sierra Madre Mountain Range. Because of the altitude, views can stretch for miles around this virtually uninhabited belt of southern Wyoming. But the altitude also causes road closures in the winter. Wyo. 70 climbs to 9,955 feet to Battle Pass, named for a nearby conflict that took place in 1841. Here it crosses the Continental Divide before descending to the small towns of **Savery, Dixon,** and **Baggs,** a trio of hamlets with a combined population of fewer than 500. Early settlers came to the area in search of gold and silver. The history of Baggs also includes a different kind of business: Outlaw Butch Cassidy pulled off several robberies here, and quick-triggered livestock detective Tom Horn frequented the area during the late 1800s.

At Baggs, turn north off Wyo. 70 onto Wyo. 789, then drive north for 51 miles through high-plains ranching country. At Creston Junction, you'll rejoin I-80. From here, you can either drive west to Rock Springs and the Utah border or return east to Laramie. You won't have traveled as far as you think, but you'll have seen a lot more along this route than you would have staring at the back of an 18-wheeler along the interstate.

CHEYENNE

93 miles N of Denver; 180 miles S of Casper

Cheyenne is located in the southeast corner of the state. Legend has it that when Gen. Grenville M. Dodge's surveying crew trudged across the prairie, picking a route for the transcontinental railroad, night came, they were tired, they stopped and said, "Good as any," and thus was born the present site of Cheyenne.

By horse or by highway, you can't miss Cheyenne, not only the largest city in Wyoming (population: 60,000), but also its capital. Visitors enjoy the many historical and political sights, from the **Capitol Building** to the **Historic Governors' Mansion.** But Cheyenne's biggest event, hands down, is that wild and woolly weeklong cowboy extravaganza, **Cheyenne Frontier Days.**

HOTELS ■
Days Inn **15**
Hampton Inn **16**
Little America Hotel and
  Resort **17**
Nagle Warren Mansion Bed
  & Breakfast **7**
Motel 6 **14**
The Plains Hotel **11**

RESTAURANTS ◆
Luxury Diner **13**
Poor Richard's **6**
Pizzeria Venti **8**

Re-O-Na Sushi **9**
Sanford's Grub & Pub **8**
2 Doors Down **8**

ATTRACTIONS ●
Cheyenne Botanic Gardens **2**
Cheyenne Depot Museum **12**
Cheyenne Frontier Days Old West Museum **1**
Cheyenne Street Railway Trolley **12**
Frontier Park **3**
Historic Governors' Mansion **5**
Nelson Museum of the West **10**
Paul Smith Children's Village **2**
Wyoming State Capitol **4**

15

SOUTHERN WYOMING | Cheyenne

Essentials

GETTING THERE   **American, United, Great Lakes,** and **Frontier** fly daily into the **Cheyenne Regional Airport** (www.cheyenneairport.com; ✆ **307/634-7071**) on East 8th Avenue, but most people choose to fly directly in and out of **Denver International Airport** (www.flydenver.com; ✆ **303/342-2000**), 101 miles south of Cheyenne in Colorado on I-25, and rent a car to drive into Wyoming from there.

By bus, you can get here with **Greyhound** (www.greyhound.com; ✆ **800/231-2222**). The **bus depot** (✆ **307/635-1327**) is at 5401 Walker Rd.

To get to Cheyenne from **Casper,** take I-25 south for 180 miles. From **Rock Springs** in the southwest part of the state, take I-80 east for 258 miles.

VISITOR INFORMATION **Visit Cheyenne** in the lovingly restored Cheyenne Depot, 1 Depot Square, 121 W. 15th St., Ste. 200 (www.cheyenne.org; (℗ **800/426-5009** outside Wyoming, or 307/778-3133), has a variety of brochures and local maps, including the "Cheyenne Historic Downtown Walking Tour" and the "Downtown Cheyenne Map." Just outside of town, you can also get information at the **Wyoming Information Center,** operated by the Wyoming Division of Tourism, located just off I-25 at College Drive.

GETTING AROUND **Avis** ((℗ **800/331-1212**), **Enterprise** ((℗ **800/261-7331**), and **Hertz** ((℗ **800/654-3131**) have airport counters. For a taxi, call **Capital City Cab** ((℗ **307/632-8294**). Expect to pay about $10 for a ride from the airport to downtown.

Cheyenne Frontier Days ★★

In the world of rodeo, there are three must-see classics: the Pendleton Round-up, the Calgary Stampede, and the "Daddy of 'em All," Cheyenne Frontier Days. Since the inaugural event in 1897, it has grown into one of the largest rodeos in the world. The Frontier Days committee and thousands of volunteers organize this 10-day-long Western spectacle of parades, a rodeo, dances, and concerts each summer, the last full week of July. It's safe to say that this is the most vivid demonstration of Western hospitality you'll encounter in the modern world.

Though the rodeo lasts for a full 10 days, picking and choosing activities carefully can save you a lot of time and money. Rodeo ticket prices range anywhere from around $12 to $40 per person, and nightly shows featuring popular country music acts cost $23 to $60.

VISITOR INFORMATION Contact the **Cheyenne Frontier Days Ticket Office** for brochures, ticket forms, and information on all shows and activities during upcoming Frontier Days celebrations at Cheyenne Frontier Days, P.O. Box 2477, Cheyenne, WY 82003 (www.cfdrodeo.com; (℗ **800/227-6336** or 307/778-7222 for tickets, or 307/778-7200 for headquarters).

GETTING AROUND DURING THE RODEO CELEBRATION Parking is provided at Frontier Park for $10 per vehicle, but shuttle parking is also available and makes much more sense. The shuttle picks up visitors at several locations and delivers them to the rodeo grounds; round-trip fare is $10 per carload. The city also runs a special bus service to Frontier Park from downtown Cheyenne that stops at nearby campgrounds and hotels. Contact **Visit Cheyenne** ((℗ **307/778-3133**) for bus stop locations and scheduled pickups.

THE GRAND PARADE With the exception of Buffalo Bill's walk through the streets of Cheyenne in 1898 and a docile march led by Theodore Roosevelt in 1910, Cheyenne's Frontier Days Grand Parade in its early days was similar to a stagecoach holdup. Guns blazed as cowboys rode through the streets with little regard to form or style. In 1925, things took a turn toward civility when the "Evolution of Transportation" theme was introduced. Today, many horse-drawn vehicles make their way through the streets of Cheyenne as part of the Old-Time Carriage section of the parade. In addition to the carriages and antique cars, marching bands, local clubs, and various Plains Indians groups march. Viewing sites are as near as the closest curb, but you'll want to claim a position 45 minutes before the start.

The parade starts at Capitol Ave. and 24th St., runs down Capitol Ave. to 17th Ave., and continues up Carey Ave. to the finish at Carey Ave. and 24th St. Free admission. During Frontier Days, parades are Sat, Tues, Thurs, and Sat, starting at 9:30am.

THE RODEO An anthropologist might see rodeo as a fading ritual to a passing way of life, but don't tell that to the fans who pack the stands at Frontier Days. It's actually one of the most popular spectator sports in the nation, as American as apple pie and baseball. Cheyenne's annual rodeo draws people from across the nation, and the best of the best cowboys.

Spectators from around the world pack into the stands to watch such events as steer wrestling, barrel racing, team roping, and the classic event—and Wyoming's state symbol—saddle bronc riding. It's enormous fun, but part of the attraction is that these men and women put themselves in harm's way, working enormous animals with a wild streak. In a world where risk is often an illusion created by entertainers, this is the real thing. Champion bull-rider Lane Frost died in the ring at Frontier Days in 1989.

Daily ticket prices start at $16 for bleachers at the far end of the arena and $30 for the center of the action—the bucking chutes. Bull riding tickets cost more, from about $30 to $40. Each night after the rodeo, country stars take the stage. Concert tickets run $23 to $60.

Frontier Park, exit 12 off I-80. *C* **800/227-6336** or 307/778-7222. Tickets $12–$24. During Frontier Days, daily at 12:45pm.

THE PANCAKE BREAKFAST Since their inception in 1952, these free breakfasts have become increasingly popular. Legend holds that a cement mixer churns up enough pancake batter to cook 100,000 flapjacks for 30,000 people. The breakfasts are held downtown at the Cheyenne Depot Plaza on the corner of Lincolnway and Capitol and served by the local Kiwanis Club, including, sometimes, an unassuming governor.

Depot Plaza, Lincolnway and Capitol. Free admission. During Frontier Days, Mon, Wed, and Fri 7–9am.

Shopping

The can't-miss retailers in Cheyenne are **Sierra Trading Post,** 5025 Campstool Rd. (*C* **307/775-8090**), for outdoor gear and close-outs of all kinds; the **Wrangler,** 1518 Capitol Ave. at Lincolnway (*C* **307/634-3048**), for cowboy boots and Western duds; and **Wyoming Home,** 216 W. Lincolnway (*C* **307/638-2222**), for Western furnishings and decor. Housed in the historic Whipple House, **Deselms Fine Art,** 300 E. 17th St. (*C* **307/432-0606**), is the city's top art gallery, featuring the work of largely local artists.

Seeing the Sights

Stop in at the **Nelson Museum of the West,** 1714 Carey Ave. (www.nelson museum.com; *C* **307/635-7670**), to see a collection of cowboy trappings, American-Indian artifacts, taxidermy trophies, and Western memorabilia. The **Cheyenne Botanic Gardens,** 710 S. Lions Park Dr. (www.botanic.org; *C* **307/637-6458**), is a showcase of lush flower beds. The gardens are home to the **Paul Smith Children's Village ★**, a first-rate kid's garden complete with a wide range of interactive exhibits. **Visit Cheyenne** (*C* **307/778-3133**) has developed free audio tours for numerous attractions in the city delivered via cellphone; contact them for information. Also call **Visit Cheyenne** for the latest schedule of **Cheyenne Gunslingers,** who put on fun shootouts downtown during the summer months.

Cheyenne Depot Museum ★ This good museum details Cheyenne's beginnings as a dusty railroad town and tells the story of how rails shaped this part of the

West. Exhibits include fascinating historical photographs, models, and the original cargo scales used when the depot was active (late 1800s–1980s). The Union Pacific Depot was restored to its original condition and is worth visiting even if you're not a railroad buff—but if you are, start here and then pick up the brochure "Tracking Trains in Cheyenne" from the information center in the depot lobby: It's a great resource for trainiacs, covering historic rail landmarks and the best places to gawk at the real thing. There are occasional excursions on a historic steam train; call for the current schedule.

121 W. 15th St., in the Union Pacific Depot. www.cheyennedepotmuseum.org. © **307/632-3905.** $5 adults, free for children 12 and under. May–Sept Mon–Fri 9am–6pm, Sat 9am–6pm, Sun 11am–5pm; Oct–Apr Mon–Sat 9am–5pm, Sun 11am–4pm.

Cheyenne Frontier Days Old West Museum Frontier Days has been around long enough that folks have become interested in its history, so sponsors established this museum to warehouse memorabilia from the rodeo and other historical artifacts. The Old West Museum, located next door to the rodeo arena, is a convenient place to take a break from the action. There are carriages, temporary exhibits, photos, a video-screening room, and a treasure trove of rodeo gear.

4610 N. Carey Ave., Frontier Park. www.oldwestmuseum.org. © **307/778-7290.** $7 adults, free for children 12 and under. Mon–Fri 9am–5pm; Sat–Sun 10am–5pm; longer hours during Frontier Days and peak summer season.

Cheyenne Street Railway Trolley No longer used as a mode of mass transit, the local trolley offers visitors a ride around Cheyenne's main tourist sites, including the Governors' Mansion, the Wyoming State Capitol, and the historic homes of the area's late-19th-century cattle barons.

Purchase tickets at the Cheyenne Area Convention and Visitors Bureau in the Cheyenne Depot, 121 W. 15th St. www.cheyennetrolley.com. © **800/426-5009** or 307/778-3133. Tour $10 adults, $5 children 4–12, free for kids 3 and under. May to mid-Sept 2-hr. tours Mon–Fri 10 and 11:30am, and 1, 2:30, and 4pm; Sat 10am and 1:30pm; Sun 1:30pm.

Historic Governors' Mansion If you're interested in the political history of the state, you should continue 6 blocks from the capitol to the Historic Governors' Mansion. Built in 1904, it housed Wyoming's first families until 1976; today, many of the rooms have been restored to their 1905 appearances. Over the years, the decorative styles mixed, and you'll find everything from Chippendale to Colonial Revival to Art Nouveau. There's even a steer-horn chair in the entrance hall.

300 E. 21st St. http://wyoparks.state.wy.us. © **307/777-7878.** Free admission. Summer Mon–Sat 9am–5pm, Sun 1–5pm; winter Tues–Sat 9am–5pm.

Wyoming State Capitol In the summer, when the streets of Cheyenne are shaded by large old oaks, it's easy to come upon the Capitol building a bit by surprise. It's not a large Capitol, as such things go, but it's a traditional one, with a gold-leaf dome and carved stone. The main structure was built in 1888; the wings were added in 1917, but otherwise, the stately building has undergone little change over the years. Inside you can admire the beautiful woodwork, stained glass, and sparkling marble floors, and view historical photos and exhibits on the state's wildlife. Outside, you can stop by three statues: a monument to the first female justice of the peace, Esther Hobart Morris; a bronze bison; and the *Spirit of Wyoming*—the wild bucking horse emblazoned on every license plate in the state.

Capitol Ave. at 24th St. ℂ **307/777-7220.** Free admission. Self-guided tours Mon–Fri 8:30am–4:30pm, except holidays. Guided tours available by appointment.

Where to Stay

Thanks to its crossroads location, there's a plethora of accommodations in Cheyenne, from basic motels to ornate B&Bs. The chain properties include the family-friendly **Days Inn,** 2360 W. Lincolnway (ℂ **307/778-8877**), with double rates of $89 to $149 ($200 and up during Frontier Days); **Hampton Inn,** adjacent to the junction of I-25 and I-80, at 1781 Fleischli Pkwy. (ℂ **307/632-2747**), offering double rates of $119 to $159 ($199 and up during Frontier Days); and **Motel 6,** 1735 Westland Rd. (ℂ **307/635-6806**), with double rates of $50 to $60 ($110–$130 during Frontier Days).

A reservation caution: Hotels fill up quickly during Frontier Days, and rack (published) rates are much higher.

Little America Hotel and Resort ★   Tucked into 1,200 acres of prairie on the outskirts of Cheyenne, this is one of the largest hotels in Wyoming and a noteworthy oasis. Surprisingly chic, the main building and low-rise brick lodges are surrounded by an executive golf course, duck pond, and mature evergreens. The main building harbors a tasteful lounge warmed by a fireplace and Navajo rugs; shops offer boutique clothing, jewelry, and Western souvenirs; there's a stuffed penguin, the hotel's unofficial mascot, in the hall. Accommodations, in five low-rise brick lodges, provide 37-inch flatscreen TVs, balconies, and bathrooms with tub/shower combos and marble counters. Rooms come in three categories: standards, minisuites with king-size beds, and executive suites. Dinner is available in **Hathaway's,** and there is also a coffee shop. The Olympic-size pool is open summer only, but a fitness center and jogging path can be used year-round.

2800 W. Lincolnway (I-80 at I-25), Cheyenne, WY 82009. www.cheyenne.littleamerica.com. ℂ **800/445-6945** or 307/775-8400. Fax 307/775-8425. 188 units. $109–$199 double; during Frontier Days $229–$289 double. AE, DISC, MC, V. **Amenities:** 2 restaurants; lounge; exercise room; 9-hole golf course; outdoor heated pool. *In room:* A/C, TV, fridge, hair dryer, Wi-Fi (free).

Nagle Warren Mansion Bed & Breakfast ★★   This gem of an inn is the centerpiece of an increasingly nice stretch on 17th Avenue. Originally built in 1888 by famed architect Erasmus Nagle (it was the first house in the state with indoor plumbing), the mansion was converted into an elegant bed-and-breakfast in 1997. Grand and spacious, the three-story structure oozes luxury, from the furnishings (almost exclusively regional antiques) to the stately spire that anchors the building's southeast corner. The rooms, named after the mansion's former residents, feature lavish, late-19th-century style, tempered by a few modern perks—CD players, televisions, and telephones. Half of the rooms are located in the main building, and half are in the adjoining carriage house (the latter have fireplaces), but they all have their own unique allure.

222 E. 17th St., Cheyenne, WY 82001. www.naglewarrenmansion.com. ℂ **800/811-2610** or 307/637-3333. 12 units. $142–$172 double; during Frontier Days $294–$324 double. Rates include breakfast. AE, DC, MC, V. Pets accepted. **Amenities:** Lounge; exercise room. *In room:* A/C, TV/DVD, hair dryer, Wi-Fi (free).

The Plains Hotel ★   Built in 1911, the stalwart Plains Hotel is once again the historic centerpiece of downtown Cheyenne. Under a stained-glass ceiling, the lobby is a multipillared space with its original tile floor and a retouched mural on the walls ringing the ceiling. Rooms run the gamut from standard (with a king-size bed or one or two queen-size), to larger parlor suites (a king-size or two queen-size), to true two-room suites, one of which is done up in high cowboy style, thanks to the help of *American Cowboy* magazine. The rooms, on the whole, are comfortable and attractive, with a subtle Western motif, with bathrooms that vary in terms of amenities and quality—some are a bit old, some have showers only, and others feature the vanities in the rooms. The elevators are also quite dinky: As the story goes, they built them that way so people couldn't take their horses up to their rooms.

1600 Central Ave., Cheyenne, WY 82001. www.theplainshotel.com. © **866/275-2467** or 307/638-3311. Fax 307/635-2022. 131 units, including 17 suites. $79–$129 double, $129–$219 suite; during Frontier Days $199–$299 double, $249–$299 suite. AE, DC, DISC, MC, V. **Amenities:** Restaurant; lounge; exercise room; spa. *In room:* TV, hair dryer, Wi-Fi (free).

CAMPING

The biggest campground is the **Restway Travel Park,** 4212 Whitney Rd., 2 miles east of Cheyenne (© **800/443-2751** or 307/634-3811). Catering to RV and tent campers alike, Restway boasts a heated seasonal swimming pool, miniature golf, and a store stocked with basic supplies; nightly rates run from about $20 for a basic tent site to about $40 for a site with full hookups during Frontier Days. For something a bit different, head to **Terry Bison Ranch,** located 6 miles south of Cheyenne via I-25, exit 2 (www.terrybisonranch.com; © **307/634-4171**), a working buffalo ranch with tent ($22 per night, $25 during Cheyenne Frontier Days) and RV sites ($36 per night, $45 during Cheyenne Frontier Days), as well as a bunkhouse, guest cabins, gift shop, and restaurant. The ranch also offers cabins, lodge rooms, and a variety of tours.

Where to Eat

On **17th Street** between Carey and Warren avenues, there is a restaurant row that will satisfy most appetites. Here you'll find **2 Doors Down,** 118 E. 17th St. (www.2doorsdown.net; © 307/634-6008), serving burgers topped with everything from green chile to horseradish to teriyaki sauce. **Sanford's Grub & Pub,** 115 E. 17th St. (www.thegrubandpub.com; © 307/643-3381), is a bar and grill with steaks, ribs, fajitas and personality to spare. For pizza and pasta, head to **Pizzeria Venti,** 112 E. 17th St. (© **307/433-1020**). Two blocks down, **Re-O-Na Sushi & Thai Cuisine,** 112 W. 17th St. (© **307/638-8820**), is another gem.

Luxury Diner 🍴 AMERICAN   A favorite blue-collar breakfast counter, the Luxury Diner is a real down-home greasy spoon. We say that affectionately, of course; the food is good, the coffee always hot, and the waitresses sassy. Breakfast is served all day. The pie: apple. The special: meatloaf. It's the real thing—no Buddy Holly posters, no 45s dangling from the ceiling for that retro look. In fact, the small dining area ran as a trolley from 1896 to 1912 before becoming a diner in 1926. Pictures of trains cover the walls, Christmas lights blink around the trim, breakfast is served all day, and the motto is, "Friendliest place in town." It's right.

1401-A W. Lincolnway. © **307/638-8971.** Breakfast and lunch main courses $4–$14. AE, DISC, MC, V. Daily 6am–4pm.

Poor Richard's ★★ STEAKS/AMERICAN   The locals' choice for a nice dinner, Poor Richard's has been serving excellent steaks, seafood, chicken, and pasta dishes since opening its doors in 1977. I recommend the blackened prime rib, but all steaks are USDA Choice Beef, aged for 4 weeks and cut fresh daily. Lunches are lighter, but include several pasta and seafood dishes beyond the sandwiches and burgers that dominate other Cheyenne eateries. The staff is efficient and sharp, working several rooms that feature stained glass, wood-backed booths, and an ambience midway between romantic and casual. This winning combination—plus the subtle Benjamin Franklin motif—attracts everyone from politicians to ranch hands.

2231 E. Lincolnway. www.poorrichardscheyenne.com. (C) **307/635-5114.** Reservations accepted for parties of 6 or more only. Lunch $8–$13; dinner $13–$27. AE, DISC, MC, V. Mon–Sat 11am–2:30pm; Mon–Thurs 5–9pm; Fri–Sat 5–10pm.

Cheyenne After Dark

The **Atlas Theatre,** 211 W. Lincolnway ((C) **307/635-0199**), is Cheyenne's prime performing arts venue, home to the **Cheyenne Little Theatre Players** (www. cheyennelittletheatre.org; (C) **307/638-6543**), mounting recent productions of *Messiah on the Frigidaire* and *Annie Get Your Gun.* The hippest watering hole in town is **Shadows Pub & Grill,** 115 W. 15th St., in the Union Pacific Depot ((C) **307/634-7625**), a sports bar/microbrewery that serves good barbecue and other pub fare. Free **concerts** are staged in front of the depot on summer Friday evenings. **Bit-O-Wyo Ranch** puts on a barn dinner show on summer weekends about 20 miles west of Cheyenne at 470 Happy Jack Rd. (www.bitowyoranch.com; (C) **307/638-6924**); the price is $40 per person ages 6 and over.

LARAMIE ★

49 miles NW of Cheyenne; 360 miles SE of Yellowstone/Grand Teton; 207 miles E of Rock Springs; 124 miles N of Denver

Though the political capital is 49 miles to the east, Laramie is the cultural and intellectual capital of Wyoming. It's home to the state's only university, public or private. Unlike Jackson, which has a prefabricated feel designed to appeal to visitors, Laramie has an earnest charm that seems to have developed by accident, and it has been this way for nearly a century. Located just east of the beautiful Medicine Bow Mountains, at an altitude of more than 7,000 feet, Laramie is sometimes buffeted by chill winds. But it has university-town amenities like bookstores and coffee shops, and a few Western features to boot, including outlying ranchlands and some rowdy downtown bars.

Essentials

GETTING THERE The **Laramie Regional Airport** (www.laramieairport.com; (C) 307/742-4164), west of town along Wyo. 130, services daily flights on **Great Lakes Aviation** from Denver.

Or go **Greyhound** ((C) 800/231-2222), which stops in Laramie at a bus depot/convenience store at 1300 S. 3rd St. ((C) 307/745-4536). The bus stops at several Wyoming cities along I-80, including Rock Springs and Cheyenne.

Laramie is an easy 49-mile drive from Cheyenne on I-80; driving from Salt Lake, it's just more than 300 miles once you hit Evanston. The fastest route from the Yellowstone–Grand Teton area is via U.S. 287 S. for 259 miles to Rawlins and I-80 east for 101 miles to Laramie.

VISITOR INFORMATION   Contact the **Albany County Tourism Board,** 210 Custer St., Laramie, WY 82070 (www.visitlaramie.org; ✆ **800/445-5303**), or the **Laramie Area Chamber of Commerce** (www.laramie.org; ✆ **307/745-7339**).

GETTING AROUND   Hertz (✆ **800/654-3131**) and **Avis** (✆ **800/331-1212**) maintain outlets at the Laramie airport.

SPECIAL EVENTS   Jubilee Days (www.laramiejubileedays.com) is a Western party that runs early to mid-July with rodeos, parades, and fireworks.

Getting Outside

Curt Gowdy State Park (http://wyoparks.state.wy.us; ✆ **307/632-7946**) named for the television sportscaster who hailed from Wyoming, is quite pleasant, if not spectacularly beautiful. Located 23 miles southeast of Laramie, the 1,645-acre park is a great spot for a picnic ($6 day-use fee). Or stay the night in one of the five camp-sites for $17 per night. There are two lakes here, but no swimming is allowed (they provide part of Cheyenne's water supply). Boating is permitted, but no rentals are available at the park. Call for further information. To get to the park, take I-80 east until you see the exit for Wyo. 210, the scenic back road to Cheyenne.

About 10 miles southeast of Laramie, on the edge of the Medicine Bow National Forest, are **Pole Mountain** and the **Vedauwoo Recreation Area** (✆ **307/745-2300**). Vedauwoo and the Happy Jack trail head, near the Summit exit of I-80, have some excellent summer and winter recreational opportunities. The name Vedauwoo (pronounced *Vee*-duh-voo) is Arapaho for "earth-born." The rock formations—soft-edged blocks shaped like stools, turtles, and mushrooms—were considered the sacred creations of animal and human spirits, and young Indian men sought visions there. Today rock climbers pursue their quests for challenging climbs here and find tough technical pitches. Other folks see a great place to mountain-bike, hike, and scan the vistas. There is a campground with sites for $10 per night. To get there, take I-80 east toward Cheyenne, past the second-biggest Abe Lincoln head in these parts (10 miles outside town) to exit 329, to the Vedauwoo turnoff.

Seeing the Sights

The **Laramie Plains Museum,** 603 Ivinson Ave. (www.laramiemuseum.org; ✆ **307/742-4448**), is housed in a gorgeous three-story Queen Anne Victorian home built by Laramie settler Edward Ivinson, with furnishings from the 1890s. Admission is $10 adults, $7 seniors, and $5 students (free for kids 5 and under).

University of Wyoming   The only 4-year college in the state, the University of Wyoming was established in 1887 with the funding of Old Main, its first building. At that time, there were five professors, two tutors, and 42 students on the 20-acre campus, which included Prexy's Pasture, where the school's first president kept his cows. Today, the University of Wyoming has more than 2,000 faculty and staff members and an enrollment of about 13,000. The university has boomed along with oil and gas prices and the coal-bed methane market, with the legislature loosening the purse strings in recent sessions.

A campus tour is worth the effort, if for no other reason than to check out the campus architecture, which ranges from the solid sandstone castles of a century ago to the spaceship designs of today (stop at the **Visitors Services Center,** 1408 Ivinson Ave., for a map). To catch a glimpse of student life in Laramie, swing by Prexy's Pasture.

Laramie

Information (i)

HOTELS ■
Hilton Garden Inn **13**
Mad Carpenter Inn **8**
Sunset Inn **3**
Travelodge **7**
Vee Bar Ranch **1**

RESTAURANTS ◆
Altitude Chophouse & Brewery **4**
Coal Creek Coffee Company **6**
Grand Avenue Pizza **10**
Sweet Melissa **5**

ATTRACTIONS ●
Laramie Plains Museum **9**
University of Wyoming **11, 12**
Wyoming Territorial Prison State
  Historic Site **2**

    With no pro sports teams in Wyoming, the college's athletic programs take on special importance. Fans drive from all over the state to root for the **Cowboys** as they compete against Mountain West Conference foes. For event information and tickets, contact the ticket office (www.wyomingathletics.com; ✆ **800/996-3261** or 307/766-4850).
    The university plays an important role with its museum spaces, and most of the exhibits are free. Located in the Knight Geology Building, in the northwest corner of Prexy's Pasture, the **Geological Museum** (www.uwyo.edu/geomuseum; ✆ **307/766-2646**) has plenty of dinosaur fossils, as well as some from mammoth, camels,

and other extinct Wyoming denizens, not to mention a life-size T. rex statue out front. It's open Tuesday through Friday from 10am to 4pm, Saturday and Sunday from 10am to 3pm; admission is free. Also worth visiting is the **Rocky Mountain Herbarium** (www.rmh.uwyo.edu; ✆ **307/766-2236**), open Monday through Friday from 8am to 5pm (7:30am–4:30pm when school is out of session). The **Insect Gallery** (✆ **307/766-5338;** in the Ag Building, just north of Prexy's Pasture) is primarily a research facility and a bit esoteric to the average visitor; call for current hours. The **Centennial Complex** (2111 Willett Dr., on the east side of campus, east of 15th St.) houses the **UW Art Museum** (www.uwyo.edu/artmuseum; ✆ **307/766-6622**), with works by Audubon, Albert Bierstadt, Thomas Moran, and even Gauguin. It's open Monday through Saturday from 10am to 5pm. Also in this building is the **American Heritage Center** (http://ahc.uwyo.edu; ✆ **307/766-4114**), a top-notch research facility with extensive collections of Western-history materials and some unexpected archives, such as some of Jack Benny's papers, open Monday 8am to 9pm and Tuesday through Friday from 8am to 5pm.

Bordered by N. 9th and N. 15th sts. on the west and east, and E. Lewis and E. Ivinson Ave. on the north and south. www.uwyo.edu. ✆ **307/766-1121.**

Wyoming Territorial Prison State Historic Site ☺ Formerly a penitentiary where Butch Cassidy served time, the Territorial Prison transmogrified into an experimental livestock station before becoming the historical park it is today. Beyond the prison, almost everything having to do with frontier life before the start of the 20th century can be found on the site's 200 acres, from a funky frontier town (open weekends only) to homesteader's cabins and farm animals. There is also an art gallery and a gift shop. Expect to spend about 2 hours here.

975 Snowy Range Rd. (just east of I-80, exit 311). http://wyoparks.state.wy.us. ✆ **800/745-6161** or 307/745-6161. Admission $5, $2.50 for children 12–17, free for children 11 and under. May–Oct daily 9am–6pm; call for winter hours.

Shopping

Since Laramie is a university town, it has its fair share of bookstores. Our favorites are the peaceful **2nd Story Books** and **Personally Recommended Books,** both at 105 E. Ivinson Ave. (✆ **307/745-4423**). To see what's hot on campus, visit the **University Bookstore,** 1 block north of Ivinson Avenue and 13th Street (✆ **800/370-2676**).

If you're looking for the gear you need for an adventure in the Medicine Bow, try **Cross-Country Connection,** 222 S. 2nd St. (✆ **307/721-2851**), for skiing and climbing equipment (you can rent skis here, too). For Western clothing and souvenirs, hit **Martindale's,** downtown at 217 E. Grand Ave. (✆ **307/721-4100**).

Downtown Laramie is also home to all kinds of artists and craftspeople. **Earth, Wind, and Fire,** 216 S. 2nd St. (✆ **307/745-0226**), is a pottery lover's dream come true. The prime antiques store is **Antique Fever,** 211 S. 2nd St. (✆ **307/721-8398**).

Where to Stay

Among the chain properties in town are **Travelodge,** 165 N. 3rd St. (✆ **800/942-6671** or 307/742-6671), with rooms for $70 to $135 double; and the **Hilton Garden Inn,** on the University of Wyoming campus at 2229 Grand Ave. (✆ **307/745-5500**), with double rates of $109 to $159. Outside of the chains, the

Sunset Inn, 1104 S. 3rd St. (www.sunsetinn-laramie.com; © **307/742-3741**), is a small motel with an outdoor pool and indoor hot tub. Doubles cost $45 to $90.

Mad Carpenter Inn ★   Before Lawrence Thomas bought this huge Victorian near the University of Wyoming Campus, it was just a "shabby old house." But Thomas, a one-time basketball player at UW, renovated the place and crafted the woodwork that earned him the nickname "the Mad Carpenter" from his daughter. The end result is a first-rate B&B with equal parts elegance and whimsy in its three guest rooms, two of them with queens in the main house. The third room is actually its own structure, the Dollhouse, with an ornate staircase leading to a sleeping loft and the adjacent balcony. In the main house, there is also one of the best game rooms I've ever seen in an inn, complete with slick hardwood floors; a piano; dartboards; and pool, Ping-Pong, and foosball tables. Breakfast includes homemade fruit crisps and occasional egg dishes.

353 N. 8th St., Laramie, WY 82072. www.madcarpenter.com. © **307/742-0870.** 3 units. $90–$125 double. Rates include continental breakfast. AE, MC, V. **Amenities:** Game room. *In room:* TV, no phone, Wi-Fi (free).

Vee Bar Guest Ranch ★★   A jewel of a guest ranch, the Vee Bar is perfect for those looking to delve into the ranching lifestyle as they get away from it all. The property itself, 800 acres in all, features lush fields, cottonwood and willow groves, and a stretch of the crystalline Little Laramie River. Alongside the historic main lodge, the accommodations here are comfortable cabins and a trio of "Riverside Suite" duplexes that manage to balance the rustic with the convenient. Two of the free-standing cabins are more than a century old, restored and furnished with antiques of local origin; the third is modern (1990) but blends into the old-fashioned atmosphere with ease. Activities such as horseback riding, cattle drives, fishing, river tubing, and overnight camp-outs are included, as are all meals. For breakfast, expect flapjacks, eggs, and bacon; for dinner, steaks, seafood, and other hearty fare. Guests can unwind in the historic John Wayne Saloon.

38 Vee Bar Ranch Rd., Laramie, WY 82070. www.veebar.com. © **800/483-3227** or 307/745-7036. Fax 307/745-7433. 9 cabins. $3,350–$3,750 per 7-night stay for 2 adults; $1,445–$1,645 per week each additional person. 3-night packages also available. Rates include all meals and activities. Fall to spring (and summer Sat), single-night stays are available for $150–$170 for a double. AE, DISC, MC, V. Located 21 miles west of Laramie via Snowy Range Rd. (Wyo. 130). **Amenities:** Restaurant; lounge; children's programs; exercise room; outdoor Jacuzzi; Wi-Fi (free). *In room:* Fridge, no phone.

CAMPING

The **Laramie KOA,** off I-80 at 1271 W. Baker St. (© **307/742-6553**), is open year-round. There are 100 pull-through sites here, as well as a rec room, small store, and unobstructed mountain views. Full hookups cost $28 to $32 in summer (lower in winter); there are also tent sites and cabins. There are also campgrounds at Curt Gowdy State Park and Vedauwoo Recreation Area (see "Getting Outside," above).

Where to Eat

Thinkers and talkers fuel up on good java at the **Coal Creek Coffee Company,** 110 E. Grand Ave. (© **307/745-7737**); there is sometimes live music in the evenings. You can get pasta or pizza at **Grand Avenue Pizza,** 301 E. Grand Ave. (© **307/721-2909**), which hides in an old corner space downtown.

Altitude Chophouse & Brewery ★ AMERICAN/MICROBREWERY   This downtown eatery, effortlessly melding woodsy and swank, features tree stumps for bar stools and blue banners hanging from the rafters to dampen the sound of friendly chatter. The atmosphere is a rich complement to the excellent fare, which includes pub standards (burgers, pizzas, and cheese sticks) as well as excellent steaks and seafood. We like the cedar plank salmon and the orange-braised pork loin, but the steaks are also held in high regard. The prices are right, and the beers aren't bad at all, either.

320 S. 2nd St. www.altitudechophouse.com. © **307/721-4031.** Reservations accepted. Main courses $8–$24. AE, DISC, MC, V. Mon–Sat 11am–10pm. Bar open later.

Sweet Melissa 🍴 VEGETARIAN   A meatless menu in Wyoming might sound like something of an oxymoron, but this funky cafe by the rail yard will satisfy most any patron, carnivorous or not. The three-bean chili is terrific and makes me long for another trip to Laramie, but the menu also includes salads, black bean burgers and hummus sandwiches, sweet potato–black bean burrito, lentil loaf, mushroom fajitas, and several pasta dishes. There are also vegan and gluten-free options. Attached is the **Front Street Bar,** a comfortable, brick-laden space to wet your whistle

213 S. 1st St. © **307/742-9607.** Reservations accepted for large parties only. Main courses $7–$10. DISC, MC, V. Mon–Sat 11am–9pm. Bar open later.

A SIDE TRIP FOR THE OUTDOOR ENTHUSIAST: THE SNOWY RANGE & CARBON COUNTY

Snowy Range: 32 miles W of Laramie

You can very quickly leave behind the dry plains around Laramie and find yourself up among lakes, forest, and substantial peaks in the north end of the Medicine Bow Mountains, known as the **Snowy Range.** Just take Wyo. 130 west, through the foothill town of Centennial, past the **Snowy Range Ski Area** (www.snowyrangeski. com; © **307/745-5750;** full-day lift tickets are $39 for adults, $34 for teens 13 to 17, $24 for children 12 and under), and up into the mountains, where peaks rise well over 10,000 feet. Though **Medicine Bow Peak** is 12,013 feet tall, it's a relatively easy day-climb, starting at the parking lot by Lake Marie and covering about 5 miles. You can loop around the west side of the hollow in which the peak stands and return on the east side among the lakes. Trails are well marked, and you'll meet people as you hike. Just keep an eye out for thunderheads, as you'll be above timberline, exposed to lightning. For **detailed trail maps,** contact the **Medicine Bow National Forest,** 2468 Jackson St., in Laramie (www.fs.fusda.gov/mbr; © **307/ 745-2300**).

If you drive on over the Snowies—it takes only about an hour—you'll drop down into the valley of the **North Platte River,** with its old mining and timber towns such as Encampment and Saratoga. **Saratoga** is the roost of several fishing outfits that guide on the North Platte, one of the finest trout fisheries in the state. If you spend the night, you'll probably enjoy the creaky, old-fashioned style of the historic (1893) **Hotel Wolf,** 101 E. Bridge St. (www.wolfhotel.com; © **307/326-5525**), with double rates of $70 to $110; or the **Saratoga Resort and Spa,** 601 E. Pic Pike Rd.

(www.saratogainn.com; $\mathcal{C}$ **800/594-0178**), with its own private hot-spring-fed pool, golf course, and double rates of $144 to $216 in summer and $117 to $177 in winter (soaking and continental breakfast included). Opened in 2011—although the ranch dates to the 1870s—the **Lodge & Spa at Brush Creek Ranch,** 66 Brush Creek Ranch Rd. (www.brushcreekranch.com; $\mathcal{C}$ **307/327-5294**), is an all-inclusive luxury guest ranch with all of the fixings, from horseback riding and skeet shooting to buffalo hunts on private ranch land and a PGA-certified indoor golf simulator. Situated on a scenic working ranch with 2,000 cattle, lodging ranges from slick guest rooms, to restored historic cabins, to luxury homes with their own staffs. Summer rates start at $1,200 for two for a lodge room and go up from there.

At the foot of the mountains in Centennial, try the **Old Corral Hotel** (www. oldcorral.com; $\mathcal{C}$ **307/745-5918**), $85 to $130 for a double with Western decor ($55–$95 double fall and spring), or the rustic **Brooklyn Lodge** (www.brooklyn lodge.com; $\mathcal{C}$ **307/742-6916**), a log-laden B&B with rockers and wagon-wheel tables; double rates are $175. Another area attraction of note is **Woods Landing** in the dinky town of Jelm (www.woodslanding.com; $\mathcal{C}$ **307/745-9638**), a historic Western dance hall built on 24 boxcar springs—when the dance floor is full, the place literally bounces. A restaurant, a complex of rustic rental cabins ($55–$100 double), and a riverside guesthouse ($150–$175 a night, with a 2-night minimum) are on-site. North of the Snowies, off of I-80, the **Historic Elk Mountain Hotel,** 102 E. Main St., Elk Mountain (www.elkmountainhotel.com; $\mathcal{C}$ **307/348-7774**), is a nicely restored hotel with double rates of $130 to $175 and a restaurant on-site.

Camping

Medicine Bow National Forest (www.fs.usda.gov/mbr; $\mathcal{C}$ **307/745-2300**) maintains a number of semiprimitive campgrounds June through September, scattered throughout the range west of Laramie. Fees at most campgrounds range from $10 to $12 per night, although a few are free or $5 per night.

Fishing

The Upper North Platte River cuts right through Saratoga, and those in the know consider it one of the state's top trout-fishing spots. **Stoney Creek Outfitters,** 216 E. Walnut, Saratoga (www.fishstoneycreek.com; $\mathcal{C}$ **307/326-8750**), charges $450 for a full-day, two-person float-fishing expedition.

ROCK SPRINGS

258 miles W of Cheyenne; 178 miles S of Jackson

Rock Springs began as a stage station on the Overland Trail, named after a natural spring that dried up after extensive mining in the area. In 1894, Jack London wrote of Rock Springs: "It seems to be the Wild and Woolly West with a vengeance." It's still true: Rock Springs shows the rougher side of Wyoming, powered by a coal-burning power plant, freight trains roaring through, and all-night truckers stopping for coffee, adding to a blue-collar sensibility.

For more than a century, boom followed bust followed boom, and in the late 1970s, oil, gas, and coal caused the area population to skyrocket. So did the crime rate, and corruption raised its ugly head, but things have improved dramatically since.

The city is not far from some fine outdoor attractions: **Fossil Butte National Monument** (see p. 407) and **Flaming Gorge National Recreation Area** (see p. 405).

Essentials

GETTING THERE Delta and United fly into **Rock Springs–Sweetwater County Airport** (www.rockspringsairport.com; ℭ **307/352-6880**), 15 miles east of town on I-80, and the **Greyhound** bus rumbles in at 1695 Sunset Dr. (www.greyhound.com; ℭ **307/362-2931**).

Rock Springs sits at the intersection of U.S. 191 and I-80. From Cheyenne, drive I-80 west for 258 miles. From Jackson, take U.S. 191 south for 178 miles.

VISITOR INFORMATION The **Rock Springs Chamber of Commerce,** 1897 Dewar Dr. (www.rockspringswyoming.net; ℭ **800/463-8637** or 307/362-3771), and **Sweetwater County Travel and Tourism,** 404 N St., Ste. 404 (www.tourwyoming.com; ℭ **307/382-2538**), put a positive spin on Rock Springs and its immediate area.

GETTING AROUND Avis (ℭ **800/230-4898**), **Enterprise** (ℭ **800/261-7331**), and **Hertz** (ℭ **800/654-3131**) maintain counters at the airport. For a cab, contact **Executive Taxi** (ℭ **307/922-6530**).

Seeing the Sights

While strolling around town, pop into the **Community Fine Arts Center,** at the Sweetwater County Library, 400 C St. (www.cfac4art.com; ℭ **307/362-6212**), which contains a few original paintings by Grandma Moses and Norman Rockwell. The **Rock Springs Historical Museum,** 201 B St. (ℭ **307/362-3138**), is housed in the city's original city hall (1894), a fine piece of Romanesque architecture featuring exhibits covering the city's rough-and-tumble past. The **Western Wyoming Community College Natural History Museum,** 2500 College Dr. (ℭ **307/382-1600**), has several dinosaur displays and a few fish and plant fossils; there are also a pair of replica Easter Island moai statues on campus. All three museums are free.

Where to Stay

With a swimming pool, free Wi-Fi, and well-maintained modern rooms, **Holiday Inn,** 1675 Sunset Dr. (ℭ **307/382-9200**), offers rooms for $109 to $135 double. The **Motel 6,** at I-80 exit 102, at 2615 Commercial Way (ℭ **307/362-1850**), has rates of $45 to $65 double.

Where to Eat

Bitter Creek Brewing MICROBREWERY LIFE IS TOO SHORT TO DRINK CHEAP BEER, reads the sign behind the oak bar. If you agree, then Bitter Creek is the place for you. In four fermenting vats adjacent to the bar, they concoct their own special microbrews, including the popular Mustang Pale Ale and the cleverly named Coal Porter, a darker beer with a slight chocolate aftertaste. The menu includes gourmet salads, pizzas, and pasta dishes.

604 Broadway. www.bittercreekbrewing.com. ℭ **307/362-4782.** Main courses $6–$14 lunch; $9–$20 dinner. AE, DISC, MC, V. Mon–Sat 11am–10pm.

FLAMING GORGE NATIONAL RECREATION AREA ★

24 miles W of Rock Springs

By May 1869, the Union Pacific had laid its tracks across Wyoming and pinned them to the eastbound rails with a golden spike. The town of Green River, 15 miles west of Rock Springs, was only a year old. And that May, 10 frontiersmen and ex-soldiers climbed off the train, led by a veteran who'd lost his arm in the Civil War. They jumped into stout wooden boats and set off down the Green River. As they slid through red canyons with the cliffs peaking high above, almost singed yellow along the rims, they named the place Flaming Gorge.

The expedition continued down the Green, which merged into the Colorado River, and then continued on into the Grand Canyon, weaving through boulders, portaging sandbars, and being sucked through rapids. Three men decided to hike out rather than risk the rapids. They were later found bristling with arrows. The remaining seven survived. The leader went on to map and record the "Great American Desert" and later helped organize and direct the U.S. Geological Survey. The one-armed Civil War veteran, a famous river runner, was, of course, John Wesley Powell.

> ## Impressions
>
> *The river enters the range by a flaring, brilliant red gorge, that may be seen from the north a score of miles away . . . We name it Flaming Gorge.*
>
> —Explorer Major John Wesley Powell, May 26, 1869

Today a 455-foot dam, 15 miles into Utah, backs the river onto itself for 91 miles, nearly to the town of Green River. Each summer, jet-boaters, water-skiers, and anglers skim the surface of the reservoir, while paddlers drop in below the dam for scenic and adventurous floats in the wake of Powell's boats.

Essentials

GETTING THERE Take I-80 west from Rock Springs for 15 miles to the town of **Green River** at the junction of Wyo. 530. (See "A Driving Tour," below, for information on driving through the area.)

VISITOR INFORMATION For information before you arrive, contact the **District Ranger** (www.fs.usda.gov/ashley; ✆ **435/784-3445**). Once you're in the area, stop at the U.S. Forest Service's **visitor center** in Green River, at 1450 Uinta Dr. (✆ **307/875-2871**), to pick up maps and brochures.

ADMISSION & REGULATIONS If you're boating, admission to the 190,000-acre Flaming Gorge National Recreation Area is $5 per vehicle per day or $15 for a 7-day pass. The Forest Service's regulations here are mostly common sense, aimed at preserving water quality and protecting the forest and historic sites. In addition, Wyoming and Utah fishing and boating regulations apply in those states' sections of the recreation area. Leashed dogs are permitted on trails.

A Driving Tour

As you drive south from Green River on Wyo. 530, the cactus-and-sagebrush-filled **Devils Playground** badlands and the rock formations of **Haystack Buttes** will be to your right. Wyo. 530 runs the length of the recreation area's west side and provides access to the Flaming Gorge Reservoir at the **Buckboard Crossing Area,** 20 miles south, where a full-service marina operates during the summer.

From Wyo. 530, pick up Utah 44 just across the state line in Manila, Utah. Utah 44 runs south, then east for 27 miles to pick up U.S. 191. Along this route, you'll catch glimpses of Utah's Uinta Mountains to the west and may see bighorn sheep in nearby **Sheep Creek Canyon,** which has been designated a special geological area by the Forest Service because of its dramatically twisted and upturned rocks. A mostly paved 11-mile loop road cuts off from Utah 44, offering a half-hour tour of this beautiful, narrow canyon, with its lavish display of rocks that have eroded into intricate patterns, a process that began with the uplifting of the Uinta Mountains millions of years ago. This loop may be closed in winter.

Eventually, you'll come to the **Red Canyon Overlook** on the southern edge of the gorge, where a rainbow of colors adorns 1,000-foot-tall cliffs. The **Red Canyon Visitor Center** (open daily in summer) is nearby, as is **Flaming Gorge Dam.**

To head back to Wyoming, take U.S. 191 away from the eastern edge of the gorge. From the junction of Utah 44 and U.S. 191, it's 16 miles to the border. Once you're at the state line, it's 30 miles to the turnoff for **Firehole Canyon,** an access to the gorge that offers views of the magnificent spires known as **Chimney Rocks.** Keep going north on U.S. 191 and you'll hit I-80 again.

Getting Outside

For more information about the Utah portion of Flaming Gorge National Recreation Area, including additional outdoor recreational activities and outfitters, lodging options, and other nearby sites of interest, see *Frommer's Utah*.

BOATING Three marinas on **Lake Flaming Gorge** provide boat rentals, fuel, launching ramps, and boating and fishing supplies. **Cedar Springs Marina** (www.cedarspringsmarina.com; 📞 **435/889-3795**) is 2 miles west of Flaming Gorge Dam; **Lucerne Valley Marina** (www.flaminggorge.com; 📞 **435/784-3483**) is on the west side of the lake, 7 miles east of Manila; and **Buckboard Marina** (www.buckboard marina.com; 📞 **307/875-6927**) is also on the west side of the lake, off Wyo. 530, 22 miles north of Manila.

CAMPING The U.S. Forest Service maintains about 20 RV and tent campgrounds in the area (about $10–$25 a night), and there are also many primitive riverside sites. Contact the **Forest Service visitor center** in Green River (📞 **307/875-2871**) for more information.

FISHING You might want to bring along a muscular friend if you plan to fish Lake Flaming Gorge, which is famous as the place to catch record-breaking trout, such as the 51-pound, 8-ounce lake (Mackinaw) trout caught in 1988; the 26-pound, 2-ounce rainbow caught in 1979; and the 33-pound, 10-ounce brown caught in 1977. You'll also see other cold-water species, such as smallmouth bass and kokanee salmon. Fishing is popular year-round, although ice-fishermen are warned to make sure the ice is strong enough to hold them. For fishing information and excursions, call **Conquest Expeditions** (www.conquestexpeditions.com; 📞 **435/784-3370** or 801/244-9948).

KILLPECKER SAND DUNES & FOSSIL BUTTE NATIONAL MONUMENT

Killpecker Sand Dunes: 40 miles N of Rock Springs; 140 miles SE of Jackson

Killpecker Sand Dunes

North of Rock Springs and east of Eden (I'm not kidding . . . it's a small town) swell the **Killpecker Sand Dunes**—the largest active dunes in North America. Here hikers can scale and descend the heaving hills of white sand, where the noon heat shimmers and the midnight cold cuts. Rock climbers trek to **Boar's Tusk,** a standing volcanic plug, ethnography buffs seek the **White Mountain Petroglyphs,** and photographers with high-powered telephoto lenses should be on the lookout for wild horses.

Bird-watchers will especially enjoy the **Seedskadee Wildlife Refuge,** where they may see geese, sandhill cranes, and great blue herons along the miles of marshes along the Green River.

GETTING THERE   To get to the dunes, drive Wyo. 191 north from Rock Springs 36 miles to Eden. Turning east, you'll bump along at least 20 miles of gravel road. Bring a compass, plenty of emergency water, and a map. It's best to contact the Bureau of Land Management (☎ **307/352-0256**) before blazing the trail on your own. *Note:* When it rains, the bentonite on these rough roads turns to glue, and smart drivers stop trying.

Fossil Butte National Monument

Standing at the base of Fossil Butte, gazing up 1,000 feet at the rust- and ocher-stained cliffs, with the crackling desert wind rattling sage and tumbleweeds, you'd never guess that aeons ago you'd have been looking up from the bottom of a subtropical ocean. Some 50 million years ago, during the Eocene Epoch, millions of fish wriggled across what's now the sky. With the ebb and flow of millennia, they sifted into the mud and fossilized.

Today, visitors join paleontologists during the summer to dig for the ancient remains of fish, insects, turtles, birds, and even bats. You can also hike (be watchful for rattlesnakes) on two short trails—the 1.5-mile Fossil Lake Trail and the 2.5-mile Quarry Trail. This is also a prime wildlife-viewing area, where you're likely to see pronghorn, mule deer, white-tailed prairie dogs, and ground squirrels, and you might be lucky enough to spot moose, elk, and beaver as well. A variety of birds are also seen here, including Canada geese, great blue herons, Clark's nutcrackers, yellow-headed blackbirds, great horned owls, and red-tailed hawks.

The excellent **Fossil Butte Visitor Center ★** (☎ **307/877-4455**) exhibits more than 75 fossils, including a 13-foot-long crocodile and the oldest-known bat, plus it offers video programs. It's open daily from 9am to 5:30pm May through September, 8am to 4:30pm the rest of the year, and closed during winter holidays and bad snow.

GETTING THERE   From Green River, head west on I-80 to U.S. 30 (exit 66), which you follow north about 40 miles. Past Kemmerer, follow the signs to the visitor center (about 3½ miles). Admission to both the monument and visitor center is free. Advance information is available by writing to Superintendent, Fossil Butte National Monument, P.O. Box 592, Kemmerer, WY 83101 (www.nps.gov/fobu; ✆ 307/877-4455).

ALSO WORTH A LOOK   No need to rush through Kemmerer, an old mining town with a pleasant central square and some fine old buildings, set along the Hams Fork River. Here you'll find the very first **JCPenney store** (✆ 307/877-3164) and the original home of the chain's founder, James Cash Penney. The store, despite being small and historic, is a regular JCPenney, open year-round. The house is open Memorial Day to Labor Day, Monday to Saturday 9am to 6pm, with free admission. The flagship store is on the town's central square, at 722 JC Penney Dr.; the home is 1 block north. Another good local attraction: **Pine Creek Ski Resort** (www.pinecreek skiresort.com; ✆ 307/279-3201) is about 50 miles northwest of Kemmerer, though calling it a "resort" is a bit of hyperbole. Full-day lift tickets are $40 for adults, $30 for children 17 and under.

PLANNING YOUR TRIP TO MONTANA & WYOMING

The summers are short and the driving distances long in Montana and Wyoming, so the difference between a room reservation and last-second lodging improvisation can mean a 100-mile moonlight drive in an unanticipated direction.

This is especially true in and around Yellowstone, Grand Teton, and Glacier national parks in peak season. Even an ounce of planning goes a long way in these parts, and can often be the difference between a dream vacation and one you'd rather forget. So think ahead and use this chapter to carefully plan your Montana and Wyoming adventure—before you realize your target campground is full for the night and your target trail is clogged with snow.

GETTING THERE

By Plane

Travelers flying into Montana from out of state can choose to land in one of six major airports: Billings, Bozeman, Great Falls, Helena, Kalispell, or Missoula. In Wyoming, Jackson, Casper, Cheyenne, Cody, Gillette, Laramie, Riverton, Rock Springs, and Sheridan have airports with commercial airline service. To find out which airlines travel to Montana and Wyoming, please see "Airline Websites," p. 424.

Montana's and Wyoming's airports are dwarfed by **Denver International Airport** in Colorado and **Salt Lake City International Airport** in Utah. However, connecting flights are available from Denver and Salt Lake to almost all of the regional airports in Montana and Wyoming, and—if you have time—renting a car in one of these larger cities can make for a nice scenic drive to your final destination.

By Bus

Greyhound (www.greyhound.com; ℂ **800/231-2222** in the U.S.; ℂ **001/214/849-8100** outside the U.S., with toll-free access) is the sole nationwide bus line. International visitors can obtain information about the **Greyhound North American Discovery Pass.** The pass, which offers unlimited travel and stopovers in the U.S. and Canada, can be obtained outside the United States from travel agents or through **www.discoverypass.com**.

By Car

In Montana, **I-90** runs west to east from St. Regis to Wyola, near the Wyoming border southeast of Billings. **I-94** goes east from Billings to Glendive and the North Dakota border. **U.S. Hwy. 2,** called the "Hi-Line," is another east–west alternative, stretching across the northern reaches of Montana from Bainville to Troy. The major interstate traversing the state from north to south is **I-15,** from Sweetgrass to Monida.

Wyoming is crossed through the southern part of the state by **I-80,** a huge trucker route from Pine Bluffs in the east to Evanston in the west. **I-90** begins in the north-central part of the state near Ranchester and comes out in the northeast near Beulah. Just outside Buffalo is I-90's junction with **I-25,** a north–south route that runs through Cheyenne. The western part of the state, north of Rock Springs, is dominated by U.S. highways and secondary state-maintained roads.

For information on car rentals and gasoline (petrol) in Montana and Wyoming, see "Getting Around by Car," below.

By Train

Amtrak's *Empire Builder* (www.amtrak.com; ✆ **800/872-7245**) provides daily rail service along the northern tier of Montana, traveling west from Chicago and east from Seattle. The train stops at Wolf Point, Glasgow, Malta, Havre, Shelby, Cut Bank, Browning, East Glacier, Essex, West Glacier, Whitefish, and Libby. There are presently no Amtrak stops in Wyoming.

GETTING AROUND

By Plane

There is regional air service between cities in Montana and Wyoming, but your options are limited, and you'll almost always need a rental car.

By Car

Most visitors to Montana and Wyoming travel the state in a car. In fact, in some areas, it's a necessity. Planes, trains, and buses do not cover many areas of these states.

Before you set out on a road trip, you might want to join the **American Automobile Association** (**AAA;** www.aaa.com; ✆ **800/222-4357**), which has hundreds of offices nationwide. The Billings office is located at 3320 4th Ave. N. (✆ **406/248-7738**) and is open Monday through Friday from 8:30am to 5:30pm. AAA also has offices in Missoula (✆ **406/829-5500**), Bozeman (✆ **406/586-6156**), Helena (✆ **406/447-8100**), Great Falls (✆ **406/727-2900**), Cheyenne (✆ **307/634-8861**), and several other locations. Members receive excellent maps and emergency road service, and AAA will help you plan an exact itinerary. AAA members may also be entitled to discounts at various hotels, stores, car rental companies, and more.

Foreign driver's licenses are usually recognized in the U.S., but international visitors who are planning to rent a car may want to consider obtaining an international driver's permit. Ask local government officials in your home country before traveling, as it is not available once you enter the U.S.

Taxes are already included in the printed price of gasoline (petrol). One U.S. gallon equals 3.8 liters, or .85 imperial gallons. At press time, gasoline cost about $3.50 per gallon in Montana and Wyoming (91¢ per liter).

RENTING A CAR

You'll find rental-car outlets at the airports and in major cities in Montana and Wyoming, but there are great swaths of land in both states where you simply can't rent a car. National companies with outlets in Montana and Wyoming include **Alamo** (www.alamo.com; ✆ 877/222-9075), **Avis** (www.avis.com; ✆ 800/3311212), **Budget** (www.budget.com; ✆ 800/527-0700), **Dollar** (www.dollar.com; ✆ 800/800-3665), **Enterprise** (www.enterprise.com; ✆ 800/261-7331), **Hertz** (www.hertz.com; ✆ 800/654-3131), **National** (www.nationalcar.com; ✆ 800/227-7368), **Payless** (www.paylesscarrental.com; ✆ 800/729-5377), and **Thrifty** (www.thrifty.com; ✆ 800/847-4389).

Car-rental rates vary even more than airline fares. The price you pay depends on the size of the car, where and when you pick it up and drop it off, the length of the rental period, where and how far you drive it, whether you purchase insurance, and a host of other factors. A few key questions could save you hundreds of dollars.

- Are weekend rates lower than weekday rates? Ask if the rate is the same for pickup Friday morning, for instance, as it is for Thursday night.
- Is a weekly rate cheaper than the daily rate? Even if you need the car for only 4 days, it may be cheaper to keep it for 5.
- Does the agency assess a drop-off charge if you don't return the car to the same location where you picked it up? Is it cheaper to pick up the car at the airport than at a downtown location?
- Are special promotional rates available? If you see an advertised price in your local newspaper, be sure to ask for that specific rate; otherwise, you may be charged the standard cost. Terms change constantly, and reservations agents are notorious for not mentioning available discounts unless you ask.
- Are discounts available for members of AARP, AAA, frequent-flier programs, or trade unions? If you belong to any of these organizations, you may be entitled to discounts of up to 30%.
- How much tax will be added to the rental bill? Local tax? State use tax?
- What is the cost of adding an additional driver's name to the contract?
- How many free miles are included in the price? Free mileage is often negotiable, depending on the length of the rental.
- How much does the rental company charge to refill your gas tank if you return with the tank less than full? Though most rental companies claim these prices are "competitive," fuel is almost always cheaper in town. Try to allow enough time to refuel the car yourself before returning it.

Some companies offer "refueling packages," in which you pay for an entire tank of gas up front. The price is usually fairly competitive with local gas prices, but you don't get credit for any gas remaining in the tank.

Many available packages include airfare, accommodations, and a rental car with unlimited mileage. Compare these prices with the cost of booking airline tickets and renting a car separately to see if such offers are good deals. Internet resources can make comparison shopping easier.

International visitors should note that insurance and taxes are almost never included in quoted rental car rates in the U.S. Be sure to ask your rental agency about additional fees for these. They can add a significant cost to your car rental.

Surfing for Rental Cars

For booking rental cars online, the best deals are usually found at rental-car company websites, although all the major online travel agencies also offer rental-car reservations services. **Priceline** (www.priceline.com) and **Hotwire** (www.hotwire.com) work well for rental cars; the only "mystery" is which major rental company you get, and for most travelers, the difference between Hertz, Avis, and Budget is negligible. Also check out **Breezenet.com**, which offers domestic car-rental discounts, with some of the most competitive rates around.

Demystifying Renter's Insurance

Before you drive off in a rental car, be sure you're insured. Hasty assumptions about your personal auto insurance or a rental agency's additional coverage could end up costing you tens of thousands of dollars—even if you are involved in an accident that was clearly the fault of another driver.

If you already hold a **private auto insurance** policy in the United States, you are most likely covered for loss of or damage to a rental car, and liability in case of injury to any other party involved in an accident. Be sure to find out whether you are covered in the area you are visiting, whether your policy extends to all persons who will be driving the rental car, how much liability is covered in case an outside party is injured in an accident, and whether the type of vehicle you are renting is included under your contract. (Rental trucks, sport utility vehicles, and luxury vehicles may not be covered.)

Most **major credit cards** provide some degree of coverage as well—provided they were used to pay for the rental. Terms vary widely, however, so be sure to call your credit card company directly before you rent. If you don't have a private auto insurance policy, the credit card you use to rent a car may provide primary coverage if you decline the rental agency's insurance. This means that the credit card company will cover damage or theft of a rental car for the full cost of the vehicle. If you do have a private auto insurance policy, your credit card may provide secondary coverage—which basically covers your deductible. *Credit cards do not cover liability* or the cost of injury to an outside party and/or damage to an outside party's vehicle. If you do not hold an insurance policy, you may want to seriously consider purchasing additional liability insurance from your rental company. Be sure to check the terms, however: Some rental agencies cover liability only if the renter is not at fault; even then, the rental company's obligation varies from state to state. Bear in mind that each credit card company has its own peculiarities; call your own credit card company for details before relying on a card for coverage.

The basic insurance coverage offered by most car-rental companies, known as the **Loss/Damage Waiver (LDW)** or **Collision Damage Waiver (CDW),** can cost as much as $20 per day. The former should cover everything, including the loss of income to the rental agency, should you get in an accident (normally not covered by your own insurance policy). It usually covers the full value of the vehicle, with no deductible, if an outside party causes an accident or other damage to the rental car. You will probably be covered in case of theft as well. Liability coverage varies, but the minimum is usually at least $15,000. If you are at fault in an accident, you will be covered for the full replacement value of the car—but not for liability. Most rental

For up-to-date information on current weather, contact the National Weather Service at ☎ **406/449-5204** in Montana, ☎ **307/772-2468** in Wyoming, or online at www.wrh.noaa.gov. For statewide road conditions, contact the Montana Department of Transportation (www.mdt.mt.gov; ☎ **800/226-7623,** or 511 in Montana) or the Wyoming Department of Transportation (www.wyoroad.info; ☎ **888/996-7623,** or 511 in Wyoming).

companies require a police report in order to process any claims you file, but your private insurer will not be notified of the accident. Check your own policies and credit cards before you shell out money on this extra insurance because you may already be covered.

By Train

International visitors can buy a **USA Rail Pass,** good for 15, 30, or 45 days of unlimited travel on **Amtrak** (www.amtrak.com; ☎ **800/872-7245**). The pass is available online or through many overseas travel agents. See Amtrak's website for the cost of travel within the western or northwestern United States. Reservations are generally required and should be made as early as possible. Regional rail passes are also available. *Note:* Keep in mind that Wyoming has no train service.

By Bus

Greyhound (www.greyhound.com; ☎ **800/231-2222** in the U.S.; ☎ **001/214/849-8100** outside the U.S., with toll-free access) is the sole nationwide bus line. International visitors can obtain information about the **Greyhound North American Discovery Pass.** The pass, which offers unlimited travel and stopovers in the U.S. and Canada, can be obtained outside the United States from travel agents or through www.discoverypass.com. **Rimrock Stages** (www.rimrocktrailways.com; ☎ **800/255-7655** or 406/245-5392) operates intrastate service in Montana.

TIPS ON ACCOMMODATIONS

Accommodations in Montana and Wyoming range from mom-and-pop motels to major chain hotels, bed-and-breakfasts to ski condos, and getaway cabins to dude ranches. See the individual chapters for recommendations.

National motel and hotel brands frequently found in Montana and Wyoming include **Best Western** (www.bestwestern.com), **Holiday Inn** (www.holidayinn.com), **Days Inn** (www.daysinn.com), **Comfort Inn** (www.comfortinn.com), and **Motel 6** (www.motel6.com). Smaller regional chains in the area include **C'mon Inn** (www.cmoninn.com), **Lexington Hotels** (www.lexingtonhotels.com), and **Shilo Inns** (www.shiloinns.com).

A **dude ranch** (also called a guest ranch) typically offers week-long stays with all-inclusive rates. Recreation almost always includes horseback riding, but usually also covers other outdoor pursuits, such as fly-fishing, hiking, or rafting. There are about 70 guest ranches in Montana and Wyoming, according to Guest Ranches of North America (www.guestranches.com).

PLANNING YOUR TRIP TO MONTANA & WYOMING

Tips on Accommodations

413

When booking a ski vacation, look into booking lodging and buying lift tickets as part of a ski-and-stay package—this is usually substantially cheaper than getting a room and lift tickets a la carte. You will always save money by staying a few miles away from the resort: Instead of Jackson, for example, look at Driggs, Idaho, and instead of Whitefish, try Kalispell.

Your best rates at the national parks will be in the shoulder seasons. Weather can be less predictable (and desirable), but you are bound to get a better room rate when schools are back in session in the U.S. Try to book your trip in May or September, and your value will also come with much more peace and quiet than the middle of the summer at Glacier, Yellowstone, or Grand Teton.

Rather than staying at a hotel, many people—especially families—opt to rent a home during their vacations. For vacation rental listings, visit **www.vrbo.com**, **www.airbnb.com**, or **www.homeaway.com**.

FAST FACTS: MONTANA & WYOMING

Area Codes The statewide area code for Montana is **406.** Wyoming's area code is **307.** Intrastate long-distance calls also require these prefixes.

Business Hours Most stores and banks open at 8am or 9am and close at 5pm, but some stores stay open until 10pm or later.

Car Rental See "Getting Around by Car," earlier in this chapter.

Cellphones See "Mobile Phones," later in this section.

Crime See "Safety," later in this section.

Customs Every visitor to the United States more than 21 years of age may bring in, free of duty, the following: (1) 1 liter of wine or hard liquor; (2) 200 cigarettes, 100 cigars (but not from Cuba), or 3 pounds of smoking tobacco; and (3) $100 worth of gifts. These exemptions are offered to travelers who spend at least 72 hours in the United States and who have not claimed them within the preceding 6 months. It is forbidden to bring into the country almost any meat products (including canned, fresh, and dried meat products such as bullion, soup mixes, and so on). Generally, condiments, including vinegars, oils, spices, coffee, tea, and some cheeses and baked goods, are permitted. Avoid rice products, as rice can often harbor insects. Bringing fruits and vegetables is not advised, though not prohibited. Customs will allow produce depending on where you got it and where you're going after you arrive in the U.S. International visitors may carry in or out up to $10,000 in U.S. or foreign currency with no formalities; larger sums must be declared to U.S. Customs on entering or leaving, which includes filing Form CM 4790. For details regarding U.S. Customs and Border Protection, consult your nearest U.S. embassy or consulate, or **U.S. Customs** (www.customs.gov).

Disabled Travelers Most disabilities shouldn't stop anyone from traveling. However, Wyoming and Montana are not necessarily ahead of the curve when it comes to accessible facilities: There are only a handful of accessible trails in the main attraction—the national parks.

The **America the Beautiful—National Park and Federal Recreational Lands Pass— Access Pass** (formerly the **Golden Access Passport**) gives visually impaired people and people with permanent disabilities (regardless of age) free lifetime entrance to federal recreation sites administered by the National Park Service, including the Fish and Wildlife Service, the Forest Service, the Bureau of Land Management, and the Bureau of Reclamation.

This may include national parks, monuments, historic sites, recreation areas, and national wildlife refuges.

This Access Pass can be obtained only in person at any NPS facility that charges an entrance fee. You need to show proof of medically determined disability. Besides free entry, the pass also offers a 50% discount on some federal-use fees charged for such facilities as camping, swimming, parking, boat launching, and tours. For more information, go to **www.nps.gov/findapark/passes.htm**.

The **Montana Independent Living Project,** 1820 11th Ave., Helena, MT 59601 (www.milp.us; ✆ **800/735-6457** or 406/442-5755), operates an information and referral service for travelers with disabilities, providing information relating to such topics as accessibility, recreation, and transportation.

Drinking Laws The legal age for purchase and consumption of alcoholic beverages is 21; proof of age is required and often requested at bars, nightclubs, and restaurants, so it's always a good idea to bring ID when you go out. Do not carry open containers of alcohol in your car or any public area that isn't zoned for alcohol consumption. The police can fine you on the spot. Don't even think about driving while intoxicated.

All liquor stores in Montana are state-controlled, with minimum hours of 10am to 6pm, although individual stores may be open longer. Most are closed on Sunday. Liquor may also be bought at bars with package licenses during their operating hours. Beer and wine are available at convenience stores and supermarkets from 8:30am to 2am. Bars in both Montana and Wyoming close at 2am.

Electricity Like Canada, the United States uses 110 to 120 volts AC (60 cycles), compared to 220 to 240 volts AC (50 cycles) in most of Europe, Australia, and New Zealand. Downward converters that change 220–240 volts to 110–120 volts are difficult to find in the United States, so bring one with you.

Embassies & Consulates All embassies are in the nation's capital, Washington, D.C. Some consulates are in major U.S. cities, and most nations have a mission to the United Nations in New York City. Montana and Wyoming have no official foreign consulates; they are usually covered by offices in Denver, Colorado. If your country isn't listed below, check **www.embassy.org/embassies** or call for directory information in Washington, D.C. (✆ **202/555-1212**).

The embassy of **Australia** is at 1601 Massachusetts Ave. NW, Washington, DC 20036 (www.usa.embassy.gov.au; ✆ **202/797-3000**). Consulates are in New York, Honolulu, Houston, Los Angeles, and San Francisco.

The embassy of **Canada** is at 501 Pennsylvania Ave. NW, Washington, DC 20001 (www.canadainternational.gc.ca/washington; ✆ **202/682-1740**). Other Canadian consulates are in Buffalo (New York), Detroit, Los Angeles, New York, and Seattle.

The embassy of **Ireland** is at 2234 Massachusetts Ave. NW, Washington, DC 20008 (www.embassyofireland.org; ✆ **202/462-3939**). Irish consulates are in Boston, Chicago, New York, San Francisco, and other cities. See website for a complete listing.

The embassy of **New Zealand** is at 37 Observatory Circle NW, Washington, DC 20008 (www.nzembassy.com; ✆ **202/328-4800**). New Zealand consulates are in Los Angeles, Salt Lake City, San Francisco, and Seattle.

The embassy of the **United Kingdom** is at 3100 Massachusetts Ave. NW, Washington, DC 20008 (http://ukinusa.fco.gov.uk; ✆ **202/588-6500**). Other British consulates are in Atlanta, Boston, Chicago, Cleveland, Houston, Los Angeles, New York, San Francisco, and Seattle.

Emergencies Call ✆ **911**.

Family Travel Montana and Wyoming are full of great family destinations, especially Yellowstone, Grand Teton, and Glacier national parks. Many properties in these areas have family cabins that include kitchens, and most motels have family rooms or suites tailored to the needs of parents traveling with their kids. To locate accommodations, restaurants, and attractions that are particularly kid-friendly, refer to the "Kids" icon throughout this guide.

Family groups should always ask about discounts for attractions and accommodations. If you plan to stay a week at a ski resort or dude ranch, you may find a better value by renting a condominium or lodge rather than multiple rooms. Ski areas often offer packages that include accommodations and lift tickets; check with a ski resort's reservation service for current prices. Before booking any type of room, event, or activity, inquire whether there are discounts for children or age restrictions.

The U.S. National Park Service offers an **America the Beautiful—National Park and Federal Recreational Lands–Annual Pass** for $80 for 1 year, which allows up to four people to enter into all national parks and federal fee areas. For more information, go to www. nps.gov/findapark/passes.htm.

Montana Kids (www.montanakids.com) is a website from Travel Montana that's for both kids (with games and such) and their parents (with information about places to go and things to do with families). As for books, *Frommer's National Parks with Kids* (John Wiley & Sons, Inc.) is an excellent resource.

To locate accommodations, restaurants, and attractions that are particularly kid-friendly, look for the "Kids" icon throughout this guide.

Gasoline   Please see "Getting There by Car," earlier in this chapter.

Health   Montana and Wyoming's extremes—from burning desert to snow-covered mountains—can cause health problems for the ill-prepared. If you haven't been to the desert before, the heat, dryness, and intensity of the sun can be difficult to imagine. Bring a hat, strong sunblock, sunglasses with ultraviolet protection, and moisturizing lotion for dry skin. Hikers and others planning to be outdoors should carry water—at least a gallon per person, per day.

Another potential problem for short-term visitors is elevation. There's less oxygen and lower humidity in the mountains, which rise to over 13,000 feet. If you have heart or respiratory problems, consult your doctor before planning a trip to the mountains. Even if you're in generally good health, you may want to ease into high elevations by changing altitude gradually. Don't fly in from sea level in the morning and plan to hike in the high country of Yellowstone or Glacier that afternoon. Spend a day or two at a lower elevation to let your body adjust.

If you suffer from a chronic illness, consult your doctor before your departure. Pack **prescription medications** in your carry-on luggage, and carry them in their original containers, with pharmacy labels—otherwise, they won't make it through airport security. Visitors from outside the U.S. should carry generic names of prescription drugs. For U.S. travelers, most reliable healthcare plans provide coverage if you get sick away from home. Foreign visitors may have to pay all medical costs up front and be reimbursed later.

Common ailments in Montana & Wyoming include:

○ **Altitude Sickness**   Because most people live at or near sea level, the most common health hazard is discomfort as they adjust to Montana and Wyoming's high elevations. Acclimation to high elevation is a process that can take a day or more. Symptoms include headache, fatigue, nausea, loss of appetite, muscle pain, and lightheadedness. Doctors recommend that, until acclimated, travelers should avoid heavy exertion, consume light meals, and drink lots of liquids, avoiding those with caffeine or alcohol.

○ **Extreme Weather Exposure**   The weather in the Northern Rockies is capricious—it can snow in July or give you serious sunburn in February. If your wilderness activity takes you to a body of water, have extra clothes available in case you get wet—preferably wool and fleece fabrics, which wick away moisture. Hypothermia occurs when the body can no longer warm itself, and you're especially susceptible if you're wearing wet wool or cotton clothing. Many Western streams, rivers, and lakes are glacier-fed and run high during spring; they can be difficult to negotiate and are extremely cold. Winter backcountry explorers should always be equipped with a shovel, a sectional probe, and an avalanche transceiver, since avalanches are common.

o **Waterborne Illnesses** Two waterborne hazards are **giardia** and **campylobacter,** with symptoms that wreak havoc on the human digestive system. If you pick up these pesky bugs, they might accompany you on your trip home. Untreated water from lakes and streams should be boiled for at least 5 minutes before consumption or pumped through a fine-mesh water filter specifically designed to remove bacteria.

o **Wildlife Concerns** Be especially cautious around wildlife, particularly with children. Bison are not big sheepdogs, and bears are not stuffed animals; they are wild animals that can turn on you suddenly if you get too close. Never—I repeat, never—get between a mother bear and her cub. If you're exploring during the summer, carry a can of pepper spray (bear mace), an effective deterrent to bears, available at local sporting goods stores. Also keep an eye out for rattlesnakes and ticks.

Hospitals Hospitals with 24-hour emergency rooms can be found in most cities and large towns in Montana and Wyoming, as well as Yellowstone National Park, which has three clinics within its borders. In the case of a medical emergency, call ✆ **911.**

Insurance For information on traveler's insurance, trip cancelation insurance, and medical insurance while traveling, please visit www.frommers.com/planning.

Internet & Wi-Fi In Montana and Wyoming's major cities and resorts, Wi-Fi is commonplace. It's harder to find in some of the less populated areas but generally not difficult to access the Internet in any conurbation. Check at libraries and coffee shops if your lodging lacks Internet access.

Legal Aid While driving, if you are pulled over for a minor infraction (such as speeding), never attempt to pay the fine directly to a police officer; this could be construed as attempted bribery, a much more serious crime. Pay fines by mail or directly into the hands of the clerk of the court. If accused of a more serious offense, say and do nothing before consulting a lawyer. In the U.S., the burden is on the state to prove a person's guilt beyond a reasonable doubt, and everyone has the right to remain silent, whether he or she is suspected of a crime or actually arrested. Once arrested, a person can make one telephone call to a party of his or her choice. The international visitor should call his or her embassy or consulate.

LGBT Travelers Wyoming and Montana do not have the reputation of being the gay-friendliest states in the Union, especially in the wake of the Matthew Shepard murder in Laramie in 1998. But larger cities tend to have a gay scene of some kind, especially Missoula and Bozeman in Montana, and there is little for gay travelers to worry about. However, some of the more rural destinations are still rife with homophobia.

The **International Gay and Lesbian Travel Association (IGLTA;** www.iglta.org; ✆ **954/630-1637)** is the trade association for the gay and lesbian travel industry and offers an online directory of gay- and lesbian-friendly travel businesses and tour operators. Many agencies offer tours and travel itineraries specifically for gay and lesbian travelers. Based in Red Lodge, Montana, **OutWest Global Adventures** (www.outwestadventures. com; ✆ **800/743-0458** or 406/446-1533) offers gay and lesbian adventure travel packages, including ranching vacations in Montana and backpacking trips in Yellowstone.

Mail At press time, domestic postage rates were 32¢ for a postcard and 45¢ for a letter. For international mail, a first-class letter of up to 1 ounce costs $1.05 (85¢ to Canada and 85¢ to Mexico); a first-class postcard costs the same as a letter. For more information, go to **www.usps.com**.

If you aren't sure what your address will be in the United States, mail can be sent to you, in your name, c/o General Delivery at the main post office of the city or region where you expect to be. (Call ✆ **800/275-8777** for information on the nearest post office.) The addressee must pick up mail in person and must produce proof of identity (such as a driver's license or passport). Most post offices will hold mail for up to 1 month, and are open Monday to Friday from 8am to 6pm, and Saturday from 9am to 3pm.

Always include zip codes when mailing items in the U.S. If you don't know your zip code, visit www.usps.com/zip4.

Medical Requirements Unless you're arriving from an area known to be suffering from an epidemic (particularly cholera or yellow fever), inoculations or vaccinations are not required for entry into the United States. Also see "Health."

Mobile Phones Just because your cellphone works at home doesn't mean it'll work everywhere in the U.S., thanks to the nation's fragmented cellphone system. It's a good bet that your phone will work in major cities, but take a look at your wireless company's coverage map on its website before heading out; T-Mobile and Sprint are particularly weak in rural areas. In Montana and Wyoming, expect good coverage in cities and towns, but do not count on it in the far-flung areas, including the national parks. While there is some coverage in all of the national parks in both states, it is far from comprehensive. Off the beaten path, expect limited coverage, if you have any at all. If you need to stay in touch at a destination where you know your phone won't work, buy a **pay-as-you-go phone** that has superior coverage in Montana and Wyoming.

If you're not from the U.S., you'll be appalled at the poor reach of our **GSM (Global System for Mobile Communications) wireless network,** which is used by much of the rest of the world. Your phone will probably work in most major U.S. cities; it definitely won't work in many rural areas. And you may or may not be able to send SMS (text messaging) home from some of these states' most secluded corners, either, including areas in the national parks.

Money & Costs

THE VALUE OF THE U.S. DOLLAR VS. OTHER POPULAR CURRENCIES

US$	A$	C$	€	NZ$	£
1	0.96	1.02	0.78	1.25	0.65

Frommer's lists exact prices in the local currency. The currency conversions quoted above were correct at press time. However, rates fluctuate, so before departing, consult a currency exchange website such as **www.oanda.com/currency/converter** to check up-to-the-minute rates.

As most parts of Montana and Wyoming are connected to the broadband backbone, you'll find **credit cards** are accepted at most lodgings and restaurants, and many attractions. **ATMs** are also fairly common in towns of all sizes, and even in the national parks. But these states also have numerous back roads that lead to out-of-the-way places with establishments that do not accept credit cards; I recommend you carry at least some cash on hand (about $200 is a good amount) while traveling in either state.

While the states are still relatively inexpensive in terms of the cost of hotel rooms and lodging, there are also many luxury establishments in places like Whitefish and Jackson

WHAT THINGS COST IN MONTANA & WYOMING   US$

Taxi from the Billings airport to downtown Billings	5.00–10.00
Double room, very expensive (Jackson, WY)	250.00–1,000.00
Double room, expensive (Whitefish, MT or Cody, WY)	150.00–300.00
Double room, moderate (Bozeman, MT)	75.00–150.00
Tent campsite in a national park	10.00–23.00
RV campsite in a national park	20.00–56.00
Three-course dinner for two without wine, moderate	50.00–100.00
Bottle of beer	1.00–5.00
Cup of coffee	1.00–3.00
Full-day adult ski lift ticket at Jackson Hole	60.00–100.00
Full-day adult ski lift ticket at Bridger Bowl	48.00
Admission to most national parks	25.00/week (per car)

Hole. You'll find plenty of $50 double motel rooms, but lodgings in Yellowstone gateway towns and ski resorts average about $150 in peak season for a standard room. Nevertheless, there are vacations for almost any budget, from camps and cookouts in the national parks to the pricey rooms at the Four Seasons Jackson Hole.

Newspapers & Magazines   Montana's major daily newspapers are the *Missoulian* (www.missoulian.com), the *Great Falls Tribune* (www.greatfallstribune.com), and the *Billings Gazette* (www.billingsgazette.com). In Wyoming, the *Casper Star-Tribune* (www.trib.com) is the only statewide paper, while the *Wyoming Tribune-Eagle* (www.wyomingnews.com) is Cheyenne's daily. Magazines of note include *Big Sky Journal* (www.bigskyjournal.com) and *Montana Magazine* (www.montanamagazine.com).

Packing   Nothing will ruin a trip faster than sore or wet feet. Take some time planning your travel wardrobe. Bring comfortable walking shoes, even if you plan to keep walking to a minimum. **Bring shoes that are broken in,** and if you plan to do some hiking, get sturdy boots that support your ankles and wick away water. Early in the season, trails might be wet or muddy; late in the fall, you can get snowed on. The more popular trails are sometimes also used by horses, which can make stream crossings a mucky mess.

In the outdoors, wear your clothing in layers, and bring a small backpack or fanny pack so that you can take those layers off and on as temperature, altitude, and your physical exertion change. Cotton is a no-no in the backcountry; synthetic fabrics are recommended because they dry much faster. Gloves or mittens are useful before the park heats up, or in the evening when it cools down again—*even in summer.* The atmosphere is thin at higher altitudes, so protect your skin. Bring a strong sunblock, a hat with a brim, and sunglasses. I also recommend bringing insect repellent, water bottles, and a first-aid kit. Take into account that elevations in Montana and Wyoming are commonly between 5,000 and 10,000 feet; in campgrounds and on hiking trails, you'll want clothing appropriate to the temperatures—in summer, 40°F (4°C) in the evening, 75°F (24°C) during the day.

For more helpful information on packing for your trip, download our convenient Travel Tools app for your mobile device. Go to www.frommers.com/go/mobile and click on the Travel Tools icon.

Passports   Virtually every air traveler entering the U.S. is required to show a passport. All persons, including U.S. citizens, traveling by air between the United States and Canada, Mexico, Central and South America, the Caribbean, and Bermuda are required to present a valid passport. *Note:* U.S. and Canadian citizens entering the U.S. at land and sea ports of entry from within the Western Hemisphere must now also present a passport or other documents compliant with the Western Hemisphere Travel Initiative (WHTI; see www.get youhome.gov for details). Children 15 and under may continue entering with only a U.S. birth certificate or other proof of U.S. citizenship.

Contact your local passport office for more information:

o **Australia   Australian Passport Information Service** (www.passports.gov.au; *C* **131-232**).

o **Canada   Passport Office,** Department of Foreign Affairs and International Trade, Ottawa, ON K1A 0G3 (www.ppt.gc.ca; *C* **800/567-6868**).

o **Ireland   Passport Office,** Setanta Centre, Molesworth Street, Dublin 2 (www. foreignaffairs.gov.ie; *C* **01/671-1633**).

o **New Zealand   Passports Office,** Department of Internal Affairs, 47 Boulcott Street, Wellington, 6011 (www.passports.govt.nz; *C* **0800/225-050** in New Zealand or 04/474-8100).

o **United Kingdom**   Visit your nearest passport office, major post office, or travel agency, or contact the **Identity and Passport Service (IPS),** 89 Eccleston Square, London, SW1V 1PN (www.ips.gov.uk; *C* **0300/222-0000**).

o **United States**   To find your regional passport office, check the U.S. State Department website (travel.state.gov/passport), or call the **National Passport Information Center** (*C* **877/487-2778**) for automated information.

Petrol   Please see "Getting Around by Car," earlier in this chapter.

Police   Call *C* **911** for emergency police help.

Safety   While there are many reasons to visit Montana and Wyoming, the two cited most often are visiting historic sites and exploring the magnificent outdoors—especially the three national parks. However, visiting historic sites and participating in outdoor activities can lead to accidents.

When visiting such historic sites as ghost towns, gold mines, and railroads, remember that they were likely built more than 100 years ago, when safety standards were extremely lax, if they existed at all. Never enter abandoned buildings, mines, or rail cars on your own. When touring historic attractions, use common sense, and don't be afraid to ask questions.

Walkways in mines are often uneven, poorly lit, and sometimes slippery due to seeping groundwater that can stain your clothing with its high iron content. In old buildings, be prepared for steep, narrow stairways, creaky floors, and low ceilings and doorways. Steam trains are wonderful as long as you remember that steam is very hot, oil and grease can ruin your clothing, and, at the very least, soot will make you very dirty.

As you head into the great outdoors, bear in mind that injuries often occur when people fail to follow instructions. Take heed when the experts tell you to stay on established ski trails, hike only in designated areas and carry rain gear, and wear a life jacket when rafting. Mountain weather can be fickle, and many beautiful spots are in remote areas. Be prepared for sudden changes in temperature at any time of year, and watch out for summer afternoon thunderstorms that can leave you drenched and shivering in minutes.

Senior Travel   Most lodging establishments and museums in Montana and Wyoming offer discounts to seniors. Mention the fact that you're a senior when you make your travel reservations. Many hotels offer discounts for seniors, and in most cities, people 60 and over qualify for reduced admission to theaters, museums, and other attractions, as well as discounted fares on public transportation.

Members of **AARP,** 601 E St. NW, Washington, DC 20049 (www.aarp.org; $\mathcal{C}$ **888/687-2277**), get discounts on hotels, airfares, and car rentals. AARP offers members a wide range of benefits, including *AARP The Magazine* and a monthly newsletter. Anyone 50 or over can join.

The U.S. National Park Service offers an **America the Beautiful—National Park and Federal Recreational Lands Pass—Senior Pass** (formerly the **Golden Age Passport**), which gives seniors 62 years or older lifetime entrance to all properties administered by the National Park Service—national parks, monuments, historic sites, recreation areas, and national wildlife refuges—for a one-time processing fee of $10. Besides free entry, the America the Beautiful Senior Pass also offers a 50% discount on some federal-use fees charged for such facilities as camping, swimming, parking, boat launching, and tours. For more information, go to www.nps.gov/findapark/passes.htm.

Smoking   Montana has a statewide smoking ban; Wyoming does not, but smoking is banned in many public places, including thermal areas at Yellowstone National Park. *Note:* Smoking is permitted in many areas of the U.S. national parks, but smokers should dispose of their used cigarette butts.

Taxes   The United States has no value-added tax (VAT) or other indirect tax at the national level. Every state, county, and city may levy its own local tax on all purchases, including hotel and restaurant checks and airline tickets. These taxes will not appear on price tags. Montana has no state sales tax, but there is a lodging tax of 7%, and certain resort communities can also charge an additional tax for goods and services. Wyoming's state sales tax is 4%, and local communities can add up to 1% more. Communities can impose a lodging tax of up to 4%.

Telephones   Many convenience groceries and packaging services sell **prepaid calling cards** in denominations up to $50. Many public pay phones at airports now accept American Express, MasterCard, and Visa. **Local calls** made from most pay phones cost either 25¢ or 35¢. Most long-distance and international calls can be dialed directly from any phone. **To make calls within the United States and to Canada,** dial 1 followed by the area code and the seven-digit number. **For other international calls,** dial 011 followed by the country code, city code, and the number you are calling.

Calls to area codes **800, 888, 877,** and **866** are toll-free. However, calls to area codes **700** and **900** (chat lines, bulletin boards, "dating" services, and so on) can be expensive—charges of 95¢ to $3 or more per minute. Some numbers have minimum charges that can run $15 or more.

For **reversed-charge or collect calls,** and for person-to-person calls, dial the number 0, then the area code and number; an operator will come on the line, and you should specify whether you are calling collect, person-to-person, or both. If your operator-assisted call is international, ask for the overseas operator.

For **directory assistance** ("Information"), dial $\mathcal{C}$ **411** for local numbers and national numbers in the U.S. and Canada. For dedicated long-distance information, dial 1, then the appropriate area code plus 555-1212.

Time   Montana and Wyoming are both in the **Mountain Standard Time Zone.** The continental United States is divided into **four time zones:** Eastern Standard Time (EST), Central Standard Time (CST), Mountain Standard Time (MST), and Pacific Standard Time (PST). Alaska and Hawaii have their own zones. For example, when it's 9am in Los Angeles (PST), it's 7am in Honolulu (HST), 10am in Denver (MST), 11am in Chicago (CST), noon in New York City (EST), 5pm in London (GMT), and 2am the next day in Sydney.

Daylight saving time (summer time) is in effect from 1am on the second Sunday in March to 1am on the first Sunday in November, except in Arizona, Hawaii, the U.S. Virgin Islands, and Puerto Rico. Daylight saving time moves the clock 1 hour ahead of standard time.

For help with time translations and more, download our convenient Travel Tools app for your mobile device. Go to www.frommers.com/go/mobile and click on the Travel Tools icon.

Tipping   In hotels, tip **bellhops** at least $1 per bag ($2–$3 if you have a lot of luggage) and tip the **chamber staff** $1 to $2 per day (more if you've left a big mess for him or her to clean up). Tip the **doorman** or **concierge** only if he or she has provided you with some specific service (for example, calling a cab for you or obtaining difficult-to-get theater tickets). Tip the **valet-parking attendant** $1 every time you get your car.

In restaurants, bars, and nightclubs, tip **service staff** and **bartenders** 15% to 20% of the check, tip **checkroom attendants** $1 per garment, and tip **valet-parking attendants** $1 per vehicle.

As for other service personnel, tip **cab drivers** 15% of the fare, tip **skycaps** at airports at least $1 per bag ($2–$3 if you have a lot of luggage), and tip **hairdressers** and **barbers** 15% to 20%.

For help with tip calculations, currency conversions, and more, download our convenient Travel Tools app for your mobile device. Go to www.frommers.com/go/mobile and click on the Travel Tools icon.

Toilets   You won't find public toilets, or "restrooms," on the streets in most U.S. cities, but they can be found in hotel lobbies, bars, restaurants, museums, department stores, railway and bus stations, and service stations. Large hotels and fast-food restaurants are often the best bet for clean facilities. Restaurants and bars in resorts or heavily visited areas may reserve their restrooms for patrons.

VAT   See "Taxes," earlier in this section.

Visas   The U.S. State Department has a **Visa Waiver Program (VWP)** allowing citizens of the following countries to enter the United States without a visa for stays of up to 90 days: Andorra, Australia, Austria, Belgium, Brunei, Czech Republic, Denmark, Estonia, Finland, France, Germany, Greece, Hungary, Iceland, Ireland, Italy, Japan, Latvia, Liechtenstein, Lithuania, Luxembourg, Malta, Monaco, the Netherlands, New Zealand, Norway, Portugal, San Marino, Singapore, Slovakia, Slovenia, South Korea, Spain, Sweden, Switzerland, and the United Kingdom. (***Note:*** This list was accurate at press time; for the most up-to-date list of countries in the VWP, consult http://travel.state.gov/visa.) Even though a visa isn't necessary, in an effort to help U.S. officials check travelers against terror watch lists before they arrive at U.S. borders, visitors from VWP countries must register online through the Electronic System for Travel Authorization (ESTA) before boarding a plane or a boat to the U.S. Travelers must complete an electronic application providing basic personal and travel eligibility information. The Department of Homeland Security recommends filling out the form at least 3 days before traveling. Authorizations will be valid for up to 2 years or until the traveler's passport expires, whichever comes first. Currently, there is a US$14 fee for the online application. Existing ESTA registrations remain valid through their expiration dates. ***Note:*** Any passport issued on or after October 26, 2006, by a VWP country must be an **e-Passport** for VWP travelers to be eligible to enter the U.S. without a visa. Citizens of these nations also need to present a round-trip air or cruise ticket upon arrival. E-Passports contain computer chips capable of storing biometric information, such as the required digital photograph of the holder. If your passport doesn't have this feature, you can still travel without a visa if the valid passport was issued before October 26, 2005, and includes a machine-readable zone; or if the valid passport was issued between October 26, 2005, and October 25, 2006, and includes a digital photograph. For more information, go to **http://travel.state.gov/visa**. Canadian citizens may enter the United States without visas but will need to show passports and proof of residence.

Citizens of all other countries must have (1) a valid passport that expires at least 6 months later than the scheduled end of their visit to the U.S. and (2) a tourist visa.

For information about U.S. visas, go to **http://travel.state.gov** and click on "Visas."

Australian citizens can obtain up-to-date visa information from the **U.S. Embassy Canberra,** Moonah Place, Yarralumla, ACT 2600 (✆ **02/6214-5600**), or by checking the U.S. Diplomatic Mission's website at http://canberra.usembassy.gov/visas.html.

British subjects can obtain up-to-date visa information by calling the **U.S. Embassy Visa Information Line** (✆ **09042-450-100** from within the U.K., at £1.20 per minute; or ✆ **866/382-3589** from within the U.S., at a flat rate of $16 and payable by credit card only) or by visiting the American Embassy London's website at http://london.usembassy. gov/visas.html.

Irish citizens can obtain up-to-date visa information through the **U.S. Embassy Dublin,** 42 Elgin Rd., Ballsbridge, Dublin 4 (http://dublin.usembassy.gov; ✆ **1580-47-VISA [8472]** from within the Republic of Ireland, at €2.40 per minute).

Citizens of **New Zealand** can obtain up-to-date visa information by contacting the **U.S. Embassy New Zealand,** 29 Fitzherbert Terrace, Thorndon, Wellington (http://newzealand. usembassy.gov; ✆ **644/462-6000**).

Visitor Information Travel Montana, P.O. Box 200533, 301 S. Park St., Helena, MT 59620 (www.visitmt.com; ✆ 800/847-4868 or 406/841-2870; TDD 406/841-2702), provides information about Big Sky country and specific locales in Montana. It puts out two well-designed vacation planning kits—one for summer and one for winter—that include maps and the *Montana Vacation Planner.* The planner includes contacts with agencies that can provide information and travel services, such as airlines and rental-car agencies; it also has listings, by town, of places to stay and eat, with charts specifying price ranges and such amenities as hot tubs and access for travelers with disabilities. Travel Montana will also send you separate guides to some of Montana's more popular sports activities: snowmobiling, fishing, and skiing; as well as site-specific guides for each of the six travel regions: Glacier Country in the northwest, Gold West Country in the southwest, Russell Country in north-central Montana, Yellowstone Country in south-central Montana, Missouri River Country in the northeast, and Custer Country in the southeast.

For additional information about attractions, facilities, and services at specific Montana destinations—national parks, cities, or towns—contact the **Montana Chamber of Commerce,** P.O. Box 1730, Helena, MT 59624 (www.montanachamber.com; ✆ **406/442-2405** or 443-7888), for the address and phone number of the nearest chamber office.

The **Wyoming Business Council Travel & Tourism Division,** 1520 Etchepare Circle, Cheyenne, WY 82007 (www.wyomingtourism.org; ✆ **800/225-5996** or 307/777-7777), distributes summer and winter editions of the *Travelers Journal,* an informative guide with information about sights and towns in the state's five travel areas—Devils Tower/Buffalo Bill Country in the north and east, Oregon Trail/Rendezvous Country in central Wyoming, Medicine Bow/Flaming Gorge Country along the southern border, Jackson Hole/Jim Bridger Country in the west, and Grand Teton and Yellowstone—as well as special features on everything from geology to adventure travel. They also furnish maps, cultural and park guides, and other information.

Water Although tap water is generally safe to drink in Montana and Wyoming, hikers should avoid drinking untreated water from lakes and streams, which can cause **giardia** or **campylobacter,** with symptoms that wreak havoc on the human digestive system. See "Health," earlier in this section, for more information.

Wi-Fi See "Internet & Wi-Fi," earlier in this section.

Women Travelers Founded in 1982 and the first of its kind, **AdventureWomen** in Bozeman, Montana (www.adventurewomen.com; ℂ **800/804-8686,** or 406/587-3883 outside the U.S.) offers customized trips to just about anywhere in the world for active and adventurous women age 30 and older. In Montana, the company guides hiking trips, as well as skiing and guest-ranch trips.

AIRLINE WEBSITES

Alaska Airlines/Horizon Air
www.alaskaair.com

Allegiant Airlines
www.allegiantair.com

American Airlines
www.aa.com

Delta Air Lines
www.delta.com

Frontier Airlines
www.frontierairlines.com

Great Lakes Airlines
www.greatlakesav.com

Gulfstream International Airlines
www.flygia.com

United Airlines
www.united.com

US Airways
www.usairways.com

Index

INDEX